Lecture Notes in Computer Science   **9747**

Commenced Publication in 1973
Founding and Former Series Editors:
Gerhard Goos, Juris Hartmanis, and Jan van Leeuwen

More information about this series at http://www.springer.com/series/7409

Aaron Marcus (Ed.)

Design, User Experience, and Usability

Novel User Experiences

5th International Conference, DUXU 2016
Held as Part of HCI International 2016
Toronto, Canada, July 17–22, 2016
Proceedings, Part II

 Springer

Editor
Aaron Marcus
Aaron Marcus and Associates
Berkeley, CA
USA

ISSN 0302-9743   ISSN 1611-3349   (electronic)
Lecture Notes in Computer Science
ISBN 978-3-319-40354-0   ISBN 978-3-319-40355-7   (eBook)
DOI 10.1007/978-3-319-40355-7

Library of Congress Control Number: 2016940899

LNCS Sublibrary: SL3 – Information Systems and Applications, incl. Internet/Web, and HCI

Printed on acid-free paper

This Springer imprint is published by Springer Nature
The registered company is Springer International Publishing AG Switzerland

Foreword

The 18th International Conference on Human-Computer Interaction, HCI International 2016, was held in Toronto, Canada, during July 17–22, 2016. The event incorporated the 15 conferences/thematic areas listed on the following page.

A total of 4,354 individuals from academia, research institutes, industry, and governmental agencies from 74 countries submitted contributions, and 1,287 papers and 186 posters have been included in the proceedings. These papers address the latest research and development efforts and highlight the human aspects of the design and use of computing systems. The papers thoroughly cover the entire field of human-computer interaction, addressing major advances in knowledge and effective use of computers in a variety of application areas. The volumes constituting the full 27-volume set of the conference proceedings are listed on pages IX and X.

I would like to thank the program board chairs and the members of the program boards of all thematic areas and affiliated conferences for their contribution to the highest scientific quality and the overall success of the HCI International 2016 conference.

This conference would not have been possible without the continuous and unwavering support and advice of the founder, Conference General Chair Emeritus and Conference Scientific Advisor Prof. Gavriel Salvendy. For his outstanding efforts, I would like to express my appreciation to the communications chair and editor of *HCI International News*, Dr. Abbas Moallem.

April 2016   Constantine Stephanidis

HCI International 2016 Thematic Areas and Affiliated Conferences

Thematic areas:

- Human-Computer Interaction (HCI 2016)
- Human Interface and the Management of Information (HIMI 2016)

Affiliated conferences:

- 13th International Conference on Engineering Psychology and Cognitive Ergonomics (EPCE 2016)
- 10th International Conference on Universal Access in Human-Computer Interaction (UAHCI 2016)
- 8th International Conference on Virtual, Augmented and Mixed Reality (VAMR 2016)
- 8th International Conference on Cross-Cultural Design (CCD 2016)
- 8th International Conference on Social Computing and Social Media (SCSM 2016)
- 10th International Conference on Augmented Cognition (AC 2016)
- 7th International Conference on Digital Human Modeling and Applications in Health, Safety, Ergonomics and Risk Management (DHM 2016)
- 5th International Conference on Design, User Experience and Usability (DUXU 2016)
- 4th International Conference on Distributed, Ambient and Pervasive Interactions (DAPI 2016)
- 4th International Conference on Human Aspects of Information Security, Privacy and Trust (HAS 2016)
- Third International Conference on HCI in Business, Government, and Organizations (HCIBGO 2016)
- Third International Conference on Learning and Collaboration Technologies (LCT 2016)
- Second International Conference on Human Aspects of IT for the Aged Population (ITAP 2016)

Conference Proceedings Volumes Full List

Design, User Experience and Usability

Program Board Chair: **Aaron Marcus, USA**

- Sisira Adikari, Australia
- Claire Ancient, UK
- Arne Berger, Germany
- Jan Brejcha, Czech Republic
- Hashim Chunpir, Germany
- Silvia de los Rios Perez, Spain
- Marc Fabri, UK
- Tineke (Christina) Fitch, UK
- Patricia Flanagan, Australia
- Steffen Hess, Germany
- Long Jiao, P.R. China
- Nouf Khashman, Canada
- Khalil R. Laghari, Canada
- Tom MacTavish, USA
- Judith A. Moldenhauer, USA
- Francisco Rebelo, Portugal
- Kerem Rızvanoğlu, Turkey
- Christine Riedmann-Streitz, Germany
- Patricia Search, USA
- Marcelo Soares, Brazil
- Carla Spinillo, Brazil
- Virginia Tiradentes Souto, Brazil
- Manfred Tscheligi, Austria
- Ryan Wynia, USA

The full list with the program board chairs and the members of the program boards of all thematic areas and affiliated conferences is available online at:

http://www.hci.international/2016/

HCI International 2017

The 19th International Conference on Human-Computer Interaction, HCI International 2017, will be held jointly with the affiliated conferences in Vancouver, Canada, at the Vancouver Convention Centre, July 9–14, 2017. It will cover a broad spectrum of themes related to human-computer interaction, including theoretical issues, methods, tools, processes, and case studies in HCI design, as well as novel interaction techniques, interfaces, and applications. The proceedings will be published by Springer. More information will be available on the conference website: http://2017.hci.international/.

General Chair
Prof. Constantine Stephanidis
University of Crete and ICS-FORTH
Heraklion, Crete, Greece
E-mail: general_chair@hcii2017.org

http://2017.hci.international/

Contents – Part II

DUXU in Learning and Education

Games and Gamification

Culture, Language and DUXU

DUXU for Social Innovation and Sustainability

Usability and User Experience Studies

Emotion, Motivation, and Persuasion Design

Visceral Design: Sites of Intra-action at the Interstices of Waves and Particles

Patricia Flanagan[✉]

University of New South Wales, Paddington, Australia
Patricia.flanagan@unsw.edu.au

Abstract. Quantum physics has undermined our traditional view of the world. Waves and particles that were once considered fundamentally opposed now can be both, depending how we look at them. This raises questions: How do we conceive the world beyond human-centric perception? How do we enrich experience and feel empathy for other entities human and non-human?

As we deconstruct the Cartesian logic of modernity, other borders fall under scrutiny. There is a fundamental change occurring in the theory and practice of art and design where the line between product and user, wearable and wearer, artwork and audience is blurring. This article explores visceral design approaches to human computer interaction and wearable technology drawing on theories of critical/speculative design, visceral thinking, humanistic computing and intra-action. Case studies are introduced to demonstrate approaches that are open to the perspectives presented and represent ways the sensibility described can be distributed through practice.

Keywords: Visceral design · Visceral theory · Wearables · Actants · Intra-action · Vibrant matter · Interface · Interaction · Material · Object oriented ontology · BODYecology · BIOdress · Human-centric perception · Speculative design · Critical design

1 Introduction

Excess of sorrow laughs. Excess of joy weeps... Exuberance is Beauty.

William Blake [1]

Blake's poetry captures a visceral sensibility. This paper explores the visceral from a trans-disciplinary perspective that converges arts praxis, computer and cognitive science, and philosophy that lead us to question: How can we reconfigure art and design practices to realign with the extraordinary changes in our understanding of the world? How do we conceive the world beyond human-centric perception? How do we enrich experience and feel empathy for other entities human and non-human? How do we undermine our subjective segregation of time and our commodification of labour? How can we leverage the affordances of wearables, implantables, digestibles, to augment our sensibilities and emotions to immerse the body in sustainable post-anthropocentric ways of living in the world?

© Springer International Publishing Switzerland 2016
A. Marcus (Ed.): DUXU 2016, Part II, LNCS 9747, pp. 3–15, 2016.
DOI: 10.1007/978-3-319-40355-7_1

Quantum physics has undermined our traditional view of the world and demands a radical shift in our current design practices. At the heart of visceral design is a consideration of matter, so that is where this article begins. Rather than interpret the world through language, linguistic and semiotic analysis, we shall explore interaction at a more primary level – prior to cognition. The author extends Donald Norman's ideas about Visceral Design with Steve Mann's notion of Humanistic Intelligence. They both engage pre-cognitive communication channels. The dominance of language over material within Western culture is under scrutiny as a natural progression of deconstructivist modernist theories of feminism, postcolonialism, queer theory and post-humanism. Gender politics strived for inclusivity of female activity, then gay and other gendered, displaced, disporic, animal, plant and ultimately all forms of matter.

The work of Donna Haraway on multispecies cosmopolitics for example, offer concepts to overcome this hierarchy of mind over matter [2]. A contemporary understanding of materials acknowledges that they are actants – they have agency. Resisting this notion, our traditions and culture prioritise language in the way we interpret the world where materials are viewed as dormant, passive and mute. Representationalism situates us as outsider reflecting on the world. Karen Barad posits a post-humanist performative approach which "insists on understanding, thinking, observing and theorising as practices of engagement with, and as part the world in which we have our being".

The author draws on Barat's notion of intra-action and material practices of agency such as vibrant matter (Bennett) [3] and Sunaptic sculpture (Flanagan) [4]. Rather than intellectual theory alone, Visceral Theory, along with Affect Theory and Actor Network Theory offer notions of direct entanglement and active engagement with the stuff of the world. The site of creativity can be found in the flow, in the in-between spaces that are always in motion. Art and design practices generated in the interstices, at the site of intra-action, give us a glimpse of post-anthropocentric ways of experiencing and understanding the world. The first section of this paper will describe theoretical perspectives followed by case studies of wearables and digestibles that exemplify arts praxis that are explore this shift in world view. Acknowledging entanglement with the environment promotes accountability and fosters a world where the quality and experience of design, rather than the acquisition of goods, is what determines value and quality of life.

2   HCI and DUXU

There is a growing awareness of visual and soma aesthetics in interactive systems design. In the domain of Human Computer Interaction (HCI), the modus operandi of screen and keyboard is in demise, for example, voice recognition will quickly supersede the need to type and other haptic modes of communication will follow. Contemporary HCI now operates with an expanded frame of reference that encompasses experimental new digital technologies. Methodologies within HCI and design user experience and usability are evolving to acknowledge interdisciplinary approaches and have been greatly influenced by areas of the humanities such as social science, anthropology and art. The authors focus, and that of this paper is wearable computing or wearable technologies (for expediency we will use the generic term 'wearables') that are emerging at the intersection of innovation and tradition, where scientific research, artisan knowledge and material histories mix.

Materiality is a vital notion to consider to understand the relationship between humans and digital technologies. Visceral experience is a bodily response, Jens Hauser uses the notion 'reverse othering' [5] to put forward the case that materials elicit reactions as a demonstration of their agency. Both humans, objects and materials are performative, but our social histories have enculturated us to believe we hold the seat of power in this relationship. Effectively blinkering us into ignorance regarding the dynamism and reciprocity of these networks of interactions, numbing our sense of accountability for the repercussion and consequence of what we put-out into the world.

For too long the process of design has been considered a matter of imposing our will onto materials, whereas good design is often born from traditional wisdom where the tolerances of materials and forms are tried and tested – where artisans understand that objects result from a meeting of the will of the material and the will of the maker. It is in this fuzzy zone (in a Bhabhaian sense) where effervescent peripheries intermingle that new forms generate. In other words, evolution is enabled through the intra-active reciprocity of the maker's hand and material.

Wearable technology is both physical and ephemeral, increasingly smaller or invisible, so it is disappearing into the substrates of the built and organic world around (and within) us. The next generation of wearables will not only be created from electronic components – metal, wire and silicon – but include a wide range of materials such as organic wetware, graphene, Biomedical gel and data. Good design reaches into the future to explore new material technologies and into the past where traditional wisdom has pushed the boundaries and tolerances of materials and techniques, tried and tested to create a harmonious balance between material form and function. Wearables combine digital and traditional crafting of atoms and bits, and as data is fungible can flow into different physical or visual forms. Hence, our capacity to inhabit an expanded sense of being in the world is extended beyond perceptual borders of time and space.

3 Visceral Theory

The two main approaches to aesthetic interaction can be classified as analytical or pragmatic [6]. An analytical approach typically looks at an objects appearance, attractiveness, formal physical qualities of design and the concept of the design without broader reference to the conditions of its environment. A pragmatic approach, (endorsed by the author) is experiential involving intra-action [7] between artefact and observer, subject and object, user and tool, and emerges through their entanglement with context, history and culture. "Aesthetic interaction promotes bodily experiences as well as complex symbolic representations when interacting with systems" [8].

The dictionary defines 'visceral' as: 1. relating to the viscera: *the visceral nervous system*; 2. relating to deep inward feelings rather than to the intellect. Progenitors of visceral thinking are evident in the literature of design theorists such as Zdislaw Lewalski 1988, Ray Crozier 1994 and Mike Baxter 1995, each developing different terminology to express similar ideas. Lewalski describes what he refers to as "X-values," which express "the order of visual forms" [9]; Ray Crozier's research into psychological responses to design identifies the visceral as a "response to form" [10]; Mike Baxter uses the term "intrinsic attractiveness" to describe something similar [11]. Donald Norman adopted the term "visceral" when he categorized design interaction into three levels – visceral, behavioral and reflective [12].

The visceral level describes the body's immediate gut feeling eliciting subconscious reactions. The body gauges a situation and responds automatically, sending biological signals directly to the muscles to react and to the brain to be on alert. It can automatically decide whether something is dangerous or safe, bad or good, attractive or unattractive. The visceral level is intuitive but it is influenced by the surrounding environment and the other cognitive levels of perception (behavioural or reflective).

Since Norman, others have attempted to describe the visceral using different langauge such as Gerry Cupchik's "sensory/aesthetic response" [13]. More recently Cara Wrigley proffered a synthesis of the whole canon of literature as "visceral hedonic rhetoric framework" [14].

4   Affect and Embodiment

Anthropologist Thomas Csordas posits 'affect' as one of ten components of corporeality to methodologically describe embodiment. According to Csordas the other components are sensory experience, movement or mobility, bodily form, copresence, metabolism/ physiology, capacity, orientation, gender and temporality [15].

Rather than limit our interpretation of the world through the semiotic paradigm of culture as text, a phenomenological paradigm of embodiment offers a complimentary interpretation. The phenomenon of intentionality and existence can be analysed in terms of affect. Our participation in a cultural world is an embodied experience, so in order to think about the future of human computer interaction it is important that designers consider embodiment as part of their methodology. Emotion and cognition are equally influential to thought and behaviour and should not be considered as separate entities. Further, design must go beyond the limitation of human centric perception and recognise the potential of materials and bodies (not only human bodies) as actants. How can wearables draw our attention to the limitations of our current perception and expand our awareness to one that leverages our entanglement with the world around us toward sustainable ways of being? How did we come to have a liminal rather than holistic perception of the world in the first place?

5   Vibrant Materiality

Life is not life, but rock rearranging itself under the sun.

Dorian Sagan [16]

Matter can be observed to change state from a solid body, to liquid and finally gaseous and invisible as in ice, water, steam. In accordance with this observation it was believed prior to the enlightenment that the breath (Greek pneuma, Latin spiritus) seen in cold weather was evidence of the solid human body turning into gas – from body to spirit.

The etymology of 'material' follows a path that leads to our current interpretation of 'immaterial' to mean it's opposite, in other words matter as substance and immaterial as emptiness or nothingness. According to Vilém Flusser immaterial should be understood as full of stuff, meaning something more like amorphous, lacking in form but brimming with matter. The Greek term for wood 'Hylé' was used by philosophers not to refer to wood in general but the type of wood stored in carpenter's workshops. Greek philosophy came up with this term seeking a way to define what is opposite to 'morphé' (Greek for 'form'). Flusser concludes that 'Hylés' use was analogous to our use of amorphous. Greek philosophy's explanation of the world was that of an amorphous stew of phenomena (the material world) that was only revealed to us through theory. Reality consists of forms concealed behind an illusion that is the 'formal world'. "… amorphous phenomena flow into forms, occupy them in order to flow out into the amorphous once again" [17]. Hylé and morphé are opposing concepts, like the English matter/form. So material/immaterial are always the same stuff they are just in different amorphous states. Flusser suggests we think of 'matter' as 'stuff' - which gets stuffed into forms - as a more appropriate contemporary metaphor than that of the carpenter's wood blocks being cut into forms. A parallel idea within a scientific world view is to acknowledge that materials are in a constant state of entropy, where "matter is substance in its intra-active becoming —not a thing, but a doing, a congealing of agency. Matter is a stabilizing and destabilizing process of iterative intra-activity" [18].

6   Scientific Epistemology

In modern science under the influence of Cartesian thought, we took a path that led us in one direction to divide matter into infinitely smaller pieces; and in the other to the speed of light (gas viewed as high energy). Matter and energy, body and spirit, material and time, viewed as opposite to one another. An order of hierarchy fell into place in Western societies under the enlightenment modernity paradigm that placed the human mind at the top and the body below followed by animals, plants, less complex organisms, down to inanimate objects like stone. Human relations to the non-human world continue to be governed by this hierarchal order. We legitimise its structure by valorising one human-centric perspective where all else is viewed as other. Where "rational subjects remake the world as 'objects' – scientific objects, material objects, economic objects, objects of conquest, objects of desire, and so on. These objects are constructed through a gaze that is necessarily reductive since it isolates things from the complexity of systems in which they are immersed" [19].

Contemporary information technology, particularly virtual reality is enabling us to visualise concepts of matter that are closer to the original notion in Flusser's explaination – viewed as temporary filling of forms. At Ars Electronica in 1993 Peter Weibel noted this shift from "defining life as substance, material hardware or mechanism to conceiving life as code, language, immaterial software, dynamical system" [20]. But this faith in the virtual as descriptor of the real has now been unplugged, rather than flipping reality, quantum physics shows us the vibrancy of matter at an atomic level where substance, material and mechanism are viewed as temporary constellations of stuff that are always moving toward a natural state of entropy. Louise Poissant's description seems to grasp this, "the raw material, one must say is algorithmic and abstract and at the same time composed of communicational flux made of sensations, emotions, ideas and exchanges" [21].

7   Moist Media

Life began in the ocean, where water is ambient and life is an immersive experience. With the evolution to life on land, organisms emerged that found ways to mobilise the environmental functions that the ocean had once performed and marine life had taken for granted. Rather than being immersed in the life giving fluid that supports half of the living mass of the world, life on the land evolved portable irrigation systems that connected organisms [22].

"Biota has had to find ways to carry the sea within it, and moreover, to construct watery conduits from 'node' to 'node'" [23]. Over time water enacts the rising of sea level as "the land biota literally carries the sea and its distinctive solutes over the surface of the land" [24].

Following Dianna and Mark McMenamin's notion of life on land as a 'Hypersea', Sadie Plant presented the narrative above in her 1998 publication Digital Women + the New Technoculture. Plant's interest lay in the fuzzy border between land and water. This is the litteral zone, an edge that is never stable but always in a state of flux, where the intra-action of water and land fuse into beaches of silicon.

"Ninety-five percent of the volume of the earths crust is composed of silicates" they are within our bodies as well as the earth. It is this mutual materiality that makes silicon an ideal conduit for our fluid technogenisis. The mechanical limitations of computing are becoming evident, but technological and biological mutation continue the evolutionary process of wearable technology in wetware and new materials science. The tide continues to rise to quantum levels of computing in digital oceans. "What were once discreet media and separable senses have become promiscuous and entwined" [25].

The growth of wetware complements software and hardware. Roy Ascott points out that moist media describes a more coherent network at a biological level [26]. Moist media implies that technological tools and media are not viewed in opposition to humans but form a moist living ecosystem.

8   Object Oriented Ontology

If the world is made of particles and waves, parts or effects, then an object is something in between. Quantum theory posits that objects are only cognitive constructions. This sideways glance has more to do with framing experience, which then appears as a kind of shape shifting. In this light, art and design can provide ways to indirectly gain access to the object. The intense interest, growth and viability of wearables is in part due to their ability to inhabit the in-between, the intra-active space brought to life in the litteral zones of the body and world, private and public, physical and digital. Once we accept that objects are inherently unstable, we need not think of them as being pushed around by processes, particles or perception, rather the instability of objects in a state of quantum coherence is intrinsic. In defence of an object oriented ontology Timothy Morton says that objects are not static but metaphorically they seem to 'breathe', "occupying two positions, vibrating and not vibrating simultaneously" [27].

Wearables bring brain, body and environment back together in an integrated expression where both bodily and intellectual aspects of experience are equally valid. In this sense art and design take an exploratory role and act as conduit to disseminate new ideas. Following Merlo Ponty's phenomenological approach to perception, wearable design takes as its starting point 'embodied interaction' which entails a consideration of "physical, bodily, and social aspects of our interaction with digital technology" [28]. Speculative and critical wearable design practices search for new possibilities, they then test, project and distribute these new definitions.

9   Organic Intra-action

The definition of human-computer interaction traditionally refers to information exchange between human and computer but that definition is too narrow to define the future that will include more corporeal experiences and information exchange between physical world and computers. Jun Rekimoto describes future intra-active systems that aim to mimic the complexity of natural ecosystems "wall systems that will react to human gesture, be aware of the air in the room, and be able to stabilize conditions (such as temperature and humidity) in the same way a cell membrane maintains the stability of a cell environment" [29]. In a similar approach Natalie Jeremijenko's projects demonstrate interface ecologies, practices that interconnect multiple systems to form a whole. "Interfaces are the catalytic border zones where systems of representation meet, mix, and recombine. Through this recombination, interface ecosystems generate fundamental innovations of form, experience, knowledge, and technology" [30].

The title of this article proposes design creativity as sites of intra-action at the interstices of waves and particles. The term intra-action makes a direct reference to Karen Barad's theory of agential realism. The word 'interaction' is based on the assumption that two entities are separate to begin with, 'intra-action' alternatively describes the same space but with full awareness of the agential nature of each entity. In fact, the conception of the object is in some sense inverted or turned inside out. "It is through specific agential intra-actions that the boundaries and properties of the components of phenomena become determinate and that particular concepts (that is, particular material articulations of the world) become meaningful" [31]. Barad offers a theory that hinges on causal relationships between materials and practices which can be viewed as an alternative to representationalism and in this sense intra-action is a profound conceptual shift. Hers is an agential realist ontology, both posthumanist and performative. Wearables represent a media capable of inhabiting and engaging these intra-active interfaces.

"Phenomenon is a dynamic relationality that is locally determinate in its matter and meaning as mutually determined (within a particular phenomenon) through specific causal intra-actions" [32]. In this reframing sustainability becomes an inherent condition of materiality. "Responsibility is not an obligation that the subject chooses but rather an incarnate relation that precedes the intentionality of consciousness. Responsibility is not a calculation to be performed. It is a relation always already integral to the world's ongoing intra-active becoming and not-becoming" [33].

10   Case Studies

Having described a general theoretical approach, in this section three case studies are described that demonstrate speculative design approaches that are open to the perspectives presented. They represent ways that the aforementioned visceral sensibilities can be played out and tested in art and design practice.

10.1   Cross Species Adventure Club

Natalie Jeremijenko's arts practice can be described as experimental design to promote non-violent social change. The Cross Species Adventure Club leverages the visceral aesthetic experience of eating. It consists of an iPhone app, a cookbook and a series of events that explore "food webs, community structure, chemistry, nutrient cycles and the behavior of organisms within complex ecological systems" [34]. In Boston she hosted 'Lures and other Edibles – Adventures in Aquatic Ecosystems' where guests attended a banquet and the molecular gastronomy menu consisted of environmentally conscientious meals. For example, edible fishing lures containing a chelating agent, that when digested by humans or fish, binds the heavy metals in the body so that they can be passed through in a less reactive harmless form as salts. "With the lures, humans and fish share a diet engineered for environmental remediation. Sharing these particular foods promotes an active, interventionist companionship anchored in bodily processes" [35]. One can imagine Jeremijenko's approach combined with naturally occurring nano actuators such as those used by Tangible Media Group at MIT Media Lab in BioLogic. BioLogic is a breathable fabric with vents that open when bacillus subtilis natto, a substance found in fermented soya beans, expands through hygromorphic transformation induced by heat or humidity [36].

10.2   BODYecology

The author's arts practice is developed with an awareness of interconnected systems and visceral sensibility. BODYecology operates in the liminal space between unconscious sleep and material artifact illuminating our contemporary society in a critical sleep crisis. Our culture has a problematic relationship to sleep leading to chronic social jetlag and affiliated illnesses [37]. The industrialization of time, governed by productive work hours leaves sleep as something negative that our body gives-in-to when we can no longer stay awake. Sleep is eroded at each end of the day. Diurnal time is ignored, as we stimulate our bodies to stay awake way past sunset late into the night fueled by electric lights and screens, then in the morning the industrial time of the alarm clock wakes us long before our bodies are fully rested. This repeats all week resulting in social jetlag and then we binge sleep on weekends.

Flanagan's installation consists of a system of connected objects: a bed, a portable dying machine and a weaving loom. Merino lamb's wool is spun into thread and placed into one end of the dying machine, threaded through the system and connected to an empty bobbin at the other end. When set in motion, the wool is drawn through an indigo dye bath and drying box. The bobbin is connected to a pressure sensor on a pillow on the bed adjacent to the box. When Flanagan sleeps the weight of her head on the pillow engages the sensor and the bobbin starts turning. Flanagan's body is connected to the dye machine via a Fitbit. Specifically, the Fitbit communicates to an auger above the dye bath. Three phases of sleep are translated into three positions of the auger. Deep sleep = low in the indigo dye bath, restless = shallow, awake = above the dye level. By the morning the wool has been transferred from one end of the dye machine to the other resulting in a bobbin full of variegated blue thread, the visceral memory of sleep the night before. The thread is then transferred to a shuttle and to the third phase of the system, the weaving loom which sits adjacent to the dying machine. A double weave configuration on a portable loom enables the weaving to be contained in a narrow area. After approximately one month sleeping and weaving, the warps are cut and the blanket unfolded from the loom. The blanket can then be used on the bed, completing the cycle. The performance installation and resulting blanket act as catalyst for discussion and self reflection on sleep. Visitors to the installation spend time in dialogue with the artist sharing their experience of sleep. Through this dialogical methodology future research questions solidify, for example an awareness of changes in sleep patterns can be used as a diagnostic tool to warn mental health sufferers of pending relapses, in bipolar disorder [38]. A future research study proposition is to investigate woolen textiles and their effect on sleep quality in menopausal women (Fig. 1).

Fig. 1. BODYecology 2015 Tricia Flanagan (video still)

10.3   BIOdress

BIOdress is a body-worn interface designed to enhance empathy between human and non-human entities "facilitating interspecies communication with a goal to create an expanded network of embodiment. The overall objective is to encourage human empathy beyond the anthropocentric towards more sustainable development" [39]. BIOdress connects the body to plant and environmental data through visceral and visual communication to evoke awareness and responsibility by human agents for their role in the ecosystem. The BIOdress augments the body's awareness and sensitivity to the life of plants by responding to three parameters (Fig. 2).

Fig. 2. BIOdress 2014, Sara Adhitya, Beck Davis, Tricia Flanagan, Raune Frankjaer, Zoe Mahony, (alphabetically listed).

EMG readings and particulate sensors on a plant induce movement, temperature and color changes on the BIOdress so wearers develop an emotional response to conditions affecting their companion plant. Thermochromatic dyes change the color of the leafy structure of the dress according to particulate levels in the air. Clean air gives a green-brown reading and red-magenta is the response to pollutants. The color change is produced by heating conductive thread embroidered onto the dresses surface, so the color change is felt through the wearers skin as well as witnessed externally by others. The shoulders of the dress are made from thermally pleated organza that expand and contract, metaphorically breathing. Actuators set into the shoulders respond to the particulate sensor reading on the plant. Heavier breathing, i.e. faster motion indicates poorer air quality. Movement of fabric leaves are engineered using shape memory alloy embedded in vein like structures on the dress. The movement reflects the plants activity as gauged by the EMG sensor attached to the surface of one of it's leaves.

"The impact works on a number of levels. As a wearer, one is able to embody the state of the plant and its surrounding environment. As an observer, this information is broadcast to the public domain" [40].

11 Conclusions

Wearables exist in intra-active zones. The living body provides mobility and the frame of reference changes as they enter new environments – cultural, social, climatic, environmental etc. They are open to transformation by media and discourse and are developed with critical interaction in mind – in terms of user/wearer experience. As digital media becomes increasingly intuitive and hidden away within the structures of our clothing and built environments, wearables speak out as a reassertion of the body's haptic, visceral sensibilities in the digital world, an extension of the body's organic and dynamic interface aesthetics [41].

Two perspectives emerge as profound, from one the sensory deterritoralization is conceived as an ontological shift in the materiality of our culture "a necessary consequence of the historically unprecedented interpenetration of the body and media" [42]. The other imagines an unprecedented fluidity between the human body and computer. Steve Mann's humanistic computing for example draws on this formulation where there exists a mutual embedding of both 'body and space' in the primary 'medium' of sensation. Mark Hansen acknowledges these shifts and hypothesises 'the affective body' – "the role of the body as, at once, a *source* for and *activator* of a rich affective constitution of space" [42]. In this way space itself is an attribute of wearables. "Whilst media make space flexible and invisible, it is the body that allows mediated space to be experienced sensorily, precisely as space made wearable" [43].

A visceral approach to design could be viewed as an extra parameter to extend standard approaches to human computer interaction and design user experience and usability, but rather its full potential could be the reinvigoration of current design practices to address anthropocentricism and promulgate sustainable design approaches.

Acknowledgements. Presentation of this research at HCI International 2016 was made possible with the kind support of the University of New South Wales Australia. BODYecology coding by Dr. Kenning Zhu, City University Hong Kong. BIOdress was created at Haptic InterFace workshop at the Wearables Lab, Academy of Visual Arts, Hong Kong Baptist University Hong Kong with technology support by Seeed Studios, Shenzhen. Patricia Flanagan Orcid.org/ 0000-0003-2605-7630.

References

1. Blake, W.: Proverbs of hell. In: Sampson, J.(ed.) The Poetical Works, Including the unpublished French Revolution together with the Minor Prophetic Books and Selections from The Four Zoas, Milton & Jerusalem, p. 247. Oxford University Press, London (2011)
2. Haraway, D.: Multispecies Cosmopolitics: Staying with the Trouble, *2013* Distinguished Lecture, Arizona State University, 5 March 2013. http://syntheticzero.net/2013/07/29/haraway-on-multispecies-cosmopolitics-staying-with-the-trouble/. Accessed 5 Mar 2016
3. Bennett, J.: Vibrant Matter: a Political Ecology of Things. Duke University Press, Durham (2010)
4. Flanagan, P.: The ethics of collaboration in Sunaptic Sculpture. Ctr + P J. Contemp. Art **14**, 37–50 (2011)
5. Hauser, J.: Whose afraid of the in-between? In: Hauser (ed.) Sk-interfaces: Exploring Boarders _Creating Mambrains in Art Technology and Society, pp. 6–7, 11–13, 15–17. Liverpool University Press (2008)
6. Shusterman, R.: Pragmatist Aesthetics: Living Beauty, Rethinking Art, 2nd edn. Rowman and Littlefield, Boston (2000)
7. Barad, K.M.: Meeting the Universe Halfway: Quantum Physics and The Entanglement of Matter and Meaning, p. 139. Duke University Press, Durham (2007)
8. Petersen, G.M., Iversen, O.S., Call, P., Ludwigsen, N.: Aesthetic interaction: a pragmatist's aesthetics of interactive systems. In: Proceedings of the 5th ACM Conference on Designing Interactive Systems Processes, Practices, Methods, and Techniques, p. 274 (2004)
9. Lewalski, Z.: Product Aesthetics: An Interpretation for Designers. Design & Development Engineering Press, Carson City (1988)
10. Crozier, R.: Manufactured Pleasures: Psychological Responses to Design, Manchester University Press, Manchester (1994)
11. Baxter, M.: Product Design: A Practical Guide to Systematic Methods of New Product Development. Chapman & Hall, London (1995)
12. Norman, D.: Emotional Design; Rosalind Picard, pp. 125–162. Affective Computing. MIT Press, Cambridge (1998)
13. Cupchik, G.: Emotion and Industrial Design: Reconciling Means and Feelings (paper presented at the 1st International Conference on Design and Emotion), Delft, The Netherlands, (1999)
14. Wrigley, C.: Design dialogue: the visceral Hedonic Rhetoric framework. Des. Issues **29**(2), 82–95 (2013)
15. Csordas, T.: Somatic modes of attention. Cult. Anthropol. **8**(2), 135 (1993)
16. Sagan, D.: Biospheres. Arkana, London (1980)
17. Flusser, V.: The Shape of Things: A Philosophy of Design. Reaktion, London (1999). Form and Material (1991); trans. Anthony Mathews
18. Barad, K.: Posthumanist performativity: toward an understanding of how matter comes to matter. Signs: J. Women Cult. Soc. **28**(3), 822 (2003)
19. Woods, F.: Hybrid Formations: an Alternative Topology of Human/Animal Relations. http://fionawoodsmusings.blogspot.com.au/2012/10/hybrid-formations-enacting-alternative.html. Accessed 5 Mar 2016
20. Weibel, P.: Life – the unfinished project In: Genetic Art – Artificial Life, pp. 9–10. Vienna: Ars Electronica, PVS (1993)
21. Poissant, L.: The passage from material to interface. In: Grau, O. (ed.) MediaArtHistories, p. 244. The MIT Press, Cambridge (2007)
22. Plant, S.: Zeros and Ones, pp. 248–249. Fourth Estate Limited, London (1997)

23. McMenamin, M., McMenamin, D.: Hypersea: Life on Land, p. 5. Columbia University Press, New York (1994)
24. McMenamin, M., McMenamin, D.: Hypersea: Life on Land, p. 25. Columbia University Press, New York (1994)
25. Plant, S.: Zeros and Ones, vol. 225. Fourth Estate Limited, London (1997)
26. Ascott, R.: Technoetic territories. Perform. Res.: Digit. Resour. **11**(4), 39–40 (2006). Allsopp, R., Delahunta, S. (eds.)
27. Morton, T.: An object orientated defence of poetry. New Literary Hist. **43**(2), 205–224 (2012). Spring 23
28. Svanaes, D.: Interaction design for and with the lived body: some implications of Merleau-Ponty's phenomenology. ACM Trans. Comput.-Hum. Interact. **20**(1), Article 8, March 2013
29. Rekimoto, J.: Organic interaction technologies: from stone to skin. Commun. ACM **51**(6), 44 (2008)
30. Jeremijenko, N., Schiphorst, T., Mateas, M., Strauss, W., Wright, W., Kerne, A.: Extending interface practice: an ecosystem approach. In: Appolloni, T. (ed.) SIGGRAPH 2002, p. 90. ACM (2002)
31. Barad, K.: Meeting the Universe Halfway, Quantum Physics and the Entanglement of Matter and Meaning, vol. 139. Duke University Press, London (2007)
32. Barad, K.: Posthumanist performativity: toward an understanding of how matter comes to matter. Signs **28**(3), 820 (2003)
33. Barad, K.: Diffracting diffraction: cutting together-apart. Parallax **20**(3), 183 (2014)
34. Jeremijenko, N.: The X-Species Adventure Club brochure. http://goo.gl/1SpJNJ. Accessed 5 Mar 2016
35. Kelley, L.: Digesting wetlands. In: Third International Conference on Transdisciplinary Imaging at the Intersections of Art, Science and Culture, Cloud and Molecular Aesthetics, Istanbul, Turkey, 26–28 July 2014
36. Tangible Media Group. https://vimeo.com/tangiblemedia. Accessed 9 Feb 2016
37. Wittmann, M., Dinich, J., Merrow, M., Roenneberg, T., Jetlag, S.: Misalignment of biological and social time. Chronobiol. Int. **23**(1–2), 497–509 (2006)
38. Foster, R.G., Peirson, S., Wulff, K., Winnebeck, E., Vetter, C., Roenneberg, T.: Sleep and circadian rhythm disruption in social jetlag and mental illness. Prog. Molec. Biol. Trans. Sci. **119**, 325–346 (2013)
39. Adhitya, S., Davis, B., Frankjaer, R., Flanagan, P., Mahony, Z., The BIOdress: a body-worn interface for environmental embodiment. In: TEI 2016 Proceedings of the TEI 2016: Tenth International Conference on Tangible, Embedded, and Embodied Interaction, 14–17 February, pp. 627–634 (2016)
40. Adhitya, S., Davis, B., Frankjaer, F., Flanagan, P., Mahony, Z., The BIOdress: a body-worn interface for environmental embodiment In: TEI 2016 Proceedings of the TEI 2016: Tenth International Conference on Tangible, Embedded, and Embodied Interaction, 14–17 February, pp. 627–634 (2016)
41. Ryan, S.E.: Social fabrics: wearable + media + interconnectivity. Leonardo **42**(2), 116 (2009)
42. Hansen, M.: Wearable space. Configurations **10**(2), 322 (2002)
43. Hansen, M.: Wearable space. Configurations **10**(2), 369 (2002)

A Study of Attributes of Affective Quality Affecting Judgment of Beauty for Simple Graphic User Interfaces

Shih-Miao Huang[1(✉)], Wu-Jeng Li[1], and Shu-Chu Tung[2]

[1] Department of Mechanical Design Engineering, National Formosa University, Yunlin, Taiwan
{smhuang,wujeng}@nfu.edu.tw
[2] Department of Environmental Engineering, Kun Shan University, Tainan, Taiwan
shuchu@mail.ksu.edu.tw

Abstract. This article argues that aesthetic preference judgment might not depend on aesthetic prototypes, but on object's affective qualities. That is, when an object is presented, one perceives not only its feature organization, but also the perceived affective quality where it presents in some specific situations. Therefore, this study tries to find out the attributes of affective qualities which would be factors influencing user aesthetic preferences for system interfaces. Item analysis, Factor analysis and Regression analysis, were conducted to find the typical attributes of affective quality which could significantly explain the variances of aesthetic preferences. The results showed that six adjective terms of affective quality can be used to predict beauty: "Delicate", "Unique", "Robust", "Tight", "Fierce", "Mysterious", "Assertive" and "Traditional". The outcomes indicate that a delicate appearance of interactive skins is most important to design an aesthetic skin. The skin with the feelings of "Assertive", and "Robust" are well received. However, designers have to avoid design a skin with a tight feeling.

Keywords: Affective quality · Aesthetic preferences · Simple skins

1 Introduction

1.1 Factors Affecting Aesthetic Preferences

Aesthetics, which refers to "beauty" in this study, pertains to a sense of what is beautiful and visually pleasing. Previous studies tried to find out factors which influenced human judgment of beauty. However, physical features, aesthetic prototypes and the arousal theory do not properly explain the factors that influence audience aesthetic preferences. An interface does not only include one attribute; on the contrary, it includes many attributes with varied levels. Huang et al. classified interface attributes into six categories [1]. They are "Form elements", "Form organization", "Interactive features", "Stylistic quality", "Feeling quality", and "Emotional quality" from low to high construct. The previous discussion of physical features, aesthetic prototypes and the arousal theory on aesthetic preferences focuses on the influences of "Form elements", "Form organization", "Interactive features", "Stylistic quality". However, when an object is presented, one perceives not only its form quality, but also the perceived affective quality even audiences do not know the content, or knowledge, of the object [2]. For example, one

© Springer International Publishing Switzerland 2016
A. Marcus (Ed.): DUXU 2016, Part II, LNCS 9747, pp. 16–24, 2016.
DOI: 10.1007/978-3-319-40355-7_2

admired the beauty of a sunset scene not because of the knowledge of the scene, but the scene itself elicited an affective quality, "glory". Possibly jumping off the inherent frameworks of object configuration into knowledge of emotion involved might be a feasible way to find factors of aesthetic preferences. It is worth to explore if affective qualities of system interfaces would be factors influencing user aesthetic preferences.

Among these six levels of attributes, "affective quality" referred to object's attributes to arousing human feelings which can be expressed with affective terms, such as cute, vivacious, hard, soft ... etc. Affective quality is a stimulus' ability to cause a change in core affect which is a neurophysiological state [3]. One feels an object is cute because it just causes him a cute feeling without any reasons. "Emotional quality" referred to object's attributes to arousing one's emotional responses. This kind of attributes is to describe human emotional responses, such as, sad, happy, exciting ..., etc. The terms belonged to this attribute also includes affective adjectives which imply good or bad values, such as sad, scared, bored or excited. The terms belonged to this attribute could be arranged with two approaches: the discrete emotion approach, and the dimensional approach [4]. Compared with Norman's [5] three levels of emotional responses, "Form elements", "Form organization", and "Stylistic quality" would arouse visceral emotional responses; "Interactive features" would arouse behavioral responses. In addition, affective quality is the feeling description of both visceral and behavioral responses evoked from the object. Emotion quality is a kind of mood description reflecting from objects in a reflective level. Both affective quality and emotional quality influence emotional responses in the reflective level.

1.2 Varied Rating Consistency for Different Attribute Levels

As rated to describe the same object, the terms in lower level of constructs, i.e., attributes, such as, "clean," or "symmetrical" belonged to form elements, are rated more consistent than those in higher construct (ex. Cute in affective quality category). The judgment of a low level product attribute (e.g. colorful) was clear and predictable for all audiences; however, the judgment of a high level product attribute (e.g. cheerful) was varied from different audiences. Besides, a low level attribute of a product might induce a high level affect. For example, the objects with "order" (form organization) feeling might arouse audience's feeling of legibility (interactive quality).

It was found that previous studies did not find the identical affective dimensions to predict aesthetic preferences after reviewing the articles related to affective dimensions. It is possibly that those studies mixed up all attributes in different levels and did not discriminate affective meanings from the other product attributes when searching for key affective dimensions. For example, Hsiao and Chen [6] extracted four fundamental dimensions in the affective responses: "trend factor", "emotion factor", "complexity factor" and the "potency factor" from 28 adjective pairs. However, the adjective pairs used in their study include Excited–calm, Elegant–not elegant, Avant garde–conservative, and Streamlined–rugged, belonged to the attributes of emotional quality, affective quality, stylistic quality and form elements, respectively. Besides, Lavie and Tractinsky [7] also found a two-dimensional structure for perceived aesthetics: classical and expressive aesthetics. The classical aesthetics refers to orderliness in design, including descriptions such as "clean," "pleasant," "symmetrical" and "aesthetic". The expressive aesthetics indicates designers' creativity and originality, and can be described by "sophisticated," "creative," "uses special effects" and "fascinating." "Clean," "pleasant," "symmetrical" are belonged to different attributes. Moreover, Kim and Moon [8] found that the emotion space is defined by seven dimensions including attractiveness, symmetry, sophistication, trustworthiness, awkwardness, elegance, and simplicity to evaluate immediate affective feelings about cyber-banking system interfaces. Obviously, their outcomes are not consistent because they mixed up all attributes in different levels. Therefore, this study will explore the affective dimensions only with the terms in affective quality, excluding the other levels of object attributes.

1.3   Effects of Affective Quality and Emotional Quality on Aesthetics

Huang et al. [9] explored both effects of affective quality and emotional quality on aesthetic preferences of complicate skins by using path analysis. He found that all the attributes in emotional quality did not well predict interactive skin aesthetics, but the attributes in affective quality could predict skin aesthetics well by judging R-squares of their regression models. He found seven key attributes of feeling quality selected into the aesthetic predicted model, Delicate, Hi-tech, Formal, Fierce, Unique, Tight and Robust. The outcomes implied that skin appearances with the feelings of "Hi-tech", "Formal", "Fierce", "Unique" and "Robust" were well received. A delicate appearance of interactive skins was most important to design an aesthetic skin, but the skins with a tight feeling were the worst. He also explained why emotional quality did not influence subject aesthetic preferences. He argued that one's emotional feelings evoking from an objects would be translated into affective quality he felt, in light of the reflective level of emotional responses. For example, a dreadful skin might be deemed as a fun skin because subjects perceive the "fun" meaning of the dreadful skin and enjoyed its fun. That is, subjects received a fun feeling which belonged to affective quality, but no more than emotional quality. Therefore, this paper would only focus on effects of affective quality on aesthetic judgment; the other levels of attributes are excluded based on Huang's findings.

1.4   Complexity vs. Simplicity Skins

Osgood [10] found that the E-P-A structures of affective meanings might be not existed when the rated objects were not "noun". It implies that the affective structures would be identical when the rated objects are the same whoever the subjects are. Therefore, affective structures of complex skins might not be the same as those of simple one if different levels of complexity of interactive skins could not be deemed as the same "concept". Therefore, it is worth to explore if different levels of complexity of interactive skins share the same affective structures. Huang et al. [9] had used complex skins selected from Windows media player to explore the affective structures of complex skins. This study will only focus on the findings of affective structures of simple skins. Besides, both affective structures will be compared to explore if they have the same structures.

1.5 Purpose

To sum up, the main purpose of this paper is to find the typical attributes of affective quality which could significantly predict aesthetic preference of skins. Before that it is necessary to find out the affective structures of simple skins of interactive interfaces. Besides, this paper also tried to explore the similarity of both affective structures to describe simple and complex skins, respectively.

2 Methods

Item analysis was performed to selection adjective terms which could be used to describe objects' attributes of affective quality firstly. Secondly, Factor analysis was used to find out affective structures from those adjective terms which could describe simple interactive skins. Finally, Regression analysis was conducted to find those affective structures could significantly predict aesthetic preferences of skins.

2.1 Item Analysis

Firstly, 628 feeling terms were written respectively on cards in Chinese and divided into five card groups. They were collected from resources including studies related to affective design in journals, catalogues, books and websites. Those adjectives not written in Chinese were translated into Traditional Chinese. Afterwards, five female teachers who have five year experiences at least in teaching Chinese in Junior High school arranged each one of card groups with kin diagram, respectively. Kin diagram refers to a diagram in which the terms with close conceptual affinity are put closely. Finally, those adjective terms were condensed into 296 adjective pairs.

Next, item analysis was used to discard the affective adjectives which cannot distinguish subject affects evoked from skins among 296 pairs. There are two steps to perform item analysis: semantic differential and screening with criteria.

Semantic Differential. Sixteen windows media player skins selected from Ms-office official website were rated with the 296 adjective pairs. Considering the reliability of subject ratings, the "independent" pair and "familiar" pair are replicated. Totally, 298 adjective pairs were used in the experiment. If the correlations between original pairs and replicated pairs are high, the reliability of subject ratings is high to accept the outcomes of the Semantic differential. Forty-six subjects rated the skins with a 7-point Likert scale. The test was programmed with Director 8.0 and performed on a 20" TFT LCD screen. There are 736 (46 × 16) rating scores, called Raters' opinions, for each adjective pair.

Criteria Screening. Six criteria were used to screen out the adjective pairs which cannot discriminate differences among skins according to the rating scores of semantic differential. First, the selection score of each adjective pair was added 1, respectively, when three criteria, Mean, Variance and skewness of each affective meaning are between 1 and −1, Variance > 0.1.5, or Skewness < 0.7, respectively. Next, Correlation of Internal

Consistency (CR) was performed. The 736 rating scores were arranged from low to high scores for each adjective pair, and divided into four groups. The group with the higher scores than other groups was called High Score Group (HSG); the group with the lower scores than other groups was called Low Score Group (LSG). The selection score of each adjective pair was added 1 when its rating scores of HSG significantly differed from those of LSG at a significant level, 0.01, which could discriminate Raters' opinions significantly. Besides, The selection score of each adjective pair was added 1 if their item-to-total-score correlations or factor loadings were larger than 0.3. Finally, the adjective pairs were selected if their selection scores were larger than 3. Consequently, 123 adjective pairs were remained. Furthermore, the previous five Chinese teachers were recruited again to pick up the adjective pairs belonged to the attributes of affective quality from the 123 adjective pairs. Finally, 75 adjective pairs were chosen.

2.2   Factor Analysis

Factor analysis was used in this experiment to condense the 75 pairs into typical attributes of affective quality. Twelve simple mobile phone skins with different color combinations were used as interactive skins shown in Fig. 1. There are named as simple skins because the icons in the skins are presented only with varied both figure and background colors as compared to the skins of Windows Media Player.

Fig. 1. Twelve simple mobile phone skins with different color combinations (Color figure online)

These twelve icons and color combinations were selected from the experimental material of Huang [11] who evaluated 3306 color combinations with their rating consistency and aesthetic preference. Huang [11] believed that the best color combinations do not only get high aesthetic preference scores, but also have high rating consistency among subjects. The twelve interfaces includes those that have high, middle and low preference rating consistence with high and middle aesthetic rating respectively in his study. For example, in Fig. 1 HH01 and HH02 have a higher aesthetic score and the highest rating consistency.

43 undergraduate students were recruited and asked to perform ranking tests which were programmed with Director 8.0 for all adjective pairs shown in Fig. 2. If feeling the skin is closer to the adjective on the bottom, subjects dragged it into the gray block closer to left on the bottom row. The skins can be moved in or out the blocks with time, or

frequency, limited. For reducing fatigue effect, subjects spent three days to complete the rankings. Each day only performed 25 ranking tests.

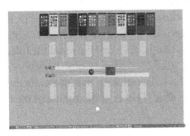
(a) An initial rakning test page

(b) Test page after finished

Fig. 2. The screens used in the experiment

The outcomes found that there were 8 factors which eigenvalue are larger than 1. They are "Delicate", "Unique", "Robust", "Tight", "Fierce", "Mysterious", "Assertive" and "Traditional". The 8 factors can explain 63.81 % variance of the model. Huang et al. [9] found the 11 typical attributes of affect quality for complex skins: "delicate", "unique", "robust", "Hi-tech", "tight", "saucy", "fierce", "mysterious", "exaggerated", "formal" and "pure". Obviously, the number of attributes of affective quality for complex skins is more than that of simple skins. The outcome seems to suggest that complex skins could present more typical attributes than simple ones.

2.3 Regression Analysis

Regression analysis was to find out the typical affective meanings which could predict aesthetic preferences of simple skins. Like experiment 2, subjects performed ranking tasks programmed with Director 8.0. 12 simple skins in Fig. 2 were used again in this experiment; however, the adjective pairs as scales to rate simple skins were a "beauty-ugly" pair plus 8 typical attributes of affective quality from experiment 2.

43 undergraduate students performed ranking tasks which are the same as experiment 2 shown on computer screen. Believing that the feeling evoked from the skin is closer to the adjective on the top, subjects dragged the skin into the gray block closer to left on the top row. Likewise, if they believe their feelings evoked from the skin is closer to the adjective on the bottom, subjects dragged the skin into the block closer to left on the bottom row. The scores of the skins on the blocks from top left to top right are 12 to 7, respectively; from bottom left to bottom right are 1 to 6, respectively.

The scores of beautiful pair were regarded as the scores of aesthetic preferences of the skins. Moreover, aesthetic preference is as a dependent variable; the other adjective pairs are deemed as independent variables. Each model has an R-square to describe the variances of aesthetic preference explained by the terms in affective quality. The model with larger R-square than the other could be a better model to predict aesthetic preference.

3 Results and Discussions

The Regression model shows that the six typical attributes of affective quality can significantly predict skin aesthetic preferences shown on Table 1. They are "Delicate", "Unique", "Robust", "Tight", "Fierce", "Mysterious", "Assertive" and "Traditional". The adjusted R-square is 0.474. The Collinearity diagnoses also show that the tolerances of "Delicate" (0.860), "Unique" (0.775), "Tight" (0.673), "Mysterious" (0.805), "Assertive" (0.891), and "Robust" (0.766) are close to 1. It indicates that these attributes of affective quality do not depend linearly on each other. That is, the estimate of the regression model is more stability.

Table 1. Regression model of simple interfaces

Variables	Un-standardized		Standardized	t	Sig	Tolerance
	B-estimate	Standard error	Beta			
Constant	5.338	.565		9.446	.000	
Delicate	.418	.040	.418	10.457	.000	.860
Unique	−.115	.042	−.115	−2.736	.007	.775
Tight	−.248	.045	−.248	−5.492	.000	.673
Mysterious	−.177	.041	−.177	−4.280	.000	.805
Assertive	.225	.039	.225	5.727	.000	.891
Robust	.153	.042	.153	3.623	.000	.766
Fierce	−.077	.042	−.077	−1.826	.069	.772

Besides, "Delicate" (β-weight = 0.418) is the most important attributes of affective quality to influence aesthetic preference. The second important feeling term is "Assertive" (β-weight = 0.225). However, "Tight" has a negative β-weight (−0.248). The outcomes indicate that a delicate appearance of interactive skins is most important to design an aesthetic skin and that the skin appearances with the feelings of "Assertive", and "Robust" are well received. However, designers have to avoid design a skin with a tight feeling.

Huang et al. [9] found the 7 typical attributes of affect quality for complex skins. This study finds 6 typical attributes of affect quality for simple skins. Both path diagrams of attributes predicting aesthetic references are shown in Fig. 3. Four attributes can significantly predict aesthetic preferences for both simple and complex skins: "delicate", "unique", "tight", and "robust". These evidences showed that the skins should present more intensity of delicate feelings, but not tight feelings for creating aesthetic appearances for both complex and simple skins.

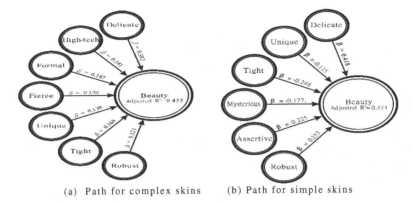

(a) Path for complex skins   (b) Path for simple skins

Fig. 3. Both path diagrams of attributes predicting aesthetic references

The similarity of both Regression analysis models of aesthetic prediction for complex skins and simple skins were calculated as below:

$$\left[\left(\frac{4}{7}\right) + \left(\frac{4}{6}\right)\right] \div 2 = 61.90\,\%$$

The score of similarity (61.90 %) for both models is moderate. It indicates that the affective structures of both complex and simple skins are not entirely identical.

The outcomes show that the number of attributes for complex skins is more than for simple skins. The reason might be that subject's affective responses to both skins are different. For experiment tasks of complex skins, subjects had to operate the skins to play music before they rated the skins. However, for experiment tasks of simple skins, subjects only looked at the skins and judged their affective quality. In other words, the responses of subjects to complex skins involved two affective levels: visceral responses and behavioral responses in light of Norman's views of affective responses [5]. However, their responses to simplex skins only involved visceral affective responses. Therefore, the outcomes show that only four attributes of affective quality could affect aesthetic preferences for both complex skins and simple skins. This outcome seems to imply that factors affecting aesthetic preferences would be varied when affective responses are in different levels (i.e. visceral responses and behavioral responses). However, four attributes would commonly affect skin aesthetic preferences whether subjects' responses are in visceral or behavioral levels. These four attributes are "Delicate", "unique", "tight", and "robust". It suggests that these four attributes might have to be satisfied in skin design.

Acknowledgments. The authors would like to thank the Ministry of Science and Technology, Taiwan for financially supporting this research (MOST 103-2221-E-150-051).

References

1. Huang, S.-M., Li, E.-J., Lin, J.-C.: Investigating the typical affective meanings influencing interactivity of interactive products for Chinese-speaking users. Appl. Mech. Mater. **311**, 316–321 (2013)
2. Huang, S.-M.: A study of affective meanings predicting aesthetic preferences of interactive skins. In: 2015 IEEE International Conference on Industrial Engineering and Engineering Management, pp. 1781–1785. IEEM Press, Bangkok (2013)
3. Russell, J.A.: Core affect and the psychological construction of emotion. Psychol. Rev. **110**(1), 145–172 (2003)
4. Scherer, K.R.: What are emotions? And how can they be measured? Soc. Sci. Inf. **44**(4), 695–729 (2005)
5. Norman, D.A.: Emotional Design: Why We Love (or Hate) Everyday Things. Basic Books, New York (2004)
6. Hsiao, K., Chen, L.: Fundamental dimensions of affective responses to product shapes. Int. J. Ind. Ergon. **36**, 553–564 (2006)
7. Lavie, T., Tractinsky, N.: Assessing dimensions of perceived visual aesthetics of web sites. Int. J. Hum.-Comput. Stud. **60**, 269–298 (2004)
8. Kim, J., Moon, J.Y.: Designing towards emotional usability in customer interfaces – trustworthiness of cyber-banking system interfaces. Interact. Comput. **10**(1), 1–29 (1998)
9. Huang, S.-M., Tung, S.-C., Li, W.-J.: Relationships between aesthetic preferences and both affective quality and feeling quality of graphic user interfaces. In: 2015 International Conference on Applied System Innovation, Osaka, Japan, 22–27 May 2015
10. Osgood, C.E.: Studies on the generality of affective meaning systems. Am. Psychol. **17**, 10–28 (1962)
11. Huang, S.-M.: Rating consistency of aesthetic preference for various icons-background color combinations. Appl. Ergon. **43**, 141–150 (2012)

A Scheme for Representing Beneficial Inconvenience

Hiroshi Kawakami[1]([✉]), Toshihiro Hiraoka[1], and Yuichi Hasebe[2]

[1] Kyoto University, Kyoto, Japan
kawakami@design.kyoto-u.ac.jp
[2] Sony Corporation, Tokyo, Japan

Abstract. This paper proposes a representation scheme of human-machine interaction that provides users with beneficial inconvenience. The scheme consists of three layers. The top layer represents user-dependent subjective matters, and the middle layer describes inconvenience as an objective phenomenon that creates opportunities to get objective benefits. The bottom contains a task-achievement model whose basic structure is a triangle relation among user, object, and system, based on Vygotsky's insight into human activities. This paper demonstrates the performance of our scheme by representing typical situations for obtaining beneficial inconveniences in a uniform construction. This scheme can also be used as a testing ground of *fuben-eki* designs. *Fuben-eki* stands for the benefits of inconvenience, and a *fuben-eki* design means a design that appreciates the concept of *fuben-eki*.

Keywords: Representation scheme · System design · Human machine system · Benefit of inconvenience

1 Introduction

Assuming that convenience means saving time and reducing effort, efficiency and high functionality provide convenience to users, but the disadvantage of solely pursuing it has been an open question for some time [1]. One typical way for pursuing convenience is automatization. But the US federal aviation administration reported that the continual use of autoflight systems could lead to the degradation of a pilot's ability to quickly recover aircraft from undesired states [2]. The recent developments of vehicle automation systems will remove the fun of operating vehicles from drivers and shift their responsibility from active operators to passive observers [3].

This paper focuses on human-machine interactions. Interactive tools require time and effort. In this sense, one aspect of the research on interactions is investigating beneficial inconveniences, some of which are beneficial for interactions, even though not every one provides benefits.

To investigate the conditions for beneficial inconveniences, we collected positive and negative examples. The former include

© Springer International Publishing Switzerland 2016
A. Marcus (Ed.): DUXU 2016, Part II, LNCS 9747, pp. 25–33, 2016.
DOI: 10.1007/978-3-319-40355-7_3

- a cell production system instead of a line production system
- barrier-aree (aree is a Japanese word that means existence) instead of barrier-free.

Compared with a line production system, a cell production system is superficially inconvenient because it requires that workers have the skills to assemble such complex productions as automobiles in small groups. But it does allow them to be skilled and encourages them to understand production. Compared with barrier-free, barrier-aree introduces such minor obstacles as differences in floor levels on purpose to maintain physical abilities [4].

The collected examples can be classified into two groups:

G-1 interactions between artifacts and users
G-2 methods, rules, or policies.

A cell production system and barrier-aree belong to G-2. Positive examples provide users opportunities to get the following benefits of inconvenience [5]:

- fostering affirmative feelings
- providing motivation for tasks
- reassurance
- enhanced awareness
- prompting system understanding
- personalization.

2   Representation Scheme

Our proposed scheme is for G-1 and can represent all of its positive examples and eliminate all of its negative examples. The scheme consists of three layers (Fig. 1). The top layer represents user-dependent subjective matters: perceived efforts and benefits. The middle layer states an inconvenience as an objective phenomenon that creates opportunities to get objective benefits. The bottom layer contains

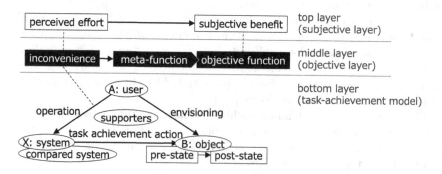

Fig. 1. Basic structure of proposed scheme

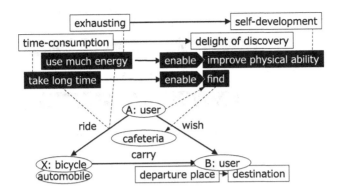

Fig. 2. Example that represents benefits of inconvenience

a task-achievement model (TAM), whose basic structure is a triangle relation among A (user), B (object), and X (system). TAM is based on Vygotsky's insight into human activities [6] and the abstracted action model [7].

Figure 2 shows an example of G-1. Compared with an automobile, a bicycle is superficially inconvenient in the sense of time-consumption when the task is moving over long distances. But it enhances the awareness of several things along the way. It may enable bicycle users to find a cafeteria, which is overlooked when traveling by car. If the user perceives time-consumption as a matter of inconvenience and feels that it is beneficial to find her favorite place to eat, this situation is a positive example of *fuben-eki*, which denotes a viewpoint that embraces the benefits of inconvenience.

2.1 Top and Middle Layers

Since the benefits of inconvenience are emotional, e.g., reassurance, affirmative feelings, and motivation, they cannot be scaled in a quantitative manner. So this paper measures them by an ordinal scale. Humans can directory perceive the quasi-order of emotions without physical scales [8].

The positive aspects of inconvenience are classified into two groups:

– Objective functions
– Subjective benefits

Subjective benefits are represented in the top layer, but they cannot be directory related to inconveniences. As an explanatory mediator between them, the middle layer introduces objective functions and represents objectively observable inconveniences and functions. The top layer consists of subjectively perceived efforts and benefits.

In the top and middle layers of Fig. 1, arrows denote causal relations and their directions are from causes and effects. By inconveniences (the left part of the middle layer), users perceive their own consumption efforts (the left part of the top layer), and objective functions (the right part of the middle layer) are

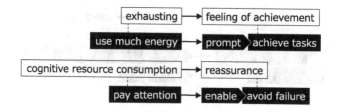

Fig. 3. Examples of top and middle layers

also derived by inconveniences. When users recognize subjective benefits with the help of perceived efforts and objective functions, such subjective benefits are called *fuben-eki*.

Even though taking a long time is generally inconvenient, it allows users to make long-term commitments to systems that might provide opportunities for discovery. Figure 2 shows this situation. In this case, the delight of discovery is enhanced by time-consumption.

The upper part of Fig. 3 shows a situation where inconveniences impose a great energy expenditure on users to achieve a task, and she perceives it as exhausting. However she might be filled with a sense of achievement, which is not only derived by the fact that the task is achieved but by recognizing her contribution to it. The feeling cannot be obtained without the subjective perception of an effort.

The lower part of Fig. 3 shows another example. Focusing on avoiding failure is inconvenient when users feel that their cognitive resources are being consumed, but the situation where failures are avoided not by a black box but by themselves reassures users.

Meta Functions in the Middle Layer: Objective functions are classified as follows:

- enabling (allowing) investments of time and effort
- enabling (allowing) collateral functions
- prompting action
- prompting task-achievement

Each objective function is composed of a noun phrase and such a meta-function [9] as enable or prompt.

2.2 Bottom Layer

In the bottom layer, a task-achievement model (TAM) or a combination of TAMs is represented. The basic structure of TAM is a triangle relation among A (user), B (object), and X (system), based on Vygotsky's insight into human activities [6]. By introducing the notions of the abstracted action model [7], arrows from A to X, from A to B, and from X to B denote an operation, its envisioning, and a task-achievement action, respectively. The task-achievement is

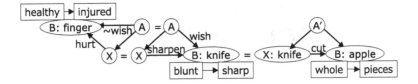

Fig. 4. Combinations of TAMs

represented by the state transition of B. Additionally, for representing inconvenience, another system belongs to B. Inconvenience can only be defined by comparing an inconvenient system with a convenient one.

3   Representation of Beneficial Inconveniences

Inconvenience requires users to invest time and effort for the following reasons:

- operating systems
- envisioning task-achievement
- just waiting for task-achievement by systems
- preparation for achieving tasks
- conscious attention to possible mistakes.

The differences of such types of investigation are represented by the differences of the destination of the links from the objective layer (dashed lines in middle part of Fig. 2) to the arrows in TAM (solid arrows at bottom part of Fig. 2):

Arrow from A to X denotes time and effort for operations,
Arrow from A to B denotes time and effort for envisioning,
Arrow from X to B denotes time and effort for just waiting.

Other types are drawn by combinations of TAMs (Fig. 4). The center triangle is the preparation of the main task, which is represented by the right triangle. By unifying the B of the center triangle with the X of the right triangle, two triangles are joined and the scheme sketches for sharpening a knife take the position of preparing the main task: cutting an apple. By unifying A and X of the center triangle with A and X of the left triangle, conscious attention to possible mistakes is represented, where user A does not wish to cut himself while sharpening a knife.

3.1   Inconvenience of Operation (Between A and X)

Typical inconveniences when interacting with a system arise while operating it. In this case, the inconvenience described in the middle layer is linked with the operation arrow between A and X (user and system) in the bottom layer

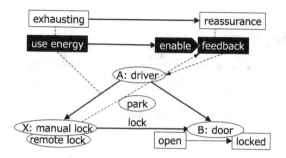

Fig. 5. Locking a door: example of A-X driven inconvenience that leads to reassurance

(Figs. 1 and 2). Figure 2 shows an example where riding (operating) a bicycle is more inconvenient than driving an automobile.

Figure 5 shows another example of inconvenience for operating systems. Compared with remote locking, manual locking is inconvenient because it requires relatively difficult operations. However, it concretely informs users that the lock worked by the reaction force of the twisting hand and by the noise as each door is locked. Such feedback is represented by dashed arrows between the middle and bottom layers in Fig. 5

3.2   Inconvenience of Envisioning (Between A and B)

Other than operations, envisioning task-achievement also consumes time and effort. Consider sharpening a pencil by a knife; users need to think about the desired shapes of the pencil. Convenient electric sharpeners do not require such thought. In other words, the convenience does not allow users into sharpen pencils in their favorite shapes.

In this case, the inconvenience described in the middle layer is linked with the envisioning arrow between A and B (user and object) in the bottom layer.

3.3   Inconvenience of Waiting (Between X and B)

Consider the task of sending a message over a long distance. Compared with e-mail, postal mail is inconvenient because it takes much longer. This inconvenience is different from that shown in Fig. 4, where an operation takes time. In this case, what takes time is not the operation but the task achieved by an action by X (system). The inconvenience described in the middle layer is linked with the arrow of the task-achievement action between X and B (system and object) in the bottom layer (Fig. 6).

3.4   Other Inconveniences

Preparation: For relaxation at a hot spring, we need to travel to a hot spring inn. For cutting ingredients with a knife, we need to sharpen it. Moving to an

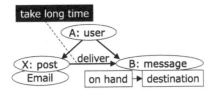

Fig. 6. Postal mail: example of *X-B* driven inconvenience

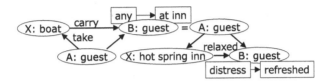

Fig. 7. Example of preparation-tasks driven inconvenience

inn and sharpening a knife are preparations for the main tasks. Generally, they are said to be inconvenient, but the difficulty of reaching inns is beneficial for attracting guests to secluded hot springs.

Inconvenient preparations are represented by combining TAMs. Figure 4 shows an example of knife sharpening, and Fig. 7 shows a secluded inn. The inn is surrounded by a channel, and guests need to take a boat to get to it. In the figure, by unifying the *A* of the main task with the *B* of preparation, two TAMs are combined.

Conscious Attention of Possible Mistakes: Conscious attention of possible mistakes is also represented by combining TAMs. Figure 4 shows an example how knife sharpening might cut fingers. The state transition of *B* of the left most triangle is imagined and *A* (user) wants to avoid it.

Figure 8 shows another example. Compared with digital cameras, traditional cameras are inconvenient because film must be loaded into them and the number of pictures is also limited. Therefore, user need to concentrate on camera-

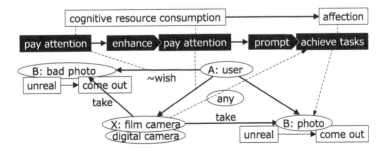

Fig. 8. Camera: example of conscious-attention driven inconvenience that leads to affection to photos

operation to avoid mistakes. In the middle layer of the figure, attention to avoid mistakes enhances the attention to operate the camera.

4 Discussion and Conclusions

This paper proposed a model for representing human-machine interactions that provides the benefits of inconvenience and demonstrated its ability by representing typical cases. The main purpose of the present paper is to provide a uniform grammar to describe each case, but the ability of our proposed scheme is not confined to representation. It can be applicable to a *fuben-eki* design.

Design Support by Analogical Reasoning: Since the structure of our proposed scheme is simple, the scheme enables comparisons among completely different systems. Such comparison leads to analogical reasoning of the latent benefits of normal systems based on known *fuben-eki* systems. For example, sharpening pencils by a knife takes longer than by an electric sharpener, and moving by bicycle also takes longer than by automobile. Considering travel by bicycle provides the delight of discovery, and sharpening by knife has the potential of designing a tool that enables users to discover the latent features of pencils.

Negative Example Elimination: Our proposed scheme can be used as a format to check whether an inconvenience provides subjective benefits. It explains how the activity, which is described in the bottom layer, leads to subjective feelings of inconveniences and benefits described in the top layer.

If an interaction between systems and users cannot be represented by the proposed scheme, the interaction cannot provide the benefits of inconvenience. For example, single-lens reflex cameras are more inconvenient than compact cameras because they require difficult operations, but they also provide high-quality images. When the delight of getting high-quality pictures is placed in the slot of the subjective benefits in the top layer and the slot of the perceived effort is filled with the difficulty of operations, there are no causal relations between them. Such a situation is unacceptable. On the other hand, when intense cerebrations lead to understanding the mechanism of cameras, and cerebration efforts lead to emotional attachment to photos, this situation can be represented by the scheme and is acceptable.

References

1. Norman, D.A.: Human centered design considered harmful. Interactions **12**(4), 14–19 (2005)
2. Federal Aviation Administration: Safety Alert for Operators, vol. 13002 (2013)
3. Endsley, M.R.: Automation and Situation Awareness: Automation and Human Performance: Theory and Applications, pp. 163–181. Lawrence Erlbaum, Mahwah (1996)
4. Fujiwara, S.: No need to be strong, all you have to be not-weak. Toyo Keizai Inc. (2010) (in Japanese)

5. Hasebe, Y., Kawakami, H., Hiraoka, T., Naito, K.: Card-type tool to support divergent thinking for embodying benefits of inconvenience. Web Intell. **13**(2), 93–102 (2015)
6. Vygotsky, L.S.: Mind in Society. Harvard University Press, Cambridge (1978)
7. Sumita, K., et al.: An ontological consideration on essential properties of the notion of "service". Trans. Japan. Soc. Artif. Intell. **27**(3), 176–192 (2012)
8. Gibson, J.: The Senses Considered as Perceptual Systems. Houghton Mifflin, Boston (1983)
9. Kitamura, Y., Mizoguchi, R.: A framework for systematization of functional knowledge based on ontological engineering. J. Eng. Des. **15**(4), 327–351 (2004)

The Emotion and Personality User Perception in Multi-screen Interaction

In-Chu Liao[1(✉)], Yi-Shin Deng[1], and Hsiao-Chen You[2]

[1] Institute of Creative Industries Design, National Cheng Kung University, Tainan, Taiwan
forevelyn@gmail.com, yishin.deng@gmail.com
[2] Department of Multimedia Design, National Taichung University of Science and Technology, Taichung, Taiwan
hcyous@gmail.com

Abstract. With the emergence of multi-screen services, this new technological advancement allowed users to consume their desired content according to their needs and through different contexts. Prior research from the field have shown that users were able to identify specific personalities for products. However, personality was determined mostly by product appearance and the single device approach was not adequate in explaining the experiences with multiple devices. Therefore, this study aimed to explore three multi-screen interaction experiences, tackle users' emotional responses and investigate what kind of interaction personality they perceived during interaction. The result of this study demonstrated the relationship between user perceptions and multi-screen experiences, which is useful for future design reference in multi-screen services.

Keywords: Multi-screen service · Interaction experience · Emotion responses · Personality trait · User experience

1 Introduction

Report has shown that consumer owns an average of four digital devices [1], which means that the number of touchpoints has expanded with the rise of device ownership. Multi-screen services like Netflix, Allrecipes and Fitbit have broken usage boundaries and allowed users to freely shift from one device to another. Multi-screen services involve consumer interacting with multiple devices and is characterized by the different location, duration and purpose of use compared to single screen services. Multi-screen services have formed new kinds of interaction experiences: consistent, continuous and complementary experiences [2]. Thus, the user-device relationship now involves more than one device and has become even more complex. According to CASA (Computers are social actors) paradigm, users tend to interact with computers as if they are human beings and apply social rules (e.g. politeness) to them [3]. This study aims to take it further by investigating the relationship between users and multi-screen interaction experiences, with emphasis on users' emotional responses to the experiences and personality traits they assign to the interactions.

© Springer International Publishing Switzerland 2016
A. Marcus (Ed.): DUXU 2016, Part II, LNCS 9747, pp. 34–45, 2016.
DOI: 10.1007/978-3-319-40355-7_4

2   Literature Review

2.1   Interaction Experience

When devices operate within a multi-screen service, the relationship on how devices connect with each other to accommodate different services or to conform to the users' behavior, have formed new kinds of interaction experiences. How people interact with multi-screen is different from the traditional way of interaction with single device. Levin has revealed three kinds of interaction experiences: consistent, continuous and complementary experiences [2]. Consistent interaction refers to the same experience interacting with similar contents, visual effects and main functions with different kinds of devices. These characteristics decrease people's learning curve when migrating through devices, and people can intuitively and easily adopt the best available device to be used according to their wishes. Continuous interaction emphasizes on its continuation in accomplishing a single or sequential of activities across various devices; therefore, the coordination between devices is determined through users' activity flow, duration of the activity, context of the activity and the number of subtasks needed to be accomplished. Activities like cooking, trip planning or reading books on multiple devices can be done in a more seamless and sophisticated way of interaction. Complementary interaction is the most representative interaction of the multi-screen ecosystem. Two or more devices in an activity work together, or complement with each other or control one another to elevate the overall experience. It is the most accessible for users since users can use their own device as a starting point and extend the experience beyond what was already in existence. For instance, using one's own smartphones as a way of input in a multi-player game so everyone who owns a smartphone has the opportunity to participate in the game and thus promote social connections. Also, devices could serve as second-screen to provide additional information to enrich the main activity such as receiving movie description and viewers' comment on a tablet that corresponds to the movie that is currently being watched [4].

These three kinds of multi-screen interactions have provided various impacts, and the experiences can only be amplified and accommodated when users' behaviors have been identified and when the actual needs were fulfilled. Prior research have emphasized on multi-screen user behavior such as energy intake [5] or human activity for system recommendation [6]. There is a deficiency in the understanding of the interplay between multi-screen interaction and user perceptions. Höök et al. stated that the overall experience of interaction could not be explained fully by the knowing of only traditional human factors; however, users' perceptions such as emotion, understanding, and interpretation are also as equally as important [7]. Therefore, this study aims to identify the emotions and personality traits perceived from multi-screen interaction, which has never been done in this aspect before and to provide more information from the user perception point of view.

2.2 Emotion in Multi-screen Interaction

Emotions play an important role in human-machine interaction as stated by Norman [8], and this has been extensively studied and analyzed in HCI (Human-computer interaction). From a user experience point of view, emotional responses can be influenced and determined by interpreting the iterative interplay between the context and the continuous actions [9]. The emotions identified and analyzed in this study are the results and consequences of interactions with multiple devices, which is different from the concepts of seeing emotion as an antecedent or mediator to product use [10]. Most often, emotional responses are associated with the needs and goals of an individual. In an information-seeking context, if the user interfaces that users interacted with can help to navigate or facilitate in finding desired information, users' emotions are often positive. That is, users' emotional experience can be directly impacted by the user interfaces to the extent of conforming to their needs and goals [11]. Therefore during the context of multi-screen services, interaction experiences occurred with the desire to accomplish certain goals, so users' emotional responses would be determined by whether the interaction could successfully assist users toward those goals. Although it is hard to say what kind of emotions users would experience from these multi-screen experiences, but certainly they would influence users' emotions [12]. For this reason, this study assumed that different emotions would be elicited from the different interactions in consistent, continuous and complementary experiences. Identifying the emotions from interactions in multi-screen services can help to determine which interaction to assign to a given activity that is consistent with users' emotional expectations or the demand of the services. The study of the non-instrumental aspects through emotions and personality traits enriches the current field of research with more knowledge on how people perceive this kind of newly emerged interaction experiences.

2.3 Personality in Multi-screen Interaction

Based on different contexts of use in multi-screen services, people tend to personify their devices with certain personalities and roles that go beyond their instrumental power. For example, tablets are interpreted as an on-the-move professional assistant in formal business context [13], and devices are described as companions [14, 15]. Personality traits applied to products are originally used in describing human beings, and users are able to differentiate them among products [16]. Since people interact with devices similarly to how they interact with human beings, being aware of their device personalities can help them better mange tasks successfully, just like how people in social interactions with each other [17]. Most often, a person's personality can be assessed from his or her facial expressions, personal styles or postures, and a product's personality can be perceived from its shape [18] or material choices [19]. Since appearance is an important determinant in the perception of personality in products, user interfaces and computers, it is unclear whether the same theory applies to multi-screen interaction where more than one device are involved. Desmet et al. have analyzed the relationship between interaction, appearance and personality in physical interactions, which demonstrated that appearance is strong in interaction personality, but personality is not merely the sum of product appearance and the effect of interaction [20]. Therefore, it would be interesting to probe into the attributes constituting personality in multi-screen interactions. This study aims to understand people's perception toward multi-screen interaction, comprehend whether the interactions can be described with personality traits, and to explore the relationship between user perception and the three kinds of interaction experiences.

3   Method

In order to get users' real feedback, the experiment simulated the real world setting, and invited participants to physically interact with the devices. The purpose was to find out users' perception towards consistent, continuous and complementary interaction experiences through post-interaction questionnaire and a follow-up interview to answer whether personality traits can be discovered in multi-screen interactions and the relationship between user perception and three kinds of multi-screen interaction in respect of emotion and personality.

3.1   Participants

A sample of 16 participants (9 male and 7 female, mean age = 28.63) participated in this experiment. Majority of them had experiences in using two to three devices along or in conjunction with one another in completing a task. On a daily basis, participants owned and used smartphones (100 %), tablets (44 %), laptops (81 %), desktops (81 %), Internet-enabled TV (13 %), smart-watches (6.3 %) and other wearable devices (6.3 %).

3.2   Questionnaire

A paper-based post-interaction questionnaire was used to collect participants' impressions after completing each task. The questionnaire includes questions regarding emotion and personality descriptions. For personality assessment, a set of 24-item personality traits was adopted from previous studies [20–23]. Participants' emotional responses were assessed with the positive and negative affect schedule (PANAS) [24]. Questionnaire data were analyzed using Ward's hierarchical clustering method, and selected by means of the cluster and variation. Therefore, ten items in total were retained to be used in the experiment: cheerful, open, relaxed, easy-going, cute, interesting, dominant, boring, gentle and preference for personality scale; and strong, enthusiastic, inspired, determined, attentive, active, interested, distressed, hostile and irritable for emotional scale.

3.3   Apparatus

The hardware used in this experiment includes an Apple iPhone 4 (iOS version 9.2.1), a 42-inch TV, a 13-inch MacBook Pro and a 13-inch Asus laptop. The user interface images shown in the experiment were designed previously in graphic design software.

Since appearance is a major determinant in product personality [18], in this experiment the appearance of user interfaces were controlled, so the design elements in all images remained identical in terms of color, icon and style. The images were then imported to and simulated on smartphones with POP prototyping application (Woomoo Inc.), which enables the simulation of applications participants would interact on their smartphone. For the simulation on laptops and TV, Microsoft PowerPoint was used to simulate webpage browsing and TV watching. One of the essential features of multi-screen interaction is that it is context sensitive. Therefore, the experimental setting divides the room into three distinct areas: living-room area, study room area and an outdoor area (Fig. 1). Participants were informed about the purpose of each area before the experiment took place.

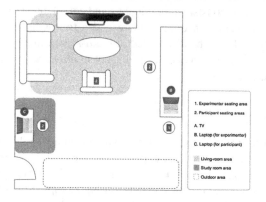

Fig. 1. Experimental setting

3.4 Task Procedure

The scenario of the experiment was developed based on the topic: exercise. With the emerging number of people using multiple devices like smartphone, laptop or wearable devices (e.g. Nike fuelband, Fitbit, Apple watch, etc.) to record, keep track and share their physical activities, exercise is a good example to demonstrate the multi-screen service therefore it was chosen for this study. Based on the scenario, three tasks were designed according to three multi-screen interactions of consistent, continuous and complementary design. In order to simulate the interaction and usage between two to three devices together, the Wizard of Oz (WOz) technique was applied. During the experiment, participants were told that the devices they are using were all connected together in the multi-screen ecosystem by a service called Myworkout, and in the following three tasks they were going to interact with different kind of interaction provided by the service (Table 1).

Table 1. Task description

Experience	Device	Task	Simulated UI
Consistent	Smartphone, TV, Laptop	Task 1: Add one exercise video to my collection, then go to "my collection" page and check whether the video has been successfully added (Same task need to performed on three devices)	
Continuous	Latop→ TV→ Smartphone	Task 2: Watching exercise video on laptop in the study room, and continue watching the same video on TV in the living-room, then added the saved video to "my collection", and showed the saved video to his/her exercise peers from smartphone in the gym.	
Complementary	TV+ Smartphone	Task 3: Select one video to watch on TV by using a smartphone as remote controller, and while the video is playing, participants were asked to look at the video comments left by other viewers on the smartphone.	

As the experiment was a within-subjects design, participants were required to perform all three tasks. The experiment was carried out in an individual basis. Participants were assigned to three different task sequences (e.g., ABC, BCA, CAB). The entire experiment lasted approximately 30–40 min.

4   Result

The method by Ward's hierarchical clustering was used to analyze the post-interaction questionnaire. The cluster analysis was later ascertained by one-way ANOVA to see if there was significance among the clusters and to determine the level of the clusters.

4.1 Personality Clustering

In consistent interaction, the items regarding personality are grouped into four clusters: 1st cluster (cute, boring), 2nd cluster (interesting), 3rd cluster (cheerful, easy-going, gentle) and 4th cluster (relaxed, preference, open, dominant). In continuous interaction, the items regarding personality are grouped into four clusters: 1st cluster (cheerful, relaxed, easy-going, preference), 2nd cluster (open, dominant), 3rd cluster (cute, gentle) and 4th cluster (boring). In complementary interaction, the items regarding personality are divided into four clusters: 1st cluster (open, easy-going, relaxed, cheerful), 2nd cluster (dominant, interest, preference), 3rd cluster (cute, gentle) and 4th cluster (boring).

4.2 Personality in Multi-screen Interaction

In consistent interaction, the clusters differed significantly in terms of personality $(F_{3,156} = 31.914, P = 0.000 < 0.001)$. With the LSD post-hoc test applied, it was revealed that cluster 4 is larger than the other three clusters. Participants thought consistent experience had a relaxed, preference, open and dominant personality. In continuous interaction, the clusters differed significantly in terms of personality $(F_{3,156} = 40.195, P = 0.000 < 0.001)$. With the LSD post-hoc test applied, it was revealed that cluster 2 is larger than the other three clusters. Participants thought continuous experience had an open and dominant personality. In complementary interaction, clusters differed significantly in terms of personality $(F_{3,156} = 37.72, P = 0.000 < 0.001)$. With the LSD post-hoc test applied, it was revealed that cluster 1 is larger than the other three clusters. Participants thought complementary experience had an open, easy-going, relaxed and cheerful personality (Fig. 2).

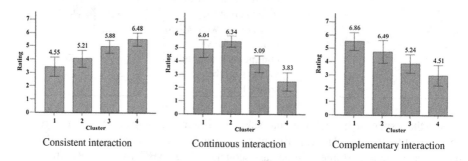

Consistent interaction   Continuous interaction   Complementary interaction

Fig. 2. Personality clusters in multi-screen interaction

4.3 Emotion Clustering

In consistent interaction, the items regarding emotion are grouped into four clusters: 1st cluster (determined, active, attentive, interest), 2nd cluster (enthusiastic, inspired, strong), 3rd cluster (distressed, irritable) and 4th cluster (hostile). In continuous interaction, the items regarding emotion are grouped into four clusters: 1st cluster (determined, attentive, enthusiastic, inspired), 2nd cluster (active, interest), 3rd cluster (strong, distressed) and 4th cluster (irritable, hostile). In complementary interaction, the items regarding emotion are grouped into three clusters: 1st cluster (inspired, interest, active, enthusiastic, determined), 2nd cluster (strong, attentive) and 3rd cluster (irritable, hostile, distressed).

4.4   Emotion in Multi-screen Interaction

In consistent interaction, the clusters differed significantly in terms of emotion ($F_{3,156} = 53.122, P = 0.000 < 0.001$). With the LSD post-hoc test applied, it was revealed that cluster 1 is larger than the other three clusters. Participants felt determined, active, attentive and interested. In continuous interaction, the clusters differed significantly in terms of emotion ($F_{3,156} = 103.52, P = 0.000 < 0.001$). With the LSD post-hoc test applied, it was revealed that cluster 2 is larger than the other three clusters. Participants felt active and interested. In complementary interaction, the clusters differed significantly in terms of emotion ($F_{2,157} = 127.38, P = 0.000 < 0.001$). With the LSD post-hoc test applied, it was revealed that cluster 1 is larger than the other two clusters. Participants felt inspired, interested, active, enthusiastic and determined (Fig. 3).

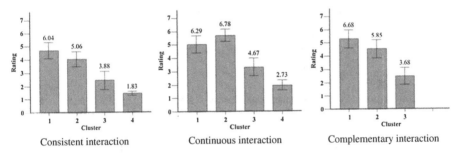

Fig. 3.   Emotion clusters in multi-screen interaction

5   Discussion

The purpose of this study is to understand user perception in multi-screen interaction experiences, in particular what emotions would be perceived as well as the personality traits that users would assign to the interaction. From the result of the experiment, similarities were discovered among three interaction experiences: consistent, continuous and complementary. Participants thought all multi-screen interactions possessed an open personality that is perceived to be curious, creative, flexible and more opportunities. An open personality is part of the openness trait in the five-factor model described by Carver and Connor-Smith [25]. They demonstrated that openness trait is related to engagement coping, which refers to problem solving and cognitive restructuring. That is, the three multi-screen interactions have the tendency to provide positive impacts as the interactions serve to assist participants in accomplishing their goals and accommodate stressor in the activity process. In terms of emotion for the three kinds of interactions, similarities were also found as participants thought all multi-screen interactions elicited emotions that are active and interested. It was found that all of the interactions have been mentioned to be impressive, and participants felt interested and attracted toward the interaction they thought to be the most impressive and wanted their devices to interact in the same way. Overall, the multi-screen interactions are perceived to be open, active and interested.

The results of the experiment showed that different multi-screen interactions tend to associate with certain personality traits and emotions (Table 2). In consistent experiences, preference and attentiveness are the most representative personality and emotion in this experience. Preference usually occurred when the design elements are in concordance with the characteristics of its user group [22]. It can also be explained from the interview conducted, as participants' prefer consistent design in icon position, layout and style that facilitate easier searching and positioning across multiple devices. The experience was perceived to be deliberate and provide users with a sense of familiarity. Therefore, consistent experience is suitable to apply to services dealing with enormous information content or complex information architecture when users are expecting simple, familiar interaction experience with minimum adjustment required across multiple devices.

Table 2. User perception in multi-screen experience

Experience	Personality trait	Emotion
Consistent	Open, relaxed, dominant, preference	Determined, attentive, active, interest
Continuous	Open, dominant	Active, interest
Complementary	Cheerful, open, relaxed, easy-going	Enthusiastic, inspired, determined, active, interest

Result showed that continuous experience is perceived to be open, dominant, active and interested. The term dominant is used to describe a person exhibiting tendencies to command, control or lead others to take action, and a dominant interaction is usually perceived from the order of interaction, the confidence level and the language displayed on the computer [26]. In the services where continuous experience takes place, users often got asked to make certain decisions for the actions to be performed across multiple devices for continuation of the tasks. A too dominant interaction may make users feel imposing and forceful, while a less dominate interaction may be too weak and disorganized. It is therefore vital for designers to take into consideration the personality traits of the experience and their impact since these may interfere with users' reaction to an activity. Services dealing with user behaviors and contextual information such as scheduling or quantified self movement, the spontaneous and convenient characteristics of continuous experience may be preferable to enhance such services. The term "convenience" has been emphasized several times by participants to address the freedom of the interactions. The technical foundation of continuous experience thus needs to be well designed so that every device can work smoothly with on another to provide the freedom of device shifting for the users.

In the complementary scenarios, users perceived this kind of experience as cheerful, easy-going, enthusiastic and inspiring, which were perceptions not perceived in either consistent or continuous interaction experiences. In an information-seeking approach, an easy-going person usually prefers easy access to information that requires less effort and thoroughness [27]. Therefore, complementary interaction experiment is perceived with a spontaneous, uncomplicated and relaxed feeling. Users could utilize their existing devices to collaborate or control other devices. This low entry barrier reinforce the anytime, anywhere concept, which makes users feel emotionally positive and inspires them to pursue further activities with other devices. Moreover, the combination use of multiple devices not only deepened the content knowledge in a service, but also elevated users' experiences to another level that are novel, attractive, smart and well-executed. With these perceived characteristics, complementary interaction experience is best adopted to enhance the fun experiences in entertaining services, and to enrich with constant inspiration and motivation in exercising or productivity services.

6   Conclusion

In multi-screen services, interaction experiences were the results derived from the contexts of activities, the number of available devices, and users' personal goals. The results of this study showed that user perception could be elicited from multi-screen experiences, and variations of emotions and personalities can be found among consistent, continuous and complementary interactions. As mentioned earlier in this study, users interact with computers through social norms similarly to human interactions. As a consequence, future research could investigate relationships among user interfaces, interaction emotions and personality traits in the multi-screen services. This would verify the effects on whether the attributes of user interface such as color, input/output, message route, or information content are compatible with the types of interaction experiences.

The characteristics of the different interaction experiences may serve as a criterion to be adopted in an activity, as it is undeniable that certain interaction is more suitable for certain activity. This study wants to aggregate on top of what has already known and provides additional insights from user perspective for designers to adopt the appropriate interaction to match with their design goals. It is also useful to enhance existing services so that the conveyed interaction emotion and personality is in consistence with the purposes of the services. Furthermore, it can be utilized as an evaluation tool to examine the discrepancies between user perception and the services they use. Even though the subject of this study focused on the issue of exercise, the experiment was conducted through simulating real world situations under well-controlled experimental conditions. Therefore, results from this study can be further analyzed and used in different subject matters, providing further insight in the field of multi-screen interactions.

References

1. Nielsen: A Nielsen report on the digital consumer (2014). http://goo.gl/Af7vI2
2. Levin, M.: Designing Multi-Device Experiences: An Ecosystem Approach to User Experiences Across Devices. O'Reilly Media, Sebastopol (2014)

3. Nass, C.I., Stener, J.S., Tanber, E.: Computers are social actors. In: Proceedings of CHI 1994, pp. 72–78 (1994)
4. Cesar, P., Knoche, H., Bulterman, D.C.A.: From one to many boxes: mobile devices as primary and secondary screens. In: Marcus, A., Roibás, A.C., Sala, R. (eds.) Mobile TV: Customizing Content and Experience. Human-Computer Interaction Series, pp. 327–348. Springer, London (2010)
5. Marsh, S., Mhurchu, C.N., Jiang, Y., Maddison, R.: Modern screen-use behaviors: the effects of single- and multi-screen use on energy intake. J. Adolesc. Health 56(5), 543–549 (2015)
6. Schweizer, I., Schmidt, B.: Kraken.me-Multi-device user tracking suite. Presented at the 2014 ACM International Joint Conference, New York, USA, pp. 853–862 (2014)
7. Höök, K., Persson, P., Sjölinder, M.: Measuring experience of interactive characters. In: Green, W.S., Jordan, P.W. (eds.) Pleasure with Products: Beyond Usability. Taylor and Francis, London (2002)
8. Norman, D.: Emotional Design: Why We Love (or Hate) Everyday Things. Basic Books, New York (2004)
9. Battarbee, K.: Co-experience: understanding user experiences in social interaction. Unpublished doctoral dissertation, University of Art and Design Helsinki, Helsinki, Finland (2004)
10. Hassenzahl, M., Tractinsky, N.: User experience - a research agenda. Behav. Inf. Technol. 25(2), 91–97 (2006)
11. Brave, S., Nass, C.: Emotion in human–computer interaction. In: Jacko, J., Sears, A. (eds.) The Human-Computer Interaction Handbook, pp. 81–93. Lawrence Erlbaum Associates, Mahwah (2003)
12. Chorianopoulos, K., Spinellis, D.: User interface evaluation of interactive TV: a media studies perspective. Univ. Access Inf. Soc. 5(2), 209–218 (2006)
13. Zamani, E., Giaglis, G.M., Nancy, P.: Dad bought another toy: meaning making and emotions with tablets. In: 2012 International Conference on Mobile Business, Paper 16 (2012)
14. Turkle, S. (ed.): Evocative Objects: Things We Think with. MIT Press, Cambridge (2007)
15. Van Dijck, J.: Mediated Memories in the Digital Age. Stanford University Press, Stanford (2007)
16. Jordan, P.W.: The personalities of products. In: Green, W.S., Jordan, P.W. (eds.) Pleasure with Products: Beyond Usability. Taylor and Francis, London (2002)
17. Janlert, L.E., Stolterman, E.: The character of things. Des. Stud. 18, 297–314 (1997)
18. Govers, P., Hekkert, P., Schoormans, J.P.L.: Happy, cute and tough: can designers create a product personality that consumers understand? In: McDonagh, D., Hekkert, P., Van Erp, J., Gyi, D. (eds.) Design and Emotion, The Design of Everyday Things, pp. 345–349. Taylor and Francis, London (2004)
19. Van Kesteren, I.E.H., Stappers, P.J., Kandachar, P.V.: Representing product personality in relation to materials in a product design problem. In: 1st Nordic Design Research Conference, Copenhagen, Denmark (2005)
20. Desmet, P.M.A., Ortíz Nicolás, J.C., Schoormans, J.P.: Product personality in physical interaction. Des. Stud. 29(5), 458–477 (2008)
21. Govers, P.C.M.: Product personality. TU Delft, Delft University of Technology (2004)
22. Fogg, B.J.: Persuasive Technology: Using Computers to Change What We Think and Do. Morgan Kaufmann, San Francisco (2002)
23. Schenkman, B.N., Jönsson, F.U.: Aesthetics and preferences of Web pages. Behav. Inf. Technol. 19, 367–377 (2000)

24. Watson, D., Clark, L.A., Tellegen, A.: Development and validation of brief measures of positive and negative affect: the PANAS scales. J. Pers. Soc. Psychol. **54**(6), 1063–1070 (1988)
25. Carver, C.S., Connor-Smith, J.: Personality and coping. Annu. Rev. Psychol. **61**, 679–704 (2010)
26. Moon, Y., Nass, C.: How, "Real" are computer personalities? Psychological responses to personality types in human-computer interaction. Commun. Res. **23**(6), 651–674 (1996)
27. Heinström, J.: Five personality dimensions and their influence on information behaviour. Inf. Res. **9**(1), 165 (2003)

Cuteness Design in the UX: An Initial Analysis

Aaron Marcus[1](✉) and Xiaojuan Ma[2]

[1] Aaron Marcus and Associates,
1196 Euclid Avenue, Berkeley, CA 94708, USA
Aaron.Marcus@AMandA.com
[2] Department of Computer Science and Engineering,
University of Science and Technology, Hong Kong, China
mxj@cse.ust.hk

Abstract. The authors conducted initial research/analysis of cuteness, especially in East Asian countries, and its existing/potential use in computer-based products/services worldwide. They provide a taxonomy of cuteness to guide developers and offer initial recommendations.

Keywords: Appeal · Asia · China · Culture · Cuteness · Design · Development · Emotion · Engineering · Experience · Information · Interface · Mobile · Persona · Social networks · Usability · Usefulness · User

1 Introduction

For many decades, cute toys, animations, publications, and images have been used in many cultures. They are often associated with and used widely in products/services for children. As an example, at one point in time Walt Disney's Mickey Mouse character, introduced in 1928, became the most widely known image/character in the world, surpassing even images of Santa Claus [18]. In the past few decades, cute products/services, images, icons, *etc.*, have appeared extensively in east Asian countries (China, Japan, South Korea, Taiwan, in particular). In part, this increased use of cuteness may stem from the popularity of *animé*, comics, and electronic games in east Asia, the audiences for which are no longer limited to children, teenagers, and young adults. Cuteness has been used to define and brand computer-based products/services (*e.g.,* the MIUI themes of recent Xiaomi phones in China). While cuteness has less impact in Africa, Europe, India, South America, and the USA, the globalization of products/services (*e.g.,* the Hello Kitty brand, Line, and Wechat) coming from east-Asian countries makes it likely that cuteness will be incorporated more and more into many products/services, their devices, user interfaces, and branding. An example is the extensive use of emoticons in the Japanese Line product and the Chinese WeChat product. Now, even Skype, which was founded in 2003 by Swedish and Danish persons with Skype software from Estonia, and which is currently owned by Microsoft in the US, features numerous cute icons (see Fig. 1) some of which seem very culture-bound.

All of these products/services possess user experiences (UXs), that is, user interfaces, user touch points, etc., which must be usable, useful, and appealing, and which

A. Marcus (Ed.): DUXU 2016, Part II, LNCS 9747, pp. 46–56, 2016.
DOI: 10.1007/978-3-319-40355-7_5

Fig. 1. Example of cute emoticons (some very culturally biased) in Skype (December 2015), including a dancing turkey for use during the Thanksgiving (US) holiday. The emoticons are also designed with too-small components, making them difficult to identify. (Figure permission assumed through fair-use circumstances).

can meet the needs/preferences of major stakeholders (the user community, engineering, marketing, business management, government, investors, and journalists). We believe cuteness can contribute to the UX by increasing appeal and memorability, and by helping to clarify concepts. There is now a challenge to create successful UXs that are cute. Exploring UX cuteness can cover country/culture criteria, design philosophy, methods, evaluation criteria for stakeholders, and relations among stakeholders.

Computer-based (especially mobile and consumer-oriented) products/services are produced/consumed worldwide. Designers/developers must be aware of culture differences in thinking about cute UX designs, even for diverse domestic markets. The focus on cuteness is especially important for Asian cultures, which give increased attention to aesthetic appeal and fun in the UX in comparison to Western cultures, as shown by Frandsen-Thorlacius et al. [4]. Cuteness engineering or design, culture theory, and design theory in relation to applying cuteness to products/services in many different cultures and contexts are all inter-connected. Culture theories and models and user-centered design theory can serve as a basis for analyzing cuteness in, for example, mobile devices, publications, and Websites. Cuteness can be connected to time orientation, spatial relations, family structure, gender roles, beauty, happiness, health, money/wealth, age/aging, groups/individuals, privacy/security, trust, and persuasion/behavior change. In this paper we shall have an initial opportunity to comment on cuteness of Asian products/services in relation to personas, use scenarios, information architecture (metaphors, mental models, and navigation), and look-and-feel (appearance and interaction) for products/services.

We believe it reasonable to consider several issues of cuteness design, or cuteness engineering, in UX design:

- What is the taxonomy of cuteness?
- Where has cuteness been used in computer-based products/services?
- How does cuteness work or become effective?
- What guidelines exist for cuteness design?
- What information resources exist for the cuteness designer?
- How can local developers create successful cuteness user-experience for domestic and foreign products and services?
- How can foreign software/hardware developers create a successful user-experience for products and services in other countries/cultures?

- Is there a significant difference in Asian (*e.g.,* Chinese cuteness), as opposed to Western cuteness?
- What is the nature of the cuteness in China, Japan, South Korea, and/or Japan?
- Are there any significant design patterns for cuteness?
- What information resources exist to help designers of cuteness?

We explore a few of these issues and base our hypothesis of emerging cuteness design on examination of hundreds of images gathered over 10 years by Marcus and five years by Ma, and by previous qualitative and quantitative research. We hope to raise usable, useful, and appealing issues to consider further.

2   User-Interface, User-Experience, and User-Centered Design

We do not elaborate on these concepts and terms, because they are familiar to most readers, are widely understood, and are explained in numerous resources, for example, [2, 5, 9–11]. All such terms must all be reconsidered in the light of cuteness design. We consider a few specific topics below.

3   Cross-Cultural UX Design

Theorists of culture, anthropologists, ethnographers, and professionals in the UX field have devised descriptions of culture, proposed models of culture, dimensions of culture, and explored similarities/differences of patterns of feelings, opinions, actions, signs, rituals, and values, as studied by [2–4, 6, 7, 9, 11–15, 17, 19]. Especially important: researchers noticed differences between Eastern (Chinese, Japanese) and Western (European and North-American) users in terms of learning strategies, navigation behavior, *etc.* Frandsen-Thorlacius *et al.* [3] studied Danish *vs.* Chinese users to determine that the very concept of usability differed between the two cultures. Chinese users consider that "usability" more strongly possesses the attributes of "fun" and "aesthetically pleasing" built into the concept than Danish users. Based, in part, on studies of Japanese and US participants staring at fish tanks and describing what they saw (Japanese viewers tended to describe relationships, US viewers tended to describe objects), Nisbett [15] postulated that there were major cognitive differences between the East and West; people in these two regions think differently.

4   Cuteness Taxonomy

Cuteness relates to all the above UX issues. We propose an initial, simplified definition of cuteness: a characteristic of a product, person, thing, or context that makes it appealing, charming, funny, desirable, often endearing, memorable, and (usually) non-threatening. Cuteness as a concept is nuanced and complex. The authors present an initial taxonomy below to help future researchers/designers.

4.1 Evolution of Cuteness

Cuteness-Historical Changes: For example, the evolution of the look of Mickey Mouse, Garfield, and other cartoon characters over decades of time.

Cuteness-Social Influence: For example, the Otaku phenomenon, a Japanese term for people with obsessive interests, commonly used for fans of Japanese animé and manga. See: http://en.wikipedia.org/wiki/Otaku.

Cuteness-Technology Orientation: From just the appearance (e.g., icon design) to more extensive characteristics of functions and services (See Fig. 2, Yamaha's Hatsune Miku singing synthesizer https://en.wikipedia.org/wiki/Hatsune_Miku).

4.2 Dependence of Cuteness (with Acknowledgement to Wentao Wang of Baidu, Who Includes Some Cuteness Guidelines in the Baidu UX Design Guidelines [1])

Cuteness-Age Dependence: Baby, child, teenager, senior, etc.

Cuteness-Context Dependence: Advertising, education, medical, government, sport, entertainment, etc.

Cuteness-Culture Dependence: European, North American, Indian, Asian, Chinese, Japanese, Korean, etc.

Cuteness-Education Dependence: Advanced education may reduce sensitivity to cuteness.

Cuteness-Gender Dependence: Men, women, other genders.

Cuteness-Profession Dependence: Designers may be more sensitive.

4.3 Elements of Cuteness

Cuteness-Medium: Emojis/emoticons, mascots, ACG (animation, comics, games).

Cuteness-Appearance: Color, *e.g.,* pink and other pastels), shapes (rounded, blobs), face treatment (baby-like, large eyes), anthropomorphism (*e.g.,* hammers can become human-like characters), expression (hyperbolic, ritualized), *etc.*). See for example [8].

Cuteness-Sound: Voice, sound *(e.g., Pikachu), etc.* Pikachu are Japanese fictional Pokemon creatures that appear in comics, animations, agames, and movies/television. See: https://en.wikipedia.org/wiki/Pokémon_Pikachu.

Cuteness-Language: Slangs and symbols, e.g., 萌萌哒 ("so cute," frequently seen in Chinwaw social media), 么么哒 ("kiss kiss"), the tilde symbol ("～"), *etc.*

Cuteness-Behavior: Gesture, posture, *etc*. The term "acting/playing cute" means someone deliberately attracts others by showing off (or pretending) to be cute, such as the leading character in the 2011 movie *Puss in Boots* (Fig. 3). The use of *kaomoji* in Japanese social media is one example. See http://kaomoji.ru/en. The Website notes that the emoticons are uniquely Japanese and that the Japanese consider the eyes the source or chief denoter of emotion. Another example is found at the Youtube video https://www.youtube.com/watch?v=iwxYV6y7Cl4. A young man (a lawyer, see Fig. 3) is playing cute while the girl standing behind is also supposed to be cute. The "cuteness" of "the guy" demonstrates another type of cuteness. Figure 4 shows a cute animal with large eyes, furry body, round forms.

Fig. 2. Yamaha synthesizer

Fig. 3. Cute lawyer

Fig. 4. Cute animal

4.4   Styles of Cuteness

Sexy-Cute: Examples of this style are plentiful, including some of the gestures and behavior of Marilyn Monroe in the movie *Some Like it Hot*.

Cuteness-by Contrast: (反差萌 in Chinese, *i.e.*, something that is conventionally considered serious, dangerous, scary, *etc*. is playing cute.) An example is the lawyer, the man in suit that is dancing in the court in the image above.

Cuteness-by Association: Some other characteristics, not negative, that may evoke the perception of cuteness, *e.g.*, the following adjectives:

- Lolita-cute: (Moe (萌え, pronounced [mo.e]) in Japanese) is the most common style of cuteness in ACG young girl characters. The girl in Fig. 5 is dressed in the Lolita-cute style. See: https://en.wikipedia.org/wiki/Moe_%28slang%29).
- Stupid: (蠢萌), *e.g.*, *Minions* characters (Fig. 6).

Fig. 5. Lolita-cute style

Fig. 6. Minions characters

Fig. 7. Cute Ice Age Squirrel

- Slow-witted: (呆萌, 囧萌) *e.g.*, the squirrel in the *Ice Age* movie (Fig. 7)
- Naïve: (天然萌) such as Baymax in Big Hero Six (Fig. 8).
- Angry: (Fig. 9)
- Ugly, lurid, vulgar, or anarchic: (丑萌, 贱萌) when something is sensationally displeasing to a certain extent, it can become cute, as in Garfield (Fig. 9) and selected *baozou* stickers (Fig. 10). Baozou comics/animations in China are popular character stickers on Tencent's Wechat messaging application, which seem to be derived from other Internet memes.

Fig. 8. Baymax character.

Fig. 9. Cute-Angry Garfield.

Fig. 10. Example of baozou stickers

In Fig. 10, the left character says "Dear Police, I lost my wallet (top)" but he actually means "Give it back to me (bottom)." The right character says "No problem. I will handle it (top)" but really means "Are you kidding me?"

4.5   Value of Cuteness

Cuteness-Psychological Value: Keeping people curious, interested, and engaged.

Cuteness-Social Value

Cuteness-Economic Value: Brand value.
Cuteness-Culture Value:
See: http://www.56.com/u53/v_MTI5OTE2ODE4.html.
See: http://www.bilibili.com/video/av1701475/.
The following examples, primarily of social value, bring something that used to be distant, serious, formal, and/or cold more close to ordinary people and everyday life.
One example is playing "Little Apple" for the Chinese People's Liberation Army (PLA) recruitment video (Figs. 11, 12 and 13).
In Fig. 14, the Nanjing, China, police department uses baozou stickers for anti-fraud campaign:
http://news.sina.com.cn/s/wh/2015-10-02/doc-ifximeyw9480918.shtml.

Fig. 11. The original music video of Little Apple

Fig. 12. Performance at the 2014 American Music Awards

Fig. 13. The Little Apple version of the PLA recruitment video

Fig. 14. Cuteness in anti-fraud campaign

Fig. 15. China border control cuteness

Fig. 16. China border control greeting

In Figs. 15 and 16, images show the mascot (a cute mix of sun and shield) of the Chinese Border Control Immigration Inspection guards welcoming everyone to China.

The souvenir store (both online and offline) of the Forbidden City Museum in Beijing, China, uses cute characters (Figs. 17, 18 and 19).

Fig. 17. "Buy it, and then we are friends."

Fig. 18. "Kiss Kiss ~ (the product is a mobile phone stand)."

Fig. 19. Qing Dynasty-style Baymax.

Cuteness and Culture; Storytelling; Beauty/Aesthetics:

Culture biases
Historical patterns

Cuteness and Emotions:

Cuteness and happiness

Cuteness and helplessness
Cuteness and childishness

Other Cuteness Topics (Health, Nutrition, Exercise; Wealth, Money Management; Age; Privacy; Security; Storytelling; Innovation; Travel; Work; Entertainment; Manners and Social Norms):

Theories
Culture biases
Historical patterns

5 UX Design Topics

The following UX cuteness-design topics seem especially relevant and worth considering regarding patterns of differences/similarities in countries and cultures:

- Personas and use scenarios
- Metaphors
- Mental models and navigation, *i.e.,* information architecture
- Appearance and interaction, *i.e.,* look-and-feel

6 Examples of Cuteness in UX of Computer-Based Products/Services

The following examples show cuteness incorporated into different aspects of computer-based products and services, including appearance and functions.

6.1 Product Images

See Figs. 20, 21, 22, 23, 24, 25 and 26.

Fig. 20. Branding/aesthetics of Miui themes for phones from Xiaomi, China.

Fig. 21. Error messages: free cloud service, video demo, China

Fig. 22. Cloud service cuteness.

Fig. 23. Cute imagery for 360 backup wizard, Baidu backup progress, China.

Fig. 24. File-transfer cuteness.

Fig. 25. Cute penguin mascot for TenCent QQ, China. Image source: [7].

Fig. 26. Loading cycle from Bilbili, China.

Fig. 27. Cute Guidelines in [1].

6.2   Design Guidelines for Cuteness

Many companies that produce cute products, services, publications, brands, such as Disney and Hello Kitty, do not regularly publish detailed information about the cuteness-design guidelines that make their designs so effective. One known major high-technology company that has published design guidelines is Baidu [1] (Fig. 27).

Another, limited source of cuteness guidelines is Preuss' "The Elements of Cute Character Design" [16]. Space does not permit extensive recitation of the recommendations, but topics include the following:

Definition of cuteness: childlike, sweet, helplessness

Childlike characteristics: large round heads; large eyes; small or absent mouths

Arms and legs: short, round, soft, unmuscular

Roundness: used throughout

Simple: avoid complexity

Little and lovable: small-sized, sociable

Colors: warm, friendly, soft contrasts

For all such guidelines, it remains to be determined how culturally biased such prescriptions are. Metrics are yet to be determined; much research remains.

6.3   Cautions and Future Challenges

The authors believe the characteristics described here can provide guidance and stimulation to others who may research these topics more thoroughly and design specific guidelines and solutions to demonstrate the impact of cuteness on UX design.

Acknowledgements. We acknowledge Wang, Wentao, Senior UX Designer, Baidu; Baidu [1]; Preuss [16].

References

1. Baidu UX Department: Baidu UX Design Guidelines, p. 234. Baidu, Beijing (2014)
2. Brejcha, J.: Cross-Cultural Human-Computer Interaction and User Experience Design: A Semiotic Perspective. CRC Press, Boca Raton (2015)
3. Dong, Y.: A cross-cultural comparative study on users' perception of the webpage: with the focus on cognitive style of Chinese, Korean, and American, 113pp. Master's thesis, Department of Industrial Design, Korea Advanced Institute of Science and Technology, Seoul, Korea (2007)
4. Frandsen-Thorlacius, O., Hornbæk, K., Hertzum, M., Clemmensen, T.: Non-universal usability? A survey of how usability is understood by Chinese and Danish users. In: Proceedings of Conference on Human Factors in Computing Systems 2009, pp. 41–58 (2009)
5. Hartson, R., Pyla, P.S.: The UX Book. Morgan-Kauffmann, New York (2012)
6. Hofstede, G., Hofstede, G.J.: Cultures and Organizations: Software and the Mind. McGraw-Hill, New York (2005)
7. Kyriakoullis, L., Panayiotis, Z.: Culture and HCI: a review of recent cultural studies in HCI and social networks. Univ. Access Inf. Soc. J. **14**(4), 1–14 (2015)
8. Lang, A.: 24 Tech Mascots with Eyes, Spikes or Wings. Rewind and Capture, 20 August 2014.   http://www.rewindandcapture.com/24-tech-mascots-with-eyes-spikes-or-wings/. Accessed 5 Jan 2016
9. Marcus, A.: Globalization, localization, and cross-cultural communication in user-interface design (Chap. 23). In: Jacko, J., Spears, A. (eds.) Handbook of Human-Computer Interaction, pp. 441–463. Lawrence Erlbaum Publishers, New York (2002)
10. Marcus, A.: Mobile Persuasion Design. Springer, London (2015)
11. Marcus, A.: HCI and User-Experience Design. Springer, London (2015)

12. Marcus, A., Baradit, S.: Emerging Chinese user-experience design. In: Proceedings of Design, User Experience, and Usability Conference, HCII 2015. Springer, London (2014). http://2015.hci.international/proceedings

13. Marcus, A., Baumgartner, V., Chen, E.: User-interface design and culture dimensions. In: Proceedings, Human-Computer Interface International Conference, Crete, Greece, June 2003, pp. 300–320 (2003)

14. Marcus, A., Baumgartner, V.: Mapping user-interface design components vs. culture dimensions in corporate websites. Vis. Lang. J. **2004**, 1–65 (2004). MIT Press

15. Nisbett, R.E.: The Geography of Thought: How Asians and Westerners Think Differently ... and Why. Free Press, New York (2003)

16. Preuss, S.: The Elements of Cute Character Design, 12 April 2010. http://design.tutsplus.com/articles/the-elements-of-cute-character-design–vector-3533. Accessed 5 Jan 2016

17. Schwartz, S.H.: Mapping and interpreting cultural differences around the world. In: Vinken, H., Soeters, J., Ester, P. (eds.) Comparing Cultures, Dimensions of Culture in a Comparative Perspective, pp. 43–73. Brill, Leiden (2004)

18. Suddath, C.: A Brief History of Mickey Mouse. Time, 18 November 2008. http://content.time.com/time/arts/article/0,8599,1859935,00.html. Accessed 8 Nov 2015

19. Sun, H.: Cross-Cultural Technology Design. Oxford, New York (2012)

The Visceral Voice

Breath and the Politics of Vocalization

Frank Millward[1](✉) and Heather Keens[2]

[1] University of Newcastle, Newcastle, Australia
Frank.Millward@newcastle.edu.au
[2] The Art of Voice, Newcastle, Australia
heather@theartofvoice.com.au

Abstract. There are many factors that influence the sound of a 'visceral' or emotive affect vocalization. This discussion develops ideas about how we hear and understand emotive content in the human and the synthetic voice, particularly in relation to affect utterances and nonverbal and paralinguistic vocal gestures. This is important for areas of affective computing and for developing human computer interactive voice processes. Focus is given to how the breath or vocal energy and the affordance of sound, along with socio-political and cultural factors have impact on interactive vocalizations and what that implies for the development of the artificial emotionally intelligent voice of the future.

Keywords: Visceral · Voice · Affect utterance · Artificial emotional intelligence · Interactive · Synthetic voice · Paralinguistic · Voice empathy · Voice qualities

1 Introduction

The interactive synthetic voice is designed and positioned to respond and function in particular scenarios. The manner and form of a synthetic vocal response may be described in a variety of ways - task activation, confirming, instructional, informative or responsive to particular physical or timed events to name a few. "Human-centered" or "experience-centered" design has 'opened up deeper investigations of the meaning of affect, emotion, and experience' [1]. This discussion will look at the role played by political, cultural and social aspects involving interaction where the 'visceral voice' or emotive vocal interactive processes are in play. This is particularly relevant in understanding how the empathetic voice can be further developed into the interactive synthetic voice and for exploring the nature of a vocal interactive experience with a free talking artificial emotionally intelligent voice.

Synthetic voices read text and are designed to deliver an emotive position dependent on the environment of delivery. In listening to the instructional voice during a Google Map journey, the synthetic voice is delivered in a neutral voice. The interactive response to the driver taking an alternate route is to remap the alternate route and deliver the subsequent vocal instruction that follows with a similar neutral vocal tone. In a gaming situation however, the use of affect or emotive expressions are freely used to heighten

© Springer International Publishing Switzerland 2016
A. Marcus (Ed.): DUXU 2016, Part II, LNCS 9747, pp. 57–66, 2016.
DOI: 10.1007/978-3-319-40355-7_6

the emotive response and the sense of a constructed reality, usually presented in a neo-filmic sonic environment where the synthetic voice may be underscored with music to assist in creating an emotive soundscape.

Vocal qualities and attributes can be described and aligned with identifiable emotive states. A voice can be described as happy, sad, angry and so on. These emotional positions can be transferred and represented through the voice in responsive and listening modes. Much of the work to date regarding human technology interaction involving emotion has been multi-modal in approach, using a number of indicators in tandem such as facial, skin response, gestural, pulse, respiration and the like when 'analysing emotions as an aspect of the user experience' [2].

Our discussion will focus on a paralinguistic approach involving the sounds that are voiced but generally not included in text-based readings. Affect utterances such as the 'ums', 'ahs', 'sighs' 'growls' and 'breath marks', indicators of passing emotive states, will be considered in suggesting how these affects might be used to give emotive color to a vocal delivery, real or synthetic. The intention will be to better understand the links between the human voice, the visceral, the breath and the politics of expression in our social, cultural and networked world. To look towards an artificially transacted vocal future when the free speaking synthetic voice may (or perhaps may not) be imbued with the ability to convincingly read and express human emotions using an artificial emotionally intelligent voice.

2   The Visceral

The James–Lange theory 'focuses on bodily change in the muscles and viscera as causing the feeling component of the overall emotional experience rather than being concomitant of it' [3].

> These early theories were typically found to be incorrect or, more commonly, not sufficient in themselves to explain the motivational states in question ... and theories focusing on the central nervous system (CSN) control are now more common. Nonetheless these theories remain about the body' [3].

There is still some worthy discussion to be had here regarding the 'visceral voice'. Lavine in his book *In An Unspoken Voice* presents the thought that 'many of our most important exchanges occur simply through the "unspoken voice" of our bodies'.

> The visceral sense is our capacity to directly perceive our gut sensations and those of other organs, including our heart and blood vessels. Most medical texts state that a refined visceral sense is not possible, that "gut feelings" are just a metaphor and that we are only able to feel pain "referred" from the viscera to more superficial body regions. This is ... wrong in fact, without the visceral sense we literally are without the vital feelings that let us know we are alive; it's our guts that allow us to perceive our deepest needs and longings. [4]

The visceral voice, as an expressive medium, might be seen as coming at the end of a body-located internal communicative process. We feel a physiological sensation. The voice responds with an affect utterance, a 'sigh' of discomfort or the 'scream' of fear motivated by the intensity of a pain. The lungs support the breath that flows through vocal folds after the brain sends a message to respond. The enactment, a compressed timeline sequence, starts with a physiological sensation and ends with an affective emotive vocalization. A visceral rhythmic motif is produced as a result of the timing of the sequence of these events. The spectrum of the rhythm being directly dependent on the time period enunciated between the physiological sensation and the end of the affect utterance.

The Attack, Decay, Sustain, Release (ADSR) aspect of this rhythmic/sonic envelope may be considered as a form, as used with music synthesizers when shaping the formation of a musical sound, a fundamental building block in the structuring of a single note, syllabic or phoneme like. The idea of a sonic envelope can be thought of either as a micro and macro descriptor, a single note, phrase or as the envelope of an entire discussion or musical piece. A vocal affect utterance might be thought of as a sonic envelope, a sigh or a cry for example.

A baby's visceral vocalizations, a scream motivated by hunger, may be considered to have a short attach and release time with an extended sustain and decay time, the length of which is contingent upon satisfying the hunger. A baby's visceral voice rhythms might be attributed to a number of motivating physiological causes - pain, discomfort, hunger and so on. The timing of the flow of the envelope develops rhythmic motifs that when repeated provides a way of recognizing or identifying particular visceral vocalizations of the baby. Empathies between mother and child are complex and are commonly acknowledged as formations that commence in the womb as the fetus develops a familiarity and bonds with the sound of the mother's voice [5, 6].

While the suggestion about the rhythmic analysis is speculative it offers an idea for framework development in considering ways in which a synthetic voice might be modeled or programed, with designed rhythmic cells to reflect coded visceral or affect responses. 'Crying has its internal rhythms, which can be discerned based on an aesthetic sensibility that attends to and interprets sound, tone, intensity, volume, pitch and pace' [7].

The driving notion here lies with the idea that the rhythm of a vocalisation could be seen to be at the centre of political considerations regarding such expression. If we moderate or temper a visceral vocal expression, we may be making a political choice - should I say what needs to be said or what I know will be acceptable to this listener - or perhaps we are confronted with adopting accepted lines of social behaviour, such as if we were to not express a pain through a vocal expression but rather hide the pain and not show that we are hurting.

The nature of the choices for a baby is uninhibited and without censorship, the expression comes straight from the sensation via a direct unimpeded pathway to the voice. For an older person the sensation is more than likely to be tempered with considerations of appropriateness and codes of behavior encouraging a more sanitized vocal expression - particularly when issues involving passionate or viscerally motivated belief are involved – the visceral voice is then tempered and contained, it becomes aware adapts to of social conventions or correctness of behavior. In situations of primal utterance the flow also may be uninhibited such as is fight or flight circumstances.

The visceral utterance may be replaced with an acceptable euphemism. The angry response, "That is impossible!" may become, "Umm … that will be a challenge". In these circumstances metaphor plays a role, as does personal identity and the connectivity of that identity to the individual sound of the expressive voice. This supports the Jõemets idea that

> as soon as voice becomes verbal, it ceases to be voice and becomes language, conveying linguistic meaning by acoustic means ... in order to study voice in its nakedness, it must be viewed from beneath the verbal and musical decorations that have their own modes of creating meaning and that dominate over the purely vocal means of signification. [8]

It is here that the tensions are to be interrogated, where the clarity of an emotion becomes tempered with linguistic considerations and the expressive emotion pushed into managing the breath, connected to the politic of utterance and verbal expression, vocalization.

The 'visceral voice' is something the uninhibited child has little problem with until language is acquired, [8] but is constrained in the adult voice as it speaks to be compliant in a socially and culturally coded language. Life itself could be thought of as a journey that commences in the clarity and resonant qualities of the directness of a visceral, emotive voice to evolve through a number of different stages of sounding, into the matured wisdom of a well-considered vocalization. If a synthetic voice is to be believable and useful in free talking discussions with people, should not this evolutionary and developmental ageing process be incorporated into the artificial emotionally intelligent voice of the future?

3   Breath and Voice Quality

Emotive indicators such as anxiety, fear, joy, sadness, anger, surprise, disgust can be variously read as indicated in the sound of a voice, emotive experiences subliminally contained within the vocal sound, not dependent on the linguistic content, delivered by a particular set of vocal qualities or indicators. In early research involving the voice and emotive expression, Scherer suggested that 'the key to the vocal differentiation of discrete emotions seems to be *voice quality*' [9].

Since then there has been massive amount of research done in analyzing and understanding the emotive voice [23–25], especially involving fundamental frequency F0, range and pitch and how these indicators are rendered or read as emotive signaling. More recent studies involving voice qualities suggest 'that there is no one-to-one mapping between voice quality and affect: individual qualities appear rather to be associated with a constellation of affective states, sometimes related, sometimes less obviously related'. [10]

'Whoa-oa-oa!' - the opening scream from the song 'I Feel Good' by James Brown is an example of a heartfelt voice expressing joy. 'Whoa-oa-oa!' is also an example of vocal constriction (pharyngeal constriction). This occurs when the Vestibula folds (false vocal folds) act as a dampener on the true folds, due to excess or under-excess breath flow combined with laryngeal and physical body tension. When the vocal folds (or vocal chords) - the fleshy structures in the larynx that produce the sound of the voice - have been compromised. Instead of vibrating freely, the folds slam together in a compressed space producing a distorted sounding voice. If the voice is consistently constrained in this manner - through continual shouting for example - damage can occur where a callous or nodules form. As a result, the voice produces a hoarse or 'raspy' sound, or sometimes no sound at all.

'Hoarseness' is used to describe the sound of a voice with damaged vocal folds, oedema (swelling) caused by constriction or vocal fatigue, or folds in a state of pharyngeal constriction, sometimes the sound is referred to as 'harsh' voice. This is one of a number of terms used to describe voice qualities, in speech and singing, including - breathy voice, whispery voice, creaky voice and lax–creaky voice, cry, twang, and for the sung voice; speech quality, opera quality, belt, siren, 'vocal fry' and so on. The exact meaning of such terms is often problematic as word descriptions of a vocalized sound can mean different things to different listeners. Nevertheless these terms, as currently developed by voice practitioners and specialists, form a common language for voice quality descriptors and moreover often assume associated emotive qualities.

The idea of character is perhaps more relevant than a distinctive definable emotive quality, in as much as the sound afforded by a 'hoarse' or damaged voice brings with it certain notions of a life of experience. A truth, worldliness, a wisdom not present in an emotionally neutral voice. Just as we might consider that a higher pitched (young sounding) voice may project the idea of innocence. Focusing on the sonic quality of a voice, the idea is that the breath drives a number of factors when the voice communicates emotion, mood or attitude. Breath is a fundamental visceral component in producing the sound of a voice. Its function also signals the rhythm of a vocal delivery, as 'gaps in speech necessary for breathing are governed by syntactic structure of the language' [11].

The idea of experiencing the rhythmic affordance of sound is relevant in the sense that many emotive utterances and paralinguistic vocalizations come as embedded human knowledge. Further, such sounds are learned as a result of social interaction and the development of codes of behaviour throughout a person's lifetime.

> sounds are not lived in isolation, but experienced through the lived context of social representations that govern how we listen and hear. As Hayes-Conroy and Hays-Conroy (2008:467) [12] remind us: "In the visceral realm, representations affect materially". Following this lead, the historical weight and orientation of social norms aligned to sounds become part of new intensities, memories and emotions-sounds mobilise visceral mechanisms that help particular political subjectivities to temporally fluoresce. [13]

In our technologically socialized world the mediated and processed real and synthetic voice has shaped the way we hear and perceive the sound of the disconnected and the visually aligned 'voice'. This is particularly relevant when considering spatial context, consonance, dissonance, rhythmic flow, factors associated with social behavior and what could be described as embedded knowledge – relevant here is embedded sonic knowledge that makes it intuitive for humans to decide on a course of action such as fight or flight as described above, the ability to differentiate between 'between distressed and other kinds of cry' [7].

The Scherer model of *time-frequency-energy measures* [9] could be added to and repositioned as - *duration, pitch variation, breath, visceral rhythmic indicators along with a range of considerations to do with social context and cultural understandings –* translated, codified or modelled this becomes a complex array of layers that interact within and between layers in a voice as well as between voices in discussion, nested rhythms - rhythms within rhythms, within rhythms. Fractal formations, when looked into reveal another within, then another, and another and so on. The connection to be made here is with neuroscience investigations involving the rhythms of the brain where the idea of nested rhythms is associated with notions of consciousness, processes within processes within processes considered as rhythmic units, the rhythms of living, the rhythm of 'being'.

The *AjoChhand Artificial Brain Building* project is an example of where this idea is being used - 'we believe that we need a completely new geometric language of nested rhythm to process information in the fractal architecture' [14]. Other approaches being used such as 'Neuromorphic Engineering', seek 'to build artificial nervous systems which mimic the functions of biological nervous systems' and aim to 'replicate the performance of the brain' and also to contribute to 'better brain-machine interfaces' [26]. Feinberg's article explores

> fundamental questions about the nature of consciousness and the nervous system, and attempts to reconcile certain philosophical positions with neuroscience. In particular I focus on the relationship between consciousness and hierarchical neural structure, emergence, scientific reduction and ontological subjectivity [27].

The connections being made between the idea of 'nested rhythms' and 'consciousness' is where current research is being used to connect the neural with understandings about emotion and its manifestations physical, psychological and verbal [28]. In this neuroscience environment modeling the visceral voice is within its infancy, but nevertheless there are signs that significant connections are being made in understanding the relationship between, consciousness, the visceral, the computational, the developmental and the evolutionary phases of our life cycles and how that might translate to the sound and nature of the artificial emotionally intelligent voice.

4   Empathy and Affect Utterance

While Mirror Neuron research is also in early stages of development, there was an interesting observation made about the way in which a monkey responded to a 'noisy action' (any action that produces a sound) and later responded to the sound of that action. 'The results showed that a large number of mirror neurons, responsive to the observation of noisy actions, also responded to the presentation of the sound proper of that action, alone' [15]. Is there some thread here for speculating that there is a basis for the idea that empathy can be signaled through vocal sound alone, without the confirming view of a facial expression?

In studies where conversations with virtual human voices have been conducted, synthetic emotions have been used to evaluate responses from the perspective of the human interactive experience. In a study conducted by Qu, Brinkman et al., outcomes relevant to this discussion were noted:

> The analyses on the data for valence and discussion satisfaction suggest that positive compared to negative synthetic emotions expressed by a talking virtual human can elicit a more positive emotional state in a person, and create more satisfaction in the conversation [16].

This suggests that the virtual speaking voice is more attractive to the human listener when the virtual voice speaks in a positive, supportive or conformational way.

Responding to this research outcome, designers seeking to 'elicit emotions' in a virtual voice should concentrate on making the virtual voice able to speak (and listen) to the human in a positive way.

Another outcome noted that 'participants seemed less satisfied with the conversation when the virtual voice showed negative instead of positive emotions during the listening phase'. What one might expect, most people would prefer to be acknowledged by positive conformational emotive interaction rather than experience a negative presence. This supports the idea that the politic of expression is best framed with positive emotions that present empathy through engagement, the negativity of aggression, fear or anxiety with a virtual or real person of course is much less appealing.

Currently HMM (Hidden Markov Model) based speech synthesis is used to produce stronger emotional readings in synthetic speech where existent speaker emotions are modeled and transposed onto a synthetic voice [17]. The study conducted by Lorenzo-Trueba et al. tested four learned emotions - anger, happiness, sadness and surprise in their 'emotion transplantation' project to produce an 'increase in the perceived emotional strength' [18] of a synthetic voice – when reading texts. The emotion transplantation method is described as a

> method capable of learning the paralinguistic information of emotional speech, control its emotional strength and transplant it to different speakers for whom we do not have any expressive information. We decided to focus on emotional speech as a particularization of expressive speech … we can expect the transplantation method to be able to support different expressive domains [18].

Changes in the response of the listening and the speaking virtual voice may be enhanced by programing the virtual voice with conformational affect or visceral utterances during the listening and speaking phase; sounds such as the positive 'Umm', the confirming 'ah', the 'sigh' of acknowledgement and so on. The inclusion of such affect signaling in the virtual speaking voice would provide paralinguistic sonic material to make the prosody familiar to the human listener.

Modes of speaking have been drawn through positions on a cultural hierarchy, tribal division or identified as a politic expressed through ways of speaking. For example the affect utterances of particular dialects or accents or cadential forms such as the upward inflection in ending a sentences or ways of speaking that can be identified as a cultural identifier, are now readable in a globally connected socially networked world.

The breath in combination with voice quality identifies emotive sonic attributes in a voice. To know ourselves through how we speak, to identify who we are, what we know and connect to the visceral sense that 'arises through receptors in the gut', as an intrinsic part of that knowing. The 'gut' feeling vocalized or heard in another person's voice. 'The most intimate sense we have of ourselves is through proprioception, kinesthesia and visceral sensation' [4]. The visceral sensation translated as reaction, the scream, the sigh, the expletive all sustained by the life sustaining breath.

But is it possible for a synthetic or virtual voice to be visceral? Where do we stand with tampering with the line between reality and fiction or comfortable truth, e.g. being supportive or annoyingly positive, reflecting and speaking only what wants to be heard. This begs the consideration of a more profound position put by Boddam-Whetham

'Voice' can be taken as a phenomenon that takes quite a privileged place; what it utters are not words or phrases as such, but it is rather a voice that speaks in between our words, it contaminates them. In short, the voice of the friend speaks the truth of our Being-with others, it calls from a relation between us which is arguably beyond both the phenomenological subject *qua* philosophical one. The voice opens us up to each other from in-between in a relation of resonance. [19]

Such thoughts point to questions about how we are to achieve social and political understandings when the metaphoric is crossed within and between the boundaries of conflicting realities, synthetic, conceptual and actual. 'Heidegger's radical thought in Being and Time was that sociality is a primordial part of existence' [19]. How can we harness this idea in the networked world where the sincere virtual voice may need to be distinguished from the number of purpose built or *designed voices*. Might it be as simple as making the political decision to 'un-friend' the annoying or dishonorable voice?

5   Concluding Questions

How can these ideas be made meaningful for the development and improvement of the free speaking interactive synthetic artificial emotionally intelligent voice of the future? If we are to have meaningful, creative and useful dialogues with machines, with synthetic voices, perhaps we need to consider and understand the possible framework in which such dialogues might take place. What should be the role of the synthetic voice? Should that be something that the human is able to choose as a descriptor of interactive persona? - the helpful voice; the cynical voice; the joker; the advisor; the self-designed voice?

Considering the free speaking, emotively sensitive synthetic voice, we might benefit through being able to discuss the creative development of ideas, complex problem solving, philosophical or critical analyses to name but a few possible interactive discussions. A voice that would effectively communicate and read emotions, visceral, tempered or uninhibited, and respond with a number of different, choose-able degrees where 'visceral' and 'logical' occupy opposite ends of a complex nested set of spectra. A voice that is able to combine advising, discussing and counseling. A voice that would be able to interact with a person who may be stressed or emotionally unstable,

A new USC study suggests that patients are more willing to disclose personal information to virtual humans than actual ones, in large part because computers lack the proclivity to look down on people the way another human might [20]

The idea of a socially and culturally informed voice, one that matures with a life relationship with a human voice, or might be educated to be culturally, socially and politically informed and be aware that these aspects of the communication process are important. Should the synthetic voice be imbued with such qualities and abilities? Should that include a social, cultural and political intelligence, an identity, and a mindfulness of its power to communicate an emotive presence in conversations with real people, one to one or networked? If such a voice were networked how could this contribute to bringing cultures together? How are we to negotiate the political ramifications of designing such a voice? How would that voice be heard? It is clear that we are always on the cusp of another possible great leap forward. That leap will involve the role the mind plays in direct control or instigation of interactions with technology.

What seems clear is that keyboard/screen-mediated human-computer interaction will be a thing of the past. Communication through brainwaves or other somatic sources will be able to create changes, movements, colors, and sounds in our fully-fashioned future. [21]

How will we manage a world 'in which computational power is also directed at the emotional and psychological dimensions of existence' [22]? We can only pose questions that may influence the politic of our socially interactive future, where the relationship between the thought and the utterance speak in genuine tones of respect and peaceful co-operation.

References

1. Lim, Y.-K., Donaldson, J., Jung, H., Kunz, B., Royer, D., Ramalingam, S., Thirumaran, S., Stolterman, E.: Emotional experience and interaction design. In: Peter, C., Beale, R. (eds.) Affect and Emotion in Human-Computer Interaction. LNCS, vol. 4868, pp. 116–129. Springer, Heidelberg (2008)
2. Mahlke, S., Minge, M.: Consideration of multiple components of emotions in human-technology interaction. In: Peter, C., Beale, R. (eds.) Affect and Emotion in Human-Computer Interaction. LNCS, vol. 4868, pp. 51–62. Springer, Heidelberg (2008)
3. Cameron, O.G.: Visceral Sensory Neuroscience: Interoception. Oxford University Press, New York (2002)
4. Lavine, P.A.: An Unspoken Voice: How the Body Releases Trauma and Restores Goodness. North Atlantic Books, Berkeley, California (2010)
5. Michelle, N.A., Dorothy, S.M.: The formation of the maternal-fetal relationship: a reflection on the findings of modern medicine. Natl. Catholic Bioeth. Q. 15(3), 443–451 (2015)
6. Welch, G.F.: Speech and song in childhood: a symbiotic development. Perspect. Voice Voice Dis. 12(2), 7–11 (2002). doi:10.1044/vvd12.2.7
7. Hopwood, N.: The rhythms of pedagogy: an ethnographic study of parenting education practices. Stud. Continuing Educ. 36(2), 115–131 (2013)
8. Jõemets, V.: Human voice: its meaning and textuality outside the verbal and the musical. Semiotica 2014(198), 305–320 (2014)
9. Scherer, K.R.: Vocal affect expression: a review and a model for future research. Psychol. Bull. 99, 143–165 (1986)
10. Gobl, C., Ní, A.: The role of voice quality in communicating emotion, mood and attitude. Speech Commun. 40(1), 189–212 (2003)
11. Henderson, A., Goldman-Eisler, F., Skarbek, A.: Temporal patterns of cognitive activity and breath control in speech. Lang. Speech 8(4), 236–242 (1965)
12. Hayes-Conroy, A., Hayes-Conroy, J.: Taking back taste: feminism, food, and visceral politics. Gender Place Culture 15(5), 461–473 (2008)
13. Waitt, G., Ryan, E., Farbotko, C.: A visceral politics of sound. Antipode 46(1), 283–300 (2014)
14. AjoChhand Brain Building Project: Artificial Brain Building: A New Approach to Induce Another Industrial Revolution: A White Paper, NIMS www.anirbanlab.co.nr, www.nanobraintech.com
15. Rizzolatti, G., Craighero, L.: Mirror neuron: a neurological approach to empathy. In: Changeux, J.-P., Damasio, A.R., Singer, W., Christen, Y. (eds.) Neurobiology of Human Values, pp. 107–123. Springer, Heidelberg (2005)
16. Qu, C., Brinkman, W.P., Ling, Y., Wiggers, P., Heynderickx, I.: Conversations with a virtual human: synthetic emotions and human responses. Comput. Hum. Behav. 34, 58–68 (2014)

17. Yamagishi, J.: An Introduction to HMM-Based Speech Synthesis. Technical report, Tokyo Institute of Technology (2006)
18. Lorenzo-Trueba, J., Barra-Chicote, R., San-Segundo, R., Ferreiros, J., Yamagishi, J., Montero, J.M.: Emotion transplantation through adaptation in HMM-based speech synthesis. Comput. Speech Lang. **34**, 292–307 (2015)
19. Boddam-Whetham, J.: The authentic voice of truth and the resonance of being. J. Interdisc. Voice Stud. **1**(1), 41–55 (2016)
20. Lucas, G.M., Gratch, J., King, A., Morency, L.P.: It's only a computer: virtual humans increase willingness to disclose. Comput. Hum. Behav. **37**, 94–100 (2014)
21. Flanagan, P.: 2029 fashion futurism. In: User Experience, vol. 13, issue 2, 2nd Quarter (2013). http://uxpamagazine.org/fashion-futurism/
22. De Botton, A.: Artificial Emotional Intelligence Will Put Old Heads on Shoulders of All Ages: The World in 2016. In: Wired, London, pp. 50–53 (2015). http://www.wired.co.uk/magazine/archive/2015/11/features/wired-world-2016-alain-de-botton-artificial-emotional-intelligence. (online version subtitled – Six areas that artificial Intelligence will revolutionise)
23. Scherer, K.R.: Vocal communication of emotion: a review of research paradigms. Speech Commun. **40**(1), 227–256 (2003)
24. Bänziger, T., Hosoya, G., Scherer, K.R.: Path models of vocal emotion communication. PloS ONE **10**(9), e0136675 (2015)
25. Koelsch, S., Jacobs, A.M., Menninghaus, W., Liebal, K., Klann-Delius, G., von Scheve, C.: The quartet theory of human emotions: an integrative and neurofunctional model. Phys. Life Rev. **13**, 1–27 (2015). doi:10.1016/j.plrev.2015.03.001. Epub 7 April 2015
26. Orchard, G., Basu, A., Thakor, N.: Building a silicon nervous system: neuromorphic engineering. Innovations Mag. **12**(1) (2013)
27. Feinberg, T.E.: Neuroontology, neurobiological naturalism, and consciousness: a challenge to scientific reduction and a solution. Phys. Life Rev. **9**(1), 13–34 (2012)
28. Fingelkurts, A.A., Fingelkurts, A.A.: Mind as a nested operational architectonics of the brain: comment on "Neuroontology, neurobiological naturalism, and consciousness: A challenge to scientific reduction and a solution" by Todd E. Feinberg. Phys. Life Rev. **9**(1), 49–50 (2012)

User-Interface Supporting Learners' Motivation and Emotion: A Case for Innovation in Learning Management Systems

Hana Ovesleová[✉]

Information Science and Librarianship, Charles University, Prague, Czech Republic
hana.ovesleova@gmail.com

Abstract. Lately, elearning has been making a comeback not only in business education of global corporations but in academia as well. Offer of classes for masses of population, regardless of time, place or social status, has become a norm in great world centers of learning. One of the most respected MOOC portals, Coursera, joins 138 partners from over 28 countries in its portfolio. Majority of universities offer a comprehensive portfolio of open or paid courses of wide range of specialization, from technical fields to humanities. Rising popularity of this type of education is well documented by the number of students, which reaches 17.5 million [1]. This way, even those whose life circumstances do not allow them to become full-time students can take part in classes. This form of education also enables suitable social conditions for inclusion, which is a welcomed bonus in current situation of population exodus. In the Czech Republic, MOOC projects are among top priorities of the Ministry of Education for 2016 [2]. Design of education systems and applications has undergone distinctive changes lately. Modern technologies, such as mobile and wearable technologies, cloud services and global expansion of the Internet make education accessible for almost anybody and make it largely available. Structure of users and their learning activities expand, which logically brings about a call for better personalization of learning environment. This paper examines what role the user interface plays in the learning process and what requirements on management system the education process reflects.

Keywords: Learning management system · elearning · Massive open online courses · Education systems and applications · User interface · Evaluation · Design guidelines · Human computer interaction · Motivation · Emotion · Semiotic · Effective learning

1 Learning, Emotion and Motivation

Based on a number of studies by Marcus [26], Marzano [14], Stuchlíková [8] and others, it is obvious that effective learning process relates combination of previously gained knowledge (alternatively existing cognitive schemes) with new subject matter, which is acquired through different contexts of individual's knowledge fond, active knowledge and motivation support, which creates emotional background to the educational process.

© Springer International Publishing Switzerland 2016
A. Marcus (Ed.): DUXU 2016, Part II, LNCS 9747, pp. 67–75, 2016.
DOI: 10.1007/978-3-319-40355-7_7

Out of effective pedagogic approaches, which work with emotions as with the bearer of motivation, Maria Montessori's educational program can be mentioned [3]. According to Stuchlíková [8], UNESCO International Commission on Education emphasizes "four pillars of education" in "learning society", learn to become aware, learn to act, learn to live together with others, and learn to be (authentic integrated individual). Emotional literacy is one of essential prerequisites leading to fulfillment of these requirements – it is a prerequisite of positive self-acceptance and effective and sensitive conduct in social environment [18].

In our paper, we are focusing on emotions and emotional conditions related to the learning process and on methodological tools that can work with emotions. Emotions can be both positive and negative and either increase or decrease motivation towards accomplishment of a learning activity. In life and in the learning process as well, pleasant emotions perform especially motivational and cognitive functions (assessment of incoming stimuli as good or bad), supply energy for realization of activities, speed up our reactions, enhance efficiency, and nurture belief in our capabilities. Good feeling as a positive emotion can be created e.g. by accomplishment of our duties, overcoming of weaknesses and strengthening of our will, discovering of correct solutions or sharing of our successes. And on the contrary, unpleasant emotions lead us away from certain activities and focus our attention in different direction. Feelings of anger, lack of interest, disgust, frustration, envy, fatigue or shame caused by failure, uncertainty or stress are uncalled for in the learning process. However, even these negative feelings can have, under certain circumstances, favorable implications for the learning process. Mild stress (caused by higher level of cognitive stimuli) can be given as an example. This stress will help us recollect certain pieces of information because this situation is seen as a threat from our inner criteria viewpoint. What level of stress is still beneficial for an individual and what stress level is harmful remains a question. Stress hinders performing of creative activities because these are tied to a state of relaxed concentration, which is preclusive of psychical state of stress [6]. Stress and negative emotions induce series of changes in cognitive processes. At first, it manifests itself in reduced ability of concentration; other qualitative changes arrive later: The individual loses cognitive capacity, speed, concentration, and attention, serious problems with memory come about, the person loses ability to perform more complex tasks or absorbs new facts with difficulties, interpreting of subject matter as well as its structuring is difficult; decision making process (simplified analytical approach) is inhibited as well. Distinctive changes in motivation towards learning arise, the individual does not feel like doing anything.

2   Role of Interface in the Learning Process

Specifics of user interfaces of learning systems lie in providing support to the learning process, which brings about distinctive mental strain of the user. While focusing on the content of the subject matter and the process of acquiring the knowledge, there is not much mental capacity left to be used on the system itself. In ideal case, the user interface of the elearning system should be an invisible companion providing right tools for desired activities in right time. User interface should actively influence users' behavior and effectively motivate and support them in the learning process.

Proceeding from beforehand determined evaluation rules for LMS user interface [27], it is possible to build on agreement among aims of several main pedagogical movements for the work with emotions and motivation, which is linked to them. Our research is therefore based on Robert Gagné's research [4] and his model Nine Events of Instruction (Fig. 1), on Skinner's operant conditioning theory (orig. Programmed Instruction Educational Model) [13], on Keller's Personal System of Instruction [9], on Bloom's Taxonomy of Learning Domains [5], and on Keller's [16] ARCS Model (Fig. 2). All of these theories assign a prominent role to the work with motivation during the learning process and insist on effort to avoid a failure in students' learning process.

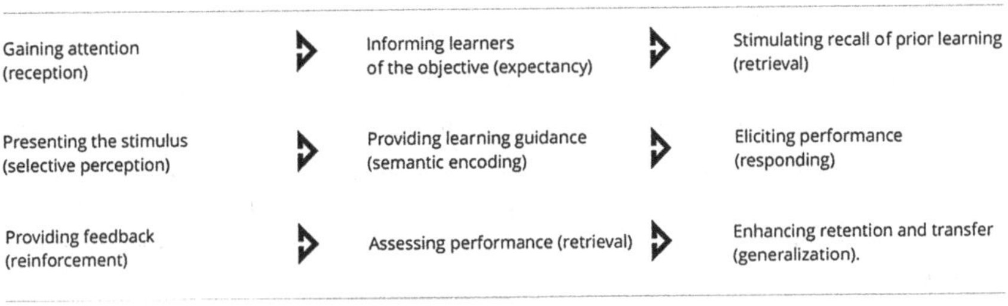

Gaining attention (reception)	▷	Informing learners of the objective (expectancy)	▷	Stimulating recall of prior learning (retrieval)
Presenting the stimulus (selective perception)	▷	Providing learning guidance (semantic encoding)	▷	Eliciting performance (responding)
Providing feedback (reinforcement)	▷	Assessing performance (retrieval)	▷	Enhancing retention and transfer (generalization).

Fig. 1. Robert Gagné: Nine Events of Instruction

Motivational Concept	Motivational Strategies	Motivational Concept	Motivational Strategies
Attention	Incongruity and conflict Concreteness Variability Humor Inquiry Participation	Confidence	Learning requirements Difficulty Expectations Attributions Self-confidence
Relevance	Experience Present worth Future usefulness Need matching Modeling Choice	Satisfaction	Natural consequences Unexpected rewards Positive outcomes Negative influences Scheduling

Fig. 2. J. M. Keller: Motivational Concept of ARCS Model

3   Requirements of the User Interface in LMS Environment Based on Effective Learning Methodology

Gaining Attention. Arousing of students' interest is the main goal of the first event. This pre-learning activity does not require any kind of effort, it is up to the lecturer what kind of tools and method he or she chooses to provoke students' curiosity. It is the students' first encounter with the topic. When comparing with the work in the system, it is possible to compare this activity to the first encounter with the system and its interface. That is why we place high demands on simplicity, comprehensibility and attractiveness. From the viewpoint of interface grammar [25] and information architecture, it is desirable to use for interface layout design patterns derived from users' mental models and respecting mental consistency and intuitiveness. Many experimental studies were carried out in the field of design approaches, defining relationships between objective and subjective factors of interactive systems aesthetics perception, e.g. Seckler et al. [7]. However, the results show that universal principals for design patterns cannot be unambiguously defined. Our recommendation therefore is to respect common typographical rules and composition solutions, which harmonize the complex in dependence on the number and mutual relationship of individual components, and sociocultural customs of target audience. First impression is often crucial and determines further motivation of users to work with the system.

Informing Learners of Objectives. Informing of objectives allows the learners to organize their thoughts on what they will learn and perform. This works by helping to cue the learners on the goals of the instruction and how they will be able to use their new skills in the workplace. Marzano [14] reported an effect size of 0.97 (which indicates that the achievement can be raised by 34 percentile points) when goal specification is used. When students have some control over the learning outcomes, there is an effect size of 1.21 (39 percentile points) [10]. From the standpoint of the system, there is a requirement for structure transparency and clarity, possibility of linear and non-linear classification, visibility and control. Grammar of interaction is emphasized, "where to go" is suppressed at the expense of "what to do". Every tool, which the students have to their disposal, must be uniquely identifiable with respect to function and use. For this purpose, mental models and design pattern are use yet again.

Stimulating Recall of Prior Learning. Support through "proctors" [9] or, more likely, "scaffolding" - building upon the learners' previous knowledge and skills [15]. In the learning process, it is deliberate collecting of existing information with relation to given issues, search activities within one's knowledge fond, and directive creative activity pointed to action preparation. With respect to system requirements, it is directed use of analytical capabilities of the system recording history and attributes of user action, and offer of functions and tools required for search and creative activities (notes, tags and flash cards systems, tools for creation of mind maps, lexicons, collaborative wiki systems, cloud services, etc.).

Presenting the Stimulus. Methodology of learning materials presentation covers wide range of looking at information, its presentation and interpretation. According to Marzano [14] all information that is perceived via the senses passes through three processors that encode it as linguistic, nonlinguistic, or affective representations (Fig. 3). In the educational and training world, knowledge is most commonly presented linguistically, so perhaps this mode receives the most attention from a learning standpoint [17]. The linguistic mode includes verbal communication, reading, watching (e.g. learn the rule of chess through observation), etc. [10]. The nonlinguistic mode includes mental pictures, smell, kinesthetic, tactile, auditory, and taste. And finally the affective mode can be thought of as a continuum of feelings, emotions, and ultimately moods. Possibilities of distribution and perception of information (alternatively personal preferences in dependence on student's study type [11] and personality) are therefore one of the key topics. The amount of information in time also plays an important role in the learning process. To prevent cognitive overload, it is necessary to serve information sequentially. This is related to Skinner's sequenced learning events - allowing the learners to receive feedback on individualized tasks, thereby correcting isolated problems rather than having little idea of where the root of the learning challenge lies [10].

Fig. 3. Robert Marzano: The Three Representational Modes

First of all, learning management system must provide wide range of tools for distribution and content structuring. There we perceive a large space for experiment on content distribution so that it combines traditional linguistic mode with nonlinguistic and affective modes. This will support easier saving and subsequent retrieval of information from memory. As the form is concerned, it is possible to highlight incorporating of modules that integrate gamification components (virtual environment). Variability of content form makes choice according to personal preferences possible. We also consider essential technological shift from currently common interface to less traditional forms that permit use of more senses, such as haptic or kinetic interfaces [19].

Providing Learning Guidance. Often, when students interact with new subject matter, they lose motivation due to negative emotions [6]. In this study phase, it is essential to arouse or boost positive emotions and suppress the negative ones. This phase is the most demanding on students' mental load, on support of their motivation and interaction with the lector of the system. It is therefore a subject of utmost importance to sustain (preferably automatically) early feedback concerning students' actions (action - reaction). There might be many forms of reaction, from a positive message through reward (e.g. very popular system of badges, which makes possible sharing of success or reaching of certain level of understanding or knowledge) to regulation of students' behavior (e.g. repeated use of wrong path to the outcome). Collective problem solution can be an important type of feedback. Another request on the system consequently is a module of social connections (linking with social media, discussion forums or other means of communication, such as videoconferences, etc.).

Eliciting Performance. Opportunity to apply newly acquired knowledge, findings and skills in different contexts is desirable for their consolidation and retrieval later. These activities cover eliciting student activities with asking deep-learning questions, eliciting recall strategies, facilitating student elaborations (elaborate or explain details) and helping students integrate new knowledge (provide content in a context-rich way) [12]. There is a wide range of tools serving to this purposes, such as control questions, auto-corrective exercises, auto-tests, educational games, quizzes, etc.

Providing Feedback. There are many forms of feedback; its form depends on the phase of the learning process and what aim it has. It can be generally stated that feedback works effectively with users' emotion only when its frequency and form are chosen aptly. For example, we can confirm correctness of chosen course of action, correct it or make instructions more specific, without revealing the correct procedure. We can evoke feeling of active listening or participation by informative addition or suggest analytically new solutions for correction of unsuitable solution [12]. Feedback can be provided by a lector, system or by another student. On the other hand, some forms of feedback are highly individualized and thus difficult to automate. However, in the requirements on the system, we can boldly mention automated mailing of feedback messages about reading a message, about control or completion of a task, about meeting all the requirements and so on. System of reminders and motivating messages can be added among the requirements on the system because they enable linking of the system to other media and devices. This way, better accessibility is reached (mobile technologies, wearable technologies etc.).

Assessing Performance. In order to evaluate the effectiveness of the instructional events, one must test to see if the expected learning outcomes have been achieved. Performance should be based on previously stated objectives. Methods for testing learning include pretest for mastery of prerequisites, post-test to check for mastery of content or skills, embed questions throughout instruction through oral questioning or quizzes, objective or criterion-referenced performances which measure how well a student has learned a topic and identification of normative-referenced performances which compares one student to another student [12]. Assessment scores may cause motivation drop in further learning; it is therefore important to pay due attention to selection of the right form of assessment. Verbal comments or activities that make assessment by fellow students possible (for example evaluation of a presentation according to given criteria) are a welcomed addition to commonly used written tests (filling in the blanks, multiple choice, etc.) [20]. Tools for advancement assessment or learning process outcome must be variable, so that assessment of students in all phases is possible (using fitting form and scale).

Enhancing Retention and Transfer. Transfer of training is effectively and continuing applying the knowledge, skills, and/or attitudes that were learned in a learning environment to the job environment. Closely related to this concept is Transfer of Learning—the application of skills, knowledge, and/or attitudes that were learned in one situation to another learning situation [22]. This increases the speed of learning [21]. Virtual environment can be a convenient help in such a situation, because it can simulate use of gained knowledge and skills in "real" world [23]. The system can contain modules of "test applications", simulations and games, can be interconnected with commonly used applications from public life, use real data from publically accessible databases, etc.

Fig. 4. Czechoslovakia 38-89: a complex educational simulation (http://cs3889.com) (reproduced with permission).

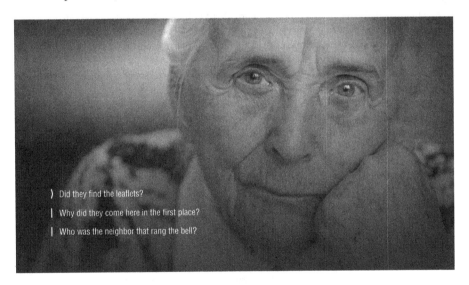

Fig. 5. Czechoslovakia 38-89: a complex educational simulation (http://cs3889.com) (reproduced with permission).

4 Summary

The process of user interface design is a communication process among the system designers and the users. According to de Souza's account [24], both designers and users are interlocutors in an overall communication process that takes place through an interface of words, graphics, and behavior. The designer of the learning management system communicates with two groups of users through the interface. There are the lectors on one side, being the content creators, and the students, the content consumers, on the other side. Learning process and its methodology become a basic strategic starting point, from which framework for both the designer pattern and user behavior comes to being. Course methodology determines measure and type of user interaction with study content. Through the system, the designer gives the content creator a set of tools for effective content presentation and distribution.

Respected theories of learning are ground for this paper, in which we are trying to define all aspects of effective learning process that set requirements on the LMS interface. Apart from general rules for LMS [27], we are completing the criteria with aspects related to the support of motivation. Resulting set of criteria will be used as a ground for analysis of current learning management systems used at Czech universities and as basis for their innovation. The aim of the research is the design of experimental modular system of plug-ins, which will be arbitrarily combined and will be easily included into existing learning management systems.

References

1. Meet our partners. https://www.coursera.org/about/partners. Accessed 10 Feb 2016
2. Fryč, J.: O masové on-line otevřené kurzy je ve světě zájem, neměli bychom zůstat pozadu. http://www.msmt.cz/vzdelavani/stredni-vzdelavani/o-masove-on-line-otevrene-kurzy-je-ve-svete-zajem-nemeli. Accessed 09 Feb 2016
3. Základní principy pedagogiky Montessori. http://www.montessoricr.cz/principy-montessori-pedagogiky/. Accessed 21 Jan 2016
4. Gagné, R.: The Conditions of Learning and the Theory of Instruction, 4th edn. Holt, Rinehart, and Winston, New York (1985)
5. Bloom, B.S., Engelhart, M.D., Furst, E.J., Hill, W.H., Krathwohl, D.R.: Taxonomy of educational objectives: the classification of educational goals. In: Handbook I: Cognitive Domain. David McKay Company, New York (1956)
6. Nývltová, V.: Psychologie učení. Praha 2014. http://kuhv.vscht.cz/cinnosti/inspec. Accessed 09 Feb 2016
7. Seckler, M., Opwis, K., Tuch, A.N.: Linking objective design factors with subjective aesthetics: an experimental study on how structure and color of websites affect the facets of users' visual aesthetic perception. Comput. Hum. Behav. **49**, 375–389 (2015)
8. Stuchlíková, I.: Základy psychologie emocí. https://is.muni.cz/www/344438/7159323/Iva_Stuchlikova_Zaklady_psychologie_emoci.pdf. Accessed 01 Feb 2016
9. Keller, F.S.: Goodbye teacher.... J. Appl. Behav. Anal. **1**, 79–89 (1968)
10. Clarke, D.: Robert Gagné's Nine Steps of Instruction. http://www.nwlink.com/~donclark/hrd/learning/id/nine_step_id.html. Accessed 02 Feb 2016
11. Learning Styles. https://en.wikipedia.org/wiki/Learning_styles. Accessed 01 Jan 2016
12. Gagnes nine steps of instruction. http://www.niu.edu/facdev/_pdf/guide/learning/gagnes_nine_events_instruction.pdf. Accessed 02 Feb 2016
13. Skinner, B.F.: Teaching machines. Science **128**(967–977), 137–158 (1958)
14. Marzano, R.J.: A theory-based meta-analysis of research on instruction. Regional Educational Laboratory, Mid-Continent Aurora, Colorado (1998). http://eric.ed.gov/?id=ED427087
15. Collins, A., Brown, J.S., Holum, A.: Cognitive apprenticeship: making thinking visible. Am. Educ. **15**, 6–46 (1991)

16. Keller, J.M.: Development and use of the ARCS model of instructional design. J. Instr. Dev. **10**(3), 2–10 (1987)
17. Chomsky, N.: Language and the Problems of Knowledge: The Managua Lectures. MIT Press, Cambridge (1988)
18. Goleman, D.: Emotional Intelligence: Why It Can Matter More Than IQ. Columbus Press, Boston (1997)
19. Educause Learning Initiative. 7 things you should know about… Haptics. http://net.educause.edu/ir/library/pdf/eli7029.pdf. Accessed 12 Feb 2016
20. Infogram. Hodnocení vzdělávací činnosti. http://www.infogram.cz/article.do?articleId=1328. Accessed 23 Jan 2016
21. Clarke, D.: Transfer of Learning. http://www.nwlink.com/~donclark/hrd/learning/transfer.html. Accessed 19 Jan 2016
22. Perkins, D.N., Salomon, G.: Transfer of Learning. Contribution to the International Encyclopedia of Education, 2nd edn. Pergamon Press, Oxford (1992)
23. Czechoslovakia 38-89: Assassination. Complex educational simulation for high school students. http://cs3889.com/article.do?articleId=1148. Accessed 12 Feb 2016
24. De Souza, C.S.: The Semiotic Engineering of Human-Computer Interaction. Acting with Technology. MIT Press, Cambridge (2005)
25. Brejcha, J.: Cross-Cultural Human-Computer Interaction and User Experience Design: A Semiotic Perspective. CRC Press, Boca Raton, Taylor & Francis Group, LLC, London (2015)
26. Marcus, A., Peng, Y., Lecca, N.: The learning machine: mobile UX design that combines information design with persuasion design. In: Marcus, A. (ed.) DUXU 2013, Part II. LNCS, vol. 8013, pp. 247–256. Springer, Heidelberg (2013)
27. Ovesleová, H.: E-learning platforms and lacking motivation in students: concept of adaptable UI for online courses. In: Marcus, A. (ed.) DUXU 2015. LNCS, vol. 9188, pp. 218–227. Springer, Heidelberg (2015)

Affective Design with Kansei Mining: An Empirical Study from Automotive Industry in Indonesia

Amalia Suzianti[✉], Septy Apriliandary, and Nabila Priscandy Poetri

Department of Industrial Engineering, Faculty of Engineering,
Universitas Indonesia, Depok, Indonesia
suzianti@eng.ui.ac.id,
septyaprilliandary_ti2010@yahoo.com,
nabilapriscandy@yahoo.com

Abstract. Automotive industry delivers a great contribution to Indonesia by accounting high percentage in gross domestic product. As automotive industry is developing, especially for car industry, the competition between car companies is highly increasing. This condition resulted in a situation where products from different car companies having the same standard for quality. Therefore, customers are triggered to consider another factor beside functional specification and quality, which is affective perception. This research focused on how customers of city car in Indonesia evaluate the product from its exterior shape by considering their affective side. Method of this research is *Kansei* Engineering, specifically its *Kansei* Words. Data from customers are processed with the method of association rule mining and conjoint analysis. From the output of this research, there are five groups of *Kansei* Words that represent customers' affective perception (i.e., classic and sleek, robust and powerful, sporty and formal, cute, and modern). The final output from this research are five recommended designs for city car exterior shape that describe all the *Kansei* Words above.

Keywords: *Kansei* Engineering · *Kansei* Words · City car · Car exterior shape · Association rule mining · Conjoint analysis

1 Introduction

Automotive industry is one of the fastest-growing industrial sectors in Indonesia. According to The Association of Indonesia Automotive Industry, in the second quarter of 2013, the manufacturing industry accounted for 23.64 % of the gross domestic product of Indonesia with the largest contribution coming from automotive manufacturing, amounted to 50.37 %. This leads the automotive industry to be one of the industries that support the three pillars of industrialization in the country (i.e., increasing added value, maximizing the impact in the country, and positioning Indonesia in the global supply chain). The third pillar in this term refers to the opportunity for Indonesia to become a part of global network by evolving Indonesia as a global automotive industry producer.

© Springer International Publishing Switzerland 2016
A. Marcus (Ed.): DUXU 2016, Part II, LNCS 9747, pp. 76–85, 2016.
DOI: 10.1007/978-3-319-40355-7_8

From the various types of car that are available in the Indonesian automotive market, city car is the type of car with the most rapid development. City car is the notion of four-wheeled vehicles powered from 1000 cc to 1300 cc that brings the concept of light and compact vehicle. According to The Indonesian Automotive Industry Association, the trend of city car sales in the last five years increased five-fold in 2012.

As automotive industry is developing, especially for city car, the competition between car companies is highly increasing. This condition resulted in a situation where products from different car companies having the same standard for quality. Consumers will be more selective in choosing a car when all brand products offer the same quality, price, design, comfort, performance, security, and after sales service. Therefore, customers are triggered to consider other factors beside functional specification and quality, which is affective perception; given the fact that car's exterior is the first thing that is recognized when looking at car products.

Therefore, when designing a product, the consumer affection needs to be considered [1]. Based on previous study, six different roles of product appearance for consumers are identified (i.e., communication of aesthetic, symbolic, functional and ergonomic information, attention drawing and categorization) [2]. From those six appearance roles, it can be concluded that a product's appearance can have aesthetic and symbolic value for consumers, can communicate functional characteristics and give a quality impression (functional value), and can communicate ease of use (ergonomic value). However, they are much more difficult to measure and understand compared to product assessment through the specification and technology owned.

This research focused on how customers of city car in Indonesia evaluate the product from its exterior shape by considering the affective factors. In order to guide the designers in designing products that consider the customer affection, this study used the concept of *Kansei* mining. This method utilizes available design of products in the market to run the product design process. Therefore, the product development process does not have to start from scratch. This research aims to propose the exterior design of city car based on the affective perception of consumers. The proposed designs will be useful for designers in the automotive industry in running their product development process.

The rest of the paper is organized as follows. Section 2 describe the data and methodology used in this study. Section 4 presents the analysis based on the result of data processing and also shows the proposed designs. The paper ends with conclusions and suggestions of the overall study, mainly from the results and analysis. In addition, the suggestions will include input for further research.

2 Methodology

This section explains about the data and methodology used in the study. This study used two types of data, namely primary data, which was gained through questionnaires, and secondary data, such as data gained from reports, journal, etc. The method used in this research are *Kansei* Engineering, Data Mining and Conjoint Analysis. *Kansei* Engineering was chosen because it is one of the most implemented method in emotional design and engineering methodology that translates impressions, feelings, and demand of customers on existing products or on the concept of design solutions and concrete design parameters.

Primary data needed are the consumer's perception mapping data in the form of *Kansei* Words against city car exterior shape, and the consumer's perception data against a combination of city car exterior components. Therefore, this research collected customer's perception in the form of two questionnaires. The consumer's perception mapping data in the form of *Kansei* Words against city car exterior shape was obtained through first questionnaire.

Table 1 below shows *Kansei Words* that represents the exterior shape of city car, while Fig. 1 shows several type of city car's exterior shape. Respondents were asked to choose their favorite type of car based on *Kansei Words* given and match it with the cars in the picture. The first questionnaires were processed using association rule mining in order to find the pattern of the data. From the data processing using Magnum Opus software, five groups of *Kansei Words* that represents city car's exterior shape were obtained (i.e., classic and sleek, robust and powerful, sporty and formal, cute, and modern) (Table 2).

Table 1. Kansei Words of city car's exterior shape

No.	*Kansei* Words
1	Cute
2	Sporty
3	Classic
4	Formal
5	Powerful
6	Modern
7	Robust
8	Spacious
9	Sleek
10	Luxurious

The next step of this study is collecting the consumer's perception data against a combination of city car exterior components through the second questionnaire. Of the eight types of city car exterior components from previous study, five were chosen as the most influential exterior components for the consumer as shown in Fig. 2. Then, those five city car exterior components, namely headlights, front bumper, rear light, fog lamp, and door handle, were combined with five groups of *Kansei* Words that represents city car's exterior shape obtained from the first questionnaire.

Data was collected by distributing the second questionnaires in the form of rating by respondents towards the stimuli presented. Rating was given using a *Likert* scale of 1 to 5 where higher values indicate higher preference (Table 3).

Afterwards, the questionnaires were processed using conjoint analysis. Conjoint analysis was used because it is a technique specifically used to understand the desire or

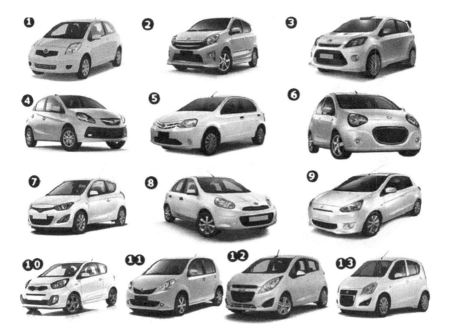

Fig. 1. Exterior shape of city car from various brands

Table 2. Descriptive statistics of the first questionnaires

		Sample
N		1000
Age	20–24	39 %
	25–30	33 %
	31–35	22 %
	36–40	6 %
Gender	Male	65 %
	Female	35 %
Occupation	Student	31 %
	Employee	56 %
	Entrepreneur	7 %
	Teacher	1 %
	Lecturer	2 %
	Others	3 %
Car ownership	Yes, I have owned a car	5 %
	Yes, I have and still own a car	70 %
	I have never owned a car	25 %

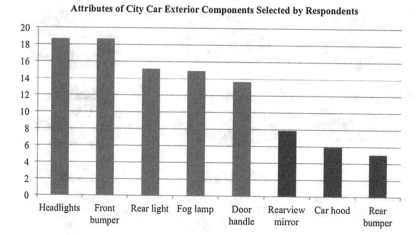

Fig. 2. Percentage of city car's exterior components selected by respondents (Color figure online)

Table 3. Descriptive statistics of the second questionnaires

		Sample
N		100
Age	20–24	70.3 %
	25–30	17.82 %
	31–35	7.92 %
	36–40	3.96 %
Gender	Male	55.45 %
	Female	44.55 %
Occupation	Student	62.38 %
	Employee	24.75 %
	Entrepreneur	1.98 %
	Others	10.89 %

preference of consumers towards a certain product or service by measuring the level of usability and the relative importance of various attributes of the product [3].

3   Results and Discussions

This section explains about interpreting the results and analyzing the results obtained in this study. From the data processing before, the consumer's perception mapping data in the form of *Kansei* Words was obtained in the form of rules based on the association rule-mining concept. *Rules* is a pattern that shows the relationship of consumer perception–in this case is Kansei Words–with the exterior shape of the associated city car. The *rules* can also shows the probability of *Kansei* Words to emerge which followed by the appearance of the exterior form of a particular city car that represent consumer preferences. The probability in this term can be seen from the value of strength. The *rules* gained have a strength value between 0.030 and 0727. Those *rules* data obtained with Magnum Opus software are to be filtered based on the strength value in order to group *Kansei* Words that has several similarities in term of exterior shape of city car. The higher the strength value indicates the higher probability of *Kansei* Words to appear in consumer's preference data. Therefore, *rules* that have the strength value between 0.0 and 0.1 are to be considered insignificant. Table 4 below shows several groups of *Kansei* Words that have similarities in terms of the exterior shape of related city car.

Table 4. Kansei Words that have similarities in terms of the city car's exterior shape

Kansei Words	Exterior shape elements
Sleek, Classic	Car 7, Car 9
Robust, Powerful	Car 7, Car 8
Sporty, Formal	Car 4, Car 9
Cute	Car 4, Car 6
Modern	Car 10, Car 12

In order to determine the most preferred combination of attributes, the authors measured the level of each utility value of each component of the exterior for every combination obtained from the second questionnaires.

The combination that most represents the consumer's perspective on classic and sleek cars is the combination of components that have rear lights, door handles, and front bumper from the car 9 and headlights and fog lights from the car 7. As for the robust and powerful cars, the best combination is the combination of components that have rear lights and door handles from the car 8 and headlights, front bumper, and fog lights from the car 7. The combination that most represents the consumer's perspective on sporty and formal cars is the combination of components that have rear lights, headlights, and fog lamp from the car 9 and door handles and front bumper from the car 4. On the other hand, the combination that most represents the consumer's perspective on cute cars is the combination of components that have rear lights, front bumper, and fog lamp from the car 6 and door handles and headlights from the car 4. Lastly, the combination that most represents the consumer's perspective on modern cars is the combination of components that have rear lights, headlights, and fog lamp from the car 12 and door handles and front bumper from the car 4.

Table 5 below shows the relationship of *Kansei* Words that represent consumer perception with the exterior shape of the associated city car. It can be seen that there are some exterior components that do not only represent one *Kansei* Words alone.

As it is previously stated, this study aims to propose the exterior design of city car based on the affective perception of consumers. Therefore, those combinations above will be used as inputs to design the new city car's exterior shape. Each group is of Kansei Words is represented by one exterior design of city car.

Table 5. Combination of city car's exterior components against *Kansei* Words

Kansei Words	Rear light	Door Handle	Headlights	Front Bumper	Fog Lamp
Classic, Sleek					
Robust, Power-ful					
Sporty, Formal					
Cute					
Modern					

For the classic and sleek city car, consumers are more likely to choose long rear light, lift-back type for door handles, and headlights with oval shape on the right side and pointy on the other. As for the front bumper, consumers tend to choose the one with a slightly curved shape at the bottom and straight line at the top. Lastly, the diamond shaped fog lamp is more preferred by the classic and sleek seeker (Fig. 3).

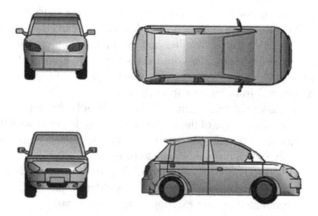

Fig. 3. 2D design of classic and sleek city car

The headlights and fog lamp chosen for the robust and powerful city car are the same with the classic and sleek city car. The robust and powerful seeker tends to prefer the rear light that is longer vertically and pull-type door handles. As for the front bumper, consumers are more likely to choose the one with trapezoid shape (Fig. 4).

Fig. 4. 2D design of robust and powerful city car

For the sporty and formal city car, consumers' preference is the same with the classic and sleek city car for the rear light component. Consumers of this type of car prefer to have pull-type door handles, headlights with oval shape on the left side and pointy on the other, and a rectangular front bumper with slightly curves at the top and bottom. The fog lamp for the sporty and formal city car is a little bit similar with the previous two types of city car (Fig. 5).

Fig. 5. 2D design of sporty and formal city car

For the cute city car, consumers are more likely to choose tiny rear light with triangle shape, pull-type door handles, and long headlights. As for the front bumper, consumers tend to choose the oval shaped type. Lastly, the round shaped fog lamp is more preferred by the cute city car seeker (Fig. 6).

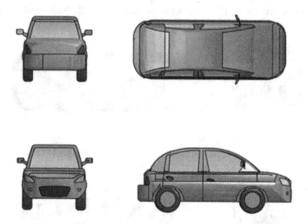

Fig. 6. 2D design of cute city car

The last type of city car, which is modern city car, has the same type of door handles with the previous three. As for the rear light, consumers are more likely to choose the one that is longer vertically, but a little more complicated compared to the robust and powerful city car's. For the modern city car seeker, they prefer to have a car with diamond shaped headlights, long front bumper, and diamond shaped fog lamp with sharper corner (Fig. 7).

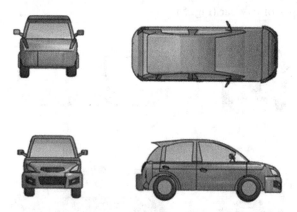

Fig. 7. 2D design of modern city car

4 Conclusion

Along with the increasing the competitiveness of the car manufacturers, particularly for the type of city car, functional specification is no longer the only factor of consideration for consumers to purchase a car. Car's exterior is the first thing that is recognized when looking at car products, thus becomes a significant impact on the consumer's decision to buy a car. This study aims to provide a draft proposal of the car's exterior shape that represents affective perception of the consumer in the form of *Kansei* Words.

The early stage of this study was determining what kind of existing exterior shape of city car that represents the affective perception of consumers. By mapping *Kansei* Words of the car's exterior shape with a certain type of car, several *Kansei* Words associated with car's exterior were obtained.

Afterwards, the study continued to know specifically what kind of exterior components according to consumer that represent their affective perception. The determination of the most representative exterior components based on consumer perceptions was conducted by calculating the utility value of every combination of exterior components. Combination with the highest total value of utility will be proposed as a draft form of city car's exterior shape. It can be concluded that the proposed designs for the shape of city car's exterior will fulfill affective needs of consumers.

This study resulted in five designs of city car's exterior shape. These proposed designs are the result of combination between the five most significant components (i.e. rear lights, door handles, headlights, front bumper and fog lamps) and five groups of *Kansei* Words (i.e. classic and sleek, robust and powerful, sporty and formal, cute, and modern). For the future research, a similar research can be conducted with other types of car, such as family car, SUV, or sport car.

References

1. Creusen, M.E., Schoormans, J.P.: The different roles of product appearance in consumer choice. J. Prod. Innov. Manag. **22**, 63–81 (2005)
2. Hair Jr., J.F., Anderson, R.E., Tatham, R.L., Black, W.C.: Multivariate Data Analysis with Readings. Prentice Hall, Upper Saddle River (1995)
3. Jordan, P.W.: Designing Pleasurable Products. Taylor & Francis, London (2000)

Conflict Interfaces

Mediated Meditations on Desire, Fear and Anxiety

Matthew Wizinsky[(✉)]

School of Design, University of Cincinnati, Cincinnati, USA
matthew.wizinsky@uc.edu

Abstract. Personal computing interfaces have so fully integrated into contemporary life that their impacts on everyday choices often go unnoticed. The discipline of User Experience Design operates a user-centric methodology that similarly dissipates the designer's sense of responsibility for the social effects produced by such systems. This situation doubly masks the potential for personal computing interfaces to operate with goals hidden from and potentially contradictory to those of their users. By situating personal computing interfaces and User Experience Design within various theoretical contexts, I will describe a growing body of critical HCI work that I identify as Conflict Interfaces and share pedagogical techniques for teaching interaction design through the lens of political conflict.

Keywords: Interaction design · Critical Design · User Experience Design · Speculative Design · Design pedagogy · Political theory · Mediation · Agonism

1 Introduction

As our myriad machine companions become more intelligent and more embedded in our everyday lives, we tend to lose sight of the fact that we are interacting with complex systems designed by other human beings for a multitude of intentions. Our daily and mundane interactions with systems and interfaces of mobile and personal computing produce a new natural order to life that belies the potential for these systems to harbor goals that are contradictory, conflicting or simply tangential to our own. We make choices about our daily movements based on real-time and predictive data from the city. Location-based "recommendations" influence choices in everything from shopping to dining to choosing a doctor. Social media systems and their distributed interfaces produce spaces that define and mediate relationships with our friends and families and even play the role of romantic matchmaker. The news we receive about local or global events is filtered and sculpted by our tracked and calculated preferences and behaviors. Even our cultural experiences are affected by algorithmically-determined suggestions for books, films, music, and entertainment. All this is to say nothing about the nature of contemporary work, which has radically altered the human experience from email to video conferencing to specialized software of all varieties.

This comfortable proximity of mediated information and feedback as an apparently supportive companionship (*thanks, friend!*) holds the potential for—and maybe even masks—coercive sway in the tiniest nooks of everyday life. Of course, such systems

© Springer International Publishing Switzerland 2016
A. Marcus (Ed.): DUXU 2016, Part II, LNCS 9747, pp. 86–97, 2016.
DOI: 10.1007/978-3-319-40355-7_9

are all products of human efforts and are borne of the human intentions that brought them into our new social, cultural and work experiences.[1] While often useful or convenient, these systems and their interfaces are not exactly adapting themselves seamlessly into our daily lives. Instead, we are often so enamored by their utility and convenience that we willingly bend toward their languages, prompts and rituals. By allowing even trivial decisions to be swayed by algorithmic determinations, we are, in effect, limiting our own choices and, perhaps, overlooking the possibility of coercion.

The design of everyday human interactions with computing systems has ushered in something akin to a meta-category of design practice called User Experience Design. Transcending traditional distinctions made by domain, media or discipline, User Experience Design draws on methodologies known from product design, communication design, software design and others, producing techniques and methodologies to materially and experientially situate computational experiences within human lives.

Within this context, I will describe a growing body of critical HCI work that I am identifying as Conflict Interfaces. Conflict Interfaces foreground and make palpable the reality that personal computing interfaces are the sites of mediated political relations. Often presented as prototypes, one-offs, installations, performances or other means of provocation, these projects are not typically intended for mass production, nor do they propose a *should be* vision of technologically-driven social organization. Instead, their purpose is to make the personal computing interface understood as a complex site of desire, fear and anxiety. By doing so, they make visible the often imperceptible social or political forces that produce such interfaces to suggest they could be re-imagined or even re-configured. These works traverse diverse sub-categories of Critical Design practices, including Speculative Design, [3] Adversarial Design [1] and Tactical Media [12]. They emanate from university research labs, experimental media collaboratives, exhibitions, student projects, conferences, competitions and other liminal spaces in the great global network of technology experimentation. They are inherently political in their ambitions and use design's power to make complex—even contradictory—ideas materially manifest.

To understand how Conflict Interfaces operate, I will first build the theoretical and practical contexts that situate them within various contemporary design practices. From that grounding, I will share my preliminary experiences in expanding this territory—theoretically and practically—through teaching interface design as a critical practice. These pedagogical approaches are supplemented by case studies of projects by university students to exemplify the territory of Conflict Interfaces that I am defining.

2   Context

What do I mean when I claim that personal computing interfaces are the sites of *mediated political relations*? To further define these terms and give Conflict Interfaces a theoretical grounding, I will draw on positions from political theory, social theory, systems theory and critical practices in design.

---

[1] Bruno Latour tells us, "Technical action is a form of delegation that allows us to mobilize, during interactions, moves made elsewhere, earlier, by other actants" [8, p. 52].

2.1   The Political

Political theorist Chantal Mouffe distinguishes "the political" from "politics" in this way: "By 'the political' I refer to the dimension of antagonism that is inherent in human relations, antagonism that can take many forms and emerge in different types of social relations. 'Politics,' on the other side, indicates the ensemble of practices, discourses and institutions which seek to establish a certain order and organize human coexistence in conditions that are always potentially conflictual because they are affected by the dimension of 'the political.'" [10, p. 101] If we follow this *agonistic* view of political theory [9], an interface between two systems negotiating independent—and, therefore, potentially competing—goals becomes the site of *political* negotiation.

Political negotiations are an inescapable aspect of human social relations. Any space that produces territory for negotiations is an opportunity for inquiry, debate and re-configuration of the relations that produce that space. Given the vast quantity and diversity of human relations that unfold within human-computer interfaces today—from personal to institutional to corporate to governmental communications and exchanges—personal computing interfaces produce a multi-dimensional space in which contemporary power relations are configured, established and operated.

2.2   Mediation

Inspired by Bruno Latour, I will take up a definition of *mediation* as the action-and-effect of human actors (*makers*) producing the signs or objects that engage and shape the lived experiences of other human actors (or *users*). Latour gives us the wonderful example of the speed bump [8]. The driver's intention to *get from point A to point B* is subtly interrupted by the mediation of the speed bump and becomes *slow down to protect nearby children or pedestrians*. Or, perhaps more cynically, *slow down so as not to damage my car*. Either way, the driver's behavior is modified. We can understand mediation as a complex entanglement in which techniques, production systems and human intentions are translated into an inseparable mix of materiality and social relations.

Generally speaking, design operates at this point of *translation*—turning intentionality into a complex blend of matter and experience. From Latour's example, the speed bump is not just a lump of painted concrete, but it is "full of engineers and chancellors and lawmakers, commingling their wills and their story lines with those of gravel, concrete, paint, and standard calculations" [8, p. 41]. In this way, mediation describes the scenario in which "we hourly encounter hundreds, even thousands, of absent makers who are remote in time and space yet simultaneously active and present" [8, p. 40]. In our everyday encounters with speed bumps, cultural etiquette, kitchen utensils and so on, the makers of these signs and objects—unlikely to be present with us in person—are actively shaping our experiences based on some prior set of goals.

Certainly, personal computing interfaces operate from a breadth and diversity of social and material techniques at least equivalent to those of a speed bump. Designers play a mediating role when domesticating technologies to make them useful, viable and desirable, in turn, transforming our daily experiences.

2.3   Learning Systems and Choice

Setting out to characterize different types of interactions, Dubberly, Pangaro, and Haque have developed a matrix of couplings between different orders of systems [2]. For example, a human operating a steam engine is seen as a "learning system coupled to a self-regulating system" [2]. The complexity of interactions between coupled systems increases as each system moves from Reacting (linear) to Self-Regulating (first order) to Learning (second order). In the "Conversing" model, two Learning systems are engaged. Each system takes input from the other, yet each system "has the choice to respond to the other or not" [2]. The element of *choice* is critical as it allows each system to maintain or re-adjust its goals in response to the other system's feedback—or ignore that feedback altogether.

This systems view of interaction helps better articulate the nature of mediation in most contemporary personal computing interfaces. It states that *intention*, the capacity for independent goals and malleable decision-making, is a necessary condition for a Learning system. The author—i.e., designer, developer, distributor—of the system is no longer directly involved in the ongoing and changing actions of the system, delivered through its interface with the human user. Rather, the Learning system is encoded with its author's (or authors') intentions during production, then left to continually adjust its goals and subsequent actions autonomously toward those intentions. This complicates and obfuscates any clear view of the author's agenda. The author is both anonymous and absent while the system—through its interface—takes on its own authority to mediate the political relations between absent maker and present user.

2.4   User Experience Design

The term *interface* defines that point (or system of touch-points) where two or more systems, orders, or logics intersect and interact. An interface makes manifest the social, material and experiential nature of that interaction. Given that Human-Computer interfaces are the product of human labor and intention, we can recognize that an interface is actually a mediated space for human-human social relations. In other words, an interface produces space within which social and power relations unfold. Personal systems that utilize computation and algorithms to inform, prompt, nudge or assist humans in everyday life play an integral role in decisions we make from the grand to the mundane: from my filtered and curated local, global and political news to the neighborhood where I decide to live or where to pick up dinner. The customization of modern technologies has embedded them so deeply into our daily rituals that they seem a natural extension of our own most personal needs and desires.[2]

The last few decades have seen human-computer interfaces move to center stage of almost all cultural experiences. With this transition, many communication and product designers have focused their efforts on creating fluid and extensible languages and

---

[2] According to Latour, the adjective *modern* "does not describe an increased distance between society and technology or their alienation, but a deepened intimacy, a more intricate mesh, between the two" [8, p. 47].

scenarios for human-machine systems to interface in disparate locations, asynchronously and across multiple touch-points. The discipline of User Experience Design has emerged with its battle cry: "Know your user!" [11] Designers are trained to practice User Centered Design processes to understand the needs, desires, contexts and motivations of potential users in order to align new products or services with their aspirations, behaviors and daily rituals. These techniques have helped produce many successful personal computing products and services. Yet, with these new disciplinary techniques come new questions: What role do personal computing and communication technologies—including the people who labor to produce them—play in producing or maintaining social relations and even power struggles through the everyday experiences they generate? Based on Michel Foucault's historical analysis of power structures and disciplinary techniques, we see that disciplines produce knowledge at the same time that they produce new sites for exercising power and asserting authority [4].

If designers view their decisions about how to shape other humans' experiences as directly informed by qualitative and quantitative research based on the *needs* of other people (*users*), designers are less likely to understand their work as guided by any personal subjectivities, desires or judgments. It would be very easy for the interaction designer to feel that she is merely operating the controls of a dynamic (maybe even *altruistic*) system and overlook the authority she is surely investing in the process and product. While the autonomy of the interface and its supporting systems seems to disappear into its banal role in everyday life on the *user* side, the designer's authority and responsibility similarly fade into a sense of simply satisfying needs on the *maker* side.

2.5   Critical Design

It is interesting that the term "Critical Design" was coined in the 1990s—the early days of personal computing and the dawn of the internet. "It grew out of our concerns with the uncritical drive behind technological progress, when technology is always assumed to be good and capable of solving any problem" [3, p. 34]. It was the increasing prevalence of personal experiences with computation that clarified design's capacity to problematize the relationship between design and technology.

Critical Design is distinguished by intentionality rather than methodology. The intention of Critical Design is to *use* design—its processes, techniques and outputs—to embed critical or social commentary within objects, communications, environments or, indeed, interfaces. Rather than writing a critical assessment of design's complicity in technically-driven social conditions (as I am partially doing here), Critical Design produces that commentary within design's own modes and materials of engaging an audience. This immanent form of critique uses the languages and techniques of the same systems they confront to let us materially experience opposition to, exaggeration of, or simply a refusal of design's role in perpetuating the status quo. Such critique is "not necessarily negative," [3, p. 34] but can serve to offer alternatives, highlight hidden agendas or simply examine "weaknesses within existing normality" [3, p. 35].

Because design operates across many domains, Critical Design produces material and experiential critique that is topical while also questioning design's role in that topic. For example, a designer working on a kitchen utensil must consider a variety of factors, including: the functional needs of the tool for cooking or baking, the human form as it relates to using that tool, material demands related to heat, durability or cleanliness, feasibility concerns such as manufacturing and unit cost, as well as the cultural context within which this utensil must be perceived as useful and desirable. Meanwhile, a Critical Design approach considers these same factors but might add to them a questioning of gender roles associated with that product. Rather than ignoring or reinforcing normalized gender views for the purpose of functional and commercial success, the designer of a *critical* kitchen utensil might exaggerate, invert or distort these views to help us understand how they are folded into the design of any object—either inadvertently or to capitalize on them.

2.6   Speculative Design

As a category of Critical Design, Speculative Design uses design methodologies to expand beliefs about what is possible—often through imaginative future worlds or alternate versions of reality. After coining the term Critical Design, designers Anthony Dunne and Fiona Raby became evangelists of Speculative Design, demonstrating its potential and techniques through their own practice and as educators. They describe the aims of Speculative Design as such: "This form of design thrives on imagination and aims to open up new perspectives on what are sometimes called *wicked problems*, to create spaces for discussion and debate about alternative ways of being, and to inspire and encourage people's imaginations to flow freely. Design speculations can act as a catalyst for collectively redefining our relationship to reality" [3, p. 2]. They assert that conceptual acts of design produce social value by opening up new spaces and experiences for critical dialogue. "It is not enough that it simply exists and can be used to experiment or entertain; we also want it to be useful, to have a sort of social usefulness, specifically, to question, critique, and challenge the way technologies enter our lives and the limitations they place on people through their narrow definition of what it means to be human…" [3, p. 34].

With the explicit intention of promoting debate, this work is grounded in a democratic ideology. Speculations may vary from optimistic utopias to dystopian cautionary tales. Regardless, these radically imaginative proposals give us something tangible to advance dialogue on where we are and where we're going—or where we'd like to go.

3   Conflict Interfaces

Building from these theoretical positions and critical approaches to design, I identify Conflict Interfaces[3] as a body of research and creative production directly pointed at critical investigations *of* and *within* Human-Computer Interfaces—particularly,

---

[3] "It's such a gamble when you get a face" [5]. It's also a gamble to put a face—or a name—on any emerging and as-yet unnamed body of creative or technical work.

interfaces of personal and everyday use. The ubiquity of computer-interfaces for personal use in daily life creates a robust and capacious space for critical inquiry into political contestations at the scale of a "micro-physics" of power operations [4]. From an agonistic political perspective, conflict is inevitable in all social relations, and this certainly extends to one of the most populated sites of contemporary human relations.

By design, Conflict Interfaces induce and make manifest a sense of conflict within the human participant in relation to the goals and prompts of the interface itself and/or the human actors responsible for the interface. Rather than making attempts to hide, neglect or flatten those conflicts, Conflict Interfaces demonstrate that intractable contemporary political and cultural differences can be uniquely engaged *in* and *through* personal computing interfaces.

Conflict Interfaces produce a point of tension by rupturing the dream of seamless (*responsive! intuitive!*) computer-mediated communications. They encourage reflection on the myriad ways in which human-human power relations are mediated through human-computer interactions and invite us to reflect upon and critique the nature of these relations. Conflict Interfaces don't critique specific technologies but the social organizations produced through interactions with computational devices. By disrupting the trust we place in our daily, routine and even mundane interactions with personal computing interfaces, these projects ask how we might maintain, sustain or gain some autonomy—maybe even *human-ness*—in our continually evolving relationships with computer-mediated social systems.

4 Interaction Design as Critical Inquiry

One of the dominant pedagogical models of contemporary design education—particularly within Interaction Design—is that of User Centered methodologies. Interaction Design students are tasked to balance technical, conceptual and aesthetic decisions with a clear understanding of the *needs of the user* of the system they are creating.

While recognizing the value and opportunities of this model—sharing authority in the normative process of design—there is a challenge in teaching these methodologies without compromising an understanding that the designer is still ultimately responsible for the social effects of her productions. How can students engage in effective user-research methodologies to generate an empathetic understanding of *users' needs* while simultaneously using this process to evaluate the power structures embedded in the resulting social interactions? Further, how can students inscribe their work with an articulation of those evaluations—laden as they must be with the students' own desires, fears, anxieties and intentions? In other words, how can teaching these methodologies produce interaction designers who are critical and reflective producers of mediated social interactions, taking stock of their own accountability in the process?

4.1 Pedagogy

My position is that Conflict Interfaces offer an excellent method for bringing criticality to teaching interaction design. Based on preliminary attempts at blending User

Centered and Speculative Design processes, I have observed rich potential for encouraging students to see their work as naturally coercive—rather than missing or overlooking the broader political implications inherent in any system of mediation. By doing so, students are forced to take stock of the fact that *their* goals merge with the perceived *user's needs* to produce interfaces that are the sites of political negotiation. Students must explore the tensions, paradoxes and conflicts inherent in mediated political relations to understand how those relations are played out through Human-Computer interfaces. Their interaction projects become more focused, and I believe it invests them with a heightened sense of responsibility (perhaps, the starting point of an *ethics*) for their work as designers.

User Centered Processes. From the User Centered Design model, students are asked to investigate social issues via a combination of Secondary Research (essays, articles, current events, social/cultural/political trends), Primary Research (direct observation, discussions, surveys, interviews, expert testimonials), Creative Inspiration (contemporary conditions observed through trends in products, services, fashion, media, entertainment, etc.) and to research New and Emerging Technologies to understand what new things are coming out of research labs and what impacts they are proposed to have on contemporary life. From this matrix, students map, align, identify and hone in on a particular topic space, which is then articulated as an opportunity for design to intervene. The typical extension of the User Centered Design process from this point of identifying a problem/opportunity space would be to ideate, prototype, test and refine until arriving at a "solution." Hardly a straight line, yet the intention of *resolution* drives these activities forward as a unified force.

Speculative Processes. Following this first leg of the User Centered Design process, my approach has been to extend beyond a "solution" into *possible* future conditions. This Speculative Design approach willfully admits the intention of proposing, provoking and making critique rather than resolving. Having identified a problematic issue within its systemic contexts, students engage in written and visual exercises to imagine an array of *possible* future scenarios by extending these contexts into the near future— usually 20-30 years out. For example, imagine that the problematic issue becomes as bad as you can possibly imagine. What would happen if all of society hinged on this one issue? This act of reduction crystallizes the various social and material forces driving the issue, letting us examine it from the level of object to system to network of systems to society. Next, imagine if the problematic issue disappears completely tomorrow. What new social organizations—but also challenges—might result to occupy those objects, spaces or rituals currently defined by the problematic?

To connect social conditions with techniques of mediation, students are next asked to play out writing and visualization experiments imagining similarly divergent future scenarios based on a single example of emerging technology. What do the inventors claim this technology can do to make life better, safer, healthier, more efficient or more pleasant (after all, this is how new technologies are often *sold* to the general public)? Imagine these utopian promises were to come true and change life as we know it. Now, imagine the unforeseen but *always also present* negative impacts this technology holds. What dystopian future worlds are also possible within the promises of emerging technologies? These mental and visual exercises quickly produce a matrix of speculative future scenarios in which we can articulate our contemporary desires, fears, and anxieties at the same time that we identify the social, cultural, political or technological twists that could create new versions of reality. We can then ask what artifacts, communication systems, environment or interfaces would that world reality produce, and how might we read the proposed social conditions within those designed outputs.

Hybrid Model. By blending User Centered Design processes with a Speculative Design approach, highly imaginative proposals are paired with rigorous methodologies to keep the research and its outputs lively, critical, reflective and relevant [13]. In order to make work that is critical yet still situated in design's normative functions, projects must present enough desirability to imagine *wanting* as part of a new daily life, yet also produce an anxiety that reveals the political tensions at play. The closer the proposal lies to my everyday desires and fears, the more power it has to disturb my understanding of current—and possible future—social relations that shape my daily life.

4.2   Student Case Studies

The Algorithmic Automation of Politics: *Google Vote*. Smartphone users are familiar with the moment of decision to be made when installing a new app: *Do you accept the terms and conditions?* The conveniences afforded by "useful" apps make it easy to often shrug off what might normally be concerning requests for information such as your location, personal contacts, etc. Meanwhile, our tastes and preferences are increasingly "accommodated" by smart systems that analyze behaviors such as online searches, purchases, likes, and so on. But, how far are we willing to hand over personal and privates choices to algorithmically determined patterns?

Google Vote is a project by Nicole Krause, produced while she was a student at the University of Illinois at Chicago. As a graduate student in Communications, Nicole studied the affects of media on political discourse, the polarization of political rhetoric in the United States and the emergence of a phenomenon called the *Spiral of Silence,* the quieting of centrist political views and accompanying reduction in voter participation, particularly by young people. To explore these tensions in an experiential manner—beyond the reach of essays and empirical research—Krause produced a Speculative Design project to engage contemporary audiences in critical dialogue about the future of democracy in the United States.

Krause imagines a near future in which voter participation is so low that it threatens to undermine the most basic principle of democracy: voting. The only solution is for the U.S. Government to partner with a private technology corporation (*guess who!*) to make voting "smarter" and "easier" for the whole population. *Google Vote* extends the potential of algorithmic determinations based on users' preferences and behaviors by suggesting this data could also translate citizens' interests and actions into votes for pending legislation or candidates for public office. The system asks the user to complete a brief series of abstract philosophical puzzles in order to produce a custom worldview. Having established the user's worldview, the app makes voting recommendations for local, regional or national issues and candidates (Fig. 1).

Fig. 1. Google *Vote* by Nicole Krause, University of Illinois at Chicago

The anxiety of your vote being determined for you is exacerbated by the proposal of this as an Opt-Out system. Unless you adjust your worldview to alter the recommendations of the system, it will automatically cast its algorithmically-determined votes for you. These tensions at the intersection of politics, algorithms of choice and personal computing are beautifully summarized by the button labeled, "Build my Worldview."

Vote with Your Wallet: PollWatch. University of Cincinnati Graphic Design student Evan Hoffman took a Speculative Design approach to antagonize the relationship between politicians, corporate donations and American consumerism in his project *PollWatch*. Hoffman envisions a future in which citizens no longer cast ballots to elect political leaders or enact legislation. Rather, votes are cast based on each citizen's shopping habits. Proposed as an interactive personal data system for a wearable device, the user's purchase history is tracked to reveal the political causes supported by those corporations or businesses from whom the user buys products. Over time, the user's profile generates a political "stance," situated between six poles that quantitatively represent the political leanings of the products and corporations patronized. This act of *reductio ad absurdum* crystallizes the relationship between politics and corporate political influence in order to focus on how it might produce new forms of political life —simultaneously asking us to question the current state of this relationship (Fig. 2).

By contrasting the political "stance" supported through consumption against a desired political "stance," users can identify the gap between ideals and purchase-derived actions. "Anyone can track their spot on the political spectrum and adjust purchases accordingly or change their own platform to better coincide with their stance. When changing platforms, users may even choose a template based on a favorite politician, celebrity, or religion" [7].

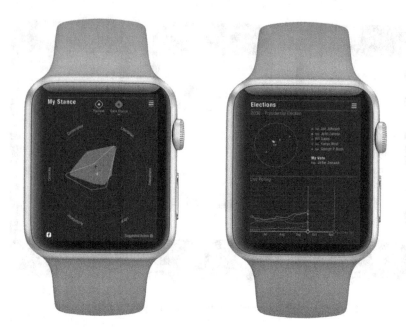

Fig. 2. *PollWatch* by Evan Hoffman, University of Cincinnati

The problematic moment arises when a user can choose to adjust spending to match political ideology or let the system "recommend" a more appropriate ideology. This conflict, derived as it is within a wearable and personal computing interface, creates the perfect point of anxiety in which the reach of such systems can be experientially understood and considered.

5 Conclusion

As we have been acclimating to the complete integration of personal computing interfaces into everyday life, the human efforts to produce such systems have congealed into new disciplinary techniques for deigning interfaces between humans and computational systems. Most designers would readily admit their work holds the potential for persuasion. Yet few would likely recognize that the experiences they produce between human actors and computational Learning systems also produce sites of political conflict simply by making manifest new spaces for communication and exchange. As a category of critical HCI work, Conflict Interfaces offer new perspectives on the social impacts of personal computing interfaces plus opportunities for teaching interaction design as a method of critical inquiry.

Can these stabs at the status quo make real change? Is a prototype or installation enough? Dan Hill would likely tell us no [6]. He urges designers to engage in policy-making and public service for real change. Yet, where to begin?

I believe this begins by developing positions on current conditions, by making informed and intelligent speculations about where things could be going, then using design to share that vision materially and experientially. Critical Design is only possible *in relation to* the discipline's standard operations. The two work in tandem, pushing and pulling one another. Critical Design practices create new visions of society while demonstrating design's normative role within it. By offering tangible views of the next horizon of social organization, Conflict Interfaces clarify our contemporary desires, fears and anxieties to help us imagine where we'd like to go next.

I have a wild hunch that human-computer interactions will continue to evolve into more dynamic, more complex, more unpredictable and probably far more provocative scenarios—scenarios in which traditional notions of human agency will be increasingly challenged, compromised and transformed. With those changes, I hope there will be a parallel evolution of Critical Design practices to continually provoke and challenge us to question the ways that technologies produce and mediate the human experience. This is what design is so good at doing: normalizing today's version of everyday life while simultaneously imagining radically different possibilities for what's next.

References

1. DiSalvo, C.: Adversarial Design. MIT Press, Cambridge (2012)
2. Dubberly, H., Pangaro, P., Haque, U.: What is interaction?: Are there different types? http://www.dubberly.com/articles/what-is-interaction.html
3. Dunne, A., Fiona, R.: Speculative Everything: Design, Fiction and Social Dreaming. MIT Press, Cambridge (2013)
4. Foucault, M.: Discipline and Punish: The Birth of the Prison. Random House, New York (1995)
5. Hell, R., The Voidoids: Blank Generation [LP]. Sire Records, New York (1977)
6. Hill, D.: Dark Matter and Trojan Horses: A Strategic Design Vocabulary. Strelka Press, Moscow (2012)
7. Hoffman, E.: PollWatch. http://studiojunglecat.com/speculativecity/pollwatch/
8. Latour, B.: On technical mediation: philosophy, sociology, genealogy. Common Knowl. **3** (2), 29–64 (1994)
9. Mouffe, C., Wagner, E.: Agonistics: Thinking the world politically. Verso, New York (2013)
10. Mouffe, C.: The Democratic Paradox. Verso, New York (2000)
11. Norman, D.: Human-Centered Design Considered Harmful. http://jnd.org/
12. Raley, R.: Tactical Media. University of Minnesota Press, Minneapolis (2009)
13. Speculative City: An Interdisciplinary Design Studio, curriculum by Matthew Wizinsky. http://studiojunglecat.com/speculativecity/

Research on Appearance Design of Outdoor Cabinets Focusing on User's Emotional Experience

Le Xi, Jianxin Cheng$^{(\boxtimes)}$, Junnan Ye, and Wangqun Xiao

School of Art, Design and Media, East China University of Science
and Technology, M. BOX 286 NO. 130, Meilong Road,
Xuhui District, Shanghai 200237, China
xilutar@sina.com, cjx.master@gmail.com,
yejunnan971108@qq.com, xiaoyao-1916@163.com

Abstract. The appearance design of products is a complicated issue that concerns multiple factors relating to materials, structures, functions, colors, etc. Product modeling is an important medium for the communication between designers and clients. It is also an effective way to satisfy user's emotional experience. In terms of products' appearance modeling, designers have always been dedicated to the creation based on their own experience, inspirations and techniques. Due to the lack of effective evaluation system, it is difficult to deal with user's emotional experience accurately and effectively.

On the basis of the theory and methodology concerning Kansei engineering and imagery cognition, the paper conducts research on design procedures concerning the extraction and application of characteristic elements of product modality focusing on user's emotional experience. It also achieves the systematic expression of user's emotional experience on the level of imagery cognition, and conducts relevant experiments and analysis aiming to set up the evaluation system focusing on the effective expression of product modeling features. The paper takes the design case of outdoor cabinet as an example. Through the virtual construction of product modeling, the paper conducts analysis of perceptual image based on virtual reality from the perspective of user's emotional experience, thus constructing the model of image descriptions on form elements. It extracts characteristic semanteme influencing users emotional experience by utilizing semantic differential method and principal component analysis, analyzes and summarizes perceptual image factor. It analyzes product form elements by using morphology analyzing method, and finds out the corresponding relationship between perceptual image factor and product form. In order to provide theoretical reference to the form designer, this paper also offers a proposal to the issue of "how to conduct product form design and optimization through perceptual image factor".

Keywords: User's emotion experience · Product design · Kansei · VR · Imagery cognition

© Springer International Publishing Switzerland 2016
A. Marcus (Ed.): DUXU 2016, Part II, LNCS 9747, pp. 98–109, 2016.
DOI: 10.1007/978-3-319-40355-7_10

1 Introduction

As market competition is getting increasingly fierce, clients have began to show diversification and individuation in their requirements on product appearances (Zhou 2011). Utilitarian functions or values of products are no longer the most primary factor in user's requirements (Zhou 2011). They attach greater importance to emotional experience. Meeting users' complicated and multiple element individualized requirement, designing the products conforming to users' desire and expectation are a crucial task to product design developer (Zhou 2011). Product form design is a multifactorial complexus, which is connected with various factors, such as structure, function, visual sense, material, color, psychology, etc. (Zhou 2011). For products' form design, designer creates it according to their own experience, inspiration and skill all the time. With the development and change of consumption pattern, the development design thought of current products has switched from technology and function orientated to emotion and experience orientated (Zhou 2011). Because lacking of the effective evaluation system reference, it is difficult to accurately and efficiently respond to users' emotional experience demand.

Therefore, in view of the user needs and expectations, it requires both preliminary qualitative analysis and objective quantitative analysis. Accurately grasping users' emotional demand, hobby and tendency has a very important significance to enterprise wining the market.

2 Research Background

Self-driving tour rises in the United States. At first, people called the weekend driving tour as "Sunday Drive", afterwards, it became "Drive Travel". In 1990s, automobile started to enter in Chinese families. Up to this day, Chinese automobile consumption has transformed from high-end to mass consumption. According to China National Tourism Administration (CNTA) China Self-driving Tour Annual Development Report (2014–2015), the national every hundred households possesses 25 private cars, with the total person of self-driving tour in 2014 being about 2.2 billion.. Chinese self-driving tour industry develops prosperously, and the products sales related to self-driving tour is also in the strong growth (Xiao 2010).

Different from western countries' self-driving tour form of taking estate car as principal, China is high population density, and has a lot of road facility limitations, with urban and rural environment being difficult to meet the parking and driving of travel saloon car (Yu and Wu 2011). Therefore, Chinese self-driving tour mainly gives priority to family small automobile. However, Chinese dining habit is essentially different from foreign dining habit, with a great diversity of Chinese cooking methods. Therefore, it must research the operational method and culture of Chinese dining if we want to meet Chinese dining demand outdoors, developing miniaturization, integration and multifunctional vehicle-mounted outdoor cabinet. The products in this research are exactly researched ad developed under this background (Fig. 1).

Outdoor cabinet is designed for solving outdoor dining problems of self-driving tour users. In addition to provide the necessary table and stool functions, it also

Fig. 1. Outdoor cabinets design

integrates and takes stoves and kitchen utensils and appliance, tableware, tool and others, which makes users can conveniently take it in the trunk of the automobile, unfolding at any time any where, in order to solve the outdoor dinning problem. Therefore, based on fully researching users' demand in emotional experience, aesthetic taste, etc., it designs the truly "heartstrings" products in accordance with users' expectations. On the basis of this objective, designers need to grant products with more emotional factors when they consider the products form.

The perceptual image of products is a kind of mental feelings of people to object and a deep-seated affective activity. It mainly uses the relative theory and methods of Kansei Engineering to research perceptual image (Zhou 2011). Kansei Engineering is a technology combined with sensibility and engineering, which mainly designs products according to people's sentimental demand and manufactures products according to people's habit (Zhou 2011). It quantitatively expresses all feelings (amount of perceptual) of people to object (products, environment, etc.,) through engineering technology means (Zhou 2011). And then, it tries to find out the internal connection between amount of perceptual and the physical quantity (product feature) used in the product design (Zhou 2011). Moreover, it takes this kind of connection as the basis of product's design and development, analysis and research. The research objective of Kansei Engineering is "people", and its serving objective is the design process and object (products) (Zhou 2011). It establishes the logical relation between people and object through a series methods, to help designers to design the "object" which meets the "people's" feeling and expectation.

3   Literature Review

Professor Mituo Nagamachi systematically discussed the effect and application method of Kansei Engineering in product design in Kansei Engineering in Consumer Product Design, which researched people's emotional factors in products. Simmon Schutte further investigated and discussed to the products' emotional problems in Designing

Feelings into Products—Integrating Kansei Engineering Methodology in Product Development, and also researched the emotional engineering research methods at product's developing and designing stage. Norman made an in-depth research to the product's emotional experience in Emotional Design, which has an important significance to product's emotional research. Akinori Takamasa explored vehicle systems in A Kansei Engineering Approach to a Driver/vehicle System by utilizing various Kansei Engineering methods. Rajkumar researched the customer-centered design methods and approaches in User-centric Design and Kansei Engineering by utilizing Kansei Engineering methods. Zhou Meiyu and Dai Guangliang analyzed their relationship through image scale and Kansei Engineering methods in the Yacht Form Imagery Cognitive and Perceptual Design Research, built the model of semantic space and sentimental design, which provided reference basis for product's design. Huang Cheng et al established the mathematical model of styling features and image semantic by utilizing morphological analysis method to extract design elements in Smart Watches Modelling Study Based on Consumer Psychology and Kansei Engineering, thus to accurately grasp consumers' psychological perceptual image. Yao Ziying and Wang Siping found out the principal component factor influencing users' perceptual cognition through factor analysis method in Projector Modeling Design Based on Perceptual Image, and found out the weight factor influencing product's appearance through morphological analysis method, which has reference significance to this research's methods.

In conclusion, the research to users' emotion is an important content to the research of Kansei Engineering. The varied methods application can effectively improve the products form of users' emotional demand. However, it can find that in the current research, the sensibility evaluation to products mainly relies on 2D images, which is relatively week to products' intuitive experience. So, the investigation results' degree of reliability is generally, and its influence to subsequent design research is relatively significant. Therefore, in Kansei Engineering research, "how to improve the experience reliability in research" is a problem demanding prompt solution.

4   Research Methods

4.1   Questionnaire of Combining VR Technology

Questionnaire is a method to collect research objects' research material and data through the strictly designed measuring projects or problems in written form. In consideration of requiring test to get closer to the participants' experience data of real product form to improve the accuracy and reliability of data, this paper's questionnaire survey adopted VR technology platform, which can carry out immersive user experience to the virtual concept form of outdoor cabinet. The G-MAGIC six-channel virtual reality system of ECUST is the domestic leading VR experiential platform. Restoring through cavernous product form, it can intuitively reflex product's future actual shape and functional characteristics. Comparing to plane display device, it possesses a more real and straightforward visual experience, and has reliable supporting effect to users' emotional determination.

4.2   Semantic Differential Method (SD)

SD method is an attitude measurement technology proposed by American psychologist, Osgood, and it is a test method researching participants' mental imagery. SD method takes adjectives as basis, which requires participants to make an evaluation to things or concepts on some measure gauges of opposite meaning. SD method applied to product design shall firstly determine the measure gauge grade of the measured object (product), and generally, it is divided into seven continues grades (Fig. 2). It requires participants to evaluate each attribute according to their feelings and opinions to the measured object, and mark in the corresponding grade position.

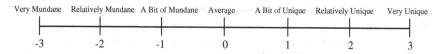

Fig. 2. Semantic difference measure gauge

4.3   Principal Component Analysis Method (PCA)

PCA method is a multivariate statistical method which changes multiple variables into a few aggregate variables. During the research process, in order to comprehensively and systematically analyze problems, it must consider the influence of many factors, but too many variables will increase the problems' complexity degree. Therefore, people hope to get more information with fewer variables. PCA is an ideal method solving this kind of problems. After importing the data extracted through SD method into professional statistical software SPSS, this paper gets the related conclusion through data processing.

4.4   Appearance Analysis Method

The characteristic of Appearance analysis methods is that dividing research objects or questions into some basic components, and then making a separate analysis to a certain basic component. It respectively provides various solutions or methods. In the end, it forms the general plan of the whole problem. Through questionnaire, this paper lists the main factor's score of influencing product's form image, and gets the internal relation of product's each form components through analyzing the factor score between product form samples, then puts forward suggestions to product's form design optimization.

5   Research Process

This paper applies the principles and methods of Kansei Engineering, and combining with the example of outdoor cabinet product design, it researches and reflects the corresponding relation between product form characteristics and users' experience, and then, it extracts morphological characteristic factors of influencing users' psychological feelings to products. In order to get the relatively reliable data in experiment, it respectively organizes two groups of respondents in this research: Group A and Group B. Group A is constituted by 5 senior product designers and 5 outdoor players; Group B is constituted by 30 industrial design students, 10 personnel of having cooking experience, and 10 personnel of without cooking experience.

5.1 Emotional Semantic Space Establishing Based on VR Technology

Through the relevant information searching to Chinese food and beverage, outdoors dining and self-driving tour dining, and the interview to outdoor players and picnic users, it collects the perceptual image description vocabulary to the modeling and function of outdoor cabinet. Screening and finishing these collected vocabularies, it gets 36 pairs of perceptual vocabulary, and then it builds semantic dictionary. Formulating semantic differences questionnaire, asking the respondents of Group A to carry out subjective judgment. Classifying 36 pairs of perceptual vocabulary and selecting 9 words with highest votes, and combining its corresponding antonym to take it as sample. In the end, it gets 9 pairs of perceptual adjectives (Table 1).

Table 1. Perceptual vocabulary pairs

Vocabulary pair	Code
Complex - Concise	Y1
Retro - Modern	Y2
Normal - Personality	Y3
Decoration - Functional	Y4
Heavy - Light	Y5
Tough - Soft	Y6
Formal - Leisure	Y7
Ugly - Beautiful	Y8
Difficult to clean - Easy to clean	Y9

After extensive research, the outdoor cabinets of similar type in the market are relatively rare. Therefore, this research collected 16 styles of concept outdoor cabinet designed by professional designers as samples. Because of a relative complex product structure, too many components, and being difficult to research with solid model, this research applied G-MAGIC system to carry out product display and experience. In G-MAGIC, combining the virtual 3D products with outdoor environment, it can unfold and operate the real-time product function module, and can fully show product's details (Fig. 3). It makes respondents can experience product's modeling and functions more real, which not only reduces experiment cost, but also improves respondent's experience reliability. All the 16 product samples in this research adopt the unified match colors to reduce the color influence factors. As shown is Fig. 4.

Applying SD method to combine the selected 9 pairs of perceptual image vocabulary with 16 styles of product sample and formulate it into questionnaire. The questionnaire is

Fig. 3. Using products in G-MAGIC VR system

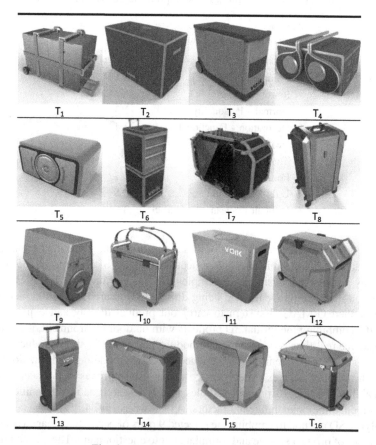

Fig. 4. Outdoor cabinets design sample

formulated according to seven measure gauges (−3, −2, −1, 0, 1, 2, 3) of SD method. Carrying out G-MAGIC system test by combining the respondents of Group B, and filling in the questionnaire. Carrying out statistics to all questionnaires, Adding the image description evaluation value of the respondents of Group B to product samples together, and averaging it, then it comes the evaluation average value. The results are shown in Table 2.

Table 2. Mean scores of the evaluation

Sample	Vocabulary pair								
	Y_1	Y_2	Y_3	Y_4	Y_5	Y_6	Y_7	Y_8	Y_9
T_1	0.231	0.473	−1.120	0.654	0.213	−1.534	−0.539	−1.612	1.072
T_2	1.191	−0.275	−1.017	1.057	0.222	−1.136	−1.496	−1.664	1.271
T_3	0.015	1.145	1.024	1.312	0.376	0.261	0.453	0.307	0.183
T_4	−0.143	1.514	1.982	−1.183	0.337	1.611	1.322	0.636	−0.567
T_5	0.452	1.276	0.574	−0.435	0.164	1.312	0.373	0.723	1.051
T_6	−0.432	0.741	−1.052	0.726	−0.438	−1.718	−1.283	−1.212	−0.172
T_7	−1.302	1.665	1.317	−0.269	−0.163	0.071	1.275	1.143	−1.203
T_8	−0.527	0.342	−0.715	1.112	−0.249	−0.334	−0.054	1.301	0.130
T_9	0.279	0.413	0.174	−0.214	0.043	−1.682	−0.331	−0.121	0.189
T_{10}	0.306	0.222	0.096	1.203	1.322	0.654	0.358	0.603	0.048
T_{11}	1.874	1.143	0.172	−0.332	1.351	−0.026	1.636	1.236	1.895
T_{12}	−1.175	−0.328	−1.311	0.703	−1.076	−0.836	0.007	−1.732	−0.217
T_{13}	0.442	1.175	−0.667	0.052	−0.737	0.760	0.464	0.923	1.013
T_{14}	0.241	−0.217	0.032	−0.416	−1.411	−1.376	−1.582	−1.875	0.651
T_{15}	0.526	1.251	0.227	−0.541	0.101	0.304	1.104	0.154	0.382
T_{16}	0.213	−0.402	−1.162	0.633	0.238	−0.236	−0.061	−0.173	−0.013

Taking 9 pairs of perceptual image vocabulary as variable Y, carrying out PCA analysis in SPSS, taking factors of its eigenvalues being greater than 1, getting 3 PCA factors of relative great contribution rate, with its cumulative contribution rate being 82.932 %. According to the results outputted by SPSS, it sorts PCA analysis results into Table 3.

Table 3. Results of factor analysis

Factors	Code	Factor load			Eigenvalues	Contribution rate %	Cumulative contribution rate %
Factor1	Y_8	0.896	−0.006	0.061	4.205	46.720	46.720
	Y_7	0.882	−0.034	0.235			
	Y_6	0.814	−0.011	0.221			
Factor 2	Y_1	0.086	0.977	0.030	2.141	23.790	70.510
	Y_9	−0.160	0.937	−0.003			
Factor 3	Y_4	−0.197	−0.072	−0.932	1.118	12.422	82.932

According to the rotated PCA matrix, it is known that high load variables on factor 1 are Y_8, Y_7, Y_6, and it concludes them as style factors according to their perceptual image. The high load variables on factor 2 are Y_1, Y_9, and it concludes them as quality factors. The high load variable on factor 3 is Y_4, and it concludes it as value factor. Figure 5 is three factors rotating space composition three-dimensional diagram. So far, it finds out 6 groups of typical perceptual image vocabulary, as shown in Table 4. It shows that users' perceptual awareness to these vocabularies is relatively high, and these vocabularies represent users' perceptual image to product.

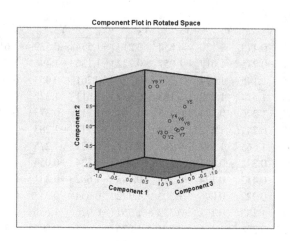

Fig. 5. Component plot in rotated space

Table 4. Typical image vocabulary pairs

Vocabulary pair	Code
Ugly - Beautiful	Y_8
Formal - Leisure	Y_7
Tough - Soft	Y_6
Complex - Concise	Y_1
Difficult to clean - Easy to clean	Y_9
Decoration - Functional	Y_4

5.2 Appearance Design Analysis

Product form has direct influence to users' image cognition. In order to further grasp the form features of designing scheme, it needs to carry out form elements decomposition to products. Finding out the internal relation between form elements through investigating typical perceptual image factors to users, so that designers can carry out the targeted revise and perfect to the form of product.

Firstly, it investigates the respondents of Group A. It respectively experiences it by aiming at the product form, and determines 5 main products' form elements according to experience investigation results, namely, these five elements are cabinet body, side

Table 5. Product form decomposition questionnaire

Parts	Code	Pic	Y_8	Y_7	Y_6	Y_1	Y_9	Y_4
							Difficult	
			Ugly	Formal	Tough	Complex	to clean	Decoration
Main	T_3		• • •	• • •	• • •	• • •	• • •	• • •
			Beautiful	Leisure	Soft	Concise	Easy to clean	Functional
Cabinet Body	T_3-a		o-3 o-2 o-1 o 0 o 1 o 2 o 3	o-3 o-2 o-1 o 0 o 1 o 2 o 3	o-3 o-2 o-1 o 0 o 1 o 2 o 3	o-3 o-2 o-1 o 0 o 1 o 2 o 3	o-3 o-2 o-1 o 0 o 1 o 2 o 3	o-3 o-2 o-1 o 0 o 1 o 2 o 3
Side Panel	T_3-b		o-3 o-2 o-1 o 0 o 1 o 2 o 3	o-3 o-2 o-1 o 0 o 1 o 2 o 3	o-3 o-2 o-1 o 0 o 1 o 2 o 3	o-3 o-2 o-1 o 0 o 1 o 2 o 3	o-3 o-2 o-1 o 0 o 1 o 2 o 3	o-3 o-2 o-1 o 0 o 1 o 2 o 3
Cover Plate	T_3-c		o-3 o-2 o-1 o 0 o 1 o 2 o 3	o-3 o-2 o-1 o 0 o 1 o 2 o 3	o-3 o-2 o-1 o 0 o 1 o 2 o 3	o-3 o-2 o-1 o 0 o 1 o 2 o 3	o-3 o-2 o-1 o 0 o 1 o 2 o 3	o-3 o-2 o-1 o 0 o 1 o 2 o 3
Drawer	T_3-d		o-3 o-2 o-1 o 0 o 1 o 2 o 3	o-3 o-2 o-1 o 0 o 1 o 2 o 3	o-3 o-2 o-1 o 0 o 1 o 2 o 3	o-3 o-2 o-1 o 0 o 1 o 2 o 3	o-3 o-2 o-1 o 0 o 1 o 2 o 3	o-3 o-2 o-1 o 0 o 1 o 2 o 3
Handle	T_3-e		o-3 o-2 o-1 o 0 o 1 o 2 o 3	o-3 o-2 o-1 o 0 o 1 o 2 o 3	o-3 o-2 o-1 o 0 o 1 o 2 o 3	o-3 o-2 o-1 o 0 o 1 o 2 o 3	o-3 o-2 o-1 o 0 o 1 o 2 o 3	o-3 o-2 o-1 o 0 o 1 o 2 o 3

plate, cover plate, drawer, and handle. Because of schedule time limit of investigation work, this research emphatically selects two products of T_3 and T_7 to carry out morphological decomposition research, and it respectively formulates products' form decomposition questionnaire. Taking T_3 as an example, and as shown in Table 5. The respondents of Group B carry out perceptual evaluation scoring, summarize and formulate Table 6.

Analyzing according to the results shown in Table 5: firstly, for style factor, the form separating degree between the side plate of T_3, the form of the drawer and other components is relatively big, which shows that the style difference is obvious. Of course, in consideration of taking the side plate as outdoor table top to design, its form is relatively regular, and we can consider to add the curve line (round form style controlled by Y_6) in later design to improve the consistency of its style; the style consistency of T_7 maintains a relatively consistent. Secondly, for quality factor, the deviation degrees of the cabinet body, cover plate, side plate and handle of T_3 are very

Table 6. Product design form evaluation

Code	T_3					T_7				
	T_3-a	T_3-b	T_3-c	T_3-d	T_3-e	T_7-a	T_7-b	T_7-c	T_7-d	T_7-e
Y_8	0.131	0.207	0.026	−0.122	0.410	1.673	1.416	1.101	0.733	0.213
Y_7	1.051	−0.778	0.141	−0.357	1.021	0.878	1.158	1.483	1.207	−0.035
Y_6	0.532	0.021	0.172	−0.655	1.123	0.113	0.352	−1.660	−1.701	0.342
Factor 1(Σ)	**1.714**	**−0.55**	**0.339**	**−1.134**	**2.554**	**2.664**	**2.926**	**0.924**	**0.239**	**0.520**
Y_1	−1.301	1.863	−1.516	−0.584	1.725	−1.833	−0.144	−0.707	−0.832	−1.522
Y_9	−1.015	2.031	−0.363	1.301	−0.210	−1.905	−0.463	−2.215	−2.228	−0.317
Factor 2(Σ)	**−2.316**	**3.894**	**−1.879**	**0.717**	**1.515**	**−3.738**	**−0.607**	**−2.922**	**−3.06**	**−1.839**
Y_4/Factor 3	**−1.037**	**1.603**	**−0.470**	**−1.204**	**−0.873**	**−1.851**	**−1.078**	**−2.011**	**−1.870**	**−0.331**

significant, which shows that quality contrast is relatively obvious; the quality consistency of each component of T_7 is relatively balanced, however, the orientation is negative, which shows that on the whole, the design quality is unsatisfactory. Last, for value factor, two styles of design scheme do not show the obvious practical characteristics, meanwhile, it also shows the next step's improvement direction.

6 Summary and Discussion

Introducing VR technology in users' emotional experience research is a creative attempt. With the help of Kansei Engineering research method, it can carry out quantitative and qualitative analysis and improvement to the image form of design scheme. Because the samples in this research are still the conceptual products, users' perceptual knowledge to it is still relatively unfamiliar. It still has form and function misunderstanding in experience, therefore, at a certain degree, it influences the statistical result. It still needs to further sort and develop the operation mode of Chinese food and beverage and the tool function research. It also needs to further increase the quantity of samples, and further refine and separate the components of sample form analysis. In the future, we can consider to carry out comparative and analytic research to the added new improved design scheme and the early design scheme. All of these are the problems which need to be solved in the subsequent research.

References

Nagamachi, M.: Kansei engineering in consumer product design. Mag. Hum. Fact. Appl. 1(10), 5–9 (2002)

Schutte, S.: Designing feelings into products-integrating Kansei engineering methodology in product development. Linkoping Studies in Science and Technology Thesis (2002)

Norman, D.A.: Emotional Design (Chinese). Zefang Fu. Publishing House of Electronics Industry, Beijing (2005)

Akinori, H., Takamasa, S.: A Kansei engineering approach to a driver/vehicle system. Int. J. Ind. Ergon. 15(1), 25–37 (1995)

Rajkumar, R., Michael, G., Kieran, K.: User-centric design and Kansei engineering. CIRP J. Manuf. Sci. Technol. **1**(3), 172–178 (2009)

Zhou, M.: Kansei Design (SSTEPH), pp. 90–95. Shanghai Scientific and Technological Education Publishing House, Shanghai (2011)

CNTA: China Self-driving Tour Annual Development Report (2014–2015)

Xiao, J.: Analysis on self-driving tour development in China. Econ. Manag. **11**, 273 (2010)

Yu, H., Wu, B.: Research progress of oversea self-driving tour. Tourism Tribune **26**(3), 55–61 (2011)

Guo, F., Liu, G., Chen, C., Li, S.: Customer-oriented study on design support technology based on perception of car style. J. Northeast. Univ. (Nat. Sci.) **5**(30), 741–744 (2009)

Xia, Y., Tang, W., Du, Y.: Application of Kansei engineering on form design of domestic oxygenerator image. Mach. Des. Manuf. Eng. **11**(43), 15–20 (2014)

Huang, G., Tang, W., Shao, J.: Research on the consumer psychology and Kansei engineering on form design of smart watch. Mach. Des. Manuf. Eng. **11**(43), 32–37 (2014)

Yao, Z., Wang, S.: Projector form design based on perceptual image. J. Donghua Univ. (Nat. Sci.) **4**(39), 529–534 (2013)

Lai, C., Zhu, W.: Determination of optimal product styles by Kansei engineering for bathroom faucets. Ind. Eng. Manag. **6**(17), 122–127 (2012)

Chen, Z., Guan, H.: Evaluation of furniture design schemes based on Kansei engineering. J. Eng. Graph. **30**(4), 150–155 (2009)

Zhou, M., Dai, G.: Research of Yacht form image cognition and kansei design. J. Donghua Univ. (Nat. Sci.) **4**(39), 539–544 (2013)

Emotion-Aware Music Recommendation

Jinhyeok Yang[1], WooJoung Chae[2], SunYeob Kim[2],
and Hyebong Choi[2(✉)]

[1] School of Computer Science and Electronic Engineering,
Handong Global University, Pohang, South Korea
yjh2067@gmail.com
[2] School of Creative Convergence Education,
Handong Global University, Pohang, South Korea
{21100706,21100096,hbchoi}@handong.edu

Abstract. Emotion is one of the major factors for users to determine service preference. Especially online music streaming services are in trend-sensitive industry, hence largely affected by user's experience and reputation. Conventional music streaming services provide users keywords-based search for music. Accordingly it strongly relies on user's prior knowledge and experience. It often fails to expose non-expert users to the music that the users are not familiar with. In this paper, we suggest an emotion-aware music recommendation system that proposes songs and artists based on the mood of each user.

First, we infer user's emotion using real-time weather information. Second, we classify songs and artists which are favorable in different weather conditions. To do so, we collect and combine daily chart of K-pop music and weather history data to find the music preference in different weather. It is used to recommend timely and favorable music to users after capturing their mood implcitly.

Moreover the emotion-aware music recommendation system is extensible to provide a personalized service by using user's social media, heartbeat, time, location, and so on. We expect this would enrich user experience noticeably. Being aware of user's emotion will enable broad areas of industry to provide intelligent services in a user-friendly way.

Keywords: Emotion-aware system · Recommendation system · Data mining

1 Introduction

In music industry, the main service media has been rapidly shifted from tangible devices such as magnetic tape and optical disc media (CD and DVD) to intangibles. It heavily relies on online music streaming service as one major source of revenue. Due to its trend-sensitive nature, user experience and reputation are keys to be successful in the music streaming service market. Traditional music streaming service provides keyword-based search to users which is straightforward to find songs and artists in their mind or memory. However, it limits its service within users' expectation and prior knowledge where it leaves non-expert users inaccessible to a large portion of service. It often fails to create a new experience that exposes users to the songs that they have never heard of, yet are enjoyable to them.

© Springer International Publishing Switzerland 2016
A. Marcus (Ed.): DUXU 2016, Part II, LNCS 9747, pp. 110–121, 2016.
DOI: 10.1007/978-3-319-40355-7_11

To overcome the limitations, personalized recommendation has been proposed [4–6]. It finds out user's preference of music from user historical behavior or service consumption pattern assuming that a user group who consume the same patterns of music has a higher change to have a similar music preference than the other group who consume different types of music. It often captures a useful insight of service consumption pattern and broadens the opportunities in music streaming market.

However, it somehow ignores that users' music preference might change as their emotions change over time. Emotion reflects various factors such as weather condition, personal relationship, work-related matters, and social issues. Emotions are also latent factors that affect which type of music user prefer at that moment which may fluctuate irregularly.

Based on the assumption, we attempt to derive the latent emotion factors from historical weather data and daily music chart. Specifically, we co-analyze K-pop daily chart from online music streaming service and Korean weather history for the last few years, assuming that the latent emotion factors collaboratively affect music preference and are affected by the weather condition. According to IFPI 2014 annual report [1], South Korea has the 8th largest music market in terms of total retail value. The climate in Korea is relatively uniform across regions and consistently changes as season changes from spring to winter.

The key contributions of our study are summarized as follows.

1. We characterize K-pop music streaming service industry and Korean weather by analyzing historical records of music chart and weather.
2. We reveal correlations between weather condition and music preference pattern.
3. We devise a model that recommends songs and artists based on latent emotion factors. The emotion factors are inferred from weather condition using collaborative filtering method.
4. Through comprehensive tests and validations, we show the emotion-aware recommendation system noticeably outperform the baseline model that always recommends the most popular music.

2 Preliminary Study

2.1 Dataset Description

We have obtained the dataset from Weather Underground and Bugs Music Chart [2, 3]. Bugs Music, a popular K-pop music streaming web-sites, provides various music chart daily and weekly. The chart provides a list of top 100 songs with artist most frequently enjoyed on each day.

The main Bugs music chart counts all population who subscribes their music streaming service. However, the main chart tends to be influenced strongly by the fandom culture of K-pop which makes the chart skewed toward songs that are performed by a boy band or girl band and songs newly released. Figure 1(a) shows the probability density of how many days each song takes to rank in the chart after song release date during the period from 2012 to 2015. About 65 % of songs in the chart are released within a month. Songs that older than one year take place less than 7 %. Moreover, 35 out of top 100 artists who ranked in most frequently during the period are either a boy band or girl band. We expect this mitigates the effect of weather condition and its related emotion factors.

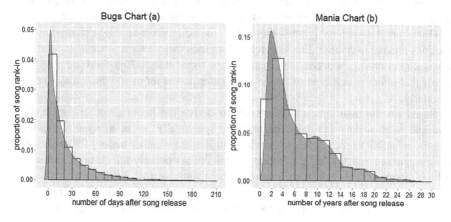

Fig. 1. Number of days after song release for the songs in Bugs Music Chart

On the other hand, the Bugs Music provides another type of daily chart called "Mania Chart" that only counts top 2 % of users who use their music streaming service most often. It also removes songs not older than 1 year, which helps disentangle the new song impact from relation between music preference and weather effect. As shown in Fig. 1(b), it took a song about 6.5 years to rank in the Mania Chart on average. Furthermore, boy bands and girl bands take only about 10 % of portion in the chart. For the rest of this paper, we only use "Mania Chart" as daily music chart data.

For the historical weather data, we have retrieved daily temperature (min, max, and average), humidity (min, max, and average), dew point, air pressure, wind speed (min, max, and average), visibility, and weather events (rain, fog, snow, and thunderstorm) from 2012 to 2015 from Weather Underground [2]. Furthermore, we added up 3 more weather variables of wind chill, heat index, and discomfort index that indicate coldness, heat, and discomfort more directly related to human feeling [7–9]. It consists of weather parameters of Seoul, the capital city of South Korea that account for 1/4 of total population of Korea where the weather is relatively uniform across its regions.

For the next two Sects. 2.2 and 2.3, we overview the two datasets to understand general characteristics of Korean weather and K-pop music market before proceeding to recommendation models.

2.2 Weather Data Analysis

Figure 2 illustrates daily temperature change from 2012 to 2015 in Korea. The temperature goes up around 30 °C in summer and drops to 0 ~ −10° in winter. As in Figs. 3 and 4 rainfall is concentrated during summer season hence increase the humidity and discomfort level combined with high temperature.

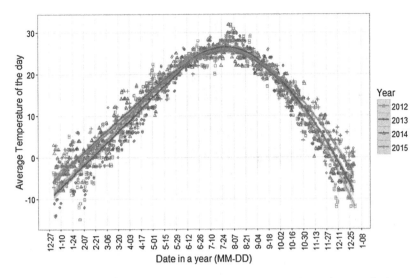

Fig. 2. Daily average temperature from 2012 to 2015 (Color figure online)

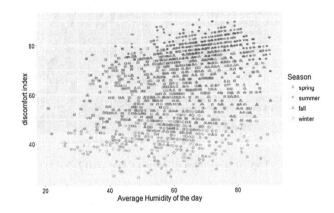

Fig. 3. Seasonal discomfort level and humidity (Color figure online)

With that said, it is expected that songs that compensate the displeasure feeling of hot and humid weather will be preferred during the summer season whereas different types of music will be preferred in other seasons.

2.3   Music Chart Analysis

Figure 5 shows a list of song titles that appears most frequently in the Mania Chart from 2012 to 2015. We expect the music preference may differ in accordance with weather condition. To reveal the correlation, we define *event preference index* as follows:

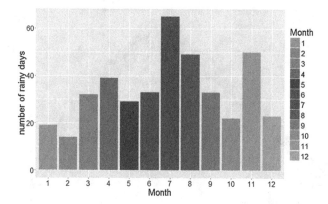

Fig. 4. Average monthly rainy days in Seoul (2012–2015) (Color figure online)

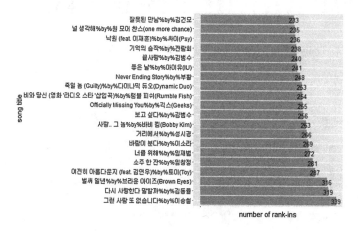

Fig. 5. Top 20 song titles of Mania Chart (2012–2015)

Given weather event W, the preference index of song S_i is

$$P_{index(X,W)} \equiv P(X \mid W)/P(X \mid \sim W)$$

where X denotes an event that the song S_i shows up in the chart. $P(X \mid W)$ and $P(X \mid \sim W)$ can be calculated from the Mania Chart dataset. If p index value for a song over event "Rain" is near to 1.0, it implies the songs preference is marginally affected by the event. If the value is larger than 1.0, say 2.0, then the song is considered to be twice more preferred on a rainy day than other day. Values near to zero mean the song would not be listened on a rainy day on the contrary.

Figure 6 shows top 20 songs with highest p index value on Rain and Snow event that appear to be different with the list in Fig. 5. On a rainy day, songs that tell mostly loneliness after break-up are found to be preferred. Songs in a romantic mood tends to be listened more on snowy days. This infers that emotion factors make an impact on

p index over Rain event		p index over Snow event	
Title	p_index	Title	p_index
Rain Drop%by%아이유(IU)	2.18	한사람을 위한 마음%by%럼블 피쉬(Rumble Fish)	2.72
Bubble Pop!%by%현아 [포미닛]	2.08	아시나요%by%조성모	2.48
비오는 압구정%by%브라운 아이즈(Brown Eyes)	1.98	Hello%by%허각	2.40
정%by%영텍스클럽(YTC)	1.93	바래진 기억에%by%박지윤	2.32
비행기%by%거북이	1.86	취중진담(醉中眞談)%by%전람회	2.22
사랑은 봄비처럼... 이별은 겨울비처럼%by%임현정	1.84	I Love U, Oh Thank U (feat. 김태우)%by%MC 몽	2.08
우산 (feat. 윤하)%by%에픽 하이(Epik High)	1.73	라라라%by%이수영	2.08
좋은 사람 (feat. 김형중)%by%토이(Toy)	1.70	시간이 흐른 뒤 (As Time Goes By)%by%t윤미래	1.99
그녀와의 이별%by%김현정	1.58	오래된 노래%by%김동률	1.97
술이야%by%바이브(Vibe)	1.57	With Coffee...%by%브라운 아이즈(Brown Eyes)	1.88
빗소리%by%윤하(Younha/ユンナ)	1.55	사랑에 빠지고 싶다%by%김조한	1.84
파도처럼%by%유엔(UN)	1.55	With Me%by%휘성	1.83
슬퍼지려 하기 전에%by%쿨(COOL)	1.52	I Don't Care%by%투애니원(2NE1)	1.82
비가 오는 날엔%by%비스트(Beast)	1.49	좋아해%by%요조(Yozoh)	1.80
취중진담(醉中眞談)%by%전람회	1.48	내게 오는 길 (Bonus Track)%by%성시경	1.74
너에게 난, 나에게 넌%by%자전거 탄 풍경	1.45	Second First Date (feat. Ritha K) (Bonus Track From Jazz Set)%by%디제이 아키(DJ AKI)	1.73
러브 레시피%by%거미	1.42	BK Love%by%MC 스나이퍼(MC Sniper)	1.71
정말로 사랑한다면%by%버스커 버스커(Busker Busker)	1.40	차마...%by%성시경	1.59
벚꽃 엔딩%by%버스커 버스커(Busker Busker)	1.40	바람이 불어오는 곳%by%제이레빗(J Rabbit)	1.52
안녕이라고 말하지마%by%다비치	1.39	거기서거기 (Without You)%by%다이나믹 듀오(Dynamic Duo)	1.51

Fig. 6. Songs preferable on Rain and Snow events

user's music preference. We will proceed into deeper study on this correlation in the later sections.

3 Methodology

3.1 Hypothesis

We suppose that latent emotion factors are affected by weather conditions and affect favorite music kinds. Hence, it is prudent to test the hypothesis by predicting preferable music based on weather condition and comparing the predicted music with the actual music chart. Furthermore, we took a deeper look at our recommendation model to comprehend the factors in it.

3.2 Preprocessing

We only consider songs that showed up in the music chart more than 50 times to build our model, which are 628 songs out of 9422. For the rest, we assumed that they do not have enough information to figure out the weather effect.

From weather dataset, we picked daily average temperature, average humidity, wind speed, dew point, air pressure, wind chill, heat index, and discomfort level as variables of our recommendation model. The variables are either z-normalized or discretized using quantile-based range partitioning (see Sect. 4 for more details). The discretized variables are converted into dummy variables with one-hot encoding.

To further characterize the daily weather features, we partitioned all the records (from 2012 to 2015) into eight groups using k-means clustering with the weather variables [13]. Each cluster and its centroid represent one weather condition group as described in Table 1. For instance, the first cluster represents cold and dry weather condition group, which mainly corresponds to winter season. The last one denotes hot

Table 1. Description of 8 weather condition clusters

cluster ID	centroids												number of days	weather description
	meanT	avgH	pressure	avgW	wind_chl	heat_idx	discomf_idx	Rain	Fog	Snow	Thrstrm	daily.T.range		
1	-1.07	51.6	1025.07	8.08	-7.99	3.87	44.13	0.01	0	0	0	9.94	331	Cold, Dry
2	22.97	74.9	1007.04	9.22	7.88	28.24	75.69	1	0	0	0	5.9	150	Hot, Rain
3	21.44	76.3	1008.07	10.44	5.91	27.43	74.25	1	0	0	1	6.7	71	Hot, ThStrm
4	14.24	53.7	1017.24	7.4	0.49	20.86	66.43	0.01	0	0	0	13.08	273	Warm
5	10.88	73	1017.33	6.09	-0.7	17.12	60.82	0.25	1	0	0.01	11.13	103	Warm, Fog
6	8.37	65.9	1015.62	10.41	-2.19	12.12	54.58	0.95	0	0	0	7.77	132	Cool, Rain
7	-2.15	62.5	1021.43	9.93	-8.8	2.08	40.35	0.34	0.1	1	0.03	8.47	88	Cold, Snow
8	23.8	66.3	1009.37	7.27	7.66	31.91	78.49	0	0	0	0	9.26	310	Hot

weather with high discomfort level mainly in summer season. The second and third cluster represents monsoon season in Korea, which is hot and rainy in summer. This cluster information is added into our model according to its configuration as described in Sect. 4.

3.3 Recommendation Model

We build two different music recommendation models, multi-class logistic regression model and alternating least square, ALS for short, model [10, 11]. For comparison, we design a baseline model that always recommend the same 100 songs that showed up in the chart most frequently. To evaluate the performance of each model, we randomly split the data of weather and music chart into test set and training set with ratio of 2:8. The training set is used to train our models. The test set is to measure the performance of each model.

For the multi-class logistic regression, we devise one logistic regression model for each song. The target variable is a binary variable that has value of 1 when the song is in the music chart and 0 when the song is not in the chart. Each logistic regression model predicts the probability of the song being in the chart on each day using weather variables. Given probability of each song, we pick top 100 songs with the highest probability and recommend those songs to user. Figure 7 illustrates the multi-class logistic regression model for song recommendation.

Figure 8 shows ALS model for music recommendation model. We first construct *n* by *m* input matrix, where *n* is the number of combinations (cluster, season) and *m* is the number of songs we use for recommendation. Each element of input matrix represents the normalized number of times that each song ranked in the chart within the pair of cluster and season. By ALS algorithm [12], the input matrix decomposed into two matrices, A and B. Each row of A represents the cluster and season pair and each column represents magnitude of an emotion factor toward the cluster. For transpose of B, each row implies a song, and column means the magnitude of an emotion factor for the song. Given k emotion factors, if an emotion factor has a large positive number for a song and a cluster, then it increase the probability of the song being preferred in the cluster. On the contrary, an emotion factor that has large negative values for a song and cluster decreases the probability of the song being in the chart. For prediction, it first determines to which cluster the input weather condition belongs, and output the 100 songs with the highest values of the cluster in the matrix A × B.

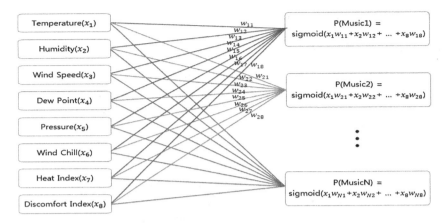

Fig. 7. Multi-class logistic regression model

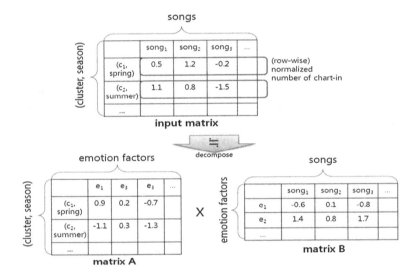

Fig. 8. ALS for music recommendation

Considering our recommendation models more focus on the weather-effect than song's popularity whereas baseline model only consider popularity, we construct a hybrid model of ALS and baseline with weight parameter α, where we compute the score of each song as in Eq. 1. It recommends 100 songs with the highest scores.

$$S(song) = \alpha \times S_{ALS}(song \mid cluster, season) + (1 - \alpha) \times S_{baseline}(song) \qquad (1)$$

4   Result and Discussion

4.1   Experimental Settings

We have used R and Python for preliminary study, modeling and testing. We used Scikit-learn library of Python for logistic regression model, and Pandas library for data preprocessing and management [12, 14]. Hardware and software specification are described in Table 2.

Table 2. Hardware and software configurations

Processor	Inteli5(4-core 2.50 GHz)
Memory	DDR3(L) 8 GB
Hard disk	500 GB, 7200 RPM
OS	Windows7 (64 bit)
IDE	Canopy1.6, Minitab
Language	R, Python2.7
Main Python Library	Pandas, Scikit-learn

For model training, we use weather variables of daily average temperature, average humidity, wind speed, dew point, air pressure, wind chill, heat index, and discomfort level. For logistic regression model, we normalized the variables for LR1 and discretized for LR2 as in Table 3. For LR3 and L4, we put additional variables of cluster ID and season to LR1 and LR2, respectively.

Table 3. Model configurations

Model label	Model	Training
BaseLine	Base Line Model	N.A.
LR1	Logistic Regression Model	Normalized variables
LR2	Logistic Regression Model	Discretized variables
LR3	Logistic Regression Model	LR2 + Season + Cluster
LR4	Logistic Regression Model	LR1 + LR3
ALS	ALS Model	Season + Cluster
Hybrid	Base Line Model + ALS Model	Season + Cluster

4.2   Evaluation Measure

Our recommendation models and the baseline model recommend 100 songs given weather condition. To evaluate the accuracy of each recommendation, we define *hit ratio* for each prediction as the number of songs in both prediction and actual music chart of the day. We use the test set for evaluation, which we separated before model training. For example, we predict 100 songs for given weather condition, and 10 songs actually hit in the chart, then hit ratio is 10. For performance comparison, we calculate the average hit ratio for each recommendation model.

4.3   Result and Discussion

Figure 9(a) shows average hit ratio on the test set for each recommendation model according to the configuration in Table 3. The baseline model hits 13.32 songs on average. Logistic regression models outperform the baseline model up to 20.4 %. ALS increase the hit ratio 13.21 %. The result shows that the weather variables contribute to the music preference significantly.

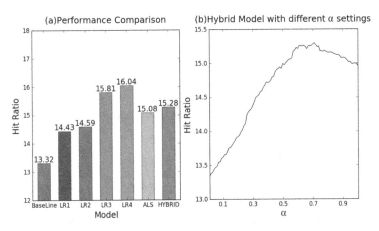

Fig. 9. Comparing model performance (Color figure online)

On the other hands, it also implies there are other factors that affect to user emotion or music preference itself. As LR3 and LR4 introduce additional variables, season and cluster ID that capture more information about users, it models more accurately the music preference than LR1 and LR2. For example, the season variable may infer effect of annual events such as graduation ceremony, thanks-giving day, and sports event, which may not be captured by weather information. Accordingly, we include the season variable into ALS model as well.

Considering ALS model mostly focuses on variables related to the date, weather and season whereas Baseline model fully relies on the popularity of each song. Mixing them together would be a chance to improve our model. Hybrid model slightly improves the performance up to 1.3 % depending on the weight parameter α. Figure 9(b) shows the performance of hybrids model with different α settings. The performance is maximum near the point of $\alpha = 0.7$.

Figure 10 shows the average hit ratio in each month. In winter season, December, January, and February, the difference is marginal as weather effect becomes less significant. In summer season, June, July, and August, the weather effect becomes stronger as the weather changes more drastically than other seasons because of monsoon and typhoon. It can be also thought that hot and humid weather is more crucial for human emotion since summer season in Korea has high discomfort level, which indicates the actual discomfortness of weather to people's activity.

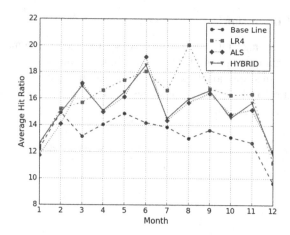

Fig. 10. Average hit ratio in each month

5   Conclusion and Future Work

We have proven that associating weather condition with user emotion factors notice-ably improves music recommendation system. It has a great chance to enrich the user experience in online music streaming service by reflecting factors that change dynamically. The finding are extendable to recommend music artists and music genre as well as songs alone to users.

Many other factors affect user emotion and music preference as well as weather condition. There are more chances to improve the recommendation by integrating personal and social factors such as social media activity, residential area, age, gender and social issues to the system. It is also challenging to recommend new songs and artists with no historical record.

Acknowledgement. This research was supported by Advancement of Collage Education (2016) funded by Ministry of Education.

References

1. RIAJ Yearbook 2015: IFPI 2013, 2014. Global Sales of Recorded Music, p. 24. Recording Industry Association of Japan (2015)
2. Weather Underground. http://www.wunderground.com/history/
3. Bugs Music Chart. http://music.bugs.co.kr/chart?wl_ref=M_left_02_01
4. Nanopoulos, A., et al.: Musicbox: personalized music recommendation based on cubic analysis of social tags. IEEE Trans. Audio Speech Lang. Process. **18**(2), 407–412 (2010)
5. Lu, C.-C., Tseng, V.S.: A novel method for personalized music recommendation. Expert Syst. Appl. **36**(6), 10035–10044 (2009)

6. Chen, H.-C., Chen, A.L.P.: A music recommendation system based on music data grouping and user interests. In: Proceedings of the Tenth International Conference on Information and Knowledge Management. ACM (2001)
7. Steadman, R.G.: The assessment of sultriness. Part I: a temperature-humidity index based on human physiology and clothing science. J. Appl. Meteorol. **18**(7), 861–873 (1979)
8. Steadman, R.G.: The assessment of sultriness. Part II: effects of wind, extra radiation and barometric pressure on apparent temperature. J. Appl. Meteorol. **18**(7), 874–885 (1979)
9. Thom, E.C.: The discomfort index. Weatherwise **12**(2), 57–61 (1959)
10. Hosmer Jr., D.W., Stanley, L.: Applied Logistic Regression. Wiley, New York (2004)
11. Takács, G., Tikk, D.: Alternating least squares for personalized ranking. In: Proceedings of the Sixth ACM Conference on Recommender Systems. ACM (2012)
12. Scikit-learn Library. http://scikit-learn.org/
13. MacQueen, J.: Some methods for classification and analysis of multivariate observations. In: Proceedings of the Fifth Berkeley Symposium on Mathematical Statistics and Probability, vol. 1, no. 14 (1967)
14. Mckinney, W.: Python for Data Analysis: Data Wrangling with Pandas, NumPy, and IPython. O'Reilly Media, Inc., Sebastopol (2012)

Toward Long-Term Persuasion
Using a Personified Agent

Akihito Yoshii[(✉)] and Tatsuo Nakajima

Waseda University, Shinjuku, Japan
{a_yoshii,tatsuo}@dcl.cs.waseda.ac.jp

Abstract. People sometimes treat a nonliving object including a computer as if it is a living one. Today, we can interact with them regardless of location or time and we are sometimes affected by computers to decide something. Thus, strategies for weaving virtual experience generated by a computer into the real world are needed because of the prevalence of computers compared to the past. However, a room for discussion is still exist in an aspect of relationship between motivation for specific behavior and representation of information related to the behavior. In this paper, we discuss the design implications for choosing a virtual agent representing a personified object for long-term persuasion. Based on the previous experiments, we conducted a group study regarding design aspects of a personified agent. We describe the details and findings of group study; and then discuss design implications and future directions for personified agents which can construct preferable relationship with a user.

1 Introduction

People sometimes treat a nonliving object as if it is a living one. Reeves and Nass stated that people sometimes interact with computers as if they are living things [10]. When people treat computers as a living entity, they are conscious that computers are lifeless; however, they still communicate with computers socially [5]. As another example, an automated sweeper is reported to be seen as a "cute thing" as if it is a companion animal [8].

Computers are so prevalent that we can interact with them regardless of location or time. In addition, we are sometimes affected by computers to decide something. For example, computer products support our daily exercising using technologies (e.g. Nike+[1]), or websites encourage visitors to buy products using techniques such as recommendation. Fogg defined persuasion as "an attempt to change attitudes or behaviors or both" [3] and proposed Captology (Computers as Persuasive Technologies) as related realms, for example, designing, analyzing or understanding persuasive computer products [3].

Thus, strategies for weaving virtual experience generated by a computer into the real world are needed because of the prevalence of computers compared to the past. For example, in the Human-Agent Interaction (HAI) field, researchers

---

[1] https://secure-nikeplus.nike.com/plus/products/#all_day_section.

© Springer International Publishing Switzerland 2016
A. Marcus (Ed.): DUXU 2016, Part II, LNCS 9747, pp. 122–131, 2016.
DOI: 10.1007/978-3-319-40355-7_12

attempt to discuss interactions between people and general artificial objects not limited to a computer and a robot [15]. Captology covers persuasive computer systems and points out roles of computers as a persuader [3]. Although Captology and HAI are different research field, both are related to interaction between artificial objects and users affecting them sometimes.

Computers can behave as social entity in persuasion as well. Multiple forms of a social behavior can be considered for persuasive computer systems. For example, social entity can be expressed as text messages or speech-based assistant like Apple Siri[2]. As another way, computers can also present embodied character to a user.

Still, people can be familiar with daily things represented as a character. The authors examined an agent as a personified object shown to a user and discussed the possibility of persuasion by such agent in the previous study [17]. In this study, we designed a "cleaning" task and then ask participants to move objects to the initial locations. This task incorporated a prototype application and this application show an agent as a personified object. Using this setting, the agents can interact with a user as if an object itself is directly talking to the user [17]. The future direction of this study included the possibility of encouraging users to be interested in real-world problems by receiving messages from an agent as a "proxy" of an object.

However, a room for discussion still exists in an aspect of relationship between motivation for specific behavior and representation of information related to the behavior. Positive impressions of an agent can lead to encouraging users to be interested in the agent and real-world problems such as beautification of public spaces or environmental problems. Moreover, sustained motivation leads to the possibility of long-term intervention by persuasive computer systems in a daily life.

In this paper, we discuss the design implications for choosing a virtual agent representing a personified object for long-term persuasion. Based on the previous experiments, we conducted a group study regarding design aspects of a personified agent. We describe the details and findings of group study; and then discuss design implications and future directions for personified agents which can construct preferable relationship with a user. We use the word "personification" when an agent behaves as a "proxy" of a daily object. Although we sometimes intend a meaning similar to "anthropomorphism", we also intend the broader representation of an object than human-like things.

2   Related Work

Design of personified artificial objects has been discussed by researchers from the past. Owada pointed that people treat a Roomba produced by iRobot[3] as if it is a living thing and he discussed personification required for electrical appliances in the future [8]. In his book, he mentioned Media Equation proposed by Nass and

---

[2] http://www.apple.com/ios/siri/.
[3] http://www.irobot.com/For-the-Home/Vacuum-Cleaning/Roomba.aspx.

Reeves [10] and explain that people sometimes interact with nonliving things as if they are living ones. Besides, he introduces organic and sympathetic natures of an object referring to related work [8]. Personification has the possibility of emotional attachment to an object. For example, affection for personified daily objects is mentioned in [14] with some examples.

Yamada et al. stated that the degree of reality should not exceed the level of functions for the successful design of personification [14]. They called the difference between functions modeled by a user and actual ones as Adaptation Gap [14]. This aspect corresponds to the discussion by Shedroff and Noessel. They explained that if an application provides a user of excessive expectation compared to actual functionality, the user can be annoyed [12]. They mentioned to Knowledge Navigator which was created by Apple in 1987 and explained that the agent deployed in Knowledge Navigator worked because of its suitability for the actual ability [12]. Conversely, they also pointed out an example of an unsuccessful assistant agent drawing the story of Clippy deployed in Microsoft Office [12].

Although discussions of the effectiveness of embodiment exist from the past, the possibilities of an embodied agent are suggested. For example, Lester et al. applied animated agent to an interactive learning environment [4]. Their work suggested that the existence of an animated agent had positive effect on perception of learning experience in an interactive learning environment (persona effect) [4]. DiSalvo and Gemperle discussed applying anthropomorphism to product design. In their work, two types of quality of anthropomorphism: "seduction" and "fulfillment" [2]. Seduction means that a product leads people to consume it by anthropomorphism and fulfillment leads to meaningful understanding of the product. Seduction can still be accepted because of enjoyable and rewarding nature [2].

Moreover, researchers are trying to examine essential elements for anthropomorphism. Osawa et al. attempted to anthropomorphize a daily object by attaching eyes-like and arms-like parts to it [7]. They examined reaction of a user when s/he received an explanation of functions of a printer from different object. One is a printer with eyes and arms and the other is an independent robot. As a result, they reported that a user more concentrated to the target and remembered the functions explained [7].

3   Previous Studies

We used a prototype application named Fairy Agent [16]. This prototype can show a 3D virtual character superimposed on an object using augmented reality. Each character was intended to behave as a personified object and interact with a user as if the object itself has obtained life [17]. We examined combinations of objects and characters using questionnaires and a task based study.

We chose appearances of the agents using keywords associated with each object. Especially, we focused on keywords related to an occupation and then we prepared existing 3D models which can be associated with the keywords.

Keywords were collected in the Object-Image questionnaire; and then, agents were chosen referring to the results of the Object-Image questionnaire in the Agent-Image questionnaire. Based on the results of questionnaires, we experimented with Fairy Agent to examine the perception of personification and the effect of persuasion.

From the results of each surveys, the condition where different agents chosen for each object were shown on near the objects suggested the possibility of persuasion using a personified agent [17]. In this case, we have chosen an agent based on keywords associated with an object regardless of the preference of a user. However, the consideration of an impression of an agent can still be needed if the agent tries to construct relationship with a user.

4   Group Work

We arranged a group work to collect ideas for personification regarding the preference of users. The main purpose of this group work was to specify essences of personification of nonliving objects referring to existing pop cultures such as games and anime. The group work was divided into two parts and each part is followed by a sharing and discussion session (Fig. 1). This kind of findings can be utilized for designing personified agent.

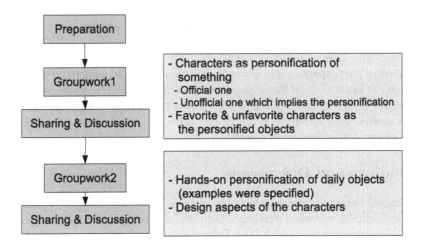

Fig. 1. Group work flow

4.1   Participants

Ten participants from our laboratory attended the group work. The participants consist of seven males and three females; and all participants were Japanese. Participants of previous studies [17] were included. They are paired with another participant and then each participant is supposed to discuss themes with the partner.

4.2   Task 1: Essence of Personification

In the first part, we discussed the main features of personified (anthropomorphized) characters referring to existing examples. We asked participants to consider characters which they know and then find the favorite or not-favorite points of them. Especially, we asked each participant to enumerate existing personified characters from multiple aspects: official ones, not-official ones, favorite ones, and not-favorite ones. Then, participants were asked to discuss the main elements for personification and favorite/not-favorite attributes of the characters.

We separated official and not-official characters because an official character may not always suitable for an original object to which was referred by the character.

4.3   Task 2: Personification of Familiar Daily Objects

We have chosen two daily objects: a camera tripod and a box of tissue paper. We asked participants to choose one or both of them and designing personified characters and its personalities. When proceed with the task, participants can choose one of two options: generate a 3D model using SIMS3[4] or sketch an image of the personified agent. However, the number of the vacancy was limited for the SIMS3 option, most of participants

Before the task, we announced example aspects to the participants: genders, ages, hair style, clothes and accessories. Also, other types of an aspect can be accepted.

Tables 1 and 2 show a part of keywords answered by participants. Keywords from a part of participants could not collected clearly. Some participants designed a character of both a box of tissue paper and a camera tripod; however, the others designed for either of them. Each keyword was translated to English while the original words were specified in Japanese. The "-" means that difficulty was existed in extracting keywords clearly.

5   Findings and Discussions

We extracted clues regarding preferences and perception of personification in the Task1. In addition, we asked participants to explain the process of personification of the daily objects in the Task2. The Table 3 shows the sentences extracted from the discussion in the Task1 and new aspect of personification in the Task2.

Table 1. Keywords of a character for a box of tissue paper

Participant	Color	Clothes/Accessory	Hairstyle	Gender	Other characteristic
P1	White	White coat	Longish	Male	-
P2	White	Red ribbon, dress	Long	Female	Caught a cold
P3	White	Dress	Long, fluffy	Female	-
P4	White	-	Curled brown hair	-	-

---

[4] http://www.thesims3.com.

Table 2. Keywords of a character for a camera tripod

Participant	Color	Clothes/Accessory	Hairstyle	Gender	Other characteristic
P3	Black	T-shirt, glasses, wrist band	Short	Male	Supports a camera (personified camera character is implied)
P5	-	Square-like cap, belt	Short/ponytail, with a fluffy tip	Male	Loyal to a camera person
P6	Black	Cap	Ponytail	Female	-
P7	Black	Glasses	-	Male	-

Table 3. Extracted sentences of attributes for personification from the group work

Task	Subject	Keywords
Task1	Personification	Resemblance to, or consistency with an original entity
	Preference	Unreal abilities, effect of learning, desire, commonness
Task2	Considered aspects	Functions, an attribute of a user, specific situations

5.1 Task1

Resemblance to, or consistency with an original entity to which a personified agent refers includes contexts or episodes around the entity. That is, "effective personification" can be derived from natural translation of, for example, an original image, a history, and uniqueness. In an aspect of preferences, an agent's fictional nature can be important characteristics. For example, if an ability of an agent matches the desire of a user or commonness between the agent and the user, the user can be attracted to the agent. Existing work suggest that people prefers a computer whose personality is similar to them [6]. When a characters from pop cultures concern, a certain amount of unreality can be accepted.

Certain amount of incompleteness can be accepted with affection [8]. Owada discussed combination of the scenario of a character and an electric appliance (iRobot Roomba). Roomba sometimes sweeps a room in a less sophisticated manner and this can be incompleteness [8]. He pointed the similarity of a hero/heroine of a story and the behavior of Roomba [8].

5.2 Task2

Keywords related to a color for each daily object were almost same. This commonness was considered to be affected by a color of a daily object. Clothes, accessories, and hairstyle had a partial commonness and some of them are related to texture of an object.

From the keywords from the Task2, we find interesting keywords for personification process. For example, one participant mentioned a function of a tripod. The personified character can have a camera as a friend because a tripod supports a camera. As another example, another participant said that a personified character, which derived from a box of tissue paper, catches a cold because of an image of those who blow their nose.

As another result, some participants specified characteristics depend on a model object or particular use. For example, one participant introduced red color for an agent of a box of tissue paper because she associated tissue paper with nosebleed. Thus, keywords can be derived from specific situations.

5.3 Summary

In summary, we propose key implications for designing agent characters as a personified object. First, user's preferences have the possibility of being adjusted by drawing fictional settings. Second, different types of keywords can be utilized for designing agent. That is, an agent derived from keywords according to common understandings and image of a model object can be easily understood. In contrast, certain amount of "accents" can also be introduced to make an agent interesting.

When long-term persuasion using personified agent is considered, positive impression and attractiveness of an agent can play a role. Balancing between consistency with the original and fictionality should be introduced.

6   Future Direction

In this paper, we mentioned the possibility of long-term persuasion using interaction with personified agent and existing pop culture. Especially, an agent can be embodied form and it can be combined with existing fictional stories or worldview; therefore, an application can provide users of the extended experience during the use. In addition, if an application let users choose their favorite agent for a companion, they can be affected by the agent because of their preference. We call such agents as customizable personified agents.

However, when a developer try to apply the customizable personified agent to general persuasive application, the customizable personified agent needs to be combined with other persuasive methods because of multiple issues. We have proposed the Tailorable Persuasive Agent (TPA) framework, a conceptual framework for development of a persuasive application with an agent for a long-term period. TPA consists of three elements: Adaptive Persuasion (AP), Intention Adjustment (IA), Preference-Based Internalization (PBI).

Adaptive Persuasion (AP). This element is related to variable persuasion based on estimated behavior status of a user. We can use existing theories for modeling of individual current behaviors. As one of behavior models, we referred to Transtheoretical model proposed by Prochaska et al. [9] as a staged behavior change process.

Intention Adjustment (IA). An application can adjust expectations by users to actual abilities of an agent and encourage users to continue to use the application. This element is described in two aspects.

Augmenting use intentions. For example, an application can let a user stop interaction with an agent preventing annoyance [12]. As Henriette et al. examined [13], visual appearances can be chosen to reduce disappointment by users.

Encouraging interest in persuasion. Agent properties can be arranged to encourage a user to take persuasion seriously. For example, Zanbaka et al. compared different characters in different gender, species, and reality [18]. According to their experiment, people tend to be persuaded by a person in different genders (male/female). In addition, nonhuman characters were seen more bold than real human ones [18].

Preference-Based Internalization (PBI). This element contains virtual experiences provided by customizable features from an application. The customizable personified agent is included in this element. Using the customizable personified agent, application can attempt to prevent users from ceasing behavior change if they are bored in the needed task. This functionality is intended to trigger intrinsic motivation. Intrinsic motivation is caused by enjoyment and challenge while extrinsic motivation is outcome-oriented, and provided by external pressures and rewards [11].

TPA is intended to be utilized across modeled time frames from the beginning of application use to being accepted and continued use. Figure 2 shows an overview of the TPA framework.

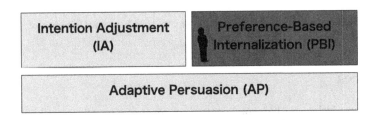

Fig. 2. Conceptual framework

Although different combinations of elements are used for each time frame, the AP element is fundamental part of persuasive application and this element is applied during most of the use period.

7   Other Issues

In relation to the proposed framework, some aspects are yet to be discussed. The perception of personification and embodiment can be varied among cultures. When people are familiar with embodied personification because of fictional stories, we may able to accept the personification. However, embodiment is not required for personification [14] and developer can choose a design among multiple options.

If a persuasive application is intended to be internationalized, the preference of attributes for designing agents should be discussed from a multiple-culture or multiple-generation aspect. For example, a game character on a package design is known to be changed suitable for a country in which the game is sold [1]. A visual or nonvisual attributes for a virtual agent should be adjusted according to countries or districts where the persuasive agent is used.

8   Conclusion

In this paper, we explained the room for discussion of persuasive agent in an aspect of personification and introducing existing pop cultures. Based on the previous experiments, we described a group study consists of two parts. In the first task, we attempted to extract characteristics of personified agents referring to existing characters. Then, we examined attributes of viewpoints of designing personified agent through the hands-on task.

Based on the findings from the group work, we discussed design implications and future directions for personified agents which can construct preferable relationship with a user. As a summary of the group work, we proposed two implications. First, user's preferences have the possibility of being adjusted by drawing fictional settings. Second, keywords for designing agent must be carefully chosen according to common understandings of image of a model object.

Acknowledgments. The authors would like to thank to participants of the group work.

References

1. American kirby is hardcore. http://tvtropes.org/pmwiki/pmwiki.php/Main/AmericanKirbyIsHardcore
2. DiSalvo, C., Gemperle, F.: From seduction to fulfillment: the use of anthropomorphic form in design. In: Proceedings of the 2003 International Conference on Designing Pleasurable Products and Interfaces, DPPI 2003, pp. 67–72. ACM, New York (2003). http://doi.acm.org/10.1145/782896.782913
3. Fogg, B.J.: Persuasive Technology. Morgan Kaufmann Publishers, San Francisco (2003)
4. Lester, J.C., Converse, S.A., Kahler, S.E., Barlow, S.T., Stone, B.A., Bhogal, R.S.: The persona effect: affective impact of animated pedagogical agents. In: Proceedings of the ACM SIGCHI Conference on Human Factors in Computing Systems, CHI 1997, pp. 359–366. ACM, New York (1997). http://doi.acm.org/10.1145/258549.258797
5. Nass, C., Moon, Y.: Machines and mindlessness: social responses to computers. J. Soc. Issues **56**(1), 81–103 (2000). http://dx.doi.org/10.1111/0022-4537.00153
6. Nass, C., Moon, Y., Fogg, B., Reeves, B., Dryer, D.: Can computer personalities be human personalities? Int. J. Hum.-Comput. Stud. **43**(2), 223–239 (1995). http://www.sciencedirect.com/science/article/pii/S1071581985710427
7. Osawa, H., Ohmura, R., Imai, M.: Using attachable humanoid parts for realizing imaginary intention and body image. Int. J. Soc. Robot. **1**(1), 109–123 (2008). http://dx.doi.org/10.1007/s12369-008-0004-0

8. Owada, S.: Moe-Home Electrical Appliances. Discover Twentyone (2015). (In Japanese, title is also translated)
9. Prochaska, J.O., DiClemente, C.C., Norcross, J.C.: In search of how people change: applications to addictive behaviors. J. Addictions Nurs. J. Prev. Manag. Addictions **5**(1), 2–16 (1993). Spring
10. Reeves, B., Nass, C.: The Media Equation: How People Treat Computers, Television, and New Media Like Real People and Places. CSLI Publications, Stanford, Cambridge University Press, New York (1996)
11. Ryan, R.M., Deci, E.L.: Intrinsic and extrinsic motivations: classic definitions and new directions. contemp. educ. psychol. **25**(1), 54–67 (2000). http://www.sciencedirect.com/science/article/pii/S0361476X99910202
12. Shedroff, N., Noessel, C.: Make It So: Interaction Design Lessons from Science Fiction. Rosenfeld Media, LLC, Brooklyn (2012)
13. Van Vugt, H.C., Hoorn, J.F., Konijn, E.A., de Bie Dimitriadou, A.: Affective affordances: improving interface character engagement through interaction. Int. J. Hum.-Comput. Stud. **64**(9), 874–888 (2006). http://www.sciencedirect.com/science/article/pii/S1071581906000589
14. Yamada, S.: Designing "Relationship Between" Human and Robot. Tokyo Denki University Press, Tokyo (2007). (In Japanese, title is also translated)
15. Yamada, S.: Originality in human-agent interaction. Jpn. Soc. Artifi. Intell. **24**(6), 810–817 (2009). http://ci.nii.ac.jp/naid/110007467976/. (In Japanese)
16. Yoshii, A., Nakajima, T.: Fairy agent: a persuasive application encourages behavior changes using conversations with an agent representing a daily object. In: DICOMO 2014 Symposium (2014). (In Japanese)
17. Yoshii, A., Nakajima, T.: Personification aspect of conversational agents as representations of a physical object. In: Proceedings of the 3rd International Conference on Human-Agent Interaction, HAI 2015, pp. 231–234. ACM, New York (2015). http://doi.acm.org/10.1145/2814940.2814983
18. Zanbaka, C., Goolkasian, P., Hodges, L.: Can a virtual cat persuade you?: the role of gender and realism in speaker persuasiveness. In: Proceedings of the SIGCHI Conference on Human Factors in Computing Systems, CHI 2006, pp. 1153–1162. ACM, New York (2006). http://doi.acm.org/10.1145/1124772.1124945

Mechanism of Persuasive Experience-A New Design and Evaluation Framework of Persuasive Systems

Kaixiang Yu and Huiyang Li[✉]

State University of New York at Binghamton, Binghamton, NY, USA
{kyu7,hli}@binghamton.edu

Abstract. Persuasive technology has drawn increasing attention from researchers. However, only a few studies in the literature have proposed theoretical frameworks for the design and evaluation of persuasive systems. The current theories are not fully developed because they provide neither insights into users' persuasive experience while using the persuasive systems nor the appropriate methods to effectively evaluate the persuasiveness of each design element. This paper first reviews current literature on behavior change theories and the design of persuasive systems, and then presents a new framework of persuasive systems that emphasizes the concept of persuasive experience.

Keywords: Persuasive systems · Persuasive technology · Persuasive experience framework · User-behavior relationship stages · Behavior change · Persuasive design · Health information technology

1 Introduction

Persuasive technology (also called "persuasive system") has drawn increasing interest from researchers in the past decade and has been used to modify human behaviors in the fields of health, sustainability and more [1]. However, few studies in the literature have proposed theoretical frameworks for the design and evaluation of persuasive systems, and most theories currently available are not fully developed. A recent evaluation of a famous persuasive systems design framework pointed out that the model does not explicitly describe how to include persuasive design principles and user context in the content development process [2]. A recent literature review of persuasive systems found that many studies of persuasive systems investigated the behavior change effects of the designed persuasive system as a whole instead of analyzing how individual design features and functions of the system caused intended behavior changes [1]. These findings show that current literature does not fully investigate the mechanism by which the user changes behavior or attitude after interacting with the persuasive system, or in other words, the users' persuasive experience occurring when a persuasion is attempted by the system. Without a framework to describe the details about the interaction between the users' persuasive experience and components of persuasive systems, it is impossible to fully evaluate and compare the persuasiveness of different persuasive systems as each system would be a "black-box."

© Springer International Publishing Switzerland 2016
A. Marcus (Ed.): DUXU 2016, Part II, LNCS 9747, pp. 132–143, 2016.
DOI: 10.1007/978-3-319-40355-7_13

The goal of this paper is to investigate the mechanism of users' persuasive experience and the implication of the persuasive experience in the design and evaluation of persuasive systems. Famous health behavior change theories were reviewed to conceptualize persuasive experience, and a new framework for designing and evaluating persuasive systems was developed accordingly. The framework can be used for defining successful persuasive systems and for developing meaningful metrics for evaluating the persuasiveness of systems.

2 Method

Recent literature on health behavior change theories was searched on the PMC database and used to identify the most widely adopted theories for behavior change in the health domain. Identified theories were then reviewed, and content that may explain the persuasive experience of users was summarized. Current definitions of persuasive systems and limitations of currently available theoretical frameworks were also summarized. Keywords that were used to search persuasive systems design frameworks were "persuasive system/technology," "persuasive design," "frameworks of design persuasive systems" and "design principles of persuasive systems."

3 Results

3.1 Health Behavior Theories Identified

A literature review in 2015 found that the most widely studied behavior change theories are the Transtheoretical/Stages of Change Model, the Theory of Planned Behavior/Reasoned Action, the Social Cognitive Theory, the Health Belief Model and the Self-Determination Theory [3]. Among these theories, the Self-Determination Theory describes the nature of motivation, and the Transtheoretical Model describes the behavior change process of a target audience being persuaded while other theories mainly describe the factors that cause the behavior change. The Precaution Adoption Process Model (PAPM), which also attempts to explain the behavior change process and closely very resembles the Transtheoretical Model, was also identified during the process of reviewing relevant literature that describes the Transtheoretical Model [4]. In addition, Fogg's Behavior Model (FBM) and the Behavior Grid [5, 6] are also considered health behavior theories in this paper.

3.2 Self-Determination Theory (SDT)

The Self-Determination Theory (SDT) introduced by Ryan and Deci is the only theory among all reviewed theories that addresses the nature of motivation and how different types of motivations are influenced. In this theory, two major types of motivation, intrinsic and extrinsic, are identified. The former is defined as "the doing of an activity for its inherent satisfactions rather than for some separable consequence;" the latter is defined as "doing something because it leads to a separable outcome" [7]. Authors also explain that when a person lacks an intention to act, he or she is said to be in the state of a motivation. Extrinsic motivation is further divided into four taxonomies: external regulation (performing behaviors or complying because of extrinsic rewards or punishments), introjection (performing behaviors to "enhance or maintain self-esteem and the feeling of worth"), identification (recognizing the importance of the activity to one's personal values), and integration (fully assimilating identified regulations into one's personal values and needs). When the state of one's motivation changes from amotivation to extrinsic motivation to intrinsic motivation, the process is called internalization. The authors argue that internalized motivation promotes more persistent and engaged behaviors [7]. The theory suggests that internalization can be facilitated by increasing one's sense of relatedness, perceived competence and a feeling of autonomy.

3.3 Stage Theories of Behavior Change

The Transtheoretical Model (TTM) and the Precaution Adoption Process Model (PAPM) use the stage model to describe the behavior change process. The TTM model is the most widely used and studied theory in health behavior change [3], and it mainly consists of four constructs: the Stages of Change, the Processes of Change, the Decisional Balance and the Self-Efficacy. The Stages of Change construct states that when a person changes his or her behavior, he or she will linearly or non-linearly progress through a series of six stages: precontemplation (having no intention of taking action anytime soon), contemplation (intending to change behaviors in the next six months), preparation (intending to take actions soon, measured as within the next month), action (having made specific, observable modifications in lifestyle within the past six months), maintenance (having made additional specific, observable modifications in lifestyle and trying to prevent relapse) and termination (perceiving no need for further behavior change and maximum self-efficacy achieved) [4]. The Processes of Change, Decisional Balance and Self-Efficacy constructs describe the principles that promote behavior change.

The TTM model is criticized for a number of reasons. First, when it is used to produce complex behaviors (i.e. behaviors that consist of multiple behavior patterns instead of a single behavior), such as physical activity and low fat intake, the assessment of stage allocation may become imprecise as people may think they are in line with the proposed complex behaviors while their actual behavior patterns differ from the recommended patterns. Similarly, if people think they are not in line with the recommendation when they actually are, the model categorizes people under the precontemplation stage. A second criticism of the TTM is that the difference between the action stage and the maintenance stage can be measured only by arbitrary methods. Third, future behavior change (i.e. behaviors that occur after completing the initial behavior change) may be produced by psychological changes, such as having a more positive attitude towards a particular behavior, rather than the progression of the stages only. Fourth, the effective behavior change process needs not only stage-based intervention but also individually tailored intervention [8].

In contrast to TTM, which uses days and the state of the behavior change process as the stages of change, PAPM identifies seven stages or mental states: S1-Unaware of

Issue, S2-Unengaged by Issue, S3-Undecided About Acting, S4-Decided Not to Act, S5-Decided to Act, S6-Acting and S7-Maintenance [4]. The main difference between TTM and PAPM is that PAPM can distinguish between those who are unaware of the behavior change opportunities and those who are aware of the issue but undecided about changing behaviors. The theory suggests that different communication strategies should be taken to approach the two different populations because the former may not hurry to make a conclusion from the information provided while the latter is ready to make a decision of acting or not [4].

3.4   Constructs of Health Behavior Change

Reviewed health behavior change principles identify what causes a behavior change. The Integrated Behavior Model of the Theory of Planned Behavior/Reasoned Action, the Social Cognitive Theory and the Health Belief Model suggest that the key constructs that influence one's decision to behave include one's actual behavioral capability (knowledge and skills to perform the behavior), self-efficacy (perceived confidence in successfully performing the behavior), perceived control (perceived control over the behavior), social norms (others' expectations and behaviors), attitude (feelings and beliefs about the behavior), perceived susceptibility (perceived likelihood of acquiring the proposed condition), perceived severity (perceived risk of maintaining the current condition), expectations/perceived benefits (perceived positive consequences that the behavior would produce) and cues to action (something that triggers the action) [4].

Fogg's Behavior Model (FBM) simplifies behavior change by suggesting that a specific behavior would easily occur if one's level of motivation, ability to perform the behavior and the right trigger were merged [5]. Fogg emphasizes that if the behavior is simple enough to be performed, one will need only basic motivation and an adequate trigger (cues of action) to start the behavior. He argues that the general strategy to behavior change is to start with a very simple behavior change that needs little effort to perform and gradually build on small successes of behavior change to achieve the ultimate behavior change goals.

Fogg's Behavior Grid identifies 15 types of behavior (lowered from its original 35 types) categorized according to the duration that each behavior needs to be performed and the nature of the behavior being performed [6]. As Fogg explains, there are dots (behaviors done one-time and measured in seconds, minutes or hours), spans (behaviors performed for days and weeks) and paths (habits or permanent behavior changes). It is suggested that dot behaviors are the easiest to perform. The difficulty of performing the behavior increases when the duration of the behavior change period increases.

3.5   Frameworks for Persuasive Systems

The literature search identified three widely adopted frameworks that intend to guide the design and evaluation of persuasive systems. Fogg's original work that conceptualized persuasive technology is very well known, and the work has been cited by many scientists who study persuasive systems [9]. In 2009 Fogg also provided an eight-step design process of persuasive technology that was integrated with FBM [10]. A more systematic design and evaluation framework, Persuasive Systems Design (PSD) framework [11], was developed by Oinas-Kukkonen and Harjumaa in 2009, and this framework has been used and evaluated by many other studies [3]. Later, Oinas-Kukkonen called PSD-based systems a Behavior Change Support System (BCSS) [12]. Lastly, the concept of motivational affordance was promoted by Zhang, which emphasized that persuasive systems should incorporate the design features and functions that fulfill the needs of user motivation [13]. Karanam et al. later listed types of motivational affordances that are used in a health game [14].

3.6   Design and Evaluation Framework

In Fogg's framework of persuasive technology, Fogg identified the major persuasion principles that are used in persuasive technology, but he did not provide specific guidance on how to implement these principles into the actual design of the system [9]. Fogg addressed this issue in his eight-step design process [10]. The process suggests that designers need to identify the behavior to cause, the audience of the persuasion and what FBM factor prevents the target behavior. Then designers select a technology channel based on the analysis. After initial analysis of the context and selection of the technology channel to be used, the process suggests the design team find relevant persuasive technology examples and imitate effective design patterns of the examples. Then the team should test and iterate the system quickly to improve and comprehend the system. It should be noted that what makes Fogg's approach unique from other methods is that the design process does not directly generate system features and functions based on existing persuasion principles but instead, first identifies the existing design patterns that are already successful in terms of applying the persuasion principles (i.e. design patterns that already have generated persuasion effects, preferably). Fogg says this approach is taken because "there is no need to reinvent the wheel." Therefore, Fogg's approach focuses more on building successful persuasive technology products than on investigating the general cause and effect of developed persuasive systems.

Oinas-Kukkonen and Harjumaa provide more of an "academic" framework for the design and evaluation of persuasive systems in their PSD model. The model suggests that key steps for designing persuasive systems are to identify the intent; analyze use and user and technology context, choose direct or indirect routes to deliver the persuasion message, select appropriate persuasion principles to implement, translate principles into system quality requirements and implement a design based on the requirements [11]. To evaluate the system, designers can use checklists to evaluate if the system quality requirements are fulfilled. Problems with the PSD model were later identified by Harjumaa and Muuraiskangas when they implemented the PSD model in two persuasive systems [2]. First of all, some persuasion principles provided by the PSD model were perceived to be overlapped by the participants of the study, and the list of persuasion principles might be incomplete. Secondly, the model appeared to be too generic as it did not offer thorough guidance to designers on how to perform the design activities suggested by the model.

Oinas-Kukkonen later identified critical questions that need to be answered in future research of Behavior Change Support Systems (BCSS) developed using the PSD model [12]:

- How does one measure (behavior) changes caused by the system?
- How does one conduct experiments to pinpoint a change to a specific software feature?
- Which software features, or combinations of software features, have the greatest impact in different settings?
- Which modes of interaction are more persuasive than others? How does one measure the fit between the modes and persuasion effects so that different modes can be compared?

Lastly, motivational affordances refer to "the properties of an object that determine whether and how it can support one's motivational needs" [13]. This is more of a supplemental concept that can be used to identify the design principles and features that satisfy generic motivational needs of users [13, 14].

4   Persuasive Experience Framework

4.1   Necessity of Persuasive Experience Concept

Discussion of persuasive experience is necessary because the currently available frameworks of persuasive systems do not address the change process occurring to users when being persuaded. When designers determine what intention to realize by persuasive systems, some may propose to change complex behaviors, such as weight-loss management and chronic disease management, while others may propose to change simple and specific behaviors, such as sharing a document and clicking the order button. If the intention is about changing simple behaviors that occur only once, the design and evaluation of persuasive systems may be easy because the effects of the system are easily observable, e.g. measured the frequency of the behavior. However, if the intention is about changing complex behaviors or forming habits, which consist of multiple behaviors performed in different situations over long periods, the previous approach may not be applicable for two reasons. First, multiple design features or functions may work together to cause different behaviors in different situations. This makes it difficult to observe the interaction between specific features or functions and the occurrence of target behavior change. Second, forming a habit or mastering complex behaviors is a process that takes time. Designing a system that intends to change complex behaviors requires a design framework that explains how design features and functions of persuasive systems interact with and change users over time, which is not provided by current frameworks. Therefore, it is important to incorporate behavior change theories such as SDT, TTM and PAPM into the current design framework of persuasive systems as they describe the needs of users at different stages of behavior change and how the nature of users' motivations influences their behavior.

4.2 Persuasive Experience Model

Persuasive experience is an incremental or decremental transition that occurs in between the user-behavior relationship stages. In other words, a persuasive experience occurs when the nature of a user's relationship towards specific behaviors changes. The Persuasive Experience Model (PEM) illustrates the mechanism of persuasive experience using stage-based theory (Fig. 1). The model is developed by integrating SDT, TTM and PAPM.

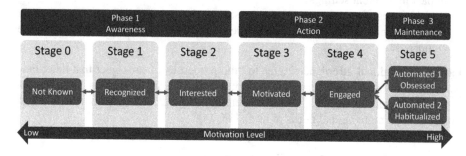

Fig. 1. Persuasive Experience Model

The PEM consists of two components: the user-behavior relationship stages and the persuasive experience phases. The concept of the user-behavior relationship stages posits that there are six stages in one's psychological relationship with the defined behaviors when the behavior change process occurs. They include (S0) not known, (S1) recognized, (S2) interested, (S3) motivated, (S4) engaged, (S5-1) obsessed and (S5-2) habitualized. When user relationship stage moves towards a later stage, the user's level of motivation towards performing a behavior also increases. The persuasive experience phases describe the nature of the persuasive experience occurring. The phases are divided into three parts: awareness, action and maintenance.

The PEM model explains all psychological outcomes that users will gain through interaction with specific design features and functions of persuasive systems. The PEM model divides ultimate behavior change (usually complex behaviors) into multiple simple behaviors that can be achieved at different stages of the user-behavior relationship. Each design feature and/or function is intended to achieve a certain simple behavior or attitude change to move users forward in the behavior change process. Therefore, the PEM model posits that persuasive design features and functions may not necessarily cause the ultimate behavior change directly, but as long as they support incremental stage transitions, the ultimate behavior change will occur eventually. To determine whether particular design features and functions are effective, the designer needs only to know whether they contribute to particular persuasive experience. Persuasive experience can be measured by the frequency of particular behavior or user perception of and attitude towards specific behavior/opinion. Therefore, this approach differs from the traditional approaches that directly connect all design features and functions to the ultimate behavior change(s) and thus are less helpful for explaining which features, functions, or combinations of them caused the occurrence of the ultimate behavior change.

The definitions of the user-behavior relationship stages are described below:

- **Stage 0: Not known.** Target users are unaware of the opportunity to change behaviors. At this stage, designers should focus on strategies to reach and get the attention of the target audience and deliver the information that is relevant to the behavior.
- **Stage 1: Recognized.** Target users recognize the opportunity to change behaviors. They may already know the pros and cons of the proposed behaviors as they may have learned about them via the Internet, social interactions, or other channels unintentionally. At this stage, target users may still remain uninterested in the behavior. The users at this stage will not proactively search for information relevant to the behavior if they do not find anything further interests them (i.e. behaviors are relevant to their personal lives, values and benefits, etc.). Thus, persuasion strategies at this stage should focus on increasing users' interests to either perform the behavior or learn more about the behavior. Of note is that users may recognize the proposed behaviors to be either positive or negative at this stage. If they perceive the behaviors to be strongly negative, they may refuse to perform the behaviors.
- **Stage 2: Interested.** Target users are interested in learning about the opportunity for performing the behavior. If the target users have an opportunity to perform the behavior, and the behavior is simple enough, users may try the proposed behavior once even if they are not strongly motivated. Otherwise, users at this stage may proactively search for relevant information about the behaviors if the interest level is high and there are opportunities to do so. However, interest can fade soon if no effective reinforcement strategies are implemented, and users may experience decremental persuasive experience (i.e. their user-behavior relationship retreats to Stage 1) when they lose interest in performing the behavior.
- **Stage 3: Motivated.** Target users are ready to or getting ready to perform the proposed behaviors. Users at this stage are usually motivated enough to perform the behavior once or for certain periods, but such motivation may decrease rapidly if the difficulty of performing the behaviors increases. Hence, persuasive systems should simplify the behaviors, aid the removal of barriers or improve a user's ability (knowledge and skills) so that the proposed behaviors are performed at least once. Persuasive systems may persuade users to start from some simple behaviors instead of complex behaviors at this stage. For example, if the proposed behavior is to form a habit of running, the system may encourage users to start forming such habit by trying to run for only short amounts of time with moderate intensity in the beginning to help users avoid experiencing muscle pains and feeling uneasy.
- **Stage 4: Engaged.** Target users are willing to integrate the proposed behaviors into their habitual/daily life routine, or at least they are willing to perform the behaviors for a period of time as long as they have a passion for the behaviors. Users are highly motivated at this stage, and they can perform the behaviors even if they face some obstacles to do so. However, users may gradually discontinue performing the behavior if they fail to integrate the new behaviors into their current lifestyles and rely on external sources to maintain their motivation. Possible cases of failure may include situations when users are no longer supported socially, or their lives get busier, and they fail to manage time for running. To increase engagement and move to the next stage, designers should propose persuasion strategies that facilitate the

internalization of users' motivation and promote sustainability of the behaviors at this stage.

- **Stage 5-1: Automated 1-Obsessed.** Target users are obsessed with the proposed behaviors. This type of motivation largely depends on the internal feeling of users. If users find target behaviors enjoyable, they will automatically perform the behaviors even if there are obstacles to doing so. However, the behaviors may not be performed permanently if users perceive the behaviors to cause negative impacts on their lives (i.e. the behaviors are useless, meaningless and/or harmful). Also, if users find the behaviors to be no longer enjoyable, they may stop performing them.
- **Stage 5-2: Automated 2-Habitualized.** Target users have successfully integrated the behaviors into their lifestyles (i.e. formed a habit), so they will no longer need to deliberately maintain their motivation. Users may not stop performing the behaviors easily at this stage. Users may no longer need persuasive systems to facilitate the behavior change anymore. However, persuasive systems can still provide value to users by continuously facilitating the internalization of users' motivation.

The definitions of the persuasive experience phases are described below:

- **Awareness phase** refers to the process of raising awareness among target users. Persuasive experience that occurs within the range of Stages 0 to 2 belongs to the awareness phase. Critical factors that raise awareness of users may include attention, curiosity, emotion and rational judgment of benefits and risks.
- **Action phase** refers to the process of engaging users in the proposed behaviors. Persuasive experience that occurs within the range of Stages 2 to 4 belongs to the action phase. Persuasion strategies used in this phase focus on removal of barriers, simplification of behaviors and improvement in users' knowledge and skills to perform the behaviors. Perceived usefulness, meaningfulness and enjoyment may also play key roles at this phase as they facilitate the internalization of motivation.
- **Maintenance phase** refers to the process of aiding users in sustaining the behaviors. Persuasive experience that occurs within the range of Stages 4 to 5-1 or 5-2 belongs to the action phase. This phase promotes the automation of behavior by either largely enhancing the enjoyment of the behavior or supporting the habit formation. Some behaviors are inherently enjoyable while others may not generate that much fun. However, it is possible that persuasive systems can alter the nature of the behavior by gamifying the behavior.

The PEM model suggests that during the behavior change process, as users' motivation levels increase, users may not only perform the proposed behaviors but also other relevant behaviors that are not specified by designers. For example, users may be motivated to care for their health more when they try to form a habit of running. This increased motivation turns users into proactive entities pursuing better health, and thus, they may also start performing other health-related behaviors such as eating more vegetables and playing tennis.

It should be noted that a persuasive system may not necessarily cause all phases of persuasive experience. Some persuasive systems may be designed to mainly raise awareness instead of engaging users in the behaviors. The decision of which phases to include in a single persuasive system largely depends on the context of the users who use the system and the technology the system is built upon.

4.3   Advantages of PEM over TTM and PAPM

The PEM model visualizes users' psychological relationship with the proposed behaviors during behavior change whereas the TTM and PAPM attempt to visualize stages of the behavior change process without accurately describing the actual psychological status of users.

The TTM model suggests that an individual in the precontemplation stage has no intention of taking action anytime soon, but the model does not specify "why" one has no intention. This issue is addressed later in the PEPM by dividing the precontemplation part into the "Unaware of Issue" stage and the "Unengaged by Issue" stage. There is a major difference between users who already know the benefits and risks of certain behaviors and users who do not recognize the problems, and those users will need different interventions to raise awareness. The PEM model addresses this issue better, because it labels each user differently to accurately and precisely describe their psychological statuses (not known, recognized and interested).

Another issue of the TTM and PAPM is that they do not differentiate users who are performing the behaviors at different levels. In the case of running, some may run once a week with no intention of increasing the frequency after the behavior change process, while other users may run three times a week and are still interested in increasing the frequency and improve their running. The former and latter groups both changed their behaviors, but the TTM and PAPM may either categorize both of them under the same action stage or put the former back to the precontemplation stage as they do not meet the required level of activeness. However, users who have already performed the behaviors are different from those who have never performed the behavior or are unaware of the issue. The PEM addresses this issue by differentiating users who are acting and by identifying whether they are motivated or engaged in the behavior.

The PEM also separates two different psychological statuses of users at the maintenance phase (described as one single stage in the TTM and PAM). Users may maintain the behaviors either because they feel inherently satisfied or enjoy performing the behavior, or because they have successfully made the behaviors their habit. Original models do not specify such differences in the nature of maintenance.

Therefore, stages described in the PEM model clarify the psychological statuses of users themselves during the behavior change process. This approach yields more relevant information about users compared to the approach of just identifying the behavior change processes that users are experiencing. The PEM has the potential to help designers better tailor specific interventions to appropriate user populations.

4.4   Designing and Evaluating Persuasive Systems Using PEM

The design process of persuasive systems using the PEM model differs slightly from Fogg's eight-step design process and the PSD model. Designers may still analyze the context of persuasion by researching users and technology, but they may also identify which persuasion experience(s) should be generated by the system before they directly apply persuasion principles to the context. Designers should then identify the measureable outcomes that characterize the success of each persuasive experience the system aims to generate and match persuasion principles to achieve the identified outcomes. After this process, designers should translate the persuasion principles into design elements (design features and functions). With these three steps, documenting each design element, clarifying persuasion principles an element is implemented upon, and defining what measureable user outcomes a design element should yield, designers can clearly see the effectiveness of each design implementation when they evaluate the system. When evaluating the system, designers may check whether each design element and the persuasion principles match the context of users and the technology the system is built upon, and check if the design elements are effectively yielding the predicted outcomes, as well as measuring if the persuasive experience has occurred while users interact with the system. Possible methods to collect data may include system logs, observations, surveys and interviews.

5 Conclusion

This paper reviewed the current literature on behavior change theories and persuasive systems and described a new framework of persuasive systems. As a result, the Persuasive Experience Model is developed to guide design and evaluation of persuasive systems. Further investigation into the concept of persuasive experience is needed, and the PEM is subject to testing through empirical studies to examine its validity. However, the persuasive experience framework certainly brings a new perspective to the understanding and development of persuasive systems.

References

1. Hamari, J., Koivisto, J., Pakkanen, T.: Do persuasive technologies persuade? - a review of empirical studies. In: Spagnolli, A., Chittaro, L., Gamberini, L. (eds.) PERSUASIVE 2014. LNCS, vol. 8462, pp. 118–136. Springer, Heidelberg (2014)
2. Harjumaa, M., Muuraiskangas, S.: Building the persuasiveness into information systems. In: International Conference on Information Management and Evaluation, Article No. 58. Academic Conferences International Limited (2013)
3. Davis, R., Campbell, R., Hildon, Z., Hobbs, L., Michie, S.: Theories of behaviour and behaviour change across the social and behavioural sciences: a scoping review. Health Psychol. Rev. 9, 323–344 (2015)
4. Glanz, K., Rimer, B.K., Viswanath, K. (eds.): Health Behavior and Health Education: Theory, Research, and Practice. Wiley, San Francisco (2008)
5. Fogg, B.J.: A behavior model for persuasive design. In: 4th International Conference on Persuasive Technology, Persuasive 2009, Article No. 40. ACM (2009)
6. Fogg, B.J.: The behavior grid: 35 ways behavior can change. In: 4th International Conference on Persuasive Technology, Persuasive 2009, Article No. 42. ACM (2009)
7. Ryan, R.M., Deci, E.L.: Intrinsic and extrinsic motivations: classic definitions and new directions. Contemp. Educ. Psychol. 25, 54–67 (2000)

8. Brug, J., Conner, M., Harré, N., Kremers, S., McKellar, S., Whitelaw, S.: The Transtheoretical Model and stages of change: a critique Observations by five Commentators on the paper by Adams, J. and White, M. (2004) Why don't stage-based activity promotion interventions work? Health Educ. Res. **20**, 244–258 (2005)
9. Fogg, B.J.: Persuasive Technology: Using Computers to Change What We Think and Do. Elsevier, San Francisco (2002)
10. Fogg, B.J.: Creating persuasive technologies: an eight-step design process. In: 4th International Conference on Persuasive Technology, Persuasive 2009, Article No. 44. ACM (2009)
11. Oinas-Kukkonen, H., Harjumaa, M.: Persuasive systems design: key issues, process model, and system features. Commun. Assoc. Inf. Syst. **24**, 485–500 (2009)
12. Oinas-Kukkonen, H.: Behavior change support systems: a research model and agenda. In: Ploug, T., Hasle, P., Oinas-Kukkonen, H. (eds.) PERSUASIVE 2010. LNCS, vol. 6137, pp. 4–14. Springer, Heidelberg (2010)
13. Karanam, Y., Filko, L., Kaser, L., Alotaibi, H., Makhsoom, E., Voida, S.: Motivational affordances and personality types in personal informatics. In: 2014 ACM International Joint Conference on Pervasive and Ubiquitous Computing: Adjunct Publication, pp. 79–82. ACM (2014)
14. Zhang, P.: Technical opinion motivation affordances: reasons for ICT design and use. Commun. ACM **51**, 145–147 (2008)

DUXU in Learning and Education

The Use of OUP E-learning System in Teaching English Language in the Preparatory Year at the University of Dammam, Issues and Challenges

Saad S. Alamri[✉]

English Language Department, Preparatory Year Deanship,
University of Dammam, Dammam, Saudi Arabia
salamri@uod.edu.sa

Abstract. E-learning has been around for quite some time. There have been different implementations of e-learning in different learning and teaching contexts ranging from blended learning to fully online delivery. Learning language online has been a new experience to preparatory year students at the University of Dammam. They have been given access to Oxford University Press Online e-learning system that has a complete language course called (QSkills) online where students can fully study online or supplement that with their face to face instructions. However, there have been some issues in this implementation and some pedagogical and technical challenges. This paper highlights these issues and challenges and attempts to propose some practical solutions. The results showed some technical and pedagogical issues and challenges that should be addressed properly by the environment; yet, there was some positive feedback that should be capitalized on to facilitate more the learning process.

Keywords: Elearning · English language teaching · Qskills · Preparatory year · Dammam

1 Introduction

ICT has revolutionize the learning and teaching arena. Not only that but it has expanded the horizons of teaching and learning practices. Educational technologies encompassing e-learning tools have enriched the language learning and teaching. E-learning as identified by Wikipedia to "includes an array of approaches, components, and delivery methods". E-learning has been introduced to the field of language teaching to offer many advantages like abundant teaching resources, ease of access to information, the effect of direct interest, and teaching students according to their aptitudes [1]. The Internet possibly will offer a defining moment in English language teaching methodology [2]. E-learning in English language teaching has started since the first days of the invention of the internet. Then it evolved exponentially to start using all online technologies such as streaming services like YouTube and social media like Twitter and Facebook. E-learning impacted the learning styles as well as the teaching strategies.

© Springer International Publishing Switzerland 2016
A. Marcus (Ed.): DUXU 2016, Part II, LNCS 9747, pp. 147–156, 2016.
DOI: 10.1007/978-3-319-40355-7_14

The preparatory year decided to introduce E-learning part in its intensive English language program as a blended learning initiative to empower its students in their learning process. The English language program in the preparatory year is composed of two semesters where a dedicated course is taught for 20 h a week. General English course is offered in the first semester whereas the English for specific purposes is taught in the second semester for the same duration and contact hours. The preparatory year has around 2000 male and female students in its program. Students are admitted into four tracks: health, engineering, science and arts tracks. They are required to obtain an average grade (C) in order to pass to the second year in their respective colleges. They are also empowered by intensive proficiency language test preparation like IELTS and TOEFL in order to prepare the students for their proficiency tests once decided to attend them.

For the last two years, the preparatory year English language program has been using QSkills Course from Oxford University Press. Such a course is a skill based course where language skills are taught separately. QSkills comes with its E-learning companion to enable students access more exercises and foster some learning autonomy. This E-learning part is offered as a blended learning part. This QSkills E-learning platform is a fully fledged language course structured in a way that enables the student to enroll him/herself in his/her designated class and start the course materials wherever he/she wants. It also offers the teacher fully detailed administrative functions where he/she can track the progress of their students and have a full monitor over their learning process.

2   Literature Highlights

2.1   E-learning and Language Learning

According to [3] "the terms online learning, e-learning, multimedia learning, computer-based learning, Internet-based learning and virtual education can be used when talking about computer-assisted language learning". [4] cited in [3] points out that blended learning offers good potentials to education in general and adult education in particular. Advantages such as saving time and travelling costs, helping students to study according to their own base at their own convenient time. E-learning can be employed by talented and creative teachers to boost teaching and learning conditions [5]. These are used to make learning more interesting, motivating, stimulating and meaningful to the students.

[6] cited in [3] has mentioned some characteristics that blended learning can offer like personalizing learning experience and learning support, encouraging autonomous and cooperative learning as well as increasing student engagement and accommodating variety of learning styles. Not only that but also allowing the students to practice the target language outside the classroom in a less stressful more enjoyable ubiquitous environment.

2.2 E-learning and Language Teacher's Role

In such a new dynamic teaching environment away from the passive approach where students are passive recipient, both teachers' and students' roles have drastically changed. Teachers are obliged to transform their teaching practices in a blended learning context and move from being a knowledge master to a facilitator so students can engage more and take over their learning process. [7] neatly outlines the pedagogical roles and competencies required in a teacher performing in an e-learning environment. They summaries the roles of the teachers to eight main roles. First and most important pedagogical role as the teacher should be aware of instructional designing and development. He should be a content expert, a tutor, an organizer and a facilitator, and a professional practitioner. Then, comes the other roles as social and evaluator, administrator, technologist, counselor, personal and researcher. [8] points out that the role of the teacher today could be an advisor since he is supposed to be an expert in the field in order to support the student's learning progress. Such a role is more resourceful and much more demanding compared to the traditional role. [9] cites in [8] points out that teachers are powerful *"motivational socialisers"*.

Learners' responsibility is a major part in e-learning environments. Their learning roles should shift from being passive recipient to an active participant. [10] emphasize that successful e-learners should often be self-directed, have good organization and study skills, and have a high level of learning autonomy where they feel comfortable working independently.

3 Methodology

This study aims to answer the following research questions and support or refute these hypotheses. The research questions are:

1. What are the technical and pedagogical issues faced preparatory year students when using OUP e-learning platform?
2. What are the technical and pedagogical challenges faced prepare year students when using OUP e-learning platform?
3. To what extent these issues and challenges have hindered the learning process?

We also formulated the following research hypotheses:

1. Students will find it difficult to study online!
2. Students will have time management issues!
3. Computer literacy won't affect students when using OUP e-learning system!

3.1 Instruments

To answer these research questions and test the hypotheses, we devised two research instruments, i.e. semi-structured surveys and interviews.

Survey. To collect required data for this study a semi structured survey was constructed. This survey have 6 objective questions using a Likert scale with three responses: disagree, don't know and agree and bad-to-excellent scale. We decided to use two scales to simplify the process and obtain more accurate results. Two open ended questions were also used to ask about technological and pedagogical issues and challenges regarding OUP system to give the students more freedom to explain and add further to their responses should the researcher miss any related part. The survey was written in simple English and students face no issues in responding in English as well.

Interviews. The interview questions where the same as the survey question however it was a more of students responding to these questions by explaining and elaborating more on their survey responses.

3.2   Participants

The participant of this research are volunteers from all tracks. The purpose of this research was explained to all students via a post on the university E-learning portal Blackboard and they were encouraged to participate in this study by answering a straightforward survey. The response rate was acceptable where 230 responses have been collected. This represents about 15 % from the overall preparatory year intake. Then to further validate the collected responses, a group of 10 students were randomly selected and interviewed.

3.3   Procedure

The survey questions were presented to OUP coordinators at the preparatory year to take their feedback and approved them. Then the survey questions were automated using an online survey system QuestionPro used and approved by the university. After that, the link of the survey was posted on the BlackBoard with a detailed explanation of the study so the students are fully aware of the purpose of this research. The availability of the survey online was timed to one week. The students were invited to voluntarily take part in this study. Then after collecting the responses, a random sample of ten students was selected for the interview process. They were scheduled for interview in their spare time. Their consents were obtained in order to record their responses for analysis purposes.

4   Analysis and Discussion

We used both quantitative and qualitative analyses to analyze the output of this research. The descriptive statistics (mean and percentages) where utilized to explain the survey objective questions and the responses of the open ended questions were analyzed qualitatively. Below are the responses to the research questions followed by data analysis to test the hypotheses. The students reaffirm their responses in the individual interviews. The selected interview participants were asked corresponding questions to address their replies in the survey to clarify and validate their responses. Due to paper space limit, the survey and interviews responses will be analyzed and discussed concisely and precisely together in each section afterwards.

Technical and Pedagogical Issues Related to OUP E-learning System. Students have responded thoroughly to the survey question asking them about the technical and pedagogical issues from their experience when they used OUP e-learning system. From the total number of participants, 125 (about 54 %) did not state that they have neither technical nor pedagogical issues when they used the system. Only 105 Out of 230 (about 46 %) replied to this question in detail. They mentioned various technical and pedagogical issues. Some students mentioned issues like slowness of the system and freezing some of its sections when choosing the certain responses in the assigned exercises. They also mentioned usability issues like some faulty links and buttons. Furthermore, the system might freezes or even shut down accidently which causes the loss of students' responses. Some students complained that some exercises in certain language skills such as listening did not function properly. There was also further complaints about some hardware defects which led to unpleasant user experience. In addition, the system uses activation codes to enroll students, yet some students mentioned that some codes were incorrect therefore they had to wait for some time to get the new code. By the time they got the new code, their classmates have progressed in their course materials which have slightly impacted such students.

Time limit was a noticeable complain where exercises are time limited and thus some slow students have experienced a difficulty submitting their homework on time which led to losing some homework grades. There was a slight complain about weak Wi-Fi connection for those people relying heavily on their mobile and tablets devices to access the system. This caused them temporary disconnection and prevented them from punctually turning in their assignments. There was one complain about the accuracy of the system to record grades where an incident happened with a student after submitting his homework and getting the grades, when he revisited the system the grade was not stored correctly. Some students also mentioned that sometimes the OUP e-learning platform is not accessible due to either internet disconnection or the platform being offline. There was a complain about the accuracy of the marking in certain parts of the system where the system deducts mark for awkward irrelevant reasons like capitalization or spacing. There was also a pedagogical issue related to the difficulty of the exercises especially the listening exercises and a student complained about the confusion caused to him by the online exercise and the classroom course book. Some students complained about the lack of connectivity at home and the shortage of time while they are in the university to do the required exercises. Some frequent technical problems such as unavailability of the system and the corrupted links were repeatedly mentioned. Some students raised the issue of the lack of notification alerts when there is a new assignment added or a deadline to meet. Moreover, some students mentioned that the system is not user friendly and they found it difficult to navigate through the system.

An issue was reported by some students related to the usability of the system where it was hard to follow what tasks already accomplished in the reporting and monitoring section so called the "planner". Furthermore, some students mentioned the complexity of the process needed to access the required exercises where students have to go through many steps to reach their target. There was a common complaint about the sound tracks that are frequently not functioning which in turn impacted the base of the students' progress. Some students mentioned that the lack of monitoring the students' performance allowed some cheating cases where students share their answers with each other. Based on these responses, we can notice that there are serious technical and pedagogical issues. Technical issues such as system unavailability, inaccurate links, navigation complexity, user's interfaces design, invalid access codes, and freezing and hanging system, lack of notification functionality as well as the slowness of the system raise a question about the technical capabilities of the platform. This go further to impact the student's experience which inhibits the learning from occurring or could adversely demotivate the students. The system also has a technical bug which is saving students responses so when they hit the back button they can view their previous response. In such a case, when the students browse back on the screen, his responses disappear.

In addition to the technical issues, there were important pedagogical issues stated throughout the responses. For example, the shortage of time designated for the e-learning exercises, the inaccuracy in recording the obtained grades, and the mismatch between the hard book and its soft electronic counterparts are counterproductive. These issues might hinder the learning process and cause a mistrust in the system and its capabilities which will impact the learning outcome. It will also reflect inaccurate performance about the students if their grades are misreported or stored. Not only is that but the cheating issue is something that requires attention so it will not impact the learning environment.

Technical and Pedagogical Challenges Related to OUP E-learning System. The second question in the survey tackled the technical and pedagogical challenges faced by students when using OUP e-learning system. They responses varied from no response to positive responses about the system where the students' experience were good. However, some serious challenges were reported by 60 students (26 %) of the participants. There was a challenge of time management when doing exercises online. Some students reported that it was challenging doing the exercises because of time constrains challenge though they know the responses. This could demotivate the students and hinder the learning process. It might also impact their engagement in the learning activities since they already experienced such unpleasant practice. Some students mentioned the difficulty level of the exercises where some exercises do not consider the students competency level though the students are placed in the system based on their proficiency level. This might be slightly individual and subjective opinion because we could not validate such a complaint through the interview process. There was a technical challenge which was faced by some students related to the quality of sound recorded tracks related to some reading and listening exercises. Students complained that the sound was low and this impacted their listening comprehension. Furthermore, the slow internet connection made some students bored of continue using the system and became frustrated about this experience. There was a technical challenge that was raised by one students which is related to the absence of on-screen timer where the remaining time is displayed. Most students were complaining about finding time for e-learning activities where they have a very intensive language program comprising different disciplines courses. Some students expressed a challenge of using the system on their tablets and smart phones and requested the company to have a mobile application to ease the accessibility of the system. There were some challenges related to the way the system works with marking writing exercise since it pays more attention on the accuracy rather than the competency such as capitalization and indentation not coherence and argument as such.

These findings yield an answer to the third question about the level of the impact created by these technical and pedagogical issues. They also show that there are some issues and challenges that have impacted the learning process since these issues were encountered by (26 %) of the participants. Furthermore, technical issues such as system unavailability and inaccuracy of grade keeping could seriously impact the learners and discourage them from learning online. Additionally, the pedagogical issues like unmatched difficulty with corresponding materials in class would hinder the learning from occurring and might confuse the students and consequently affect their performance.

To test the first hypothesis, we formulated the following four questions. The students' experience about the OUP e-learning system was addressed by asking them about the difficulty of the system. Their responses were as follows (Table 1):

Table 1. Responses to question 1

I find Oxford Learning System difficult to use	Responses
Agree	17.45 %
Don't know	16.04 %
Disagree	66.51 %

The results above show that the majority of the students (66.5 %) and a mean of (2.5) perceive the system as an easy usable system. However, the remaining (33.5 %) should not be ignored. This validates their responses to the issues they mentioned earlier and should be addressed by the English language department and preparatory year management in coordination with OUP to address the issues causing such a negative perception. The overall results of this question refuted the first hypothesis. This question was validated by a further question about the impression of studying online in general to distinguish that students' responses was not affected by the OUP system. The responses were as follows (Table 2):

Table 2. Responses to question 2

Studying online is difficult!	Responses
Disagree	63.38 %
I don't know	17.84 %
Agree	18.78 %

These responses (63.4 %) with a mean of (1.6) reaffirms the previous responses that the students experience was positive in general whether studying online in general or using a particular system like OUP platform. Student's impression about the system in general was also captured in the second question through asking them how they feel about the system. The responses were (Table 3):

Table 3. Responses to question 3

Oxford Learning System is:	Responses
Excellent	21.03 %
Very good	24.30 %
Good	46.73 %
Poor	4.67 %
Bad	3.27 %

Summing up the good to the excellent responses will give a total of nearly (92 %) and a mean of (2.45) perceiving the system positively. This is a good feedback which entails that the issues and challenges mentioned can be overcome (Table 4).

Table 4. Responses to question 4

Disagree	54.46 %
I don't know	29.11 %
Agree	16.43 %

About (54.5 %) with a mean of (1.6) disagreed about the difficulty of blended learning mode. They mentioned in the interviews that this mode is more useful and it reinforces what they study in the classroom. This is encouraging and should be utilized by the preparatory year management to promote learning autonomy and encourage learners' engagement.

To test the second hypothesis, there following question related to the students' ability to manage their time efficiently online to explore if that affects their perception and experience when using the OUP system. The responses were (Table 5):

Table 5. Responses to question 5

I can't study online because I can't manage my time efficiently!	Responses
Disagree	46.23 %
I don't know	18.40 %
Agree	35.38 %

About (55 %) with a mean of (1.9) has no issue with managing in general their time efficiently online. This could explain the reason about time constrain in OUP exercises and why some students failed to deliver their homework in the due dates. This also refutes the second hypothesis. The difficulty of studying in a blended learning mode is quite important and this was tackled by the following question.

To eliminate the technology illiteracy impact and test the third hypothesis, we asked a question about whether the student knowledge of technology did affect their online study experience. The responses are discussed below (Table 6):

Table 6. Responses to question 6

I can't study online because I don't know how to use technology!	Responses
Disagree	92.06 %
I don't know	4.67 %
Agree	3.27 %

It is quite obvious that the students (92 %) with a mean of (1.1) are computer literate and familiarity with technology did not interfere with their online learning experience. This additionally confirm and validates their responses about the technical issues they faced during their online learning experience and shows the importance of addressing these issues to facilitate more the learning process. This positively supports the third hypothesis and shows that there is no effect of computer literacy on students experience when studying online.

5 Conclusion

This research highlighted the technical and pedagogical issues and challenges face by the students in the English language program students at the preparatory year at the University of Dammam. The study used a semi-structured survey and interview to collect data required to answer the study questions. The total participants was 230 in the survey and 10 in the interview. The results revealed some important technical and pedagogical issues and challenges that should be carefully addressed by the preparatory year team in order to facilitate the learning process and keep students engaged. However, the overall users' experience and willingness to use elearning technologies and study in a blended learning environment was positive and encouraging and the preparatory year management should capitalize on that. It is also recommended to assess the efficacy of the elearning environment including all of its components before and after the students commencing their study to measure accurately the interference of elearning in the learning process. We also encourage the preparatory year management to pilot any future solution before introducing that to the environment and prepare professionally the students and faculty by raising their awareness and offering them proper practical training sessions.

References

1. Cai, H.: E-learning and English teaching. In: Proceedings of International Conference on Future Computer Supported Education, vol. 2, pp. 841–846 (2012). Elsevier, IERI Procedia
2. Yang, S., Chen, Y.: Technology-enhanced language learning: a case study. Comput. Hum. Behav. **23**, 860–879 (2007). Elsevier
3. Linna, M., Valo, A.: The use of HILL online e-learning environment in language teaching. In: MIPRO, Opatija, Croatia (2015)
4. Meisalo, V., Sutinen, E., Tarhio, J.: Modernit oppimisymparistot. In: Juva, pp. 154–156
5. Chhbra, P.: Use of e-learning tools in teaching English. In: Proceedings of I-Society, pp. 2229–6166. GKU, Talwandi Sabo Bathinda, Punjab (2012). International Journal of Computing & Business Research
6. Marsh, D.: Blended Learning: Creating Learning Opportunities for Language Learners, pp. 3–6. Cambridge University Press, New York (2012)
7. Carril, P., Sanmamed, M., Sellés, N.: Pedagogical roles and competencies of university teachers practicing in the e-learning environment. Int. Rev. Res. Open Distance Learn. **14**(3), 462–487 (2013). Athabasca University
8. Mullamaa, K.: ICT in language learning - benefits and methodological implications. Int. Educ. Stud. **3**(1), 38–44 (2010). CCENET, Canada
9. Dörnyei, Z.: Teaching and Researching Motivation. Pearson Education Limited, Harlow (2001). Malaysia, LSP
10. Coryell, J., Chlup, D.: Implementing e-learning components with adult English language learners: vital factors and lessons learned. Comput. Assist. Lang. Learn. **20**(3), 263–278 (2007). Routledge

Human-Centered Design with Autistic University Students: Interface, Interaction and Information Preferences

Marc Fabri[1][(✉)] and Penny C.S. Andrews[2]

[1] Leeds Beckett University, Leeds, UK
m.fabri@leedsbeckett.ac.uk
[2] University of Sheffield, Sheffield, UK
pcsandrews1@sheffield.ac.uk

Abstract. This paper reports on a study aimed at creating an online support toolkit for young autistic people to navigate the transition from school to university, thereby empowering this group in developing their full potential. It is part of the Autism&Uni project, a European-funded initiative to widen access to Higher Education for students on the autism spectrum. Our particular focus is on the Human-Computer Interaction elements of the toolkit, namely the visual design of the interface, the nature of interactions and navigation, and the information architecture. Past research in this area tended to focus on autistic children, often with learning difficulties, and their preferences in terms of interface and interaction design. Our research revealed that the preferences of young autistic adults who are academically competent and articulate, differ considerably from those of autistic children. Key findings are that text is preferred over visual material; visual design should be minimal; content ought to be organized in a logical and hierarchical manner; the tone of language ought to be genuine yet not too negative or patronizing; and images or video are only useful if they illustrate places or people, in other words information that cannot easily be conveyed in other ways.

Keywords: Interface design · Information architecture · Participatory design · Design Thinking · Autism · Asperger syndrome

1 Introduction

Autism is a pervasive development disorder that presents difficulties in the social use of communication and unusual patterns of behavior, due to e.g. interests of unusual intensity or focus, or unusual reactions to sensory input. Young people on the autism spectrum, like any other young people, want to grow up and lead full and independent lives. But whilst autism on its own is not an indicator of academic ability, many young people on the autism spectrum find it difficult to enter university. And those who do start a degree course are prone to dropping out early.

Autism&Uni is an EU-funded project with partners in the United Kingdom, Finland, Poland, Netherlands and Poland. The project aim is to support greater numbers of young

© Springer International Publishing Switzerland 2016
A. Marcus (Ed.): DUXU 2016, Part II, LNCS 9747, pp. 157–166, 2016.
DOI: 10.1007/978-3-319-40355-7_15

adults on the autism spectrum to gain access to Higher Education (HE) and to navigate the transition successfully.

2   Initial Research

We conducted a multi-national survey across 5 European countries to investigate current provisions, aspirations and means by which autistic students are supported on their journey into Higher Education (cf. Fabri et al. 2016). Participants included students, parents, teachers, tutors, disability advisors and autism support professionals. The purpose of this initial research was to gain a deeper understanding of the challenges students face so that any new support tools would help students overcome the most pertinent of these challenges.

Students and graduates were asked whether or not they had been diagnosed with autism and who had made the initial diagnosis, alongside the challenges they face(d) and support they may have received, but were not expected to describe the 'severity' of their disability. 'Functioning labels', describing autistic people as 'high-functioning' or 'low-functioning', can be misleading and even offensive to autistic adults and their families (Kenny et al. 2015; Feminist Aspie 2015). However, all students in this study were either realistically considering higher education or had some experience of higher education study, and therefore did not have a co-morbid intellectual impairment.

The research, based on 280 survey responses and 16 student case studies that looked in detail into individual experiences, revealed a number of key challenges faced by young autistic people, with five themes emerging:

(1) The social and physical environment
  - difficulty picking up unwritten social rules when interacting with tutors and fellow students
  - difficulty tolerating background noise, lighting, crowding or other sensory aspects of the university environment
  - handling the social isolation that often comes with living in a new environment
(2) Lack of appropriate support
  - lack of access to appropriate support right from the start
  - a focus on the 'deficits' of autism, rather than the strengths students can bring
  - lack of consistency in reasonable adjustments, autism-specific services and personal support
(3) Unrealistic expectations
  - what university study is really like
  - content of study subject or course
  - performing at the same high standard as in secondary education
  - fellow students' interests and dedication
(4) Challenges concerning assessment (even when mastering the subject matter)
  - difficulty interpreting ambiguous and open assignment briefs correctly
  - lack of understanding why something needs to be done
  - difficulty planning studies and revision
  - uncertainty how much time to spend on a given task

(5) Transitioning to adult life requiring more effort than it would for the average student
- moving away from home for the first time
- time management and establishing routines
- an unfamiliarity with advocating effectively for oneself

Arguably these are challenges for any new student. But while most can adapt reasonably quickly and draw from the support of their friends, for autistic students these challenges can rapidly lead to anxiety, further isolation, depression and eventually drop out from university (Liew et al. 2014).

3   Early Design Considerations

A key aim of the Autism&Uni Online Tool was to support autistic students in navigating the transition to university. To provide some pointers towards the information and design preferences of the toolkit's target group – students on the autism spectrum – the survey included a question regarding the websites they liked, and what they liked about them. 26 out of 77 eligible participants responded to this question. The most popular sites were wikis (6 times) and the Google family of sites such as website search, image search and YouTube (6 times). Other sites tended to appeal to people's special interests e.g. web comics, chemistry, food, sports or the British Dr Who television series.

The comments made about preferred sites had a strong bias towards simple and logical design, clear and easy navigation, organization of content in threads, lists or groups, the absence of non-functional sound or animation, and the ability to personalize the experience. This is somewhat in line with Grynszpan et al. (2008) who found that simple interfaces are preferred by autistic learners. Complex interfaces that stimulated other users were found to be confusing and abstract, and they can have a negative impact on task performance and choice-making. Similarly, Biju et al. (2013) argued that interfaces ought to be clean and unambiguous, without too many choices. Further, the link between interface elements and modalities, and the task at hand, must be made explicit (Grynszpan et al. 2008).

4   Design Methodology

In creating the online toolkit for students on the autism spectrum, we followed a human-centered Design Thinking approach. Design Thinking uses co-research, co-design and intuitive problem-solving techniques to match people's needs with what is technologically feasible and logistically viable (Brown 2008). The methodology is based on the premise that by combining empathy, creativity and analytical processes, true innovation can emerge.

This was considered a suitable approach because there are multiple variables involved, notably a large number of highly individual personal accounts of students who have told us what worked for them, and what stopped them from fulfilling their full potential in higher education.

A number of frameworks are available to help with the execution of a Design Thinking approach, including IDEO's Field Guide (DesignKit 2015) and Stanford University's d.school resources (d.school 2013). For this study, we chose the established five step d.school model with the steps: Empathize, Define, Ideate, Prototype and Test.

5   Procedure

What follows is a brief description of each step of d.school's model, how it was applied in this study and a summary of findings:

1. **Empathize:** To gain a deep understanding of end users' needs and how their lives are affected, we conducted the surveys and interviews outlined above. The focus was on collecting stories about real events – problem cases and success stories, rather than speculate on what may be possible.
2. **Define:** The aim during this step to identify what is needed, in which context, and why. We looked for patterns in responses and, amongst others, identified the following recurring core themes:
   - An awareness of one's autism condition but reluctance to talk about it
   - High levels of anxiety due to support not being in place when needed
   - Some coping strategies worked really well for interviewed students
   - Uncertainty about how to behave in certain university situations
   - Managing one's expectations of what university is "really like".

   What stood out during consultations was the need for reliable information that went beyond universities' marketing material and which could be accessed by students in their own time, at their own pace. There was also little mention of a need for academic support – students generally felt on top of their subjects and worried more about the non-academic aspects of student life.
3. **Ideate:** Considerable time was spent on generating ideas about how to meet end users' needs. In a brainstorming session that included academics, designers, developers, psychologists, support service staff and people on the autism spectrum, all stakeholders proposed toolkit content themes. Through a gradual selection process, the most promising content ideas were shortlisted and content was developed further. Eventually, the following were agreed on as being the most pertinent topics to take back to the end users for feedback and co-design activities:
   - Choosing the right subject and university
   - Managing expectations about study and social life at university
   - Typical study situations
   - Managing difficult social interactions
   - How to talk about one's autism – the strengths and the difficulties
   - How to get support in place early
   - Finding your way around campus
4. **Prototype and Test:** A number of toolkit prototypes were created to obtain feedback from end users on their design preferences and to carry out co-design activities during three workshops. The first workshop (held in the UK) focused on content and information hierarchy, the second (UK) and third (Finland) workshop focused on visual

design and toolkit navigation. The remainder of the paper describes these workshops and discusses the findings.

6   Workshops

Several researchers have considered how best to design creative workshops and design activities with participants on the autism spectrum. Benton et al. (2014) provide a framework for working with neuro-diverse people, considering the preparation of the physical environment and the planning of activities. They also put a strong emphasis on tailoring activities to the individual. Benton et al. (2012) report that younger autistic people tend to have a strong preference for, and well-developed skills in, visual thinking. Braz et al. (2014) examine the use of paper prototyping of interactive systems, which can pose challenges due to the un-finished nature of the prototype material itself, and the "what-if" nature of questions surrounding the prototype. Martin (2015) points out that activities ought to be presented as optional open invitations, thereby reducing demand pressure on participants. The language with which participants are addressed can also play an important role, e.g. considering them "experts" who are there to advise is preferable to "participants" who have come to test a new idea the researchers had. This body of research was considered in the design and execution of both workshops.

For the first co-design workshop, content was carefully prepared based on the list of topics resulting from the Ideate stage. This consisted of background text, practical activities, prompts for reflection, image and video material. The toolkit consisted of loosely related toolkit items, each covering a different topic. Videos were commissioned to cover disclosing disability, myths and facts about university and an introduction to the library of the university campus where the workshop took place.

For the second workshop a visual design 'skin' was applied to the toolkit, informed by the initial design considerations and navigation preferences expressed by survey respondents.

A guiding principle for creating these artefacts was Wass and Porayska-Pomsta (2013) suggestion that the focus of future interventions for autistic learners should not be on teaching new skills (social, communication, emotional) but instead on how to apply these skills in real and complex situations. This is supported by studies of observational learning and its challenges for learners with autism (Plavnick and Hume 2014), and by the assertion that activities should be specialized and situated in real practice, not general role play (Gulikers et al. 2008).

3 participants took place in the first workshop, 5 in the second and another 4 in the third. Most were students who had either enrolled on a course but not yet started, were already studying or had recently graduated. The one exception was a person at the final workshop who was the mother of a young autistic female in the process of enroling into university (without her daughter being present at the workshop). During all three workshops, participants went through a series of planned activities which were designed to provide feedback on toolkit content, information hierarchy of toolkit items, image material, video content, navigation and visual design. Feedback was recorded partly through

the activities (post-it notes, drawn wireframes, paper prototyping) and by recording and taking notes of responses and discussions.

7   Results

An analysis of the activities and feedback obtained revealed recurring preferences by this group of autistic people, specifically relating to interface design, interaction design and the nature of the information presented. Below are key findings from all three workshops:

7.1   Interface Design Related

The general conception that autistic people think visually was clearly challenged. Participants preferred well-structured text information to illustrations, infographics or videos. They did not wish to have visual elements added just to improve the look of the website, but approved of visual content when it provided information that text alone could not achieve, e.g. in connection with directions to a building on the campus, or the photograph of a real person they were likely to meet. However, a comic strip featuring quotes from survey responses by autistic students was received positively (see also observations below regarding using quotes).

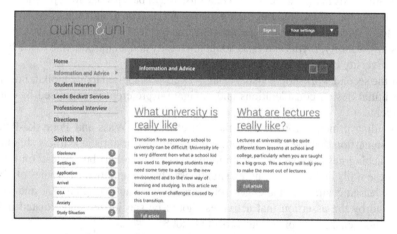

Fig. 1.   Toolkit interface

The graphic design skin was well received, and comments revolved around how it was basic, muted and did not distract from the content. There were individual preferences regarding colours, fonts and the style in which the text was displayed (Fig. 1).

7.2 Interaction Related

Participants liked a flat navigation structure and ways to group and order content according to their needs. Animations and transitions were not rejected outright, but they needed to add a clear benefit to the interaction they supported (e.g. additional information sliding in when hovering over an image).

A simple interactive feature that appealed to all participants was the option of viewing longer text either as a single page or divided into smaller sections, with quick links at the top of the toolkit item (Fig. 2).

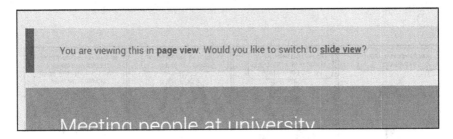

Fig. 2. Ability to switch between page view and slide view

An important message was that the students did not wish to have certain choices made for them, as their preference might depend on content and context (we had the option of pre-setting this choice based on a user's previous behavior, but decided against it following the feedback).

7.3 Information and Language Related

Participants told us that they tend to think logically, and that information needs to be presented in a clear and objective fashion for it to be both informative and believable. They liked the idea of having easy access to large amounts of information – and accessible ways to get at that information and process it at their own speed. The concept of introductory 'tasters' or 'teasers', which we presented in the form of videos, was less popular.

Having large amounts of information at one's disposal creates challenges, e.g. how to guide the user through the wider narrative and information architecture. During the workshops, various suggestions were made about topics that should be added, but at the same time there was a sense of concern about keeping the toolkit navigable. This was expressed in the UK workshop as a wish to have related toolkit items linked or grouped, making connections more visible, and in the Finnish workshop as a request for a toolkit-wide search mechanism, as well as the option of customizing the toolkit to only show selected items on the basis of the student's location and the current stage of their study career.

Participants challenged wording that made assumptions that they would find things difficult, preferring a more neutral tone that provided information without judgement.

Negative depictions of autism and 'doom-and-gloom' scenarios were generally not well-liked. Rather than raising awareness and willingness to find out more, they increased anxiousness and discouraged engagement with the toolkit material. The same applies to generalizations about autism – participants were keen to see the individual nature of their experiences acknowledged and liked to hear about other autistic students' accounts, and about variations of such accounts.

Quotes and case studies must be genuine – authenticity is paramount, not just in the writing but also regarding the use of photographs of students, study situations and places. Any typographic errors, repeated content or inappropriate language was immediately picked up and we were told that this would severely distract from the rest of the toolkit (Fig. 3).

Fig. 3. Comic strip showing genuine quotes from the survey

Participants liked prompts that encouraged reflection or taking action, e.g. how to get support, where to ask, who to ask and how. Anything that promoted self-advocacy was considered positive. However, some called for more concrete advice on how to proceed in solving a problem, rather than the general thoughts and questions to ponder that were offered in some of the toolkit items. Such proposed action needs to be specific, practical and pragmatic – e.g. *"try to buddy up with another student"* is clearly too vague.

8   Discussion

The feedback received from workshop participants was relatively consistent, despite students being located in two countries (UK and Finland) and coming from a range of academic disciplines. There are strong indications that a considerable proportion of autistic students share similar preferences with regard to certain design features, particularly a clean and minimal overall look, architecture that allows easy navigation of large amounts of data, and the opportunity to adjust the amount of information displayed on the screen. Further, the uniformity of the feedback suggests that participants were able to express their views effectively in the workshops, and were thus contributing to the design process in a meaningful way.

However, there are validity concerns considering the limited number of participants. It is not clear how representative these were of the autism community in general, and where contradictory preferences were expressed, it is difficult to determine which ones are the most likely to serve the needs of other autistic people. The use of a control group in future co-design activities could be a useful way to determine whether autistic participants are actually taking the design process in a direction where it might not otherwise go.

One of the most ubiquitous oversimplifications concerning autistic people is that they are predominantly 'visual thinkers', combined with the assumption that they are likely to prefer images rather than text to convey information. The results of our study suggest the opposite is true for autistic people who are academically capable and of average of higher intelligence. While many may share perceptual strengths such as visual reasoning, they consistently preferred text with a minimum of visual distractions. This has clear implications on future work, especially in the area of interface design and user experience design for people on the autism spectrum.

Acknowledgements. We would like to thank the survey and workshop participants for dedicating their time and sharing their experiences. The research leading up to this paper has been made possible thanks to the AUTHEW (Autism&Uni) project, part of the Erasmus Lifelong Learning Programme.

The Autism&Uni project has been funded with support from the European Commission. This publication reflects the views only of the authors, and the Commission cannot be held responsible for any use, which may be made of the information contained therein.

Lifelong
Learning
Programme

References

Benton, L., Johnson, H., Ashwin, E., Brosnan, M., Grawemeyer, B.: Developing IDEAS: supporting children with autism within a participatory design team, p. 2599. ACM Press, New York (2012). doi:10.1145/2207676.2208650

Benton, L., Vasalou, A., Khaled, R., Johnson, H., Gooch, D.: Diversity for design: a framework for involving neurodiverse children in the technology design process, pp. 3747–3756. ACM Press, New York (2014)

Biju, S.M., Todd, C., Tchantchane, L., Yakoob, B.: E-Learning software for students with autism. In: Sobh, T., Elleithy, K. (eds.) Emerging Trends in Computing, Informatics, Systems Sciences, and Engineering, vol. 151, pp. 403–410. Springer, New York (2013)

Braz, P., Felipe David, V., Raposo, A., Barbosa, S.D.J., de Souza, C.S.: An alternative design perspective for technology supporting youngsters with autism. In: Schmorrow, D.D., Fidopiastis, C.M. (eds.) AC 2014. LNCS, vol. 8534, pp. 279–287. Springer, Heidelberg (2014)

Brown, T.: Design Thinking, in Harvard Business Review, June edition, pp. 84–95 (2008)

DesignKit: The Field Guide to Human-Centered Design. IDEO Publishing (2015). ISBN: 978-0-9914063-1-9

d.school: Design Thinking Bootcamp Bootleg (2013). http://dschool.stanford.edu/wp-content/uploads/2013/10/METHODCARDS-v3-slim.pdf

Fabri, M., Andrews, P.C.S.: Hurdles and drivers affecting autistic students' higher education experience: lessons learnt from the multinational Autism&Uni research study. In: Presented at 10th Annual International Teaching, Education and Development Conference (INTED), 7–9 March 2016, Valencia, Spain (2016)

Feminist Aspie (2015). https://feministaspie.wordpress.com/2015/03/13/functioning-labels-101-whats-the-big-deal/

Grynszpan, O., Martin, J.-C., Nadel, J.: Multimedia interfaces for users with high functioning autism: an empirical investigation. Int. J. Hum.-Comput. Stud. **66**, 628–639 (2008)

Gulikers, J., Kester, L., Kirschner, P., Bastiaens, T.: The effect of practical experience on perceptions of assessment authenticity, study approach, and learning outcomes. Learn. Instr. **18**(2), 172–186 (2008)

Kenny, L., Hattersley, C., Molins, B., Buckley, C., Povey, C., Pellicano, E.: Which terms should be used to describe autism? Perspectives from the UK autism community. Autism (2015). doi:10.1177/1362361315588200

Liew, S.M., Thevaraja, N., Hong, R.Y., Magiati, I.: The relationship between autistic traits and social anxiety, worry, obsessive–compulsive, and depressive symptoms: specific and non-specific mediators in a student sample. J. Autism Dev. Disord. (2014). doi:10.1007/s10803-014-2238-z

Martin, J.A.: Research with adults with Asperger's syndrome–participatory or emancipatory research? Qual. Soc. Work **14**, 209–223 (2015). doi:10.1177/1473325014535964

Plavnick, J., Hume, K.: Observational learning by individuals with autism: a review of teaching strategies. Autism **18**, 458–466 (2014). doi:10.1177/1362361312474373

Wass, S.V., Porayska-Pomsta, K.: The uses of cognitive training technologies in the treatment of autism spectrum disorders. Autism (2013). doi:10.1177/1362361313499827

Information and Universal Design
in Online Courses

Luciane Maria Fadel[1], Viviane H. Kuntz[1(✉)], Vania R. Ulbricht[1],
and Claudia R. Batista[2]

[1] Post Graduate Program in Knowledge, Engineering and Management, Federal
University of Santa Catarina (UFSC), Florianópolis, Santa Catarina, Brazil
liefadel@gmail.com, vkuntz@gmail.com,
vrulbricht@gmail.com
[2] Expressão Gráfica Department, Federal University of Santa Catarina (UFSC),
Florianópolis, Santa Catarina, Brazil
claudiabatista@gmail.com

Abstract. This paper aims to identify how the interface design of a Massive Open
Online Course can incorporate the seven Principles of Universal Design. In order
to do that, this paper begins with a literature review on Universal Design and
interface design. This review is followed by a review on the WCAG 2.0 and a
verification instrument is designed. The verification is then performed on a
Coursera Course and aims to identify how the seven Principles of Universal Design
are applied in this environment. The results suggest that the Coursera platform is a
good example of Universal Design because the guidelines were followed. Therefore, Universal Design is a challenge that is possible to be implemented.

Keywords: Universal Design · Online course · Information design

1 Introduction

According to the UN there are 7.2 billion people in the world and 10 % of this
population has at least one disability. In addition, the World Health Organization
(WHO) addressed that this percentage tends to increase due to population growth and
the advances in medicine that prolong the aging process. Furthermore, the report of the
United Nations Regional Information Center [1], points out that in countries where life
expectancy is over 70 years, each individual will live with a disability for eight years on
average. This is 11.5 % of his/her lifetime. These data emphasize the importance and
magnitude of a greater dissemination of Universal Design (UD) [2].

Universal Design allows the products and environments to be used without the need
for adaptation or specialized design. Therefore, Universal Design should be considered
an efficient approach for distance learning environments because the users come from a
wide variety of social backgrounds and there are increasing numbers of students with
disabilities pursuing education [3]. Meyer and Rose [4], for example, addressed
questions about understanding learner differences and how technology can augment
and streamline a teacher's ability to give students timely, personalized, balanced and
varied attention. In addition, a broad range of users requires a high quality interface [5].

© Springer International Publishing Switzerland 2016
A. Marcus (Ed.): DUXU 2016, Part II, LNCS 9747, pp. 167–177, 2016.
DOI: 10.1007/978-3-319-40355-7_16

Thus, this paper aims to identify how the interface design of a Massive Open Online Course can incorporate Universal Design.

This paper begins with a literature review on Universal Design and interface design. This review is followed by a review on the WCAG 2.0 guidelines and the design of the UD verification instrument. This instrument is then used to identify how the Principles of Universal Design[1] could be applied in the design of this environment. Finally, this paper discusses how Universal Design can assist users with disabilities using a distance learning environment. This paper highlights the importance of research about Inclusive Design and Universal Design, especially in the context of information design because it is a duty and an act of social justice to make information accessible to all people. In addition, it is an attitude of respect to others considering the differences between users in terms of their capabilities.

2   Universal Design and Accessibility

Toward the design of an instrument to verify the Universal Design in an interface this paper begins by establishing the relationship between Universal Design and accessibility. According to the definition of Mace [6] the intent of Universal Design is to generate environments, products, services, programs, and technologies available to meet the greatest number of people, to the largest extent possible, without the need for adaptation or specialized design.

On the other hand the Brazilian Federal Decree no. 5,296/2004 (1), in its Article 8, I, establishes a definition for accessibility as being "… condition for use, with security and autonomy, total or assisted, of spaces, furniture and equipment urban, of buildings, in transport services and device, systems and communication media and information, for a disabled person or person with reduced mobility".

Based in these definitions this paper assumes that the Universal Design encompasses accessibility since this focuses on designing for people with some kind of disabilities while UD focuses on designing for a greater number of people (including people with disabilities). The seven Principles of Universal Design are as follows [6]:

1. **Equitable Use:** The design is useful and marketable to people with diverse abilities;
2. **Flexibility in Use:** The design accommodates a wide range of individual preferences and abilities;
3. **Simple and Intuitive Use:** Use of the design is easy to understand, regardless of the user's experience, knowledge, language skills, or current concentration level;
4. **Perceptible Information:** The design communicates necessary information effectively to the user, regardless of ambient conditions or the user's sensory abilities;
5. **Tolerance for Error:** The design minimizes hazards and the adverse consequences of accidental or unintended actions;

---

[1] The Principles of Universal Design were conceived and developed by The Center for Universal Design at North Carolina State University. Use or application of the Principles in any form by an individual or organization is separate and distinct from the Principles and does not constitute or imply acceptance or endorsement by The Center for Universal Design of the use or application.

6. **Low Physical Effort:** The design can be used efficiently and comfortably with minimum fatigue;
7. **Size and Space for Approach and Use:** Appropriate size and space is provided for approach, reach, manipulation, and use regardless of user's body size, posture, or mobility.

Focusing on learning, the so called Universal Design for Learning (UDL) is a new way of thinking about education that has the potential of curricular reform and makes learning experiences more meaningful and accessible to all students. The recommendations and current specifications available that involve online learning are the W3C Web Accessibility Initiative (WAI), the IMS and DublinCore [7].

3 Information and Interface Design of UDL

The significance of the interface design of learning environments has been documented in several studies, which seek to establish how the design can support learning [8] contribute to user satisfaction [9] or develop design methods [10]. Similarly, there are many research that stress qualities of Information Design (ID) and learning materials, such as the design principles addressed by Pettersson [11]: Functional Principles, Administrative Principles, Aesthetic Principles, and Cognitive Principles. These principles might add depth to the Principles of Universal Design because they seek for clarity of communication. For example, Simple and Intuitive Use – UD might benefit from Providing Clarity and Simplicity principles (Functional Principles – ID) and Harmony principle (Aesthetic Principles – ID; or Low Physical Effort – UD might benefit from Facilitating Attention, Perception, Mental Processing and Memory principles (Cognitive Principles – ID).

In addition, the effects of implementing universal design in systems that are dedicated to education are object of many studies [3, 12]. For Gregga, Chenga and Toddb [3] the Principles of Universal Design are one of the key factors for the success of the BreakThru (platform of teaching at a distance from the University of Georgia) in addition to the virtual access, tools for social contact, e-mentoring, encourage persistence, resources for reasoning based on cases. In BreakThru, the UD was related to the shortcomings of literacy and for each deficiency detected it was chosen to apply the principles that could help to overcome this deficiency.

For Rose and Meyer [13] there are three principles of a universal design that can be applied to educational technologies (UDL). These principles are based on the idea of flexibility in relation to the means of representation, forms of expression and engagement and are summarized below.

1. Multiple means of representation - to present the content using different modes of representation enables the students to choose the mode that most favors them. In addition, the more senses are stimulated better the assimilation of content.
2. Multiple forms of engagement strategy - it is well known that students learn better if they are actively engaged in an activity [14]. Then the system needs to offer key concepts and provide guidance to students to think independently.

3. Multiple means of expression - the system must offer different ways for students to express themselves, whether through multimedia projects, texts, or different forms of assessment.

Similarly, Rose, Hernándeza and Hilera [15] listed the main accessibility standards for the preparation of courses in virtual learning environments. These standards were established by agencies such as AENOR (2003, 2009, 2012), ANSI (2008), CAN-CORE (2009), IMS (2003, 2004, 2005), ISO (2008), ISO/IEC (2008), W3C (2000, 2008, 2009). Based on some of these standards, Akoumianakis and Stephanadis [16] reported the efforts of the scientific community to bring universal design for the area of interaction human-computer. After analyzing these efforts the authors reported that the universal design applied to interfaces is more a challenge than a utopia.

One of these challenges is to understand the criteria that are used by these standards. For example, the WCAG 2.0 (standard that specifies accessibility for web) reports criteria, which are presented as testable statements that, according to the document, are not for a specific technology. Due to the complexity of applying the criteria, it is possible that there is some difficulty in understanding the operation of the document. This is because the WCAG 2.0 introduces several levels of approach, which include principles, recommendations of a general nature, testable success criteria and a large set of techniques. In addition, the document shows common failures documented with examples, links to resources and source code [17].

At the top of this hierarchy are four principles that represent the foundation of Web accessibility: noticeable, operable, understandable and robust. For each one of these principles there are recommendations that gather 12 basic objectives that Web designers must achieve in order to make your content accessible.

In addition, for each recommendation there are testable criteria of success, which can be used when there is a need for compliance tests. The document provides three levels of compliance depending on the group to be answered (A to the lowest, AA and AAA for the highest level).

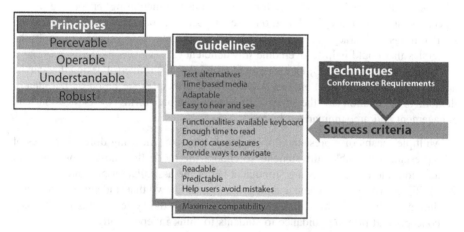

Fig. 1. Levels of approaching - WCAG 2.0 (based on [13])

In addition to the recommendations and success criteria, the W3C documents techniques of an informative character into two categories: Sufficient techniques and techniques are advisory. The sufficient techniques meet the criteria of success established by WCAG 2.0; the type recommended go beyond what is required in each one of the criteria for success and allows authors to a better compliance with the recommendations, approaching the barriers of accessibility not yet covered by the testable criteria of success (see Fig. 1). The Center for Universal Design has also established guidelines for each Principle of Design [2]. These guidelines are shown in Fig. 2 associated with the WCAG 2.0 guidelines.

4 MOOCs

For Grunewald, F. et al. [18] the origin of the concept Massive Open Online Course (MOOC) is commonly assigned to an experiment in 2008 carried out by educational researchers from Canada, George Siemens and Stephen Downes. They developed a theory for the digital age, called connectivism, which conceives learning as the creative and social process of connecting nodes of knowledge. This means that all material created by the professors was optional with students free to choose their path. Because of the large class size it is expected that a bigger connectivist "class" emerge with a greater potential for the quantity and variety of modal connections. David Cormier, another Canadian and manager of web communications and innovations at the University of Prince Edwards Island and the host of the weekly EdTechTalk webcast coined the term "MOOC". He came up with the name during an EdTechTalk interview with Siemens and Downes in 2008 [19].

"The course content and instructions frequently are hosted on different platforms, such as EdX, Coursera, Udacity, Udemy, MOOC^{2}Degree, from online learning, such as BlackBoard Learn, Moodle" [20].

This paper chose the Coursera platform as the object of study. This is a non-probabilistic and intentional sample. Coursera is an online education platform founded at Stanford by Andrew Ng and Daphne Koller [21]. This platform was accessed on 26 October 2014 and the course was called Design: Creation of Artifacts in Society by Karl T. Ulricht.

5   Close Reading of a Massive Open Online Course

This paper aims to identify how the interface design of a Massive Open Online Course can incorporate the seven Principles of Universal Design. In order to that, a close reading of the course was performed to allow detailed notes to be taken about the interface design. Close reading is a detailed examination, deconstruction and analysis of a media text and adapted to other media forms such as interface design [22]. For Inman [23] close reading of digital media implies that reading is much about the "shape of the page" as it is about any other element.

Thus, a verification instrument was designed based on the Principles of Universal Design and the guidelines of WCAG 2.0. Figure 2 shows how each UD principle was

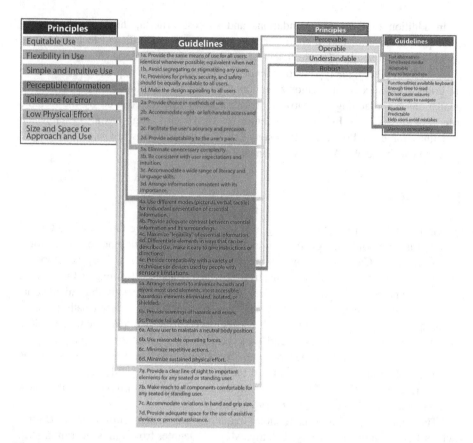

Fig. 2. UD's guidelines (Copyright 1997 NC State University – The Center for Universal Design) and WCAG 2.0's guidelines (based on WCAG 2.0)

linked to the correspondent WCAG 2.0 principle. The content analysis of each principle created this correspondence.

The notes taken from the close reading analysis were tabulated among with the Principles of Universal Design and WCAG 2.0. A total of 9 tables were designed to investigate if the Principles of Universal Design and the guidelines of WCAG 2.0 were supported by the interface design. The first 5 tables correspond to the first 5 Principles of Universal Design and the last 4 tables correspond to the 4 principles of WCAG 2.0. Principles 6 and 7 of Universal Design neither were considered because they deal with physical interaction, which does not pertain to the scope of this paper. In addition, this paper restricts the investigation to the visual design of the interface. Thus, the final instrument is composed of a list of interface elements that are designed to support the Principles of Universal Design and the guidelines of WCAG 2.0.

This paper argues that providing simplicity on interface design might support Universal Design, which will create an environment for a greater number of people. As declared by Pettersson "simplicity in a message will result in a easier and more efficient perception, processing and memory of that message" [11]. For Pettersson simplicity is achieved through readability of text, pictures and graphic forms (layout, symbols, numerical values, maps, color). Readability is determined by content and formulations and how well they are adapted to a greater number of readers.

The tables were filled out looking for elements of Coursera interface that could establish whether the guideline was followed or not. It was considered the following legend:

✓ - Observed on pages | x - Not observed on pages | NA - Not Applicable, because the functionality was not implemented.

Tables 1 and 2 show the results for the first Principle of Universal Design – Equitable Use and for the first principle of WCAG 2.0's - Perceivable. The others 7 tables follow the same structure and were omitted because of space constrains.

Table 1. Results of principle Equitable Use

UD | **Principle 1- Equitable Use**: The design is useful and marketable to people with diverse abilities. Equitable means just and impartial	Results
Provide the same means of use for all users: identical whenever possible; equivalent when not; so that it can be changed into other forms people need	✓
Content based on text	✓
Video with close caption	✓
Avoid segregating or stigmatizing any users	x
Pictures with description	x
Provisions for privacy, security, and safety should be equally available to all users	✓
Login	✓
Make the design appealing to all users.	✓
Interface design simple	✓
Good contrast	

Next session discuss the results and explores how simplicity is applied to support Universal Principles.

6 Discussion

The results suggest that the Coursera course named Design: Creation of Artifacts in Society by Karl T. Ulrich follows the Universal Design guidelines. This is based on the analyses of the interface that supports the principles 'Equitable Use', 'Flexibility in Use', 'Simple and Intuitive Use', 'Perceptible Information' and 'Tolerance for Error'. The result of the principle Equitable Use pointed out that pictures did no have description, which might create difficulty for some users. The principles 'Flexibility in Use', 'Simple and Intuitive Use', and 'Perceptible Information' had al their guidelines supported by the interface design. But the principle 'Tolerance for Error' could have

Table 2. Result of principle perceivable

WCAG 2.0 Principle 1: Perceivable - Information and user interface components must be presentable to users in ways they can perceive.		Results	
Text Alternatives: Provide text alternatives for any non-text content so that it can be changed into other forms people need		50	
	Non-text Content		✓
		Controls, Input	✓	
		Time-Based Media	✓	
		Test	NA	
		Sensory	NA	
		Decoration, Formatting, Invisible	NA	
Time-based Media: Provide alternatives for time-based media.		x	
	Audio-only and Video-only (Pre-recorded)		NA
		Pre-recorded Audio-only and Video-only	NA	
		Pre-recorded Audio-only	NA	
	Captions (Pre-recorded)		✓
	Pre-recorded Video-only		NA
	Audio Description or Media Alternative (Pre-recorded		NA
	Captions (Live)		x
	Audio Description (Pre-recorded)		x
	Sign Language (Pre-recorded)		NA
	Extended Audio Description (Pre-recorded)		x
	Media Alternative (Pre-recorded)		NA
	Audio-only (Live)		NA
Adaptable: Create content that can be presented in different ways (for example simpler layout) without losing information or structure			
	Info and Relationships		✓
	Meaningful Sequence		✓
	Sensory Characteristics		NA
Distinguishable: Make it easier for users to see and hear content including separating foreground from background.		100	
	Use of Colour		✓
	Audio Control		✓
	Contrast (Minimum)		✓
		Large Text	✓	
		Incidental	✓	
		Logotypes	✓	
	Resize text	✓	✓
	Images of Text		✓
		Customizable	NA	
		Essential	NA	
	Contrast (Enhanced):		✓
		Large Text:	✓	
		Incidental	✓	
		Logotypes	✓	
	Low or No Background Audio:		✓
		No Background:	✓	
		Turn Off:	✓	
		20 dB	✓	
	Visual Presentation:		✓
		Foreground and background colours can be selected by the user.	✓	
		Width is no more than 80 characters or glyphs (40 if CJK).	✓	
		Text is not justified (aligned to both the left and the right margins).	✓	

		Line spacing (leading) is at least space-and-a-half within paragraphs, and paragraph spacing is at least 1.5 times larger than the line spacing.	✓	
		Text can be resized without assistive technology up to 200 percent in a way that does not require the user to scroll horizontally to read a line of text on a full-screen window.	✓	
		Images of Text (No Exception)		✓

been applied in to a broader approach because it was not found evidence of warnings of hazards and errors.

The last two principles 'Low Physical Effort' and 'Size and Space for Approach and Use' were not applicable because they refer to physical interaction, which were not in the scope of this paper.

The results of the accessibility based on the guidelines of WCAG 2.0 suggest that the principle "perceivable" that recommends that "the information and the components of the user interface has to be presented to users in ways that they can understand" is being met in almost all guidelines but miss to provide text alternatives for any non-text content.

The results of the principle "operable" indicate that only the option to use the keyboard to act on the functionality of the interface does not seem to have been accomplished.

The results of the principles "understandable" and "robust" indicate that both principles are in accordance with the guidelines.

The elements of interface that support many of these guidelines are: text, pictures, layout and colors with a good readability. The readability of these elements supports simplicity as discussed next.

Readability of text is achieved by using clear contrast, clear hierarchy, balance between text and white space, and balance among length of words, sentences and paragraph.

Readability of pictures is achieved because the few pictures complete the ideas explained in the text. They miss legends though.

Readability of layout and text are the most impressive in this work. The layout follows a specific pattern, where heading, paragraphs, pictures and general concept of the structure is clear.

Readability of colors is used to emphasize links, or to show differences and similarities. Few colors with a clear contrast were used.

Simplicity is achieved by focusing on the essential to inform and elementary form. The result is a dynamic form language with all the elements having a clear reason to be in the page. The interface design design returns to the basic [24] with a sophisticated aesthetic. This supports the Akoumianakis and Stephanadis [16] statement that Universal Design is more a challenge than a utopia. The challenge resides on understanding the principles and most of all implementing them.

References

1. United Nations Regional Information Center (2013). http://www.unric.org/
2. Centre for Excellence in Universal Design. http://universaldesign.ie/What-is-Universal-Design/The-7-Principles/
3. Gregga, N., Changa, Y., Toddb, R.: Social media, avatars, and virtual worlds: re-imagine an inclusive learning environment for adolescents and adults with literacy barriers. Procedia Comput. Sci. **14**, 336–342 (2012)
4. Meyer, A., Rose, D.: Universal design for individual differences. Educ. Leadersh. **58**(3), 39–43 (2000)
5. Lidwell, W., Holden, K., Butler, J.: Universal Principles of Design. Rockport Publishers, Gloucester (2003)
6. Mace, R.: About UD. Retrieved Junho 12, from the Center for Universal Design (2014). http://www.ncsu.edu/ncsu/design/cud/about_ud/about_ud.htm
7. Macedo, C.M.S.: Diretrizes para criação deobjetos de aprendizagem acessíveis. Tese para obtenção do título de Doutor no programa Pós Graduação em Engenharia e Gestão do Conhecimento –PPEGC, da Universidade Federal de Santa Catarina, Florianópolis (2010)
8. Ramakrisnana, P., Jaafarb, A., Razaka, F.H., Rambaa, D.A.: Evaluation of user interface design for leaning management system (LMS): investigating student's eye tracking pattern and experiences. Procedia Soc. Behav. Sci. **67**, 527–537 (2012)
9. Izzo, M.V.: Universal design for learning: enhancing achievement of students with disabilities. Procedia Comput. Sci. **14**, 343–350 (2012)
10. Wong, M., Khong, C., Thwaites, H.: Applied UX and UCD design process in interface design. Procedia Soc. Behav. Sci. **51**, 703–708 (2012)
11. Petterson, R.: It Depends: ID - Principles and Guidelines. Institute for Infology, Tullinge (2007). http://www.iiid.net/PublicLibrary/Pettersson-Rune-ID-It-Depends.pdf
12. Türk, Y.A.: Planning-design training and universal design. Procedia Soc. Behav. Sci. **141**, 1019–1024 (2014)
13. Rose, D., Meyer, A.: Teaching Every Student in the Digital Age: Universal Design for Learning. Association for Supervision and Curriculum Development, Alexandria (2002)
14. Csikszentmihalyi, M.: Flow: The Psychology of Optimal Experience. Harper Perennial Modern Classics, New York (1991)
15. Rose, H.R., Hernándeza, R., Hilera, J.R.: Implementation of accessibility standards in the process of course design in virtual learning environments. Procedia Comput. Sci. **14**, 363–370 (2012)
16. Akoumianakis, D., Stephanidis, C.: Universal design in HCI: a critical review of current research and practice. Universal Design: Towards a Universal Access in the Info Society (2001)
17. Web Content Accessibility Guidelines. https://www.w3.org/WAI/intro/wcag
18. Grunewald, F. et al.: OpenHPI-a case-study on the emergence of two learning communities. In: 2013 IEEE Global Engineering Education Conference (EDUCON), pp. 1323–1331. IEEE (2013)
19. Harber, J.: MOOCS. The MIT Press, Caparral (2014)
20. Tu, C.-H. et al.: A cycle of online education ecstasy/agony: to MOOC or not to MOOC. In: IEEE 63rd Annual Conference International Council for Educational Media (ICEM) (2013)
21. Midha, A.: Credit crisis: the need for student inclusion in MOOC decision making. The Stanford Review (2013). Retrieved from http://stanfordreview.org/article/credit-crisis-the-needfor-student-inclusion-in-mooc-decision-making/

22. Bizzocchi, J., Tanenbaum, J.: Well read: applying close reading techniques to gameplay experiences. In: Davidson, D. (ed.) Well Played 3.0. ETC Press, Pittsburgh (2011)
23. Inman, J.: Electronic texts and the concept of close reading: a Cyborg anthropologist's perspective. In: Walker, J.R., Oviedo, O.O. (eds.) TnT: Text and Technology. University of Toronto Press, Toronto (2003)
24. Hellers, S.: Less is More: The New Simplicity in Graphic Design. NorthLight, Cincinnati (1999). Anne Fink

The Design of Guidelines for Teachers and Parents in the Use of iPads to Support Children with Autism in the Development of Joint Attention Skills

Chrysoula Mangafa[1(✉)], Louise Moody[1], Andrée Woodcock[1],
and Alex Woolner[2]

[1] School of Art and Design, Coventry University, Coventry, UK
mangafac@uni.coventry.ac.uk,
{aa0445,adx974}@coventry.ac.uk
[2] AdsReality, London, UK
alex@pandigital.org.uk

Abstract. Children with autism have an affinity with technologies, which imposes the need to keep abreast of new digital technologies [1]. The benefits of mobile devices and interactive technologies in providing structure and predictability [2] and the vast variety of apps that can facilitate social communication makes it imperative to effectively incorporate iPads in the teaching of joint attention. Despite the increase use of mobile devices there is a lack of guidance for parents and teachers on how to use these devices in home and school environments for young children with autism. This study fills this gap. This paper reports on one of the final stages of the project, in which focus groups with teachers, parents, academics and children were conducted to discuss the development of guidelines on how to use the iPads with children with autism to improve their joint attention skills.

Keywords: Social communication · Joint attention · iPads · Guidelines

1 Introduction

Joint attention (JA) is described in a variety of ways in education, psychology and human computer interaction may provide different definitions. In this study joint attention is defined as the act of sharing, sustaining and shifting attention between two social partners - teachers or parents with a child with autism - and a task or toy [3]. It is achieved when the child can recognize the other's presence and intention in sharing interest with them for a task or activity they do together. Joint attention skills include the child's ability to follow gaze, point, keep eye contact, take turns and initiate or respond in social interaction. In typical development these skills are usually mastered by the age of 18 months but in children with autism these skills may be impaired or delayed [4].

The overall aim of the study is to develop guidelines on the ways in which tablet computers can be used to foster joint attention skills in children with autism based in

A. Marcus (Ed.): DUXU 2016, Part II, LNCS 9747, pp. 178–186, 2016.
DOI: 10.1007/978-3-319-40355-7_17

part on the experience and input of parents and teachers. The purpose of the guidelines is to help parents, teachers or those who work with the child to structure their 'iPad time' and provide them with more confidence to use the iPad as an education tool that can facilitate social communication and joint attention. The research is divided into five studies; interviews with teachers, observations in schools, interviews with parents, focus groups with stakeholders and an evaluation of the guidelines. This paper will present the results of the fourth study.

The results from the first three studies (i.e. the interviews with teachers, parents and classroom observations) have shown that the design of guidelines will be a useful tool for teachers and parents as there is lack of training and experience in using the iPads for learning purposes [5].

In the first study sixteen teachers were interviewed in three UK primary schools (one mainstream and two special needs) in order to examine the ways in which educational interventions, strategies and iPads are used in schools to support children with autism in the area of JA. The findings showed that teachers used a variety of evidence-based strategies in their daily teaching practice to promote JA, such as using children's personal interests as motivators, sharing and turn-taking play activities, visual prompts, social skills groups and role models. iPads were used less often to teach the curriculum and turn taking skills. The need for iPad training was considered important by all participants in terms of getting technical support and learning more about the pedagogical value of the device [5].

Complimentary classroom observations were undertaken to examine how technology was embedded in learning activities to promote joint attention skills. Twelve children with eight teachers were observed using the iPad in conjunction with visual aids and other teaching resources to teach the curriculum, sharing, eye contact and turn-taking skills. A similar set of challenges were faced by all teachers, such as children not sharing the iPad with peers or not staying on the particular app their teacher assigned them work to do [5]. Interviews with ten parents of children with autism showed that they would like to use the iPad more often with their children if they felt themselves more confident in using the device.

Current methodologies are techno-centric [6] and there is a lack of consideration in research papers of the interlink among content of technology, pedagogy and context; indeed, research papers not very often refer to interdisciplinary work [7]. This may be because a lack of communication between different disciplines such as education, psychology, computer science as well as between users (teachers/parents/therapists) and academics [8, 9].

2 Methods

As an attempt to bridge the gap between user community and academics, this study involves focus groups with teachers, parents, children and academics, where different perspectives on how the guidelines should be designed are explored. Academics from a UK Higher Education institution, primary school teachers, parents of children with a diagnosis of autism and primary school aged children were recruited. The focus group with the academics was arranged at the university grounds while the focus groups with school staff, parents and children were conducted in the school. During the focus groups with the adults (n = 10) participants were firstly reminded of the purpose of the meeting and the definition of joint attention was discussed to reach a common understanding of the term. The main part of the focus groups considered the content of the guidelines, their format and importance. Table 1 shows the content of guidelines discussed.

Table 1. The content of guidelines

The content of guidelines	
Technical section	Educational section
• Preparations before using the iPads	• Teachers' and parents' attitude towards the iPad
• Checklist of criteria for choosing suitable apps	• The structure of the environment
	• Teacher's and parent's strategies: (a) how to overcome challenges and (b) how to promote joint attention skills

The focus groups were audio recorded and thematically analyzed. In addition to this, during the focus group with the parents, a member of the school staff was present in the room taking notes on a flipchart as shown in Fig. 1.

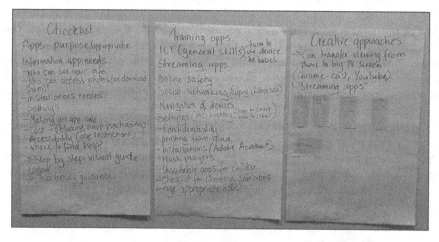

Fig. 1. Flipchart notes taken during the focus group with parents

The focus group with the children followed a more child friendly format. The children (n = 19) were aged 8–11 years old and were members of the school's student council. The teacher who led the student council meeting was also present and contributed to the smooth running of the focus group. The researcher told the children that the meeting had been arranged to capture their voices in relation to how iPads helped them in their learning and development of communication skills as well as how they could be improved in the future. Their teacher captured their comments while they were talking. Later, the children completed a questionnaire about their personal views and experiences as shown in Figs. 2, 3, 4 and 5. For ethical reasons, the focus group with the children was not audio recorded but the written feedback from the flipchart and questionnaires were analyzed.

Fig. 2. Drawing showing that iPads could be used in different places in class

Fig. 3. Drawing showing a child wishing that the iPad had been fully charged before they used it

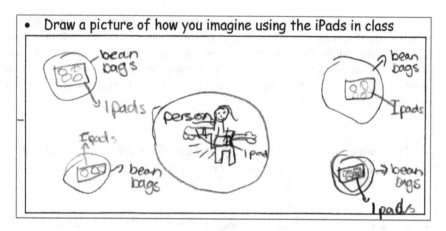

Fig. 4. Drawing showing that iPads could be used while sitting on beanbags

Fig. 5. Drawing showing that the iPad screen could be projected on the interactive whiteboard

3   Results

Through the analysis of the data (transcripts, questionnaires and field notes) derived from the focus groups, five major themes were developed: 'The format of guidelines', 'Technical Preparations', 'Checklist of Apps', 'Attitude to the iPad', and 'JA Teaching Strategies'.

3.1   The Format of the Guidelines

All participants mentioned that the guidelines will be an invaluable tool for teachers, parents and children that can be used as a reference point whenever they are using the iPad for learning purposes and choosing apps. In particular, it was discussed that the guidelines should be written on an A4 poster with an accompanying booklet where all the information should be simply demonstrated with many visuals and step by step instructions. Bullet points with headings and checklists of the steps to follow were also mentioned. The language used should be simple and child friendly as well as jargon should be avoided. Participants made clear that even though they understood the term joint attention when it was explained and discussed during the focus group, the term social communication should be used instead as it is the term that teachers and parents widely use and understand.

3.2   Technical Preparations

The intersection between the technological and pedagogical aspect of the guidelines was frequently mentioned in the focus groups among participants. It was widely mentioned that it is equally important not only to use the iPad to teach joint attention skills but also to know how to use it and make necessary preparations beforehand. The children commented that the guidelines should include advice on making sure the iPad was fully charged as many of their peers were frustrated when the iPad runs out of battery. Also the parents mentioned that the reason why iPads are still not as frequently used as the laptops is the lack of printing facility. So, it was suggested that the guidelines should include step by step instructions on how to connect the iPad with the printers on the wireless network. A major concern among participants was ensuring that online safety settings are activated on the iPad before giving it to the child. Particularly, parents mentioned that it would be helpful if the guidelines included how to set up firewall filters and monitor their child's navigation history. Teachers also mentioned that online safety tips should be included as they feel that children can more easily access inappropriate content on the iPad due to its small screen size and portability.

3.3   Checklist of Apps

The selection of applications was a recurring theme in all studies and it was also thought mandatory by the participants to be included in the guidelines. The academics mentioned that even though teachers and parents would prefer to have a list of recommended apps for teaching their children joint attention and social skills, they suggested that adding a checklist on how to choose suitable apps would be better since new apps are advertised in the market daily. Teachers said that a checklist reminding them of what to look for when choosing an app would be useful. For example, all participants mentioned that the app should be linked to learning outcomes so that the teachers, parents and children know what they are using them for. There should be a purpose for choosing to use a particular app with the child, whether it is to teach turn-taking, to record their work and discuss it later or sustain their attention. Also, parents mentioned that the checklist can include some criteria, such as whether the app has in-app purchases, a user guide to refer to when needed and whether it is safe and age appropriate.

3.4   Attitude to the iPad

The children mentioned that the iPad has helped them improve their communication skills because they can present in front of the classroom confidently, they can learn more things about their learning partner and be able to problem solve. They also mentioned that they can work better with others on the iPad rather than using other resources and they would like their teachers to use the iPads more in the classroom as they make learning more fun and interesting. On the contrary, teachers and parents said that they do not feel confident in using the iPad as they would like to receive training to learn the basics of how it operates and then its educational value. Parents suggested that their child's school could organize after school iPad clubs where parents are invited in the classroom to play with their child on the iPad while looking at the guidelines for tips.

3.5   JA Teaching Strategies

After discussing technical issues the focus groups addressed how iPads could be used to teach joint attention skills. The first issue raised was that adults need to overcome some challenges in order to be able to encourage initiation and response to joint attention. For example, children with autism very often do not like to share or have someone very close to them. In addition, researchers mentioned that the iPad was not designed to be shared due to its small screen size. Parents recommended that streaming apps and hardware can be used to project the iPad screen to the TV screen and IWB. They said that it would be useful to include in the guidelines different ways of projecting the iPad screen, such as using AirPort Express or Chromecast. This would give the opportunity to teachers, parents and children to comment on what a child is doing on the iPad and encourage joint attention opportunities. In addition, children mentioned that choosing their learning partner, who they are working with, would help them interact more and work better while on the iPad. The dynamics of peer work was also mentioned by the teachers, who said it was important to let the child with autism choose who they feel more comfortable working with. In terms of the structure of the environment, children added that they would like to share the iPad with others beyond the school desks, such as on beanbags or around the school. Finally, parents mentioned that it is essential to remind teachers and other parents that using positive reinforcement and showing interest in what the children are playing on the iPad can help children with autism boost their self-esteem and participate more in joint attention opportunities. Taking turns in educational games, sharing enjoyment and rewarding the child when completing a task on the iPad were the main strategies mentioned by participants for improving joint attention skills. Table 2 summarizes the key findings of the focus groups.

Table 2. Summary of the key findings of the focus groups

Summary of key findings	
Themes	Recommendations
The format of the guidelines	• A4 poster with accompanying booklet • Simple language and visuals • Headings with bullet points and step by step instructions
Technical Preparations	• iPads to be fully charged before use • Connect the iPad to wireless printers • Online safety settings

Checklist of Apps	To include:
	  • Purpose of the app
	  • User guide available
	  • Block in-app purchases
	  • Age appropriate

Attitude to the iPad	• iPad training • After school iPad clubs with parents
JA Teaching Strategies	• Project iPad screen to the TV and IWB • Dynamics of learning partners • Moving around and sitting on bean bags • Positive reinforcement and rewards • Sharing enjoyment • Taking turns in games

4   Discussion

This study was the fourth in a sequence that explored the need for guidance on how to use the iPads with children with autism to teach joint attention skills. The aim was to bring together different stakeholders with the common purpose to explore the technical and educational characteristics of the device. Focus groups with academics, teachers, parents and children were conducted to discuss the guidelines on how to use the iPad for joint attention purposes. The results showed that it is important to know how the device operates as well as how to use it for learning purposes. Participants mentioned that before giving the iPad to the child, there are a number of challenges and steps that should be addressed, such as the child's difficulty in sharing, choosing suitable apps and ensuring that online safety settings are activated. In addition, the iPad can be used to promote joint attention skills as long as parents and teachers are willing to use the device with the child by sharing with them what they enjoy doing on the device, joining in when they are playing games and providing positive reinforcement. It is suggested that the iPad's contribution in the educational process can be successful only if a holistic approach of iPad's use for JA purposes is followed not only from teachers individually, but from the whole school as an institution and the parents with their children at home.

5   Conclusion

The guidelines will inform teachers' practice and be used as material for professional development. Teachers should keep ahead of the technological and pedagogical innovations, so the guidelines can help them instil the habit of using the iPad as a teaching tool to develop joint attention skills in their everyday teaching practice. Also parents can try using the tablet in collaboration with their child in order to interact and communicate more often. This paper supports the view that the device should only be used as a facilitator in the learning process and should not overtake what the teacher or parent already have in place. What is important is the mutual understanding and sharing of interest between the adult and the child by using a medium which in this study is the iPad.

The guidelines are proposals rather than definite answers on how to use the iPad for joint attention. In order for the guidelines to be effective in promoting joint attention, researchers, teachers, parents and app developers should work in partnership. This study will be followed by the development and evaluation of the guidelines that will be created according to the results of the studies.

References

1. Durkin, K.: Videogames and young people with developmental disorders. Rev. Gen. Psychol. **14**(2), 122–140 (2010)
2. Boucenna, S., Narzisi, A., Tilmont, E., Muratori, F., Pioggia, G., Cohen, D., Chetouani, M.: Interactive technologies for autistic children: a review. Cogn. Comput. **6**(4), 722–740 (2014)
3. Patten, E., Watson, L.: Interventions targeting attention in young children with autism. Am. J. Speech-Lang. Pathol. **20**, 60–69 (2011)
4. Loveland, K.A., Landry, S.H.: Joint attention and language in autism and developmental language delay. J. Autism Dev. Disord. **16**(3), 335–349 (1986)
5. Mangafa, C., Moody, L., Woodcock, A., Woolner, A.: Teachers' experiences of developing joint attention skills in children with autism using iPads. In: 7th Edulearn International Conference on Education and New Learning Technologies, pp. 6170–6179. Edulearn Press, Barcelona (2015)
6. Mercader, C., Pozos, K.: Conditioning factors for pedagogical integration of technologies in higher education teaching: a cross case analysis of two studies in Mexico and Spain. In: 7th Edulearn International Conference on Education and New Learning Technologies, pp. 1955–1967. Edulearn Press, Barcelona (2015)
7. Fletcher-Watson, S.: Evidence-based technology design and commercialisation: recommendations derived from research in education and autism. TechTrends **59**, 84–88 (2015)
8. Pellicano, E., Dinsmore, A., Charman, T.: A Future Made Together: Shaping Autism Research in the UK. Centre for Research in Autism and Education (2013). http://newsletters.ioe.ac.uk/A_Future_Made_Together_2013.pdf
9. Parsons, S., Guldberg, K., MacLeod, A., Jones, G., Prunty, A., Balfe, T.: International Review of the Literature of Evidence of Best Practice Provision in the Education of Persons with Autistic Spectrum Disorders. National Council for Special Education (2009). http://www.aettraininghubs.org.uk/wp-content/uploads/2012/05/NCSE-report-2009-Parsons.pdf

Mobile Devices as Assistive Technologies for ASD: Experiences in the Classroom

David Roldán-Álvarez[1]([⊠]), Javier Gomez[1],
Ana Márquez-Fernández[2], Estefanía Martín[2], and Germán Montoro[1]

[1] Universidad Autónoma de Madrid, Madrid, Spain
{david.roldan, jg.escribano, german.montoro}@uam.es
[2] Universidad Rey Juan Carlos, Móstoles, Spain
anamarqfer@gmail.com, estefania.martin@urjc.es

Abstract. Information and Communication Technologies offer new opportunities to people with disabilities to develop their autonomy and independence in their daily life activities. However, more research should be done in order to comprehend how technology affects this collective of people. This paper presents two experiences where participants with cognitive disabilities and Autism Spectrum Disorder used AssisT-Task to perform job related activities and DEDOS to perform educational activities. Their performance is improved along the sessions using both tools. Combining visual and textual information help students with cognitive disabilities and ASD to focus on the contents presented, avoiding usability and accessibility issues, and therefore improving their learning process while they are having fun interacting with new technologies.

Keywords: ASD · ICT · Mobile · Learning

1 Introduction

Information and Communication Technologies (ICTs) are becoming very popular among people with cognitive disabilities and Autism Spectrum Disorder (ASD) [1, 2]. Besides, they are excellent tools to help them in their daily life activities. However, the number of research studies related to this topic is still limited [3]. In this sense, Holzinger et al. [4] discussed the tolerance of individuals to introduce new devices in their lives and discovered that the acceptance. The authors concluded that acceptance is related to previous exposure to technology. Therefore, popular technologies such as smartphones and tablets remain as optimal choices for this kind of studies, since the previous or future exposure is guaranteed by the society. In fact, choosing a device of high acceptance level decreases the risk to become an abandoned device through time, as studies pointed out [5].

Touch devices are making computing more accessible for a wide variety of population. The simplicity and benefits of the touch interaction and their portability have lowered the barriers for interacting with ICTs [6]. These devices allow users to interact through natural gestures and manipulate the content directly, allowing them to express themselves in a more physical way, generating better comprehension [7]. This way of interacting help users to focus on the content while they enjoy doing the activities, which helps them acquire a deeper knowledge of the topic presented [8, 9].

© Springer International Publishing Switzerland 2016
A. Marcus (Ed.): DUXU 2016, Part II, LNCS 9747, pp. 187–197, 2016.
DOI: 10.1007/978-3-319-40355-7_18

Two particular areas of interest related to assistive technologies for cognitive disabilities are job insertion [10] and education [11]. Technologies in general, and mobile technologies in particular, seem to fit perfectly in the formation and training process of both. Traditionally, the necessary skills to promote the job insertion of these people are acquired by repeating the typical tasks several times. During these sessions, educators usually provide oral instructions and help but also paper manuals with the list of instructions [12]. In some cases, these manuals are enriched with pictograms or diagrams. This approach presents some challenges such as difficulties to relocate when they get lost or to look for a certain instruction [13]. Moreover, during the learning process caregivers have to monitor their performance, which is time and human resources consuming. To solve this issue, we chose smartphones as a platform to develop an adapted system to support activities of daily living, AssisT-Task, an application that provides pervasive assistance thanks to the use of smartphones in combination with QR codes.

Regarding the education area, the use of tablets for people with special needs has produced lots of excitement among the education community and their preference for touchscreens has long been documented [14]. However, this excitement has brought developers to build hundreds of apps to help people with cognitive disabilities, making it difficult for teachers to identify the useful ones [15]. Moreover, sometimes teachers do not achieve their educational objectives since they are not able to provide suitable multimedia content [16], mostly due to the lack of flexibility of the available tools. Therefore, we also designed DEDOS-Project, a system to design and play educational activities for multiple platforms, such as personal computers, digital whiteboards, tablets and multitouch tabletops.

This paper is organized as follows: after this introduction, we describe our two approaches in detail. Then, we present our experiences in the classroom and finish with the conclusions extracted from them.

2 Mobile Technologies

2.1 AssisT-Task

AssisT-Task is a mobile system that provides adapted and pervasive guidance to do sequential tasks. Thanks to the use of smartphones in combination with QR Codes, users can receive assistance at any time and place. Moreover, this help is adapted to the user, her needs and context. To do that, caregivers have to design the sequence of steps that composes the task. Then, all the necessary information to identify the task is coded into a visual mark (the QR Code) that should be printed and put near the place where the task should be done. This way, users only have to start the application and point with their phones to the tag to receive the assistance.

The guidance is provided by means of sequential instructions supplemented with photographs. In order to ease the process, the system can be configured to automatically read the instruction aloud. This way, users receive the information by multiple modes and channels. Besides, AssisT-Task offers an alarm mechanism to prevent users from being blocked. In case users do not interact with the smartphone for a period (configurable), the system automatically reads aloud the instruction again to warn them and recover from the block. Finally, it records a detailed registry so users' performance can be analyzed afterwards.

Caregivers can create, edit and adapt the sequences for their users. To do that, AssisT-Task counts with a PC authoring tool. This software has been developed considering users' needs (no necessary technical profiles), so its functioning is very similar to standard office software. Figure 1 shows a screenshot of the interface. It is divided in two parts: on the left side, there is a navigation bar including all the available tasks in the system. The main frame contains all the steps that composes a task. In this example, the sequence corresponds to the "make toasts" task. As can be seen, it is composed of 12 steps, each one contains a text (the action) and an image. In this case, some of the images are pictograms while others are actual photographs. Depending on users' needs and preferences, caregivers may decide to include one or another or, even more, to edit the images (with any external image editor) to highlight a detail or the most important elements of the picture.

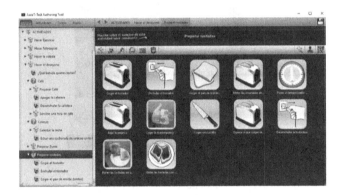

Fig. 1. AssisT-Task authoring tool. In the example the "Make toasts" tasks is shown

This software also allows caregivers to adapt the sequence to users' needs by removing the amount of help provided. They can choose any step or steps from the original sequence and remove them for a particular user. This way, the assistance is adapted to users' progress.

Both the interface and the interaction of the client have been developed in collaboration with therapists and educators. The main objective was to design a simple interface, easy to understand. Therefore, we designed the interfaces shown in Fig. 2(a) Presents the user selection screen. In order to provide a personalized experience, we included it so users could look for themselves using the arrows. Thanks to the names and photographs displayed, the task is easier, according to experts' opinion. Once the user is selected, a QR capturing screen is displayed. It shows an actual view from the camera. When a QR Code is detected, it is captured and decoded automatically. This way, all the available information of the task is loaded and the sequence of steps starts. In Fig. 2(b) a screenshot of a step is presented. On the top of the screen there is a title bar. The three dots on the right access the configuration options. Right under it, we included the instruction. As can be seen the font is big and clear enough to be easily read. Regarding the text, task designers are in charge of making it simple, direct and easy to understand. The image is under the text. As can be seen, it takes most of the available space of the screen. This way, users may not miss any detail. Finally, at the bottom of the screen there are two buttons to navigate through the sequence. They have different colors, colorblind-proof and with a subtle intention: the next button is green, as a metaphor of positive reinforcement. Pressing it means advancing within the whole task, whereas the previous button is yellow, meaning a neutral connotation – it is not negative to go back and retry if you feel lost but you have not advanced in the process. The arrow symbols printed on them gives the meaning of both buttons. Educators explained that users tend to respond well to arrow indications representing directional messages.

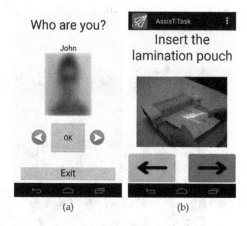

(a)   (b)

Fig. 2. Screenshots of AssisT-Task mobile client. (a) Presents the user selection screen. (b) Shows a step interface (Color figure online)

2.2   DEDOS

The main objective of DEDOS-Project was to provide educators with the suitable tools to design and play educational and collaborative activities for any student. It is composed of two different tools: DEDOS-Editor and DEDOS-Player. On the other hand, DEDOS-Editor is an authoring tool designed to allow teachers to create educational activities in a simple and flexible manner. Our aim was to leverage the design potential of the teaching community by empowering it to create, adapt and modify educational activities. This process can be done in traditional computers and novel touch devices, including collaborative tabletops. Moreover, the application as specifically designed to be used by users with little technological expertise and disregarding the device where the activities will be performed (DEDOS-Player will adapt the content designed by the teacher to the device where the students will solve the activities).

With this idea in mind, we decided to design DEDOS-Editor as a card-based metaphor where each activity is a card-based game. It offers four types of simple activities: single and multiple choice, pair-matching, point connection and mathematics, but they can be combined to design more complex exercises.

The elements used to create the activity are dragged from the toolbar and dropped into the edition area. Designers can use all the elements at hand to create the activity they want and by reusing concepts, elements and operations to create multiple educative activities we favor the users' learning curve, making them more confident on their mastery and making it easier to learn further concepts. Finally, in order to provide a familiar interface to teachers, we based DEDOS-Editor interface on standard office software, since most teachers know and use it in regular basis. Figure 3 shows the user interface of DEDOS-Editor.

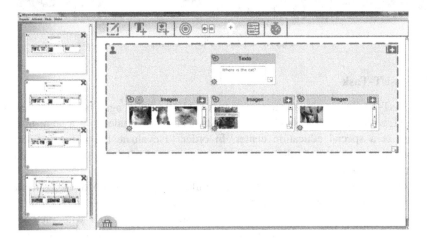

Fig. 3. User interface of DEDOS-Editor

Once the educational project is designed, the students can solve it using DEDOS-Player. As can be seen in Fig. 4, the player runs in multiple devices, such as digital blackboards (left) and tablets (right). Before starting the activities, teachers can configure it depending on the educational objectives they want to achieve and the students' needs. In addition, DEDOS-Player allows, (a) to configure the number of students that will perform the project, (b) how the feedback is going to be given, (c) if students will solve the activities by turns or all at the same time, (d) how many students should answer the activity, (e) if students must answer correctly the activities and, (f) if they have to give the same answer.

3   Experiences in the Classroom

We strongly believe that including mobile technologies in job training and special education will greatly help them to acquire important competences that will improve their autonomy. In order to test how technology influences students in the both aforementioned main areas, we carried out two trials where mobile technologies were used to help in the learning processes of job related and educational skills.

Fig. 4. DEDOS-Player example

3.1 AssisT-Task

The AssisT-Task educational experience involved 10 people, aged between 16 and 19 years old, with cognitive disabilities and ASD. They were students of a labor-training program at a special education center. In order to evaluate the impact of mobile technologies as a catalyst in their formation process, we included a smartphone loaded with AssisT-Task as part of the materials of the course.

In order to develop an interesting and useful activity (in regards to the educational process), educators suggested working on the lamination task. As we said before, these tasks are usually trained by means of oral instructions or cards with pictograms. Although many users are able to follow the instructions, they have to be continuously supervised by the educator, which is time and human resources consuming. Therefore, we designed the "lamination" task. It consisted of a set of six instructions supplemented with actual photographs of the process. During the experiment, participants only received the assistance of the smartphone and indirect supervision from their educator. In every session, the educator took notes and registered if the user finished the activity correctly or not.

The study consisted of 90 sessions and took approximately two months and each user did the task 9 times. From the records (both the smartphone and educator's notes) we found that all of the participants did the activity correctly during the experiment. Therefore, we have a 100 % completion rate. This is a very important factor since the educational process tries to make them capable to do the tasks and, afterwards, work on it to do it in the less possible time. In this sense, we also measured the completion time. In Fig. 5 we have plotted the average time needed to do the task for every session. As can be seen, there is a decreasing tendency, which means an improvement in users' efficiency. According to educators, this time could not be reduced much more, since lamination machine takes a time to heat up and the lamination process is slow. These issues were also reflected on the registries: the steps corresponding to heat up and laminate took longer than the others in general. Moreover, in many cases the alarm sounded although users were not blocked. In order to provide a view of users' progress regarding blocking situations, we cleaned up the registries by removing these alarms (false positives) and plotted the average number of alarms per session in Fig. 6. As can be seen, there is also a decreasing tendency, reaching the 0 value at the end of the experiment. Regarding session 4, and its larger standard deviation, educators reported that one of the users was very nervous and did not pay any attention. Therefore, the alarm triggered several times (10 times according to phone's registries) and provoked this mislead.

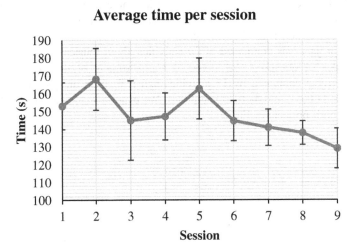

Fig. 5. Average time needed per session to do the lamination task

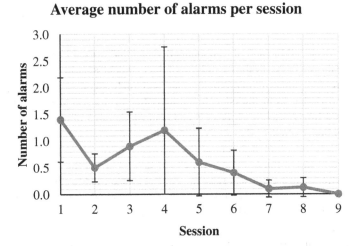

Fig. 6. Average number of alarms per session

Finally, regarding the use of the smartphone, they did not present any serious trouble and the interaction was fluent. Moreover, it was motivating and made them more willing to participate in the activity.

3.2   DEDOS

The DEDOS experience involved 15 students (10 boys and 5 girls) from 12 to 20 years old with cognitive disabilities. Some of them were also diagnosed with Autism Spectrum Disorder (ASD). In addition, more than a half of the participants presented low reading skills. The study was carried out in three sessions during three weeks and each participant had to perform two educational projects using tablets. Each student completed both projects at least once a week during three weeks total. The duration of each session was not fixed beforehand in order to prevent participants to get nervous. In total, each activity took from 7 to 15 min.

The first project was composed of 24 activities about musical instruments. There were two types of questions: the name of an instrument or its type. The second educational project contained by 17 activities and it focused on questions related to Theory of Mind (ToM) and daily life activities. We can see an example of the activities designed for both projects in Fig. 7.

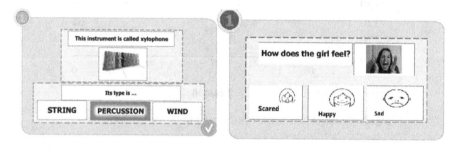

Fig. 7. Left: activity about musical instruments/Right: example activity about ToM

In both projects, all the activities contained visual and textual information. Besides, texts were easily readable, so they would not affect student's performance. The images provided were real musical instruments and real pictures in order to improve the transfer of knowledge from the educational activities to the real world. Finally, since some users had lower reading skills, we included pictograms in addition to the texts.

Regarding the sessions of this study, although we observed a general increase in the number of correct answers throughout the sessions, some participants' performance dropped severely in the third session, which led us to analyze the data gathered using direct observation. During this last session, some students tried to solve the activities as quickly as possible since they wanted to perform better than their partners did. This fact added up to their low reading skills, resulted in many unwanted mistakes.

In order to analyze the answers given by the participants, we checked if there were any activities (A) that posed problems to them, so we could identify if they gave wrong answers in the same activity due to the activity itself or if the mistakes were different in each participant. This will help us to understand if there are any topics that were troublesome for the students or if there were any flaws in the design of the activities. Tables 1 and 2 show the number of wrong answers given for each activity and each session (the maximum number of mistakes per activity and session could be 15 since

Table 1. Wrong answers in musical instruments' project. Part 1

	A1	A2	A3	A4	A5	A6	A7	A8	A9	A10	A11	A12
S1	3	0	1	3	1	2	0	9	6	3	3	4
S2	1	0	1	4	0	1	4	8	2	5	3	7
S3	0	0	0	2	0	0	2	8	2	3	1	5
Total	4	0	2	9	1	3	6	25	10	11	7	16

Table 2. Wrong answers in the musical instruments' project. Part 2

	A13	A14	A15	A16	A17	A18	A19	A20	A21	A22	A23	A24
S1	7	1	4	2	1	5	1	3	2	5	3	2
S2	8	5	6	4	1	6	1	3	1	5	5	0
S3	5	5	1	0	2	6	1	3	1	4	1	0
Total	20	11	11	6	4	17	3	9	4	14	9	2

there were 15 participants). We found that the activities which caused more problems to the students where A8, A13 and A18 so we decided to analyze what could be wrong.

In activity A8, we asked the name of an instrument called "*bandurria*", which is in form, very similar to guitars. Since guitar was one of the answers, the participants mistook the instrument and most of them chose that answer, failing the activity. In A13 we asked for the type of instrument of the piano and as commonly happen when not having too much knowledge about musical instruments, most of the students chose the percussion option instead of string. The participants made the same mistake in A18, where they were asked again about the type of instrument the piano is. When asked again about this instrument in A24, they the right answer. The rest of errors where distributed among all the participants and they were only due to each participant knowledge of this topic, since as one chose the right answer in the first session, the chose it wrongly in the second session, and the other way around. This happened because they sometimes got distracted or they wanted to finish the project as fast as possible, not paying enough attention to the questions asked.

We also wanted to check if students had any problems with a specific activity of the second project. The data gathered is shown in Table 3. As expected, since the students performed well when working with this project, we could not find any specific activity that was difficult for them. However, we would like to note that the participants could not distinguish well between the pictograms that represent being scared and being surprised, which in some cases made them to finally choose the wrong answer (A2, A12). In addition, most of the students guessed the correct answer by discarding those answers that they knew for sure they were wrong. For instance, and using the example of Fig. 7 they guessed the correct answer because they knew that the face was not expressing neither happiness nor sadness.

Table 3. Wrong answers in emotion and daily life activities' project

	A1	A2	A3	A4	A5	A6	A7	A8	A9	A10	A11	A12	A13	A14	A15	A16	A17
S1	1	1	0	2	0	0	0	0	0	0	0	1	0	0	0	0	0
S2	1	1	1	1	0	0	1	0	0	0	0	0	0	0	1	0	0
S3	1	2	0	0	0	0	0	0	0	1	2	3	0	0	2	0	0
Total	3	4	1	3	0	0	1	0	0	1	2	4	0	0	3	0	0

4   Conclusions

From both of the studies, we can conclude that participants increased their performance as the sessions progressed. Combining visual and textual information help students with cognitive disabilities and ASD to focus on the contents presented, avoiding usability and accessibility issues, and therefore improving their learning process while they are having fun interacting with new technologies.

From the results of both experiences, we can conclude that the use of technology could have a positive influence in students when performing learning activities. Moreover, the use of technology motivates them and, combined with traditional methods and other learning sources, tutors, teachers and students can achieve better and more easily their objectives. The portability and accessibility provided by smartphones and tablets make them interesting tools to be used in learning environments for students with special needs. By promoting smooth and direct interaction with tactile devices, we facilitate the students to engage with the activities they have to solve, reducing their frustration and increasing their willingness to interact with a certain application or device.

Acknowledgments. This work has been funded in part by the Spanish Economy and Competitiveness Ministry under project "e-Integra: e-Training y e-Coaching para la integración socio-laboral" (TIN2013-44586-R) and by the Region of Madrid under project "eMadrid – Investigación y Desarrollo de tecnologías para el e-learning en la Comunidad de" Madrid (S2013/ICE-2715). Thanks to the participants who were involved in the experiences presented in this paper.

References

1. Gell, N.M., Rosenberg, D.E., Demiris, G., LaCroix, A.Z., Patel, K.V.: Patterns of technology use among older adults with and without disabilities. The Gerontologist **55**(3), 412–421 (2013)

2. LoPresti, E., Bodine, C., Lewis, C.: Assistive technology for cognition [understanding the needs of persons with disabilities]. IEEE Eng. Med. Biol. Mag. **27**(2), 29–39 (2008)

3. Dawe, M.: Understanding mobile phone requirements for young adults with cognitive disabilities. In: Proceedings of the ACM Conference on Human Factors in Computing Systems (CHI 2007), 30 April–03 May 2007, pp. 179–186. ACM (2007). doi:10.1145/1296843.1296874

4. Holzinger, A., Searle, G., Wernbacher, M.: The effect of previous exposure to technology on acceptance and its importance in usability and accessibility engineering. Univ. Access Inf. Soc. **10**(3), 245–260 (2011)

5. Chang, Y.-J., Chou, L.-D., Wang, F.T.-Y., Chen, S.-F.: A kinectbased vocational task prompting system for individuals with cognitive impairments. Pers. Ubiquit. Comput. **17**(2), 351–358 (2013)

6. Hourcade, J.P., Williams, S.R., Miller, E.A., Huebner, K.E., Liang, L.J.: Evaluation of tablet apps to encourage social interaction in children with autism spectrum disorders. In: Proceedings of the SIGCHI Conference on Human Factors in Computing Systems, pp. 3197–3206. ACM (2013)

7. Cantón, P., González, Á.L., Mariscal, G., Ruiz, C.: Applying new interaction paradigms to the education of children with special educational needs. In: Miesenberger, K., Karshmer, A., Penaz, P., Zagler, W. (eds.) ICCHP 2012, Part I. LNCS, vol. 7382, pp. 65–72. Springer, Heidelberg (2012). doi:10.1007/978-3-642-31522-0_10

8. Inkpen, K.M., Ho-Ching, W., Kuederle, O., Scott, S.D., Shoemaker, G.B.: This is fun! we're all best friends and we're all playing: supporting children's synchronous collaboration. In: Hoadley, C.M., Roschelle, J. (eds.) Proceedings of the 1999 Conference on Computer Support For Collaborative Learning (CSCL 1999). International Society of the Learning Sciences (1999). Article 31

9. Roldán-Álvarez, D., Márquez-Fernández, A., Rosado-Martín, S., Martín, E., Haya, P.A., García-Herranz, M.: Benefits of combining multitouch tabletops and turn-based collaborative learning activities for people with cognitive disabilities and people with ASD. In: 2014 IEEE 14th International Conference on Advanced Learning Technologies (ICALT), pp. 566–570. IEEE (2014)

10. Taylor, J., Hodapp, R.M.: Doing nothing: adults with disabilities with no daily activities and their siblings. Am. J. Intell Dev. Disabil. **117**(1), 67–79 (2012)

11. Radford, J., Bosanquet, P., Webster, R., Blatchford, P.: Scaffolding learning for independence: clarifying teacher and teaching assistant roles for children with special educational needs. Learn. Instr. **36**, 1–10 (2015)

12. Robinson, W., Syed, A., Akhlaghi, A., Deng, T.: Pattern discovery of user interface sequencing by rehabilitation clients with cognitive impairments. In: 2012 45th Hawaii International Conference on System Sciences, pp. 3001–3010. IEEE (2012)

13. Lazar, J., Kumin, L., Feng, J.: Understanding the computer skills of adult expert users with down syndrome: an exploratory study. In: The Proceedings of the 13th International ACM SIGACCESS Conference on Computers and Accessibility, ser. ASSETS 2011, pp. 51–58 (2011)

14. Gómez, J., Alamán, X., Montoro, G., Torrado, J.C., Plaza, A.: AmICog–mobile technologies to assist people with cognitive disabilities in the work place. ADCAIJ: Adv. Distrib. Comput. Artif. Intell. J. **2**(7), 9–17 (2014)

15. Abinali, F., Goodwin, M.S., Intile, S.: Recognizing stereotypical motor movements in the laboratory and classroom: a case study with children on the autism spectrum. In: Proceedings of the 11th International Conference on Ubiquitous Computing (Ubicomp 2009), pp. 71–80. ACM, New York (2009)

16. Lloyd, J., Moni, K., Jobling, A.: Breaking the hype cycle: using the computer effectively with learners with intellectual disabilities. Down Syndr. Res. Pract. **9**(3), 68–74 (2006)

Evaluating Play-Personas of an Educational 3D Digital Game for University Students to Learn Portuguese as a Foreign Language

Roberta C.S. Salomão[1,2(✉)], Francisco Rebelo[3],
and Fernando Gamboa Rodríguez[4]

[1] Erasmus Mundus Grant in Engineering of Digital Media for Education,
University of Lisbon, Lisbon, Portugal
rocarolsalomao@gmail.com
[2] Universidad Nacional Autónoma de México, Mexico City, Mexico
[3] FMH – Ergonomics Laboratory – University of Lisbon,
Research Centre for Architecture, Urbanism and Design (CIAUD),
Lisbon, Portugal
frebelo@fmh.ulisboa.pt
[4] CCADET - Universidad Nacional Autónoma de México, Mexico City, Mexico
fernando.gamboa@ccadet.unam.mx

Abstract. This work is part of a user centered design development research with 106 international university students from 27 nationalities who were living in Brazil, Mexico and Portugal, which resulted in the game design and programming of the 3D Adventure Game to learn Foreign Languages "Back to the knowledge – the foreign student and the book of language and culture". With the proposal of exploring a new approach of learning a foreign language in autonomy through an educational game and its development according to the needs and expectations of its targeted audience; this two years project started in 2014 by conducting interviews for creation of university students' Personas. This article presents the last users evaluations in the perspective of Play-Personas. The quantitatively and qualitative analysis of ten students *play ways* compiled player preferences and behaviors in terms of interaction and navigation in five Play-Personas and allowed to contrast them to the initial Persona.

Keywords: Educational digital game design · Play-Personas · Foreign languages · Portuguese as a foreign language · University students

1 Introduction

During the process of educational games design, besides the main challenge of balancing fun and learning [1, 2] and proposing high quality content in one significant approach [3], there is as well a challenge to adapt story, environment, mechanics (interactions) and learning content to the largest range of users as possible part of the targeted audience, embracing variety of users preferences [4, 5]. Once established the main goals of the game according to the audience; the game gender definition, the story choice, scenarios and mechanics should be based on real user information.

© Springer International Publishing Switzerland 2016
A. Marcus (Ed.): DUXU 2016, Part II, LNCS 9747, pp. 198–207, 2016.
DOI: 10.1007/978-3-319-40355-7_19

The methodology of Personas [6–8] constructed from potential user's interviews is a possibility to guide the development. The comparison between Play-personas originated from users evaluation of final product with Personas previously created allows verifying the robustness of those Personas along with the game's degree of adaptation to the variety of user-players. Since players not only follow rules, but constantly push against them, testing and demanding more from the system and that there is never just one game (as players experience it differently [9]); play-Personas is one important source for game design improvement and adaptation. Considering the design of educational digital games to learn languages, the 3D environment is one lever to promote the environmental – interactive storytelling [10, 11] and embodied learning [12], favoring learning in context. The player has the possibility of attaching words and expressions to actions, goals and dialogues [1], to see the consequences of his actions and to relate them to environment [13, 14]. In addition, player has the possibility to have the help of spatial memory related to the story when remembering certain content. Context in communication in real life can be defined as what is contained in this scenario: people, dialogues, gestures and the implicit cultural knowledge shared by agents [1]. Making a parallel with a game, it is possible to understand that each scenario of a game: part of the story in one specific environment with its mechanics provided by the system, with characters actions and dialogs, managed by the rules of the game, is a different context. In a foreign language learning game, this context should be as close as possible to the real use of the language to be learned [15], while understanding real not as necessarily a realistic game, but as a source of information able to be used in the real life. To evaluate the adequacy of educational content and missions, potential users' game evaluations are one important source of information [16] as well as the definition of patterns and identification of players' behaviors and preferences.

1.1 Play-Personas

Play-Personas are the models of players created from the evaluation of real users playing experiences. For their construction, players are observed and patterns are identified in terms of players' navigation and their interaction with game mechanics. Temporal and spatial criteria are some of the metrics used [4]. In the case of educational games, the interaction related to learning content of each different context presented is also analyzed.

2 Methodology

According to principles of Research Design in Education [17] and User Centered Design [18, 19], during all game design process of the 3D Adventure Game "Back to the knowledge the foreign student and the book of language and culture", university students contributed voluntarily to the project, totalizing 106 university students from 27 nationalities who were living in Brazil, Portugal and Mexico. After defining Personas to guide the design process [20], narratives creation, establishment of pre requirements [21], game design, programming and usability and user's experience evaluations; real users playing performances/experiences were analyzed. Ten (10) players, students of Universidad Autónoma de Mexico – UNAM were chosen from the targeted audience (university students Spanish speakers) and then observed. The invitation was made at Language Center of UNAM and at CCADET of UNAM. They were invited to play the game for an average of one and a half (1.5) h in one monitored room. Before the evaluation, they had to complete a consent and a user profile form. Results were analyzed quantitatively over 111 questions of the 10 game missions with metrics set as either right/wrong/wrong answers followed by second try/absence of answers. Scenarios were compiled based on screens' video recording, aiming to verify navigation behaviors. The qualitatively study was based on after game-playing interviews in order to identify preferences in terms of game interactions-mechanics proposed. Questions were open: "How was the play experience?", "What are the positive aspects of the game?", "What are the negative aspects of the game?", "Do you have any suggestion?". Interviews were transcribed and content analyzed in order to identify most mentioned items.

2.1   Participants

Students were on average 27,9 years old, five (5) male, five (5) female. Five of them had studied Portuguese as a Foreign Language during one semester at the Language Center from UNAM and self-evaluated themselves as "basic level knowledge of the language" while the remaining five (5) affirmed had never studied Portuguese in a formal way before. Out of the last five (5), four (4) of them self-evaluated themselves as without any knowledge of the language and one (1) as "basic level of the language" (learned Portuguese in an informal way with online apps). In regards to their playing digital games habit, one (1) was not used to play digital games, one (1) played occasionally and the others were considered familiar to digital games. Classification was as follows: almost never/2 or 3 times per month/once a week/2 or 3 times a week/daily.

In resume, students profile were: Student 1 (S1)- 37 (Age), female, bachelor in literature, studied Portuguese, not used to play digital games; S2- 24, female, bachelor in biology, studied Portuguese, played digital games 2 or 3 times per month; S3- 24, male, bachelor in mechanical engineering, didn't studied Portuguese, played digital games once a week; S4- 36, male, bachelor in psychology, studied Portuguese, played digital games daily; S5- 23, male, bachelor in biology, studied Portuguese, played digital games 2 or 3 times per week; S6- 25, female, bachelor in computer science, didn't studied Portuguese, played digital games once a week; S7- 29, male, bachelor in computer science, didn't studied Portuguese, played digital games once a week; S8- 25, female, bachelor in mechanical engineering, didn't studied Portuguese, played digital games 2 or 3 times per week; S9- 22, male, bachelor in mechanical engineering, didn't studied Portuguese, played digital games daily; S10- 34, female, master in dance, studied Portuguese, played digital games once a week.

3   Results and Discussion

3.1   The Game Design

In brief the game design (which will be detailed in another article currently in progress), allows the understanding of the evaluations, where 111 questions with multiple choice (between two and three options) and word/sentences typing answers were part of 10 story main missions-scenarios. According to the persona chosen, the game was built to international students Spanish speakers without previous knowledge of Portuguese or basic level of the language who aimed to learn Portuguese in autonomy (self-directed learning). The 3D environment is the city of Sao Paulo, Brazil including a university campus. The main missions were: 1- Rent a room, Interact with characters; 2- Discover objects in the house, find objects with audio, respective written name and cultural information by clicking on them; 3- Arrive at university's library, interact with characters, ask for directions, check the map, check text with direction instructions; 4- Discover following missions by texts interpretation, read texts at library and answer questions about their meaning; 5- Buy food and drink at the Coffee Shop, interact with characters; 6- Find street signs, walk around to find street signs and interpret them; 7- Find advertisements, walk around to find advertisements, texts interpretation; 8- Go back home, find the way back to home; 9- Find out the meaning of the message left by flatmates, words used to order food and drinks and interpretation of informal expressions; 10- Arrive at the bar, interact with characters, ask for directions, informal expressions interpretation.

3.2   Patterns Definitions

Patterns to guide both quantitative and qualitative analysis and to build Play-Personas were chosen: habits of playing digital games and existence or not of previous knowledge of Portuguese. This choice aimed to verify the adaptation of each game mission to students from those groups given that one big challenge in the design process of educational games to learn languages in autonomy is to balance content to students without previous knowledge of the language and, in the present research, as well without making it less challenging to students with basic level of the language.

3.3   Quantitative Analysis

To identify the navigation experience of each student, the percentage of questions' completion of each mission was analyzed. Results are in Table 1.

According to the habits of playing digital games, students with highest percentage of game completion played digital games either daily or 2/3 times per week. Student 1 (S1) with lowest level of total game completion (didn't do 3 of the missions proposed) didn't have the habit of playing digital games. S4 with a daily habit of playing digital games and S7 with habit of playing once per week discovered in the final mission unexpected ways to complete the mission, without doing all activities required (*pushing against the system* [9]). Students 3, 6 and 10 didn't do mission 3 because they

Table 1. Navigation – percentage of completion/student per mission

	M1 %	M2 %	M3 %	M4 %	M5 %	M6 %	M7 %	M8 %	M9 %	M10 %	Total %
S1	60	100	100	100	0	0	0	100	100	100	66
S2	67	100	100	100	100	54	72	100	100	100	89
S3	67	100	0	100	0	69	100	100	100	100	74
S4	100	100	100	100	100	100	100	100	100	20	92
S5	67	100	100	100	100	100	88	100	100	100	95
S6	100	84	0	100	100	100	100	100	100	80	86
S7	100	100	100	100	100	100	72	100	100	20	89
S8	67	100	100	100	100	100	88	100	100	100	95
S9	33	100	100	100	100	85	100	100	100	100	92
S10	67	95	0	100	100	100	100	100	100	100	86
Total	73	98	70	100	80	81	82	100	100	82	

chose a second way to solve this mission, already expected in the game design (not asking characters but following text instructions or checking the map). The design of mission 1 also wasn't linear, giving liberty to players, which explain the variety of completion percentages. S3 didn't see the Coffee shop or wasn't interested in doing this activity. As the game has predominantly a linear story, 100 % of the students did mission 9. Also since this mission (9) had the highest level of difficulty, some students tried to guess the answer and therefore it took longer than expected. One (1) student without previous knowledge of Portuguese asked to the evaluation monitor to pass to the following mission. To evaluate the level of difficulty of each mission and its relation with previous knowledge of Portuguese, Figs. 1, 2, 3, 4, 5, 6, 7, 8, 9 and 10 were created with the quantity of right/wrong/wrong answers followed by second try/absence of answers for each students over the 10 missions.

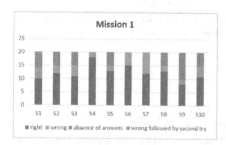

Fig. 1. Game metrics per student mission 1. (Color figure online)

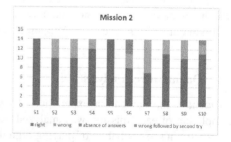

Fig. 2. Game metrics per student mission 2. (Color figure online)

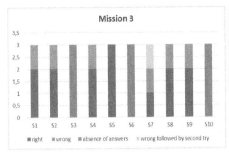

Fig. 3. Game metrics per student mission 3. (Color figure online)

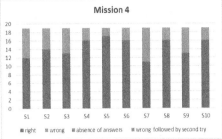

Fig. 4. Game metrics per student mission 4. (Color figure online)

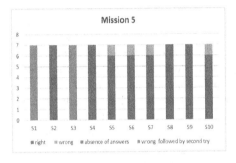

Fig. 5. Game metrics per student mission 5. (Color figure online)

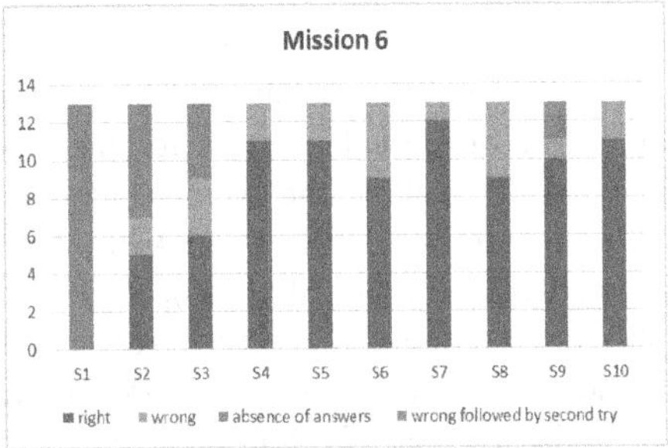

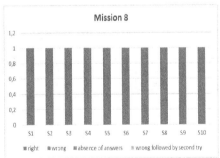

Fig. 6. Game metrics per student mission 6. (Color figure online)

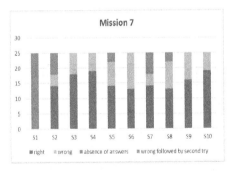

Fig. 7. Game metrics per student mission 7. (Color figure online)

Fig. 8. Game metrics per student mission 8. (Color figure online)

S6 and S7, without previous knowledge of Portuguese made more errors than other students, as it is also shown in Table 2, with the comparison of percentage of the players' right answers to the average percentage of right answers per missions.

Fig. 9. Game metrics per student mission 9. (Color figure online)

Fig. 10. Game metrics per student mission 10. (Color figure online)

Analyzing results from the graphs and Table 2, it is possible to observe that the percentage of correct answers for S4, with previous knowledge of Portuguese, was always equal or above the average. When comparing students with previous knowledge of Portuguese S1 (1), S2 (4), S4 (0), S5 (3), S10 (2), and students without previous knowledge S3 (3), S6 (6), S7 (6), S9 (3), it is possible to see (highlighted in the table in grey) results where the percentage is lower than the average from students of the second group. S8, who learned Portuguese in a non-formal way, had less answers below the average (2) than students of the second group. With exception of S7 in mission 3, percentages of correct answers were not lower than 50 %, indicating that students from both groups were able to do activities and missions proposed, leading to a consequently initial adaptation of the game design to both groups.

Table 2. Percentage of right answers per mission

	Portug uese	M1 %	M2 %	M3 %	M4 %	M5 %	M6 %	M7 %	M8 %	M9 %	M10 %
S1	yes	89	84	67	63	---	---	---	100	100	80
S2	yes	80	74	67	74	100	71	78	100	75	80
S3	no	80	68	---	68	---	67	72	100	100	80
S4	yes	87	89	67	84	100	85	76	100	100	---
S5	yes	80	100	100	89	86	85	64	100	50	80
S6	no	73	75	---	84	86	69	52	100	100	75
S7	no	60	53	33	58	86	92	78	100	75	---
S8	Non formal	80	84	67	84	100	69	59	100	100	80
S9	no	80	74	67	68	100	91	64	100	100	80
S10	yes	80	78	---	84	86	85	76	100	75	80
Avera ge		79	78	67	76	93	79	69	100	87,5	79

3.4 Qualitatively Analysis

The content analysis of interviews showed cultural information presented in the game as the most positive aspect mentioned (mentioned by 6 students), followed by presence of informal expressions (by 5 students), street signs and advertisements interpretation (by 5 students), text interpretation of library books (by 4 students), dialogs with characters (by 3 students), audio presence in the second scenario-mission (by 3 students) and the purchase of typical food and drink at the Coffee (by 2 students). Negative aspects and suggestions about missions and interactions were (A) the absence of possibility in other scenarios to interact to objects, hear audio and see written form of word as in scenario 2 (mentioned by 3 students - 2 with and 1 without previous knowledge of Portuguese), (B) the difficulty in mission-scenario 9 (by 2 students - without previous knowledge of Portuguese), (C) absence of audio in all of dialogs (by 2 students), (D) not many activities to write/type the answer (by 1 student - without previous knowledge of Portuguese), (E) many texts in the library (by 1 student - without previous knowledge of Portuguese) and (F) not much action in the second scenario (by 1 student - without previous knowledge of Portuguese, played digital games 3 times per week). Students who suggested the interaction of scenario 2 in other scenarios as well (find the object, hear its pronunciation and see the correspondent word) reinforce the premises of environmental storytelling and embodied learning in terms of memory relating to environment and story. From the group of students who played the game, it was possible to identify five play-personas. Play-Persona 1: not used to play digital games, with previous knowledge of Portuguese (formal learning); Play-Persona 2 and 3: used to play digital games 3 times per month, with/without previous knowledge of the language. Play-Persona 4 and 5: used to play digital games 2 or 3 times per week/daily, without previous knowledge of Portuguese. A Play-Persona not used to play digital games and without previous knowledge of Portuguese wasn't in the sample. Characteristics of Play-Personas identified were the appreciation of cultural information, informal expressions, original texts interpretation (street signs, advertisements and library books), dialogs with characters, audio and typical food vocabulary. When comparing those aspects to the pre-requirements of the game design (discovered during the construction of Personas at the beginning of its research [20]), it was possible to find the same items (items in bold in the below text): For a Spanish speaker university student persona, the most important Portuguese learning content are: ask for directions, ask questions, buy, **food vocabulary**, expressing plans, house vocabulary, **informal vocabulary and typical informal expressions**, vocabulary to rent a room, phonetics. The learning strategy for this persona was to **learn with authentic audio and original texts**. The negative aspects and suggestions identified will help the improvement of game design such as changing the design of the Coffee Shop to make it more attractive/visible, moving from a linear to a nonlinear story in mission 4 and 9, (allowing students with no previous knowledge of Portuguese to choose the missions' order or to avoid them), adding more audio and more exercises of writing/typing.

4 Conclusion

The persona created at the beginning of this research, from qualitative content analysis of 30 interviews with potential users (international students who were living in Brazil and Portugal interested in learning Portuguese as a Foreign language) had elements repeated as most mentioned items in the content analysis by the group of students (Spanish speakers interviews living in Mexico) who evaluated the final game version. This evidence indicates the robustness of the Persona that guided the game design. From quantitatively and qualitatively game-playing evaluations, it was possible, among others, to observe lower total missions completion percentage by Student 1 (S1) who hadn't the habit of playing digital games, decided to reduce his game experience by not doing the middle missions. S1 indicated as well, during the interview, the belief that the game could help with learning Portuguese in parallel of classes. The other students indicated they could learn with the game in autonomy if repeating it and continuing the levels, without the necessity of classes. This difference in opinions is one interesting association between digital games playing habits and the belief about teaching/learning capacity of digital educational games. The evaluations showed that missions were adapted to both students' groups with and without previous knowledge of Portuguese independent of their digital game playing habits and indicated suggestions of improvements in the game design.

References

1. Gee, J.P., Hayes, E.R.: Language and Learning in the Digital Age, 1st edn. Routledge, New York (2011)
2. Winn, B.M.: The design, play, and experience framework. Handb. Res. Eff. Electron. Gaming Educ. **5497**, 1010–1024 (2007)
3. Hense, J., Mandl, H.: Learning in or with games? Quality criteria for digital learning games from the perspectives of learning, emotion and motivation theory. In: CELDA, pp. 19–26 (2012)
4. Tychsen, A., Canossa, A.: Defining personas in games using metrics. In: Proceedings of 2008 Conference on Future Play: Research, Play, Share - Future Play 2008, p. 73 (2008)
5. Canossa, A., Drachen, A.: Play-personas: behaviours and belief systems in user-centred game design. In: Gross, T., Gulliksen, J., Kotzé, P., Oestreicher, L., Palanque, P., Prates, R. O., Winckler, M. (eds.) INTERACT 2009. LNCS, vol. 5727, pp. 510–523. Springer, Heidelberg (2009)
6. Cooper, A.: The Inmates are Running the Asylum. Macmillan Publishing, Indianopolis (1999)
7. Miaskiewicz, T., Kozar, K.A.: Personas and user-centered design: How can personas benefit product design processes? Des. Stud. **32**(5), 417–430 (2011)
8. Queirós, A., Cerqueira, M., Martins, A.I., Silva, A.G., Alvarelhão, J., Teixeira, A., Rocha, N.P.: ICF inspired personas to improve development for usability and accessibility in ambient assisted living. Procedia Comput. Sci. DSAI 2003 **27**, 409–418 (2014)
9. Klopfer, E., Osterweil, S., Salen, K.: Moving learning games forward. Flora **3**, 58 (2009)
10. Jenkins, H.: Game design as narrative architecture. Comput. (Long. Beach. Calif.) **44**(3), 118–130 (2004)

11. Crawford, C.: Chris Crawford on Interactive Storytelling. New Riders, Indianapolis (2012)
12. Gee, J.P.: What video games have to teach us about learning and literacy. Comput. Entertain. **1**(1), 20 (2003)
13. Biesta, G.: Pragmatism's contribution to understanding learning-in-context. In: Edwards, R., Biesta, G., Thorpe, M. (eds.) Rethinking contexts for learning and teaching: communities, activities and network. Routledge, New York (2009)
14. Russel, D.R.: Texts in contexts: theorizing learning by looking at genre and activity. In: Edwards, R., Biesta, G., Thorpe, M. (eds.) Rethinking contexts for learning and teaching: communities, activities and network, pp. 17–30. Routledge, New York (2009)
15. Prensky, M.: Enseñar a nativos digitales. Ediciones SM, Naucalpan (2011)
16. Nacke, L.E., Drachen, A., Goebel, S.: Methods for evaluating gameplay experience in a serious gaming context. Int. J. Comput. Sci. Sport **9**(2), 31 (2010). Darmstadt, Germany. http://iacss.org/index.php?id=96
17. Beck, D., Perkins, R.: Review of educational research methods in desktop virtual world environments: framing the past to provide future direction. J. Virtual Worlds Res. **7**(1), 1–27 (2014)
18. Norman, D., Draper, S.: User Centered System Design: New Perspectives on Human-Computer Interaction. Lawrence Erlbaum Associates Publishers, London (1986)
19. Chamorro-Koc, M., Popovic, V., Emmison, M.: Human experience and product usability: principles to assist the design of user-product interactions. Appl. Ergon. **40**(4), 648–656 (2009)
20. Salomão, R., Gamboa-Rodríguez, F., Rebelo, F.: Defining *personas* of university students aiming the development of one digital educational game prototype to learn Portuguese as a foreign language. AHFE, Las Vegas (2015)
21. Salomão, R., Gamboa-Rodríguez, F., Rebelo, F.: Diseño de un juego digital educativo para el aprendizaje autónomo del portugués como lengua extranjera. In: SOMI XXXII Congreso Nacional de Instrumentación, Durango, México. ISSN 2395-8499. Ref. Electrónica: FG-90 (2015)

Prototyping and Interface Design of an Automated Screening Test to Evaluate the Linguistic Processing Abilities of School Children

José Guilherme Santa Rosa[1(✉)], Tito Henrique Borges[1], João Bosco Santos[1],
Mário Sergio Filgueria[1], Thiago Oliveira[1], Leonor Scliar-Cabral[2],
Mauricio Martins[3], Antonio Pereira Junior[4], and Beatriz Stransky[5]

[1] Departamento de Design, UFRN, Natal, Brazil
jguilhermesantarosa@gmail.com, chitostito@gmail.com,
jbsantosxd@hotmail.com, mariofilgueira@gmail.com,
thiago.s.oli@outlook.com
[2] Departamento de Lingua e Literatura Vernáculas, UFSC, Florianópolis, Brazil
leonorsc20@gmail.com
[3] Departamento de Arquitetura, UFRN, Natal, Brazil
maurimartins@gmail.com
[4] Instituto do Cérebro, UFRN, Natal, Brazil
pereira@neuro.ufrn.br
[5] Departamento de Engenharia Biomédica, UFRN, Natal, Brazil
beatriz.stransky@ct.ufrn.br

Abstract. The performance of Brazilian students in reading tests, both national and international, have been worrisome lately. However, it is widely known that fluency in reading is essential for both personal growth and national development. In this study, we present a prototype of a digital system platform, based on a UCD (User Centered Design) approach, to detect language impediments that can negatively impact literacy acquisition in schoolchildren. This system is based on a battery of tests created earlier by one of the authors (Leonor Scliar-Cabral). The initial results indicate that this digital system has the potential to improve on the original tests battery, making it more effective and easy to deploy, with the promise to help improve the competence and reading fluency of Brazilian elementary school students.

Keywords: Prototype · Design · Ergonomy · Linguistic

1 Introduction

Brazilian students perform poorly in reading tests, both domestic and international (PISA - Program for International Student Assessment). Sadly, the most recent results from the PISA do not show a trend towards improvement and the number of low performance students is about half the sample [8]. Since poor reading performance has long-term negative impacts on both individuals and nations, something effective has to be done if the country wants to level the playing field for its citizens and allow the social

© Springer International Publishing Switzerland 2016
A. Marcus (Ed.): DUXU 2016, Part II, LNCS 9747, pp. 208–215, 2016.
DOI: 10.1007/978-3-319-40355-7_20

inclusion of traditionally marginalized sectors of its society. While the task is not easy, one alternative is to make use of new Technologies, such as digital games, to effectively engage children and teenagers during screening and intervention.

The main goal of this study is to develop a screening test to detect possible language problems of Brazilian schoolchildren to be assessed by specialists. The test is designed to be used in the school setting administered by teachers with the minimal amount of training. The test will be deployed in the form of a computational system based on commercially available portable operating systems, such as the Android or iOS systems. It's our intention that this system could be helpful in detecting possible language impediments that can prevent early literacy acquisition in Brazilian schoolchildren to be assessed by specialists. Specifically, we intend to, after the assessement by specialists: (1) allow the early identification of difficulties in language skills; (2) offer more detailed information to both parents and teachers about the nature and extension of these difficulties; (3) help designing individually tailored intervention measures. The system will be based on scientifically proven methods and will include a battery of 9 tests [2]:

(1) Auditory Reception: evaluates the perception of phonemic distinction of words;
(2) Phrase comprehension: evaluates working memory's capacity;
(3) Oral production of items: evaluates the precision of phono-articulatory expression;
(4) Oral production of phrases: evaluates fluency of oral production;
(5) Phrase pairing: evaluates perception of grapheme contrasts in minimal pairs;
(6) Grapheme-to-phoneme: uses pseudowords to evaluate understanding of relationships between graphemes and phonemes;
(7) Phoneme-to-grapheme: uses pseudowords to evaluate understanding of relationships between graphemes and phonemes;
(8) Oral reading: evaluates fluency;
(9) Reading Comprehension: evaluates understanding of the text.

The system will be composed of two interfaces: one for the children and another for the examiner. In the examiner's interface, test results will be displayed in real-time in graphic format and there will be the option to log comments. Depending on the individual scores obtained, the system will indicate whether the child needs to be referenced to a specialist for further professional evaluation. In the children's interface the tests will be deployed using a gamified narrative, with the help of cartoon characters.

The present work will describe the development of a paper prototype using the following techniques: (1) prototyping on paper; (2) high-resolution prototyping. The prototype will be used in a pilot experiment to obtain user feedback about the interface, including opinions about interaction dynamics and aesthetics. Paper prototyping is a variation of usability testing where selected users perform realistic tasks by interacting with a paper version of the interface that is manipulated by a person "playing computer", who doesn't explain how the interface is intended to work [6].

Following the definition of screen design and interface elements, the material was printed on paper and cut to allow the moderator to present the elements in response to the intention manifested by the participants while they pointed the paper elements with their index finger. The moderator acted as an "incredibly intelligent computer" [6], manipulating the printed elements in accordance with the rules, interaction models and navigation flow established in the project, i.e., responding to the user's commands and simulating screen transitions, dialogues, spoken words, sound elements and animation.

2   Methods

We used the User Centered Design (UCD) approach to design and prototype the application. The prototype will be tested with a sample of children with socioeconomic and educational levels similar to the target group. The prototype was designed in four steps: (i) identification of needs and requirements of the system; (ii) definition of characters and narrative; (iii) fluxogram and wireframes; (iv) prototyping. This workflow helped everyone in the creation team to better understand the system's goal, user specificities and even the difficulties encountered during implementation of the prototype.

3   Results and Discussion

3.1   Definition of the System's Requisites

First, children were observed while performing the original paper version of the test [2]. This was important to identify the main difficulties children faced during the test and try to present solutions to them in the interactive application. Sessions were video-recorded and the material was used in discussions with the team members (Fig. 1).

Fig. 1. Observation of a student performing a Scliar-Cabral test

In particular, the following steps during the application of the physical version of the test to the children were considered troublesome: (i) the examiner could be overwhelmed and confused while trying to manipulate test objects and simultaneously give instructions to the child; (ii) difficulty to maintain the engagement of the respondent during the time necessary to manipulate and arrange the test objects; (iii) difficulties associated with the filling of the forms with the test results; (iv) problems due to possible human error during all the above steps.

Based on these observations, the team established a strategy of putting the user (student) at the center of the design process. The first step was to guarantee the user's engagement by using the following approaches: (1) use of gamification strategies to create an engaging plot and characters in order to draw the children's attention; (2) make heavy use of multimedia resources to bring the characters to life. This second approach aimed at optimizing the system's dynamics, including the presentation of each test and data management, in order to avoid human error. The proposed solution was to develop the application in two layers: the first one would play out in the user's tablet, and the other in the examiner's, which in turn would be able to control and send instructions to the children's device. After definition of this basic architecture, we proceeded to create the game's plotline and develop the characters responsible for presenting the narrative to the children (item 3.2); establish the navigation Fluxogram and wireframes (item 3.3) and Prototyping (item 3.4).

3.2 Plotline and Characters

We created 9 short stories to accompany each test. The development of characters was based on a psycholinguistics approach [1, 2], with elements and strategies usually employed in videogames (gamification). The characters will interact with the children and follow them through the completion of the test. Besides the obvious purpose of engaging the children to perform the tests, gamification also helped with the delivery of clear instructions to the children.

The characters were based on animals found in the Brazilian fauna and with anthropomorphic characteristics. The goal was to make the characters come to life with characteristics which are harmonic with the goals of each test. The scripts were created to convey the feeling of an interactive challenging adventure. Below, we present the plots and characters used in the test battery.

1 – Bat photographer 1
Summary: at the beginning of the test, the children is presented to a child bat: Morce Guinho. He is a photographer, but his eyesight is not so good and he ends up mixing the photographs he just made after having a fruit for lunch. Guinho then asks the child for help, saying that he will say which object is in each picture and the child indicates which one it corresponds. After the task is done, Guinho thanks the child and go on to take other pictures.

Morce Guinho: *"Hi! How are you? This is a big forest, isn't it? I almost got lost taking my pictures after lunch and... I can't believe! I was so absorbed taking pictures that I ended up mixing them!... Listen, would you help me find and organize them? I don't see well and would be happy if you could help me."*

The pictures show up on the screen

Morce Guinho: *"It is very simple, I tell you what the picture is about and you point to the correct one. Then, I take it and put it in my backpack... Isn't it easy?... Shall we begin?"*

After the test

Morce Guinho: *"Gee, thanks! You helped a lot. I appreciated it. Now, I'll go back to taking my pictures. See you!"*

2 – Bat photographer 2

Summary: When he is leaving, the bat stumbles and fall to the ground (He is afraid of heights and avoids flying), spreading again the pictures that fall off from his backpack. Thus, the child will help the bat to reorganize his pictures, again. This time, however, he points to the picture and asks the child what is depicted on it. Then, he puts it back in his backpack. After it is finished, he thanks the child, again, and apologizes before returning to take pictures.

Morce Guinho: *"Look, a cardinal! It's being so long since... Ouch!"*

*The batch stumbles and falls to the ground. The pictures are shown flying around *

Morce Guinho: "I can't believe it! Again?! Oh, no! Now, I'll have to organize everything, again. At least you helped me before and I won't have trouble finding them... My glasses... I broke them! What's happening, today?! It's definitely not my lucky day. Look, since I can't see without my glasses, if I point to the pictures, would you tell me what they show?"

the test begins and ends

3 – Tamarin friends

Summary: While he is distracted taking pictures, the bat leaves its backpack open and a folder falls off spilling some photographs on the floor. Two tamarin monkeys, Dodô and Marrom, are observing the scene and ask the child to organize them back in the folder. After, the bat asks them to deliver the photos to one of his friends, a sea turtle.

4 – Parrot family– Papai Gaio and the little Aya

Summary: the father is teaching his daughter about phonemes, the units of sound that differentiate words. He then asks the child to help them by pronouncing words after removing their first phoneme. At the end, the father thanks the child for helping teaching his daughter.

3.3   Fluxograms and Wireframes

In this part, we defined the models of interaction of the application considering the two target layers of the system: child's and examiner's. Figure 2 shows an example of a wireframe - the schematic and visual representation of a screen, with its respective elements of interaction and information. In Fig. 3 we show an example of a wireframe of a screen from the examiner's layer, which contains the results and information regarding the performance of the child on Test 2 "oral production". This screen allows the recording and playback of the children's speech for offline analysis– a resource that was not available in the print version of the test. It should be emphasized that the interface allows the examiner to input his/her considerations about the child's performance and observations about eventual interferences during the test.

Fig. 2. Wireframe with Guinho character

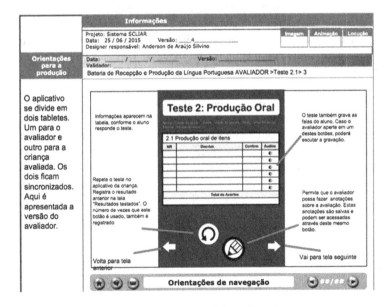

Fig. 3. Wireframe interface of the assistant's system.

3.4 Prototying

Initially, we developed a general wireframe of the examiner's layer – with schematics of the interface and its elements of interaction and information. After definition of this wireframe, based on the observations of the sessions with the children, analysis of the print version of the instrument (Paper Prototyping), we established the goals, restrictions and characteristics necessary to implement the application.

The paper prototyping allowed the team to establish the objectives and evaluate constraints and needs without having to devote many hours working with coding in a specific computer language.

From the prototyping sessions it was possible: (a) to redefine the position and size of certain elements on the screen; (b) to discuss the advantages and disadvantages of using specific interfaces elements; (c) to identify gaps in the consistency of the navigation and the microinteractions adopted by the interaction model.

4 Final Comments

Even though the print version of the Scliar-Cabral battery has been tested successfully before in several schools, we believe our system has the potential to bring considerable improvement to the test battery and help it being more effective. One crucial improvement is related to the engagement and motivation of the users with the help of gamification. Since videogames are very pervasive in the demography targeted by the system, the use of elements associated with game playing, such as interactivity with characters following a fictional narrative, has the potential to motivate the users and increase the odds of them successfully completing the test battery. This helps to improve both the sensitivity and specificity of the test. Besides, our system helps diminish the possibility of inadvertent errors by the examiner.

One important early decision in our efforts was to use a participatory design approach, seeking to include a crucial stakeholder, the child, in the design process. The reliance on high definition prototyping was time consuming, but gave the creative team a better comprehension of the desirable characteristics of the system. The next steps will include testing the paper prototype with schoolchildren of variable degrees of literacy, development of a high definition prototype with the full version of the system, including both the user's and examiner's systems, development of an artificial intelligence system to recognize and analyze oral production, and definition of distribution strategies.

References

1. Scliar-Cabral, L.: Princípios do sistema alfabético do português do Brasil. Contexto, São Paulo (2003)
2. Scliar-Cabral, L.: Guia Prático de Alfabetização - baseado em Princípios do Sistema Alfabético do Português do Brasil. Contexto, São Paulo (2003)

3. Nielsen, J.: Usability Engineering. Academic Press, Boston (1993)
4. Rogers, Y., Sharp, H., Preece, J.: Design de interação [recurso eletrônico]: além da interação humano-computador. Tradução: Gasparini, Isabela; revisão técnica: Pimenta, Marcelo Soares, 3rd edn. Dados eletrônicos. Bookman, Porto Alegre (2013)
5. Rosa, J.G.S., Moraes, A.: Design Participativo - técnicas para inclusão de usuários no processo de ergodesign de interfaces. Rio Book´s, Rio de Janeiro (2012)
6. Synder, C.: Paper Prototyping: The Fast and Easy Way to Design and Refine User Interfaces. Morgan Kaufmann, San Francisco (2003)
7. Eisner, W.: Quadrinhos e Arte Sequencial: princípios e práticas do lendário cartunista, 4ª edn. Editora WMF Martins Fontes, São Paulo (2010)
8. The Organization for Economic Co-operation and Development (OECD). Program for International Stuent Assessment (PISA). https://www.oecd.org/pisa/aboutpisa/. Accessed 15 May 2016

User Experience in the Era of O2O - Service Design Revolution of the Online Education

Ruixiang Shen[✉]

Baidu IxD, Beijing, China
shenruixiang@baidu.com

Abstract. With the high-speed development of China Internet and great impact of advanced worldwide design minds, Baidu's UED Department design work has developed from traditional interface design to product innovation design based on qualitative research. At the same time, we are carrying out experience measure strategy which is more efficient and more quantitative. To better explain the core concept "experience measure strategy", an application example is described in detail. "Service design" is mentioned and supported to be the key of future user experience in the time of O2O. Two interesting experiences are shared to back up a view that Service design is not only to design a specific "service", from a higher point of view, it should be a systematic product design, including brand, users, products and service, all these connections makes up into a new pattern of optimizing service value.

Keywords: DUXU in developing countries · Education/training for DUXU · Service design

1 Introduction

Based on years of design practices of Baidu products, this article discusses the importance of the experience measurement in the current Chinese Internet. An example is given for explaining how Baidu makes design innovation that is driven by data measurement. Moreover, it brings the thinking and inspiration of the design education in current China, as well as the value of Baidu's promotion of design education. This article sums up practical experiences on service design under China's O2O trend by means of innovative explorations in the area of design education. The following is the structure of this article:

1. User experience redefinition:Experience measure strategy
   (a) The Development of Baidu's User Experience;
   (b) The Evolution from Design to Experience;
   (c) The Application Example of Experience Measure Strategy - The Searching Revision of Baidu Chuanke (www.chuanke.com);
   (d) The future of user experience
2. Internet Trend in China: O2O Is the Trend
   (a) The Emerging of O2O Generation;

© Springer International Publishing Switzerland 2016
A. Marcus (Ed.): DUXU 2016, Part II, LNCS 9747, pp. 216–226, 2016.
DOI: 10.1007/978-3-319-40355-7_21

(b) Setbacks and Blocks of Design Education;
(c) O2O Revolution in Design Education;
3. The Future of User Experience: Service Design Revolution

2   User Experience Redefinition Experience Measure Strategy

2.1   The Development of Baidu's User Experience

Founded in 2005, User Experience Design Department of Baidu has constantly grown with the development of Baidu Company and China internet in the past decade. In the first 2–3 years, we were mainly responsible for visual graphics, such as sort of searching advertisements and business systems which are similar to Google Adwords and Baidu Ecom. The work value of User Experience Design Department was about basic design category, including graphic, color beautification, format design and so on. We also did parts of front-end development. At that time, we were named as "art worker", not designer (Fig. 1).

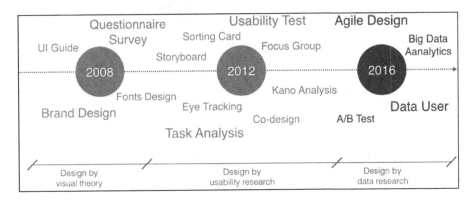

Fig. 1. The development process of user experience in Baidu

With the high-speed development of Baidu and great impact of advanced design concepts and minds from foreign countries (especially, Nielsen's Ten Usability Heuristics, Norman's Availabilities and the Design of Everyday Things), design work of User Experience Design Department has developed from traditional interface design to product innovation design based on qualitative research, which is not only including mature user research, market analysis, interaction design, visual design, but also involving product concept innovation and business program design. At the same time, we are carrying out experience measure strategy which is more efficient and more quantitative.

2.2   The Evolution from Design to Experience

What is experience measure strategy? To put it simply, it aims to use special automa-ticdatabase platform to analysis a large number of samples efficiently, guide and evaluate products' usability and innovativeness. Through this method, it is objective to reflect products' user experience in current data trend. In addition, compared with traditional qualitative measure methods, automatic database platform could reduce time-cost and resource investment. It is significant for Internet to reduce time-cost because internet may happen revolutions and information explosion in any time.

In Baidu, there are three automatic database platforms help designer to do product analysis and design Innovation. The most important platform (code name: Hunter) is used by User Experience Design Department, which could seasonable monitor users' behavior. Hunter's core system metrics containclick distribution of page elements, the number of clicks, sequence of clicks, browsing depth etc. Moreover, Hunter could make visual analytical graph (The image below is a thermodynamic chart of users' On Clicks, which introduces users' click distribution of page elements and product module) (Fig. 2).

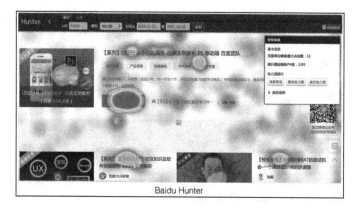

Fig. 2. The product interface of Baidu hunter

Besides, the other two user experience database platforms: Baidu Tongji and Baidu UFO. Firstly, Baidu Tongji platform has many data analysis functions, for example it could analysis the PV, UV, bounce rate, browsing time of full station. There are three important KPI involved with user experience: user source, distribution of user properties, degree of users' contribution. In addition, Baidu UFO platform is a on-line collection of experience advices and error feedback system. User could submit experience problems by feedback entrance of product to system server. And these feedbacks are collected key words and statistic analysis by UFO, which helps designer to improve product interaction and product tactic. Meanwhile, user experience researcher can select helpful and valuable users to do qualitative research (Figs. 3 and 4).

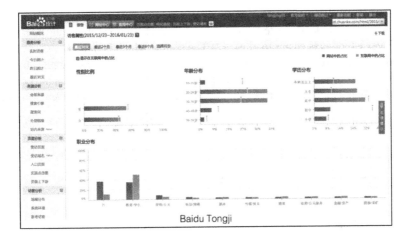

Fig. 3. The product interface of Baidu Tongji

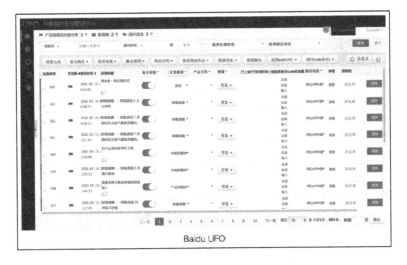

Fig. 4. The product interface of Baidu UFO

2.3 The Application Example of Experience Measure Strategy - The Searching Revision of Baidu Chuanke (www.chuanke.com)

To better explain experience measure strategy, there is an example about visual data directing revision design. Baidu Chuanke is one platform for sharing education videos. On this platform, users can search various interesting education content, watch on-line videos, study and discuss knowledge, submit assignments on-line. According to data accumulation in the past, it is can be see that there are more than 20 % users prefer to looking for content by searching entrance on the site. In September 2015, our designers used on-line data system of Hunter to check the data of search engine results page. From on-line data chart, designers found some serious experience problems: (1) Thermodynamic diagram of clicks indicated that headlineclick rate was much higher than that of course cover which was easier to click. (2) The course which is ranking first could not attract users intensively click it and its visual guide was too intense, while the other courses' click area were intensive. (3) Simple list type visual design made the order too important, which result in the click rate of ranking first course much higher than others (Fig. 5).

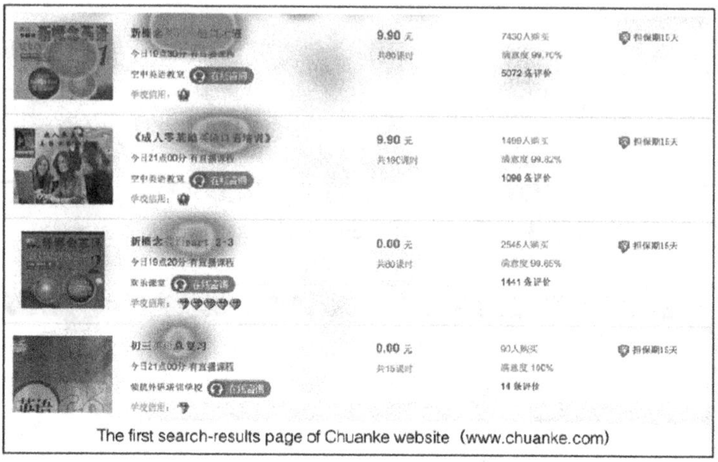

The first search-results page of Chuanke website (www.chuanke.com)

Fig. 5. The data of search engine results page of Chuanke website; the color represents the number of clicks (Color figure online)

According to the visual data monitoring, we accurately analysis user experience problems rapidly and output optimization scheme: (1) the design defect of the first question was that relevant elements used different design patterns. In view of gestalt principles, adjusting the positional relation between words and pictures could deal with this problem. (2) The second question was that one course had different types of information, which space distributions were too scattered and visual focus could not keep connection. Designers used card type design to order the title, price, satisfaction, the number of users by importance ranking to solve this problem. (3) It is easier to optimize the third question, based on using card type design to arrange information, designers make sure the rationality of card quantity and consider card quantity on the first screen (According to the experience, four cards in one row, two lines of card in one vertical screen) (Fig. 6).

2.4   The Future of User Experience

Could user experience become better in the future? In the view of the business value and Innovation thought created by user experience, I look forward to user experience. If you ask me how long time will new revolution of experience use, I could not answer this question accurately. However, design education may be one method to guide and

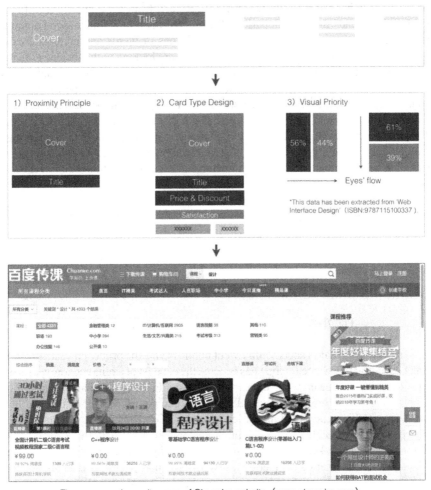

The new search-results page of Chuanke website (www.chuanke.com)

Fig. 6. The design idea of new search-results page

stimulate us in the experience future. We analysis the environment of China Internet and the situation design education, which might help us to touch experience future.

3 Internet Trend in China: O2O Is the Trend

3.1 The Emerging of O2O Generation

In the time of PC, the Internet companies in both U.S. and China shared a lot in common, e.g. product forms, business models, key technology. Many people think Google and Baidu are the same or twin brothers due to the similarity of their home pages. And a lot of people say that Baidu copied Google because Google was established before Baidu

(Google was established in 1998, Baidu 1999). In fact, from my point of view, this is the impact of "trend" in a certain period of time. Internet brought high-speed communication and explosive information, there are millions of words and pictures created every day. How to get access to the information you are looking with efficiency? In this case, the birth of searching engine is a corollary. Different user behavior and culture variation lead to different regional market environment. Therefore, the existence of similar searching engines like Baidu, Yahoo, Naver, Google, can be reasonable. There are many companies focusing on the same business, not only in searching field, social and e-commerce as well. In the time of PC, Internet companies in China are playing a role of learning, changing and catching up. Even thought we bring in new concepts from outside, we still pushing the pace of innovation and revelation in this region (Fig. 7).

Fig. 7. The screenshots of Baidu, Yahoo, Naver, Google

The decade after Baidu successfully went public is also the prime ten years of China Internet development. Since Internet has become the catalyst of China economy, in 2015, China government came up with "Internet +" strategy. In short, the goal is to encourage Internet enterprises to reform traditional industries and get rid of inefficiency and low-marketization. China traditional industries have two characteristics, which makes O2O fit all needs: at first, high cost of obtaining customers. Advertising investment from traditional industries takes up more than 50 % of Baidu's annual revenue, while their understanding of Internet stays superficial as website display pages stand for all. Suppose user A wants to learn English, if he or she searches key words "English training", and gets into a website of English Training School B, online service IM and promotion information show up, customer service Rep needs to use all the means to lead user to offline experience, and it is not 100 % certain that this user will actually pay. No matter how is the conversion rate, the expense of a big service team is a huge cost. Secondly, information asymmetry between online and offline, which is harmful to competitiveness of the product on marketplace. Suppose user A wants to apply for a 100,000 CNY loan, he or she needs to go to each bank and consults in person, then compares various offers. If user A can get on to a financial platform and search loaning plans accordingly, fill in and submit application forms online for banks to evaluate risks, and receive feedback plus loaning offers, at the end, user A can quickly go through decision making process, goes to the chosen bank offline and to finish last step of withdrawing money.

With the development of mobile end in the time of O2O, online service can solve multiple-scenario problems, improve conversion rate, match up offline service, and reduce operation cost while enlarging margin. The core value of O2O is to expand user behavior chain, and impact every steps alternately, to improve user agglutinant, to bring more "cross-subsidies" value, to build a certain product ecosystem.

3.2 Setbacks and Blocks of Design Education

We stepped into many design colleges and universities, such as Tsting hua University, the China Academy of Art, Renmin University of China, for discovering the design education was walking in front of the industry development, which would give us new surprises. However, design education in China is moving forward very slowly, there's a big gap between school education and needs from coperations. As I mention in the first part above, our professional knowledge structure is evolving with the developing and reforming of user experience. Nowadays, it's common of designers working in different disciplines from their college majors. Meantime, curriculum is mainly based on traditional graphic design and art education, theory is more than practice, especially lacking adaptive abilities. The urgent demand of user experience talent caused by Internet development makes this contradiction even more intense.

How about user-experience-oriented professional education? Will it fix the missing part of current design education? I'm afraid it only backfires. Tarena, a NASQ public company, its expertise is internet-related training, it is also the biggest design training organization in China. The main part Tarena's UI training class is Adobe, teachers train students how to use all kinds of design softwares with product case studies. In this way, Tarena attracts students with Adobe certification test. Mastering design software is only a basic technique of a designer, adaptive capability and professional enhancement cannot be acquired via short-term immersive and speculative training. A more severe question is the lectures in design training industry are not Internet practicers, do they really understand the true demand and changes of market (Fig. 8)?

3.3 O2O Revolution in Design Education

We have done a cool thing in 2015. We established online school "Baidu UE Classroom", to explore innovation of online education and promote reform of design training. Within a short time of 3 months, more than 40,000 students enlisted, this is the number of students in a tier-one China university. How did we accomplish this? First: the rising of online education platform. Baidu is an enormous platform product, Baidu Chuanke.com was given birth to focus on online education along vertical process. As C-end designers, we provide high qualify content, and complete teaching functions on the platform, which enables Chuanke.com to enclose user value loop with high speed and low cost. Second: shareable Economic Storm. There is a set of mature criteria of position ranking inside Baidu, it requires designers to sort out and summarize concepts, methods and innovation in work on annual base in order to participate job evaluation. Besides, Baidu offers designer improvement classes for the growth of design team. As long as we convert these useful materials into videos (record + live) and share on online platform, users can learn with us on Internet. Of course we are trying a deeper engagement solution, we are going to make a set of standards and matching system, open upload interface, to let designers get access to related content. It's a win-win for both designer

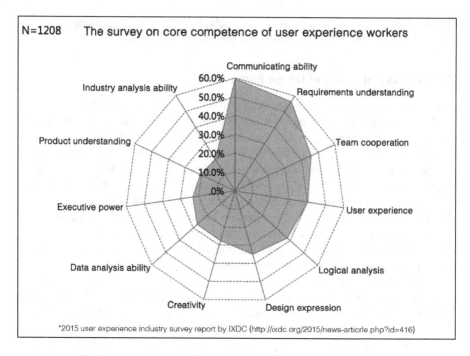

Fig. 8. The survey on core competence of user experience workers

and learners, they can optimize value of obtained knowledge and maximize market response. On the other hand, it urges designers to refine and systemize work experience. If we can achieve profit realization value based on this experiment, it would be a success of shareable economy (http://zt.chuanke.com/html/2015/daue/index.html).

But our breakthrough cannot change the whole industry fundamentally. According to the analyst above, traditional education won't collapse in one second and markets won't shuffle the cards automatically. "Everything real is rational", it's not always true. So we use O2O solution to extend user scenario, to find complementary points between online and offline. The biggest hardship of schools and training organizations is content, second teachers quality. Their biggest advantage is quality control of offline teaching, second immediate and customized teaching services. Baidu export personalized course outline and content, lectures from training organizations to teach, learners use online lessons for complementary review, or taking part in live class teaching by Baidu designers at spare time. To deliver class offline, to complete lessons online, add up into a comprehensive O2O education solution. Baidu has signed frame work agreement with several universities and training organizations, to export knowledge and capability models (divided into 3 levels) of various disciplines. Content is standardized into: key knowledge definition, explain sample, adaptive sample, combined knowledge sample, practical case study, etc. Modularized and standardized solution brings in better online design training, and easier to connect to offline services. For instance, we implant lots of case explanation in live lessons, C-end users can share more practical case study as well.

Fig. 9. The brand VIS of Baidu UE classroom

Baidu UE Classroom is inspiring and motivating to in both near and longer future. We will insist to input more resource, and striving to do a better job. What's more, the process of starting from zero, of building and furnishing this Classroom, is another surprising achievement along the way. We believe service design is the core motivation of O2O time by exploring profitable value of user experience and bringing in innovative design solutions. Service design is the "Destination" of user experience's path.

4   The Future of User Experience: Service Design Revolution

Service Design is not a new concept, it came up earlier in the 90s of 20th Century. At the beginning of 20th Century, a famous American user experience design firm IDEO promoted its methods and drove it into a system with methodologies like emotional design and experience design research. What I'm going to share now is basic experience, not specific application of methodologies. I cannot create a completely different way, my experience is based on the thinking of rebuilding product ecosystem by using service design, in this way to create new service touch points and paths, to search for new possibility of better service design.

Experience One: focus on brand, but focus more on brand operation. As we all know, service design is targeting to a multi-role and multiple scenario system, especially during the constant jumping between online and offline. Users with different natures will have differentiated feedback, emotions and feelings, no matter how, we need to ensure that all recognition of value is concentrated on the brand, rather than get diluted by complex scenario and multiple individuals. At the begging of Baidu UE Classroom, we spent big amount of time and money to establish our visual identify system (VIS), to set the tone of brand via basic colors, logo, slogan etc. and utilize the asset in all service touch point and operations. In order to upgrade service touch points into brand touch points, VIS is implanted both online and offline, from cover page of lessons, video posters, to campus campaigns, U fans open days, design experience classes, covering all the user interactive media (clicks, visual rest, conversation) (Fig. 9).

Experience Two: Channelization and Digitalization of User Information. It's necessary to build channels "arrive to" users, the ultimate goal off all design is to increase users' amount via channels. The premise of create better participatory service design is to get to know your users, be more accurate on users needs and feedback, use design to improve service quality and status. Digitalization stresses data dimensions, which helps to evaluate user loyalty, and to build user pyramid. We abandoned traffic and PV/PU as product benchmark from the very first day of UE Classroom, instead, we leverage numbers of learners (users that actually watched video), numbers of loyal users (users that collected schools), numbers of active users (users that comment on lessons) as three index, and we built three channels accordingly: in-station mail, Wechat public account, and QQ group. These three channels lead us to actual users, helps collect user feedback and suggestions, and validate new service and product design.

Service design is not only to design a specific "service", from a higher point of view, it should be a systematic product design, including brand, users, products and service, all these connections makes up into a new pattern of optimizing service value. Brand brings spreading of reputation, and attracts more users, while users come through an all-dimensional user-arriving channel. Participatory design will lead us to a treasure vault of business value by the path of consistent interactive product and service design.

References

1. Chuanke Website. http://www.chuanke.com
2. 2015 user experience industry survey report by IXDC. http://ixdc.org/2015/news-articrle.php?id=416
3. Zhang, F., Luo, Q., Gong, X.: Web Interface Design (ISBN 9787115100337)

Games and Gamification

Analyzing Playability in Multi-platform Games: A Case Study of the Fruit Ninja Game

Çakır Aker[1]([✉]), Kerem Rızvanoğlu[2], Yavuz İnal[3], and Alan Sarp Yılmaz[2]

[1] Faculty of Communication, Bahcesehir University, Istanbul, Turkey
cakir.aker@comm.bahcesehir.edu.tr
[2] Faculty of Communication, Galatasaray University, Istanbul, Turkey
krizvanoglu@gsu.edu.tr, alansarpyilmaz@yahoo.fr
[3] TÜBİTAK-BİLGEM Software Technologies Research Institute, Ankara, Turkey
yavuz.inal@tubitak.gov.tr

Abstract. Video games offer new perspectives for discussions and studies on user experience, which results in a change of the relevant terms in the context of gaming; replacing 'usability' with 'playability' and 'user experience' (UX) with 'player experience' (PX). PX can be inspected in various gaming platforms, which present diverse interaction methods through different peripherals, consequently uncovering the complex nature of video games. Therefore, it is critical to understand the nature of PX through user research. However, limited number of studies investigated PX and playability in detail in order to create an analysis framework for entertainment systems by referring to former UX and usability methodologies. Majority of those studies presented a set of playability heuristics on theoretical basis, which still required to be tested through empirical research in various gaming platforms. In this context, this study focuses on the qualitative analysis of multi-platform PX through a proposed playability heuristics framework derived from relevant literature. This study aims to test the proposed framework in a multi-platform game setting and thus seek ways to contribute to the establishment of a new comprehensive analysis framework to understand multi-platform PX. For this purpose, a qualitative multi-method study based on game platform diversity is designed to measure player experience with 8 users in two different gaming platforms which is based on mobile and full body gesture based interaction. Besides revealing the effect of "On-Screen" elements on PX such as game interface, mechanics and gameplay, the study also presents promising findings for the effect of "Off-Screen" aspects such as the environmental and social factors.

Keywords: User experience · Player experience · Usability · Playability · Gesture based · Game controllers

---

This study was realized through the coordination of Assoc. Prof. Kerem Rızvanoğlu with the support of Galatasaray University Scientific Research Fund (Project ID: 15.300.003).

© Springer International Publishing Switzerland 2016
A. Marcus (Ed.): DUXU 2016, Part II, LNCS 9747, pp. 229–239, 2016.
DOI: 10.1007/978-3-319-40355-7_22

1   Introduction

Technological improvements and novelties have not only provided us with new hardware options including mobile devices, bigger screens and diverse peripherals such as game controllers, but also inevitably led to the adoption of a more user-oriented approach to design more user-friendly platforms. From the first conventional keyboards to the advanced gesture-based interactive technologies, the need for a high-quality user experience has emerged and increased. In the last decade, in order to cope with this transition adopting a user-centered perspective, numerous studies have been conducted making the term user experience (UX) one of the pinnacles of technological evaluation and progression.

The ever-changing and rapid developments in technology can also be observed in the context of video games, which are considered one of the leading indicators of technological advancement. Video games offer new perspectives for discussions and studies on UX; however, conventional UX and usability methodologies are not sufficient to provide a full understanding of the video game experience, since they mostly focus on productivity in digital platforms rather than entertainment which underpins the gameplay experience. This major difference even leads us to change the terms we use in the context of gaming; replacing 'usability' with 'playability' and 'user experience' (UX) with 'player experience' (PX) [1, 2].

PX can be observed in different gaming platforms from consoles to mobile devices and from peripheral-based to gesture-based games requiring novel interaction mechanisms including different screens and peripherals, thus revealing a complex structure at various levels [2]. It is critical to understand the complex nature of PX through user research. However, there are only a limited number of studies investigating PX in detail and therefore, this study aims to create a framework for the analysis of this phenomenon based on previous work on usability and UX in the relevant literature.

The available studies on gaming experience only present a set of PX and playability heuristics on a theoretical basis; therefore, there is still a need to conduct empirical research collecting data from various gaming platforms. This study focuses on the analysis of multi-platform player experience based on a PX and playability heuristics framework derived from the literature on usability and UX. The proposed framework is also tested in a multi-platform game setting to seek ways to contribute to the improvement and enrichment of the framework.

2   Playability and Player Experience

Sánchez et al. (2009) proposed a new approach to PX with their playability model (PM) revealing the differences of evaluative goals in several specifications [4]. The term playability is used in the analysis of a video game or its design aspects. Sánchez et al. identified playability as, "a set of properties that describe the Player Experience using a specific game system whose main objective is to provide enjoyment and entertainment, by being credible and satisfying, when the player plays alone or in company" [6].

Several authors [e.g. 1, 3, 7, 8, 10] have offered numerous heuristic models to evaluate playability as well as genre-specific models such as heuristics for mobile games [3] or advanced table top games [9]. However, none of these models were validated through tests and/or comparison with other methodologies. We believe that these models need to be validated with user tests in multiple platforms. Usability focuses on utilitarian aspects such as task completion, elimination of errors, external rewards and reducing workload whereas playability is concerned with hedonic aspects such as entertainment, fun to beat obstacles, intrinsic rewards and new things to learn. [5]. Therefore, conventional usability approaches and heuristics cannot be used alone to describe PX.

The first set of heuristics specific to the structure and model of video games were created by Federoff [8]. To identify playability heuristics, Federoff gathered traditional usability heuristics from literature review, observed the game development procedures of a company and conducted interviews with the game team of the company. Focusing mostly on game engagement and storyline, Federoff suggested that video games have the following three features; 'game interface', 'game mechanics' and 'game playability'.

Another set of heuristics, Heuristics of Playability (PLAY), were proposed by Desurvire (2009) based on the evaluation of usability. The PLAY heuristics were developed with the help of game industry professionals and grouped into three categories: The first category, Gameplay, contained heuristics related to players' feel of control, challenges, goals, consistencies, balance and the notion of fun; the second was concerned with coolness, entertainment, humor and emotional immersion; and the final category, Usability and Game Mechanics, consisted of the heuristics on documentation, status and score, feedback, terminology, burden on player (as in not putting unnecessary burden on player), screen layout, navigation, error prevention and game story immersion [10].

Korhonen and Koivisto [3] developed another approach to PX, called 'Playability Heuristics for Mobile Games', which is closely related to other methodologies regarding playability. The authors proposed a model focusing on mobile technologies and their use in entertainment applications with an emphasis on mobility. They suggested, "The mobile context has some unique characteristics, which require special attention during the evaluation" and discussed these characteristics in detail. Korhonen and Koivisto supported the previous studies in the literature in that traditional usability heuristics lack comprehension and cannot be directly applied.

Even though Korhonen and Koivisto [3] indicated that usability heuristics cannot be applied to video games, similar to Sánchez et al. [1], they based their heuristics mostly on user interface. In addition, they pointed out that the former playability approaches were not feasible for mobile platforms and did not offer a novel perspective. Therefore, in their proposed heuristics model, in addition to gameplay and game usability, they included the mobility module. In mobile interaction, users often have environmental distractions such as lighting, weather conditions or noise. There can also be other people in the vicinity, affecting the gaming experience of users. Therefore, Korhonen and Koivisto identified three main mobility heuristics as 'the game and play sessions can be started quickly', 'the game accommodates with the surroundings' and 'interruptions are handled reasonably' [3].

All the above-mentioned methodologies and approaches are viable; however, one [11] has recently integrated the various definitions and categories of playability heuristics into the framework of 'playability'. The PM framework developed by Sánchez et al. provides an easy-to-manage and well standardized set of heuristics to understand PX and its relation with UX.

The PM framework is inspired from the three heuristics of usability; effectiveness, efficiency and satisfaction as well as their correlation with playability. As a result, seven different heuristics are proposed as follows: effectiveness, learnability, satisfaction, immersion, motivation, emotion and socialization.

3   Methodology

In this study, the framework of analysis is based on the PM framework of Sánchez et al. (2009, 2012) and the parameters of effectiveness, learnability, satisfaction, immersion, motivation, emotions and socialization. In the tests, we also utilized the mobility heuristics developed by Korhonen and Koivisto [3].

Since playability analysis is a complex process due to various perspectives, Sánchez et al. suggested "Playability Facets" into consideration, in which they used those facets to categorize different elements of video game architecture. Each facet of playability identify different attributes of playability. The notion of playability facets is to function as a tool to study playability across different video game elements. Along with other methodologies and categorizations, playability facets cover categories of interpersonal and intrapersonal playability.

Mobility heuristics devised by Korhonen and Koivisto [3], and Interpersonal and Intrapersonal Playability categories proposed by Sánchez et al. are relatively new to the literature (Fig. 1). We acknowledge that they have brought a novel perspective to the playability analysis. In our study, for a better analysis of playability, we introduce a comprehensive approach not only in terms of game features but also concerning the separate evaluation of various complex game elements assessing the parameters in two categories; 'On-Screen' and 'Off-Screen'.

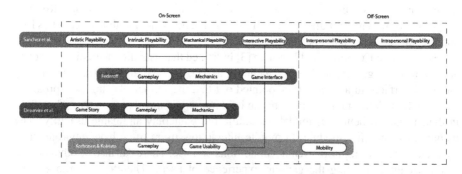

Fig. 1. Relations between video game elements for the analysis of Playability/PX

The notion of On-Screen represents the game elements that have been extensively examined in the literature, such as game interface, mechanics, gameplay and storyline. Off-Screen represents the aspects that have only been partially explored to date. These are the environmental and social factors affecting the video game experience of individuals. With the development of cross-platform and multi-platform games, there is a need to consider these social and environmental conditions for a better assessment of PX. The framework we propose allows us to holistically scrutinize all internal and external environmental elements of PX by incorporating the most recent yet incomplete approach by Sánchez et al. and the mobility heuristics developed by Korhonen and Koivisto. In addition, the division between the Off-Screen and On-Screen elements contributes to the comprehensive and complementary structure of this framework. In order to provide an in-depth analysis of multi-platform PX, two different gaming platforms were evaluated; a mobile device (HTC smartphone) and a video game console offering full body gesture-based interaction (Microsoft Xbox 360). The latter platform was selected for testing, not only because there are limited number of studies regarding the novel interaction possibilities that it provides, but the experience provided might offer physical, mental and social benefits and offer a transition from success oriented play to playing only for fun [13].

The qualitative differences between these two platforms were examined using the Fruit Ninja game which is available for both Xbox 360 and mobile platforms. The Fruit Ninja game was originally designed for mobile gaming platforms specifically targeting the mobile phone users. Therefore, the gesture-based version on the Xbox 360 console is only an adapted version of the original game. The game focuses on 'gameplay' rather than other game elements such as narrative. This property has been anticipated to facilitate the comparative data gathering and analysis during the study. Both versions for the platforms had the same game mechanics, in our case using an imaginary sword (finger in mobile version, gestures for the Kinect version) to cut objects. The similarity in gameplay and mechanics enabled us to observe and focus on the experiential differences caused by the gaming platforms.

For the tests, a 50 in. LED TV and Xbox 360 including the Kinect peripheral and a HTC 820 smartphone with a 5.5 in. screen were used. For a more realistic experience, a naturalistic test environment was prepared. Representing one of the major user segments in mobile and console game ecosystem in Turkey, the participants were eight university students from Turkey, dimidiated in terms of gender, with prior experience in using smartphone technologies and ages differing between 19 and 23. Majority of the subjects have played the Fruit Ninja game on mobile platform before and only one of them had prior, but limited experience with Kinect peripheral. The test procedure was based on three steps: In the first step, a semi-structured pre-test interview was conducted to collect demographic information about the participants, their gaming background and their experience in relation to using technology and particularly gaming platforms/controllers. The second step was the task observation phase, in which each participant was asked to play the Fruit Ninja game on an Android phone and Xbox 360 game console sequentially. We adopted usability testing for understanding and analyzing playability in detail which provided the possibility of witnessing specific quotations from players, which validate real experiences [12]. With the taskflow which reflects a default gaming experience and incorporate essential game attributes so that the players could have realistic experience of the game. Tasks were to enter the game selection screen (task 1), starting the game in classic mode (task 2), going back to the main menu via stopping/

pausing the game (task 3), re-entering game selection screen (task 4) and starting and playing the game in arcade mode (task 5). Behavioral data was collected via video recording and mobile eye-tracking equipment. The final step was a post-test interview. This last phase consists of an in-depth interview to understand and analyze player experience in detail. This phase also enabled an attitudinal analysis. The findings of the study were expected to provide an in-depth understanding of PX in two different platforms with a solid framework containing the parameters of usability and UX.

4   Results and Discussion

Effectiveness: The effectiveness of the platforms was evaluated in terms of how easy the game was to play and how much effort it required. All the players stated that the game was easier to control and the tasks were easier to achieve in the mobile platform. Figure 2 presents a comparison of the two platforms in terms of the average completion time of tasks for each player (Task 4 was removed from the dataset in the table since it was not included in the Android platform as a new action). The task completion times being less on the mobile device indicates that this platform better facilitated the achievement of specific goals, in our case, the tasks explained in the previous section.

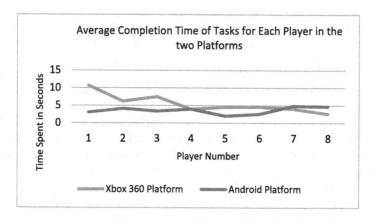

Fig. 2. Average completion time of tasks for each player in the two platforms (Color figure online)

The third task was about stopping or pausing the game and was not completed by any players in the Xbox 360 platform. This was expected to be found via the trial and error method but none of the actions of the players stopped the game from running. Some players were frustrated and gave responses such as "Do you really believe that we can find a way to exit this game?" (P1), "I think there is no option for it" (P1 & P2), "Would it stop if I turn my back to it?" (P3), and "Stop Kinect stop!" (P4). Participants also gave non-verbal reactions such as turning their back against the screen (P3), waving hands (P3) or even ignoring the task and keeping on playing (P6, P7, P8). Post-tests also showed that the players found the Kinect peripheral much more confusing.

Learnability: This refers to the player's ability to comprehend and master the game system and mechanics. The learnability heuristics are characterized by game knowledge, player skill, difficulty, frustration, speed of learning and discovery.

All the participants were able to understand the game mechanics and had no problems or questions about it. The action of slashing fruit came naturally to all players in both platforms (using arms gestures on Xbox and swiping fingers across the screen in the mobile platform). In terms of the player skills, in the Xbox 360 platform, some players experienced peripheral-related problems caused by system feedback. Even when the players were able to react quickly, the system received the input with a delay, which frustrated the players. However, the players tried to adapt to this defect during play and master the game.

The difficulty aspect of the game can be considered in direct relation to the game completion performance since the Fruit Ninja game is mostly based on game mechanics and dynamics. The mobile platform was found to be less difficult to interact with compared to Xbox. The players expressed their frustrations with the difficulty of playing the game as follows: "I needed to cut the fruit with my left hand!" (P1) and "I tried hard, but maybe next time!" (P7). Furthermore, they responded to negative situations by blaming themselves rather than the system although the main reason was the problems with the peripherals.

Regarding the interaction mechanics of the game in the mobile platform, the players mostly acted intuitively and considered it familiar due to prior experience with similar applications. As a result, the participants could quickly relate to the interaction methods. However, in the Xbox 360 platform, the players found the interaction methods to be new, which made space for discovery. During gameplay, some participants tried to improve their skills using different interaction methods such as making a door knocking gesture (P3).

Immersion: The immersion heuristics are concerned with conscious awareness, absorption in the game, game realism, control dexterity and socio-cultural proximity with the game. Players acted like 'ninjas' mimicking generic martial art movements (such as using the side of their hand to make a cutting gesture to score points). This demonstrated the realism aspect of the system. In other words, the Kinect peripheral provided the players with an opportunity to mimic gestures similar to the observed socio-cultural actions. Furthermore, environmental distractions such as other people talking in the room and noise from the street allowed us to observe some players losing their concentration while some others taking no notice of what was going on in their surroundings.

In the study, the players seemed to be under stress when playing the game on Xbox 360. Unlike the mobile platform, many players tended to react anxiously to the loading screens of the Xbox 360 system, biting their nails and/or loosing focus. However, few players responded in the exact opposite way, enjoying the company of the other participants and even dancing during the loading of the game. Therefore, it can be concluded that in the Xbox 360 platform, there is a certain degree of correlation between social capabilities and immersion in the game.

Satisfaction: The satisfaction heuristics refer to the gratification or pleasure derived from playing the game. It is characterized by game fun, disappointment with content and attractiveness. During post-tests, the majority of the players stated that they would like to play the game again. Players who preferred Xbox 360 considered this platform to be more fun to interact with due to the novel interaction methods and the bigger screen offered by the system. It was also observed that during gameplay, not only the player but also the other participants had fun since they enjoyed watching or commenting on the active player's effort. This finding may be evaluated in the context of sociability. In terms of aesthetics and content, both platforms offered very similar aspects, rendering it impossible to make a comparison between the two.

Motivation: The results regarding motivation give an idea about the game character-istics prompting the player to undertake and continue to perform specific actions until they are completed. The motivation heuristics are characterized by encouragement, curiosity, players' self-improvement and the diversity of game resources. In the current study, six players were eager to play the game again after the tests. The only reason for the loss of players' motivation and encouragement was the errors and unresponsiveness of the system which mostly occurred in the Xbox 360 platform. On the other hand, playing in front of other participants increased the motivation to play the game again.

The players were mostly responsive to the different types of fruit appearing on the screen when playing the game on Xbox 360. The players were curious about how the Kinect peripheral worked, experimenting with several different gestures to achieve the goals and asking other participants about their opinions. However, to play the mobile version of the game, the players only had to swipe their fingers across the screen.

Emotion: The emotion heuristics indicate the players' involuntary impulses in response to the stimulus of a video game. The characteristics of emotion are player reaction, game conduct and sensory appeal for game elements. The emotion heuristics are analyzed via observation. The players who played the Fruit Ninja game before tended to get more excited when they realized that they could play the game using the Kinect peripheral but after experiencing certain problems with the platform, there was a signif-icant loss of excitement among these players.

In the classic mode of the game, when a big fruit appeared on the screen (as an object to be slashed), the players reacted with enthusiasm, even yelled. One player got so excited that she accidentally pressed the volume button of the mobile phone just after seeing a bigger fruit appearing on the screen. Such actions are examples of impulsive reactions to the given stimulus. In both platforms, the players had fun and control over the game in general and clearly understood the objectives. In the Xbox platform, the participants were more responsive to the actions of the active player and their reactions were also louder when the active player made a mistake.

Socialization: The socialization heuristics refer to the set of attributes, elements and resources that promote the social dimensions of the game experience in a group scenario. They have the characteristics of social perception, group awareness, personal implica-tion, sharing of social resources, communication techniques and interaction rules. In this study, the players were in constant social interaction during the tests since they were allowed to watch each other play and talk during gameplay. This was to observe the social interactions and provide a natural environment to conduct the tests. In addition, we had the chance to explore whether there were any differences between the two platforms in terms of the socialization aspect.

The observations and interviews showed significant differences between the two platforms with Kinect providing a significantly more sociable environment. In the Xbox 360 platform, the players were able to comfortably watch and comment on each other when playing whereas the mobile platform rather isolated the active player. The Xbox 360 platform was observed to encourage group awareness more than the mobile platform. In Xbox 360, at first, the players were competitive but then they quickly shifted to a more cooperative communication resulting in increased personal implication, group awareness and sharing of social resources. Some players shared their ideas about their interaction with Kinect, asking for other participants' help to discover more features of the system. For instance, one player asked the spectators, not the test supervisors, whether he had made a mistake saying, "did I press the wrong button?" (P1). Even though the active and passive players could watch and interact with each other as a group also in the mobile platform, they continued to talk about the Kinect peripheral during the mobile test and how they would try to interact with it next time. In addition, the bigger screen offered by the Xbox 360 platform made it more comfortable for the other players to watch the active player during gameplay.

Mobility: In several occasions, in the Xbox 360 platform, the Kinect peripheral needed re-calibration, significantly delaying the start of the game. These calibration problems also caused errors in the system response such as the game starting itself and/or receiving wrong input during gameplay. The length of time the loading screen was displayed was similar in both platforms. Regarding the game accommodation with the surroundings; circumferential elements such as lighting or outside noise affected the game experience in the Xbox 360 platform more than in the mobile platform.

The Kinect peripheral needed to be precisely setup to work flawlessly and even then, caused several problems during the tests since the natural light in the room changed from time to time. Having other players in the vicinity also had an adverse effect on some players, causing them to lose concentration as explained in the immersion heuristics section. However, during the mobile platform tests, the players were also distracted by other players in the vicinity when they heard them talk to each other. This was not particularly a problem for the Xbox 360 platform since all the players watched the game being played and provided feedback to the active player. In terms of interruptions being handled reasonably; the mobile platform was easy to pause and allowed the players to easily go in and out of the game as opposed to the Xbox 360 platform in which none of the players were able to stop or pause the game when asked.

5   Conclusion and Future Work

This study analyzed multi-platform PX based on a playability heuristics framework derived from the literature on usability and UX. The proposed framework was tested on the same game in two different platforms to seek ways to contribute to the enrichment and improvement of the existing PX frameworks. Based on the results, it can be concluded that the players were glad that they experienced playing the game on Xbox 360; however, they lost interest in the game due to the playability problems they encountered. At the end of the tests, most players stated that they preferred to play the game on the mobile platform rather than on Xbox 360 with the Kinect peripheral.

Despite both platforms offering identical game mechanics, the players had problems reaching certain areas of the screen using the Xbox 360 system due to the bigger screen size. Furthermore, the big screen size negatively affected the players' reaction time to game stimuli. In terms of playability, the mobile platform was more preferable in general but the novelty of the peripheral included in the Xbox 360 platform enhanced the experience. The motivation heuristics were improved since the peripheral encouraged the players to experiment with other possible interaction methods. The results on the immersion heuristics were better for the Kinect peripheral due to its intrinsic quality of rendering the player a direct input and increasing realism going beyond the limitations of the game.

The results on the socialization heuristics indicated that the Xbox 360 platform with a bigger screen size and the Kinect peripheral better enhanced the social experience. However, in terms of effectiveness, the mobile platform players achieved the goals faster and scored better. The Xbox 360 version of the game lacked the necessary tutorials and/ or indicators for players regarding some aspects such as pausing the game, thus resulting in frustration. The players stopped interacting with the game from time to time and therefore lost interest in the game. The Kinect peripheral and the bigger screen size in the Xbox platform allowed more social interactions during and even after the tests. In addition, the interaction problems and system errors did not affect the socialization aspect. With its quality of being new in terms of the interaction method used, the Xbox 360 platform caused more excitement at the beginning. The full body gesture-based interaction also enhanced the immersiveness of the game, allowing the players to role-play during the game. However, in terms of mobility, the Kinect peripherals were susceptible to interruptions and the environmental elements were less forgiving. Yet, none of the players were observed to leave the game atmosphere. We consider that games designed specifically for the Kinect peripheral would provide better PX compared to those adapted from the mobile versions.

In the development of the proposed framework, several methodologies were taken into consideration to form a feasible and comprehensive framework to better analyze and understand PX. In this study, we introduced a new framework in which we grouped the game elements into two as Off-Screen and On-Screen elements for a comprehensive and complementary analysis of PX. We found that the mobile heuristics were specifically identified for mobile games and platforms, yet there were limited number of heuristics regarding peripherals such as Kinect and console games that are significantly different in terms of the screen sizes and/or the environment they offer.

Future research is needed to identify interchangeable and specific modules of heuristics for specific platforms. There is also the need for comprehensive comparative studies to increase the generalization and validity of our results. In future work, we aim to conduct similar tests with a bigger sample size and in comparable environments to further analyze the proposed division of On-Screen and Off-Screen elements, placing a greater emphasis on the Off-Screen aspects of the experience.

References

1. González Sánchez, J.L., Padilla Zea, N., Gutiérrez, F.L.: From usability to playability: introduction to player-centred video game development process. In: Kurosu, M. (ed.) HCD 2009. LNCS, vol. 5619, pp. 65–74. Springer, Heidelberg (2009)
2. Pagulayan, R., Keeker, K., Wixon, D., Romero, R.L., Fuller, T.: User-centered design in games. In: Jacko, J.A., Sears, A. (eds.) The Human-Computer Interaction Handbook: Fundamentals, Evolving Technologies, and Emerging Applications, pp. 883–906. CRC Press Book, Hillside (2003)
3. Korhonen, H., Koivisto, E.: Playability heuristics for mobile games. In: MobileHCI 2006, Finland, pp. 9–16 (2006)
4. Sánchez, J.L., Simarro, F.M., Zea, P.N., Gutierrez, F.L.: Playability as extension of quality in use in video games. In: CEUR-WS (2009)
5. Lazzaro, M.: Game usability: advice from the experts for advancing the player experience. In: Isbister, K., Schaffer, N. (eds.) pp. 315–345. Morgan Kaufmann (2008)
6. Sánchez, J., Zea, N., Gutiérrez, F.L.: Playability: how to identify the player experience in a video game. In: Gross, T., Gulliksen, J., Kotzé, P., Oestreicher, L., Palanque, P., Prates, R.O., Winckler, M. (eds.) INTERACT 2009. LNCS, vol. 5726, pp. 356–359. Springer, Heidelberg (2009)
7. Desurvire, H., Jegers, K., Wiberg, C.: Evaluating fun and entertainment: developing a conceptual framework design of evaluation methods. In: Facing Emotions: Responsible Experiential Design INTERACT 2007 Conference, Rio, Brazil (2007)
8. Federoff, M.A.: Heuristics and usability guidelines for the creation and evaluation of fun in video games. Master of thesis, FUN in Video Games Thesis University Graduate School of Indiana University, p. 52, December 2002
9. Köffel, C., Haller, M., Heuristics for the evaluation of table top games. In: Evaluating User Experiences in Games, Workshop at the 2008 Conference on human Factors in Computing Systems (2008)
10. Desurvire, H., Wiberg, C.: Game usability heuristics (PLAY) for evaluating and designing better games: the next iteration. In: Ozok, A., Zaphiris, P. (eds.) OCSC 2009. LNCS, vol. 5621, pp. 557–566. Springer, Heidelberg (2009)
11. Sánchez, J.L., Vela, F.L.G., Simarro, F.M., Padilla-Zea, N.: Playability: analysing user experience in video games. Behav. Inf. Technol. **31**(10), 1033–1054 (2012)
12. Desurvire, H., Wiberg, C.: User experience design for inexperienced gamers: gap – game approachability principles. In: Bernaupt, R. (ed.) Evaluating User Experience in Games. Human-Computer Interaction Series, pp. 131–147. Springer, London (2010)
13. Mueller, F.: Evaluating exertion games. In: Bernhaupt, R. (ed.) Evaluating User Experience in Games. Human-Computer Interaction Series, pp. 187–207. Springer, London (2010)

Gamification Design Based Research on Fitness Mobile Application for University Students

Fengjiao Cai, Guanyu Dai, and Ting Han$^{(\boxtimes)}$

School of Media and Design, Shanghai Jiao Tong University, Shanghai, China
hanting@sjtu.edu.cn

Abstract. The assumed deterioration of the students' health conditions in many universities of China poses challenges for the future. The prevalence of students lacking exercise in the universities has increased dramatically in recent decades, leading to increased research interest in treatment and forestallment. Among these research, gamification has been studied as an obvious advantage in motivating attitudinal and behavioral change. This study explores the use of gamification when applied to a mobile application targeted at motivating university students to do more physical activity. This paper describes the foundations of a design framework used to integrate game elements to LOOP, a gamification-based application with LBS (Location Based Service) for smart phones. The system is explained in terms of the design framework and the findings of the experiment for usability. The purpose of this study is testing the first iteration of the application, exploring how different game elements would affect user experience.

Keywords: Physical activity · Gamification design · User experience · Enjoyment · Motivation

1 Introduction

1.1 College Students' Health Conditions

The Chinese Ministry of Education has hammered the great importance of students' physical health. However, under the intervention of the Ministry of Education, schools and other relevant departments, students in different grades vary in physical performance. The 2014 National College Health Assessment reports that the health conditions of primary and secondary school students is pretty satisfying, but that of university students is becoming ubiquitously poorer. The reason might line in that the various interventions are easier to be implemented in primary and secondary schools. Compared with juvenile school students, university students spend less time exercising vastly contrasted with sedentary activities. These results indicate that a high proportion of university students' physical activity levels remain below recommended standards. The survey shows that 84.16 % of university students spend less than one hour a day in exercising, 50.2 % of college students cannot meet current recommendations of the Ministry of Health (at least 6000 steps per day,the best for more than 10000 steps per day).

There is a close relationship between health and lifestyle. Studies have revealed that the five factors closely related with college students' health conditions are: diet,

© Springer International Publishing Switzerland 2016
A. Marcus (Ed.): DUXU 2016, Part II, LNCS 9747, pp. 240–251, 2016.
DOI: 10.1007/978-3-319-40355-7_23

exercise, sleep, health habits and leisure activities [1]. Considering the particularity of university life,physical exercise is the most proper aspect to be chosen to ameliorate by design and products. Many university students are inactive or irregularly active during their leisure time. Therefore, intervention strategies, for promoting lifetime physical activity among all university students, represent a major health priority. In view of the little possibility of forcing university students to take more exercise, products can be an innovative way to motivate them to be more physically active.

1.2 "Physical Activity" and "Exercise"

"Physical activity" and "exercise" are terms that describe different concepts. However, they are often confused with one another and the terms are sometimes used interchangeably. Physical activity is defined as any bodily movement produced by skeletal muscles that results in energy expenditure. Physical activity in daily life can be categorized into occupational, sports, conditioning, household, or other activities. Exercise is a subset of physical activity that is planned, structured and repetitive and has as a final or an intermediate objective the improvement or maintenance of physical fitness [2]. It is difficult for university students to cultivate the habit of exercise, but it is not that difficult to do some interesting physical activity every day or several times a week in their leisure time. Hence our study focuses on motivating university students to do more physical activity during their leisure time. Previous studies have shown that physical activity at moderate intensity gives people the happiest experience [3]. Brisk waling and jogging are of moderate intensity for university students (boys at 7 km/h, girls at 6 km/h) [4].

1.3 Physical Activity Confers a Positive Benefit on Health

Physical activity is a key ingredient to be healthy. The benefits and importance of physical activity have been well confirmed.

Over the past half-century, scientific evidence has continued to accumulate, indicating that being physically inactive leads to major negative health consequences throughout the lifespan [5]. Health promotion programs should target people of all ages, since the risk of chronic disease starts in childhood and increases with age [6]. There appears to be a linear relation between physical activity and health conditions, such that a further increase in physical activity will lead to additional improvements in health conditions [6]. Furthermore, routine physical activity can improve musculoskeletal fitness and there is increasing evidence supporting that enhanced musculoskeletal fitness is associated with an enhancement in overall health conditions and a reduction in the risk of chronic disease and disability [6].

Routine physical activity is also associated with improved psychological well-being (e.g. through reduced stress, anxiety and depression) [6]. It has been claimed that vigorous physical activity has positive effects on mental health in both clinical and nonclinical populations. The evidence also suggests that physical activity and exercise might provide a beneficial adjunct for improving self-image, social skills, and cognitive functioning, reducing the symptoms of anxiety and altering aspects of coronary-prone (Type A) behavior and physiological response to stressors [7].

Furthermore, the intensity of physical activity also has a close relation with one's mood. People are in better emotional state after doing physical activity at small or moderate intensity [3].

2 Gamification: An Overview

Recent years have seen a rapid proliferation of mass-market consumer software that draws inspiration from video games. Usually summarized as "gamification" which is defined as "an informal umbrella term for the use of video game elements in non-gaming systems to improve user experience and user engagement" [8]. One of the most popular uses of gamification is to transform a mundane, menial, or otherwise uninspiring task into one that engages users and actively encourages them to complete the needed task [9]. The use of video game elements to enhance the enjoyment of non-game applications dates back to research as early as the 1980s [10]. Companies have widely accepted and adopted gamification as a means to increase initiation and retention of desired behaviors [11].

2.1 The Application of Gamification

Adding game elements to an application to motivate use and enhance the user experience is a growing trend known as gamification [12]. There is increasing interest in the potential use of gamification as a means to motivate attitudinal and behavioral change. Sports and fitness seems to be an area where people have a hard time of motivating themselves in [13]. If we blend the cheerful nature of games with the boring exercising process, it will enlarge the enjoyment of the process.

Mobile phone technology has recently become an area of focus for disseminating health behavior change interventions [14–16]. This technology has been used to study several health topics like physical activity [17], diabetes self-management [18], and smoking cessation [19]. Third party applications, also abbreviated as apps, are software programs that serve to expand the utility of mobile devices. Within just 6 years, Apple celebrated its 50 billionth app download, with Google only trailing slightly behind with 48 billion as of May 2013 [22]. Health apps have also become a part of this market, with over 31,000 health and medical apps available for download [17]. With the blooming of mobile phone ownership and the number and complexity of health apps likely to increase, the potential for technology-based health interventions to impact populations is expanding in ways previously not possible [11].

Using gamification in health and fitness apps has become immensely popular, and it has been estimated that 60 % of health initiatives in workplaces now include gamification elements [20, 21]. Though there are thousands of downloadable apps with the presence of gamification in the Health & Fitness category on Apple's App Store,the goal of each application is similar: an attempt to promote and encourage physical activity. Despite the inclusion of at least some components of gamification, the mean scores of integration of gamification components were still below 50 % [11]. In this usage, game components such as a scoreboard, competition amongst friends, and awards and achievements are employed to motivate users to achieve personal health goals [9].

2.2 "Gamification" and "Games"

Games are certain products or services with pure purpose of entertainment. Gamification is the use of game design elements in non-game contexts [22]. Video games are designed with the primary purpose of entertainment and since they can demonstrably motivate users to engage with them with unparalleled intensity and duration, game elements should be able to make other, non-game products and services more enjoyable and engaging as well [23, 24]. Gamification uses elements of games for purposes other than their normal expected use as part of an entertaining game and gamification has been defined as a process of enhancing services with (motivational) affordances in order to invoke gameful experiences and further behavioral outcomes [25, 26]. The purpose of our design is to motivate university students to be more physically active and make the suffering running process more interesting and enjoyable. Therefore, LOOP can be defined as a gamification-based fitness mobile application.

3 Methodology Description

3.1 Gamification Design for Sedentary University Students

There are mainly five different categories of motivations for activity engagement: fitness, appearance, competence, enjoyment, and social [27]. Prior studies have shown that adherence is associated with motivations focused on enjoyment, competence and social interaction, other than those focused on fitness or appearance. Body-related motivations are not, on average, sufficient to sustain regular exercise regimens [27]. So it is more effective to place the focus of exercise promotion on the inherent enjoyment of physical activity. Spontaneous enjoyment of an activity leads to increased persistence, decreased stress and positive psychological status. In addition, social interaction can add one's enjoyment in participating [28]. To sum up, we believe that gamification design for sedentary students to become more physically active should focus on enjoyment and social interaction.

3.2 Design Guidelines

Based on the sedentary lifestyle of university students and previous research on gamification in the field of health and fitness application, promoting lifetime physical activity through mobile apps among all university students represents a major health priority. Their needs are concluded as follows:

- Sedentary students should spend more time doing physical activity during their leisure time.
- The exercising process must be full of enjoyment to ensure students' adherence.

In accordance to the needs of sedentary students, four design guidelines for gamification-based fitness application are concluded as follows:

- The physical activity should be easily accessible.
- The intensity of the physical activity should be moderate.
- The process of the physical activity should be interesting enough to motivate students to adhere.
- Social interaction should be added to the process of the physical activity to reinforce enjoyment.

4   Case Study of Gamification Design for University Students

4.1   Prototype

Based on above research findings, a prototype of a gamification-based fitness mobile application named LOOP, has been developed. The prototype is an easily-used mobile application for sedentary university students to motivate themselves to do more physical activity at school. It is recommended for sedentary university students who want to be healthier but find it difficult to adhere to their regular exercise plan in their leisure time (Fig. 1).

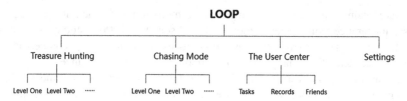

Fig. 1. Logical frame of LOOP

The Gamification-Based Fitness Mobile App. The app is designed for university students who find it difficult to stick with exercise. It has three main functions: game, social interaction, multidimensional reward mechanism.

Game. A series of game levels is designed for users. The intensity and difficulty of the physical activity (jogging & brisk walking) will increase as users proceed to harder levels. There are two game modes: Chasing Mode and Treasure Hunting Mode. No matter in which mode, users must run or move for a reasonable distance to win the game. The game scene is designed based on the real-life scenarios of the users' own campus, so that there are many various scenarios for students from different universities to choose from. The real-life scenarios will bring users a strong feeling of immersion and enjoyment. With the LBS (Location-based Service) technology, users and the game characters can move simultaneously in the similar scenarios.

In treasure hunting mode, treasures are hidden somewhere in the campus scenario. Users must move and collect more clues to find the treasure according to the given prompts. Users will be rewarded if the treasure is found (Fig. 2).

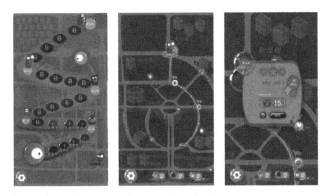

Fig. 2. Treasure hunting

In chasing mode, users can choose to be chased or to be a chaser. If one was a chaser, he or she should try the best to catch runaways as many as possible. The more he/she catches the runaways, the more rewards he/she will receive. If one was a runaway, he/she should try the best to evade capture of the chasers. The longer he/she survive in the game, the more rewards he/she will receive (Fig. 3).

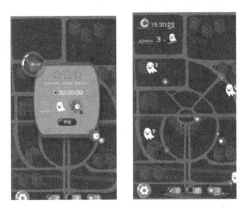

Fig. 3. Chasing mode

Social Interaction. During the chasing process, social interaction will happen when catching somebody or being caught. Thus students will meet each other and make friends offline. Meanwhile, users can also talk with their friends and check their ranking in the app (Fig. 4).

Fig. 4. Friends list & ranking page

Multidimensional Reward Mechanism. Users will be rewarded when they win the game. In addition to the game's virtual reward, users will also be rewarded with discount coupons that can be used in stores around the campus (e.g. fruit stores, book stores, supermarkets, restaurants and so on).

4.2   Experiments

On the basis of prior findings, we hypothesized that: (a) gamification-based process brings users more enjoyment than traditional process (b) adding social interaction to the gamification-based process increases users' enjoyment as well.

Comparing Access to Physical Activity. We made a survey on how and where they did physical activity among 98 college students (49 girls and 49 boys).

Comparing Enjoyment. The experiments were designed based on the design guidelines, aiming to compare three running processes: the traditional running process (just running without doing anything else), the gamification-based process and the gamification-based process with social interaction. The comparison experiments were designed to compare the enjoyment of the three processes.

Participants were 12 university students. They all ran at low frequency before and want to cultivate the habit of running regularly. They were divided into three groups by average. Group A proceeded the traditional running process as control group; Group B proceeded the gamification-based running process; And Group C proceeded the gamification-based running process with social interaction. The emotion performance of students in the three processes was recorded by experimenters with emotion scores. The scores ranged from -2 to 2. -2 means very unhappy; -1 means a little unhappy; 0 means no obvious emotion; 1 means a little happy; 2 means very happy. Experimenters took notes of what happened when emotion varied.

4.3 Results

Access to Physical Activity. We made a survey on how and where they did physical activity among 98 college students. We found that running was the most popular exercise among students and the campus was the most popular venues they would like to choose (Fig. 5). In conclusion, running or jogging in the campus was the most accessible among university students. That might reason from geographical and economic factors.

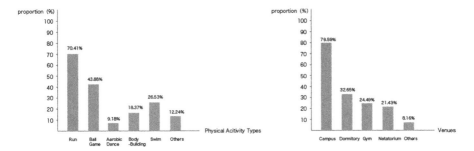

Fig. 5. How & where do you usually do physical activity? (Multiple choice questions)

Table 1. Emotion performance of three students in three training processes

	Time(min)	0	1	2	3	4	5	6	7	8	9	10	11	12	13	14
Emo-tion Score	Traditional	-1	-1	-1	0	0	0	1	1	1	1	1	2	2	2	1
	Gamification	-1	0	0	0	0	0	1	1	1	1	1	2	1	1	1
	Gamification & Social	-1	0	0	0	0	0	1	1	1	2	2	2	2	2	2

	Time(min)	15	16	17	18	19	20	21	22	23	24	25	26	27	28	29
Emo-tion Score	Traditional	1	1	1	0	0	0	0	0	0	0	0	-1	-1	-1	-1
	Gamification	1	1	1	1	2	1	1	-1	-1	-1	-1	1	0	0	0
	Gamification & Social	2	2	2	2	1	1	1	1	1	0	0	-1	0	0	0

	Time(min)	30	31	32	33	34	35	36	37	38	39	40	Average
Emo-tion Score	Traditional	-1	-2	-2	-2	-2	-2	-1	-1	0	1	1	-0.075
	Gamification	0	1	1	1	1	1	1	-1	1	1	1	0.6
	Gamification & Social	0	1	2	1	1	1	1	1	1	1	1	0.925

Enjoyment. Emotion performance of the twelve students in the three training processes was marked by emotion scores each minute. For example, the emotion performance of three object students from three groups was recorded in Table 1 and Fig. 3, according to which average emotion score of the three processes was calculated and displayed in Table 2.

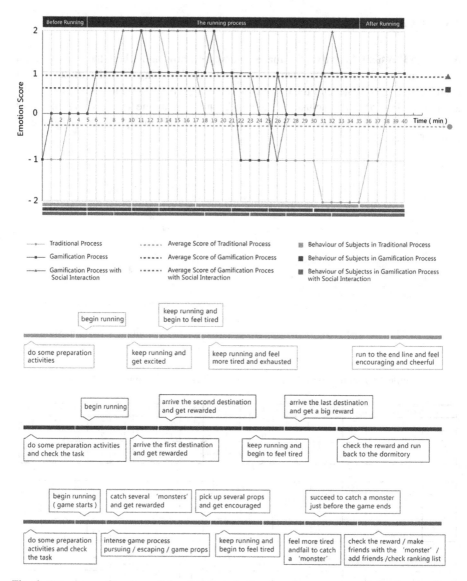

Fig. 6. Emotion performance of three students in three running processes (Color figure online)

According to the experimental data (Fig. 6), we found that (a) students from Group B and Group C were happier during the running process than those from Group A; (b) students from Group C were happier than students from Group B. This result verifies that gamification-based process brings the users more enjoyment and the experiment results have confirmed our prior hypothesis.

In traditional running process, students got excited in the beginning, but soon got tired. They were forced to keep running and running solely by their willpower, filled with tendency to give up. A long period of the process could be suffering. But when

Table 2. Average emotion scores of each student in three training processes

Group A (Traditional)	Subject No.	1	2	3	4
	Average Emotion Score	-0.075	-0.01	-0.025	-1.25

Group B (Gamification)	Subject No.	1	2	3	4
	Average Emotion Score	0.6	0.525	0.725	0.375

Group C (Gamification & Social Interaction)	Subject No.	1	2	3	4
	Average Emotion Score	0.925	1.075	1	0.725

adding gamification to the process, students' excitement extended obviously. Students' spirit got stimulated when the game feedback (the game sound, picking up props, finding the treasure and so on). When adding social interaction on the basis of gamification, the stimulation became more conspicuous. They found themselves quite amused when catching somebody or being caught especially when the interaction happened between male and female users. Though they would get disappointed when they missed the opportunity to catch somebody, users actually didn't have time to feel tired throughout the process.

5   Conclusion

In this paper, the idea of amalgamating gamification and social interaction with traditional running process has been proposed and a health & fitness mobile application LOOP is designed and developed following the 4 guidelines derived from our survey. Experiments have been performed as well to compare the three processes and the conclusions are as follows:

1. Running or jogging in the campus are more accessible physical activity compared with their counterparts. Easier access can confirm more adherence to a certain extent.
2. Gamification-based process brings more enjoyment to users and those students who feet more enjoyable would be more likely to adhere.
3. On the basis of gamification, social interaction has an effect of boosting enjoyment, which leads to relatively greater adherence.

While the results of the experiment support our general hypotheses, this study contains several limitations and shortcomings due to time limit. It is hither to based on a small population of samples and the association between enjoyment and adherence has not been firmly confirmed by experiments. The product is still being modified and iterated and future work will include more tests on larger student population from more universities.

Acknowledgement. This paper is sponsored by Shanghai Pujiang Program (13PJC072), Shanghai Philosopy and Social Science Program (2012BCK001), Shanghai Jiao Tong University Interdisciplinary among Hunmnity, Social Science and Natural Science Fund (13JCY02). Moreover, we thank to the students of Shang-hai Jiao Tong University who contributed to this research.

References

1. Li, S., Yang, L., Lin, H., Cao, Z.: The study of the relationship between college students' health and lifestyle. Sichuan Sports Sci. **01**, 113–118 (2010)
2. Caspersen, C.J., Powell, K.E., Christenson, G.M.: Physical activity, exercise, and physical fitness: definitions and distinctions for health-related research. Public Health Rep. **2**, 126 (1985)
3. Du, H.: Sports participation in research on the influence of subjective feeling of well-being. Shanxi Normal University (2010)
4. Ma, C., Qian, Y., Tian, X.: College students' fitness walking and jogging cardiopulmonary load dynamic observation. J. Beijing Sport Univ. **8**, 96–98+101 (2009)
5. Haskell, W.L., Blair, S.N., Hill, J.O.: Physical activity: health outcomes and importance for public health policy. Prev. Med. **4**, 280–282 (2009)
6. Warburton, D.E., Nicol, C.W., Bredin, S.S.: Health benefits of physical activity: the evidence. Can. Med. Assoc. J. **6**, 801–809 (2006)
7. Taylor, C.B., Sallis, J.F., Needle, R.: The relation of physical activity and exercise to mental health. Public Health Rep. **2**, 195 (1985)
8. Deterding, S., Sicart, M., Nacke, L., O'Hara, K., Dixon, D.: Gamification: using game-design elements in non-gaming contexts. In: CHI 2011 Extended Abstracts on Human Factors in Computing Systems, pp. 2425–2428 (2011)
9. Wylie, J.: Fitness gamification: concepts, characteristics, and applications. Print (2010)
10. Malone, T.W.: Heuristics for designing enjoyable user interfaces: lessons from computer games. In: Proceedings of the 1982 Conference on Human Factors in Computing Systems, pp. 63–68 (1982)
11. Lister, C., West, J.H., Cannon, B., Sax, T., Brodegard, D.: Just a fad? Gamification in health and fitness apps. JMIR Serious Games **2**(2), e9 (2014)
12. Fitz-Walter, Z., Tjondronegoro, D., Wyeth, P.: Orientation passport: using gamification to engage university students. In: Proceedings of the 23rd Australian Computer-Human Interaction Conference, pp. 122–125 (2011)
13. Stålnacke Larsson, R.: Motivations in sports and fitness gamification: a study to understand what motivates the users of sports and fitness gamification services (2013)
14. Dennison, L., Morrison, L., Conway, G., Yardley, L.: Opportunities and challenges for smartphone applications in supporting health behavior change: qualitative study. J. Med. Internet Res. **4**, e86 (2013)
15. Patrick, K., Griswold, W.G., Raab, F., Intille, S.S.: Health and the mobile phone. Am. J. Prev. Med. **2**, 177 (2008)
16. Hebden, L., Cook, A., van der Ploeg, H.P., Allman-Farinelli, M.: Development of smartphone applications for nutrition and physical activity behavior change. JMIR Res. Protoc. **2**, e9 (2012)
17. Fjeldsoe, B.S., Miller, Y.D., Marshall, A.L.: MobileMums: a randomized controlled trial of an SMS-based physical activity intervention. Ann. Behav. Med. **2**, 101–111 (2010)

18. Chomutare, T., Fernandez-Luque, L., Årsand, E., Hartvigsen, G.: Features of mobile diabetes applications: review of the literature and analysis of current applications compared against evidence-based guidelines. J. Med. Internet Res. **3**, e65 (2011)
19. Obermayer, J.L., Riley, W.T., Asif, O., Jean-Mary, J.: College smoking-cessation using cell phone text messaging. J. Am. Coll. Health **2**, 71–78 (2004)
20. Ferguson, B.: Games for wellness—impacting the lives of employees and the profits of employers. Games Health Res. Dev. Clin. Appl. **3**, 177–179 (2012)
21. Ferrara, J.: Games for persuasion argumentation, procedurality, and the lie of gamification. Games Cult. **4**, 289–304 (2013)
22. Deterding, S., Dixon, D., Khaled, R., Nacke, L.: From game design elements to gamefulness: defining gamification. In: Proceedings of the 15th International Academic MindTrek Conference: Envisioning Future Media Environments, pp. 9–15 (2011)
23. Zichermann, G., Cunningham, C.: Gamification by Design: Implementing Game Mechanics in Web and Mobile Apps. O'Reilly Media Inc., Sebastopol (2011)
24. Flatla, D.R., Gutwin, C., Nacke, L.E., Bateman, S., Mandryk, R.L.: Calibration games: making calibration tasks enjoyable by adding motivating game elements. In: Proceedings of the 24th Annual ACM Symposium on User Interface Software and Technology, pp. 403–412 (2011)
25. Huotari, K., Hamari, J.: Defining gamification: a service marketing perspective. In: Proceeding of the 16th International Academic MindTrek Conference, pp. 17–22 (2012)
26. Hamari, J.: Transforming homo economicus into homo ludens: a field experiment on gamification in a utilitarian peer-to-peer trading service. Electron. Commer. Res. Appl. **4**, 236–245 (2013)
27. Richard, M., Christina, M.F., Deborah, L.S., Rubio, N., Kennon, M.S.: Intrinsic motivation and exercise adherence. Int. J. Sport Psychol. **4**, 335–354 (1997)
28. Wankel, L.M.: The importance of enjoyment to adherence and psychological benefits from physical activity. Int. J. Sport Psychol. **24**, 151–169 (1993)

A Relational Model for Playful and Smart Game Design

Anna Priscilla de Albuquerque[(✉)], Felipe Borba Breyer, and Judith Kelner

Computer Centre, Universidade Federal de Pernambuco, Recife, Brazil
{apa,fbb3,jk}@cin.ufpe.br

Abstract. In recent years, a range of industry sectors including digital games and toys has incorporated smart tangible things into their design. This paper seeks to investigate how to integrate these physical objects associated with connectivity technologies into digital games, and how they affect the game design decisions. Therefore, the research flow consists in, systematically reviewing the literature, and then, analyzing existing market scenarios. Hence, the results of data extraction allowed to structuring a relational model of the entities that comprise different scenarios of smart play.

Keywords: Game design · Game user interface · Tangible user interfaces · Playful interfaces · Smart toys · Internet of toys · Game studies

1 Introduction

Smart things, in the context of the digital games, offer opportunities for engaging in physical play outside the virtual world. Since the things have playful aspects, such as toys, they can promote interaction independently of being linked to a digital platform. This happens because of the artifact's aesthetics, or due to the thing's own technological components, e.g., sensors and actuators. Thus, these interactions promote a connection between the physical and the digital worlds since the scenario places playful meaning on the game interface. However, to design such experience, one must first investigate how to integrate these things into the gameplay.

Although there are works focusing on these physical interactions, especially in the context of serious games [1, 2], little has been achieved concerning individual aspects related to prototyping [3] and integration of artifacts with the game design [4, 5]. For that reason, this paper aims to bridge this gap by proposing a theoretical model for game development and prototyping based on case studies. Therefore, we conducted a systematic literature review, covering related publications of the last five years resulting in 35 selected papers, and in addition, we included 30 cases from the market. During data extraction, we analyzed the systems in order to identify the agents involved in the interaction, and how these integrate the real and virtual worlds.

2 Related Work

Coulton [5] uses the game spaces [6] definition to classify IoT systems for gaming, aiming to consider how and where the interaction takes place. Moreover, the author

© Springer International Publishing Switzerland 2016
A. Marcus (Ed.): DUXU 2016, Part II, LNCS 9747, pp. 252–263, 2016.
DOI: 10.1007/978-3-319-40355-7_24

seeks to recognize when and how the interaction feedback must be presented. The author divides the scenarios into four categories: IoT object, IoT object in the player space, IoT object with tablet and IoT object with the screen. Despite that the author's model covers different scenarios of smart play taking into account the relationship between things and spaces and the types of technology that promote interactions, little is explored regarding the impact of these things on the decisions of game design, introducing only a few considerations for the last two scenarios.

Moreover in the context of smart tangible things, van de Garde-Perik et al. [7] analyzed the relationships between input and output (I/O) seeking to understand the relations involving the user information perception to create meaningful I/O experiences. The model combines two parts: the *State Change*, referring to I/O from the user perception of the physical world, and the *Information Access*, related to the smart devices, in the sense of what information the devices collect (input) and how the system translate the data (output). Connecting the two I/O models there is the cognitive dimension regarding the user's perspective, followed by the shared physical space, and the digital space. The framework, however, does not focus on gaming scenarios, but the study includes an educational game in one of the case studies.

Magerkurth [4] present a theoretical framework to describe the domains involved in hybrid gaming systems, making it based on the literature and observing aspects of board games and digital games. The author focuses on multiplayer gaming scenarios involving smart tangible things enabling to insert real-world information, with output provided by a screen and graphic-user-interface (GUI). They define that the goal of these games is to capture the traditional and co-located game experience of the physical spaces, enhanced non-intrusively using pervasive technology. The framework comprises three domains, starting with the social domain that is public, private or shared. Followed by the virtual domain associated with the social domain through the game state regarding the sharing of information. Finally, there is the physical domain accessed through the properties of the real world and tangibility.

In turn, Guo et al. [8] introduce a framework on the aspects that make a pervasive game based on literature review, and this consists of four perspectives, comprising systems such as smart-toys, affective gaming, augmented tabletop games, location-based games, and augmented reality games. The first is the temporality that classifies the game turns in closed, or open-ended where the player can join in the interaction at any time. The mobility perspective concerns games played at a fixed location, games with a large interactive environment and games with enough space to move the body. In the perception the study distinguishes how the system extracts the real-world information, and how the user and the system translate this information, also bringing an overview of the technologies. The social perspective reflects the relationship between the players, and in the social influence on the game purpose and thematic of the system. Finally, the authors use the parameters to set a score for the games, aiming to identify the pervasiveness of the each system.

3 Method

3.1 Systematic Literature Review

We conducted the systematic literature review following Kitchenham and Charters [9] guidelines, and we carried out the procedure between July and November of 2015 covering related publications between 2010 and 2015. Two researchers conducted the method, one primary researcher for select the papers, and other for validating the findings. We started with the automatic search using a search string including terms such as "tangible interface", that on account of things integrate physical form to digital information [10], "playful interfaces" that are interfaces that invite the user to engage in playful experiences [11], and sure, "game-user-interface". We applied the string in 5 search engines (ACM, Springer, IEEE, ScienceDirect, and Scopus) on 23rd July of 2015, returning a total of 483 papers, of which 62 were replicas, leaving 421 articles for the first phase of analysis. During the first stage, we applied the inclusion and exclusion criteria on the title and abstract only. We considered two criteria for inclusion, these are systems where things have playful aspects, such as toys, and gameful systems, as digital games, augmented board games, gamified multimedia applications, interactive storytelling, structured play activities, and open-ended play scenarios. So during the first phase, we classified 90 articles as "potentially accepted" and we set 68 "in doubt". Moreover, we excluded 263 articles of which 2 were non-English written, plus we regarded 33 as gray literature, 15 restricted to download, 3 were work-in-progress papers, and finally, we identified 213 out of the scope of this research, e.g., systems without playful intervention, such as wands, devices for gesture recognition, mobile phones or smartphones, and haptics devices. In the second phase, after reading both the introduction section and conclusion of the papers, only 83 articles met the inclusion or exclusion criteria.

After this stage, we started the manual search conducting the snowball of references, adding 60 articles for further quality evaluation. Also, we added another 21 full papers after manually searching the proceedings of 3 related conferences (CHIPlay, ACE, and DiGRA). In summary, 165 articles were fully read out and evaluated by 14 criteria, which 10 we extracted from the guidelines provided by [9], and we assign them weight ($N = 1$), and the other 4 criteria were regarding details of systems such as kinds of artifacts, the technologies involved and the gameplay. So, for these we designated twice the weight ($N = 2$), looking for select studies that had enough information to answer the research questions. All criteria were then scored with "0" to "no", "0.5" to "partially" or "1" to "yes", and we considered the cutoff point of 75 %. During the quality evaluation we excluded 125 articles considering the scores, and in the final selection we identified 5 papers as redundant, e.g., articles of the same authoring, and that of equal systems, resulting in 35 papers for further data extraction. Overall, the final selection of articles covers topics such as games for learning [12], games for children with special needs [2], games for health and sports [1], playful augmented training [13], interactive storytelling [14], smart and robotic toys [15, 16], tangible-augmented reality games (AR games) [17], tabletop games [3, 18], remote playful experiences [19], outdoor games [20], virtual reality games (VR games) or immersive scenarios [21], and smart devices for open-end play [22].

3.2 Market Scenarios

The study aims to extend the model's contribution to developing hybrid systems beyond the academic sphere, also including market cases. Therefore, we selected 30 cases of systems involving smart toys and digital games, doing this by analyzing the catalog of toy stores websites, and successful projects of crowdfunding. In summary, we found mostly smart toys for mobile gaming destined for babies and young children. However, we also found more complex games, e.g., Golem Arcana [23], an augmented board game with token pieces, and the tower game Fabulous Beats [24], including interactive toys for TV. Moreover, we name multiple similar cases, such as NFC collectible toys embedded with content for video games, mixed reality coloring applications as Disney Color and Play [25], touchpoints toys and stampers, and building blocks. Other common are the robot plush toys for pet management applications, e.g., the Furby Boom from Hasbro [26], and plush toy cases for smartphone and tablet, as the Didi Teddy Bear [27], including plastic toy-cases aiming for protecting the device and promoting playful tangible interaction with mini-games.

3.3 Data Extraction

Joining the 35 papers from the review and the 30 market cases, resulted in a total of 88 systems for analysis, since some papers presented more than one application or more of an artifact. Regarding the results of data extraction, we name the components that define the setup of the interaction, we started with the things, these are two kinds, the playful things, such as toys, and non-playful things, like things that we project playful appearance, or smart things able to capture information from the environment. Thus, we have the technologies associated with the things, and these are passive or active. Passive technologies include three scenarios, starting with things with markers, these are QR codes and fiducial, followed by technologies that detect things markerless, configuring a non-intrusive way, these scenarios use invisible ink [28] or detect properties of the things, e.g., shape, color, and texture. The third scenario comprises things with touch-points, consisting of conductive points positioned on the base of things that provide unique patterns for multi-touch screen, making it by the distance between points. Active technologies differ in two groups, external technology as smart tags attached to things (RFID/NFC tags) [20], and embedded technology, where the components are inside the things. These are components such as sensors used to detect an external stimulus, e.g., gyroscopes, accelerometers, color (RGB) sensors, and these vary according to the requirements of the application. In addition, there are actuators, which are responsible for the feedback of things, e.g., screen displays or LEDs, vibrating motors, or servo-motors that move parts of things, and speakers for auditory feedback. As for promoting the transfer of data between things, there are the connection modules, the most common are Bluetooth-low-energy (BLE), wi-fi module, and RFID/NFC readers. In that sense, the sensors collect information and process it into things, otherwise, the thing transfers this data to an external device to occur processing, and the feedback occurs. The feedback is visual, tactile or auditory, and can happen on things by it actuators, or in an external device, thereby promoting interaction.

Such technologies are responsible for collecting environment information to the system, and depending on the nature of the technology, these can collect a different kind. Regarding all the selected systems, we name the nature of the information collected, starting with the identification (ID), that is useful for things that have unique information and its support both active or passive technologies. The ID often is a single path, but active technologies allow updating the ID status by means of interaction. Besides, in scenarios with multiple similar objects, such as board games, individual ID is not that relevant, and then captures information such as color and shape of things is enough information to promote identification. Another recurring type of gathered information is the thing's position, there is the 2D position to capture moving up to two axes: x, y. This information is often used to recognize thing's position on the top of a display or a table, such as in tabletops, however, it also occurs off-screen. Yet another information is the 3D position, comprising moves in three axes: x, y, z, usually, the system detects such positioning outside the screen, but, researchers took efforts to recognize objects in 3D position on tabletops [18]. In scenarios that enable more free movement, usually without displaying on-screen, capturing additional information, e.g., rotation and inclination can help distinguish the 6D position of things, and of people. Although, it is noteworthy that there are no fixed rules to use the different position information, such as regard to the environment has a screen or not. In addition to this more recurring information, more specific sensors can gather a sort of data, e.g., ambient temperature, lighting, and proximity to other things. Besides, things can extract data from people, such as games that use heart rate as input.

4   A Relational Model for Hybrid Gameplay

Observing the universe of things and technologies, we realize that there are two setups of play promoted by things. There is the open-ended play, characterized by scenarios where the game rules are not predefined and the play occurs based on the interactions promoted by things and it sensors and actuators. Yet, there is the hybrid gameplay referring to scenarios where the game rules are previously established to promote interaction. Traditional toys and smart toys, when off-line, supports free-play, and the latter, when actuated, promote open-ended play, and in both cases when integrated into the game world, promote hybrid-gameplay experiences. For that reason, the study decided to focus only on scenarios with toys in the context of hybrid gameplay looking to discuss the gap of integrating things with the game design. Therefore, we propose the model presented in Fig. 1 and we done this considering the relationship between three entities: the things, people, and the environment. The model configuration enabled to fit all scenarios identified by the review. Then we explain each aspect of the model and an example is given using the model to recognize aspects of the playful system in the context of hybrid gameplay.

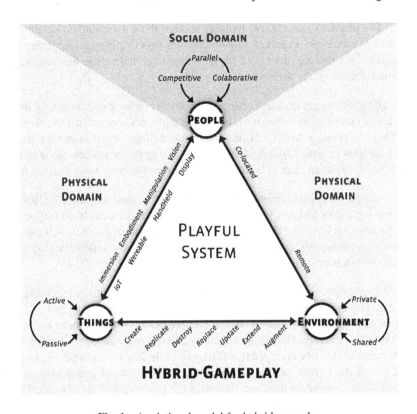

Fig. 1. A relational model for hybrid gameplay

Things are toys, and when applicable, things include the external devices connected to toys that promote the interaction. There are three types of toys and all of them can communicate with each other *actively* or *passively*. First, traditional *toys* can connect to passive or active technologies, enabling them to interact with the game environment [12]. Secondly, *smart toys* promote interaction regardless connection with an external device, and it can provide feedback concerning the game action on both toy and in the associated device [26]. Finally, *smart playground* consists of a large toy, e.g., a tower [1] or an interactive floor [29], or it consists of multiple interconnected smart toys in the same environment, featuring the Internet of toys.

Now, regarding the things and the game environment, the system review allowed classifies interactive patterns involving these connections whether this is physical or virtual. Yet, the interactions rarely occur in isolation, allowing the same toy, game, or action to associate with different interactive patterns simultaneously.

Replicate. The physical game object replicates in the game environment, doing it replicating information, e.g., positioning and orientation, as well as its physical features. For example, in the space-themed game for Portico platform [30] the ship toy has its appearance, with regard to color, shape and texture replicated in a virtual object, and the virtual ship replicates the toy's orientation in real-time.

Replace. The physical game object replaces another thing assuming its identity in the game world. For example, in games with touchpoints toys like Batman Apptivity Mattel [31], a physical toy replaces the virtual playable character in the game that interacts with other virtual objects on the screen.

Create. The physical game object creates new objects in the game world, by instantiating things or creating individual objects. For example, in Camelot [20] the players use physical toys to create a castle, but first they must collect virtual resources engaging pieces on smart toys with RFID readers, after acquiring the resources, the user is able to attach the pieces to another to build the castle before the other team finishes it.

Destroy. The physical game object destroys things in the game world. In the Ipad game Runaway using wooden blocks from Magikbee [32], the blocks can build bridges to the virtual character get from one side to the other in the game scenario, however the enemy that follows the protagonist can also use the toy bridge to trespass, then the player needs to overturn this in time, by destroying the passage.

Extend. The physical game object extends itself in the game world, by extending information, e.g., trajectory, or connecting to a virtual game object extending its real appearance, other than replicate, extended objects composes the same object. In Rope Revolution [33] a physical rope extends its trajectory and its appearance in the game to fly a kite, so the base of the rope is physical, and the end of the line where is the kite is virtual. Besides, inside the virtual gaming environment, there are wind interactions, and the microcontrollers coupled to the rope simulates the pressure and force exerted on the rope, together with fans that synchronize winds in a real environment.

Update. The physical game object sends its status or identity, to the virtual game world and receives feedback, updating its initial state. In that case, the user can update the status intentionally, or independently by interacting with other virtual or physical game objects. In the application for coloring Disney Color and Play [25], the child paints the characters in the physical coloring book, and using a tablet, the user sees the corresponding 3D virtual character and its colors updated in real-time, according to painting held by the user.

Augment. The physical game object augments information non-intrusively, referring to the rules of the game, interfering in the game challenge, and promoting social interaction between players. These include systems to play over a distance that the technology supports social interaction among participants [19], applications for playful training [13], in which uses technology to augment the rules of a traditional game scenario as the Golem Arcana [23] board game, the player uses a pen to augment character tokens by displaying information rules that guide the game through a tablet.

Moreover, the environment is where the interaction occurs, which means the place where are people and things. The environment is *private* when each player has its own information and access to the toys or *shared* when provides to all players the same information and access to things [24]. People are in two ways in the environment, *co-located*, with the players present in the same physical environment, such as in tabletop games [3]. In contrast, when players are in different physical environments they are *remote* located. In the latter, the real space of the players is private, but they share the virtual space. So, people relate to each other in three forms, first by *competition* where players compete for the same purpose in the game. Followed by *collaboration*, when players cooperate to achieve the same game goal, and may perform the same or complementary actions [33]. The third is the *parallel* play, where people interact in the same environment, but performing actions that are independent [18].

People relate to things through physical interaction mediated by technology. Observing the scenarios we recognized four main interactions, these are the *vision*, since people visually access the environment and things, followed by the *manipulation* when people use their hands to move toys or parts of things. The third is the *embodiment* where people access the environment through the body, may providing the system with information inherent to the body [20], or interacting with things that require body movements [1]. Finally, there is *immersion*, where people are inside the things, like environments with multiple interconnected objects, or large interactive installations as smart playgrounds. Such interactions increase as a scale, however, these are not mutually exclusive, but complementary.

Once, the four main interactions relate to actions that the user takes in the context of reality, then, there are corresponding technologies connecting such activities with the virtuality. In the case of vision, usually some sort of *display* present visual feedback using a screen or multiple screens, or through projection or LEDs illumination. In that sense, in manipulation the things that support action are toys or *hand-held* devices, while in the embodiment when the player uses the body as input, the *wearable* technologies are prevalent. Finally, regarding the immersive interaction considering an environment composed of multiple interconnected smart things, there are pervasive technologies related to the *Internet of Things* (IoT), in our case, the Internet of toys. Finally, perceiving the relationships between people, things, and the environment, we recognize two domains that rule such interactions. The *physical domain* comprises the interaction between things and people, and between people and the environment and the *social domain* covers the interaction between people and people, once they promote social interaction.

To guarantee applicability to the extracted model we analyze all selected systems using the proposed configuration. Here, we describe an illustrative scenario in Fig. 2. The chosen was the Age Invaders [29] consisting of a smart playground for intergenerational play promoting physical and social interaction between grandparents (GP), parents (P), and children (C). Now analyzing the game by the proposed model, we start naming things that are part of the system, these are the 45 LED tiles configuring the smart playground, the smart toys which are BLE and RFID empowered teddy bear slippers, the personal LED displays, and the BLE handheld devices, therefore things communicate with each other in an active way. On integrating things with the environment, the system replicates the virtual tiles controlled by P to the tiles on the smart playground, also occurs replacement of P for virtual avatars on-screen. The same happens in the smart playground where GP and C wearing slippers replace the virtual playable character by interacting with virtual objects on display.

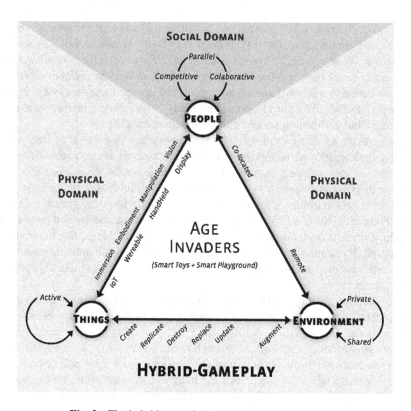

Fig. 2. The hybrid gameplay model for Age Invader [29]

The players (GP and C) also create instantiated laser shots in the game environment, by clicking on their handheld devices, and when the laser hits a player, it destroys energy points of the participants. So, the player's health status updates through collecting virtual resources or receiving hits, and the power state updates by collecting power-ups. The update also occurs in the location of players on the map by reading the RFID tags on the floor and sending this information back to the system. Finally, managing the rules of the game level the system augment information indicating possible movements for C interfering with the challenge of the game.

Thus, the environment is private for P to the other participants, and shared to the players in the smart playground. Concerning the people and the environment, people are co-located in the case of GP and C, and P is remote. Now, on the people, there is social interaction promoted by competition between the teams of GP and C, collaboration among team members and between P and the whole group, also, there is parallelism on each player's actions in the game. Yet, on the axis of things with people, we recognize the four main interactions, starting with the vision, and manipulation for all participants. Followed by the embodiment for GP and C, as well as immersion since people are inside the things (smart playground and the smart slippers). In the technology perspective, there is display on-screen for all players and display by LEDs for GP and C both in the smart playground as on the personal displays. Also, the manipulation happens through hand-held devices carried by GP and C, and by the computer interface for P. Finally, there are wearable technologies to GP and C that wear the slippers and the individual displays attached to their clothing, and IoT technology for all, since many things interconnects via BLE and wi-fi in the environment.

5   Conclusion and Future Work

In short, the study structured a relational model based on case studies from the academy and the market, able to comprise different scenarios of hybrid gameplay involving inter-action with toys in the context of digital games. The paper has succeeded in classifying the scenarios in interactive patterns regarding the interaction between three entities: things, people, and the environment. Things are toys interconnected by active and passive technologies, integrated or not with external devices. Such things can interact with the environment by replicating, replacing, extending, creating, destroying, updating and augmenting real and virtual information in the gaming environment, making it in a private or shared form to people. People interact socially with each other by collaboration, competition, and parallelism, and physically with things and the environment. Doing this through visualization of things and the environment, manipulation of things, body movement, and by movement inside outdoor or indoor environment. Finally, people act on things and things access the environment through technologies responsible for promoting interaction and providing feedback of information via displays, handheld devices, wearable, and connection through the Internet of things.

As future work, we will prototype scenarios that include 7 patterns of interaction identified by the model. The goal is to understand through a practical perspective, more details on integrating things with the gameplay and how toys influence in the game design decisions. Therefore, all prototypes must involve toys both with active and passive technologies, and so far we prototyped scenarios focused on replication, replacement, and creation, and all the games are competitive and of the same thematic. In addition, we will apply the relational model in the creative process of hybrid games, intervening in the phases of ideation, prototyping, and evaluation, over a course of four months with students of engineering, computer science, and design.

References

1. Fogtmann, M.H.: Designing Bodily engaging games – learning from sports. In: 12th Annual Conference of the New Zealand Chapter of the ACM Special Interest Group on Computer-Human Interaction, pp. 89–96. ACM, New York (2011)
2. Garzotto, F., Bordogna, M.: Paper-based multimedia interaction as learning tool for disabled children. In: 9th International Conference on Interaction Design and Children, pp. 79–88. ACM, New York (2010)
3. Marco, J., Baldassarri, S., Cerezo, E.: ToyVision: a toolkit to support the creation of innovative board-games with tangible interaction. In: 7th International Conference on Tangible, Embedded and Embodied Interaction, pp. 291–298. ACM, New York (2013)

4. Magerkurth, C.: Hybrid gaming environments: keeping the human in the loop within the internet of things. J. UAIS **11**, 273–283 (2012)
5. Coulton, P.: Playful and gameful design for the internet of things. In: Nijholt, A. (ed.) More Playful User Interfaces: Interfaces that Invite Social and Physical Interaction, vol. 1, pp. 151–171. Springer, Singapore (2015)
6. Juul, J.: A Casual Revolution: Reinventing Video Games and Their Players. The MIT Press, Cambridge (2012)
7. van de Garde-Perik, E., Offermans, S., van Boerdonk, K., Lenssen, K., van den Hoven, E.: An analysis of input-output relations in interaction with smart tangible objects. J. ACM TiiS **3** (2013). Article No. 9
8. Guo, H., Trætteberg, H., Wang, A.I., Zhu, M.: TeMPS: a conceptual framework for pervasive and social games. In: 3rd IEEE International Conference on Digital Game and Intelligent Toy Enhanced Learning, pp. 31–37. IEEE (2010)
9. Kitchenham, B., Charter, S.: Guidelines for performing systematic literature reviews in software engineering. Technical report, Keele University and Durham University Joint Report (2007)
10. Ishii, H.: Tangible bits: beyond pixels. In: The 2nd International Conference on Tangible and Embedded Interaction, pp. 18–20. ACM, New York (2008)
11. Nijholt, A.: Playful interfaces: introduction and history. In: Nijholt, A. (ed.) Playful User Interfaces: Interfaces that Invite Social and Physical Interaction, vol. 1, pp. 1–21. Springer, Singapore (2014)
12. Tsong, C.K., Chong, T.S., Samsudin, Z.: Tangible multimedia: a case study for bringing tangibility into multimedia learning. In: 12th International Educational Technology Conference, pp. 382–391. Elsevier (2012)
13. Yamabe, T., Nakajima, T.: Playful training with augmented reality games: case studies towards reality-oriented system design. J. MTAP **62**(1), 259–286 (2012). Springer, US
14. Shen, Y.T., Mazalek, A.: PuzzleTale: a tangible puzzle game for interactive storytelling. Mag. CIE, **8** (2010). Article No. 11. ACM, New York, USA
15. Faber, J.P., van den Hoven, E.: MARBOWL: increasing the fun experience of shooting marbles. J. PUC **16**, 391–404 (2012). Springer
16. Gomes, P.F., Segura, E.M., Cramer, H., Paiva, T., Paiva, A., Holmquist, L.E.: ViPleo and PhyPleo: artificial pet with two embodiments. In: 8th International Conference on Advances in Computer Entertainment Technology, Article No. 3. ACM, New York (2011)
17. Furió, D., Gancedo, S.G., Juan, M.C., Seguí, I., Costa, M.: The effects of the size and weight of a mobile device on an educational game. J. Comput. Educ. **64**, 24–41 (2013). Elsevier
18. Halskov, K., Dalsgaard, P., Stolze, L.B.: Analysing engaging experiences with a tangible 3D tabletop. In: 11th International Conference on Advances in Computer Entertainment Technology, Article No. 29. ACM, New York (2014)
19. Sakamoto, M., Alexandrova, T., Nakajima, T.: Analyzing the influence of virtuality on playful social interaction. J. MTAP, 1–29 (2015). Springer, US
20. Soute, I., Markopoulos, P., Magielse, R.: Head up games: combining the best of both worlds by merging traditional and digital play. J. PUC **14**, 435–444 (2010). Springer, London
21. Tedjokusumo, J., Zhou, S.Z., Winkler, S.: Immersive multiplayer games with tangible and physical interaction. J. IEEE TSMC **40**, 147–157 (2010). IEEE
22. Bekker, T., Sturm, J., Eggen, B.: Designing playful interactions for social interaction and physical play. J. PUC **14**, 385–396 (2010). Springer, London
23. Golem Arcana. http://golemarcana.com/
24. Fabulous Beats. http://playfabulousbeasts.com/
25. Disney Color and Play. http://www.colorandplaybooks.com/

26. Furby Boom. http://www.hasbro.com/en-us/brands/furby
27. DiDi Teddy Bear. https://goo.gl/u9nYod
28. Willis, K.D.D., Shiratori, T., Mahler, M.: HideOut: mobile projector interaction with tangible objects and surfaces. In: 7th International Conference on Tangible, Embedded and Embodied Interaction, pp. 331–338. ACM, New York (2013)
29. Cheok, A.D.: Age invaders: entertainment for elderly and young. In: Cheok, A.D. (ed.) Advances in Interactive New Media for Entertainment Computing, pp. 137–160. Springer, London (2010)
30. Avrahami, D., Wobbrock, J.O., Izadi, S.: Portico: tangible interaction on and around a tablet. In: 24th ACM Symposium on User Interface Software and Technology, pp. 347–356. ACM, New York (2011)
31. Batman Apptivity Mattel. http://www.mattelapptivity.com/
32. Magikbee. http://www.magikbee.com/
33. Yao, L., Dasgupta, S., Cheng, N., Spingarn-Koff, J., Rudakevych, O., Ishii, H.: Rope revolution: tangible and gestural rope interface for collaborative play. In: 8th International Conference on Advances in Computer Entertainment Technology, Article No. 11. ACM, New York (2011)

Questing Ruins: A Game for a Digital Inclusion

Regina Heidrich[1(✉)], Francisco Rebelo[2], Marsal Branco[1], João Batista Mossmann[1], Anderson Schuh[1], Emely Jensen[1], and Tiago Oliveira[2]

[1] Universidade Feevale, Pró-reitoria de Pesquisa e Pós-graduação, Novo Hamburgo, Brazil
{RHeidrich,marsal,mossmann,andersonrs,emely}@feevale.br
[2] Universidade de Lisboa, Faculdade de Motricidade Humana, Lisbon, Portugal
Frebelo@fmh.ulisboa.pt, t.oliveira2010@gmail.com

Abstract. The inclusion of people with cerebral palsy is not an easy path, because many of them preserve their cognitive abilities, despite being unable to speak, walk, or even both. This paper presents a study on the games applied in the education of people with cerebral palsy using Brain Computer Interface (BCI). Children affected by Cerebral Palsies have a disturbance in the control of their postures and body movements as a result of a brain injury. These injuries are the result of several causes. The most frequent is linked to the lack of oxygen flow to the brain, occurring either during or immediately after birth. The objective of the current research is to study the evaluation of the game we developed, called Questing Ruins. The methodology used was that of qualitative approach and case study. At the end we present Questing Ruins, an adventure game for entertainment and environmental awareness.

Keywords: Brain computer interface · Digital inclusion · Motor impairments

1 Introduction

1.1 Game Characteristics

All games share four characteristics, which define them: target, rules, feedback system and voluntary participation [1]. The target is the reason that justifies the player participating in any of the activities; in other words, the element by which the participants of a game concentrate their attention in order to reach the set goals. The rules adjust the player's complexity level in light of the activity to be undertaken, "releasing creativity and stimulating strategic thinking [...] therefore, they have the role of defining the way in which the player shall behave, or in which way the player will organize its actions in order to fulfill the challenges brought on by the game" [1]. The feedback system advises players as regards their relationship with the various aspects that regulate their interaction with the activity. This system is also responsible for encouraging motivation, also keeping participants aware of progress as regards themselves and their target [1]. According to the same author, in any game, whether digital or otherwise, one can observe that there is no need for an agreement between the conditions proposed and the player.

While there is yet little research, Granic *et al.* [2] point out the benefits of playing video games, the roles and benefits of which, in a more generalized manner, having been

© Springer International Publishing Switzerland 2016
A. Marcus (Ed.): DUXU 2016, Part II, LNCS 9747, pp. 264–272, 2016.
DOI: 10.1007/978-3-319-40355-7_25

studied over decades. Evolutionary psychology has long emphasized the adaptive functions of play [3], and in developmental psychology, the positive function of game has been a recurring topic for some of the most respected scholars in the field [4–6]. Erikson [5] showed that the context surrounding games allow children to simulate and experience social and emotional alternatives that can bring-on feelings of resolution outside of the game context. Similarly, Piaget [4] theorized that the game of make-believe offers children opportunities to play-out real-life conflicts, to devise optimal resolutions for their own pleasure, and to alleviate negative feelings. Both Piaget [4] and Vygotsky [6] advocated strong theoretical links between play and a variety of elements that favor the development of social cognition.

Besides social cognition, developmentalists have emphasized that the game is an emotionally meaningful context, whereby the themes of power and domination, aggression, nutrition, anxiety, pain, loss, growth and joy can be enacted productively [7]. Granic et al. [2] provided a study analysis based on existing data regarding the positive effects of playing video games. They said that these games promote well-being, including the prevention and treatment of mental health issues. The same authors also said that playing video games promotes a series of social, emotional and cognitive skills, and also assists in problem solving, in addition to enabling creativity and a persistent optimistic motivational style that contributes towards success and personal fulfillment. Researchers also acknowledged that video games are changing the way in which students and teachers approach learning, and are being used by doctors in order to improve patient's health. They suggested that video games could have a similar impact on the field of mental health, and recommended that psychologists, doctors and game designers collaborate to include video games in traditional therapies.

We now turn to the motivational, emotional and social benefits of playing video games. From an educational point of view, Johnson [8] argues that it doesn't matter what the player is thinking while playing, but the way in which the player is thinking. This statement is strengthened by Dewey [9], when arguing that the greatest of all pedagogical fallacies is perhaps the notion that a person learns only that particular thing that he or she is studying. With regard to this, he highlights collateral learning as a path to building long lasting attitudes, these often being more important than grammar lessons or geography lessons or even the history that is being learned. Thus, when playing, users are building from the collateral learning. For some time, companies have attempted to develop low cost devices, to enable use at a personal level. In this project, games and the BCI can also be classed as a type of Assistive Technology.

1.2 Brain-Computer Interface - BCI

The first BCI was described in 1964 by Walter Grey, when he implanted electrodes directly into the motor area of the cortex of a human patient. The experiment consisted of recording the patient's brain activity as he pressed a button. This action would make the slides of a projected slide show to move forward. Then the scientist developed a system that would make the slides advance whenever the patient's brain activity indicated that they wanted the button to be pressed. Interestingly, besides testing the equipment and checking its effectiveness, he also discovered that there was a need to input a small delay in presenting the slide show, as the slides were advancing slightly ahead of time of the button being pressed [10].

According to Graimann *et al.* [10], until the 90s, progress on the study of BCIs was slow. For example, in the early twentieth century, there were around 10 research laboratories, on a worldwide scale, that were devoted to this study. However, there was a rapid growth over recent years regarding research on BCIs and there are currently more than 100 related research projects worldwide. However, the most important aspect is that this area of research was able to prove that it is able, not only to rehabilitate, but also extend the capabilities of human beings. On the other hand, BCIs are not yet completely conventional, they are not easy to use and as such, there is still a need to improve systems.

A BCI provides an alternate means for natural communication of the nervous system; it is an artificial system that surrounds efferent pathways of the body. It directly measures brain activity associated with the user's intention, and translates into application control signals. Typically, it has four characteristics: it must record direct brain activity; it must have feedback; it must be in real time; and should be controlled by voluntary initiative of the user [10].

The term BCI and its definition are well accepted in scientific circles. Nevertheless, it is possible to find in literature, other ways to describe this particular form of HMI [10]. According to Wolpaw *et al.* [11] "a direct brain-computer interface is a device that gives the brain a new non-muscular communication and control channel". According to Donoghue [12] "one of the main goals of a brain-computer interface (HMI [Human Machine Interface] or BMI - brain-machine interface) is to provide a command signal from the cortex. This command serves as a new functional output to control body parts with disabilities or physical devices, such as computers and robotic limbs". In line with this, Levine *et al.* [13] states "a direct brain interface accepts voluntary commands directly from the human brain without the need for physical movement and can be used to operate a computer or other technologies".

When starting this study we sought through scientific literature regarding BCI articles and/or papers. We found many in the medical field, some in education, however none that mentioned people with physical disabilities and/or cerebral palsy that used BCI. A research study between Coventry University and the Universidad Veracruzana, conducted by Rebolledo-Mendez and Dunwell [14], presented a usability evaluation of the device known as MindSet (MS), by NeuroSky. An interesting aspect was to assess whether MS readings can be combined with the data generated by the user. Already the research group at the University of Oulu, Finland, in partnership with the Human-Computer Interaction Institute, of Carnegie Mellon University, formed by Haapalainen *et al.* [15], conducted a study on the assessment of cognitive charge. The group of researchers from the LISTEN Project at Carnegie Mellon University - Mostow, Chang and Nelson [16] - showed that EEG data from the NeuroSky device could identify the frequency bands that were sensitive to difficulty and were able to discriminate between easy and difficult sentences with, better than by chance, among samples (adults and children) and modalities (oral and silent reading). They identified frequency bands susceptible to difficulties and various properties of lexical problems, which suggests that they may detect transient changes in cognitive demand or specific aspects of lexical access. Xu *et al.* [17], from University of California, used the device to develop a Wearable Assistive System Design for the Prevention of Falls, which can detect the risk of falls by monitoring the EEG signals from users and releasing an alerts prior to the actual fall occurring. Crowley *et al.* [18], from the University College Cork, Ireland, conducted two psychological tests to assess the suitability of the headset to measure and categorize a user's level of attention and meditation while playing. Wolpaw [19] states that the brain-computer interfaces (BCIs) are a fundamentally new approach to restore communication and control to people with severe motor disorders, such as Amyotrophic Lateral Sclerosis (ALS) and spinal cord injuries as well as other degenerative diseases. And he said, in 2007, that it could be an excellent assistive technology.

Schuh *et al.* [20] developed a study and prototyped simulator of a wheelchair in a three-dimensional environment controlled by non-invasive brain-computer interface. To this effect, we used a low cost EEG, NeuroSky Mindwave, as a signal acquisition device. For the development, we used Unity, a game engine. Through the prototype developed, we were able to detect blinking, and thus use this feature as a command for the simulator.

Operation. As shown in Fig. 1, one can find that:

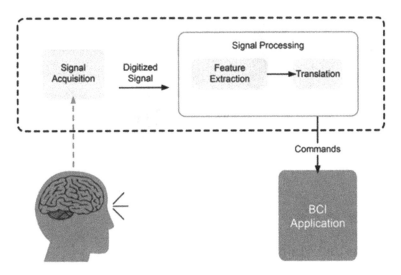

Fig. 1. BCI process diagram

- The process begins with the user's intention;
- The intention to communicate or control something triggers a complex process in certain areas of the brain;
- The activation of certain areas of the brain causes a potential difference with the adjacent areas.

NeuroSky MindWave Mobile. In the experiments we will use the NeuroSky MindWave (MW). NeuroSky is a company that was founded in 2004, in Silicon Valley, and which is focused on developing BCI devices. MW is a portable EEG machine that currently costs USD 129.90. In general terms, this machine can record brain waves, process the information and scan it. It then makes this information available to the used in applications [21].

This device is based on the NeuroSky ThinkGear technology, which consists of an electrode positioned in the Fp1 region, an electrode as point of reference in the ear clip, and an inside chip that processes all data as well as removes noise and interference. The device features a proprietary algorithm called eSense. It is through this that some features are extracted from the scanned signals, providing some alternative commands directly in the applications. One can for example, quote the attention and meditation levels [21].

Also known as neuro headset, due to its similarity in design to a headphone (earpiece), as can be seen in Fig. 2, it has a bluetooth interface with easy connectivity using serial ports, with support for Microsoft Windows platforms, OS X, Android and IOS. It does not have an internal battery and needs an AAA battery in order to operate. Other features to considered are: no need to use conducive gel on the electrode, no connection cables, extremely light, which makes it an easy to use device [21].

Fig. 2. Neurosky Mindwave

2   Methods and Materials

The research was of a qualitative approach. To develop the research we chose the case study. We justified our choice because the case study is an in-depth, multi-faceted research of a unique social phenomenon. We worked with Observational Case Studies. According to this author, the participatory work within the classroom and the new teaching methods can be object of participating observation. Stake [22] suggests that the case study is the study of the particularity and complexity of a case in understanding its activities within particular circumstances.

The purpose of the study was explained to all participants:

- Before each game there was an explanation of the purpose and mode of interaction (Attention/Meditation).
- The participants with CP performed the test individually in the presence of researcher and her interns.

The game developed is called Questing Ruins. This game has two versions: one that works with the blink of the eyes and the concentration levels (standard version) and, a version that works just with the concentration levels. Below, is shown (Fig. 3) the execution of some of the tests conducted with the sample, while playing the standard version (to the left) and with the concentration version (to the right).

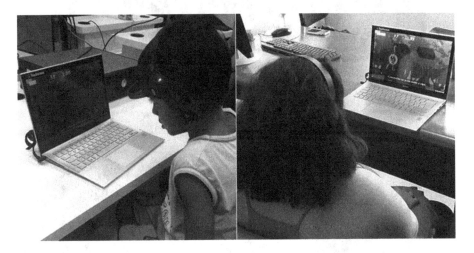

Fig. 3. User tests

In the game Questing in Ruins, the player assumes the figure of an ancient, which aims to get to the other side of town to disable a mechanism, and thus to free his people from machines that brought destruction to its once thriving kingdom. To advance in the game, one makes use of concentration and the blink of the eyes, allowing the character to interact with the objects in the scene. Below, is shown an image (Fig. 4) with these objects and scenery.

For example, when hitting an obstacle, the player must concentrate or control the intensity of his/her wink, so to overtake it. Along the way, the player encounters puzzles and only after beat them the character can continue walking. These puzzles consist of a disc that automatically rotates, having locks of different formats. When the player selects (by blinking) the correct lock and key, the game continues. At the end of each level, the player also finds another puzzle, composed of pieces that must be rotated through concentration, in order to guide a water supply inlet to its output. Below, a reference image (Fig. 5).

Fig. 4. A sample screen of the game

Fig. 5. An example of the final challenge of the game

3   Conclusions

BCI (Brain-Computer Interface) technology provides a means for interaction with machines, products, systems, and as such, its study is shown as something of major importance, because on the one hand, through BCI it is already possible to adapt machinery, products and systems to people with mobility problems in order to improve their performance, turning disabilities into mere differences of execution, but with averages of performance similar to those of ordinary people. On the other hand, the study of BCI ergonomics allows for analyzing levels of mental burden, instantly and objectively. The study on brain computed interface seeks to improve the way of interaction between humans and machines. It is important to remember that the expansion and recovery of

motor and cognitive functions are the main focus of research in this area. It can be stated that the EEG, although developed a long time ago, is still a key tool to support clinical diagnoses. However, researchers are conducting new approaches to this device. It is believed that soon we will see such approaches allied to games including educational.

It was observed after testing that this equipment has a very low precision when the game needs the input of the blink of an eye. People with motors impairments had difficulties to play. It is believed that the BCI equipment with more electrodes can solve this problem. In terms of ergonomics, materials need to be flexible so there is a better fixation on the user's head. In many people of the sample, it was not possible for the MindWave to stay steady throughout the entire test period, as it slid into smaller encephalic perimeters.

When the MindWave is used only with the concentration levels, it works better, but to our goal in assist in the education of people with cerebral palsy, MindWave was presented at this stage of testing just as a leisure tool.

References

1. Medina, B., Vianna, Y., Vianna, M., Tanaka, S., Gamification Inc.: como reinventar empresas a partir de jogos, 1st edn. MJV Press, Rio de Janeiro (2013)
2. Granic, I., Lobel, A., Engels, R.C.M.E.: The benefits of playing video games. Am. Psychol. 69(1), 66–78 (2014)
3. Piaget, J.: Play, Dreams and Imitation. Norton, New York (1962)
4. Erikson, E.H.: Toys and Reasons: Stages in the Ritualisation of Experience. Norton, New York (1977)
5. Vygotsky, L.: Mind in Society: The Development of Higher Psychological Functions. Harvard University Press, Cambridge (1978)
6. Gottman, J.M., Mettetal, G.: Speculations about social and affective development: friendship and acquaintanceship through adolescence. In: Gottman, J.M., Mettetal, G. (eds.) Conversations of Friends: Speculations on Affective Development, pp. 192–237. Cambridge University Press, New York (1986)
7. Johnson, S.: Surpreendente: a Televisão e o Videogame nos Tornam Mais Inteligentes. Campus, São Paulo (2005)
8. Dewey, J.: Experience and Education. Free Press, New York (1997)
9. Graimann, B., Allison, B., Pfurtscheller, G.: Brain-computer interfaces: a gentle introduction. In: Graimann, B., Allison, B., Pfurtscheller, G. (eds.) Brain-Computer Interfaces. The Frontiers Collection, pp. 1–27. Springer, Heidelberg (2010)
10. Wolpaw, J.R., Birbaumer, N., McFarland, D.J., Pfurtscheller, G., Vaughan, T.M.: Brain–computer interfaces for communication and control. Clin. Neurophysiol. 113(6), 767–791 (2002)
11. Donoghue, J.P.: Connecting cortex to machines: recent advances in brain interfaces. Nat. Neurosci. 5, 1085–1088 (2002)
12. Levine, S.P., Huggins, J.E., BeMent, S.L., Kushwaha, R.K., Schuh, L.A., Passaro, E.A., Ross, D.A.: Identification of electrocorticogram patterns as the basis for a direct brain interface. Clin. Neurophysiol. 16(5), 439–447 (1999)
13. Rebolledo-Mendez, G., Dunwell, I.: Assessing NeuroSky's usability to detect attention levels in an assessment exercise. In: Jacko, J.A. (ed.) Human-Computer Interaction New Trends, pp. 149–158. Springer, Heidelberg (2009)

14. Haapalainen, E., Kim, S., Forlizzi, J., Dey, A.: Psycho-physiological measures for assessing cognitive burden. In: Bardram, J.E., Langheinrich M. (eds.) Proceedings of the 12th ACM International Conference on Ubiquitous Computing, Ubicomp 2010, pp. 301–310 (2010)
15. Mostow, J., Chang, K.-M., Nelson, J.: Toward exploiting EEG input in a reading tutor. In: Biswas, G., Bull, S., Kay, J., Mitrovic, A. (eds.) AIED 2011. LNCS, vol. 6738, pp. 230–237. Springer, Heidelberg (2011)
16. Xu, W., Gong, F., He, L., Sarrafzadeh, M.: Wearable Assistive System Design for Fall Prevention (2011). http://www.ee.ucla.edu/~wxu/papers/conference/xu-hcmdss2011.pdf
17. Crowley, K., Sliney, A., Pitt, I., Murphy, D.: Evaluating a brain-computer interface to categorise human emotional response. In: 2010 IEEE 10th International Conference Proceedings on Advanced Learning Technologies (ICALT), pp. 276–278. IEEE Computer Society (2010)
18. Wolpaw, J.R.: Brain–computer interfaces as new brain output pathways. J. Physiol. **579**(3), 613–619 (2007)
19. Schuh, A.R., Lima, A., Heidrich, R.O., Mossmann, J., Flores, C., Bez, M.R.: Development of a simulator controlled using non-invasive brain-computer interface for training in the use of a wheelchair. Revista Novas Tecnologias na Educação, **11**(3), 1–9 (2013). http://seer.ufrgs.br/index.php/renote/article/view/44716
20. Neurosky. Neurosky Mindwave. http://www.neurosky.com/Products/MindWave.aspx
21. Stake, R.E.: The Art of Case Study Research. Sage, London (1995)

GEOpod: Using a Game-Style Interface to Explore a Serious Meteorological Database

Blaise Liffick[1(✉)], Gary Zoppetti[1], Sepideh Yalda[2], and Richard Clark[2]

[1] Department of Computer Science, Millersville University, Millersville, PA, USA
{blaise.liffick,gary.zoppetti}@millersville.edu
[2] Department of Earth Science, Millersville University, Millersville, PA, USA
{sepi.yalda,richard.clark}@millersville.edu

Abstract. This paper discusses the human-computer interface component of the GEOPOD project, a software system that implements an interactive, intuitive interface – the *GEOpod* – that allows student users to probe a 3-D immersive environment of authentic geophysical data (i.e. based on real observations, assimilated data, and/or simulated output from physically consistent, numerical weather prediction modeling systems), actuate virtual atmospheric devices to collect data, and record observations. The system provides a guided instructional environment in which meteorology undergraduate students can explore a given atmospheric volume in a "shuttlepod-like" virtual flying machine. Because the atmospheric data consist of real-time observations and imagery, along with simulated data from numerical models based on actual physics, the exploration environment naturally exhibits technical accuracy, scientific soundness, physical consistency, authenticity, and high fidelity.

Keywords: Game interface · Flight simulation · Visualization

1 Background

There is little doubt in academia or among the public at large about the usefulness of computer technology as a tool for learning [7]. Across many disciplines, but notably in the geosciences, computer technology as a tool for access to data and Web-based resources, and computational problem solving, is the lifeblood of the classroom. Today, students in higher education have access to real-time and legacy datasets, sophisticated visualization applications, high-bandwidth networks, and high-speed computers. The so-called "Millennials" or the Net Generation (NetGen'ers) have grown up with computers and are technologically savvy in a way prior generations could not be [15]. They are accustomed to operating in a digital environment, communicating with cell phones, text messaging, and myriad mobile and home devices. NetGen'ers enjoy being part of communities using multiple social media applications. "Millennials are putting [video games] at the center of their entertainment preferences, but it is a new kind of gaming that is more social, interactive and engaging [17, p. 9]." They are experiential learners: they prefer to learn by doing as opposed to learning by listening. By contrast, and despite huge investments in communication and computer hardware made by

© Springer International Publishing Switzerland 2016
A. Marcus (Ed.): DUXU 2016, Part II, LNCS 9747, pp. 273–283, 2016.
DOI: 10.1007/978-3-319-40355-7_26

universities and schools, most formal teaching and learning still use methods that would be familiar to a 19th century student: reading texts, listening to lectures, and participating in highly scripted laboratory exercises [9].

There is no shortage of ideas on what can be done to better understand how students learn in the digital age [1, 3, 15]. Converging evidence from educational psychology suggests that computers can play an important role in developing critical and creative thinking skills in students, such as scientific inquiry. Recent advances in learning and cognitive science research recommend individualized instruction, subject-matter experts, and rich curricular activities for improving education [17]. Unfortunately, many recommendations have not been widely adopted because they prove too expensive or are difficult to integrate into traditional teaching approaches that too often still ignore findings of learning research [10].

Applied prudently and intelligently, technology holds great promise as a means to improve education and can be implemented without unrealistic increases in spending. Prensky [16] has framed the significance of computer technology in terms of the fundamental characteristics of effective learning: active engagement; participation in groups; frequent interaction and feedback; and connections to real-world contexts [2]. Simulations can improve learning by encouraging students to "learn by doing." Advocates of electronic games suggest that gaming could increase student enthusiasm for educational materials, which could in turn increase time on task and lead ultimately to improved motivation and student performance [17].

Educators have already begun introducing games into instruction (e.g. "Discover Babylon©, Civilization II™, SimCity™, and Immune Attack™"), and will continue to benefit from commercial inroads into gaming in education so long as such applications are based on a sound understanding of which features of these systems are important for learning and why [18]. However, even if we fully understand how best to use simulated environments, the challenge of actually building technically accurate and visually compelling simulations is enormous [9].

The term "gamification" has recently been coined to describe both the use of games as tools (e.g. simulations, team-building exercises) for business, education, etc. and for the use of game techniques within a system [2, 8]. Deterding [4] suggests that gamification is "the use of game design elements in non-game contexts." He further describes one level of gamification as using game interface design patterns to incorporate common, successful interaction design components into non-game applications. It is in this context in which the GEOPOD project has been developed. While the interface elements are derived from the realm of computer gaming, game elements such as scores, levels, leaderboards, etc. have not been included. Still, the motivational factors of providing such a game-like interface are well documented [4].

2   Project Description

The GEOPOD project creates an interactive interface (GEOpod) that can probe a 3-D immersive world of authentic geophysical data using a roadmap of rich curricular materials to motivate learners to explore, query, discover, and report on geoscience concepts, processes, and phenomena. The GEOpod has the ability to navigate the data volume defined by actual geospatial coordinates and map referencing; collect and store real data by means of virtual sensors; and actuate devices for measurement and sample collection. The interface simulates a navigable pod, or 3-D vessel, with six degrees of freedom. The experience is designed for instruction that will immerse students in a 3-D exploration environment where they can explore atmospheric features such as jet streams and frontal boundaries; deploy devices to retrieve vertical atmospheric profiles; follow isosurfaces; discover relationships and connections within and between phenomena; and collect and record data for analysis.

While GEOpod is not a game, it features a game-like interactive, virtual environment with a first-person perspective, one with which many students are familiar. Such environments have the potential to enrich instruction by creating for the student an immersive environment of pictorial dynamism and sophistication that is fun, interactive, and the next-best thing to reality. Learning through performance requires active discovery, analysis, interpretation, problem-solving, memory, and physical activity [5]. "Video games are complex systems composed of rules that interact. Gamers must think like a designer and form hypotheses about how the rules interact so they can accomplish goals and even bring about emergent results. Thinking like a designer in order to understand systems is a core 21st-century skill [17, p. 12]."

The project had three main phases: (1) initial development of the data visualization and GEOpod simulator software, (2) a usability evaluation, and (3) an educational evaluation. This paper reports primarily on the second phase, describing the interface and the usability study that was conducted to evaluate and improve it.

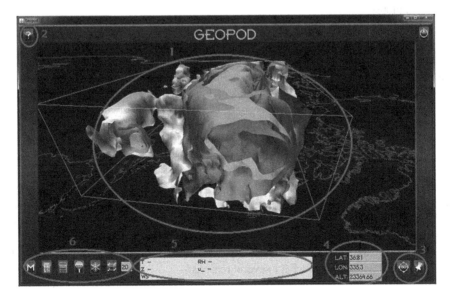

Fig. 1. Initial GEOpod interface

3 Initial Interface

Figure 1 shows the GEOpod display that was initially developed. It is meant to represent the view of the pilot out the front windshield of the pod, the various instruments providing data readings of the atmosphere, and most of the controls or operations available to the pilot. This is in addition to the controls (particularly navigational) that are provided to the user through keyboard input, which mimic those of other video flight simulators or provide additional operations.

The 6 areas of the display are configured as follows:

1. Data Volume – contains the data used to create the isosurface (a specific volume and set of conditions of the atmosphere that is currently being explored). The pod pilot can sample parameters from the data volume as they move within it. The colored surfaces within this volume represent visualizations of atmospheric data.
2. Help – displays a help page.
3. Geocode Lookup – allows the user to lookup or navigate to a specific geographic location within the data volume.
4. Navigation Panel – shows the current position of the pod in latitude, longitude, and altitude.
5. Parameter Display – displays up to 9 different atmospheric parameters on a 3 × 3 grid. Some of the default parameters are temperature (T), geopotential height (Z), wind speed (WS), relative humidity (RH), and dewpoint (Td).
6. Primary Tools – includes buttons to provide access to a calculator, notepad, measurement devices (dropsonde instrument package and particle imager), and a navigational tool for setting up grid points within the volume.

The controls of this display are meant to be accessed using a typical pointing device such as a mouse.

3.1 Navigating the GEOpod

The GEOpod is a vehicle which allows the pilot to be immersed in the 3-D data volume. When using the GEOpod, the pilot can think of themself being at a certain location inside the 3-D world that cam see on the screen (as in Fig. 1). Using any one of various navigation controls, the pilot can move the GEOpod inside this world. When the pod moves, the pilot sees the image on the screen change, because they, in the GEOpod, are moving (much as buildings appear to fly past when driving a car). The navigation controls allow the pilot to move the GEOpod within the world, not alter the world or the data volume itself. All of the controls are relative to the GEOpod's current position and orientation within this 3-D world (i.e., relative to the pod's local coordinate system). For example, moving "up" will increase the pod's altitude if the pod is level with the earth's surface, or move the pod across the surface if it were above the earth looking straight down.

A keyboard and mouse interface was used instead of using an interface device such as a joystick or game controller for several reasons:

1. Potential users may already be familiar with this style of navigation through prior experience with computer games,
2. The additional physical dexterity such devices require,
3. The expense of supplying the devices for every system in a lab, and
4. Requiring adopters of the system to buy additional hardware would decrease the dissemination potential of the system.

3.2 Keyboard Navigation Functions

The four main navigation keys are **w**, **s**, **a**, and **d**. The **w** key moves the GEOpod forward, in whatever direction it is facing. The **s** key moves the GEOpod backward. The **a** key moves the GEOpod to the left. The **d** key moves the GEOpod to the right. The **f** and **c** keys move the GEOpod "up" and "down", respectively, where these directions depend on the pods current attitude (orientation).

For a complete description of all the GEOpod controls, see [6].

4 The Usability Study

This following describes the test plan used to conduct a usability test during the development of the GEOpod software system [11]. The goals of usability testing included establishing a baseline of user performance, establishing and validating user performance measures, and identifying potential design concerns to be addressed in order to improve the efficiency, productivity, and end-user satisfaction.

It is worth emphasizing that this study is not intended as a validation test of the correct behavior of the GEOpod controls, nor as a test of the user's abilities per se, but is an evaluation of the effectiveness of the GEOpod interface from the user's perspective. Usability goals include that the user will be able, after minimal training, to perform a series of guided activities within a "reasonable" amount of time, with a minimal number of errors, instances of "dead ends," or resorting to the help menu. The reasonableness metric will be judged against the need for students to be able to accomplish a certain amount of work using the GEOpod system during a typical class lab period. A "control" study was done by having an expert user perform the timed trials as well, to provide a lower bound on the times to complete the tasks.

4.1 Methodology

Two types of usability testing were employed for this project. The first was an expert heuristic evaluation, looking for potential problems based on basic human-computer interaction (HCI) principles. The results from the expert walkthrough were used to inform some elements of the usability study, as well as to provide general recommendations for improvements to the system.

The second type of testing was a standard usability study using a small group of test participants selected from the population of potential users of the system.

The Usability Study. There were 14 primary test participants, all of whom were asked to complete the same set of four test trials – 3 short trials and one trial that approximated how the GEOpod system would ultimately be used in a class lab assignment. The order of the test trials was the same for each participant, as effects of learning bias were not a concern in this study; indeed, it was assumed that participants would learn something from each trial that could prove useful in subsequent trials. Each test participant was asked for basic demographic information including age, handedness, gender, and experience with previous 3-D navigational systems. They were also given a satisfaction assessment as a post-test to gauge their level of satisfaction with the interface.

The participants were all earth sciences students from the sophomore, junior, and senior levels, ensuring that they had at sufficient knowledge of meteorology principles and terminology; their knowledge of meteorology was not being tested, only their ability to use the GEOpod system effectively to complete the tasks. There were an equal number of male and female test participants. Participants were provided with a brief training on the use of the GEOpod controls prior to the first trial, as well as being given a short interval for experimenting with the controls in an unstructured manner.

The test system was housed in a cubical enclosed on three sides in a distraction-free research lab. One of the walls of this cubical was a 5′ high partition. The test subject was positioned at a desk within the cubical. The test facilitator sat outside the cubical on the other side of the partition, unseen by the test subject. The facilitator had a monitor that was a mirror of the test participant's monitor, as well as an active keyboard and mouse with which to interact with the system during trial setup and end-of-test housekeeping tasks. This allowed the facilitator to observe and record the action of the test without in any way being in direct contact with the test subject, either verbally or visually.

Recording was done with both a video camera trained on the mirrored monitor and through screen capture software. The GEOpod system is also equipped with a logging mechanism that records time-stamped (accurate to at least the 1/10th second) events detected by the system, including all keystrokes, button presses, etc.

Timings and error counting were done after the trials through protocol analysis of the captured video, ensuring that such measurements were consistently taken.

Results. The main usability study was conducted to primarily get a feel for the "reasonableness" of the design, i.e. were students able to successfully use the system to accomplish typical educational tasks. Inversely, the study would also point out potential problem areas with the interface, e.g. participants had difficulty completing a task.

Table 1 summarizes the timings of the 14 participants over 4 trials. In addition, the table includes the times posted by an expert user (control). A value of double the control time was used as a reference target time for the participant performance [12].

Table 1. Timed trials results

	Trial 1	Trial 2	Trial 3	Trial 4
Average	3:21	7:24	4:45	21:25
Control	1:43	2:26	1:54	10:50
2 * Control	3:26	4:52	3:48	21:40

What we see from this data is that, in Trials 1 and 4, test participants met the goal of performing the tasks in no more than double the control times. This meets the stated performance targets.

In Trial 3, participants completed the tasks in 2.5 times the control time. This is slightly worse than the target. However, there was only one time that was significantly worse than all others (nearly double the next longest time). If this time were eliminated from the average, the result is only slightly worse (4:11) than the target time.

In Trial 2, participants performed at 3 times the control time. There were 4 participants who took nearly twice as long as all other participants. Eliminating these extra lengthy participants from the average produces a result of 5:07, just slightly worse than the target time.

The conclusion for this data is that the time required for the users to complete each trial is within acceptable limits of performance.

Table 2 summarizes the participants' responses to the post-test survey which asked attitudinal questions about their experiences with the GEOpod system using a Likert scale. The full questionnaire can be found in [12].

Table 2. Questionnaire responses

Question	Q 1	Q 2	Q 3	Q 4	Q 5	Q 6	Q 7	Q 8	Q 9	Q 10	Q 11
Average	3.53	4.47	4.33	3.73	4.67	4.53	3.87	2.73	1.87	2.27	4.53

Questions 1–7 should result in agreement (at least a 4) from the user (with 5 being "Strongly Agree") if the user had a positive attitude toward the GEOpod system. Four of the seven questions resulted in average responses better than 4 (very favorable). The remaining 3 indicators showed slightly less favorable results, but still on the positive side of the scale.

Questions 8–10 should result in disagreement (a 2 or less) from the user (with 1 being "Strongly Disagree") if the user had a positive attitude toward the GEOpod system. Only one of the three indicators was clearly within the target response area (Question 9), but the other two indicators are still on the side of the scale indicating disagreement.

Question 11 asked the user directly to indicate whether they liked using the GEOpod system. An average response of 4.53 shows a strong affirmative for this question.

The conclusion for this data is that users were uniform in their positive attitude toward the GEOpod system. In general the participants liked the system and thought it was easy to use. It was clear not only from the user responses to the post-test survey but from analyzing video of the tests that navigation was a consistent problem for users. There was some indication, however, that such navigational difficulties may be temporary, as indicated both by one particular participant in the survey and from observing improved user navigational performance as the trials progressed – an expected result.

Video Analysis. The video recordings of all trials were reviewed in order to uncover problems not revealed by the data above. In particular, evidence of user confusion, execution mistakes, or misunderstandings of the state of the system was cataloged. This analysis uncovered six prominent errors by users, summarized in Table 3, in order by frequency (highest at top).

Table 3. User errors

1. User didn't hit "Enter" to set grid points
2. User became disoriented
3. User failed to successfully complete at least one step
4. User selected wrong operation
5. User moved cursor to upper right corner of a window in search of a close button
6. User used a manual process rather than an available automated one

User errors can be caused by a number of factors, not the least of which is simply inexperience with the system. User Errors (UE) 1 and 2 in particular can be accounted for by this. Such problems can usually be effectively eliminated through longer and/or more thorough training.

That being said, however, there are other issues related to user disorientation (UE 2) – a pervasive problem during the trials – including a lack of adequate feedback related to the GEOpod's orientation. This problem is discussed in more detail below.

Another indicator of concern is User Error 3, indicating a failure to complete at least one step during the trial. Usually this was because the user skipped a step (either intentionally or unintentionally), though sometimes it was because they did not perform the correct prior actions in order to successfully complete a step. Users who noticed their error and corrected their mistake were not flagged with this error.

Some of these failures can be attributed to issues not related to the system's interface. One solution, certainly, is more thorough training. Another is that the phrasing of task statements may not have been adequately understood by some participants. Examples include phrases such as "note the location" or "parallel to the isosurface." These problems can be overcome when designing assignments using the GEOpod system through a combination of training and changes in wording for certain tasks.

Table 4 shows the most frequent interface errors identified through video analysis. The most frequent error encountered is a focus problem related to the data entry fields (latitude, longitude, altitude, and gridpoints). As a consequence of this problem, users frequently ended up accidently entering command keystrokes into these data fields. While in all instances the users noticed the problem and were able to correctly fix it, this is still a significant problem of the interface as it slows users down significantly.

Table 4. Interface errors

1. Problems with selection in data fields (e.g. latitude, longitude, altitude)
2. Focus remained in data entry field
3. Insufficient feedback to user
4. User has difficulty selecting a point on the grid
5. Overlapping windows obscures important information
6. Calculator does not remain visible while using notebook

The second significant problem users had was in selecting the current values in these data fields prior to modifying the fields. It is not clear whether anything can be done about the current awkwardness of this interaction.

Recommendations. The expert review, usability study, and video analysis were all aimed specifically at identifying potential problems with the interface design. As a result of these studies, 28 specific recommendations were made for changes to the interface. The most noteworthy problems were

(1) Buttons that didn't act like buttons
(2) Data entry boxes that created confusion as a result of focus problems
(3) Navigational confusion due to lack or inconsistency of controls

As an example of the kind of navigational problems encountered, a frequent problem for users was disorientation in terms of the current position and orientation of the GEOpod. For instance, it was possible to get the pod upside-down without knowing it, since there was no feedback telling the user the pod's orientation. In such instances, many navigational commands would often do the opposite of what was expected, which both confused and frustrated users.

A complete list of recommended changes to the interface can be found at [12].

4.2   Updated Interface

Figure 2 shows a redesigned interface for the system. Most of the elements of this display were redesigned or enhanced as a result of the study. Particularly note the area designated as feature 9, the new navigational display, which now includes both a compass and a horizon (attitude) indicator. In addition, a mini-map in the upper left corner (feature 2) provides an overhead view of the volume overlaid on a world map.

Fig. 2. Updated GEOpod interface

These aids were added specifically to overcome the navigational problems experienced by users. In addition, all buttons were redesigned to be reactive, and additional controls such as a speed indicator (feature 6) were added.

5 Educational Outcomes

A detailed study of the educational benefits of the GEOPOD system for meteorology students has not yet been conducted. Plans are being made to conduct such a study.

A limited beta test of the system was conducted with 64 students in two meteorology classes. Among the results of this beta test, a post-use questionnaire asked students to respond to questions regarding whether the GEOPOD system enhanced content understanding. An "overwhelming majority of students (75 %) responded to this question in the positive... the majority felt that the GEOpod was helpful because it was visually compelling (41), some (7) expressed that it gave them a chance to explore patterns and relationships in the data displayed and gain a deeper understanding of the interrelationship among concepts. Still others (5) responded that they "enjoyed the active or kinesthetic aspects of the technology (e.g. flying around inside the jet stream and being able to set parameters)" [13].

6 Future Work

The project hopes to implement two additional studies. The first is a second usability study to determine whether the redesign does indeed correct the user problems noted in the first study. Secondly, a more comprehensive educational study of the use of the GEOPOD system in actual meteorology classes would be used to validate the overall educational benefits of the system.

7 Conclusions

Overall, student reactions to using the GEOPOD system have been overwhelmingly positive. The 3-D visualization of the system was particularly appealing to students, as was the opportunities to explore the data through directed activities. The system shows promise in assisting students to gain a deeper understanding of meteorological principles.

References

1. Beetham, H., Sharpe, R. (eds.): Rethinking Pedagogy for a Digital Age: Designing for 21st Century Learning, 3rd edn. Routledge Publishing, New York (2013)
2. Bowser, A., Hansen, D., Preece, J., He, Y., Boston, C., Hammock, J.: Gamifying citizen science: a study of two user groups. In: Proceedings of the Companion Publication of the 17th ACM Conference on Computer Supported Cooperative Work and Social Computing (CSCW Companion 2014), pp. 137–140. ACM, New York (2014)

3. Dede, C.: Immersive interfaces for engagement and learning. Science **323**(5910), 66–69 (2009)
4. Deterding, S., Khaled, R., Nacke, L., Dixon, D.: Gamification: toward a definition. In: Gamification Workshop Proceedings, CHI 2011, Vancouver, BC, Canada (2011)
5. Foreman, J.: Next generation: education technology versus the lecture. EDUCAUSE Rev. (2002)
6. GEOpod User's Guide (2012). http://millersvillecs.github.io/geopod/documents/GeopodUsersGuide.pdf
7. How People Learn. National Research Council Commission on Behavioral and Social Sciences and Education. National Academy Press. Washington, D.C. (2000)
8. Kappen, D., Nacke, L.: The kaleidoscope of effective gamification: desconstructing gamification in business applications. In: Proceedings of Gamification, Stratford, ON, Canada, 02–04 October 2013 (2013)
9. Kelly, H.: Challenges and Opportunities in Game-Based Learning Environments (2005). http://www.nae.edu/nae/caseecomnew.nsf/weblinks. Accessed 15 Apr 2006
10. Kirriemuir, J., McFarlane, A.: Literature Review in Games and Learning (2004). http://www.futurelab.org.uk/research/reviews/08_01.htm. Accessed 18 Apr 2007
11. Liffick, B.W.: GEOPOD project usability test plan (2010). http://millersvillecs.github.io/geopod
12. Liffick, B.W.: GEOPOD project usability study analysis (2011). http://millersvillecs.github.io/geopod
13. Mackin, K.J.: GEOPOD final evaluation report (2012). http://millersvillecs.github.io/geopod
14. Moore, A.H., Fowler, S.B., Jesiek, B.K., Moore, J.F., Watson, C.E.: Learners IT and 21st century learners in higher education. EDUCAUSE Res. Bull. **7** (2008). http://www.educause.edu/ecar
15. Prensky, M.: Digital Game Based Learning. Exploring the Digital Generation. Educational Technology, US. Department of Education, Washington, D.C. (2003)
16. The 2015 Essential facts about the computer and video game industry (2015). Entertainment Software Association, April 2015. Accessed 1 Sep 2015. http://www.theesa.com/wp-content/uploads/2015/04/ESA-Essential-Facts-2015.pdf
17. The Learning Federation Project (2012). http://www.thelearningfederation.edu.au/tlf2. Accessed 1 Sep 2015
18. Ziesemer, A., Müller, L., Silveira, M.: Gamification aware: users perception about game elements on non-game context. In: Proceedings of the 12th Brazilian Symposium on Human Factors in Computing Systems (IHC 2013), pp. 276–279. Brazilian Computer Society, Porto Alegre (2013)

Validation of a Gamification Design Guide: Does a Gamification Booklet Help UX Designers to Be More Creative?

Cathie Marache-Francisco and Eric Brangier[(✉)]

Université de Lorraine, PErSEUs EA 7312, Faculté des Sciences
Humaines et Sociales, Île du Saulcy, 57006 Metz, France
{cathie.marache-francisco,
eric.brangier}@univ-lorraine.fr

Abstract. Gamification is a recent concept describing a game - inspired interface design technique aimed at driving user engagement and motivation in non-game systems. Although not a new idea the gamification concept is currently very popular, since it promises happy consumers and more productive companies full of hard-working and loyal employees. Faced with constant failure and poor game design, we have tested the effectiveness of a guide initially described in Marache-Francisco and Brangier [7]. It introduces the design process based on user-centered design and also provides a tool box (gamification principles, decision trees to guide designers' choices, a grid detailing design elements by category) and examples of application. To validate this guide, 29 designers, divided into two groups (with/without guide), were given the task of gamifying a standard computer system. The results show that using the guide fostered fluidity (number of elements), flexibility (number of elements per strategy), originality (new ideas) and development (number of secondary ideas). We then discuss the contributions and limits of this research followed by suggestions for other areas of research.

Keywords: Gamification · Persuasive technology · Emotional design · Motivation · Design process

1 Introduction

The idea of applying the principles of game design to professional interfaces has been developed recently under the concept of gamification (for a synthesis, see: Marache-Francisco and Brangier [9]). In fact, gamification interaction is often considered as a challenge subject to conditions of gain, a points system, a leader board and bonuses linked to a rewards system (badges). However, Kim [2] underlines that, points, badges and leader boards are not sufficient to create a game like experience. They are in fact only feedback elements. According to Kim, game design is based on intrinsic motivation generated through three points: autonomy, mastery and purpose. Gamification is therefore not reduced to just applying surface elements (badge, level, reward challenge ...) but requires understanding player social styles, their level of expertise and manner of engagement in the task. Several authors have provided gamification

© Springer International Publishing Switzerland 2016
A. Marcus (Ed.): DUXU 2016, Part II, LNCS 9747, pp. 284–293, 2016.
DOI: 10.1007/978-3-319-40355-7_27

guides which go further than simply transposing game elements to a non-game context. Werbach and Hunter [11] provide a list of gamification elements grouped under the following ranked categories: *dynamics, mechanics and components*. They also identify six steps in gamification design: *Define business objectives; Delineate target behaviours; Describe your players; Devise activity cycles; Don't forget the fun!; Deploy the appropriate tool.* As for Kumar and Herger [3] they speak about *Player Centered Design* and describe five design stages: *Know your player; Identify the mission; Understand human motivation; Apply mechanics; Manage, monitor and measure.* They also define player persona templates, as well as lists of elements to use. Finally, Nicholson [10] highlights the concept of *"meaningful gamification"* such as the *"integration of user-centered game design elements into non-game contexts"*. Here he stresses the need for a design approach adapted to the context of application and to the types of players involved.

The aim of this article is to provide an additional contribution to these defining initiatives and to help in gamification design. To this aim, Sect. 2 will introduce the gamification guide. It includes a description of the design process which enhances user-centered design through questions of emotion and motivation, a tool-box providing principles, decision trees and a design grid as well as examples illustrating the impact of design choices on users. Section 3 raises the question of the guide's validation and related methodology. Finally, Sect. 4 will show the results of an experiment to validate a design guide involving 29 designers.

2 Design Work for a Guide to the Gamification Process

In response to the question of the poor quality of gamification, a guide to designing gamified interfaces was produced (described in Marache-Francisco and Brangier, [6]). It provides easily applicable standard approaches, fostering the creation of coherent systems adapted to the context into which they are integrated. The underlying hypothesis is that gamification design, a creative exercise, can be guided in a rational and scientific manner by a set of rules drawn from current literature and emerging practices, via a design guide which will accompany its user throughout the design process.

The guide highlights gamification design processes [3, 11] and gamification elements as well as focus points on the various negative effects encountered. In conjunction, an initial classification of gamification is included (*sensory-motor modalities, motivation and persuasion, elements, elements supporting cognitive processes*, [7]) and the results of a study carried out on the perception of gamification by designers (*cosmetic approach* with appeal and readability; *implicational approach* with social identity, freedom of choice and competing against oneself and others) described in [8]. The design guide was produced iteratively by identifying, in each source, the most important points to present to users. A pre-test on two subjects enabled us to fine-tune the guide.

The guide contains three parts:

1. A description of the design process, a two phase iterative approach: context analysis and conception
2. A «tool-box» supplying a set of design support elements:

   - *Gamification principles:* voluntary engagement, benefits both parties, personalized experience, sustain long term interaction, anticipate unwanted side effects, legality and ethics;
   - *Decision Trees:* questions guiding the selection of gamification elements; e.g., «Is there a large and reachable social community?»;
   - *Design Grid:* categories of elements (appeal, narration, avatar, task support, level, motivation, reward, gratification).

3. Examples illustrating the guide's different dimensions and variables (screen illustrations, choice of the gamification experience...).

This design choice gives an overview of the approach (design process for the steps and principles for the key concepts), an inventory of available elements (design grid), help in decision-making (decision trees), and finally, illustrated examples.

The aims of this guide are to provide designers with a body of ideas (content); guidance for the design (aim, finalisation) and resources for designing (steps, process). The guide should therefore fulfil the task of stimulating designers' creative performance.

3   Problem and Method of Validating the Gamification Guide

The guide not only aims to be educational and scientific but also features every aspect of the gamification design process. It particularly focuses on translating abstract concepts into easily understandable and operationalizable elements, the target group being an extensive one with quite varied levels of mastery of ergonomic concepts and HMI design. The designers should not be too restricted, and should be given a certain amount of freedom to ensure their compliance with the guide.

3.1   Problem

Hence the aim of this research is to determine whether the guide is useful for gamification design and how. The basic premise being that if anyone is capable of transferring game elements from existing games into a non-game system, having a guide which provides the approach to gamification and steers the designer through an extensive set of available elements would enable him/her to be more creative. For this study the general hypothesis is therefore that the guide enables interface enrichment with gamification. This is tested using the creativity indicators defined by Guilford in 1967 (cited by [5]) and Torrance in 1976 (cited by [1]), being:

- Fluidity: Refers to the number of ideas produced;
- Flexibility: How many categories of ideas are covered;

- Originality: Corresponds to the ability to produce different, new ideas;
- Elaboration: Describes the amount of detail provided by the designer.

Hence the general hypotheses are that the guide fosters simultaneously: fluidity; flexibility; originality; and elaboration.

3.2 Method

Sample. Twenty-nine designers specialized in human-machine interaction (22 men and 7 women; average age = 31, standard deviation = 9.5; 11 Masters Students and 18 professionals) took part in the experiment. They were all more or less familiar with *Business Intelligence* (3 not) and gamification (1 not) and 24 were game players.

Task and Material. The 29 participants' task was to gamify three screens of a *Business Intelligence* software, with help from the software's personas and the following material:

1. A 20-min oral presentation illustrated with slides on gamification (definition; objectives; limits);
2. For one group, guidelines to using the gamification guide (process; grid with cards and tables; examples);
3. For one group, the gamification guide containing: a booklet describing gamification principles; Design grid with 4 cards summarizing the elements in categories and 4 posters describing the content of the cards (description of elements and examples);

After answering a small questionnaire to sum up their profiles, they were given the following material to carry out their gamification task:

- A size A3 sheet of paper to make sketches on and to describe gamified screens;
- Material to be able to explain in writing the choices made for each screen;
- For one of the groups material to show the link between personas and gamification dimensions;
- A medium to enable a description of the gamification technique used;
- Pencil crayons, felt-tip pens, pencils, black pen, eraser, post-its.

Procedure. Two experimental groups were formed:

- One was a control group (g_1).
- The other group had the gamification guide (g_2).

The subjects were divided equally between the two groups according to their profiles (e.g., level of knowledge of gamification, experience or not of video games).

The procedure was as follows. Firstly the subjects (g1 and g2) were given a quick training in gamification. They were then given a questionnaire to fill in focused on their gamification and video game knowledge. The first design phase (test phase p1) lasted one hour. All the groups were given a case study which consisted in gamifying a scenario in the software. The intermediary stage was a coffee break for the control group (g1) where the subjects were asked not to discuss their ideas with each other. Group g2 were given training on the gamification guide which included: the design process, the different supports, and examples of application. During the second design phase (experimental phase p2), the groups (g1 and g2) had to go back to the initial case. They were asked to rework their gamification suggestions. Group g1 worked in the same conditions as in phase one, whereas group g2 were provided with the principles, cards and posters.

Measures. How and what are the designers going to gamify? The results analysis seeks to identify and quantify the gamification strategies and elements used by the two groups.

The strategies and elements identified are the following: *Define the functions; Plan the temporality of actions; Plan the progression; Inform on the aims pursued; Organize personalization; take into account level of experience; Develop appeal; Set the scene; Solicit other users; Enable interpersonal cooperation; Initiate social comparison; Launch individual or social competition; Motivate with high level goals; Acknowledge and reward; Contribute to group visibility; Enable self-expression; Give feedback valence; Manage perceived freedom of choice; Foster user's ethics; Reduce harmful elements or their perception.* It should be noted that the category, *Define the functions,* groups together all the elements which do not refer to gamification, an interesting element to take into consideration when conducting the analysis. The coding work carried out is illustrated in Table 1:

Once all the gamification elements were identified in the sketches, comparisons between phase 1 and 2 were made for the two groups:

- The average difference (phase 1–phase 2) in the number of gamified elements;
- The average difference (phase 2–phase 1) in the number of gamification strategies;
- The number of ideas which, in phase 2, have been re-used, changed or abandoned from stage 1 or were completely new;
- The percentage of new ideas in phase 2 compared to the total number of ideas put forward.

3.3 Operational Hypotheses

The hypotheses are the following:

- H1: The average difference (phase 2–phase 1) in the number of elements will be higher for the group which used the guide than in the group without the guide;
- H2: The average difference (phase 2–phase 1) in the number of elements per strategy will be higher for the group which used the guide than for the group without the guide;
- H3: The percentage of new ideas in phase 2 will be higher for the group which used the guide than for the group without the guide;
- H4: The average difference (phase 2–phase 1) in the number of secondary ideas will be higher for the group which used the guide than for the group without the guide.

Table 1. Examples of coding of what the designers produced

Extracts	*Strategy* : **element**
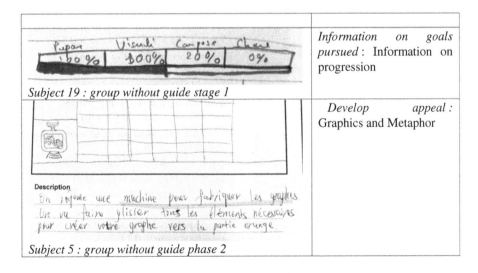 *Subject 10 : group with guide, phase 1*	*Giving feedback valence :* Congratulate *Inform on the aims pursued :* Information on progression
Subject 1 : group with guide, phase 2	*Management of perceived freedom of choice :* Acceptation of goals of the system
Subject 19 : group without guide stage 1	*Information on goals pursued :* Information on progression
Subject 5 : group without guide phase 2	*Develop appeal :* Graphics and Metaphor

4 Results Analysis

All the results were analysed statistically using comparison of averages tests. Normality and homogeneity of variances tests were conducted in order to select the type of test to conduct (parametric: student's t test; non parametric: Mann-Whitney U test).

The average difference in the number of gamified elements between phase 1 and phase 2 is much higher for the subjects who used the guide than for the others ($p = 0.03$ with $U = 55.5$ and Z adjusted = 2.14). They had on average 15.8 more gamification elements in phase 2 (standard deviation: 12.83) against 7.57 (standard deviation: 7.73) which is more than twice as many. Thus validating our hypothesis: The guide fosters fluidity.

The average difference in the number of elements per strategy is significantly different between the subjects who used the guide and the others for 7 strategies out of 20 (results in detail in Table 2). Thus validating the hypothesis: The guide fosters flexibility with enrichment in the following categories: *Plan the progression*; *Take into*

Table 2. Intermediary results summary

Hypothesis	Results in details
Fluidity: *Average difference in the number of elements between phase 1 and phase 2* **Validated (p = 0.03)**	mg = 15.8 (sg = 12.83) > mn 7.57 (sn = 7.73)
Flexibility: *Average difference in the number of elements per strategy between phase 1 and phase 2* **Validated on 7 strategies**	*Define the functions* (p = 0.03): mg = −0.07 (sg = 0.8) < mn = 0.79 (sn = 1.25)
	Plan the progression (p = 0.04): mg = 0.87 (sg = 1.25) > mn = 0.14 (sn = 0.53)
	Take into account level of experience (p = 0.02): mg = 0.6 (sg = 1.06) > mn = 0 (sn = 0)
	Set the scene (p = 0.01): mg = 0.53 (sg = 0.83) > mn = 0 (sn = 0)
	Launch an individual or social competition (p = 0.03): mg = 1.2 (sg = 1.82) > mn = 0.21 (sn = 0.8)
	Enabling self-expression (p = 0.01): mg = 1.13 (sg = 1.12) > mn = 0.28 (sn = 1.77)
	Manage perceived freedom of choice (p = 0.04): mg = 0.73 (sg = 1.39) > mn = 0 (sn = 0)
Originality: *Percentage of new ideas in phase 2* **Validated (p = 0.00)**	mg = 51.8 % (sg = 31.8) > mn = 20.1 % (sn = 21.8)
Elaboration: *Average difference in number of secondary ideas between phase 1 and phase 2* **Validated (p = 0,03)**	mg = 6.9 (sg = 5.4) > mn = 2.9 (sn = 3.4)

account level of experience; *Set the scene*; *Launch an individual or social competition*; *Enable self-expression*; *Manage perceived freedom of choice*. Conversely, the use of elements from the strategy *Define the functions* increased for the subjects without the guide whereas they decreased for those with the guide.

The percentage of new ideas out of all the ideas in phase 2 is much higher for the subjects using the guide than the others ($p = 0.00$ with $U = 41$ and Z adjusted $= 2.83$). Hence, they had on average 51.8 % of new ideas out of all the ideas put forward (standard deviation: 31.8) against 20.1 % (standard deviation: 21.8) which is more than twice as many. Thus validating our hypothesis: the guide fosters originality.

It appears finally, that the average difference in the number of secondary ideas between phase 1 and phase 2 is significantly higher for the guide users than for the others ($p = 0.03$ with $U = 56$ and Z adjusted $= 2.13$). Hence, they had on average 6.9 more secondary ideas in phase 2 (standard deviation: 5.4) against 2.9 (standard deviation: 3.4) which is more than twice as many. Our hypothesis is thus validated: the guide fosters elaboration. All the hypotheses have therefore been validated. The results are summarized in Table 2.

This study was initiated in order to verify the validity of the gamification guide described in [6]. Two groups of subjects had to carry out the task of gamifying interfaces of a *Business Intelligence* software programme. The experiment was conducted in two phases: firstly, all the subjects were given a short introduction to gamification, they then had to begin gamifying the software presented. During the intermediate phase, one group was presented with the design guide while the other group was taking a break. In the experimental phase, each group was given the task of returning to the initial case study and finishing it. The hypothesis being that the guide would enable interface enrichment with gamification, tested using four creativity indicators (fluidity; flexibility; originality; and elaboration).

All the hypotheses were validated. Hence, the subjects using the guide added more than twice as many gamification elements in phase 2 compared to the subjects without the guide (H1). Fluidity is therefore fostered by using the guide. Additionally, the subjects of the group with the guide demonstrated a more substantial enrichment in terms of elements for six gamification strategies compared to the group without the guide (H2): *Plan the progression*; *Take into account the level of experience; Set the scene; Launch an individual or social competition*; *Enable self-expression*; *Manage perceived freedom of choice*. Flexibility is therefore also fostered using the guide.

Notably, the subjects using the guide reduced the number of elements for the strategy *Define the functions* (which refers to the drawing for new useful functions, unrelated to gamification) while the subjects without the guide did the opposite. In the light of these results we can assume that the guide enables understanding of what gamification refers to, thus leading to the abandon of irrelevant strategies.

Moreover, in phase 2, the subjects using the guide put forward more than 50 % of new ideas than the subjects without the guide (H3). They were therefore much more original in their initial proposals. An in-depth analysis of the ideas put forward in phase 2 (re-used, modified, abandoned or new) also shows that only new ideas differentiate the groups. Both groups similarly decided to modify, re-use or abandon the primary ideas in phase 1.

Finally, the subjects using the guide added more than twice as many secondary ideas in phase 2 compared to the subjects without the guide (H4). They developed their ideas much more, detailing their production in a precise manner.

5 Conclusion

The results of this study emphasise the fact that the guide fosters interface enrichment when numerous gamification elements are brought in. Hence, the subjects who used the guide in phase 2 showed much more:

- Fluidity: With a higher increase in gamification elements;
- Flexibility: With a higher increase in coverage of gamification strategies;
- Originality: With more than half as many new primary ideas;
- Elaboration: With more detailed ideas.

However, it is interesting to note that the subjects who didn't benefit from the design guide did manage to submit proposals which embraced gamification elements. Thus, the designers seemed to grasp the meaning of these practises intuitively. Be that as it may, the subjects were more creative and produced more, and apparently better, having used the specially developed design guide (more strategies, more new ideas, and more details). Furthermore, we also observed more relevant design with the abandon of functionalities not linked to gamification. This study is therefore considered as an initial validation of its efficacy.

However, several limitations of the study should be noted. Firstly, the subjects were not a homogenous population group. The task was complex. They had to immerge themselves into a large case control study, the concepts being, for a certain number of them, completely unknown. Furthermore, the time allowed was relatively restricted. Moreover, the subjects using the guide in the second phase didn't get a break. They also had to learn about and understand complex material before being able to put it into application, thus shortening the time for the actual design work. The subjects in the group without the guide had time for a break and to think about what they had done. They had more time to fine-tune, and develop their ideas during the design phase. To remedy this, the subjects of the group without the guide could, for example, be trained for an unlinked task, then a break could be given for each group. Another focus of research would be to carry out an analysis of the designers' activities when using the guide to identify the improvements to be made. Presenting the guide to gamification experts could be interesting in order to identify the areas where progress is needed.

Acknowledgments. This research was supported by SAP, Levallois-Perret, France. We would like to thank SAP teams and especially Steve KOPP, Christophe FAVART and Chahab NASTAR, Ph.D., for their involvement. We wish to thank them for their numerous insightful comments on this research.

References

1. Bonnardel, N.: Créativité et conception: approches cognitives et ergonomiques. Solal, Marseille (2006)
2. Kim, A.J.: Smart Gamification: Seven Core Concepts for Creating Compelling Experiences. Récupéré le 2 février 2012 sur (2011). http://casualconnect.org/lectures/business/smart-Gamification-seven-core-concepts-for-creating-compelling-experiences-amy-jo-kim
3. Kumar, J.M., Herger, M.: Gamification at Work: Designing Engaging Business Software. The Interaction Design Foundation, Aarhus (2013)
4. Liu, Y., Alexandrova, T., Nakajima, T.: Gamifying intelligent environments. In: Proceedings of the 2011 International ACM Workshop on Ubiquitous Meta User Interfaces, Ubi-MUI 2011, Scottsdale, AZ, USA. ACM, Décembre 2011
5. Lubart, T., Mouchiroud, C., Tordjman, S., Zenasni, F.: Psychologie de la créativité. Armand Colin, Paris (2003)
6. Marache-Francisco, C., Brangier, E.: Process for gamification: from the decision of gamification to its practical implementation. In: Proceedings of CENTRIC 2013: The Sixth International Conference on Advances in Human-Oriented and Personalized Mechanisms, Technologies, and Services, Venice, Italy, October 27–November 1, 2013, pp. 126–131 (2013a). ISSN: 2308-3492; ISBN: 978-1-61208-306-3
7. Marache-Francisco, C., Brangier, E.: The gamification experience - UXD with a gamification background. In: Blashki, K., Isaias, P. (eds.) Emerging Research and Trends in Interactivity and the Human-Computer Interface. IGI-Global (2013b)
8. Marache-Francisco, C., Brangier, E.: Perception of gamification: between graphical design and persuasive design. In: Marcus, A. (ed.) Design, User Experience, and Usability, HCII, Las Vegas (2013c)
9. Marache Francisco, C., Brangier, E.: Gamification and human - computer interaction: a synthesis. Le travail humain. **78**(2), 165–189 (2015)
10. Nicholson, S.: A user-centered theoretical framework for meaningful gamification. In: Proceedings of Games + Learning + Society 8.0, Madison, WI, USA, Juin 2012
11. Werbach, K., Hunter, D.: For the Win. How Game Thinking Can Revolutionize Your Business. Wharton Digital Press, Philadelphia (2012)
12. Zichermann, G., Cunningham, C.: Gamification by Design: Implementing Game Mechanics in Web and Mobile Apps. O'Reilly Media Inc., Sebastopol (2011)

Information Design Elements in Videogames: A Proposed Classification

Rafael Pereira de Araujo and Virginia Tiradentes Souto[(✉)]

Institute of Arts, University of Brasilia, Brasília, Brazil
rafael.pereira.87@hotmail.com, v.tiradentes@gmail.com

Abstract. Some of today's videogames work with heavy cognitive loads that demand a high flow of data from the game to the user. To achieve this, games work with different visual and non-visual elements to convey information, such as heads-up display (HUD), in-game assets, subtitles and voiceovers. The choice of elements used relies not only on the game designer's choice, but also on variables including the game platform and its hardware. The aim of this study is to identify and classify different elements used in games and their relevance to the informational process. In addition, this study aims to understand the problems or solutions of such elements to reduce the noise and interference the excessive data may cause for players. This understanding may help them focus on the core activity of the game – thus improving their performance and increasing the value of the product. The classification provided is followed by a case study with the popular videogame Dota 2. By studying the game interface elements, it is possible to perceive their relevance and point out significant changes and recommendations especially considering the distinctive flow of the game and the differences in player skill level. Conclusions point, among other aspects, to the importance of information design in games, especially in helping to make complex games – or every game - more accessible and enjoyable for more players.

Keywords: Videogames · Interface · Information design

1 Introduction

Videogames are, today, part of a complex chain of electronic entertainment, being responsible for a huge impact on the industry not only in cultural but also in financial aspects. The videogames market has escalated yearly, with figures reaching US$ 83.6 billion in 2014 and projected to reach US$ 107 billion in 2017 [1].

For their considerable cultural relevance, games have also been the object of study in several different fields, ranging from computer sciences to psychology [2], design and healthcare. The field of HCI is particularly notable in this aspect, given its proximity to both computational and human aspects of games. Understanding how the user interacts with the data provided by the game might impact gaming experiences such as immersion [3].

Over the years, games have evolved and absorbed a plethora of new informational aspects in their cores. While some games stick to simple mechanics or graphics, most

© Springer International Publishing Switzerland 2016
A. Marcus (Ed.): DUXU 2016, Part II, LNCS 9747, pp. 294–302, 2016.
DOI: 10.1007/978-3-319-40355-7_28

of the current market leaders [4], such as Grand Theft Auto V [5], Batman: Arkham Night [6] and The Witcher 3: Wild Hunt [7] are games with immersive plots, realistic visuals and complex gameplay mechanics that incorporate numbers and data to be analysed by the player in a fraction of a second.

Providing an acceptable amount of information without negatively affecting the gameplay experience plays a key role in helping the player achieve a state of immersion [8]. This helps them to have a game experience in which the player will focus on his/her own performance rather than dealing with unnecessary data, ultimately achieving a state of flow [9], a state of focus in which the player dedicates full attention and commitment to the game for its own challenge.

The aim of this study is to identify and classify different elements used in games and their relevance to the informational process. In addition, this study aims to understand the problems of or solutions for such elements to reduce the noise and interference the excessive data may cause for players. For that, a review of the literature on game interface elements is carried out. After that, a case study with the game Dota 2 [10] is presented to illustrate this classification. Finally, a discussion is proposed on the relevance of information design in game design.

2   Classification of Game Information Elements

Starting from the very first games made available to the wider public (e.g. Atari, from 1977, or Nintendo, from 1983), game interfaces have always relied on similar assets to convey information to gamers: most have had characters and in-game elements that describe their current status, projected on-screen displays and additional sound effects or controller vibrations.

The uses of these assets are broadly understood by gamers and are accessible to newcomers to the gaming world, since they can be easily related to other activities and can be seen in other media or applications. One considerable example is the heads-up display (HUD), which provides information without additional distractions or eye-changing movements by the user [11]. Another example is haptic feedback (i.e. the use of vibrating, reacting surfaces that provide the player with the feeling of touch or response to a surface), seen not only in game controllers but also in mobile phones, which may be configured to react to touches on the screen with vibrations [12].

From a game developer's perspective, different game elements can be seen from a variety of points of view. This paper proposes a classification of game elements in two groups: element role and element nature. While the first is about the role the elements play in the game, the second is related to how much a given element takes part in the game world – that is, whether a given element is diegetic or non-diegetic [13]. This separation into groups aims to cover game elements from two different perspectives, considering both cultural and technical aspects of game design.

These classifications are supported by descriptions of the process of immersion and gameplay experience [8, 14]. Babu [8] argues that information processing during gameplay is affected by how game elements are presented. In line with Babu [8], Fabricatore [14] describes the role of different gameplay elements in the process of game enjoyment, pointing out their relevance in the core activity of gaming and the game learning process by the player.

These elements also influence the experience of immersion, a relevant outcome of gameplay [15]. This is because, in addition to presenting the game challenges and world elements in a playable way, they are also presented in a coherent manner that enhances the occurrence of phenomena like "flow" [9] and "spatial presence" [16], which is the perception of being "inside" the game world. Figure 1 shows the proposed classification of game elements. The two types of elements proposed are described below.

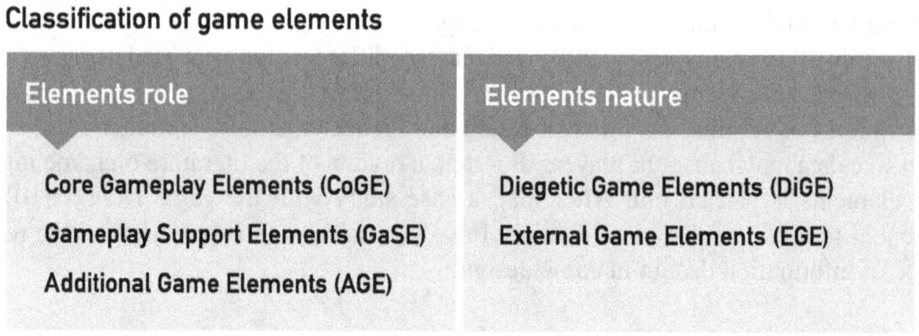

Classification of game elements

Elements role	Elements nature
Core Gameplay Elements (CoGE)	Diegetic Game Elements (DiGE)
Gameplay Support Elements (GaSE)	External Game Elements (EGE)
Additional Game Elements (AGE)	

Fig. 1. Classification of game elements proposed in this study

2.1   Element Role

From plot devices to world descriptions and gameplay mechanics, the gaming activity is often focused on receiving and analysing information and then making decisions before repeating the process as new challenges appear [14]. For a clear understanding of what these different informational elements are, it is possible to classify them not only by their design or function, but also by the role they play in the game. They are classified into three types: core gameplay elements, gameplay support elements and additional game elements. The element Role is based on the previously mentioned works [8, 13, 14], focusing on how relevant that element is to their role. The proposed classification synthesises these different works into a simplified structure to be easily compared to the next one, based on how the element is integrated into the game. Thus, a given element can be classified according to its role:

- **Core Gameplay Elements (CoGE):** These elements are related to the game world and the core activities of the game (i.e. the main objectives and activities performed by the player, such as running and jumping in an action or platform game). These include 3D models, characters, sound effects, landscape, items and some HUD elements such as health bars or countdown timers, when relevant. Without the CoGE, the game can be rendered unplayable, since the user will not have access to essential information regarding his performance and feedback for his actions.
- **Gameplay Support Elements (GaSE):** While the core gameplay elements are essential for the game activity, the support elements help the player by organising and highlighting relevant information when necessary, or by manipulating the game

world to convey additional experiences to the gamer, exceeding the gameplay mechanics. Objective highlights, additional character animations (i.e. "taunts" and "idle cycles") and on-screen notifications of player performance can be considered GaSE, depending on the game.

- **Additional Game Elements (AGE):** More than performing the core activity of the game, the user also interacts with various game elements that are related not to a game world, a plot or the game mechanics, but the game itself. Depending on the game, genre and platform, elements such as interfaces and menus, performance records, stats graphs and social media tools can be described as AGE. [17] describes the effort made by the developers of League of Legends [18] to improve player experience outside the core gameplay action, focusing on several cross-media elements (i.e. crafting and streaming systems) to enhance engagement. This is an example of AGE being used within a game.

The above descriptions of elements are related to their relevance to the core gameplay activity; that is, they do not refer to the nature of the element from an information design perspective. Hence, it is possible to classify these elements regardless of their presentation. In other words, both a 3D model and a sound effect can be classified as GaSE, for example. While this may prove useful from a developer's perspective, this classification can be complemented by another one, which covers the nature of these elements.

2.2 Element Nature Classification

Classifying the game elements by their nature – that is, pointing out if a given element is an in-game asset or a HUD projection, for example - is also a useful method of analysing and understanding the effects of information transmission in-game. It is worth noting that most of these are visual elements and, while the use of sound effects must be considered an efficient substitute for some visual assets, some gameplay conditions restrict their use. This is the case with quiet environments, mobile gaming (e.g. playing a mobile game during a commuter trip) and hearing-impaired users (although accessibility factors pose a larger field of study and must be thoroughly considered during game development) [19]. The same applies to more complex input methods (e.g. Microsoft Kinect and the Nintendo 3DS accelerometers), which may not be available at all times during gameplay.

With that in mind, this classification focuses on how much a given element takes part in the game world or, on the other hand, how much an element is detached from the context and presents itself with the sole purpose of providing information to the user. Therefore, these elements can be divided into diegetic game elements and external game elements, according to previous descriptions by Babu [8] and Saunders and Novak [13], who describe the effects of diegetics in games and point out its relevance in making the game more understandable for the player.

Saunders and Novak [13] work with two additional categories, not diegetic or non-diegetic, called Meta and Spatial. Meta category refers to elements that belong in the game world not as actual assets, but rather as projections based on the visual style of diegetic elements. Spatial, on the other hand, focuses on non-diegetic elements projected within the 3D game world (such as an exclamation mark above a character's head). The classification proposed here does not consider these types of asset as belonging to different categories, but rather as a non-diegetic, "external", game element.

- **Diegetic Game Elements ("DiGE"):** Diegetic game elements are contained within the game world as an actual part of it. Given that a character is sentient and able to observe the environment, they would be able to perceive DiGE elements, which may include characters, scenery assets and particle effects (such as "auras" or damage and debris). Essentially, every DiGE is a part of the game world and, from a broader view, it can be said that the whole game world could fall into this category. From this point of view, it can be affirmed that the whole game world describes information to be decrypted and analysed by the player.
- **External Game Elements ("EGE"):** Non-diegetic game elements take part in the game action and convey relevant information to the player, being related to the core gameplay or support activities (as seen with the CoGE and GaSE). Unlike DiGE, though, EGE are elements not visible inside the game world from a character's perspective. Examples include projections on the HUD (heads-up display), such as health bars and objective indications, but also special in-game effects that are not diegetic, such as character highlights (when selected or active) and number overlays (e.g. an enemy's loot indication when it is defeated).

2.3 Considerations About the Game Element Classification

As previously stated, classifications and definitions in the videogame context require a subjective approach to the theme, since games vary greatly in their presentations, themes and mechanics. Therefore, the developer must consider that recommendations should not be taken as completely wrong or right, and should take each project into consideration when making decisions.

While it is feasible to include special effects, graphics and audio (e.g. character voiceover or adaptive soundtrack with music matching the calm or intense moments of the match), from the users' perspective these effects may make the game very complex and therefore increase the users' challenge to both understand the game and carry out their decision-making process. By balancing diegetic and non-diegetic elements according to the flow of the game, developers can create a more interesting game world, with noticeable landmarks and effects that pose real consequences in the game. These all can happen simultaneously with the information that the player needs without compromising his/her performance. It's worth pointing out that diegetic elements are considered less distracting during the game activity [8].

Also, depending on the game's genre or characteristics adopted for a project, some data used by the player can be hidden during gameplay and presented only between matches or at specific moments. This can also be considered an exercise to evaluate if the game is offering unnecessary feedback (such as excessive data or unused figures) or cluttering the game screen with excessive noise, allowing the developer to focus on more important assets.

The next topic presents a case study with a popular game in which these elements can be seen in action and then analysed for their relevance in gameplay.

3   Case Study: Dota 2

In order to illustrate how the elements are applied in games and in addition to demonstrate the classification described above, a case study is presented with the popular videogame Dota 2. This game has been chosen because it includes a considerable variety of game elements that fall under all the categories mentioned. In addition, it is currently one of the most popular games on the PC platform – with a player base reaching peaks of over a million active players simultaneously and a monthly average of around 500,000 players [20]. The game, known for its intense competitive community, relies on a number of different gameplay elements and strategies that prove it a success after many years [21].

DotA 2 is a Multiplayer Online Battle Arena (MOBA) game which puts teams of 5 players competing for supremacy in a fixed-layout arena. Players take control of "heroes", characters with specific sets of skills that require different gameplay strategies to win, who fight their way past enemies (both human and computer-controlled), grow stronger by purchasing magical items and winning battles, and finally strike the enemy base to destroy a particular trophy-like structure that will grant them victory in the match.

Dota's complex strategies and gameplay aspects require the user to analyse an outstanding amount of data, ranging from the hero's health to complex game stats (e.g. the amount of gold collected by the team per minute, the number of enemy kills by the opposing team or skills that 'stack', requiring the player to succeed in launching a particular attack against their enemies). In order to do so, Dota 2 makes use of all types of interface elements, from diegetic graphics and effects to short audio notifications.

3.1   The Game Screen Layout

During gameplay, the player faces a screen divided into three areas. The top area is taken by the HUD, which displays the game's current situation (game time, team score and the team's heroes' situation) and AGE controls such as chat windows and the pause menu. Using the classification previously presented, the upper HUD can be described as AGE-EGE.

The lower area contains information about the player's hero, the game map, items and some core elements including skills and their cooldown timer (i.e. the time required to use a skill again, one of the core aspects of gameplay). While these elements are external to the game world from a graphic point of view, they are connected to the game's core activity, being an essential part of gameplay. Thus, the lower HUD can be clearly described as CoGE-EGE.

Most of the screen is taken up by the main game area, where the Dota world is presented to the player. Using a top-down perspective, this is where most of the game takes place – where the player will click and move his hero around, attack his foes and follow the flow of the game. Despite being a realistic representation of the game world, including the use of a fog-of-war (i.e. an effect that hides foes and items that can't be seen by the hero, despite their being visible to the game's camera), the game screen makes use of HUD-like elements and non-diegetic effects and particles. In other words, the game screen offers mostly CoGE, although they are presented in both DiGE and EGE.

3.2 DiGE vs EGE in-Game

Two examples with different characters can illustrate the difference between DiGE and EGE in-game: in the first one, the hero ("Pudge") casts an aura of rotten air that affects Pudge and the nearby foes. It can be observed that the effect fits into the game world in an effectively diegetic way, since the aura is, in fact, a cloud of rotten air surrounding the character, and its area of effect is determined by the shape and spread of that cloud. The second example is a spell cast by "Silencer". The spell, like Pudge's, affects the foes after being cast, but instead of creating a particle effect around the characters, it projects a skull right above the affected foes. Comparing the two effects, it is possible to see that both are related to the core gameplay (CoGE), though the former is part of the game world from a diegetic point of view (DiGE) while the latter presents the spell's effect using a HUD projection, thus being an EGE.

While the difference between these elements might seem clear, it must be understood that the games get more complex over time. In Dota 2, the later parts of the game usually involve intense battles between multiple players who, by that point, will have powerful spells and items that unleash the most diverse on-screen effects.

During these parts of the game, both diegetic and non-diegetic elements overlap each other, since different players are casting different spells and effects. As previously mentioned, the game makes use of different elements, including audio notifications, to keep the informational load acceptable for the player. This solution is well aligned with the recommendations previously mentioned, especially in balancing diegetic and non-diegetic elements. There is room for fine-tuning in terms of HUD elements, in order to make some information highlighted according to the in-game events, for example. On the other hand, Dota 2 relies heavily on community interaction and, for that reason, the game presents many EGE-AGE elements that may make the player stray from the core gameplay. This may affect some of the effects of engagement and immersion [15] that the game could provide, and therefore these elements could also be reviewed according to the game design strategy adopted by the developers, which may be focusing on external features and engagement strategies, as seen in similar games [17].

4 Final Remarks

Analysing the game interface is an efficient way of identifying many of the effects of gaming on players. These interfaces are in many ways similar to other computer applications, so recommendations that apply to improving user experiences with a computer might be applicable to games.

Also, by categorising game elements as related to the core gameplay (CoGE), support elements (GaSE) and non-gameplay or additional elements (AGE), the developers can evaluate if the game interface is displaying unnecessary information, giving them the possibility to lighten the cognitive load on the player. Describing each interface element and then removing or hiding the excesses is one possible way to use these classifications.

While many games focus heavily on their core gameplay, it is the developer's duty to analyse and hone elements that are not related to gameplay itself. Depending on the nature of the project, this might have an effect on creating an immersive experience for the player – keeping in mind that immersion can be either related to the challenges of the game or to the world it presents via various stimuli [22].

The classification proposed here, thus, allows developers to have a quick, easy look at how graphic elements behave according to their role within the game. This quick-reference is important in quick iteration scenarios, where designers have to point out design changes in short times. By grouping role and nature of interface elements this task is simplified, and the use of short names may help in quick documentation processes.

Also, by studying games from a technical point of view the field of Game Studies also grows in importance, and while people less familiar with games might consider that they are merely simple entertainment, society in general is slowly improving their perception of the countless possibilities that games offer in providing fantastic, engaging experiences to gamers.

References

1. Campbell, C.: Worldwide video games market will grow 9.4 percent this year, says report (2015). http://www.polygon.com/2015/4/22/8471789/worldwide-video-games-market-value-2015. Accessed 23 Dec 2015. Polygon
2. Boyle, E., et al.: The role of psychology in understanding the impact of computer games. Entertainment Comput. **2**, 69–74 (2011)
3. Fagerholt, E., Lorentzon, M.: Beyond the HUD: User Interfaces for Increased Player Immersion in FPS Games. Chalmers University of Technology, Gotemburgo (2012)
4. Morris, C.: The top 10 selling video games of 2015 (so far) (2015). http://www.fortune.com/2015/07/23/top-10-selling-video-games-2015-so-far/. Accessed 23 Dec 2015. Fortune
5. Take-Two: Grand Theft Auto V [Software]. Take-Two Interactive, United States (2015)
6. Bros, W.: Batman: Arkham Knight [Software]. Warner Bros, USA (2015)
7. CD Projekt Red: The Witcher 3: Wild Hunt [Software]. CD Projekt RED, Poland (2015)
8. Babu, J.: Video Game HUDs: Information Presentation and Spatial Immersion (2010). https://ritdml.rit.edu/handle/1850/15948. Accessed 23 Dec 2015. Rochester Institute of Technology
9. Csikszentmihalyi, M.: Flow: The Psychology of Optimal Experience. Harper and Row, New York (1990)
10. Valve: Dota 2 [Software]. Valve, USA (2013)
11. Liu, Y., Wen, M.: Comparison of head-up display (HUD) vs. head-down display (HDD): driving performance of commercial vehicle operators in Taiwan. Int. J. Hum.-Comput. Stud. **61**, 679–697 (2004). Elseiver
12. Hildebrand, J.: Android A to Z: Haptic feedback (2012). http://www.androidcentral.com/android-z-haptic-feedback. Accessed 23 Dec 2015. Androidcentral
13. Saunders, K., Novak, J.: Game Development Essentials: Game Interface Design. Delmar Cengage Learning, New York (2013)

14. Fabricatore, C.: Gameplay and game mechanics design: A key to quality in videogames (2007). http://www.oecd.org/edu/ceri/39414829.pdf. Accessed 29 Dec 2015. Centre for Educational Research and Innovation – CERI
15. Jennett, C., et al.: Measuring and defining the experience of immersion in games. Int. J. Hum. Comput. Stud. **66**, 641–661 (2008). Elseiver
16. Weibel, D., Bartholomäus, W.: Immersion in computer games: the role of spatial presence and flow. Int. J. Comput. Games Technol. **2011**, 1–14 (2011). Hindawi Publishing Corporation
17. David, E.: League of Legends dev on improving player experience outside of core gameplay (2015). http://siliconangle.com/blog/2015/12/14/league-of-legends-dev-on-improving-player-exprience-outside-of-core-gameplay/. Accessed 23 Dec 2015. SiliconANGLE
18. Riot Games: League of Legends [Software]. Riot Games, United States (2009)
19. Yuan, B., et al.: Game accessibility: a survey. Univ. Access Inf. Soc. **10**, 81–100 (2010). Springer
20. Steam Charts: DotA 2 (2015). http://steamcharts.com/app/570. Accessed 28 Nov 2015. STEAM CHARTS
21. Cohen, M.: Why is Dota 2 The Biggest Game on Steam (2013). http://www.rockpapershotgun.com/2013/09/11/why-is-dota-2-the-biggest-game-on-steam/. Accessed 5 Nov 2015. Rock Paper Shotgun
22. Ermi, L., Mäyrä, F.: Fundamental Components of Gameplay Experience: Analysing Immersion. In: Changing Views: World in Play. Selected Papers of the 2005 Digital Games Research Association's Second International Conference. Digital Games Research Association DiGRA (2015)

Digital Game for Teaching and Learning: An Analysis of Usability and Experience of Educational Games

Rennan Raffaele[1]([✉]), Breno Carvalho[2], Anthony Lins[2],
Luiz Marques[2], and Marcelo Márcio Soares[3]

[1] University of Beira Interior, Covilhã, Portugal
rennan_updown@hotmail.com
[2] Catholic University of Pernambuco, Recife, Brazil
breno25@gmail.com, thonylins@gmail.com,
prof.luizcmarques@gmail.com
[3] Federal University of Pernambuco, Recife, Brazil
soaresmm@gmail.com

Abstract. Desbravadores is a 3D game, available for web, which is about History. The game is in first person, with focus on survivor, where the player is a time traveler and needs to save old artifacts, which was lost in our history. To achieve this goal the team proposed an artifact whose interface simulates a time machine, able to take students/players to meaningful moments of different historical periods, immersing it in a realistic environment, initially in 3D and future in "virtual reality". Both are educational games for awake the interest of Brazilian students and be an interactive tool for teachers in classroom. This study set out to investigate the gameplay and usability of these two games, grounded on the concepts set out by Huizinga, Preece, Rogers and Sharp, and by observation the interactions that users engaged on laboratory tests.

Keywords: Educational games · Usability and gameplay · User's experience · Interaction · Desbravadores · Fun · Playfulness

1 Introduction

Educational games are designed specifically to teach people about a certain subject, expand concepts, reinforce development and understanding of a historical or cultural event, or help in learning some skill while playing. Educational games can have various configurations, from board games, card games or even video games. These games, in short, are intended to pass to the children some ethical foundation or life values. Can be presented in different ways, and depending on their primary context, can be used even by teachers in schools. According to the researchers DR Godden and Baddeley AD neuroscience, learning from training is usually specific to the trained skill and training of the context [1]. However, in areas such as education, it is of greatest interest that learning extends beyond specific training. For example, it is more important that a student learns to use mathematical reasoning to solve various problems outside the classroom, rather than just knowing how to use certain mathematical operation in visas

© Springer International Publishing Switzerland 2016
A. Marcus (Ed.): DUXU 2016, Part II, LNCS 9747, pp. 303–310, 2016.
DOI: 10.1007/978-3-319-40355-7_29

contexts in school. Importantly, these cognitive benefits from playing video games can be purchased by anyone, even in adults who have no previous experience with video games. One mechanism that has been adopted by teachers is the use of multimedia and computer games to stimulate and engage the student's participation in the construction of knowledge collectively.

Professor John Buck, Atlanta, United States that saw the game Angry Birds a perfect tool to teach the laws of motion of projectiles to its students, the method makes children absorb more quickly the two great movement of ideas of a projectile: the horizontal component of the movement is constant speed, while the vertical component with respect to acceleration [2].

Another example is the 3D computer game to teach physics. The game's plot is in the style of adventure, discovery and rewards. The character aims to survive the many traps around the stage and this will have to solve physics problems. The setting is a castle, where the player will undergo different spaces as secret rooms, basement, etc. [3].

Another application example is the game "Legends of Alkhimia" developed by Learning Laboratory Sciences of the National Institute of Education of Singapore. The digital game supports the chemistry curriculum for high school and students learn the subject through research, conducting chemical experiments, while working as chemical apprentices [4].

The need to prepare the new generations for its intensive use, keeping that critical skills in reading the data coming from the reality that has always been dear to the traditional education quality, given that, in our day, we can see the declining interest of students to interact with the teacher in the classroom, when organized according to the traditional "banking" in which the teacher passes a content through alphanumeric characters for the student to learn by reading and exercising sectioned activities by subject, either math, history or biology. This mismatch has brought problems in the teacher/student and in the dynamics of learning in the classroom. The possible "remedy" offered by modern communications technologies, has just not working because often, it is the teacher who does not dominate, be it technology, is the instrument of language.

In a classic definition of what are games, they are presented as a voluntary activity or occupation, performed during certain limits of time and space, to rules freely consented and obligatory, accompanied by a feeling of tension and joy, as well as an awareness of be different from everyday life [5].

The game is older fact that culture as this, even in its less stringent definitions, always presupposes human society; but the animals do not expect men to initiate the playful life. It can be argued that human civilization has not added essential characteristics that human civilization has not added any essential feature of the general idea of the game. The animals play as men. (Huizinga 2005, p. 03).

For Vygotsky (1991) addresses the role of games in learning and child development, emphasizing the role of the game in the child to the extent that it enables the creation of a next development zone (ZDP) - level of development, in which children think and solve situations with the help of others, to later solve alone - providing the construction of knowledge and interaction between individuals [6].

To improve the education of future generations, the researchers of this article, built a recreational educational game and Interactive at denominated history area

Desbravadores, to understand what it takes to identify why educational games not work in schools, the game was developed and tested with fun concepts, effective in use and provide the user a pleasant experience. Recalling that without the concept of fun there is no game [7].

2 The Game Desbravadores

Desbravadores is a 3D game in first person, available on the Web only to the Portuguese version, developed by the researchers of this article. The story is set in the future and the past, the player itself is the protagonist of the game, the player's objective is to travel in space and time, to collect ancient artifacts that were lost throughout the history of humankind. For now the game has only one phase that goes on in the Paleolithic period, this phase is survival, where the life of Player Points decrease every second, the player will have to explore the 3D environment and figure out how to find food and water, roots and fish in order to restore hit points while performing missions to the natives of the time, asking for the player to collect stones and twigs to create a fire, having accomplished all missions, will be given the player the location of lost artifact. The player at the same stage as the Homo sapiens learns hunted, collected food, made fire, dressed, and how was the environment in which they lived (Fig. 1).

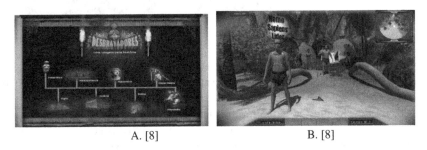

A. [8]   B. [8]

Fig. 1. A. Game level select, only the Paleolithic stage is available [8]. B. Scene where the player finds a Homo sapiens group [8].

The time traveler uses a helmet with artificial intelligence that helps him all the time, giving tips, identifying and classifying some living beings to translate words, gestures and able to communicate also has the hit points of the player, the hours of the day, battery of his flashlight, and indicates the easiest routes to the player achieve your goal. His clothes also disguises to be similar to the identified individual and let the traveler run faster.

3 Methodology Used in the Games Development and Test of Usability and Gameplay

Initially for the development of the game Desbravadores, we use the brainstorm technique for discussion and definition of thematic and visual elements of the artifact, involving undergraduate students in history and students of state schools Almirante Soares Dutra, Aníbal Fernandes, Nobrega Liceu and Oliveira Lima. As a result, we chose the first content given to the 1st year of high school students is the Paleolithic, we also believe in artifacts, items and possible characters and enemies to the game. After choosing the content did research with references (books, magazines, internet). For image production, copyright animations, which fully demonstrate the environment in which they lived Homo sapiens, and interactive approaches to teaching and learning used in other games (Fig. 2).

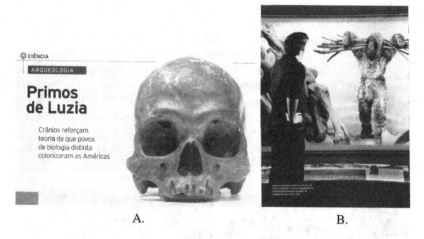

A.   B.

Fig. 2. A. Magazine shows possible locations where Homo sapiens lived [9]. B. Picture shows customs (clothing, physiology and items for survival) of Homo sapiens in the late Paleolithic [10].

To begin developing the game need to understand what would leave the playful game, which according to Huizinga, "the game is tense," that is need to have tension and awaken pleasure through fun. Based on this knowledge we implemented several factors that lead the player to have a quick wit, and at the same time have fun while achieving complete it, after giving fun in the game is to complete the challenge, and the harder the better the satisfaction after complete it.

Within the context of the discipline of history, use of usability and gameplay testing to validate the proposed analogue of the game prototype, in order to understand which elements would be required to use and which to delete, always thinking about what students should learn. Then we think of a mechanical easy and intuitive game where the player will have to explore a 3D scene to be able to find collectible items, consumables, accomplish missions and escape of animals.

In another time after the creation of the digital prototype, we conducted three tests with different schools to ascertain the dynamic version of the digital device, error correction and interface elements adjustments and phase of difficulty, until the game was ready to be used by teachers in the classroom.

For further study of usability and playability of an educational game, the concepts of Jennifer Preece diagram (Fig. 3) [11] the user experience goals were used as basis.

The goal was to understand specific criteria and explain the quality of accomplished experience.

Fig. 3. Diagram Jennifer Preece on usability goals and user experience. (Source: www.sharritt.com/CISHCIExam/preece.html)

As for used usability goals, they are connected in the user's perspective as: easy to use, efficient and pleasant. As to the objectives focused on user experience, they refer to how you will feel in human-computer interaction, considering subjective aspects as satisfaction. This interaction aims to develop projects for the application of concepts of Preece and Huizinga, based on the observation of experiments and tests with users (Fig. 4).

In the end, we observe the environment and dynamics of the classroom between teachers and students during the interaction with the game produced. The game left many questions and curiosities that are not explained, and it is up to both the students ask the teacher as the teacher take your questions. I managed to get the attention and curiosity of students making the best learning school.

At another time after the conclusion of the game and the tests we gave a lecture at the Campus Party Recife 2015 event, on how we developed the Desbravadores project idea from beginning to end of its development, explaining the methodology used, game mechanics, arts and animation, the lecture was called "Games and Education, unraveling prehistory through 3D application". After the end of the event, our talk was chosen among the best of the games that took place on Mars stage, the website of technology and entertainment BitBlog [12] (Fig. 5).

Fig. 4. A. Nobrega Lyceum school students testing the first game. B. School Student Almirante Soares Dutra completing the game for the second time

Fig. 5. A. Raffaele Rennan the microphone explaining the evolution of the game had. B. Eduardo Galdino was made explaining how the concepts of the characters and artifacts

4   Findings

After the third gameplay testing with students, thirty boys and twenty-two girls. We get more data through a questionnaire that they responded and an observation test while playing.

A total of fifty-two students, thirty-two responded that move the player was the easiest part of the game, and the other ten explained that in the beginning it was difficult, but then took the practice. 37 % said it was somewhat difficult to interact with other characters in the game, they did not know where to find him. 87 % found it very easy to understand what the Homo sapiens wanted, but 8 % were not reading the text box on what the natives wanted and this resulted in the loss of countless times game. In a matter of difficulty to locate and collect the items in the game, almost 100 % said it was average, for when the game resumes and the player does not take the mission, he is not allowed to collect the items. Twenty-one boys said it was easy to find the right way to complete your goal, and said they knew interact in a 3D environment due to other games, eight girls said it was a bit difficult because at first did not pay attention to the map and ended getting lost, after watching the map failed to understand the correct way, twelve girls and two boys they said it was very difficult, these students could not find the way because it does not pay attention where they were going, nor was guided by the map, and when they found out could be guided by the map, it was too late and ended up losing the game.

31 % of respondents were undecided about collecting items at the wrong time, but after several attempts realized it was not the current goal, then left for another approach, and after a certain time everyone knew what to do, but could not reach the goal of time. In this first stage of testing few students already played other games like this, and it said that the game is easy and managed to complete their goals. Most said that the game is difficult, because they could not complete the time, or were confused about why not pick up one item at the time he wanted.

In the second step tests the game had been simplified so that it became easier to be played based on the results obtained in the previous test. In this second test took around five boys and ten girls. Only 48 % have had experience with similar games. Even with no initial explanation of the observers about the game, all the students realized that the game is linked to prehistory and who can identify the habits of characters linked to fishing and survival, but lacked a bit of context in addition to the graphic display of game. Some girls were not used to move the mouse to play, but still managed to finish the game when they realized what was needed. With regard to learning one of the boys said that the game brings only references, but does not provide any information that might add the historical knowledge of the period. In relation to the objectives, I think that encourage going through each move a lot with the reasoning, we can actually see how the ancient people lived, it is as if we live it all, teachers could bring to the classroom is a good way to learn having fun says a girl. 20 % of boys said they want more risk in the game, more action and asks to put more enemies, another suggestion for improvement was to collect certain items, open more details about the raw material and what was its significance for prehistoric peoples. In this test the same criteria as the previous were also asked, so that we can balance and approve, that we correct mistakes and difficulties of students as, difficulty in moving, interact with characters, understand the context of the statements, locating items in the game, find the correct path for the purpose, mini map, all were corrected and simplified, 93 % of students have had no more problems and managed to complete the game.

Finally, the third and final test conducted, we ask the fifty-two students of the first test, played again the game so they notice the improvements we put in the game. In the first test few students were able to complete the game, and many were frustrated and afraid to try to play other similar games, but this time 100 % of managed to finish the game, who failed before were very excited, and we were congratulated by students and teachers with such evolution we did.

5   Final Remarks

Given the above, the Desbravadores game intended to develop a relationship of science, technology and innovation by building educational playful artifacts in a fun, interactive, motivating and challenging for construction of knowledge directed to knowledge of the history of the area through multidisciplinary study and interaction between students of the Degree in History of UNICAP, alumni Rennan Raffaele and Eduardo Galdino also UNICAP, and high school students from state schools Almirante Soares Dutra, Aníbal Fernandes, Nobrega Liceu and Oliveira Lima. The proposal was to develop at least one game to be used in tablets provided by the accessibility program to the Government of Technology of the State of Pernambuco, to assist the dynamic between teacher and students of history discipline, providing interactive content to be made available in these portable devices.

After production and phases of game tests We believe we have achieved our goals through the results and experiences with the target audience, we note an evolution not only in the game but also in ourselves about how the whole design aspect, research, development and balancing of digital games in the education sector, through that experience we finally feel like true game Designers, although we are still at graduation when the first stage of the game was complete.

The work performed leads us to the effective participation of experience in a research team, directed both to the acquisition of knowledge as to the actual production of functional digital educational materials for PCs and tablets of Pernambuco Government, the Web and Windows platforms. Allowed us, map the difficulties and the biggest challenges in the task, which will enable the continuation of the research project, with the support of undergraduate research fellows, including new technologies, and new areas knowledge. We concluded that to bring students of pedagogical teachings, the game needs to be more than a teaching tool used by the teacher with student, it must become part of everyday life for the student to learn in and out of school, educational games need to be inevitably entertaining, without fun, there is no pleasure and learning.

References

1. Godden, D., Baddeley, A.: Context dependent memory in two natural environments. Br. J. Psychol. **66**, 325–331 (1975)
2. Professores utilizam Angry Birds para ensinar física em sala de aula, G1. http://oglobo.globo.com/sociedade/educacao/professores-utilizam-angry-birds-para-ensinar-fisica-em-sala-de-aula-2787935
3. Calegari, P.F., Quirino, S.S., Frigo, L.B., Pozzebon, E.: Jogo computacional 3D no ensino de física. In: Art and Design Track do XII Simpósio Brasileiro de Games e Entretenimento Digital. SBGames, São Paulo (2013)
4. Jan, M.F., Chee, Y.S., Tan, E.M.: Learning science via a science-in-the-making process: the design of a game-based-learning curriculum. In: Martin, S. (ed.) iVERG 2010 Proceedings – International Conference on Immersive Technologies for Learning: A Multidisciplinary Approach, pp. 13–25. Iverg Publishing, Stockton (2010)
5. Prensky, M.: Digital Game-Based Learning. McGraw-Hill, New York (2000)
6. Huizinga, J.: Homo Ludens: o jogo como elemento da cultura, 4 edn. Tradução João Paulo Monteiro. Perspectiva, São Paulo (1993)
7. Vygotsky, L.S.: A formação social da mente. Martins Fontes, São Paulo (2007)
8. Facebook Desbravadores. http://www.facebook.com/Desbravadoresgame
9. SciAm: Selam - A bebê de Lucy, Edição 56, January 2007
10. SciAm: Darwin e Evolução, Edição 81, February 2009
11. Preece, J., Rogers, Y., Sharp, H.: Design de interação: além da interação do homem-computador. Bookman, Porto Alegre (2005)
12. BitBlog: Guia das melhores palestras da Campus Party Recife. http://www.bit.blog.br/guia-das-melhores-palestras-da-campus-party-recife-1123

Gamification in Education Through Design Thinking

Graziela Sombrio[1], Leonardo Enrico Schimmelpfeng[1],
Vânia Ribas Ulbricht[1], and Vilma Villarouco[2(✉)]

[1] Engineering and Knowledge Management, Federal University of Santa Catarina,
Florianópolis, Brazil
graziela.sombrio@gmail.com, leoenricos@gmail.com,
vrulbricht@gmail.com
[2] Department of Graphic Expression, Federal University of Pernambuco, Recife, Brazil
vvillarouco@gmail.com

Abstract. When thinking of inclusive education, it is necessary to consider that schools and teachers must utilize appropriate didactical materials that suit the students' needs. For some subjects, such as Geometry, the vision is the most utilized sense. However, as much as it is an important sense that helps to understand the concepts better, it can become an obstacle when the student has a visual disability. The same thing occurs with hearing disability when utilizing learning objects that contain multimedia resources. The main purpose of this work is to discuss the creation of a gamified object of accessible learning that presents the principles of design thinking. In order to achieve this goal, a literature review has been made, mainly focused on accessibility, gamification and design thinking, considering the accessibility guidelines for LOs presented by Macedo. As a result, besides the initially proposed objectives, it was also possible to relate the concepts approached by the Theory of Flow.

Keywords: Gamification · Accessibility · Learning objects · Design thinking · Theory of flow

1 Introduction

Gamification, according to [1], is the use of game design elements outside the gaming context.

According to [2], gamification in education increases the students' commitment and, by integrating game elements with the subjects, it makes the activities more attractive and engaging. With the profusion of environments focused on e-learning, there is the need of spreading gamification in education. [3] highlights that the current challenges regarding games are invitations for a knowledge adventure and a dynamic learning experience. In e-learning, articulated by HCI, the immersion process within the LMS is powered by gamification and the experience articulates interactions and knowledge sharing among the students.

The use of gamification in learning processes has been propagated, especially with the use of learning objects (LOs). According to [4], the teaching materials distributed in learning environments should be accessible to all individuals, with or without

© Springer International Publishing Switzerland 2016
A. Marcus (Ed.): DUXU 2016, Part II, LNCS 9747, pp. 311–321, 2016.
DOI: 10.1007/978-3-319-40355-7_30

disabilities. In this context, this work intends to relate: gamification concepts, design thinking and accessible learning objects, in order to produce educational content.

2 Gamification and the Theory of Flow

The insertion process of Gamification in education can help by providing a different dynamic regarding learning and mobilizing stimuli, sensations, emotions and a immersion mediated at different knowledge instances. In this context, Csikszentmihalyi's Theory of Flow sought to demonstrate how some experiences may lead the participant to a Flow state.

Mihaly has created the autotelic experience model, which is defined as "a self-sufficient activity, carried out without the expectation of some future benefit, simply because executing it is the reward itself" [5]. Figure 1 presents the Flow path.

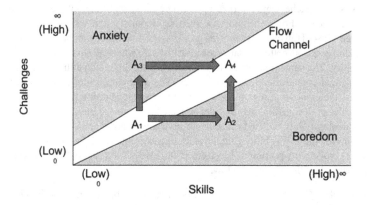

Fig. 1. Diagram showing the path for the Flow state (Source: Adapted from Csikszentmihalyi for authors, p. 74)

By associating this theory with the gamification process, it is stated that a student, when starting his gamified classes, has its challenges occurring accordingly to his ability (A1). At this point, he is probably in Flow state, though it soon turns into boredom (A2), since his skills have already increased and no longer correspond to the initial challenge. However, as soon as a new challenge is proposed, his feeling turns into anxiety (A3), as now he intends to overcome his new challenge and reach again his Flow state (A4).

According to [6], the individual reaches his Flow state in two stages: A1 and A4, both being equally pleasant. What is different in these two moments is the ability level acquired, since while achieving the full Flow state the individual realizes that his ability corresponds to level of the proposed challenge, thus transforming motivation in stimulus.

In the article "Flow in games (and everything else)", [7] lists a couple of points from the Theory of Flow. He claims that Csikszentmihalyi's research and personal observations have identified eight major components of Flow that can be associated with the gamification process: challenging activity requiring skill; a merging of action and awareness; clear goals; direct, immediate feedback; concentration on the task at hand; a sense of control; loss of self-consciousness; an altered sense of time.

In this context, gamification might be a way to make someone reach the Flow state. For such, it must be intended to provoke greater focus and concentration, stimulate the sensation of ecstasy, allow clarity and provide feedback, encourage the use of skills, provide growth, cause the loss of time sense and generate intrinsic motivation.

3 Gamification and Education

The process of inserting gamified activities into a learning object should follow the principles of game design and gamification.

The authors [8, 9] use a taxonomy of metrics of satisfaction for users and intend to extend their studies to the area of Distance Education and the studies on 'Gamification'. Thereafter, [10], from [11], brings a couple of features and recommendations to the use of gamification in learning objects. Based on the categorization made by [9], associated to what was proposed by [10, 11], it is possible to list similarities between these two approaches, through the keywords proposed by [9]. Table 1 shows how the concepts may be related to these categories.

Table 1. Relation between the concepts of Petrovic and Ivetic (2012) and Alves (2012)

	[9]	[10, 11]
Feedback	Time that the user takes to dominate the game or perform a certain task	Pleasant productivity, the players see applied efforts and energies achieving the desired results
Social	Socialization- interaction between the system and users; and duty - the system's and the generated social relations' capacity of creating and accepting the user's emotional investment	Generation of the possibility of working cooperatively, in teams and groups in order to solve problems/Construction of stronger social relationships through emotional bonds
Competition	Self-competition and effort to overcome the results	Pursuit of self-motivation to remain in the activity (intrinsic motivation)
Progression	The system's capacity of providing persistence to the user	Activities created with challenges that can be overcome
Mechanics	Pleasure that the user finds in the game	Epic meaning of achieving something expected
Context	Context of the system's actions	

Through this categorization, it is possible to use the principles above in order to produce gamified and accessible LOs. Therefore, the gamification concepts can also be inserted in the conceptual basis of a LO.

4   Gamification, Design Thinking and Learning Objects with Accessibility

According to [12], the evolution of design to design thinking is the evolutionary history of creating products for the analysis of the relationship between people and products, and finally, between people and people. Therefore, based on design concepts and "thinking through design", it was listed a few relations for the construction of several processes and activities through design theories and processes.

To [13], design thinking is an innovation process focused on the human being that emphasizes observation, collaboration, fast learning, visualization of ideas, prototyping concepts and innovation, and is also applicable in different areas.

The design thinking process is essentially human-centered and emphasizes observation, collaboration, fast learning, visualization of ideas, quick prototype building, learning from failures, and allows a project to be validated more effectively and with feedback from the public. The fact that gamification and design thinking are human-centered and respond to the students' needs meets the urge for accessibility from people with disabilities. To the development of design thinking, [14] points out that the prototype is not only a way to validate final ideas, but is also a creative process. By analyzing the design thinking approach on education and gamification process, it is noticeable the possibility of applying some of the concepts proposed by [12] as empathy, prototyping and experience design.

Another method of applying Design Thinking is the one from Bootcamp Bootleg by [15]. The approach proposed by [15] is divided into five phases: **empathy** (process centered on the user, to immerse, engage and observe the problem); **definition** (makes a synthesis, presents a focus problem or point of view); **ideation** (idea generation, exploration of solutions); **prototyping** (producing ideas in a more realistic context, bringing out the material nature); **tests** (to reset solutions and put the prototype in contact with people).

The presented phases may be related to the processes for building accessible and gamified LOs. As brought by [16], this kind of development must be collaborative and integrated, with actions oriented by the group, collective participation in making decisions, self-regulating coordination, systemically organized thoughts and building relationships through empathy. In this perspective, the gamification steps based on design thinking from their correlations can be used in the process of building accessible and gamified LOs, using steps such as discovery, interpretation, ideation, experimentation and evolution.

During the development of a gamified LO, under the principles of design thinking, it is necessary to conduct an intensive investigation on how the learning object responds to the students' needs, and also how to create added value for those who use it. Thus, it is noticeable a potential in creating gamified learning objects from design thinking, for teaching and learning processes involving disabled people.

The gamified LOs should seek the immersion and happiness present in the Theory of Flow, with the simple reward of performing the activity itself. Considering this premise, Fig. 2 presents, from the Theory of Flow, how the process of design thinking is directed in order to produce gamified LOs. However, when taking in consideration the Universal Design and people with disabilities, the only possibility of achieving a Flow stage is by including accessibility guidelines in the project. Figure 2 explains how the elements operate interdependently.

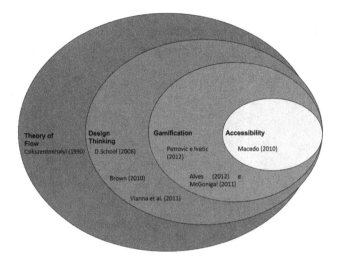

Fig. 2. Interdependence of the elements (Source: Authors)

Based on the premise that the user is the central element of the process and stages of Flow [5] - which allow an immersion state in the process- substantiate this immersion, the first steps of the design thinking process were made [15]. As shown in the model, during all stages of the DT process it was also aimed to integrate gamification theories from [9–11], and to prioritize the last layer of the diagram, from accessibility guidelines for LOs, of [4], outlined by Universal Design and the IMS GLC and W3C-WCAG 1.0 and 2.0 recommendations.

5   Gamified and Accessible LO to People with Visual and Hearing Impairment "Triangle Perimeter"

With the objective of building the LO based on the Design Thinking process, a multi-disciplinary team was organized in order to provide the contribution from different areas to the project. As part of the team, there were researchers from the design areas; programming; mathematics; communication and audiovisual, and expert consultants in LO and accessibility. Unfortunately during the first 3 steps it was not possible to include the participation of people with visual and hearing impairment, although in the process of feedback, based on UX, the tests with users will also be held with this public.

Starting from the Theory of Flow, the assumptions that could be followed in the steps of Empath, Definition and Ideation were listed, correlating to these processes the gami-fication concepts and accessibility guidelines in LOs.

Figure 3 shows the concepts correlation in these 3 steps. From this piece, the creative processes present in design thinking were utilized during the conception of the project, the correlations between the theories concepts were presented, as well as and their complementarities.

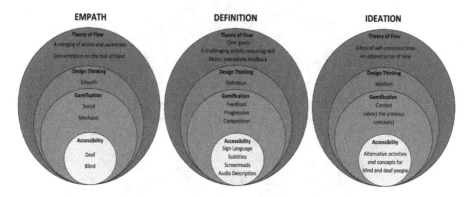

Fig. 3. Correlation of concepts (Source: Authors)

In the subsequent steps (which are not included in this study, considering that the prototype is still in construction), in Prototype, there are all the involved concepts presented, for the construction of the LO, and in Tests, the focus is on the feedback and accessibility, including all the concepts from the preceding stages.

5.1 Empath

At this stage, the process is focused on the user, in order to immerse, engage and observe. At this stage the teams utilized the bibliographic research, the mapping of gamified LOs focused in mathematical concepts and gamified and accessible LOs.

From this early stage, the experiences of each one of the professionals were taken in consideration regarding projects that have already been developed and the target audience feedback, also emphasizing the need for reflexions regarding LOs developed for people with visual and hearing impairment. The similarities between the theories were:

Theory of Flow. *Emphasized points: a merging of action and awareness; concentration on the task at hand.*

The possibility of promoting the Flow state in a gamified LO was directed to the LOs analyzes that could promote educational concepts that would lead the student to the action of starting gamified activities, through the awareness of how pleasant that activity could be. In the reflexions, it was found that many gamified LOs bring obligatory tasks and do not address the possibility of choice, which consequently removes the student from the decision-making (he is obliged to enter in the environment). Then, it was decided to go for the LO direction, in which the processes are focused on decision-making. This context lead us to the following point, the concentration on the task at hand, in which the decision-making of the tasks must be made by the student. When deciding on entering the gamified universe, he is already aware of the possibility of immersion and achieving the Flow state.

Gamification. *Emphasized points: social and mechanic.*

Social: With the work of the multidisciplinary team being done through the DT concepts, there was a direct relationship with the empathy matter, considering a product that is closely related to a social matter, in which through the system the users can promote socialization and interaction relations, and trigger phases such as competition and progression. There is also the possibility of working cooperatively in teams and groups, in order to solve problems and build stronger relationships through affective bonds.

Mechanics: From the pleasurable situations generated, it was sought the gamified LO's development, with the narrative construction from a character and his search for goals and challenges, also bringing what [10 and 11] have presented regarding the epic significance of achieving something expected.

Accessibility. *Emphasized points: Accessibility for people with visual or hearing disability.*
     In order to allow the steps above to bring accessibility tools, the empathy process begins with studies directed to dynamics utilized in gamified LOs from the stages of merging of action and awareness and concentration on the task at hand; Social and Mechanics, and accessibility and Universal Design strategies.

5.2 Definition

From the studies on empathy presented above, it was sought a first definition regarding the project, mainly summarizing the collected concepts and presenting the focus of the problem. Again, this step begins by looking for settings that can converge into solutions to the points presented by the Theory of Flow.

Theory of Flow. *Emphasized points: clear goals; A challenging activity requiring skill; direct, immediate feedback.*
     Here emerges again the user's immersion process, which directs him to challenging activities that explore his different skills, always by utilizing clear goals and immediate feedback. Exploring these possibilities allows the student, after having access to the concepts, to direct his actions towards exploring the gamified LO through the presented narrative. However, for this to occur he must be able to achieve the settled goals and, in case of failure, to be able to optimize his actions in order to continue in the immersion process. Therefore, the gamification strategies bring the directions for this.

Gamification. *Emphasized points: feedback, progression and Competition.*

Feedback: When searching for immersion, the users have different skills, and previous collected knowledge. Thus, the feedback regarding the time in which the user performs a certain task is essential, as well as the feedback regarding mistakes and successes. In the validation stage, this process should be mapped in order to provide continuity and the satisfaction of overcoming challenges. Consequently, the progression process occurs.

Progression: In order to remain in the environment, his goals and actions must be clarified as well as the key points yet to be achieved. Regarding a gamified and accessible LO (under the principles of Universal Design), all users must have a path to overcome challenges. For this to occur, the team searched for references of gamified LO with possibilities of customization according to the users profiles, in which goals are set accordingly with the presented profile. Another possibility would be the user himself setting his own tracks and challenges, by directing actions and goals according to his abilities and skills.

Competition: It was chosen to search in a VLE, besides the self-competition, also the possibility of bringing collective challenges. This feature should be explored very reflexively in learning environments. Promoting competition in gamification is one of the resources that provides the immersion and recovery process. In order to define the execution of these challenges, the team found in interactivity the possibility of the students being stimulated to stimulate, with rewards and new challenges from stimulating other colleagues.

Accessibility. *Emphasized points: Sign language, subtitle, environmental architecture for screen readers and audio description.*

The concepts presented in this work should be articulated so that people with visual or hearing disabilities can explore them. Thus, it is defined the importance of using what [4] defines as alternative media that, in the case of the gamified LO "Triangle's Perimeter" should contain the sign language resources and subtitles for people with hearing disability, and the organization of the Virtual Environment architecture in accordance with the guidelines of IMS GLC and W3C -WCAG 1.0 and 2.0, in order to be accessed by screen readers, besides the audio description resource for videos and pictures.

5.3   Ideation

It may seem that the ideation phase is present in the preceding step, however the previously articulated ideas and the presented solutions served to bring out possibilities of solutions, based on the focus of the problem. However, it was in the ideation phase that the evaluation and criticism regarding the initial solutions were applied. This option was due to the Flow state characteristics related in this stage.

Theory of Flow. *Emphasized points: A loss of self-consciousness; an altered sense of time.*

In this context, the objective of developing an accessible and gamified LO is to actually take the user into a Flow state where the full immersion occurs. By accessing the contents and starting the gamified path, the Flow experience can be associated with an immersion in which the attention level is high and the gamified process puts the user off from what is around him. For those who have lived this experience, it is known that at this moment the perception of time becomes elastic, and sometimes several hours go by during one activity, without noticing its actual passage.

Gamification. *Emphasized points: Context of system actions.*

In the ideation phase, after mapping the application possibilities, it is tried to verify the possibility of using the resources proposed in the architecture of a VLE, and how the initially planned actions may be performed. Since it is a proposal for a VLE, it is important in this process, besides the action plan of the system used in the laboratory, to settle which are the software resources and minimum hardware required to run the system, and the availability of internet connection.

Accessibility. *Emphasized points: Alternative activities and concepts for blind and deaf people.*

After bringing resources such as subtitles, sign language, screen readers and audio description, at this stage it is also aimed to develop alternative activities, based on the mapping of geometry learning process for people with visual or hearing disability. An example is the printing of Braille materials for children with visual disability, or the proposal of producing a tactile geometric board so they can handle and understand the concepts outside the computer screen. It was not presented in this topic the description of the gamified and accessible LO development, since the focus of this work is to bring directions for utilizing the presented theories towards the advancement of researches focused on the production of resources that are accessible to people with disabilities.

6 Conclusion

The ideation stage brought the direction of a gamified and accessible LO, which still has to go through stages of prototyping and feedback tests accordingly with the prescripts of UX. The target audience is geometry students with visual or hearing disability. The learning dynamic occurs from presenting educational materials accessible on the MOOBI[1] accessible platform. After accessing the accessible teaching materials regarding the triangle's perimeter, the student chooses to enter the gamified activities.

After entering the gamified LO, the student is introduced to the character Elvis (who appears in the story as an animated character; a comic character and in videos (which will be performed by an actor with similar characteristics to the character). He is the one who leads the search for the student's immersion into the Flow state, along with the accessibility guidelines (subtitles activation, sign language, audio description, presentation of challenges, activities (within the environment and at home - such as the construction of a tactile geometric board - in order to explore the perimeter concept, made with egg packagings and strings); the print of Braille materials; among other

---

[1] MOOBI is an accessible VLE (Virtual Learning Environment) that has been being developed by the group WebGD PPEGC/UFSC, and is available in http://webgd.egc.ufsc.br/.

possibilities of exploring accessibility resources, in order to bring the plane geometry's learning process closer to the universe of these children.

Besides enabling the immersion through an accessible environment, the LO stimulates through challenges, scores and awards, the search for "A loss of self-consciousness"; and "An altered sense of time". A technological tool that directs this search is the accessible environment MOOBI, which allows students to upload videos (a very useful resource for the person with hearing disability who communicates through sign language) or audio (for the person with hearing disability) and explore the interaction process along with other colleagues within the environment. With these resources, they can also interact with students without disabilities (as they are able to understand the messages), which enables the development of integrated activities.

The Flow state's main purpose in this work is directed to people with visual and hearing disabilities. The reason for this choice is due to the particularities of disabled people's learning processes, of their historical social exclusion and the limited resources available that promote learning and knowledge sharing. Lastly, it is aimed to bring this reflection to researchers, educators, developers and instructional designers, regarding the necessity of advancing in researches that seek alternatives to foster the inclusion process and the disabled people's active participation in society.

7 Future Steps

Future steps of this research should be directed to the Prototyping stages, with accessibility validation tests made with the public.

References

1. Deterding, S., Dixon, D., Khaled, R., Nacke, L.: From game design elements to gamefulness: defining "Gamification". In: Proceedings of the 15th International Academic Mindtrek Conference on Envisioning Future Media Environments, pp. 9–15. ACM, New York (2011)
2. Simões, J., Redondo, R.D., Vilas, A.F.: A social gamification framework for a K-6 learning platform. Comput. Hum. Behav. **29**(2), 345–353 (2013). Elsevier B.V.
3. Fialho, A.F.P.: From individual to social cognition: Piaget, Jung and commons, In: CSDC 2015 World e-Conference Complex Systems Digital Campus, Arizona (2015)
4. Macedo, C.M.S.: Diretrizes para criação de objetos de aprendizagem acessíveis. UFSC, Florianópolis (2010)
5. Csikszentmihalyi, M.: Flow: The Psycology of Optimal Experience. Harper & Row, New York (1990)
6. Diana, J.B., Golfetto, I.F., Baldessar, M.J., Spanhol, F.J.: Gamification e Teoria do Flow. In: Fadel, L., Ulbricht, V.R., Batista, C.R., Vanzin, T. (eds.) Gamificação na educação, pp. 38–73. Pimenta Cultural, São Paulo (2014)
7. Chen, J.: Flow in games (and everything else). Commun. ACM **50**(4), 31–34 (2007)
8. Netto, M.: Aprendizagem na EaD, Mundo Digital e 'Gamification'. In: Fadel, L., Ulbricht, V.R., Batista, C.R., Vanzin, T. (eds.) Gamificação na educação, pp. 98–121. Pimenta Cultural, São Paulo (2014)

9. Petrovic, V., Ivetic, D.: Gamifying education: a proposed taxonomy of satisfaction metrics. In: Conference Proceedings of "eLearning and Software for Education", pp. 345–350. Universitatea Nationala de Aparare Carol I, Frankfurt (2012)

10. Alves, L.: Games, colaboração e aprendizagem (Chap. 9). In: Okada, A. (ed.) Open Educational Resources and Social Networks: Co-Learning and Professional Development. Scholio Educational Research & Publishing, London, 1–7 (2012)

11. Mcgonigal, J.: Reality is Broken: Why Game Make Us Better and How They Can Change the World. The Penguin Press, London (2011)

12. Brown, T.: Design thinking: uma metodologia ponderosa para decretar o fim das velhas ideias. Elsevier, Rio de Janeiro (2010)

13. Lockwood, T.: Design Thinking: Integrating Innovation, Customer Experience, and Brand Value. Allworth Press, New York (2009)

14. Demarchi, A.P.P., Fornasier, C.B.R., Carmona, C.F., Martins, R.F.F.: Design Thinking, aprendizagem e conhecimento internalizado no processo de criação de uma mensagem educacional com linguagem visual direcionada para adolescentes. Rev. Unifamma 12, 44–67 (2014)

15. d.school: Bootcamp Bootleg. http://dschool.stanford.edu/wp-content/uploads/2011/03/BootcampBootleg2010v2SLIM.pdf

16. Amaral, S.F., Garbin, M.C.: Design Thinking: A Colaboração como Mola Propulsora da Inovação na Educação. Inova Educ. 2, 1–11 (2013)

Design of a Gamified Interface to Improve Fuel Efficiency and Safe Driving

Atiyeh Vaezipour$^{(\boxtimes)}$, Andry Rakotonirainy, and Narelle Haworth

Centre for Accident Research and Road Safety (CARRS-Q),
Queensland University of Technology (QUT), 130 Victoria Park Road,
Queensland, 4059, Australia
{a.vaezipour,a.rakotonirainy,n.haworth}@qut.edu.au

Abstract. The increasing reliance on motor vehicles has negative effects on both human health and the environment. Improving driving style has been shown to be a particularly crucial and relatively quick step to reducing fuel consumption and vehicle emissions. In this paper, a series of conceptual designs of in-vehicle gamified interfaces were evaluated, with a particular focus on the ability to use such systems to increase driver acceptance of feedback from such interfaces in order to promote eco-safe driving. Self-determination theory (SDT) was used to inform the design of the gamified interface concepts, with a particular focus on competence, autonomy and relatedness, as well as intrinsic versus extrinsic incentives and social persuasion feedback. The study adopts a user-centered design approach, utilizing focus groups to establish user needs and motivations to aid the design of a prototype system.

Keywords: Eco-driving · Safe driving · User-centered design · User experience · Gamification · Human computer interaction

1 Introduction

An increasing reliance on motor vehicles subsequently results in an increase in gaseous and particulate pollution, which has negative effects on both human health and the environment. According to the World Health Organization [1], ambient air pollution attributes to 3.7 million deaths each year worldwide. Improving driving style has been shown to be an effective way to reduce fuel consumption and vehicle emissions [2], with the adoption of fuel-efficient driving behaviors being reported as having the potential to reduce fuel consumption amongst the existing vehicle fleet by 5–10 % [3].

Whilst there are large overlaps between eco-driving and safe driving behavior, in some traffic situations they are in conflict with one another [4, 5]. In-vehicle Human Machine Interfaces (HMI) provide an opportunity to provide real-time feedback to drivers based on the immediate traffic conditions, support of the driver and navigation. These systems are developing rapidly, having recently been used to promote fuel-efficient and safe driving.

This paper employed a user-centered design approach to inform the design of a prototype eco-safe, gamified in-vehicle system. The use of game elements in the driving

© Springer International Publishing Switzerland 2016
A. Marcus (Ed.): DUXU 2016, Part II, LNCS 9747, pp. 322–332, 2016.
DOI: 10.1007/978-3-319-40355-7_31

context is becoming increasingly popular. The use of such principles as a means to influence driver behaviors has been previously explored, including a number of smart-phone, app-based approaches, such as Driving Miss Daisy [6], Learner Logbook [7] and VW Smile Drive (smiledrive.vw.com), as well as more innovative approaches such as the Speed Camera Lottery (thefuntheory.com). Furthermore, Rodríguez et al. [8] sought to prevent distractions through the use of ambient devices and haptic feedback.

The objective of the gamified interface is to motivate drivers to improve their driving performance and cooperate with other drivers in order to improve fuel efficiency and traffic safety. Of particular interest, is the acceptance and effectiveness of providing driving performance feedback to drivers through this medium, both in terms of individual feedback to the driver, as well as the exchange of social persuasion feedback among other drivers. The study investigates a number of concepts, including user perceptions of the conceptual designs (e.g., how engaging the interface is, how easily it is understood, perceived usability), as well as perceived difficulties associated with the interface and ideas for improvements.

Self-determination theory (SDT) [9] was used to inform the design of the game elements and interface concepts. According to SDT, three key needs are essential for the achievement of psychological growth: competence, relatedness and autonomy. Specifically, competence refers to an individual's need to master new tasks and learn new skills, relatedness to an individual's need to experience a sense of belonging and attachment to others, and autonomy to the need to feel in control of one's own behavior and the subsequent outcomes. Not surprisingly, these factors are often targeted in order to institute behavior change, with high levels of these factors argued to be most likely to result in intrinsically motivated behavior. In addition, the theory argues that both intrinsic (e.g., beliefs, expectations, and self-identity) and extrinsic (e.g., incentives, social norms and pressure, cultural norms) motivations can influence behavior to varying degrees. Finally, social support is argued to be important to psychological growth, such that encouraging interpersonal relationships and social interactions (e.g., through group co-operation) can harness feelings of relatedness and attachment with others.

Thus, according to SDT, a number of factors need to be considered when developing in-vehicle systems for the purpose of facilitating intrinsically motivated behaviors that are less amenable to change. These include: (i) avoiding external rewards (e.g., prizes, cash incentives); (ii) providing positive feedback to drivers regarding their behavior related to relevant tasks (e.g., eco-safe driving); and, (iii) fostering social interactions (e.g., through cooperative systems).

Therefore, this research explores the proposition that the autonomy associated with an intrinsically motivated behavior may be undermined by the provision of external rewards, such that an individual's perceived control over their behavior is diminished. In addition, this study investigates whether intrinsic motivations to perform a behavior can be promoted through the provision of positive feedback regarding task performance, aimed at improving feelings of competence. Finally, this paper draws conclusions relating to user preferences for the design and development of an in-vehicle gamified interface. The main focus is on the comparative effect of individual versus social persuasion feedback in the driving context, which may be an important element for designing in-vehicle interfaces.

1.1   Conceptual Gamified Design

In the focus groups, participants were presented with a number of conceptual designs in the form of a paper prototype. These designs were displayed as images of a smartphone depicting various screens associated with a hypothetical gamified eco-safe in-vehicle interface. Participants were informed that these screens are only accessible to drivers before the commencement or after the completion of a trip, in order to minimize distraction while driving.

In Fig. 1a, screens related to *challenges and game elements* reveal how a user is able to choose between a variety of challenges, as well as view descriptions of each challenge. The design was intended to provide users with challenges based on different levels of difficulty to facilitate feelings of enhanced competence as they progressed through levels and mastered various challenges, keeping in mind that prior research has highlighted the need to balance difficulty and user skill in order to avoid boredom (when challenges are too easy) and/or frustration (when challenges are too difficult) [10]. The design also supported autonomy by providing multiple options for challenges, allowing users to feel a greater sense of control.

In Fig. 1b, the screens display *individualized performance indicators and feedback.* Specifically, these screens highlight a user's points, level progress, achievements, as well as more specific challenge and trip information (e.g., kilometers travelled, proportion of correct/incorrect performance of the challenge behavior). Focus group participants were informed that these screens are only accessible upon completion of a trip. Furthermore, they were shown additional concept screens (i.e., a 'My Profile' screen) outlining a variety of other information, such as total scores, overall eco-driving and safety scores, a list of friends who also use the system, a list of achievements earned and tips for increasing one's total score. Given that research has highlighted the importance of positive feedback to user experiences of competence and motivation [11], these screens were designed to give primarily positively-geared feedback messages.

Finally, Fig. 1c shows the social interaction features of the system. During the trip a user can choose to have scores of other drivers also using the system in proximity of their vehicle automatically projected onto the windshield (via heads-up display, using vehicle-to-vehicle technology), showing comparative scores on overall eco-driving and safety challenges. In addition, a number of screens are accessible after a trip that reveal scores in comparison to friends and/or other drivers who use the system. These components of the system were designed to provide users with the ability to socially engage with other drivers and cooperate toward a common goal of eco-safe driving.

2   Method

2.1   Participants

A total of 34 licensed drivers from the Australian state of Queensland were recruited to participate in focus group discussions. The sample was roughly evenly split on gender (16 female, 18 males), with an age range of 19–61 years ($M = 32.11$, $SD = 10.44$). A convenience sampling approach was used, with participants being university students

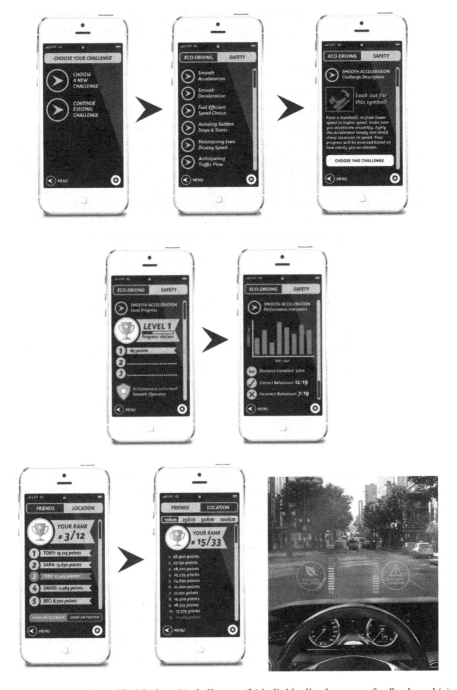

Fig. 1. Conceptual gamified design: (a) challenges, (b) individualized progress feedback, and (c) social persuasion feedback

or employees, their friends or associates. Focus groups were approximately 60 min, with participants offered a movie voucher as reimbursement for their time and contribution.

2.2 Procedure and Materials

Participants gave written consent to participate in an audio-recorded focus group discussion. In total, 6 focus groups of 5–6 participants were conducted. The facilitator began each focus group with a discussion about fuel-efficient and safe driving behavior, with participants encouraged to discuss their general concerns about eco-safe driving and the behaviors they perceived as being important to monitor while driving. The conceptualized gamified eco-safe in-vehicle system was than presented to participants (see Fig. 1), with the majority of the focus group devoted to facilitator-guided, semi-structured discussions regarding participant perceptions regarding issues such as usability, usefulness, and key effective features and areas for improvement, particularly in relation to device and feedback characteristics, gamified elements, and social persuasion feedback.

2.3 Data Analysis

Focus group sessions were audio-recorded, transcribed and coded using Nvivo. A thematic analysis was conducted to identify themes and patterns across responses and their association with research questions. Following that, familiarization and ongoing interpretation of the data allowed initial codes to be generated, which in turn were collated into a number of main themes. These included: (i) perceptions of gamified concepts; (ii) incentives and motivations to use the system; and (iii) social persuasion feedback.

3 Findings

The research findings are presented in regards to three main themes discussed in the previous section, namely: (i) perceptions of gamified concepts; (ii) incentives and motivations to use the system; and (iii) social persuasion feedback.

3.1 User Perceptions of Gamified Concepts

Overall, there were mixed perceptions regarding the use of game elements for an eco-safe in-vehicle system, with rather polarized perceptions regarding whether the inclusion of such elements was positive or negative. Those at the most extreme spectrum of less favorable attitudes suggested that the use of game elements would be potentially detrimental to the overall perceived legitimacy of the system as a safety intervention.

> *"I disagree with the game concept of it, it almost takes it away from safety and driving and makes it not as serious" (F, 53).*

More commonly, participants suggested that gamified elements simply didn't appeal to them. More specifically, many suggested that their preference would instead be for a system that provided informative and personalized feedback regarding their eco-safe driving behavior, and in particular feedback designed to help them improve their eco-safe driving. However, it is worth noting that these individuals often acknowledged that some drivers may like, and benefit from, the gamified interface.

"I think I'd use it for feedback. I wouldn't use it for gaming. But like, if it just gave me feedback after I finished driving, then yeah, I would use it" (F, 22).

"I don't think I'd use the game features. I'd be interested in it helping me drive safer and be more aware" (M, 32).

However, some people had positive perceptions towards gamified elements. Specifically, a number of participants suggested that the system could be engaging and decrease the negative effects of driving monotony.

"Probably more appealing as a game feature rather than just like "here's buttons to push to tell you something". People might get a bit more into it as a game feature" (M, 29).

"I think it's going to be fun, because sometimes a driver is going to get bored so if you have something fun, it makes your time pass smoothly" (M, 19).

It was argued that young drivers in particular may benefit from the increased engagement with the driving task associated with a gamified system.

"The game thing could possibly be good for new, younger drivers when they're first starting to go out by themselves and hone their driving skills, once they get their license" (F, 33).

"It would be good to have something a little bit fun in the car so for them [younger drivers] the game might be good for making it, sort of a little bit fun and engaging" (M, 36).

In addition, other participants highlighted that the game elements could facilitate social persuasion among family and friends, suggesting they would be motivated to challenge their peers and family.

"I could see it being engaging with the family, to see how other members of the family are behaving. From that perspective, it would be beneficial" (F, 51).

As a result, the majority of participants suggested that the gamified elements should represent more of a 'background feature' of the system, such that those users who wanted to gamify the feedback could do so, while the default was to have feedback provided in a more direct and informative manner.

"I think being able to turn that off would be good because I think personally I might be interested in the game aspect for like a week or something and then I'll probably get over it and just want the information." (F, 33).

"It would be good to have an option. If you're into the game thing, I can compete with my friends, same as any iPhone game" (M, 30).

Some participants questioned the likelihood of continued, long-term use of the system, suggesting that the novelty of the gamified elements may be short-lived. In addition, others suggested that frustration and discontinued use may result if the challenges became too difficult to master.

"I think for me, the problem will be the consistency of usage. How long are you going to use it for? There's always this period when people start using and then they are like super excited and after a point where they like, "oh, it's too much of a hassle"" (M, 22).

"I think it might improve my driving for a while but then, if I can't reach any other like challenges or achievements in the game, if it was a game, then I might just like forget it and go back to my old driving." (F, 20)

Finally, a number of participants highlighted the importance of positively-geared feedback in order to minimize the likelihood of misuse of the system and the inadvertent encouragement of poor eco-safe driving behaviors.

"I might try and see how I could push the system, like make it flash a lot that I'm doing things wrong and people would do that, like when you used to have the alcohol breath testers in the pub, you'd see who can get the highest reading, it would be similar thing with this" (M, 30)

"Good idea, if it doesn't get abused or misused. I can see my teenage son ... use it for bad behavior, instead of improving, trying to compete in bad behavior" (F, 51).

3.2 Incentives and Motivations to Use the System

Participants reported polarized views regarding the factors that would motivate them to use the system. On the one hand, a number of participants suggested that intrinsic incentives, such as the knowledge that using the system was improving their eco-safe driving behavior and helping the environment, would be sufficient to motivate them to use the system.

"I think for me personally, an estimate of how much I saved, money and emissions, that would actually be the only thing important to me. If you give me a cinema voucher after one year, great, but I wouldn't really go for it" (M, 28).

"The value has really got to come from the saving, the personal saving, not the [external] reward" (F, 35).

"I care about the environment. That would be my motivation. And any extraneous stuff like, yeah might be good, but my interest in this is from an environmental point of view" (M, 39).

"I wouldn't need exterior rewards, you can get rewarded for just being a decent driver. I'd just use it for plain curiosity" (M, 23).

Overall, the intrinsic incentives associated with game elements, such as achievements and leaderboards, appeared to have little impact on reported motivations to use the system among the participants, even though they were typically interested in receiving feedback regarding their eco-safe driving performance.

"I don't want a trophy, but I want to know when I'm driving efficiently" (M, 28).

"I don't care if my phone's saying congratulations, you got a point and a star. I don't care" (M, 29).

Interestingly, a number of participants noted that it is important to ensure that the system was accommodating, noting that different users will be motivated by different incentives, and that the system must suit an individual's needs.

"If you had a series of what the rewards are, from the point of view of I want to save money, you want to save the planet, you want to compete with your mates then you set it up into different things. The technology underneath is the same but you've got to suit you" (M, 61).

"I'd rather reward myself ... maybe you could customize it in a way that mattered to you" (M, 39).

On the other hand, a number of participants argued that intrinsic incentives would not be sufficient to motivate them to use the system. Instead, these participants suggested that extrinsic rewards would be necessary to motivate them to engage with the system.

"If you're going to use something that takes your time, and I don't feel like there's a benefit to myself or anything for using it, I don't care if I can see what kind of driver I am ... I need an incentive ... I need money or something for free or a discount" (M, 29).

"There's got to be some sort of a reward in it for me" (M, 61).

In particular, amongst those participants who advocated extrinsic incentives, many suggested the most effective rewards would be those related to the driving task, such as fuel vouchers or insurance and vehicle registration discounts. It was also noted that the rewards would have to outweigh the effort associated with using the system and altering one's driving.

"I think the incentive would have to be car-related, like insurance [discounts], because that's going to appeal to all audiences" (F, 22).

"If my insurance [company] said that if you used this you get a percentage off on your thing [premiums], I'd be like "yeah, why not"" (M, 29).

"It would have to be ongoing beneficial money value for me in fuel or rego ... it would have to be something that would keep you driving well for the points to be able to get the reward ... and the rewards need to be worth it" (M, 27).

Finally, one participant noted that the focus on extrinsic incentives may result in only short-term behavior change, particularly if there is no incentive to continue engaging in particular eco-safe driving behaviors once a challenge has been mastered. Interestingly, this individual also reported that they perceived extrinsic rewards as important to increasing their motivation to use the system, suggesting paradoxical attitudes.

"Isn't it meant to change your habits driving, not just make you try to win a game. I mean, if there's good prizes, I'm going to drive really well to get to the targets and then, that's it" (M, 27).

3.3 Social Persuasion Feedback

Participants were also divided regarding their attitudes towards the social persuasion feedback aspects of the concept system. Some drivers suggested that they would be motivated to compete with friends and family in an attempt to determine who is a better driver, while others noted that they would be curious to compare their eco-safe driving ability against other drivers. There was some evidence that having family or peers who use the system would increase the likelihood that participants would use the system themselves.

"If my friends all use it I will use it. Because I want to compete in the scores. So, I am more into the social side" (F, 25).

"I would use it to see other people's scores" (M, 29).

"People are not only trying to better themselves but they can see their friends, which more and more people are going to go see if they can out do their friends" (F, 56).

However, among these participants, some voiced concern about being judged by other drivers, highlighting that negative feedback may reduce motivation to use the system, particularly among peers and family.

"I think the social interaction part is very good. So you will see what the other person's score is, but you don't want people judging you, saying "this car is really bad and he's not a good driver"" (M, 26).

"I think if you've got an awful score, you just turn it off. You'd never do it. If you've got a great score, you'd leave it on. You don't really want all your friends to get to know you're a shit driver" (M, 61).

Other participants were less interested in the social persuasion feedback, suggesting that they were more interested in competing with themselves and focusing on improving their behavior in comparison to prior levels.

"It's only if you can beat yourself. I don't want to compare with other people" (F, 35).

4 Discussion and Design Implications

The findings from this study provide important implications for the design of future gamified eco-safe in-vehicle systems and highlight the importance of adopting a user-centered design approach from an early stage of design, through to development and implementation of any system.

Overall, participants held less than favorable attitudes regarding the gamification of an eco-safe in-vehicle system, instead reporting a preference for more informative and personalized feedback. However, the potential for such elements to increase engagement with the driving task and facilitate social persuasion feedback led many to argue that game elements should represent a 'background feature' of the system, such that those users who wanted to gamify the feedback could do so. This finding highlights that users desire a sense of autonomy and control over the system, such that they can modify the system to best suit their specific individual needs. Perhaps the most important goal is to provide feedback in an engaging manner and allowing users to choose if, and how, they want to gamify the experience for themselves. This is likely to differ dependent on user demographics and personality characteristics, such as age, gender, sociability and previous experience with games and game play. It is worth mentioning that participant responses did not show large differences between age and gender, but rather were relatively divided based on life stage (e.g., novice vs experienced drivers; parents of young children vs parents of teenagers), experience with using the technology and purpose of driving. These findings provide support for the ideas of [12] who argued that "a game element may be both intrinsically and extrinsically motivating for certain people in certain situations at certain times" (as cited in [13], p. 20). This finding therefore suggests that it is important to design in-vehicle systems in a way that allows personalization and customization, to accommodate individual users. This finding is consistent with those of previous studies [13].

Furthermore, consistent with prior research, a number of participants highlighted the importance of balancing task difficulty and user skill. Thus, careful consideration must be given to the development of challenges in order to maintain engagement and avoid situations where users become bored, such as when challenges are too easy, or frustrated, such as when challenges are too difficult.

According to SDT, intrinsic motivation is crucial for long-term behavioral change. The results of the focus study provided some evidence that intrinsic incentives would be sufficient to motivate user engagement with the system, however many participants still reported that extrinsic rewards would be necessary. Interestingly, a paradoxical attitude was noted whereby a participant reported a need for extrinsic rewards to engage with the system while also acknowledging that a focus on extrinsic incentives may result in only short-term behavior change, particularly if there is no incentive to continue engaging in particular eco-safe driving behaviors once a challenge has been mastered. Further research is required to more comprehensively understand this issue, however participants did again note the importance of autonomy and control in deciding the incentives that are most suitable to them.

The theory also argues that social support is important to psychological growth, and that encouraging interpersonal relationships and social interactions can foster feelings of relatedness. Overall, a majority of participants expressed favorable attitudes towards the social persuasion feedback aspects of the concept system. This finding suggests that the inclusion of elements such as group messages, blogs, connectivity to social networks, and chat functions may all increase a user's motivation to engage with the system.

Finally, a number of feedback characteristics were noted as being important, and should be considered in future research and system development. These included: providing positively-geared feedback in order to minimize the likelihood of misuse of the system and the inadvertent encouragement of poor eco-safe driving behaviors.

5   Conclusion

This paper presents the findings from a user-centered design focus group study which sought to investigate user perceptions of a conceptualized gamified eco-safe in-vehicle system. Results suggest that many users hold less than favorable attitudes towards gamified elements being more than a background feature to such a system, however support the functionality for users to gamify the system if they wish. Thus, consistent with SDT's concept of autonomy, users desire the ability to customize system features depend on their specific needs. Moreover, to meet a user's competence needs, challenges must be designed such that they balance task difficulty and user skill and experience levels, while the inclusion of social persuasion feedback aspects appears to be an effective method for meeting a user's need for relatedness. More research is required to comprehensively understand the role of intrinsic versus extrinsic incentives on motivations to engage with in-vehicle system. Future research should seek to develop a more realistic prototype for further evaluation in regards to usability, paying particular attention to the impact of system use on safety outcomes, such as driver distraction and the inadvertent promotion of unsafe or unlawful driving behaviors.

Acknowledgments. The Authors would like to acknowledge the funding support provided by an Australian Research Council Discovery grant (No. DP140102895).

References

1. World Health Organization (WHO): Ambient (outdoor) air quality and health. Fact Sheet No. 313. Updated in March 2014
2. Martin, E., Chan, N., Shaheen, S.: Understanding how ecodriving public education can result in reduced fuel use and greenhouse gas emissions. In: 91st Annual Meeting of the Transportation Research Board, Washington, D.C., January 2012
3. Barkenbus, J.N.: Eco-driving: an overlooked climate change initiative. Energ. Policy **38**, 762–769 (2010)
4. Vaezipour, A., Rakotonirainy, A., Haworth, N.: Reviewing in-vehicle systems to improve fuel efficiency and road safety. Procedia Manuf. **3**, 3192–3199 (2015)
5. Haworth, N., Symmons, M.: The relationship between fuel economy and safety outcomes. Monash University Accident Research Centre 0732614872 (2001)
6. Shi, C., Lee, H.J., Kurczal, J., Lee, A.: Routine driving infotainment app: gamification of performance driving. In: Adjunct Proceedings of the 4th International Conference on Automotive User Interfaces and Interactive Vehicular Applications, pp. 181–183 (2012)
7. Fitz-Walter, Z., Wyeth, P., Tjondronegoro, D., Scott-Parker, B.: Driven to drive: Designing gamification for a learner logbook smartphone application. In: Proceedings of the First International Conference on Gameful Design, Research, and Applications, pp. 42–49 (2013)
8. Rodríguez, M.D., Roa, R.R., Ibarra, J.E., Curlango, C.M.: In-car ambient displays for safety driving gamification. In: Proceedings of the 5th Mexican Conference on Human-Computer Interaction, p. 26 (2014)
9. Deci, E.L., Ryan, R.M.: Intrinsic Motivation and Self-determination in Human Behavior. Springer, New York (1985)
10. Przybylski, A.K., Rigby, C.S., Ryan, R.M.: A motivational model of video game engagement. Rev. Gen. Psychol. **14**, 154 (2010)
11. Ryan, R.M., Deci, E.L.: Intrinsic and extrinsic motivations: classic definitions and new directions. Contemp. Educ. Psychol. **25**, 54–67 (2000)
12. Deterding, S.: Situated motivational affordances of game elements: a conceptual model. In: Gamification: Using Game Design Elements in Non-gaming Contexts, a Workshop at CHI (2011)
13. Seaborn, K., Fels, D.I.: Gamification in theory and action: a survey. Int. J. Hum. Comput. Stud. **74**, 14–31 (2015)

Usability and Motivational Effects of a Gamified Exercise and Fitness System Based on Wearable Devices

Zhao Zhao[✉], S. Ali Etemad, Ali Arya, and Anthony Whitehead

Carleton University, Ottawa, Canada
{zhao.zhao,ali.etemad,ali.arya,anthony.whitehead}@carleton.ca

Abstract. Gamification of exercise has become a popular topic due to its motivational and engagement effects, which intends to result in increased exercise, activity, health, and fitness for everyday users. At the same time, wearable technologies have become a fast growing industry, providing consumers the ability to conveniently track their state of health and fitness efforts. Consequently, we propose that off-the-shelf commercial wearable technologies have great potential to be applied in gamification of fitness and exercise. In this paper, we utilize this concept through the design and implementation of a smartphone game application which uses wearable devices as input systems. The game supports two different wearable devices which are commercially available to end-users, and three types of activities were included in the gamified experience. These activities are performed as inputs to our mobile game. User tests evaluate the effectiveness of the combined use of games and wearable devices in promoting exercise. The usability of our proposed approach and effects of different factors within the system are also evaluated.

Keywords: Gamification · Exercise · Wearable device · Usability · Motivation

1 Introduction

The growing attention and interest towards exercise, health, and fitness has recently sparked the commoditization of a large number of wearable devices. These devices often range from simple activity trackers that monitor daily activities, and sleep patterns, to devices that integrate multiple sensors and can detect heart-rate, body temperature, muscle contraction intensity, hydration levels, and more [1]. Such devices, especially the activity trackers, are able to continuously collect data from the user's body and activities for analysis purposes, which not only could be used to monitor the state of health and fitness, but also help users develop better exercise routines. As wearables are becoming cheaper and more accessible, and data storage and processing capabilities improve, these devices and their associated applications are gradually becoming a part of our everyday lives.

In general, gamification is the notion of applying game design elements and mechanics to motivate and engage people in non-game contexts [2]. This practice has become a popular field of research due to increased capabilities and the wide use of smart phones and computers. Since exercise and fitness are often strenuous and

© Springer International Publishing Switzerland 2016
A. Marcus (Ed.): DUXU 2016, Part II, LNCS 9747, pp. 333–344, 2016.
DOI: 10.1007/978-3-319-40355-7_32

potentially unattractive, alternative motivators such as entertainment and persuasive technologies are considered effective ways for appealing to a wider audience [3]. Lately, the use of gamification in different fields related to exercise, fitness, and health in general, has become popular.

Wearable technologies are suitable platforms for gamified health and fitness applications. As a result, some popular wearable's original applications have started to introduce gamified elements such as community, goals, and achievements. Yet, the existing wearable based applications rarely use actual gameplay mechanisms and real game experiences. Therefore, we have proposed an approach for gamification of exercise and fitness, where off-the-shelf commercial wearable technologies are utilized for interaction with real-time exercise games [4].

In this paper, we further explore this idea through the design and implementation of a smartphone game application and integration with two wearable devices. The game has been developed on the iOS platform and currently supports two types of wearable devices: Apple Watch as an example of a wrist-band tracker, and a 3-axis wrist-worn accelerometer (TI SensorTag CC2650) as an example of a simple do-it-yourself activity tracker which can also be worn on other parts of the body like the ankle. Both of these devices are commercially available to end-users. Three types of activities were included in the study, which are running on treadmill, biking on a trainer, and rope skipping. These activities are performed as input to our mobile game. User tests evaluate the effectiveness of the combined use of games and wearable devices in promoting fitness and a healthy lifestyle. Questionnaires are used to evaluate the usability of our proposed approach and effects of different factors such as the position to wear the device, different measurements, and different activities, overall satisfaction, motivation, reception compared to regular exercise, preference of game, preference of wearable, etc.

2 Related Work

Gamification is described as the process of using game-like elements and goal-based systems to increase motivation engagement in non-game contexts [5]. Practical applications of gamification, especially in the areas of health and fitness, has been growing for the past several years. The number of available applications in the App Store and Google Play under the category of health and fitness that contain gamified elements [6] is evidence to the popularity of this concept. These applications can be lightly gamified, for example most wearables' default applications such as leaderboard and challenges (Nike+ , Fitbit, Jawbone, Misfit, etc.), or heavily gamified, for example, the application *Dungeon Run* uses the camera to detect user movement and uses it as the input to the game.

In the past few years, researchers have devoted attention to gamified exercise, especially for running. For example, the smart phone game *Zombies Run* was an example where headphones were used to interact with users while they were running. This approach proved to have a positive and motivational impact [7]. In [8], Buttussi and Chittaro used and combined a GPS and a pulse oximeter worn on the user's ear, and proposed a user-adaptive game for jogging. Their study results showed that the game motivated users, while having other benefits such as training users to jog as a cardio-vascular exercise. In [9], Mokka et al. introduced a fitness game that users could play in a virtual environment for cycling. Their user test showed that virtual environments could be a motivating factor for exercise. Campbell et al. [10] discussed the notion of everyday fitness games and suggested that for applications that people frequently use in their everyday lives, designs need to be fun and sustainable, as well as adapt to behav-ioural changes. In [11], Wyle indicated that with the use of smart phones, gamified components such as a leaderboard, achievements and challenge amongst friends are effective ways of motivating and encouraging users to reach their personal goals and track their physical fitness activities. Bradley et al. [12] proposed a game that could motivate users to exercise both physical and mental aspects through the use of wearable ECG and EEG devices.

In [13], Ilona et al. stated that gamification was important in driving user motivation in different contexts, especially in health and education. They developed a learning solution using wearables to promote healthy ageing through a fitness-oriented massive online learning course with the use of integrated fitness trackers. It was illustrated that gamification is a significant element towards user engagement. In [14], Joey et al. proposed a mobile role-playing game that could motivate users to engage in exercise through the enjoyment of a game. Results showed that there was a significant connection between real-life activity and the in-game experience. They found that the in-game virtual characters could motivate users in exercise. In [15], Whitehead et al. also indi-cated that exercise games could motivate people to participate in more physical activi-ties. Their work suggested that exercise games could be a useful solution to encourage people to exercise more, and the design should consider both incentive and physical benefits.

Most wearable devices in today's market, especially the new generation of activity trackers, are affordable and easy to purchase. Many of them even provide an application program interface (API) for third party developers to build applications. In [16], Miller has indicated that researchers are now able to study the fitness tracker as more than just a personal data-gathering tool since more interactions and social elements could be added in. In [17], Stefan et al. proposed an idea that with the prevalence of wearable devices, the input and output possibilities of smartphones can be further extended with both new sensors and actuators. New applications could be designed to enrich the inter-action experience with the development of wearable technologies.

3   Research Approach

3.1   Overview

We designed an application (game) where off-the-shelf commercial wearables are used as input devices for gamified exercise. The game was developed on the iOS platform and currently supports Apple Watch (http://www.apple.com/watch/) and TI SensorTag (www.ti.com/sensortag), both of which are commercially available. Successive to appli-cation design and implementation, the user study was designed and carried out. Finally, the results were analyzed and conclusions were made regarding the proposed concept. Figure 1 illustrates the overall process for this work.

Fig. 1. A schematic of our study: a gamified exercise application using wearable devices was designed and implemented. Subsequently, user studies were designed and carried out. Finally, the data was analyzed and interpreted to evaluate the effectiveness of our proposed approach.

With the robust and dynamic basis that was created in this work, additional wearable devices can be added to the study in the future. The three different activities tested in this study were running on a treadmill, biking on a trainer, and rope skipping. These activities were monitored by the wearable devices and respective features were used as inputs to the game through Bluetooth (BLE in our case) in real time. User studies were designed to evaluate the effectiveness of the combined use of activities and wearable devices for promoting exercise (in terms of increased activity level, enjoyment, and motivation), and understand the impact of gamification in motivating exercise and making the experience more interesting. Additionally, the usability of the system was investigated.

3.2   Application Design and Implementation

The iOS application *StrayBird* was implemented for this work. The application communicates with wearable activity trackers in real-time and uses data received from these devices as inputs for the game. The game requires that the player engages in running, cycling, or rope skipping motion to control the movements and actions of the principal character, which is a bird that has fallen behind his travelling companions. The objective is to regroup with the flock before time runs out and before the group reaches its intended destination. There are also physical and environmental parameters that may affect the movement behaviour of the bird and flock. The game features a mission-based structure and point-based system. It is based on a linear progression structure and consists of unlockable levels that increase with slight difficulty and differ to a certain degree in gameplay. Figure 2 presents snapshots from different sections of the application, namely choice of exercises, game view, and result view.

We have connected two devices to this application: Apple Watch and TI SensorTag. The former is an example of a high-end off-the-shelf product, while the latter is an example of a simple do-it-yourself system that can be adjusted for different applications. The data from the Apple Watch can be directly transferred to iOS HealthKit via Bluetooth and the app will be able to obtain data from HealthKit, though there is approximately 10 s of uncontrollable delay during the data transmission. For the TI SensorTag we could directly access the raw data from its accelerometer, so we implemented an algorithm to calculate the speed from raw acceleration data.

Fig. 2. Screen shots from our application are illustrated. From left to right: choice of exercises, game view, and result view

3.3   User Study

20 participants participated in our study, each of whom performed two sessions of exercises. The two wearable products and three different games (running, cycling, and rope-skipping) were randomly combined and assigned to participants. The Apple Watch was not used with cycling because it can only be worn on the wrists. Subjects took part in a maximum of two different trails. Each trial took 10-15 min followed by a 10-min rest and recovery period. Each exercise mode prompts the user to perform a specific exercise (run, cycle, or skip ropes). Figure 3 shows snapshots of the three exercise modes. During each game, metrics such as speed, traveled distance, and calorie expenditure are recorded from the user. Once an exercise was completed, during the rest period, participants were asked to fill a questionnaire for each game that they played. This included questions on level of enjoyment, fatigue, sense of accomplishment, motivation for more exercise, and usefulness of the application.

Fig. 3. The three types of exercises in our user study: running, cycling, and rope skipping

3.4 Data Analysis

Two-way between-groups analysis of variances (ANOVA) was conducted to analyze the main effects of different game modes (exercise and device) and different game-play parameters (perceived by users). The investigated parameters are: enjoyment, fatigue, accomplishment, motivation, usefulness, satisfaction, and preference. 7-point Likert scale was used in this study. We used R to run the analysis. The different combinations of exercise and wearable device are presented and labeled for future reference (Table 1).

Table 1. Combination of exercises and wearable devices

	Apple Watch	TI SensorTag
Running	A	B
Cycling	–	C
Rope skipping	D	E

4 Results and Discussions

20 volunteers participated in this study. 10 were males and 10 were females. Their average age was 25.25 with the standard deviation of 4.27. The average weight was 62.35 kg with a standard deviation of 11.9. The average height was 170.65 cm with a standard deviation of 6.80. Their average hours of exercise per week was 4.53 h with a standard deviation of 2.20. Their average hours of playing computer/mobile games per week was 4.95 h and the standard deviation was 4.95. 8 of the participants (40 %) previously (or currently) owned an activity tracking wearable device.

Participants were asked whether they had fun and enjoyed their experience playing the games. Figure 4 shows the average and standard deviations of the scores for this parameter where $M_A = 5.14$ and $SD_A = 0.69$, $M_B = 5.43$ and $SD_B = 0.98$, $M_C = 5.29$ and $SD_C = 1.11$, $M_D = 4.71$ and $SD_D = 1.11$, and finally $M_E = 5.57$ and $SD_E = 1.40$. ANOVA shows no significant effect for either factor ($F(2,29) = 0.07$ with $p = 0.93$ for exercise, $F(1,29) = 1.95$ with $p = 0.17$ for device, and $F(1,29) = 0.49$ with $p = 0.49$ for the interaction between them). This outcome can point to the fact that the sense of fun and enjoyment is mostly derived from the actual game content itself (digital aspect) rather the interaction and communication medium, or even the exercise.

When asked to rate the level of fatigue felt after each game, participants rated rope skipping as the most fatiguing activity among the three exercises. Figure 5 illustrates the results where $M_A = 2.71$ and $SD_A = 1.11$, $M_B = 3.14$ and $SD_B = 1.77$, $M_C = 2.86$ and $SD_C = 1.86$, $M_D = 5.86$ and $SD_D = 1.35$, and $M_E = 5.28$ with $SD_E = 2.06$. ANOVA indicates that the type of exercise has a significant effect at the $p < 0.001$ level on the feeling of fatigue, with $F(2,29) = 10.74$ and $p = 0.0003$. The results show that skipping was significantly more fatiguing than running and cycling ($M_{Skipping} = 5.57$, $SD_{Skipping} = 1.70$, vs. $M_{Cycling} = 2.86$, $SD_{Cycling} = 1.86$ and $M_{Running} = 2.93$, $SD_{Running} = 1.44$). There is no significant effect for device ($F(1,29) = 0.01$, $p = 0.91$) and the interaction of exercise and device ($F(1,29) = 0.63$, $p = 0.43$). In general, rope skipping is known to be a high-intensity exercise, which can significantly impact the amount

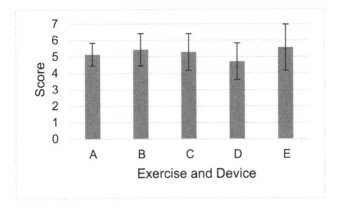

Fig. 4. User enjoyment for different modes of the game

of fatigue. The results confirm this notion. As a result, this mode of the game can be used as the *difficult* level. The wearable devices are both light in terms of weight, and do not impact the users' performance. It is therefore fair to say that non-intrusive devices such as these are potentially the right choice of device for gamified exercise.

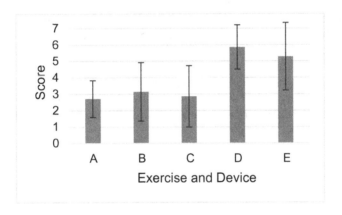

Fig. 5. The amount of fatigue for different modes of the game

Following the game session, participants were asked if they felt as if they had exercised/worked out successfully throughout the game. The results were $M_A = 5.43$ and $SD_A = 1.40$, $M_B = 5.86$ and $SD_B = 0.90$, $M_C = 5.71$ and $SD_C = 1.11$, $M_D = 5.00$ and $SD_D = 1.41$, and $M_E = 6.58$ with $SD_E = 0.53$ as shown in Fig. 6. There was a significant effect for different devices at the $p < 0.05$ level ($F(1,29) = 5.57$, $p = 0.02$), with the mean score for TI SensorTag ($M = 6.05$, $SD = 0.92$) being significantly higher than Apple Watch ($M = 5.21$, $SD = 1.37$). While the significance of this difference is not particularly strong as per the ANOVA result, we believe that the delay in the Watch could have caused participants to perceive a lack of correlation between their exercise and corresponding accomplishments in the game. This could have caused them to believe that it was not them that in fact accomplished the exercise/game goals. In addition, there is no significant effect for exercise ($F(1,29) = 0.06$ with $p = 0.94$) and the interaction of exercise and device ($F(1,29) = 1.82$ with $p = 0.19$).

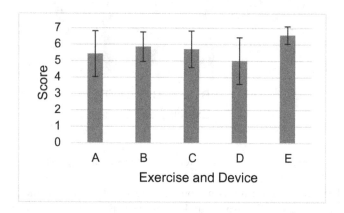

Fig. 6. Sense of accomplishment for different modes of the games

When asked whether they found this kind of application motivating for exercise, promising scores were achieved. As shown in Fig. 7, $M_A = 5.57$ and $SD_A = 0.79$, $M_B = 6$, $SD_B = 0.58$, $M_C = 5.57$ with $SD_C = 1.13$, $M_D = 5.43$ with $SD_D = 0.98$, and finally for $M_E = 6.43$ and $SD_E = 0.53$. There was a significant effect for different devices at the $p < 0.05$ level ($F(1,29) = 5.14$, $p = 0.03$), with the mean score for TI SensorTag ($M = 6.00$, $SD = 0.84$) being significantly higher than Apple Watch ($M = 5.50$, $SD = 0.85$). In addition, there is no significant effect for exercise ($F(1,29) = 0.43$ with $p = 0.65$) and the interaction of exercise and device ($F(1,29) = 0.82$ with $p = 0.37$).

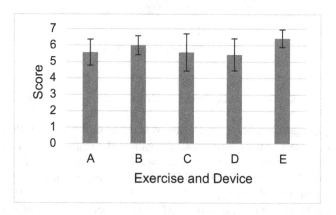

Fig. 7. Motivation for more exercise based on playing the game in different modes

Participants were asked whether they would like to use this application again. The results are presented in Fig. 8 where $M_A = 5.43$ with $SD_A = 1.27$, $M_B = 6.00$ with

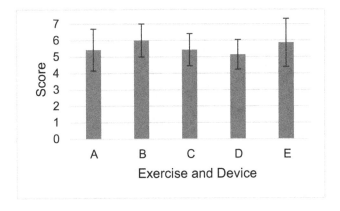

Fig. 8. Usefulness of the application based on the played game mode

$SD_B = 1.00$, $M_C = 5.43$ and $SD_C = 0.98$, $M_D = 5.14$ with $SD_D = 0.90$, and $M_E = 5.85$ with $SD_E = 1.46$. No significant effect is observed ($F(2,29) = 0.19$ and $p = 0.83$ for exercise, $F(1,29) = 2.22$ with $p = 0.15$ for device, and $F(1,29) = 0.03$ with $p = 0.87$ for the interaction between the two). Similar to the motivational aspects of the application, the results are promising and users find it useful.

Finally the overall satisfaction and preference of participants was asked. For satisfaction, $M_A = 5.29$ and $SD_A = 0.76$, $M_B = 5.86$ with $SD_B = 0.90$, $M_C = 5.71$ and $SD_C = 0.95$, $M_D = 5.0$ with $SD_D = 1.15$, and for $M_E = 5.71$ with $SD_E = 1.11$, as shown in Fig. 9. No significant effect was observed for device ($F(1,29) = 2.98$, $p = 0.10$), exercise ($F(1,29) = 0.35, p = 0.71$) and the interaction of the two factors ($F(1,29) = 0.04$, $p = 0.85$). The scores for preference were as follows $M_A = 5.14$ and $SD_A = 0.69$, $M_B = 6.0$ and $SD_B = 0.82$, $M_C = 5.86$ and $SD_C = 1.07$, $M_D = 4.86$ with $SD_D = 1.57$, and finally $M_E = 6.0$ with $SD_E = 0.82$, as shown in Fig. 10. The effect of device was significant at the $p < 0.05$ level ($F(1,29) = 6.45$, $p = 0.02$) with the SensorTag ($M = 5.95$, $SD = 0.86$) being higher than the Watch ($M = 5.00$, $SD = 1.18$. In addition, there is no other significant effect for exercise ($F(1,29) = 0.39$, $p = 0.68$) and interaction between device and exercise ($F(1,29) = 0.13$, $p = 0.72$).

The absence of a significant effect in satisfaction can be due to the fact that the concept of gamified exercise, especially through wearable devices, is quite novel and attractive for participants. As a result, relatively similar satisfaction scores were observed. Despite this similarity, preference scores were significantly higher for the SensorTag. While this significance was weak, the underlying reasons can be the lag in the Watch, which can make the experience subpar in real-time interactive applications. Software updates that enable access to the inertial measurement unit (IMU) data in real-time can alleviate this issue and increase satisfaction scores.

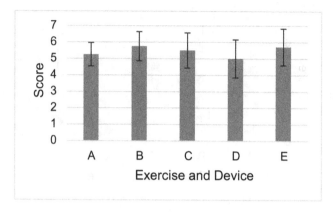

Fig. 9. Overall satisfaction of the different modes

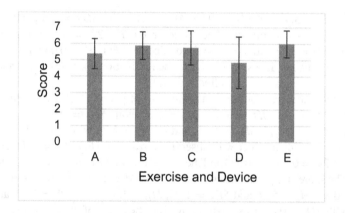

Fig. 10. Preference scores for different combinations of exercise and device

When asked which device they believed represented their movements more accurately, only 13.55 % of participants chose the Watch, while 86.45 % picked the SensorTag, mentioning the real-time performance as the key reason for their choice. This notion highlights the importance and impact of real-time interaction. While some game designs could be better suited for non-realtime applications (for example games that are based on post-workout leader boards), we believe realtime systems are more engaging and attractive for gamified exercise. It is therefore important to utilize wearable products that provide real-time access to IMU or other sensor data through their API.

5   Conclusion

We proposed the use of wearable devices for gamified exercise, towards which we designed and implemented a smart phone exercise game that communicates with wearable devices in real-time and receives user inputs accordingly. Combinations of three different exercises (running, cycling, rope skipping) and two different types of wearable devices (Apple Watch and TI Sensor Tag) are selected as different gaming modes. We performed a detailed user study to evaluate the usability and outcomes of the system. The results show that the approach is motivating and engaging. Users demonstrated high satisfaction towards the application and enjoyed the experience. Factors such as user's preferences towards different types of exercise or devices were also investigated.

In our future work, we will improve the game according to user's suggestions and feedbacks. These suggestions included adding different elements to the gameplay to make it more attractive, providing real-time multiplayer mode, and letting users input their body information so that we could assign personalized goals in the game. We will also add a control group to this study for better analysis of the results. A broader range of user needs can also be considered by adding more game modes (exercises and wearables). Furthermore, other parameters such as calories, heart-rate, and others will be monitored in order to better understand the performance and engagement of users. Finally, a long-term user study will be carried out to investigate the medium and long term effects of the proposed concept in motivating users to exercise and have a healthier lifestyle.

References

1. Barnes, K: Health wearables: early days. PwC Health Research Institute Report (2014)
2. Deterding, S., Dixon, D., Khales, R., Nacke, L.: From game design elements to gamefulness: defining gamification. In: Proceedings of the 15th International Academic MindTrek Conference: Envisioning Future Media Environments. ACM (2011)
3. Hamari, J., Koivisto, J.: Social motivations to use gamification: an empirical study of gamifying exercise. In: ECIS (2013)
4. Zhao, Z., Etemad, S.A., Arya, A.: Gamification of exercise and fitness using wearable activity trackers. In: Chung, P., Soltoggio, A., Dawson, C.W., Meng, Q., Pain, M. (eds.). AISC, vol. 392, pp. 233–240Springer, Cham (2015)
5. Lister, C., West, J.H., Cannon, B., Sax, T., Brodegard, D.: Just a fad? gamification in health and fitness apps. JMIR Serious Games 2(2), e9 (2014)
6. Deterding, S., Dixon, D., Khaled, R., Nacke, L.: From game design elements to gamefulness: defining gamification. In: Proceedings of the 15th International Academic MindTrek Conference: Envisioning Future Media Environments, pp. 9–15. ACM (2011)
7. Erenli, K.: The impact of gamification: a recommendation of scenarios for education. In: 15th International Conference on Interactive Collaborative Learning (ICL), pp. 1–8. IEEE (2012)
8. Buttussi, F., Chittaro, L.: Smarter phones for healthier lifestyles: an adaptive fitness game. In: Pervasive Computing, pp. 51–57. IEEE (2010)
9. Mokka, S., Vaatanen, A., Heinila, J., Valkkynen, P.: Fitness computer game with a bodily user interface. In: Proceedings of the Second International Conference on Entertainment Computing, pp. 1–3. Carnegie Mellon University (2003)
10. Campbell, T., Ngo, B., Fogarty, J.: Game design principles in everyday fitness applications. In: Proceedings of the 2008 ACM conference on Computer supported cooperative work, pp. 249–252. ACM (2008)
11. Wylie, J.: Fitness Gamification: concepts, characteristics, and applications (2010)
12. Trowbridge, B., Rodriguez, C., Prine, J., Holzemer, M., McCormack, J., Integlia, R.: Gaming, fitness and relaxation. In: Games Entertainment Media Conference (GEM). IEEE (2015)

13. Buchem, I., Merceron, A., Kreutel, J., Haesner, M., Steinert, A.: Gamification designs in wearable Enhanced Learning for healthy ageing. In: 2015 International Conference on Interactive Mobile Communication Technologies and Learning (IMCL), pp. 9–15. IEEE (2015)

14. Bartley, J., Forsyth, J., Pendse, P., Xin, D., Brown, G., Hagseth, P., Hammond, T.: World of workout: a contextual mobile RPG to encourage long term fitness. In: Proceedings of the Second ACM SIGSPATIAL International Workshop on the Use of GIS in Public Health. pp. 60–67. ACM (2013)

15. Whitehead, A., Johnston, H., Nixon, N., Welch, J.: Exergame Effectiveness: What the Numbers Can Tell Us. In: Proceedings of the 5th ACM SIGGRAPH Symposium on Video Games pp. 55–62. ACM (2010)

16. Miller, A.: Fitness tracers. In: XRDS: Crossroads, The ACM Magazine for Students 20.2. pp. 24–26. ACM (2013)

17. Schneegass, S., Mayer, S., Olsson, T., Van Laerhoven, K.: From mobile to wearable: using wearable devices to enrich mobile interaction. In: Proceedings of the 17th International Conference on Human-Computer Interaction with Mobile Devices and Services Adjunct. ACM (2015)

Culture, Language and DUXU

User Experience Changing Patterns
of Chinese Users

Yanan Chen[1,2], Jing Liu[3], Guozhen Zhao[1], and Xianghong Sun[1(✉)]

[1] Key Lab of Behavioral Science, Institute of Psychology,
Chinese Academy of Sciences, Beijing, China
{chenyn, zhaogz, sunxh}@psych.ac.cn
[2] University of Chinese Academy of Sciences, Beijing, China
[3] Sony Corporation, Tokyo, Japan
lorraineliul@gmail.com

Abstract. This study examined the differences between pragmatic and hedonic users for their experience changing over time. Two questions were probed in this study. We first compared two user experience changing patterns (i.e., how the quality of users' experience develops over time) between pragmatic and hedonic users in 4 weeks usage. Then, we studied how each phrase in the user experience changing patterns contributed to the overall perceived quality of products. Our results found that: (1) user experience changing patterns of Chinese users (Orientation and Identification) were different from western users (Orientation, Identification, and Incorporation); (2) user experience changing patterns were different between pragmatic (Orientation, Incorporation, and Identification) and hedonic users (Exploration and Identification); (3) changes on deciding factors to the overall products perceptions was derived by phrase transitions: utility and identification influenced long-term product perceptions by pragmatic users, while personal needs satisfaction influenced long-term product perceptions by hedonic users.

Keywords: User experience · Experience-centered design · Qualitative methods · Day reconstruction method

1 Introduction

User experience (UE) is a multidimensional cognition function that users form during their interaction with products [1, 2]. Factors, including user characteristics, expectation, product attributes, context situation, social and cultural criterion, all influence UE. With factors keep changing in different time frames, UE changes over time. A considerable amount of research has been done on this topic during the last decades to improve UE and control its formation [3, 4]. The significance of temporality has been repeatedly highlighted in UE research [1, 5]. Some studies described different dimensions of quality perceptions of products and how users form overall evaluative judgments of products on the basis of quality perceptions [5–7]. While, most of the empirical studies on temporality in the field of HCI suffer from a lack of a guiding research model.

© Springer International Publishing Switzerland 2016
A. Marcus (Ed.): DUXU 2016, Part II, LNCS 9747, pp. 347–357, 2016.
DOI: 10.1007/978-3-319-40355-7_33

An initial framework for the study [8] of prolonged user experience suggested that there were three stages in the process of technology adoption: commodification, appropriation and conversion. Commodification refers to the process through which objects and technologies emerge in a public space of exchange values. Appropriation, consumers take technologies and objects home and make them acceptable and familiar, can be divided into two respects: orientation and incorporation. Finally, conversion reflects the identification of the products.

Karapanos (2013) presented two studies that aimed to assess the differences between initial and prolonged experiences with interactive products and presented a three-stage framework of the mobile adoption (i.e., Orientation, Incorporation, and Identification [5]). The first study assessed how users formed the overall evaluative judgments of a novel interactive product. Findings suggested judgments of the overall goodness of the product to shift from a use-based evolution to an ownership-based evaluation. Judgments of beauty seemed to be dominated by perceptions of novelty during initial interactions, but this effect seemed to disappear after four weeks of use. Inspired by the framework of Silverstone and Haddon [8], the second study inquired into how users' expectations and experiences developed over time. The study revealed that product adoption contained three distinct phases. Orientation refers to early experiences that are pervaded by a feeling of excitement as well as frustration as the user experience novel features and encounter learnability flaws. As participants gradually incorporated the product in their lives, usefulness and usability became more important in the Incorporation period. Identification reflected ways in which participants formed a personal relationship with the product as it was increasingly incorporated in their daily routines and interactions, personal and social experience became more important in the latter stage.

In the past decades, most studies assume that the user were homogeneous. While, Hartmann et al. verified the user characteristic had an influence on the factors weight, that is, different users preferred different products [9]. The commercial market segmentation tools adopted in this study is widely used in fast-moving consumer goods industry provided by a professional marketing survey agency (which belongs to company secrets), it take the need of consumer for technology (traditional-progress) and consumers' attitude to products (instrument- symbolism) as the "x" and "y" axes, to subdivide the market crowd into eight categories. Among them pragmatic users (i.e. see phone as instrument) and hedonic users (i.e. see phone as symbolism) are the biggest two classes of user group in terms of market share. So we choose pragmatic users and hedonic users to investigate the user experience change rules.

The present study, inspired by the framework of Karapanos [5], examined distinct user experience changing patterns between Chinese users and western users, how different type users' experience changes across these phases, and how this impacts users' evaluative judgments about the product. This study assumes that, the user with different psychological expectations, emotional needs and functional requirements, would form different user experiences and change rules, due to their different habits and focused attention. So we put the difference of user attitude as segmentation dimension, expect different types of the user's experience will show differences over time. And explore the effect of user experiences schedule to the overall product evaluation by calculating regression relationship between the overall product evaluation and product attribute evaluation.

2 Method

2.1 Participants

Thirty-eight participants were recruited and required to answer the pre-screening questionnaire to collect the user's cell phone habits, the attitude toward technology, buying attitudes et al. and based on a 5-point scale ranging from (1) "strongly disagree" to (5) "strongly agree". Then we got 4 males and 4 females composed the pragmatic group and hedonic group. Each group has 2 male and 2 female, average age 29 ± 3 years, average time of use cell phone 9 ± 1 year. After the experiment, a certain amount of financial reward paid for the participants.

2.2 Material and Design

In the experiment, we employed the Day Reconstruction Method [10, 11], participants were asked to record the change of user experiences by self-report. We prepare 1 pre-screen questionnaire and 4 survey questionnaires: user's background information questionnaire, daily questionnaires, weekly questionnaire and AttracDiff questionnaire [6], which was used to evaluate the products attribute and overall cognition of the product. The cell phone used in this experiment was listed by Sony Ericsson (the specific model was trade secrets and public inconvenience). According to the market performance, this mobile phone belonged to the middle level. With commonly used basic functions, market positioning for the entertainment phone, the main design highlight is the appearance of its products, high-pixel camera, and multimedia capabilities.

The experiment was between group designs, independent variables was the user types, based on attitudes towards mobile phone divided into two levels, pragmatic group and hedonic group, 4 subjects in each group.

2.3 Procedure

Before the experiment, we chose one informal participant carried out one week's pre-test, the pre-test process are accord with the formal experiment. Through the pilot test, modify the ambiguous question and language of questionnaires and scales to ensure the data qualified.

In the beginning of the formal experiment, we interviewed each subjects, introduced to them about the background and purpose of the study, and informed the subjects can tried the experimental prototype then, played 2 part of advertising. Asked the user to read the product's leaflet about its specifications, price, features, according to his purchase and attention habits as usual, make the user form expectation to the experimental phone before use it.

After the introduction, asked the participants to fill out a background questionnaire. Since the day of introduction, the subjects had to use the experimental cell phone every day in accordance with their natural habits, and filled out a daily questionnaire before the end of the night. Daily questionnaire was recycling at the end of each day and week questionnaire was recycling at the end of each week.

Then, we adopted AttracDiff questionnaire [6] (see Table 1), asked the subjects to evaluate to the products attribute and overall cognition of the product, to investigate how each phrase in the user experience changing patterns contributes to the overall perceived quality of products, and explored the difference of evaluation between pragmatic participants and hedonic participants. After the experiment finished, recovered the mobile phone and paid for subjects.

Table 1. The questionnaire of product's attribute and overall evaluation

Scale	Number	Attribute
Hedonic quality–identification	1	Amateurish—professional
	2	Gaudy—classy
	3	Cheap—valuable
	4	Takes me distant from people—closer to people
	5	Unpresentable—presentable
Hedonic quality–stimulation	1	Standard—creative
	2	Conservative—innovative
	3	Lame—exciting
	4	Easy—challenging
	5	Commonplace—new
Pragmatic quality-utility	1	Technical—human
	2	Useless—useful
	3	Impractical—practical
	4	Cumbersome—direct
	5	Unpredictable—predictable
Pragmatic quality-usability	1	Complicated—simple
	2	Confusing—clear
	3	Unruly—manageable
Evaluation constructs Beauty	1	Ugly—beautiful
Evaluation constructs Goodness	2	Bad—good

Note. Order and polarity of items was randomized

2.4 Data Analysis

At the end of this experiment, totally recovered 224 daily questionnaires (7 days × 8 participants × 4 weeks, 8 background questionnaire and 32 weeks questionnaire. A total of 608 experience fragments and 224 overall experiences were collected during the 4 weeks. We use a conventional qualitative Content Analysis (CA) [12, 13].

Specific steps in CA are as follows:

1. Decomposition of experience clips. As the preparatory work of analysis of experience, each fragment of experience was split into independent experience. Among the 608 experience fragments recovered from this study, totally collected 933 independent experiences.

2. Theme extraction. Among all the 933 independent experience, extract the theme and categorized the same theme's experiences, finally extracted 80 themes in all.
3. Summarized the category of themes. We adopt the expert classification method, invited another 2 researcher of this area, and made a discussion to the 80 themes. According to the expert group's discussion, came into being 20 user experience subclasses, then they were summarized into 6 dimension of user experience.
4. Count the frequency of two groups in each of the dimensions of user experience. Their operational definitions and examples shown in Table 2 based on the resulting

Table 2. Operational definitions of the dimensions of user experience

Big theme	Theme class		Operational definition
Stimulation	Interactive aesthetic		I feel good, innovative to the interactive mode, touch and display during the interaction
	Visual aesthetic		Visually, feel beautiful, innovative, and impact
	Entertainment		Function or the game is funny and interesting
Learnability			Easy to learn or difficult to learn
Usability	Controlled		Can/can't do whatever they want
	False operational		Easy/difficult to make mistake.
	Speed		Take long/short time to complete the task
	Accessibility		Need more/less steps to complete the task
	Clear		The meaning of the phone icon, state, interface elements is clear/not clear
Utility	Property	Reliability	Is the function of the phone stable, reliability?
		Speed performance	To fulfil a task or function fast/slow
		Function implementation	To achieve the currently function good/not good
	Function	Perfect function	Have/haven't the function
		Provide intelligent support	Did it smart or automatically help users complete tasks
Personal	Extension support software		Did it provide the support of the expansion of the mobile software, good or bad
	Personalized change Settings		Set like functionality, interface, state or display
	Assisted living		The mobile better/badly assisted my life
Social	Social etiquette		This phone make me more in line with/doesn't accord with the social norms
	Distinctive		The phone can/can't make them distinctive
	Group identity		The phone can integrate them into groups or not

temporal patterns and semantic information, for pragmatic users, the 20 categories were then mapped into 3 broad themes: Orientation, Incorporation, and Identification; while, for hedonic users, the 20 categories were then mapped into 2 broad themes: Exploration and Identification.

3 Results

3.1 The Three Phases of Chinese Users in the Adoption of the Product

In order to analyze whether the Chinese users experienced the same user experience changing patterns as the western users, we use the same criterion as western researchers. This study analyze the data of Chinese subjects based to the three stages indicators.

(1) Orientation refers to users' initial experiences that are pervaded by a feeling of excitement as well as frustration as we experience novel features. With the improvement of familiarity, the feeling of excitement down. The key factors that influence user experience are stimulation and learnability in this period (see Fig. 1). (2) Incorporation. As the reliance on function, participants gradually incorporated the product into their daily life, their experiences increasingly reflected the ways in which the product was becoming meaningful in diverse use contexts. In this period, usability and usefulness becomes the major factor impacting our overall evaluative judgments. (3) Identification reflected ways in which participants formed a personal relationship with the product as it was increasingly incorporated in their daily routines and social interactions. This phase the product's social and personal becomes the major factor impacting our overall evaluative judgments.

According to the 4 pragmatic users' experiences during the 4 weeks (Fig. 1), the average frequency of stimulation and personal first decreased then increased; learnability and utility, fluctuate frequently; usability, remain unchanged; social, continued to decline. The frequency of utility ($N = 140$) and usability ($N = 93$) was the two maximums. Based on the variation trend of the 4 pragmatic users' experiences and the assumes to schedule model and criterion of the pragmatic users' experiences, we try to divided the 4 weeks into three stages; 1st week, 2nd and 3rd week, 4th week. While, for the hedonic users, the average frequency of stimulation, learnability and utility showed a sustained downward trend during the 4 weeks; usability, first increased then decreased; social, remained almost unchanged; personal, first decreased then increased. The frequency of utility ($N = 158$) and personal ($N = 108$) was the two maximums. Based on the variation trend of the 4 hedonic users' experiences and assumes to schedule model and criterion of the hedonic users' experiences, we try to divided the 4 weeks into two stages: the 1st and 2nd week, the 3rd and 4th week.

Therefore, we can test out the change rule of schedule found in pragmatic users was consistent with criterion, stimulation and learnability declined in the first week, comply with the standard of the Orientation stage, in the middle of usage, the frequency of utility become the highest dimension of user experiences, comply with the standard of the Incorporation stage, in the later period of usage, the frequency of personal increased and become the maximum dimension of user experiences, comply with the standard of

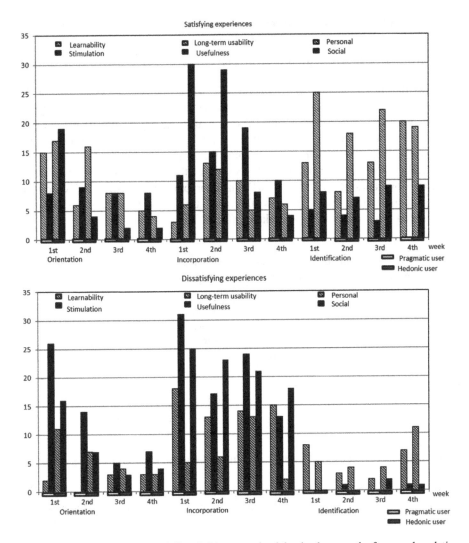

Fig. 1. Number of satisfying and dissatisfying experiential episodes over the four weeks relating to the three phases of adoption.

the Identification stage. However, for hedonic users, stimulation, learnability and utility significantly declined from the high frequency in the early stage of use, comply with the standard of the Exploration stage, in the later period of usage, the frequency of personal and social increased and become the maximum dimension of user experiences, comply with the standard of Identification.

3.2   How Does Each Phase Contribute to the Overall Perceived Quality?

Pragmatic Users. In total, 300 AttracDiff questionnaires were collected for pragmatic group.

While during Orientation of pragmatic user, Table 3 gives, the Goodness of the product was primarily influenced by identification ($\beta = 0.89$, $p < .01$). In Incorporation, the product's identification ($\beta = 0.54$, $p < .01$) and utility ($\beta = 0.40$, $p < .05$) became the primary predictor of Goodness, and in the phase of Identification the qualities of utility ($\beta = 0.94$, $p < .01$) became the most dominant qualities impacting the overall goodness of the product. The Beauty of the product in Orientation determined by stimulation ($\beta = 0.67$, $p < .01$); In Incorporation, primarily derived on the basis of Identification ($\beta = 0.39$, $p < .05$) and stimulation ($\beta = 0.53$, $p < .01$); In Identification also dominant by stimulation ($\beta = 0.89$, $p < .01$).

Table 3. Pragmatic group: Multiple Regression analysis with usefulness, utility, stimulation and identification as predictors and Goodness or Beauty as predicted (β values and significances * $p < .001$) for both satisfying and dissatisfying experiences.

	Goodness			Beauty		
	Orientation	Incorporation	Identification	Orientation	Incorporation	Identification
Identification	.89**	.54**	3.5	3.79	.39*	.89**
Stimulation			.94**	.67**	.53**	
utility		.40*	0.88			
Usability						0.78
Adjusted R2	0.79	0.85		0.43	0.8	

Note. *p < 0.05; **p < 0.01

Hedonic User. A total of 308 AttracDiff questionnaires were collected for hedonic group.

As shown in Table 4, for hedonic user, the Goodness of the product was primarily influenced by utility ($\beta = 0.84$, $p < .05$) in Exploration; In Incorporation, the product's identification ($\beta = 0.43$, $p < .01$) and utility ($\beta = 0.51$, $p < .01$) became the primary

Table 4. Hedonic group: Multiple Regression analysis with usefulness, utility, stimulation and identification as predictors and Goodness or Beauty as predicted (β values and significances * $p < .001$) for both satisfying and dissatisfying experiences.

	Goodness		Beauty	
	Exploration	Identification	Exploration	Identification
Identification		.43**	.62**	−.82**
Stimulation			.33	.76**
Utility	.84**	.51**		
Usability	.38		.32	.61*
Adjusted R2	0.7	0.83	0.38	0.42

Note. *p < 0.05; **p < 0.01

predictor of Goodness. The Beauty of the product in Exploration determined by identification ($\beta = 0.62$, $p < .01$); In Incorporation, primarily derived on the basis of Identification ($\beta = -.82$, $p < .01$), stimulation ($\beta = 0.76$, $p < .01$)and usability ($\beta = 0.61$, $p < .05$).

4 Discussion and Conclusion

The results of the present experiment testified user experience changing patterns on Chinese users are different from western users, Orientation and Identification as Karapanos [5] are verified, but not Incorporation. This study explored the stage model of pragmatic user (Orientation, Incorporation, and Identification) and hedonic user (Exploration and Identification), and revealed the effect of schedule model to the overall evaluation. The pragmatic user's long-term product evaluation depends on the usefulness and identification; hedonic user's long-term product evaluations rely on the meet to individual needs.

Based on the criteria raised by Karapanos [5] the user experience changing patterns are different between Chinese users and western users. The utility experiences of Chinese continued to decline during the 4 weeks. The usability increased in the 1st and 2nd week then declined in the 3rd and 4th week. While in western users, the utility increased from the 2nd week, increased to maximum in the 4th week, the usability experiences increased from the 1st week, reach the maximum in the 3rd week then decreased. We suspect that, Chinese participants' concerns transformed from utility and usability to personal and social in the later stage, compared to western users who always focus on utility. The social experiences remained unchanged during the 4 weeks in Chinese users, while in western users, first declined then increased. The personal experiences first declined then increased in Chinese users, while, in western users, continued to increase during the 4 weeks. Indicated that, compared to Chinese users, Western users paid more attention to personal throughout the entire process. Among the factors that may explain our findings at a more basic level are the different ways in which people from Western and Asian cultural backgrounds perceive objects [14, 15].

Hassenzahl [6] put forth two overall evaluative judgments of the quality of inter-active products, Goodness and of Beauty. Previous work suggests that goodness to be a goal-oriented evaluation, relating to the pragmatic quality of the product (usefulness and ease-of-use), and beauty a pleasure-oriented evaluation, relating to hedonic quality (stimulation and identification. We made some further discovers. In each phase, for pragmatic group and hedonic group, the product's overall evaluative judgments were affected by different attributes of the product (Tables 3 and 4). This study showed that, users experience shifted over time, for pragmatic users, under the influence of different phase, the major role in forming 'Goodness' judgments transformed from identification to utility, in terms of the judgments of 'Beauty', transformed from stimulation to identification. However, for hedonic users, the major role in forming 'Goodness' judgments transformed from utility to identification, as for the judgments of 'Beauty', largely influenced by identification at initial stage, then influenced by identification, stimulation and usability.

The research of Karapanos [5] just put forward the concept of identification. This study, we proposed the disidentification, due to we find unsatisfied experiences of social and personal in each stage, especially in the later stage. The possible reason maybe that products of Karapanos' study were IPhone which is well known to be a successful and interesting example in the market, while ours were just an ordinary smart phone. Moreover, participants of Karapanos' study were actual IPhone buyers, before actual purchase, people often have a tendency of self-affirmation in evaluation, they often know much about whether the products can meet their needs, so almost no disidentification after purchase. However, subjects of our study was young and high educated, their anticipated demand would be higher than the cell phone really was, so they presented much unsatisfied experience.

The conclusions of this study enriched the existing user experience theory from the perspective of temporality, with regard to enhancing user's satisfaction and improving prolonged experience; the present study has important practical and theoretical significance.

Acknowledgement. We appreciate the support from the National Natural Science Foundation of China (61079021 & 31300852).

References

1. Hassenzahl, M., Tractinsky, N.: User experience-a research agenda. Behav. Inf. Technol. **25**, 91–97 (2006)
2. Hekkert, P.: Design aesthetics: principles of pleasure in design. Psychol. Sci. **48**, 157 (2006)
3. De Angeli, A., Lynch, P., Johnson, G.I.: Pleasure versus efficiency in user interfaces: towards an involvement framework (Chapter 7). In: Jordan, P.W., Green, W.S. (eds.) Pleasure with Products: Beyond Usability, vol. 94. Taylor and Francis, London (2002)
4. Jetter, C., Gerken, J.: A simplified model of user experience for practical application. In: Proceedings of 2nd COST294-MAUSE International Open Workshop, pp. 106–111 (2007)
5. Karapanos, E.: User experience over time. In: Karapanos, E. (ed.) Modeling Users' Experiences with Interactive Systems. SCI, vol. 436, pp. 57–83. Springer, Heidelberg (2013)
6. Hassenzahl, M.: The interplay of beauty, goodness, and usability in interactive products. Hum.-Comput. Interact. **19**, 319–349 (2004)
7. Mahlke, S.: Aesthetic and symbolic qualities as antecedents of overall judgements of interactive products. In: Bryan-Kinns, N., Blanford, A., Curzon, P., Nigay, L. (eds.) People and Computers XX—Engage, pp. 57–64. Springer, London (2007)
8. Silverstone, R., Haddon, L.: Design and the domestication of ICTs: technical change and everyday life. In: Silverstone, R., Mansell, R. (eds.) Communicating by Design: The Politics of Information and Communication Technologies, pp. 44–74. Oxford University Press, Oxford (1996)
9. Hartmann, J., Sutcliffe, A., Angeli, A.D.: Towards a theory of user judgment of aesthetics and user interface quality. ACM Trans. Comput.-Hum. Interact. (TOCHI) **15**, 15–16 (2008)
10. Kahneman, D., Krueger, A.B., Schkade, D.A., Schwarz, N., Stone, A.A.: A survey method for characterizing daily life experience: the day reconstruction method. Science **306**, 1776–1780 (2004)

11. von Wilamowitz-Moellendorff, M., Hassenzahl, M., Platz, A.: Dynamics of user experience: how the perceived quality of mobile phones changes over time. In: User Experience - Towards a Unified View, Workshop at the 4th Nordic Conference on Human-Computer Interaction, pp. 74–78 (2006)
12. Hsieh, H.-F., Shannon, S.E.: Three approaches to qualitative content analysis. Qual. Health Res. **15**, 1277–1288 (2005)
13. Krippendorff, K.: Content Analysis: An Introduction to Its Methodology. Sage, Thousand Oaks (2012)
14. Masuda, T., Nisbett, R.E.: Attending holistically versus analytically: comparing the context sensitivity of Japanese and Americans. J. Pers. Soc. Psychol. **81**, 922 (2001)
15. Van Der Sluis, I., Luz, S., Breitfuß, W., Ishizuka, M., Prendinger, H.: Cross-cultural assessment of automatically generated multimodal referring expressions in a virtual world. Int. J. Hum. Comput. Stud. **70**, 611–629 (2012)

Health Education in Brazil

Assessment of the Understandability of Icons for the e-Books Store SAITE App

Eurides Florindo de Castro Jr.[1], Edilson Thialison da Silva Reis[1],
Camila Santos de Castro e Lima[1], Carla Galvão Spinillo[2],
and Ana Emilia Figueiredo de Oliveira[1(✉)]

[1] Federal University of Maranhão, São Luís, Brazil
euridescastro@gmail.com, edilson.sreis@gmail.com,
camilasclima@gmail.com, oliveira.anaemilia@gmail.com
[2] Federal University of Paraná, Curitiba, Brazil
cgspin@gmail.com

Abstract. The communication role of computer icons is a relevant aspect in digital interfaces, as they promote efficiency and effectiveness in the interaction between users and computer systems. This paper presents the results of a study on comprehension of computer icons for the SAITE e-Book store app of the Brazilian Health System Open University (UNA-SUS). Nine out of 39 icons designed for SAITE were assessed through online questionnaire by 139 health professionals enrolled in the distance learning courses of UNA-SUS. The results showed that five icons reached high rates of understanding and three reached low rates. It was concluded that icons may succeed in representing abstract general concepts in the health field, and that users' familiarity with an icon's graphic representation affects message comprehension.

Keywords: Computer icons · Understandability · User centered design · Information design

1 Introduction

Health education is today part of social programs in several countries as it promotes the well-being of populations. It regards the learning experience of health related contents which can be addressed to individuals as well as professionals. Among the initiatives in health education, distance learning courses and apps have been widely made available to facilitate the access of training material to health professionals.

In 2008 the federal government of Brazil founded the UNA-SUS – the National Health System Open University to offer health education training courses mainly addressed to medical doctors and nurses. To facilitate the development, publication and distribution of the e-books of the UNA-SUS e-learning courses, a platform was designed for mobile devices (e.g., tablets, smart phones): the SAITE Store. It is a virtual store that offers interactive e-books categorized into several thematic areas of health (e.g., neph-rology, pediatrics). The SAITE Store app also allows students to get their reading

A. Marcus (Ed.): DUXU 2016, Part II, LNCS 9747, pp. 358–365, 2016.
DOI: 10.1007/978-3-319-40355-7_34

material in places with limited Internet access by downloading the e-books to be read offline in their mobile devices.

E-books and apps produced for the SAITE Store employ visual resources in their digital interfaces, such as icons to represent the contents of the e-books. These are considered to aid effectiveness and efficiency in communicating content and enabling navigation in digital devices. Computer icons are valuable graphic representations of information content for both users with little familiarity with digital systems and experienced users [1, 2]. Thus, icons are important elements to design of information and interaction in GUIs-Graphic User Interfaces.

From a user centered approach, users should be involved in the design process of icons to ensure their understanding [3]. This may be at the initial stage of the process, providing inputs to make design decisions, and/or at the final stage, evaluating the designed icons. Nevertheless, there seems to be a lack of such approach to the design of computer icons. This is perhaps due to developers tending to verify the understandability of icons within their own team and/or with experts in the field, instead of with users [3]. According to Nielsen [4], the test with real users is essential to provide direct information on how people make use of and what problems they encountered when interacting with the tested interface.

By considering the relevance of users' comprehensibility of icons to the success of computer systems in health education apps, this paper presents a study on the understandability of the icons designed for the SAITE Store of the UNA-SUS (National Health System Open University) in Brazil. Before presenting the study, a literature on this topic is introduced, highlighting aspects of the graphic presentation of icons from an information design perspective.

2 Icons as a Graphic Representation of Messages

Icons are elements of graphic digital interfaces used to convey information. They directly affect the quality of interaction and user's performance. Icons represent computer system functions, what distinguishes them from other symbols/pictograms displayed on screen [5]. Moreover, icons may represent objects, pointers, controls, tools and status indicators of a computer system, and are employed to mediate user's interactions with software applications [5]. In this sense, icons are intended to convey ideas/concepts rather than spoken words in a prompt and universal manner [6]. They allow the transposition from digital and computer language to the visual language through synthetic representations accessible to people with little or no technological knowledge [2].

Thus, icons are pictorial schematic and compact representations that allow prompt visualizations of messages, and in this sense they can be said to be similar to pictograms [7, 8]. Based upon Dewar [7], the relation between an icon and its referent (things or/and concepts) can be said to be similar to those of pictograms, as follows: (a) Part – part relation in which the icon is associated to the referent through certain similar characteristics as for example a 'globe' to represent 'worldwide web'; (b) Part - whole relation in which the icon is associated to its referent through a specific characteristic, as for a 'bag' to convey 'shopping'; (c) Image-based relation in which the icon is the illustration of its referent, e.g., calculator; (d) Example-based relation, in which the icon is associated to its referent through a class of objects, as for example a 'book' to represent 'library'; and (e) Concept based relation, in which the icon has no referent, then an arbitrary image is employed to convey the intended meaning, e.g., the symbol for power on/off.

Moreover, as for pictograms, icons can represent a message through one element, i.e., simple representation or through more than one element, i.e., compound representation [8]. The number of elements of an icon may increase its visual complexity, which may affect user's perception and/or comprehension of the icon [8]. Regarding the advantages of using icons, as for pictograms [7, 8], they may be independent of words/ labels if they are part of users' visual repertoire. They also may allow the message visualization at a glance, and may be seen in adverse visual conditions, for example low resolution screens. Though, since icons are pictorial representations, they have limitations in conveying abstract concepts/ideas, but are suitable for depicting concrete/ existing objects/things [9]. Furthermore, the interpretation of pictorial representation of abstract concepts are related to individuals' familiarity with such representations, and with the graphic system to which they belong [10]. Thus, to represent computer functions and users' actions (e.g., delete, send message, save) through icons, it may be necessary to employ resources of visual rhetoric. It is also necessary to take into account users' visual repertoire, for instance, a computer disk to represent save file (visual metaphor). Thus, to known how to verify the effectiveness of icons to communicate messages seems to be a chief aspect in the design of useful icon. This is briefly presented next.

2.1 Understandability of Icons

Several testing methods and techniques are available in the literature for researchers to verify individuals' reactions to icons and pictograms/symbols, whether in the domain of perception or comprehension [11, 12]. For the latter, [3] states that understandability test is one of the most important steps in the development of symbols for public information (as computer icons), as it aims to find their correct degree of understanding. She also advocates the qualitative approach to understandability tests, as this provides support to designers to decide for the most suitable variant of a symbol, i.e., the most comprehensible graphic representation of the message.

In the scope of health education in distance learning courses, the understanding of icons in GUIs seems to be a key issue to reach satisfactory training results. Misinterpretation of the icons' meanings may make access to information difficult or even lead to unpleasant experiences in human-computer interaction by the health professional trainees. As an attempt to aid the design process of icons from a user centered design approach, [2] (2013) conducted a study on the assessment of icons of a telemedicine system interface in Brazil. As a result, the authors proposed guidelines and recommendations to develop useful icons based on the HCI literature.

Taking into account (a) the relevance of understandability tests to icons' effectiveness to communicate messages, and (b) the literature recommendations for their design, a set of icons was designed to SAITE Store platform of the UNA-SUS e-books. These were tested with health professionals to check whether the icons were properly conveying their function/role in the e-book GUIs. This is presented next.

3   The Evaluation of the Understanding of the SAITE Store Icons

The understandability test of icons of the SAITE Store was conducted in the following stages: (1) icons' selection; (2) definition of the data collection technique (online questionnaire); (3) protocol elaboration; (4) pilot testing; (5) online protocols' settings; (6) data collecting; and (7) results' compilation (Fig. 1).

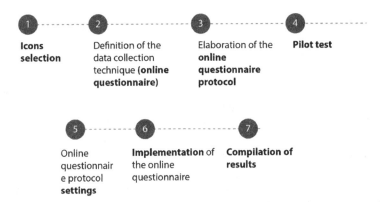

Fig. 1. Flowchart of production and application of understandability test of icons of the SAITE Store.

3.1   The Icon Sample Tested

A total of 39 icons were developed for the SAITE Store. To select the sample to be tested, the understandability of the icons (without labels) was assessed by 10 volunteer participants who were not health professionals. The results showed that the most difficult icons to understand were those for: (a) Women's Health; (b) Communicable Diseases; (c) Distance Learning; (d) Stork Network; (e) Health and Society; (f) Nephrology; (g) Health; (h) Aggravations in Health; and (i) Health Networks. Hence, the sample to be tested was composed of these nine icons, which is showed in Table 1.

3.2   Methodological Procedures

The understandability of the sample of nine icons of the SAITE Store app was assessed through an online questionnaire. The questions were closed-ended and open-ended based on the understandability test proposed by Formiga [3]. The closed-ended questions provided different meanings to an icon, and the open-ended questions provided a field for writing the answers.

A pilot test was conducted with five participants as a trial run of the main study to validate the questionnaire protocol, ensuring the reliability of the results [13].This led

Table 1. Sample of nine icons tested in the study

Icon identification	Icon	Concept	Icon identification	Icon	Concept
a		Women's Health	f		Nephrology
b		Communicable Diseases	g		Health
c		Distance Learning	h		Aggravations in Health
d		Stork Network	i		Health Networks
e		Health and Society			

to adjustments in the number of closed-ended response options to five choices for each icon, and in setting the terms provided to identify/label the icons.

The adjusted online questionnaire was made available through the Google Forms platform to 847 students of the UNA-SUS/UFMA (Federal University of Maranhão), who voluntarily responded the questionnaire. They were asked to associate the meaning of each icon to a label, and to justify their answer. The results were analyzed quantitatively and qualitatively. However, for the purpose of this article, the results herein are discussed in a qualitative manner and figures are only used to indicate trends in the participants' responses.

3.3 Overall Results

From a universe of 847 students, a total of 139 students responded the questionnaire, and most of them were healthcare professionals (n = 86). When asked to whom the nine icons of SAITE Store were addressed, 75.2 % of the participants (n = 106) correctly responded that they were for healthcare professionals. The use of elements related to the medical field in the icons was given as the main reason by the participants. Only seven participants (n = 5 %) considered the tested icons to be addressed to children (Fig. 2).

The overall results showed that five out of the nine assessed icons were satisfactorily understood by the participants. These seem to be related to their acquaintance with the graphic representations employed [10], and to the relationship between the message and its referent [7]. Two icons obtained understandability index above 90 %: Stork Network 93.6 % (n = 132) and Nephrology 96.5 % (n = 136). The responses to the former seem to be due to the participants' familiarity with the national program for pregnancy, and with the symbols for health (the cross) and for delivering babies (the stork bird). This may have led participants to easily associate the icon graphic representation to its meaning. In a sense, that was a literal representation of the concept 'Stork Network'. Likewise, the representation of 'Nephrology' (branch of medicine concerned with the kidneys) by a kidney is literal, with both part-whole and image-based relations between

In your opinion, the images above were developed for the public

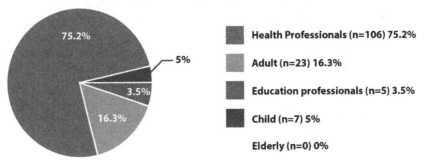

Health Professionals (n=106) 75.2%

Adult (n=23) 16.3%

Education professionals (n=5) 3.5%

Child (n=7) 5%

Elderly (n=0) 0%

Fig. 2. Results of the kind of audience the tested icons of SAITE Store were intended to. Source: Google forms. (Color figure online)

the icon and its referent [7]. The former icons employed the symbols for health and breasts (a circle with two inner circles). On the other hand, the icon for Health Network used linked dots to convey the notion of networking in a concept based relation [7].

In contrast, low understandability occurred in the participants' responses to the icons: Communicable Diseases 9.9 % (n = 14), Distance Education 28.4 % (n = 40), Health and Society, with 39.7 % (n = 56) and Aggravations in health, with 50.4 % (n = 71) as shown in Table 2.

Table 2. Results of the icons with low understandability. source: The authors

Concept	Icon	n	%
Communicable Diseases		14	9.9%
Distance Learning		40	28.4%
Health and Society		56	39.7%
Aggravations in Health		71	50.4%

Participants' difficulties in associating the icons to their intended meaning may be have been due to the abstract nature of their messages, allied to the absence of familiar symbols conveying the messages. This is demonstrated by most participants associating the Communicable Diseases icon to 'Virus' (83 %, n = 117), Health and Society icon to Primary Healthcare (52.2 %, n = 74); and the Distance Education icon to 'Archive Transfer' (62.4 %, n = 88). The misinterpretation of the latter icon, however, was perhaps due to the image of 'multiple pages' being commonly associated to the semantic domain of 'archive' rather than of 'distance learning'. As for the Aggravations in the 'Health' icon, its association to Hospital by 50.4 % (n = 71) of the participants, was probably because the cross is a symbol for hospital. Thus, the icon alone is not sufficient to represent the complexity of the concept. It is interesting to note that these icons were all in a concept-based relation to their messages, that is, they had no referent to rely on. Hence, the icons made use of visual rhetoric to represent their concepts, since images have limitations to convey abstract notions [8, 9].

4   Conclusions

Based upon the results of understandability of the icons of the e-book for the SAITE Store app, it is plausible to conclude that their success in communicating messages seem to be directly related to users' familiarity with their graphic representation. If literal depiction of a referent and/or familiar symbols are not employed, labels should be used to make clear the icons' meaning to their users, particularly when representing abstract/complex concepts. The study added empirical evidence to support the literature on the representational competence of the pictorial mode, through the results on understanding of the assessed icons. Finally, adjustments were made to the icons of the e-book for SAITE Store app according to the outcomes of this study.

References

1. Cardoso, M., Ramalho, S.: Avaliação de ícones digitais, Human Factors in Design. 1 (2012)
2. Cardoso, M.C., Gonçalves, B.S., Oliveira, S.R. R.: Avaliação de ícons para interface de um sistema médico on-line. In: Congresso Internacional de Design da Informação - CIDI, 6., 2013. São Paulo: Blucher, 2013. Disponível em: http://www.proceedings.blucher.com.br/pdf/designproceedings/cidi//CIDI-114.pdf. Acesso em: 8 abr. 2015
3. Formiga, E.: Símbolos gráficos: métodos de avaliação de compreensão, Blucher, São Paulo (2012)
4. Nielsen, J.: Usability Engineering. Morgan Kaufmann, Inc. San Francisco (1993)
5. ISO. Information technology: user system interfaces and symbols: icon symbols and functions - Part 1: Icons - General, 1979. Disponível em: www.dcs.ed.ac.uk/teaching/cs4/www/hci/guidelines/ISO-1.pdf. Acesso em: 8 abr. 2015
6. Lupton, E.: (Org). Tipos nas telas: um guia para designers, editores, tipógrafos, blogueiros e estudantes, Gustavo Gili (2015)
7. Dewar, R.: Design and evaluation of public information symbols. In: Zwaga, H., Boersema, T., Hoonhout, H. (eds.). Visual Information for Everyday Use. Design and Research Perspectives, pp. 285–304. Taylor & Francis, London (1999)
8. Spinillo, C.G.: Graphic and cultural aspects of pictograms: an information ergonomics viewpoint. Work: J. Prev. Assess. Rehabil. **41**, 3398–3403 (2012)
9. Mijksenaar, P., Westendorp, P.: Open Here: The Art of Instructional Design. Thames & Hudson, London (1999)

10. Gombrich, G.H.: Arte e ilusão: um estudo da psicologia da representação pictórica. São Paulo: Martins Fontes (1993)
11. Brugger, C.: Public information symbols: a comparison of IDSO testing procedures. In: Zwaga, H., Boersema, T., Hoonhout, H. (eds.) Visual Information for Everyday Use. Design and Research Perspectives, pp. 305–314. Taylor & Francis, London (1999)
12. Pontes, J.S., Zandomeneghi, A.L.A.O.: Ícones da ferramenta Cacuriá: comparando imagens mentais a partir do teste de produção. In: Congresso Nacional de Ambientes Hipermídia para Aprendizagem - CONAHPA, 7., São Luís, Maranhão, 2015. Disponível em: http://conahpa.sites.ufsc.br/wp-content/uploads/2015/06/ID503_Pontes-Zandomeneghi.pdf. Acesso em: 5 nov. 2015
13. Preece, J., Rogers, Y., Sharp, H.: Design de interação: além da interação humano-computador. 3. ed, Bookman, Porto Alegre (2013)

How to Improve the Overall Pre-purchase Experience Through a New Category Structure Based on a Compatible Database: Gittigidiyor (Ebay Turkey) Case

İrfan Gürvardar[1(✉)], Kerem Rızvanoğlu[2], Özgürol Öztürk[2], and Özgür Yavuz[1]

[1] Gittigidiyor (Ebay Turkey), Çiğdem Sk. No: 1/14 Ataşehir, 34746 Istanbul, Turkey
{igurvardar,oyavuz}@ebay.com
[2] Faculty of Communication, Galatasaray University, Çırağan Cad. No:36 Ortaköy,
34357 Istanbul, Turkey
{krizvanoglu,ozozturk}@gsu.edu.tr

Abstract. Customer journey mapping is a continuous process that demands end-to-end innovation through qualitative and quantitative user research. It helps to identify key points where service or communication breakdown is most likely and where they are mostly valued. Buyer journey mapping study of Gittigidiyor (Ebay Turkey) revealed the fact that the frequency of the repeat purchase was significantly limited although a high traffic and average visit time were observed. This finding pointed to the need to improve the pre-purchase experience in the web site towards motivating the users to visit more and inspiring them to buy more items. Relying on solid quantitative and qualitative research, this paper presents the action set taken for the realization of this goal. In this context the main action of the process is to renew the category structure through a focus on compatibility, which subsequently enabled the integration of a set of effective improvements. Firstly, this approach led to the improvement of a new listing creation process for the sellers by implementing an innovative and error-free experience. It also enabled to improve the search usability by presenting more relevant results, which was supported with a new smart auto suggestion feature in the search engine box and with smart compatibility filters in search results. The new compatible structure between vertical and horizontal categories brought the implementation of some persuasive features. It provided the increase in count of payment (COP) per item and average selling price (ASP) through cross-selling and up-selling features. Finally, the pre-purchase experience was supported by the integration of product rating/review mechanisms and targeted e-mailing based on previous purchase history of the customers.

Keywords: Pre-purchase · Customer journey · Compatibility · Search · Persuasive

1 Introduction

Understanding the customer journey is becoming increasingly important as the number of both digital and offline touch points increases. Consumers base their decisions on interactions across multiple media types, devices and locations [1]. This creates a

© Springer International Publishing Switzerland 2016
A. Marcus (Ed.): DUXU 2016, Part II, LNCS 9747, pp. 366–376, 2016.
DOI: 10.1007/978-3-319-40355-7_35

challenge for marketers to interact at important moments that might influence buying decisions. Customer journey mapping enables to find the the key moments that create the frustration and satisfaction in the journey of the relevant person. The buyer persona journey mapping study in Gittigidiyor (Ebay Turkey) revealed some pain points in the pre-purchase phase which resulted in the significantly low frequency of the repeat purchase for the first-time buyers. Major problems emerged from the lack of capacity to support the product search, to present complementary product recommendations and reviews in the decision-making process and finally to present targeted follow-up actions like e-mailing for retention. It was evident that the pre-purchase experience should be re-structured in detail.

This paper presents the road map through a set of actions which aimed to improve the pre-purchase experience through a new structure and relevant implementations of new features. In this context firstly the "Cellphone and Accessories" category is chosen as the experiment category, since it enabled the implementation of inter product compatibility with a huge range of items. This category is re-structured with the inclusion of new product catalogues based on compatibility specifications. The new structure subsequently enabled the integration of a set of effective improvements such as a new listing creation experience for the sellers, improved search usability and the ability to offer complementary product ratings/reviews and recommendations through persuasive features.

2   Using Customer-Journey Mapping as a Reference for UX Strategy

Understanding the customer journey is becoming increasingly complex as the number of digital and offline touch points proliferate. However, it's important to try and create an accurate map of how customers are interacting with a brand in order to optimize marketing channels and campaigns [1]. From a survey of almost 2,000 digital marketers and ecommerce professionals, 86 % of companies said that 'profitability and increased revenue' were a major benefit, while a similar proportion (83 %) said that 'identifying pain points and reducing customer struggle' were a significant benefit [2]. However, even in organizations that have been developing their digital competencies and tools, analytics and CRM have traditionally tended to be used in isolation, only 17 % of brands have the ability to fully analyze the customer journey [2].

Customer journey mapping enables the company to see things from the customers' point of view and to deliver information, messages and services at the most appropriate time through the most appropriate channels. It helps to identify moments of truth where service or communication breakdown is most likely and where they are mostly valued. In each phase of the journey, it is aimed to identify the possible actions, motivations and questions of the persona. The resulting document can be used as a reference to design the overall UX strategy.

3   Improving the Pre-purchase Experience

In this context, the "Customer Experience Strategy & Project Development Team" in Gittigidiyor (Ebay Turkey) designed and conducted a research process to map the customer journey of the buyer persona. The research process was based on both quantitative and qualitative studies. Two online surveys enabled to reach a user base of 8000 customers. Qualititative insights were derived from in-depth interviews targeting 6 different buyer personas. Interviews with a sample of 30 customers are still in progress.

The resulting map revealed significant pain-points in the pre-purchase phase. Though the web site was a leader in the market-place ecosystem with 13 millions of registered users and a high daily traffic/average visit time, the frequency of the repeat purchase after the first-time purchase was significantly low. The customers struggled to find the products they needed throughout the enormous number of listings and they were not supported in the purchase decision process with complementary offerings. Follow-up actions like e-mailing did not provide efficient results to provoke retention. There was a solid need to improve the pre-purchase experience in the web site towards motivating the users to visit more and inspiring them to buy more items by smart product recommendations. In this sense, firstly it was decided to renew the category structure by focusing on compatibility, which in long term enabled to implement new features to support UX.

4   A New Category Structure Based on a Compatible Database

Technological products are compatibility dependent, in other words, the product's relevance is determined entirely by its compatibility with another product the user already owns or plans on buying [3]. Typical compatibility dependent products include accessories (e.g., a case for a smartphone), products used in conjunction with other products (a bluetooth headphone to use with a smartphone) and spare parts (a Powerbank charger that needs to have a charger tip which matches the user's smartphone). Inter-product compatibility is essential to the user for these types of categories [3]. Unless the site provides a way to browse products based on their compatibility with the items the user already owns, the user is forced to navigate through an endless stream of noise just to find a few products that are potentially relevant to them [3]. Compatibility databases provide the basis for such navigational features and a lack of compatibility database in relevant product verticals can have hugely negative usability and business implications, resulting in lost sales, anxious customers, and returned orders [3].

The findings of the customer journey mapping overlapped with the statements provided by the study above. Each item had lots of specifications and it took a long time for the sellers to create the listing with the correct product description. Listings with incorrect product info caused difficulty for the users to find the relevant product or it contributed to the increase in the number of returns. These findings thus led the strategy team to define a road map towards renewing the category structure by focusing on compatibility. The "Cellphone and Accessories" category was chosen as the scope of the study, since that category presented the most inter-product compatibility with a huge item base.

A quantitative survey conducted with the 5700 users in different segments who previously bought from this category provided findings that emphasized the need for compatibility:

- The users, who bought their smartphones from Gittigidiyor but did not not prefer to buy a complementary accessory, declared that they would be willing to buy an accessory if they were offered any complementary products within the site.
- The users, who bought their smartphones from Gittigidiyor, declared that they gave their old phones to their family members. They told that if they were offered an efficient way of selling their old phones on the Gittigidiyor, they would be willing to do so.
- The users, who bought their previous smartphones from Gittigidiyor but preferred to buy their current phones from a different platform, declared that there were not any communication efforts in Gittigidiyor, which presented timely offers to provoke them to change their phones.
- The users, who only bought their smartphone accessories from Gittigidiyor but preferred to buy their smartphones from a different platform, declared that lack of user reviews and product videos in Gittigidiyor led them to different platforms.

	Catalogue Specs	Compatibility Specs
Cell Phone	· Make · Serie · Model · Color · Internal Memory	· Charging Input · Operating System · Max. Micro SD support · Headphone Input · Bluetooth Version
Charge, Data Cables	· Make · Model · Color · Cable length	· Connector A · Connector B
Headphone	· Make · Model · Color · Headphone Type · Microphone	· Connector · Remote · Operating System compatibility

Fig. 1. An overview from the renewed category structure based on compatibility

All the catalogues were renewed due to the principle of inter-product compatibility with the addition of new compatibility specifications in product catalogues. In a total of 44 sub-categories, brand new catalogues of the most popular brands and models were re-created by the inclusion of the correct and updated compatible specs. For the cell-phone sub-category 10000 catalogues from the last 10 years were renewed and 7000 extra catalogues were created. In the cell-phone accessories sub-category 300000 catalogues were investigated and 1000 new catalogues are recreated (Fig. 1).

4.1 A Brand New Product Definiton/Listing Experience Based on Compatibility

As mentioned above, current listing creation process in Gittigidiyor did not enable the sellers to present the detailed specifications of their products easily and thus caused frustration in the seller experience, which resulted in the incorrect presentation of the product info to the buyers. In this context, a new listing creation process, which provided a fast and error-free experience based on the new compatible category structure, was designed for the sellers (Fig. 2).

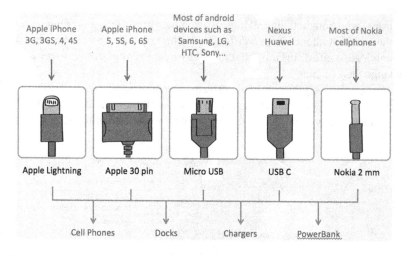

Fig. 2. Screenshot from the renewed listing creation process of a Powerbank charger

As an example, when creating a listing for a powerbank charger which enabled the charge of various smartphones by providing different tips, rather than selecting the name of the tips from a pre-defined menu, the sellers can choose through a set of the drawings of the tips that corresponded to the 90 % of cell phones in the market.

4.2 Improving Search Usability

On-site search is a key component of almost any e-commerce website. However, the poor state of search in e-commerce is industry-wide and most websites have an opportunity to gain a truly competitive advantage by offering a vastly superior search experience to their competitors'. The search usability is heavily influenced by non visible factors, such as search logic and product data integration [4]. In this context, the integration of the new compatible database into the search algorithm "Best Match" provided the opportunity to improve the end-to-end search experience both in the momentary search and post-search phases.

The compatible database enabled to improve the momentary search experience by the implementation of a smart auto-suggestion in the search engine box. The smart auto-suggestion feature enabled to present instant product recommendations specific to each user profile (Fig. 3). For example, a search query such as "white headset for iphone" generated different suggestions for the logged in users, whose previous purchase history was already known, when compared to the products offered for the anonymous visitors. In this case, logged in users who searched for "white headset for iphone" was presented with the white headset that is specifically compatible with his own smartphone, which he previously purchased from Gittigidiyor. On the other hand, an anonymous visitor who searched for "white headset for iphone" was presented with the iphone compatible white headset that had the best user rating (Fig. 4).

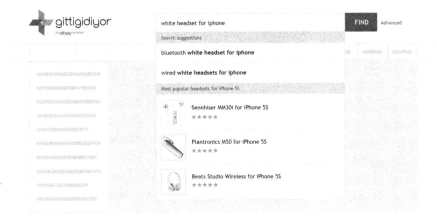

Fig. 3. Smart auto-suggestion that presented specific results for the relevant user profile

Fig. 4. Smart auto-suggestion that presented the best user rated products for the anonymous visitors.

When done right, filters enable users to narrow down a website's selection of thousands of products to only those few items that match their particular needs and interests [5]. Yet, despite it being a central aspect of the user's e-commerce product browsing, most websites offer a lackluster filtering experience. In fact, a 2015 benchmark of 19 leading e-commerce websites reveals that only 16 % of major e-commerce websites offer a reasonably good filtering experience [5]. In this sense, the compatibility specs were used as search filters in the post-search phase which let the users make fast comparisons within the listed products (Fig. 5).

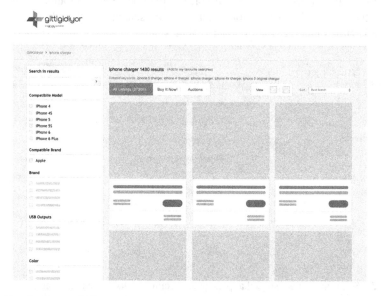

Fig. 5. Compatibility specs are presented as search filters in the left-hand menu

4.3 Persuasive Design Implementations

When creating and optimizing the ecommerce customer journey, not only do we need to ensure that we make this as frictionless as possible, but also that we make it as persuasive as possible [6]. Brands employ diverse persuasive features to support pre-purchase and retention in the customer journey.

The new compatible structure between vertical and horizontal categories brought the implementation of new persuasive features such as cross-selling/upselling, rating/review features and targeted e-mailing.

4.3.1 Cross-Selling and Up-Selling

According to Forrester research analyst Mulpuru, product recommendations through upselling or cross-selling features are responsible for an average of 10–30 % of e-commerce site revenues [7]. Upselling is when the seller encourages the customer to spend more than they had originally intended. A cross-sell is when you recommend your customer to buy a product that compliments their existing purchase, but is from a different category (or vendor) [7]. The implementation of cross-selling and upselling supported by the new compatible database in Gittigidiyor provided a solid increase in count of payment (COP) in terms of items and average selling price (ASP). Related additional items (cross-selling) or upgrades, add-ons or more expensive items (up-selling) were effectively recommended to the users in the product page (Fig. 6).

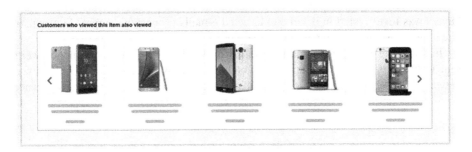

Fig. 6. The implementation of up-selling in the product page

4.3.2 Product Rating and Review

Product ratings essentially function as a type of social proof for users, letting them tap into the "wisdom of the crowd", using good ratings as a proxy for "high quality" or "value for money". The users rely on ratings to gauge a product's quality or value – especially in verticals where they lack domain knowledge or have little prior product experience [8].

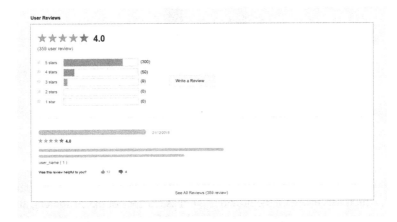

Fig. 7. Screenshot from a user review

Gittigidiyor did not have a product rating/review system and the customers oriented towards the competitors and the social media channels to find trustful reviews. In order to overcome this issue, the pre-purchase experience was supported by the integration of a product rating/review mechanism as a persuasive feature in the product page. The rating/review mechanism included the feedback on the usefulness of the review as well. In this context, one of the future goals is defined as making Gittigidiyor website a product research and review gateway for the customers (Fig. 7).

4.3.3   Targeted e-mailing

In order to provoke repeat purchase and thus retention, the purchase history of first time buyers was investigated in detail and targeted e-mails proposing compatible products due to previous purchase were sent to these users.

In this context, targeted e-mails which pushed for upselling of a new model, were sent to 2000 existing customers who bought iPhone 5s or older from GittiGidiyor between 2011−2013 (Fig. 8). An eightfold increase in open and click rates was observed.

Fig. 8.   Targeted e-mail which pushed for upselling of a new model

Referring to this positive response for the case mentioned above, a smart e-mailing template, which was supported by the new compatible database, was designed. This template, which was based on the previous purchase history of the customers, automatically generated user-specific e-mails that either offered complementary products or provoked upselling of a new model. For example, for the customers who currently used iPhone 5s were offered with highly compatible complementary products. Besides timely offers to replace their iPhone 5s with a brand new iPhone 6s could also be delivered to the same user profile via this smart e-mail mechanism. At this point, Gittigidiyor could serve as a channel in which users could both sell their current smartphone and buy a new one as well (Fig. 9).

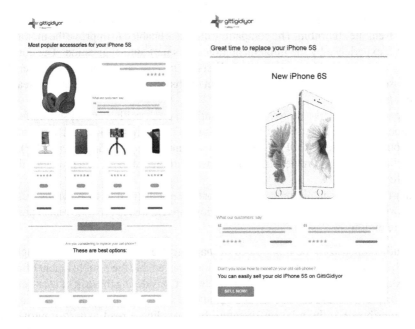

Fig. 9. User-specific e-mails automatically generated by the smart e-mail template due to the previous purchase history of the customers, which either offered complementary accessories or pushed for the upselling of a new model.

5 Conclusion

The findings of the research process to map the customer journey of the buyer persona in Gittigidiyor revealed the significant need to improve the overall pre-purchase experience towards providing a balanced increase in revisit and repeat purchase rates. Major problems were observed as the lack of support for the product search, for presenting complementary product recommendations and reviews in the decision-making process and finally for creating targeted follow-up actions like e-mailing for retention. This paper presented the set of actions which aimed to improve the pre-purchase experience through a new category structure and relevant implementations of new features in the scope of "Cell-phone and Accessories" category. The paper provided the following implications for the improvement of pre-purchase experience in Gittigidiyor.

- The category structure was re-invented due to the principle of inter-product compatibility with the addition of new compatibility specifications in product catalogues. In a total of 44 sub-categories, brand new catalogues of the most popular brands and models were re-created by the inclusion of the correct and updated compatible specs.
- A new listing creation process, which provided a fast and error-free experience based on the new compatible category structure, was designed and implemented for the sellers.

- The search usability was improved by the integration of compatibility specs into the search engine algorithm. The compatible database enabled to improve the momentary search experience by the implementation of a smart auto-suggestion. The compatibility specs were also used as search filters in the post-search phase, which enabled the users to make fast comparisons within the listed products and reach the searched item faster.
- As part of persuasive design implementations, cross-selling and upselling features supported by the new compatible database in Gittigidiyor provided a solid increase in count of payment (COP) in terms of items and average selling price (ASP).
- A reliable rating and review mechanism was introduced to act as a proxy for finding quality products.
- Smart targeted e-mails proposing compatible products due to previous purchase history of the customers were used as follow-up features to provoke repeat purchase and retention.

This study emphasized the importance of mapping the customer journey through user research to reveal key points, which in long term can enable the establishment of a solid UX strategy by prioritizing the phases to focus on. Considering the lack of user-centered studies on pre-purchase experience in e-commerce platforms specifically in Turkey, this study contributed to the relevant literature by providing a road map to improve user experience in similar environments. The implementation of the features presented in this paper are still in progress and further research will focus on measuring the impact of these features on user experience through various metrics.

References

1. Moth, D.: Do Companies Understand the Customer Journey? (2015). https://econsultancy.com/blog/66322-do-companies-understand-the-customer-journey/
2. Simpson, J.: Only 17 % of Brands have the Ability to Fully Analyse the Customer Journey (2015). https://econsultancy.com/blog/66913-only-17-of-brands-have-the-ability-to-fully-analyse-the-customer-journey/
3. Appleseed, J.: 6 Use Cases for Compatibility Databases on E-Commerce Sites (2015). http://baymard.com/blog/ecommerce-compatibility-databases
4. Holst, C.: The Current State of E-Commerce Search (2014). https://www.smashingmagazine.com/2014/08/the-current-state-of-e-commerce-search/
5. Holst, C.: The Current State of E-Commerce Filtering (2015). https://www.smashingmagazine.com/2015/04/the-current-state-of-e-commerce-filtering/
6. Pay, K.: How to Use. Persuasion throughout the Ecommerce Customer Journey (2015). https://econsultancy.com/blog/66756-how-to-use-persuasion-throughout-the-ecommerce-customer-journey/
7. Walker, T.: How To Boost eCommerce Sales With Upselling (2014). http://conversionxl.com/upselling-techniques/
8. Appleseed, J.: Users' Perception of Product Ratings (New Qualitative & Quantitative Findings) (2015). http://baymard.com/blog/user-perception-of-product-ratings

Achieving a User Friendly Error Message Design: Understanding the Mindset and Preferences of Turkish Software Developers

Yavuz Inal[✉] and Nesibe Ozen-Cinar

TÜBİTAK BİLGEM Software Technologies Research Institute, Ankara, Turkey
{yavuz.inal,nesibe.ozen}@tubitak.gov.tr

Abstract. This study investigates the preferences of software developers concerning the design of error messages and required fields in web forms and explores the factors affecting these preferences. A total of 73 software developers participated in this study and data was collected through a questionnaire and a semi-structured interview. According to the results of the study, for the error message design, the developers tended to provide solutions they considered useful not only for users but also for themselves. Therefore, the majority of the software developers chose to embed error codes in error messages; however, they stated that it was not appropriate to display the error code as the main element of the message. Furthermore, it was seen that the error message preferences of software developers were significantly influenced by the duration of developers' participation in the project, the stage at which they joined the project and the number of other experienced developers.

Keywords: Web forms · Error message design · Usability · Developers' mindset · Turkish software developers

1 Introduction

One of the main concerns of most software companies is the integration of usability activities into the software development life cycle to design and develop more user-friendly interfaces. From the literature review, it was concluded that developers are aware of the importance of usability activities in the development process; however, existing software still has low usability characteristics [1, 2], which do not meet users' needs and expectations. Usability is defined by the International Standardization Organization (ISO) as "the extent to which a product can be used by specified users to achieve specified goals with effectiveness, efficiency and satisfaction in a specified context of use" [3]. The metrics mentioned in the ISO definition were extended by Nielsen [4] to include; learnability, efficiency, memorability, errors and satisfaction. The standards of human computer interaction (HCI) and usability are not only concerned with these metrics but also focused on the user interface and interaction between user and computer [5].

The user interface is a strategic element of software projects that establishes a bridge between the users and the developed software [6]. Not only should the aesthetics of user

© Springer International Publishing Switzerland 2016
A. Marcus (Ed.): DUXU 2016, Part II, LNCS 9747, pp. 377–385, 2016.
DOI: 10.1007/978-3-319-40355-7_36

interfaces in the context of user experience [7] be taken into consideration but the usability of the developed software is also an essential factor because it is a measure of the users' performance, their effectiveness, efficiency and satisfaction [8] and directly related to the user interface quality.

Forms are significant components of web applications integrated into the interface design to ensure that users take an active part in online forums, e-commerce websites and data entry processes [9]. The completion of forms is a common way of interacting with users in web applications [10–12]. For an effective interaction with users, forms are used in various applications such as online shopping, registration and communication and online questionnaires [9, 13]. Forms not only facilitate interaction between users and the interface in web applications [9, 14], they are also an important element of design in several software products from desktop to mobile applications.

For online form completion, a user-friendly error message design is one of the important aspects of a usable interface design [14]. Users need to fully understand the message in order to achieve the particular task of filling in the form. [14] discussed the best way of presenting error messages in online forms and found that most users ignored error messages when trying to complete a form. [15] examined marking the required fields with an asterisk to prevent errors in online forms. They determined that users found marking the required field with colored asterisks was effective, efficient and satisfactory. Their study showed that low user error rates, fast form completion process and high-level user satisfaction were the important outcomes of the use of colored asterisks. [16] tested frequently-used locations of error messages in web forms finding that locating the error messages near the erroneous field resulted in a high user performance in form completion.

User-friendly error message design is critical in ensuring that the user can respond effectively and complete all the required input fields in a form. In the literature, various studies focused on user-friendly error message design from different perspectives such as location, presentation and visual design (i.e. [14–17]); however, there is only limited number research related to understanding the developers' mindset and their preferences concerning the design of effective error messages. Studies have found that there are many reasons for the lack of user-friendly design interfaces; such as developers possibly being unaware of design principles or standards and having limited or no idea about usability activities that can be integrated into the design process due to a lack of an HCI related background, insufficient training and their mindset [18–20].

The developers' mindset is one of the most prominent barriers preventing the design and development of a user-friendly interface [18]. [20] described the developer's mindset as the difficulties or barriers in understanding users and realizing usability problems in developed software by developers who lack a background of usability practice. These difficulties or barriers are the cause of not only failing to identify and fix usability problems [18, 19] in the development phase, but also have an impact on the interface design of the software resulting in low usability characteristics. It is necessary that all members of the project team, including the software developers, have a common understanding of the design of user-friendly interfaces. However, many studies that examined the design of error messages in forms were conducted with university students or volunteer participants [e.g. 14–17]. In this study, the preferences of software developers on the design of error messages and required fields in forms are investigated together with the factors affecting these preferences. The factors influencing the mindset of developers are also discussed in detail.

2 Method

2.1 Participants

There were 73 software developers with limited or no usability background who participated in this study. Their average age was 28.64 (SD = 3.64) years, they had an average software project experience of 7 years and, on average, had worked on four software projects. The education level of the participants was as follows; 16 % had a Bachelor degree, 55 % had a Master's degree and the remaining 29 % were PhD candidates. In terms of the operating system utilized, almost all (93 %) were Microsoft Windows users with only 5 % being Mac OS X users.

2.2 Design

This study was based on a questionnaire and semi-structured interview used to determine the preferences of participants concerning error message design and required fields, and the factors affecting these preferences. The questionnaire provided information on the demographic characteristics and the design preferences of the participants. For the latter section of the questionnaire, recommendations on error messages in the web form design guidelines developed by [23] and the findings of [14] concerning the design and location of error messages were taken into consideration. This process ensured that the responses of the participants were focused on the visual design, location, presentation and content of error messages and required fields in web forms. To obtain more detailed information, a semi-structured interview was conducted with participants concerning their responses in the questionnaire. The data was collected over a period of three weeks.

3 Results

3.1 Error Message Design Preferences

Concerning the error message design in forms, 44 % of the software developers (n = 32) placed them on the right of the erroneous input field, 46 % (n = 34) put them below the erroneous input field, only 10 % of the developers error messages above the erroneous field and none placed them to the left of the erroneous input field. The software developers were asked about the error message format given next to the erroneous input field; 62 % (n = 45) preferred not to repeat the information in the related field such as name, surname, password in the message, and 38 % (n = 28) chose to only repeat the name of the related field in the message (see Fig. 1).

For the pop-up window error message design, 77 % of the software developers (n = 56) used statements in the error message related to business rules to inform users

Fig. 1. Software developers' preferences concerning error message design in forms

rather than giving generic error message statements (23 %, n = 17). The developers were asked to explain the reasons behind their preference concerning the error message content. A considerable number of participants commented on the need for more explanatory and instructive business rules. The majority of participants preferred to use statements in error messages to inform users of the content of the errors and help them understand why the error had occurred.

The software developers were also asked about their preference for the presentation of error messages or statements and their location on the page. More than half the developers (n = 56) chose to place the pop-up window in the center of the screen whereas 12 developers used a thin banner on top of the page to display information or error messages for users.

The preference of 85 % of the developers (n = 62) was to use sentence case statements in error messages. The remainder of the developers used uppercase statements (12 %, n = 9) or capitalized the first letter of each word (3 %, n = 2). Almost all the software developers (95 %, n = 69) preferred to use icons for error message notifications with only 5 % (n = 4) choosing not to use icons for these notifications.

Fifty-nine percent of the software developers (n = 43) preferred to use an active sentence format in error messages and only 7 % (n = 5) used a passive sentence format. The developers stated that the active sentence format is clearer and more understandable and results in the use of simple and plain language. In terms of the location of error codes; 67 % of the developers (n = 49) placed error codes at the end of the error message in parentheses, 20 % put these codes at the beginning of the error message, and only 5 % placed the error code in the error message (See Fig. 2). The majority of the developers did not consider error codes to be the main element of the message and therefore placed them in parentheses at the end of the error message. This action was based on not distracting users and helping them focus on the message as well as making it easier for the developers to find the source of the errors. Therefore, the most preferred format of error code insertion was to give the error codes lower priority in terms of the content.

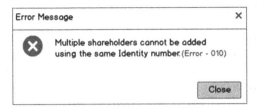

Fig. 2. Preferences of software developers concerning the error message design in pop-up windows

3.2   Required Field Design Preferences

The software developers were asked about their preference related to the display of required fields in forms, and their responses were analyzed to determine the common preferences. Twenty-six software developers stated that it was sufficient to mark the frames of required fields in red and 17 developers additionally highlighted input fields in red. Furthermore, 14 participants chose to place an asterisk at the end of required fields, 10 placed them on the right of the labels and six used them on the left of the labels. This was interesting in terms of showing that the majority of the participants chose not to use an asterisk in required fields. This may be due to their perception that colored frames or fields are eye-catching for users, thus more efficient in calling attention to the required fields (Fig. 3).

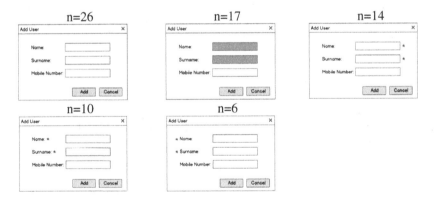

Fig. 3. Preferences of software developers on required field design in forms

When giving their opinions concerning the presentation of required fields indicating erroneous data input by users more than half the software developers (n = 43) preferred to outline the frame of the text field in red. Very few participants informed the users of an error by placing an asterisk (n = 2) or exclamation mark (n = 6) on the right of erroneous input fields. The higher number of developers using red to display erroneous input fields can be attributed to their desire to attract the attention of users to these fields.

3.3   Factors Effecting Developers' Mindset and Preferences

The results of the study showed that software developers have different preferences concerning the error message design, and in order to achieve well-designed effective error messages, it is critical to examine the factors that have an impact on the developers' mindset and their preferences. The developers selected for this study were working on five different software development projects. It was found that their mindset and preferences were mainly influenced by the project duration and number of experienced software developers engaged in the project.

Developers with extensive development experience in the same project had similar preferences regarding the error message design. This may indicate that they were influenced by the preferences adopted in the design of the project interface thus chose a similar preferences to the design of error messages. Another significant finding was that the developers who had been part of the project since the beginning gave similar responses whereas some developers that joined the project later had differing preferences. Therefore, it can be concluded that working together in a project for a long time can result in members developing similar preferences.

For software projects at the requirement or design phase (before the development phase) of the lifecycle, the software developers had differing preferences in terms of the error message design. Particularly in new projects, the lack of a specific design approach led to significant differences in the preferences of the software developers. This indicates that the project design influences the preferences of developers and contributes to the development of their mindset. Strong preferences for error messages about the same design choices were expressed in software projects, which involved more junior developers, but there was no consensus among developers in software projects comprising more senior developers.

4   Discussion

Error messages are not only a significant component of web forms [9] but also represent one of the most problematic and frustrating experiences for users [21]. It is not possible to design a web form without considering error messages [16]. Despite the significance of error messages, one of the most overlooked issues in human machine interfaces is the display of effective and high-quality messages to users when erroneous data is input [22]. Therefore, it is important to determine the design priorities and preferences of software developers and identify the related factors. However, in the literature, there is limited research on error messages from the perspective of software developers. Most studies collect data from university students or volunteer participants that are not software developers [e.g. 14–17].

In this study, in addition to determining the preferences of software developers on error messages and required fields, we identified the factors influencing the mindset of developers such as their experience, their roles and length of time working on the project. The results showed that the software developers have certain tendencies and preferences in the display of error messages. Similar to the study by [16], the participants in the current study mostly did not choose to display error messages at the top or bottom of the entire form. However, contrary to the suggestion by [16] that placing messages near or on the right side of the erroneous input field is more efficient, effective and satisfying. In the current study, the majority of the developers preferred to locate these messages very near or just under these fields.

In terms of the content of error messages, in this study, the software developers focused on providing information for not only users but also themselves. For example, a considerable number of software developers chose to include error codes in the error messages based on the idea that these codes would help themselves to correct the error. This developer preference is an interesting finding in that error codes included in error messages would not normally be of any use to users.

According to [11], the developers of web applications should attach sufficient importance to designing user-friendly forms; however, there are other factors affecting the preference of developers on error message design in forms. In recent years, several studies have been conducted to examine various factors such as the usability and user-friendliness of web forms from different perspectives [16], with some research using experimental methods and others based on the findings and experience of usability experts [23].

In terms of the presentation of required fields upon form loading or erroneous input, most software developers were found to prefer easily noticeable and eye-catching forms of display. [15] reported that using color rather than asterisks to mark required fields is more efficient in preventing errors and increasing user satisfaction. Similarly, in the current study, the developers tended to mark the frame of the required and erroneous input fields in red to make them more visible to users.

In relation to influencing the mindset of software developers, certain factors were found to play a significant role in predicting the preferences of participants particularly on the design, content and location of error messages. The software developers working in the same project for a long time were found to have similar preferences on error message design. In addition, for software projects at the requirement or design phase of the lifecycle, there was no common approach adopted by all project members and the developers' preferences differed in terms of the error message design. Therefore, it can be concluded that the mindsets of developers are influenced by various factors; the duration of developers' participation in the project the stage at which they joined the project and the number of other experienced developers. Similar to [18, 20] suggesting that the mindset of a developer precludes the design of user-friendly interfaces, in the current study, some project members had common ideas that were not in agreement with accepted design principles. Therefore, increasing the knowledge and awareness of software developers concerning usability can positively influence their mindset leading to the creation of more user-friendly designs.

To determine the preferences of software developers on the design of error messages to be displayed during form completion as well as to identify the factors affecting these preferences, it is important to collect data from a higher number of developers. We believe that the current study will guide future work to be conducted with a larger sample size. In addition, further research should focus on other factors that may influence the mindset of software developers and thus, contribute to the existing literature.

References

1. Hoegh, R.T.: Usability problems: do software developers already know? In: OZCHI 2006, 20–24 November 2006, Sydney, Australia, pp. 425–428 (2006)
2. Göransson, B., Gulliksen, J., Boivie, I.: The usability design process - integrating user-centered systems design in the software development process. Softw. Process Improv. Pract. **8**, 111–131 (2003)
3. ISO 9241-11: Ergonomic requirements for office work with visual display terminals (VDTs) - Part 11: Guidance on usability (1998)
4. Nielsen, J.: Iterative user-interface design. Computer **26**(11), 32–41 (1993)
5. Bevan, N.: International standards for HCI and usability. Int. J. Hum.-Comput. Stud. **55**, 533–552 (2001)
6. Akiki, P.A., Bandara, A.K., Yu, Y.: Adaptive model-driven user interface development systems. ACM Comput. Surv. **47**(1), 9–33 (2014)
7. Tuch, A.N., Roth, S.P., Hornbaek, K., Opwis, K., Bargas-Avila, J.A.: Is beautiful really usable? Toward understanding the relation between usability, aesthetics, and affect in HCI. Comput. Hum. Behav. **28**, 1596–1607 (2012)
8. Seffah, A., Metzker, E.: The obstacles and myths of usability and software engineering. Commun. ACM **47**(12), 71–76 (2004)
9. Wroblewski, L.: Web Form Design: Filling in the Blanks. Rosenfeld Media, New York (2008)
10. Bargas-Avila, J.A., Brenzikofer O., Roth S., Tuch A., Orsini S., Opwis K.: Simple but crucial user interfaces in the world wide web: introducing 20 guidelines for usable web form design. In: Matrai R. (ed.) User Interfaces, INTECH, pp. 1–10 (2010)
11. Seckler, M., Heinz, S., Bargas-Avila, J.A., Opwis, K., Tuch, A.N.: Empirical evaluation of 20 web form optimization guidelines. In: Proceedings of CHI 2013, pp. 1893–1898 (2013)
12. Katsanos, C., Karousos, N., Tselios, N., Xenos, M., Avouris, N.: KLM Form analyzer: automated evaluation of web form filling tasks using human performance models. In: Kotzé, P., Marsden, G., Lindgaard, G., Wesson, J., Winckler, M. (eds.) INTERACT 2013, Part II. LNCS, vol. 8118, pp. 530–537. Springer, Heidelberg (2013)
13. Bargas-Avila, J.A., Orsini, S., Piosczyk, H., Urwyler, D., Opwis, K.: Enhancing online forms: use format specifications for fields with format restrictions to help respondents. Interact. Comput. **23**(1), 33–39 (2011)
14. Bargas-Avila, J.A., Oberholzer, G., Schmutz, P., de Vito, M., Opwis, K.: Usable error message presentation in the World Wide Web: do not show errors right away. Interact. Comput. **19**, 330–341 (2007)
15. Pauwels, S.L., Hübscher, C., Leuthold, S., Bargas-Avila, J.A., Opwis, K.: Error prevention in online forms: use color instead of asterisks to mark required-fields. Interact. Comput. **21**, 257–262 (2009)
16. Seckler, M., Tuch, A.N., Opwis, K., Bargas-Avila, J.A.: User-friendly locations of error messages in web forms: put them on the right side of the erroneous input field. Interact. Comput. **24**, 107–118 (2012)
17. Mockovak, M.: Comparing the effectiveness of alternative approaches for displaying edit-error messages in web forms. In: ICES, pp. 1446–1453 (2007)
18. Bak, J.O., Nguyen, K., Risgaard, P., Stage, J.: Obstacles to usability evaluation in practice: a survey of software development organizations. In: Proceedings of the NordiCHI. ACM Press (2008)
19. Ardito, C., Buono, P., Caivano, D., Costabile, M.F., Lanzilotti, R., Bruun, A., Stage, J.: Usability evaluation: a survey of software development organizations. In: Proceedings of the SEKE. Knowledge Systems Institute Graduate School (2011)

20. Bruun, A., Stage, J.: Overcoming the Developer Mindset Barrier towards Usability Evaluations (2012)
21. Lazar, J., Huang, Y.: Improved Error Message Design in Web Browsers, Human Factors and Web Development, 2nd edn. Lawrence Erlbaum Associates, Mahwah (2003)
22. Brown, P.J.: Error messages: the neglected area of the man/machine interface. Commun. ACM **26**(4), 246–249 (1983)
23. Seckler, M., Heinz, S., Bargas-Avila, J.A., Opwis, K., Tuch, A.N.: Designing usable web forms - empirical evaluation of web form improvement guidelines. In: CHI 2014, pp. 1275 − 1284 (2014)

TIIARA: A Language Tool for Bridging the Language Gap

Nouf Khashman[1], Elaine Ménard[2(✉)], and Jonathan Dorey[3]

[1] Qatar National Library, Qatar Foundation, Doha, Qatar
nkhashman@qf.org.qa
[2] School of Information Studies, McGill University, Montreal, QC, Canada
elaine.menard@mcgill.ca
[3] School Information Studies, McGill University, Montreal, QC, Canada
jonathan.dorey@mail.mcgill.ca

Abstract. This paper presents and discusses the results of the second phase of the development of TIIARA (Taxonomy for Image Indexing and RetrievAl), a bilingual taxonomy dedicated to image indexing and retrieval. TIIARA offers indexers and image searchers innovative and coherent access points for ordinary images. Initially developed in French and English, the taxonomy has been subsequently translated in 8 languages. The preliminary steps of the elaboration of the bilingual structure are briefly described. The process used in the translation of TIIARA in Arabic language is presented, as well as the main difficulties encountered by the translator. Adding more languages in TIIARA constitutes an added value for a controlled vocabulary meant to be used by image searchers who are often limited by their lack of knowledge of multiple languages.

Keywords: Taxonomy · Controlled vocabulary · Multilingual information · Translation · Arab language

1 Introduction

The organization of visual resources such as personal photos as always been challenging. For years, traditional controlled vocabularies have been chosen for indexing and classification of images, with mixed successes. Although well developed and trying to be as enumerative as possible, these terminologies are not always precise for the pictures we take over the years with our digital cameras. Often considered too general to provide the right degree of granularity leading to precise retrieval results, most controlled vocabularies can only provide a primary subject or a broader category for images. Additionally, very good controlled vocabularies only exist in one language, limiting their use to the individuals who are familiar with this specific language.

In order to overcome this lack, TIIARA (Taxonomy for Image Indexing and RetrievAl), a bilingual taxonomy dedicated to image indexing and retrieval, was developed in order to offer a vocabulary appropriate for image indexing and retrieval. Among the many advantages of controlled vocabularies such as taxonomies, it is worth mentioning consistency and enhanced possibilities to match indexing words to search query terms. Furthermore, if the image searcher has the possibility to browse a taxonomic structure to initiate or refine queries, the retrieval will be facilitated.

© Springer International Publishing Switzerland 2016
A. Marcus (Ed.): DUXU 2016, Part II, LNCS 9747, pp. 386–395, 2016.
DOI: 10.1007/978-3-319-40355-7_37

For its initial development, TIIARA included two languages, French and English. As a logical follow-up to the initial development of a bilingual controlled vocabulary, it was decided to translate TIIARA in eight other languages to increase its international scope: Arabic, Spanish, Brazilian, Portuguese, Chinese, Italian, German, Hindi and Russian. This paper describes the initial steps of the elaboration of the bilingual structure, the process used in the translation of TIIARA in Arabic, as well as the main difficulties encountered by the translator. The last section concludes the paper and proposes future directions for improving the multilingual taxonomy.

2   Related Works

Text-based image indexing and retrieval have been studied extensively over the years [1–16]. These studies present the numerous challenges of image organization. The advantages and disadvantages of controlled and uncontrolled vocabularies used for documents or multimedia indexing, are extensively described in the literature [6, 10, 17–22]. Traditionally, some general terminologies such as the Library of Congress Subject Headings (LCSH) or specific vocabularies, including Getty's Art & Architecture Index (AAT) and the Thesaurus for Graphic Materials (TGM) have been chosen for describing visual resources such as images. As an alternative to these conventional vocabularies, taxonomies can be considered as innovative usable means for image indexing and retrieval. They can simplify the searching process and facilitate finding the "right" information near effortlessly. Unfortunately, very few studies described the basic processes of their development [23–26].

Most controlled vocabularies often present shortcomings. For example, they are often not exhaustive enough [13] to provide adequate descriptive information or access points suitable for all uses. In addition the neologisms and terminological changing usage will not be integrated quickly. This slow updating will be definitively frustrating for indexers or image searchers that rely on an up-to-date terminology.

Nor do most controlled vocabulary allow for the use of specific queries, so search results are less accurate than they need to be, a problem compounded when it comes to multilingual information. Some interesting projects exist, especially in Europe, where multilingualism is a requirement. For example, the UNESCO Thesaurus is a quadrilingual controlled and structured list of terms used in subject analysis and retrieval of documents and publications in the fields of education, culture, natural sciences and social and human sciences. With more than 7,000 terms in English and in Russian, 8,600 terms in French and in Spanish, this thesaurus offers terms from the fields of education, culture, natural sciences, social and human sciences, communication and information [27]. However, these multilingual vocabularies are rare and often very limited in the choice of languages offered. This can be explained by the fact that high-quality multilingual controlled vocabularies (thesauri, taxonomies, etc.) take a long time to be developed. Their construction can be long and expensive processes, and their maintenance time-consuming.

3   Objectives

Taxonomies are increasingly being used to organize content within organizations and to support navigation of digital content [28–30]. The review of the literature completed in the initial phase of this research project [31] revealed that there is a gap in our understanding of image searchers' expectations and what is available in terms of searching functionalities. Initially, TIIARA was developed in French and English, the two official languages of Canada, where this research is taking place. Once TIIARA was updated and retested, it was decided that it could be interesting to add other languages to TIIARA. For this first expansion phase, eight languages were selected: Arabic, Spanish, Brazilian Portuguese, Chinese, Italian, German, Hindi and Russian. This section summarizes the development of TIIARA, the translation process in Arabic, and the main difficulties translators faced.

Multilingual information processing has gained more and more attention in recent years. However very few research really explained the hit and miss of elaborating a bilingual controlled vocabulary and how other languages can be thereafter integrated in the making of a thoroughly multilingual vocabulary. This study proposes to fill this gap and answer the following research questions:

1. What are the general steps of the development of a bilingual taxonomy?
2. What are the main steps of the translation of TIIARA in Arabic?
3. What difficulties were encountered during the Arabic translation process?

4   TIIARA Development

4.1   The Bilingual Structure

The initial structuring of the taxonomy involved choosing top-level categories and their subcategories. Two approaches were chosen: starting from the narrowest terms possible and moving to the more generic ones (bottom-up approach) or the selection of general concepts within the taxonomy which are then subdivided (top-down approach). As mentioned previously, TIIARA was simultaneously structured in English and French to keep the taxonomy as parallel as possible. Both languages come from related Indo-European language families and have common origins [32]. The Indo-European family comprises languages largely used throughout Europe, Western and South Asia, and other parts of the world as a result of colonization. This group of languages refers to the easternmost extension of the family from the Indian subcontinent to its westernmost reach in Europe [33].

It was decided that the number of top-level categories and the depth of the taxonomic structure would be kept to a minimum. At first, TIIARA included nine top-categories. This initial version was tested in order to validate and refine the vocabulary and its organization. For the first validation phase, the card-sorting technique was used. Data gathered revealed difficulties encountered using the taxonomy structure and dynamically suggested ways to improve it [26]. Following this first evaluation, the preliminary nine main groupings were reduced to seven top categories (Table 1):

Table 1. TIIARA main categories (English and French)

Main category	Definition
Abstract Ideas Idées abstraites	Related to an idea of something formed by mentally combining all its characteristics or particulars; a concept.
Arts and Entertainment Art et divertissement	Related to people, tools, equipment and products specifically associated with dance, design, visual arts, writing, music, television and film, and stage.
Daily Life Vie quotidienne	Related to the activities and experiences that constitute a person's normal existence.
Nature Nature	Related to the phenomena of the physical world, including plants, animals, the landscape and other features and products of the Earth, as opposed to humans or human creations.
Places Lieu	Related to a building or a physical environment used for a special purpose.
Objects and Equipment Objet et équipement	Related to unique objects or pieces of equipment (not in active use by a person).
Work Travail	Related to people doing a job, other than those listed in "Arts and Entertainment."

These main categories were then developed to include second-, third- and, in some cases, fourth-level subcategories, in French and English. Two indexers, one English-native and one French-native speaker, used TIIARA to describe a small image database (IDOL [Images DOnated Liberally]. This custom-built database includes 6,015 images offered voluntarily by photographers. The indexing terms assigned by the two indexers were evaluated and compared to identify potential gaps in the taxonomy.

A second round of testing took place with a representative sample of image searchers. We asked the participants to complete retrieval tasks of images indexed using the revised taxonomy TIIARA to measure its degree of effectiveness and efficiency. During this experiment, a sample of 60 respondents were asked to indicate where in the taxonomic structure they thought they would find each one of the 30 images shown. Participants were also asked to fill a questionnaire intended to obtain their general opinion on TIIARA and to report any difficulties encountered during the retrieval process. The quantitative data was analyzed according to statistical methods, while the content of open-ended questions was analyzed and coded to identify emergent themes. The results of this phase of the research project indicated that, despite the fact that some categories still need further refining, TIIARA already constitutes a successful tool that provides access to ordinary images. The bilingual taxonomy constitutes a definite benefit for image searchers who are not very familiar with images indexed in English, which still dominates the Web.

Once fully tested and updated according to feedback received from indexers and image searchers, TIIARA was translated in eight different languages. Arabic was a logical choice since this language is "the largest member of the Semitic branch of the

Afro-Asiatic language family" that comprises all descendants of Classical Arabic spoken primarily across the Middle East and North Africa. It is one of the six languages of the United Nations, and serves as the first language for 22 Arab countries, and as a second language in over a dozen more. With over 375 million native speakers [34], it is one of the most spoken languages [33], mainly in the Middle East, North Africa, and some Muslim countries such as Iran, Malaysia, and Indonesia.

As a Semantic language, Arabic shares similarities with other Semitic languages, such as Aramaic and Hebrew. In terms of writing, several languages use the Arabic alphabet, such as Farsi, Urdu, Pashto and Kurdish [35].

4.2 The Arabic Translation Process

The Arabic alphabet contains 28 letters, most of which change form depending on whether they appear at the beginning, middle or end of a word, or on their own. Arabic uses eight main diacritic marks that can change the meaning of a word drastically based on their positions on those letters. When those diacritics are excluded or omitted, homonymy problem may arise [36].

Moreover, the language has around 5 million words that are derived from around 11,300 roots compared to 400,000 keywords in English, which has total of 1.3 million words. This makes the language rich of terminology and has a complex morphology compared to English and European languages [37]. Arabic is also a major source of vocabulary for other languages such as Kurdish, Spanish, Persian, Urdu, and Swahili.

Arabic language can be classified into three main variants: the formal Arabic language, known as Classical Arabic or Fus-ha, is the language in which the Qur'an is written. This is relatively a difficult form of Arabic, which is considered today more of a written language than a spoken one.

The second form is Modern Standard Arabic (MSA), which is similar but easier than Classical Arabic. It's understood across the Arab world and used on television and media, as well as to teach Arabic as a foreign language.

The last form is the Colloquial Arabic (local dialects), which differs from one Arab country to another, and even within each country. Those dialects differ from MSA and each other in terms of phonology, morphology, lexical choice and syntax. The translation of the TIIARA was primarily based on MSA; for example, translating clothes into ملابس (malabis) rather than هدوم (hudoum), which is used locally in Egypt.

4.3 The Difficulties Encountered

While some difficulties encountered in translating the TIIARA from English to Arabic will be discussed based on the particularities of the Arabic language previously discussed [36], others will be based on the translator's experience working with the TIIARA.

The peculiar morphology of Arabic might render methods used for English retrieval inappropriate. An example from TIIARA would be "beauty and hygiene", which translated to Arabic as جمال ونظافة "jamal w nathafa". In this case, the letter "waw" (meaning and) has been slightly transformed and linked with the following word; this would create problems were it decided to treat "and" as a stop word.

There was also the question whether the definite article the ال (Al) should be included or not in the translation, since the 'al' and a number of conjunctions and prepositions, are not separated from their following word by a space. Examples include الناس (people), إسلام (Islam), المنسوجات (textiles). These terms were treated based on the context and not one single rule was followed.

It is common to find many Arabic words that have different pronunciations and meanings but share the same written form (homonyms), making finding the appropriate semantic occurrence of a given word a problem. An example would be كتاب and كُتّاب, where the first word means a book, while the second means authors. Another example would be حـب (love), as it can be written as intended حُب, or as حَب (grains). The reason for this confusion is the omission or misplacement of the diacritical marks, which are also not usually indexed in online information retrieval systems.

Arabic plurals are formed more irregularly than in English depending on the root and the singular form of the word. The plural form might be produced by the addition of suffixes, prefixes or infixes, or by a complete reformulation of the word. An example from the TIIARA would be translating elephants into أفيـال or فيلة, sheep into غـم or أغنــام, canyons into وديان or أودية. The latter translation in these cases was chosen to simplify the process.

Every Arabic letter is pronounced as a word and cannot be used to represent one character like in English. Therefore, in Arabic, acronyms and abbreviations are not found. Therefore, the term Sport utility vehicles (SUVs) was translated into ســيارات دفع رباعي, and Recreational vehicles (RVs) into سيارات ترفيهية without adding acronyms.

Moreover, it appears that MSA orthography has largely been standardized for a long time now [37]. However, few variations persist across and within different Arab countries. In TIIARA, for example, golf was transliterated into غولف, but it could also be written as جولــف because the /g/sound does not occur in MSA and is replaced with the closest letters to that sound, غ and ج in this case.

There were a few instances where the politically correct terms needed to be included rather than using the literal translation of the word. For example, disabled people was translated into ذوي الاحتياجات الخاصة (people with special needs) rather than معاقون, which literally means "handicapped".

Finally, it was noted [38] that some terms related to innovations and borrowed words might not be regulated. In TIIARA, there were a number of terms that are not found in the Arabic language. To overcome this challenge, the terms were transliterated into Arabic. For example, curling was transliterated into الكيرلنج, accompanied by the word sport رياضــة to indicate it is a sport, and doing the same for hockey هـوكي الجليـد and lacrosse رياضة الكروس. Other foreign terms were directly translated into Arabic, such as مشغلات أقراص فيديو رقمية (DVD players), ماسحات ضوئية (scanners), مسجل فيديو شخصي (personal video recorders) and مراكز تجارية (malls). However, people tend to use the English term whenever they refer to these inventions.

5 Discussion and Conclusion

According to the Working Group on Guidelines for Multilingual Thesauri [39], several possibilities may be considered in the development of multilingual controlled vocabularies such a taxonomy: building a new vocabulary from the bottom up, starting with one language and adding one or more languages, starting with more than one language simultaneously, combining or merging existing monolingual controlled vocabularies, connecting existing controlled vocabularies to each other or translating a controlled vocabulary into one or more other languages. For TIIARA, the development was made in parallel in French and English. To add more languages, we selected the last of the aforementioned options (translation). Translated version of TIIARA now exists in multiple languages (French, English, Arabic, Spanish, Brazilian Portuguese, Italian, Chinese, German, Hindi and Russian). Other translations are also being considered (Polish, Japanese, Greek, etc.).

Several linguistic questions arose in the development of a multilingual controlled vocabulary. For its initial development, TIIARA only included French (from the Romance branch) and English (from the Germanic branch); two languages that are not different theoretically, being from the same Indo-European language family and having common origins [32]. However, problems with the structural hierarchy could arise in multilingual controlled vocabularies, particularly when the different languages show crucial discrepancies in the hierarchical levels where concepts are organized.

It is worth mentioning that the individuals that participated in the TIIARA translation, including the Arabic translation, could not be considered as "professional translators," nor "professional taxonomists". The different translations were rather produced by volunteers with sufficient knowledge of the source languages (English or French) and the chosen target languages. Consequently, the translators faced many difficulties, at many levels, but mainly at the semantic and syntactic level [40]. Semantic and syntactic ambiguities remain unquestionably one of the main problems that could have potentially serious consequences on the intrinsic structure of the taxonomy.

Several situations were reported by the Arabic translator: (1) some terms could be exactly translated; (2) some translated terms were inexact or nearly equivalent; (3) some translated terms only corresponded to a partial equivalence; (4) some translated terms could be matched to one-to-many equivalents, where to express the meaning of the preferred term in one of the languages, two or more preferred terms were needed in the other language; and finally, (5) some terms from the source language did not match equivalent term in the target language.

It is without surprise that the other translators also reported similar experiences. As all linguistic entity conceptualises the world from their own perspectives, meanings are rarely symmetrical across languages. Therefore, the aim for TIIARA has not been to pursue exact equivalence between languages but, instead, to lead the information retriever towards relevant search results regardless of which language is used. The multilingual nature of any controlled vocabulary, including TIIARA, poses a number of language- and culture-related challenges, and building harmonious and understandable hierarchy in more than one language is definitively a complex process that may require compromises. Nevertheless, constructing multilingual controlled vocabularies is a crucial factor in the context of information globalization. This cannot be achieved without acknowledging and respecting the differences that exist between the specific characteristics of different languages.

The next step of this research will be the testing of the translated versions with real image searchers. We also planed to include the multilingual TIIARA in SINCERITY (Search INterfaCE for the Retrieval of Images with a TaxonomY), a bilingual search engine that has been developed in parallel with the present project. The suggestion of integrating a taxonomy to assist image retrieval was expressed by many image searchers who participated in the exploration of the roles and usefulness of functionalities for image searching in a bilingual context [41]. For the moment, even if most image searchers prefer searching with keywords related to the content of the image they are looking for, the events taking place or people that appear in the picture, most search engines still do not offer their users the opportunity to browse a taxonomic structure to initiate their queries.

Moreover, most image searchers prefer searching in their own language. Giving them a hierarchical structure they can navigate seems the perfect solution to facilitate the retrieval process. Moreover, if the taxonomic structure includes several languages it will consequently give different linguistic communities equivalent opportunities and subsequently bridge the information divide that still exists. Especially for image searchers who have difficulties formulating a query using words from another language.

References

1. Panofski, E.: Meaning in the Visual Arts: Papers in and on Art History. Doubleday, Garden City (1955)
2. Krause, M.G.: Intellectual problems of indexing picture collections. Audiov. Librarian **14**, 73–81 (1988)
3. Markey, K.: Access to iconographical research collections. Libr. Trends **37**, 154–174 (1988)
4. Armitage, L.H., Enser, P.G.B.: Analysis of user need in image archives. J. Inf. Sci. **23**, 287–299 (1997)
5. Jörgensen, C.: Attributes of images in describing tasks. Inf. Process. Manag. **34**, 161–174 (1998)
6. Jörgensen, C.: Image Retrieval – Theory and Research. Scarecrow, Lanham (2003)
7. Markkula, M., Sormunen, E.: End-user searching challenges indexing practices in the digital newspaper photo archive. Inf. Retrieval **1**, 259–285 (2000)
8. Goodrum, A.A., Spink, A.: Image searching on the excite web search engine. Inf. Process. Manag. **37**, 295–311 (2001)
9. Choi, Y., Rasmussen, E.M.: Searching for images: the analysis of users' queries image retrieval in American history. J. Am. Soc. Inf. Sci. Technol. **54**, 498–511 (2003)
10. Matusiak, K.K.: Towards user-centered indexing in digital image collections. OCLC Syst. Serv. **22**, 283–298 (2006)
11. Enser, P.G.B., Sandom, C.J., Hare, J.S., Lewis, P.H.: Facing the reality of semantic image retrieval. J. Documentation **63**, 465–481 (2007)
12. Enser, P.G.B.: The evolution of visual information retrieval. J. Inf. Sci. **34**, 531–546 (2008)
13. Greisdorf, H.F., O'Connor, B.C.: Structures of Images Collections: from Chauvet-Pont d'Arc to Flickr. Unlimited Libraries, Westport (2008)
14. Ménard, E.: Image retrieval: a comparative study on the influence of indexing vocabularies. Knowl. Organ. **36**, 200–213 (2009)

15. Chung, E.K., Yoon, J.W.: Categorical and specificity differences between user-supplied tags and search query terms for images. An analysis of Flickr tags and Web image search queries. Inf. Res. **14** (2009)

16. Stvilia, B., Jörgensen, C.: User-generated collection-level metadata in an online photo-sharing system. Libr. Inf. Sci. Res. **31**, 54–65 (2009)

17. Markey, K., Atherton, P., Newton, C.: An analysis of controlled vocabulary and free text search statements in online searches. Online Rev. **4**, 225–236 (1980)

18. Muddamalle, M.R.: Natural language versus controlled vocabulary in information retrieval: a case study in soil mechanics. J. Am. Soc. Inf. Sci. **49**, 881–887 (1998)

19. Savoy, J.: Bibliographic database access using free-text and controlled vocabulary: an evaluation. Inf. Process. Manag. **41**, 873–890 (2005)

20. Arsenault, C.: L'utilisation des langages documentaires pour la recherche d'information. Documentation et Bibliothèques. **52**, 139–148 (2006)

21. Macgregor, G., McCulloch, E.: Collaborative tagging as a knowledge organisation and resource discovery tool. Libr. Rev. **55**, 291–300 (2006)

22. Rafferty, P., Hidderley, R.: Flickr and democratic indexing: dialogic approaches to indexing. Aslib Proc. **59**, 397–410 (2007)

23. Lambe, P.: Organising Knowledge: Taxonomies, Knowledge and Organisational Effectiveness. Chandos Publishing, Oxford (2007)

24. Whittaker, M., Breininger, K.: Taxonomy development for knowledge management. In: World Library and Information Congress: 74th IFLA General Conference and Council, Québec, 10–14 August 2008

25. Hedden, H.: The Accidental Taxonomist. Information Today, Medford (2010)

26. Ménard, E., Smithglass, M.: Digital image description: a review of best practices in cultural institutions. Libr. Hi Tech. **30**, 291–309 (2012)

27. UNESCO: UNESCO Thesaurus (2016). http://databases.unesco.org/thesaurus/

28. Gilchrist, A., Kibby, P.: Taxonomies for Business: Access and Connectivity in a Wired World. TFPL Consultancy, London (2000)

29. Kremer, S., Kolbe, L.M., Brenner, W.: Towards a procedure model in terminology management. J. Documentation **61**, 281–295 (2005)

30. Uddin, M.N., Janecek, P.: Performance and usability testing of multidimensional taxonomy in web site search and navigation. Perform. Meas. Metrics **8**, 18–33 (2007)

31. Ménard, E., Smithglass, M.: Image retrieval in a bilingual context: a review of best practices. Libr. Hi Tech. **32**, 98–119 (2014)

32. Walter, H.: Honni soit qui mal y pense. Robert Laffont, Paris (2001)

33. Ethonlogue Languages of the World: Explore the Languages of the World (2015). https://www.ethnologue.com/

34. Internet World Stats (2016). http://www.internetworldstats.com/stats19.htm

35. British Broadcasting Corporation (BBC): A guide to Arabic – 10 facts about the Arabic language (2014). http://www.bbc.co.uk/languages/other/arabic/guide/facts.shtml

36. Moukdad, H., Large, A.: Information retrieval from full-text Arabic databases: can search engines designed for English do the job? LIBRI **51**, 63–74 (2001)

37. Habash, N.Y.: Introduction to Arabic Natural Language Processing. Morgan & Claypool Publishers, San Rafael (2010)

38. Azmi, A.M., Aljafari, E.A.: Modern information retrieval in Arabic - catering to standard and colloquial Arabic users. J. Inf. Sci. **41**, 506–517 (2015)

39. International Federation of Library Associations and Institutions - IFLA. Guidelines for Multilingual Thesauri (2009). http://www.ifla.org/files/assets/hq/publications/professional-report/115.pdf

40. Braschler, M.: Combination approaches for multilingual text retrieval. Inf. Retrieval **7**, 183–204 (2004)
41. Ménard, E., Khashman, N., Dorey, J.: Two solitudes revisited: a cross-cultural exploration of online image searcher's behaviors. In: Marcus, A. (ed.) DUXU 2013, Part II. LNCS, vol. 8013, pp. 79–88. Springer, Heidelberg (2013)

Localized Website Design Advisor: A Web-Based Tool Providing Guidelines for Cross-Cultural Websites

Abdalghani Mushtaha[✉] and Olga De Troyer

WISE Research Group, Vrije Universiteit Brussel, Pleinlaan 2, 1050 Brussels, Belgium
{abdalghani.mushtaha,Olga.DeTroyer}@vub.ac.be

Abstract. This paper describes the Localized Website Design Advisor "LWDA" tool. It is a web-based tool that uses a localization ontology and knowledge about cultural markers to provide website localization guidelines. LWDA captures expertise on how to design websites for different cultures and at different levels of localization. LWDA generates dynamically website localization guidelines for a given localization level (1 to 5), society, language, and domain. As such the tool is helpful for organizations and individuals involved in the development of cross-cultural websites.

Keywords: Localization · Guidelines · Localized website design · Cultural markers · Localization ontology · Cultural markers knowledge

1 Introduction and Background

There is a growing acknowledgement in the Web community that the user's cultural background is, to some extent, essential and need to be taken into consideration during the design process of localized websites (i.e., websites adapted for a specific country, region, society, ...) [1–4]. Therefore, we have done several studies aiming at verifying and investigating the relationship between features of the website and the users' cultural background in terms of web usability [5–8]. Our experiments showed that it is not possible to have an absolute and clear-cut set of cultural markers to be used for designing localized websites. In addition, one single set of anthropological cultural dimensions could, in fact, be a poor choice because different levels of localization may be needed in different situations. Therefore, 5 different levels of cultural markers organized as a pyramid has been proposed [8]: (1) the e-culture level – for non-localized (thus rather international) websites, (2) the settled cultural level – for semi-localized websites, (3) the broad cultural level – for localized websites, (4) the variable cultural level – for highly localized websites, and (5) the vista cultural level – for fully cultural localized websites. For each level of localization, a group of cultural markers for a set of website design elements is provided, as well as a specific number of anthropological cultural dimensions to be considered for a specific localization level.

The website design elements considered for the different levels are: (1) Text on websites; (2) Layout and Organization; (3) Colors; (4) Pictures, Graphic Elements, and Sound; (5) Interaction; and (6) Navigation. The anthropological cultural dimensions considered are 16 existing cultural dimensions: Human Nature Orientation,

© Springer International Publishing Switzerland 2016
A. Marcus (Ed.): DUXU 2016, Part II, LNCS 9747, pp. 396–406, 2016.
DOI: 10.1007/978-3-319-40355-7_38

Individualism vs. Collectivism, Internal vs. External Control, Time Orientation, Authority Conception, Context, Gender Roles, Power Distance, Uncertainty Avoidance, Universalism vs. Particularism, Achievement vs. Ascription, Affective vs. Neutral, Specific vs. Diffuse, Experience of Technology, Face-Saving, and International Trade and Communication.

In [9] we described the Cultural Conceptual Model (C2M) (expressed in Object Role Modelling (ORM) [10]) based on the Cultural Markers Pyramid. And did transformation of C2M to Ontology (OWL [11]) and called it Localization Ontology for a more practical oriented format [12].

In this paper, we describe how the Cultural Conceptual Model (C2M) is used to develop the Localized Website Design Advisor tool. The tool uses the Localization Ontology and a Cultural Markers Knowledge Base extracted before and explained in [9].

The paper is structured as follows. In Sect. 2, we explain the Localized Website Design Advisor (LWDA) and why such a tool is needed. We then explain in Sect. 3 the technical details of LWDA. In Sect. 4, we describe how to use the Localized Website Design Advisor in practice. Conclusions are drawn in Sect. 5.

2   Localized Website Design Advisor (LWDA)

LWDA is an acronym for Localized Website Design Advisor. It is a web-based tool that uses the Localization Ontology [9] as well as a knowledge base, called the Cultural Markers Knowledge Base, which contains information and cultural markers specifications for different target societies.

LWDA tool is not a website design tool; rather it is an advisor-tool that provides guidelines that developers should take into consideration when designing a localized website for a given localization level, society, language, main website domain, and some website related domains. This means that the main input for the tool is: (1) Localization level that one wants to achieve "1 to 5", (2) Target society "Country", (3) Website language, (4) Main website domain, and (5) Related website domains.

2.1   Necessity of a Localized Website Design Advisor Tool

Knowledge about the localization of websites is scattered over many different (mostly academic) resources. This impedes the proper development of localized web sites in practice. Website developers tend to rely on their common sense and on what others did to localize a website. However, such an approach is not always resulting in an appropriate solution, as what works in one context may not work in another context. Therefore, LWDA was developed to provide a central repository for knowledge about designing localized websites. To make the repository easy to use in practice, it was designed as an advisor tool that gives to-the-point guidelines to web developers for localizing a website in a specific context. When specific information is not yet available in the repository, the tool can be used (by experts) to fill in this information. Furthermore, LWDA can also be employed for the evaluation of the localization of existing websites by using the guidelines to verify whether the website satisfies the guidelines.

3   Localized Website Design Advisor (LWDA) Technical Details

LWDA was developed using ASP.NET (Microsoft web application framework) [13] and AJAX (Asynchronous JavaScript and XML) [14] is used for the communication between the browser and server, which removed the need for a whole page to be reloaded after each interaction.

In order to communicate with the ontology, LWDA makes use of XSLT [15], to dynamically generate a questionnaire based on XML documents. Furthermore, LWDA is connected to a Microsoft access database, which is used for the cultural knowledge base to store information about the cultural markers of target societies.

3.1   LWDA Architecture

As illustrated in Fig. 1, the LWDA application is subdivided into six processes. This section describes these processes, as well as the internal relationship between them.

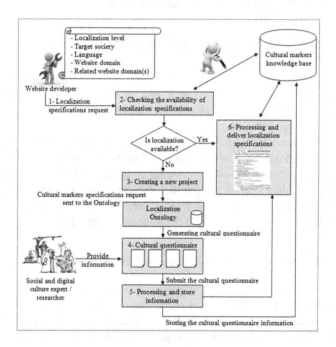

Fig. 1. Localized Website Design Advisor (LWDA) Architecture

LWDA contains two information repositories: (1) the Localization Ontology, and (2) the Cultural Markers Knowledge Base.

- The Localization Ontology is used to provide a common and unambiguous understanding of the website design elements and cultural dimensions and their interdependencies for the different localization levels. It actually contains all information provided by the Cultural Markers Pyramid.

- The Cultural Markers Knowledge Base contains information and cultural markers information about specific societies and specific website domains.

We separate between those two information repositories for the following reasons:

1. The Localization Ontology is used for the abstract guidelines as specified in the Cultural Markers Pyramid. The Localization Ontology should only be changed by a researcher specialized in culture. For example, somebody who can decide whether or not the "number of links in a group" is a cultural marker for a specific localization level. This kind of information should come from research and long-lasting investigations.
2. The Cultural Markers Knowledge Base is a information repository containing information about (1) a particular country, (2) a specific website domains, and (3) a specific localization level. The stored information can be considered as an instantiation of the abstract guidelines provided by the Localization Ontology. The Cultural Markers Knowledge Base (or parts of it) can be maintained by somebody who is a culture expert for a particular target culture.
3. The social as well as the digital culture are changing constantly [8, 16]. Therefore, information in the Cultural Makers Knowledge Base may change over time. For example, maybe today the maximum number of links in a group has to be 7 for Chinese people in a Health website, and maybe after a while this needs to be changed to 8. As long as the number of links is still a cultural marker, the value can be updated in the Cultural Markers Knowledge Base. If the number of links would no longer be a cultural marker, then the Localization Ontology needs to be updated (separation between the marker itself and the value of the marker).
4. Having the cultural markers characteristics in a knowledge base makes it easy and flexible for external application to use this data.

In order to provide a better understanding of LWDA, the following section describes the different processes of LWDA, as well as the roles of the two cultural repositories.

3.2 LWDA Processes

Here we describe the LWDA processes using a real example. Suppose we need to design a localized website, then (as shown in Fig. 1), the following processes are involved:

1. Localization specifications request:
   In this first step, the website developer needs to give some information about the website he or she wants to design. Suppose that a website developer wants to design a health website for China, wants to achieve the localization level 4 (Variable), and the website language is Chinese. After providing this information to LWDA, the tool takes over the process and passes to the second process.
2. Checking the availability of localization specifications:
   In this process, the tool checks the Cultural Markers Knowledge Base trying to find out whether the knowledge base contains information about such a request.

Suppose that there is no such information yet available then the tool passes to process 3.

3. Create a new project:

   The LWDA tool contacts the Localization Ontology asking for cultural markers specifications for the information entered by the website developer.

   For example, the ontology generated the following specifications: `"Variable-Navigation contains at most NavigationDepth"`; `"Navigation-Depth is accepted by TargetCultureGroup"`. This means that, in the variable level, the navigation depth is important to take care of and it is important to identify the depth of website navigation as accepted by the target culture.

   The information collected from the "Localization Ontology" is still abstract and no values are assigned (e.g., the actual value of NavigationDepth is not provided). For that, a questionnaire is generated from the Localization Ontology to be given to social and digital cultural experts/researchers to fill-in. This is explained in the following process, process 4.

4. Cultural questionnaire:

   In this process, all the specifications obtained from the Localization Ontology are formulated in the form of a questionnaire. The generated questionnaire is easy for non-computer specialists to deal with. For the example, the questionnaire will contain a question on the maximal navigational depth accepted by Chinese people for Health websites. The answer to this question is expected to be provided by social and digital cultural experts/researchers who have deep knowledge about the target country China.

   After the questionnaire has been filled in, the answers are processed by the tool. The tool ensures that the mandatory questions in the questionnaire are answered. Next, the information is processed and stored (process 5).

5. Processing and store information:

   The tool will pass the answers on the questioner to the Cultural Markers Knowledge Base to store it. In this way, the information can be reused for later projects (e.g., somebody needs to have website localization specifications for a similar website). But it could also be used for querying the knowledge base by other applications.

   The next process is the process with number 6.

6. Processing and deliver localization specifications:

   Based on the information in the Culture Markers Knowledge Base, the tool generating a report contains the requested localization specification guidelines.

   Note that when the requested information was already in the Culture Markers Knowledge Base at the time of the request (process 2), processes 3 to 5 are skipped.

4   Using LWDA

In this section, we illustrate the use of LWDA in practice. For example, suppose we need to design a localized website for China in the domain of Health. Also suppose that the relevant information is not yet in the Culture Markers Knowledge Base.

First, the website developer provides LWDA with the required information about the target website. This is entered at the start page (Fig. 2).

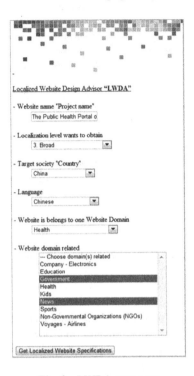

Fig. 2. LWDA start page

As an example, suppose the user has entered the following information:

– Website name "Project name": The Public Health Portal of China
– Localization level required: level 3, Broad
– Target society "Country": China
– Language: Chinese
– Website is belongs to one Website Domain: Health
– Website domain related to: Government and News

Next, the system checks if the Cultural Markers Knowledge Base already contains the requested information. Remember that we suppose that this is not the case. Therefore, the LWDA tool will generate a "Cultural questionnaire" from the information in the Localization Ontology. This questionnaire should be filled-in by a social or cultural expert and needs to be returned to LWDA for processing. Figure 3 shows the structure of the generated questionnaire for the target website.

Fig. 3. Generated cultural questionnaire

The questionnaire is divided into two main categories. The first category is for collecting information about website design elements, and the second category is to collect information about anthropological cultural dimensions.

Figure 4 shows an example of collecting information about one of the website design elements "Colors". The questionnaire provides information and raises questions about colors. Figure 4 shows that the expert gave three notes about colors; these notes are cultural markers values.

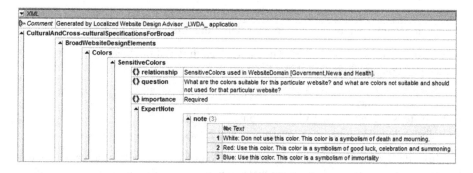

Fig. 4. Generated cultural questionnaire: question about colors

The following figure, Fig. 5, shows examples of the anthropological cultural dimension questions. The expert has added notes in the "ExpertNote" field.

◢ GenderRolesCulturalDimension							
	◢ InformationAboutCulturalDimension						
		◇ Keyquestionue...	Refers to the value placed on traditional male and female roles				
		◢ Information					
			◇ note	Refers to the value placed on traditional male and female roles			
	◢ AffectedWebsiteDesignElements						
		◢ Colors					
			◇ Information	If there is a preference for colors			
			◢ ExpertNote				
				◢ note (3)			
					Nbc	Text	
					1	Website need to be used red color. The red color is symbolic of festivals	
					2	Warm reds and yellows are colors symbolic of festivity in China	
					3	Provide FAquestions	
		◢ PicturesGraphicAndSound					
			◇ Information	In various societies in which feminine roles are clearly visible, there is a preference for pictures, news and activities related to social life (e.g. pictures of family, pictures of teams of employees).			
			◢ ExpertNote				
				◇ note	Preference for pictures, news and activities related to social life		

Fig. 5. Generated cultural questionnaire: question about the gender roles anthropological cultural dimension

After answering the questions, the expert should return the questionnaire to the LWDA tool for processing. Afterwards, LWDA stores the information for later reuse and uses it to automatically generate specific guidelines for the target web-site.

The following snapshots: Figs. 6, 7 and 8, are a part of the specification report generated. The generated guidelines are in a pseudo natural language (English).

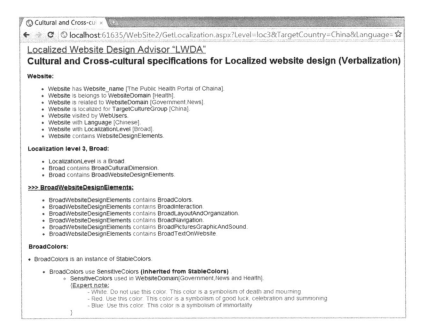

Fig. 6. Target localized website specification guidelines

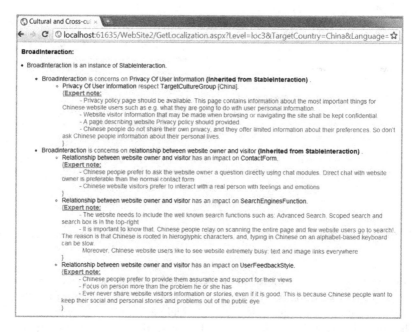

Fig. 7. Target localized website specification guidelines for interaction

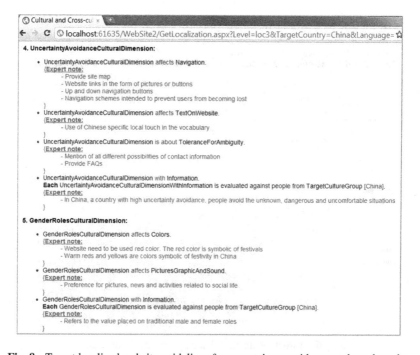

Fig. 8. Target localized website guidelines for uncertainty avoidance and gender roles

Figure 7 shows a part of the specification report for "Interactions".

Figure 8 shows a part of the specification report for two anthropological cultural dimensions (1) Uncertainty avoidance and (2) Gender roles.

Every (pseudo natural language) sentence appearing in the report is clickable and is a hyperlink to an explanation page with more details. For example, the sentence "Website with LocalizationLevel [Broad]" (shown in Fig. 5) is a clickable hyperlink to a particular page explaining this role, shown in Fig. 9.

Fig. 9. Page providing more information

5 Conclusion

In this paper, we proposed the Localized Website Design Advisor (LWDA) tool. LWDA dynamically generates advice on how to localize a website for a target country, language, level of localization, and website domain.

LWDA is based on two cultural information repositories, (1) The Localization Ontology and (2) the Cultural Markers Knowledge Base. We distinguished between them because each one has its own contribution and role. The ontology is used for providing abstract cultural specifications, while the knowledge base is used for storing the values and the description of these specifications for a particular website domain, a particular target country, and a specific website localization level. Distinguishing between the two makes the system more flexible and easier to maintain as it distinguish between information that may change over time (the knowledge base) and information that is more stable (the ontology) and only should be change when research proves that it is outdated.

LWDA was developed because there was a lack of a consolidated single source describing the cultural markers that need to be taken into consideration for the design of localized websites. Furthermore, LWDA's locaization guidelines can also be used to evaluate existing websites.

References

1. Jeong, K.-Y., Wu, L., Hong, J.-D.: IDEF method-based simulation model design and development framework. J. Ind. Eng. Manag. **2**, 337–359 (2009)
2. Sapienza, F.: Culture and Context: A Summary of Geert Hofstede's and Edward Hall's Theories of Cross-Cultural Communication for Web Usability. Usability Bull. (2008)
3. It, D., Drupal, W.: Creating usable websites. New York Times (2008)
4. Lee, I., Kim, J., An, Y.: Cultural Dimensions for User Experience: Measurement (2008)
5. Stengers, H., De Troyer, O., Baetens, M., Boers, F., Mushtaha, A.: Localization of web sites: is there still a need for it? In: International Conference on Web Engineering (held conjunction with ACM HyperText 2004 Conference), St. Cruz, USA (2004)
6. Mushtaha, A., De Troyer, O.: Cross-cultural understanding of content and interface in the context of E-learning systems. In: Aykin, N. (ed.) HCII 2007. LNCS, vol. 4559, pp. 164–173. Springer, Heidelberg (2007)
7. Mushtaha, A., De Troyer, O.: Cross-culture and website design: cultural movements and settled cultural variables. In: Aykin, N. (ed.) IDGD 2009. LNCS, vol. 5623, pp. 69–78. Springer, Heidelberg (2009)
8. Mushtaha, A., De Troyer, O.: A pyramid of cultural markers for guiding cultural-centered localized website design. In: CATAC 2012, Beyond Digital Divide New Media (2012)
9. Mushtaha, A., De Troyer, O.: The cultural conceptual model for simplifying the design of localized websites. In: Marcus, A. (ed.) DUXU 2014, Part II. LNCS, vol. 8518, pp. 158–169. Springer, Heidelberg (2014)
10. Halpin, T.: Object-role modeling (ORM/NIAM). Handb. Archit. Inf. Syst. CSCI-84, 141 (2006)
11. Wikipedia, F., Dean, M., Schreiber, G., Description, R., Web, S.: Web Ontology Language (2009). http://www.w3.org/2004/OWL/
12. Hodrob, R.: ORM to OWL 2 DL Mapping, pp. 131–137 (2010)
13. Microsoft: ASP.NET MVC Overview (2014). http://msdn.microsoft.com/en-us/library/dd381412(v=vs.108).aspx
14. Zakas, N., Fawcett, J.: Professional Ajax, pp. 1–380 (2007)
15. Kay, M.: XSL Transformations (XSLT) Version 2.0 (2007). http://www.w3.org/TR/xslt20/
16. Reed-Swale, T.W.: Engaging digital natives in a digital world. Connect **22**, 22–25 (2009)

Understanding Chinese Internet Users

Nan Wang[(⊠)]

User Experience Department, Baidu, Beijing, People's Republic of China
wangnan01@baidu.com

Abstract. User experience as an exotic concept has introduced into in China for about a decade, however, it have had a profound impact on Chinese Internet and the Chinese people and attracted more and more attention from academia and industry. From three aspects, this article discusses the user experience in China's evolution and development: first, it's the birth of the user experience and history in China, and Chinese practitioners' efforts for promoting it; Second, with the rapid development of China's society and Internet industry, Chinese people have changed a lot both in their thoughts and life. Meanwhile Chinese Internet companies also take actions on new design and products forcing on these changes; Third, it's about the potential chances and challenges for user experience and its practitioners in traditional industry as well as emerging industry.

Keywords: User experience · Chinese internet · UX practitioners

1 Introduction

User experience (UX) has become more and more fashionable in China in the tide of Internet+ and entrepreneurship. In all industries, UX plays an important role in product development and design. People focus on the user's characteristics and analyze user's habits. As for what the user experience really is, however, the answers are open. Some people think that the user experience is inviting users to try and experience products. Some people think that the user experience is the design of the user interface. Some people think that the user experience is the user-centered development process. In 2008, ISO defined UX as user experience is a person's perceptions and responses that result from the use or anticipated use of a product, system or service, which is widely accepted and recognized. One survey of UX practitioners also found that practitioners believed that the user experience was "dynamic", "the context - dependent" and "subjective" which is pretty consistent with this definition of ISO (Law et al. 2009).

The concept of UX was introduced into China for about ten years, however, in the decade, UX changed from an academic, foreign word gradually into a more Chinese characteristic one. In all these efforts, the practitioner of Chinese Internet user experience make an important contribution to promote and popularize it, which also makes Chinese Internet industry the least different compared with the international level. For Chinese user experience, however, the related literature is relatively scarce, so in this article, the author will systematically discuss the development of UX in China. From three aspects, this article discusses the user experience in China's present situation and the future:

A. Marcus (Ed.): DUXU 2016, Part II, LNCS 9747, pp. 407–415, 2016.
DOI: 10.1007/978-3-319-40355-7_39

first, birth of the user experience and history in China; Second, in the tide of China's Internet, user experience localizes in China and the product and design focus on Chinese people; Third, it's the opportunities and challenges for China UX practitioners in future China.

2   The Concept of UX and Its Localization

2.1   The Birth and Development of UX

UX is still a relatively young concept. From an academic perspective, it is an interdisciplinary subject covering design, psychology, human computer interaction and many other subjects. However, looking back, the development of the user experience is not simple and can be divided into three stages (Yuan 2015).

The first stage is UX's germination. The earliest concept can be traced back to the Second World War in last century 40s. In this stage, user experience research focuses on physical human-computer interaction, which is also called ergonomics. The results of these researches were also used in military industry and other public areas. For example, in the design of aircraft instrument panel, different color of the characters and background had different effects on instantaneous memory, which was a famous finding of this period.

The second stage appeared in the 1980s, during which time personal computers became popular. At that time, UX was on large screen products. Besides, human-computer interaction was concerned about not only physiology issues but psychology ones as well. The concept of user interface design was raised in this period. Although the exact word 'UX' was not clearly put forward then, what people thought and felt was taken into consideration in the process of product designed and developed.

The third stage is from the end of the twentieth century up to now. The start point is the definition of UX. About the appearance of UX, academic, American designer Donald Arthur Norman is recognized as the originator. Norman joined apple in 1995 as a User Experience Architect, which was the first position of UX. Norman thought that UX was a user's purely subjective feeling built in the process of using products and accepting services. Later, American economist B. Joseph Pine II and James H. Gilmore put forward the theory of experience economy. Their writings "Experience Economy", points out that under the fierce market competition pressure, in order to pursue the unique selling point, a new economic form, experience economy is separated from the service economy. It is the fourth stage after the product economy, commodity economy and service economy. The arrival of the experience economy means a further improvement of people's needs and it is the inevitable result of social productivity development to a certain extent. And one of the most critical milestone for UX is the appearance of iPhone. At MacWorld 2007, Mr. Jobs introduced the iPhone, which was with the most advanced capacitance screen technology and excellent software experience. The birth of iPhone was a revolutionary change to the mobile interaction pattern of physical buttons at the time and it also made apple once again become a successful company. Apple's success let the world see the tremendous power of the user experience. Since then, UX is no longer a vocabulary in the field of design and UX began to enter all walks of life.

As three stages of UX's development, UX practice in people's life also has experienced changes from public areas to personal areas. In the initial stage of public use, UX was in military industry, aerospace and other special areas. When used in personal area, UX first occurred in the computer field, then turned to the manufacturing, services, etc.

User experience is gradually appearing in China at the beginning of this century. Unlike the west, UX first appeared in China's electrical appliance industry, which was affected by west companies' UX practice such as Siemens and IBM. Lenovo, Haier and other large electrical appliance companies set up the user experience related department, introducing UX theory and methodology. Due to the openness and popularity of Chinese electrical appliances industry, UX roots and grow in China. Later, the Internet industry, IT industry and communication industry also gradually introduce and slowly attaches great importance to UX. "User experience" has become a fashionable word in China. The most intuitive performance is the Baidu index. Since about 2011, "user experience" and related queries from Baidu have been in a state of rapid growth, which suggests that more and more people want to learn and understand UX. The wind of UX blows in all walks of life in China. One of the most famous cases is Haidilao hotpot. As a traditional food and beverage services brand, one of the best-known features of Haidilao hotpot is its user-centered service. Haidilao provide many interesting services when costumers are waiting tables such as nail arts and shoeshine service. And when they seated on, elastic, apron and cell phone sets are provided. It is the service that makes many customers would like to wait for hours for dinner at Haidilao. Although UX entered in China for only a decade or so, its development is very breathtaking to which Chinese Internet companies make a great contribution.

2.2   UX's Localization and UXer in China

Although UX was not first introduced into China by Internet industry, the concept of UX gains a great growth benefiting from Chinese Internet industry. With the explosive growth in the Chinese Internet in the last five years, Internet user experience practitioners have proliferated and the Internet industry has become professional schools for UXers. By now, the Internet industry has become synonymous with "user experience" in China and when mentioning user experience, people always think about Internet. Not only does Baidu, Alibaba, Tencent and other Internet giant set up UX department, but many emerging, young Internet companies put UX on the very important position as well. They focus on user research and experience design, bringing a lot of amazing products for Chinese users.

Although Internet UX has developed rapidly, it is a young discipline indeed. Besides, UX has a complicated background across design, psychology, human computer interaction. By now, there has been no complete UX training system or a course in Chinese colleges and universities and even relevant content is rare. Fortunately, thanks to the natural openness and sharing spirit of Internet, Internet UXers volunteer to promote UX and provide the young with professional trainings. Internet giant's UX team publishing UX related writings and websites, such as Tencent CDC's "Around you, design for you" and Baidu UED's "Experience & Du". These books not only introduce professional UX methods and theories which are accumulated during years of product research and development by these successful teams but also present cases of outstanding Internet products. In addition to writings, the Internet giants have various practices. They hold professional salons and record online courses. All these efforts are to help the young to understand UX and start their career.

When Internet giants spare no effort to promote UX, Chinese UXers have also taken actions. They establish practitioners association, such as UXPA, HBUED, UXREN etc. These organizations build professional websites, release information about UX knowledge, UX recruitment, translation of foreign UX passages. At the same time, they carry out offline activities such as forum and seminar. These organizations not only provide young people with the chance to understand UX, but also provide UXers to communicate with each other. In addition, UX related competitions also played an important role in UX's promotion and popularization. UXD Award, is a very famous domestic user experience design competition for college students. In the competition, college students will join the whole process of product innovation, which is no doubt a valuable experience for them.

3 Internet Development in China and UX

3.1 Chinese User in Changing and Internet

On May 21, 1994, in the computer network information center, Chinese academy of sciences, scientists completed the server settings of Chinese national top-level domain names (.cn), which changed the history that Chinese national top-level domain names relied on the foreign server. Since then, Internet has been in China officially. The development of Internet in China can be divided into three stages.

The first stage is from 1994 to 2002 years or so. The commercial value of Internet rapidly developed. Forces from private sector, commercial capital, and application began to join aggressively into the Internet. Internet showed vigorous development trend. Represented by Sina, Sohu, Netease, Internet portals was created and listed. Tencent, Alibaba and Baidu also began to sprout. Internet giants that constitute China's current Internet business structure were all founded in this period. According to statistics, from 1997 to 2000, China has the largest site quickly from 1500 to 260000. The rapid growth of the Internet has brought huge bubbles, because there is no mature profit model in China. Influenced by the United States, starting in 2000, the bursting of the dotcom bubble started the Internet winter that continued until 2002 when China Mobile carried out value-added service making the Internet companies make profit and get through the winter.

The second stage is from 2001 to 2008, which is often called that the Web 2.0 era. Spent the winter, Chinese Internet companies has formed mature profit pattern of network advertising, network game, search engine and e-commerce and BAT, the big three were listed, which developed a new pattern of the Chinese Internet. More importantly, during this period, the Internet has entered a period of prominent social value. Different from the users at the first stage who is of small amount and passively accepted information, users in this period gradually expand the scale and content, and began to produce content. BBS, blogs and other network media became popular. The influence of network media extended and the citizen-leading Internet culture was taking shape. And Internet also received national attention. President Hu and Premier Wen both had online communications with citizens at this time, which also reflected the trend of Internet that gradually entered the mainstream media.

The third stage is from 2009 to the present and Internet has entered the era of Instant Internet in which time mobile Internet begins to spread. During this period, the Chinese Internet had a full-blown. In many indicators China has become the world's first and China's Internet companies have also begun to rank among the world's top Internet Co. In 2015, "the Internet+" policy develops a favorable environment for Internet and the Internet began to enter traditional industries, changing the Chinese society. With the era of Instant Internet, SNS sites raised. Weibo and WeChat became the representative products and lead a new Internet culture of universal participation. Grass root, post 90s, goddess, fresh meat, Chinese Dama and many hot words and groups became popular because of Internet. With the Internet, people show their personality and express their views. Thus, how to grasp the mentality and characteristics of different users is an important issue for Chinese UXers.

3.2 Design for Chinese Internet Users

Complex users and Internet culture make it difficult to design one product for all. So Chinese Internet companies have to aim at the different user groups and design for them. Among all the user groups, Diaosi and Dama are two important groups, and each has its own character.

Diaosi originated in the Baidu Tieba, referring to those who were born mediocre, and live at the bottom of the society without future and love. The antonym of Diaosi is "GaofuShuai", of which the literal means is someone tall, wealthy and handsome. In terms of its own meaning, Diaosi is a derogatory and indecent word, but with the fermentation of the Internet, Diaosi slowly is endowed with a self-deprecating spirit and significance of resistance. People claim to be a Diaosi and "the success of Diaosi" has also become an inspirational synonymous. In fact, the portrait of Diaosi just represents the characteristics of most Internet users in China now. Three lows – low age, low education, low income – is the typical characteristics of Chinese Internet users as well as Disoasi. The popularity of Diaosi reflects the lost and struggles of the young people in the era of dramatic changes in the value. So how to guide and make use of this value is not only the chance for the Internet but a major event related to the future of the society. As the birthplace of Diaosi culture in China and the gathering spot for grassroots, Baidu Tieba has launched Diaosi festival, letting Disao voice out and set Diaosi right, which triggers a social attention. With Diaosi culture, electronic business platform and hardware vendors play the feelings cards. They use the 'youth', 'dream' as a packaging, creating a classic case of Internet marketing. Some people say that Chinese users are most willing to pay for the feelings.

Different from hot-blooded Diaosi, Dama represents the other side of Chinese characteristics that is conservative but a little blind impulse. Unlike the Poor Diaosi, Dama hold the family finances and are well off. In recent years, Dama become famous for their buying gold and square dance and their actions and their purchasing power is surprising.

Another feature of Dama is that they are new to Internet and smartphones. They are not used to complicated operations and they are used to wind and rain. For them, dream means far less than the discount toilet paper. In 2014 and 2015, with half off of the money, Alipay's double 12 shopping carnival had a success in making Dama install and use mobile Alipay. After the gold rush, Dama begin to interest in Internet finance services. Data shows that per capita investment of women over 55 years is 43 %, higher than the average, which is nearly three times of the post 80s. Not only are the Internet financial products aimed at Dama, in health, beauty, tourism and many other areas, the 'square dance entrepreneurs' have begun Dama design. At present, China has about one hundred million square dance Dama, behind whom, it is likely to be the next one trillion marketing opportunity.

4 Chances and Challenges for Chinese UXers

4.1 New Changes in Internet Products

In the past 20 years, Internet has had a growth from zero to the world level in China. Complete business models and product systems have been formed in social products, e-commerce products, entertainment products and so on. However, we can still find these new chances in these fields for the future.

From the earliest to the BBS time to the WeChat era of instant communication, changing of social products in China can be divided into three stages: the first is the BBS time, represented by Tianya and Mop, which is the beginning of social products realizing the information collection and precipitation instead of the point-to-point communication; moving real interpersonal relationship from offline to online is the next form of social products, such as renren.com, Kaixin001, QQ Zone; the next stage is the current social product and that is micro era. WeChat is for acquaintances social-networking while Weibo for the Public information. In addition, online community and strangers' social networking maintain active. With the changing social product, users also change their habits and preferences. People become open and conservative, which brings many opportunities. First of all, it is about the entertainment of social products. Most of social products users are young people who are pretty curious and chasing for fun features. To be fun is a start point to impress them most. Many social products such as Xiaoka Show and Footprints, which use videos and photos, have ever created popularity. However, how to maintain this fresh attraction, continue it, and ultimately make it an irreplaceable product, is the most critical issue. In addition, population subdivision is another golden mine for social products. According to the characteristics and interest of the population to do the operation of the communities is a trend in the future.

Another important area is the e-commerce platform. After many years of double eleven carnivals, online shopping has become a lifestyle of Chinese users, and is playing a more and more important role. According to CNNIC statistics, until June 2015, China's online shopping users has reached 3.74 billion and the penetration rate of online shopping is up to 55.7 %, which has already surpassed the United States in the scale, becoming the world's largest online retail market. From the birth of e-commerce platform to now, e-commerce products keep a rapid development and finally reach a mature and stable stage. Getting through the price war and logistical war, e-commerce products are also gradually changed and the bred variety of new opportunities in patterns. An important trend is the development of second and third class cities and rural markets. At present, people in first-tier cities are so familiar with online shopping and habits is already very mature. While in less developed areas lacking of resources in, the potential purchase power is really strong, especially in the rural areas. Limited by the network and logistic restrictions, the rural market has been unable to develop. Along with the construction of infrastructure and the popularity of smart phones, the vitality of rural consumers are gradually inspired, which requires a higher slandered of the logistics supporting, after-sales services and other services. Another opportunity is the vertical fields. An array of integrated e-commerce platform has been unable to meet the people deeper shopping needs so a professional platform is undoubtedly a better choice. Whether the new cross-border platform or the relatively mature maternal and beauty makeup platform, both prove the potential energy of the vertical markets.

4.2   Internet+ Traditional Industries

On March 2015, Premier Li Keqiang at the third session of the Twelfth National People's Congress proposed the development of a large table "Internet plus" action plan, the report pointed out that the formulation of "Internet plus" action plan, to promote mobile Internet, cloud computing, big data, networking and modern manufacturing industry combination, to promote e-commerce, Internet and Internet industry the healthy development of Internet financial, guide enterprises to expand the international market. "Internet plus" action plan released, the Internet is no longer confined to the IT industry, will penetrate into the broader field. "Internet plus" the combination of Internet and traditional industries, promote the development of all walks of life. O2O, finance, health care, education… The Internet is quietly changing.

O2O is the most close to the lives of people with the "Internet plus", catering, travel, beauty, massage… In all aspects of people's lives, the Chinese Internet is also experiencing the O2O's entrepreneurial boom, a large number of O2O companies appear, there are a large number of O2O enterprises to die. For O2O products, a good online experience is necessary, however, O2O as a business model, it is more important to provide consumers with quality products and services. Consumers can buy high quality and inexpensive goods always hope, hope can get value for money or value for money services. Therefore, the Internet should become a powerful tool for O2O, O2O cost savings, improve efficiency, to provide excellent support for the line service.

The first combination of financial and Internet should be online banking, but the role of online banking is nothing more than the Internet means to operate the banking business. At present, Internet finance services in China have been extended to the field of banking, lending, credit and other multiple fields. In early 2015, China experienced a stock mania, which brought a very large growth of financial tool products. Except for Internet financial products' nature itself, when people use Internet financial services, what they are most concerned about is nothing more than two points. The first is security. Financial security and the security of personal information are the biggest concerns when people using the Internet financial service. The second is the usability, which is the distinguishing feature between the Internet financial service and traditional financial institutions. For example, Yuebao let people use and become familiar with Internet fund products by simple purchasing process. Future Internet financial products are obligated to make financial services simple and easy to use under the premise of ensuring the security.

In the field of more relationship to the people's livelihood, like education and medical treatment, Internet is no longer just a tool, but a part of the social productive forces, playing a role in resource coordination and promoting the development of the industry. Online education and wisdom health care provide solutions to problems in receiving education and seeing a doctor, so that social resources can be used more efficiently and the community can be more equitable. We can imagine that more problems can be solved with the combination of the Internet and these areas.

4.3 Chances and Challenges for UXers

Currently, Internet industry is becoming a sunrise industry in China, many passionate young people devote to Internet companies. Because of development potential and challenging work, Internet companies are favored by many job hunters, especially those who lack of computer professional background. We have several advices for those who have engaged in the work of UX and those who are going to join the UX:

For new recruits, we recommend that you should choose company or platform as large as possible. As a new area, education of UX industry gets behind, UX is not on the major list in universities of China. Small companies lack of professional UX growth systems due to their size. By contrast, large companies have to pay more attention to UX for the brand strategy and long-term interests. For large companies, the game between commercial interests and UX is a big issue concerning survival and development, if a deviation occurred, it may have unpredictable consequences. In large companies, new recruits can not only be access to best products in the industry, participating in product design process with millions or billions scale, but also harvest rapid growth in professional UX training system of large companies, becoming professionals who can stake a claim.

For colleagues in the industry, we suggest that we continue to maintain the state of learning and improving. UX is an interdisciplinary subject, involving product design, operations, user research, technology development, etc. It requires practitioners to be proficient in one area and grasp relevant knowledge as much as possible. This advice is to solve the growth problem of each individual practitioners, allowing practitioners to realize that outstanding UX design is a multi-disciplinary work and need different professional colleagues to work together. Only balanced synthesis of all aspects of knowledge, we can get the most suitable, the best solution to provide the best experience for users.

Finally, for the development of the entire industry, we hope that colleagues do not forget the beginning of the heart and grasp the fundamental. UX is born with the rise of the Internet industry, new direction and new products appears everyday. In the face of new changes, practitioners are often confused, following blindly. We recommend that UX practitioners need to pay close attention to needs of users and specific product forms in different social periods. In case of social products, for a decade, user's social and other basic demands did not change much, but in different stages of Internet development, the product could be BBS, QQ, happy network, micro blogging or micro channel. Although products like adorable face or foot note caused a boom, but when their heat retreat, these products did not touch users or stimulate users' demand deeply, now it seems to be a flash in the pan. In a word, consider users as the center and understand users better is still the most basic work for UX.

References

Law, L.C., Roto, V., Hassenzahl, M., et al.: Understanding, scoping and defining user experience. Proc. CHI 4–9 (2009)

Kremer, S., Michailidou, I., von Saucken, C., Lindemann, U.: User experience milestones. In: Marcus, A. (ed.) DUXU 2014, Part IV. LNCS, vol. 8520, pp. 308–318. Springer, Heidelberg (2014)

Hassenzahl, M., Tractinsky, N.: User experiencea research agenda. Behav. Inf. Technol. **25**(2), 91–97 (2006)

百度用户体验部. 体验·度: 简单可依赖的用户体验. 清华大学出版社 (2014)

申玲玲, 李炜. 中国网络文化研究综述. 社会科学战线 (7), 159–162 (2011)

诺曼. 情感化设计. 电子工业出版社 (2005)

诺曼. 设计心理学. 中信出版社 (2003)

陈建功, 李晓东. 中国互联网发展的历史阶段划分. 互联网天地 (3) (2014)

梁小杰, 袁涛. 浅析产品设计中的用户体验. 商场现代化 (21), 43–44 (2011)

林钦. 重新定义用户体验—形而下和形而上的融合. 设计 (9), 42–42 (2015)

刘毅. 中国市场中的用户体验设计现状. 包装工程 (4), 70–73 (2011)

The Utilization of Chinese Traditional Elements in Social Media Marketing of Indigenous Mobile Terminals

Li Zhang[✉] and Xin Chang

Baidu, Beijing, People's Republic of China
{zhangli27,changxin03}@baidu.com

Abstract. This paper mainly discusses the phenomenon in recent years that many brands are using traditional Chinese elements in the mobile terminal marketing so as to integrate creativity. The full text has a classic CCTV advertisement "ink" as an index, the classification of Chinese traditional elements, the interpretation of the Chinese mainland's popular mobile marketing methods that are prevailing nowadays, Baidu and McDonald's "Chinese style" case and its marketing effect, and the comprehensive analysis of this marketing phenomenon, and the forecast of its development trend.

Keywords: Chinese traditional elements · Chinese style · Mobile equipment · Marketing · Brand · Culture · Consumption

1 Introduction

Due to the gradual increase of national power, the strengthening of national self-confidence, the public's interest in their traditional culture as well as other factors, the cultivation of aesthetic taste is changing from a western style to one which more authentically Chinese. Popular mobile terminal marketing in the last two years (which mainly refers to smart phones and tablet PCs) and consumer preferences directly reflect in the forefront of the new media. How can the integration of traditional elements in mobile marketing helps businesses spread better? What can we learn from the marketing paradigm? What kind of cross-border innovative ideas can we employ in there? These are worthy of our considerations.

2 The Composition of a Typical Chinese Style Advertisement

Case: The image of a Chinese CCTV publicity film *Ink.*

Brief introduction: In 2009, China Central Television which dominates the Chinese traditional social media launched a new image of the *Ink* in order to tie in with an earlier proposed strategy which was *Enhancing Professional Levels and Implementation of brand advertising business* and fit with the image of the slogan which is *Believe in the Power of the Brand.* As shown by its name, the promo uses Chinese ink painting as the core carrier, and combines Chinese ink painting with advanced CG technology together

© Springer International Publishing Switzerland 2016
A. Marcus (Ed.): DUXU 2016, Part II, LNCS 9747, pp. 416–423, 2016.
DOI: 10.1007/978-3-319-40355-7_40

with the effect of changing and expansions of the form by putting ink into water to show famous landscapes and other elements of Chinese culture. It also presents the developmental history of CCTV and China as well as reflecting that Chinese culture has a long history, it is profound and all-encompassing and has the ability to change in accordance with the changing situation.

Composition: The *Ink* propaganda film constitutes three main parts which are the style of Chinese painting, traditional Chinese culture symbols and a text of traditional Chinese philosophy.

2.1   The Style of Chinese Paintings

Chinese paintings originated during the Han Dynasty (202 BC–AD 220). The main tools used are brushes, inks, painting colors and papers.

The artist dips a brush into water, ink and different colors, which together with the use of a number of strong or light-colored pens will give rise to vivid images of figurative and freehand figures, landscapes, flowers and birds among other things that are painted on the paper. These images are reflective of the ancient Chinese people's understanding of the cosmos, nature, society and other associated political, philosophical and religious ideas. The CCTV advertisement lays out esthetic and fantasy conceptions with the help of Chinese paintings' agile and smooth ink textures, simple but long lasting appeal of grey black and white colors, and ethereal and transparent composition. Also, the ink and water for black implies the ancient Chinese philosophy of *Yin* and *Yang*. The effect of ink diffusion is memorable to audiences and gives them multiple and implicit impressions.

2.2   Selection of Traditional Chinese Cultural Symbols

There are various images in the film that are characteristic of Chinese features. Such as landscape paintings, China carp, crane, dragon, the Great Wall, Tai Chi, etc. In the eyes of the Chinese people, each of them are associated with profound implications. For instance, Chinese landscape symbolizes elegance and tranquility, carp denotes continual upward progress, cranes represent longevity, the dragon often symbolizes noble auspicious prospects and Tai Chi means Yin and Yang and so on. When these cultural symbol which imply best wishes and good will are combined with modern CG technology, traditional Chinese culture shows its new vitality in a new way. As a result, the audience can truly feel the profound connotations of the CCTV brand.

2.3   Analysis of the Text of Traditional Chinese Philosophy

The text of the promotional film begins with the idea of *from the invisible to the visible* and *from the bounded to no border*. It ends with the idea of *believing the power of the brand*. These ideas are all presented in the form of Chinese calligraphy which has the typical features of Chinese philosophy. In my opinion, the text aims to show how the brand established itself and became popular from scratch. Once a brand is formed, commodity is no longer a specific concept but is endowed with intangible values and possesses enormous energy. When the brand has the power to influence other brands, it is able to bring huge benefits to them. Moreover, *Wuji is Taiji* in the ancient Chinese philosophy. *Taiji bears the masculine essence in motion and rests in still at its utmost, whereas it bears the Yin in stillness and comes back to motion at its utmost again. As Yang and Yin illustrated, motion and stillness bear one another and are both roots to each other.*

3 What Are the Traditional Chinese Elements

3.1 Definition by *Baidu Baike* (Baidu Encyclopedia)

The elements of traditional Chinese culture are generally referred to most of the Chinese people (including the identity of overseas Chinese) and the condensation of the traditional culture of the Chinese national spirit. These elements are reflective of national dignity and ethnic interests, symbols or customary habits.

In addition, traditional Chinese elements that are formed during the process of national integration, evolution and development were created by the Chinese people who inherited and reflected Chinese humanistic spirits and folk psychology. They are cultural achievements with Chinese characteristics. Moreover, those elements include tangible material symbols and invisible spiritual contents. In other words, they are material and cultural elements and cultural and spiritual elements.

3.2 Classification of Chinese Traditional Elements

Examples of Chinese Classical Literatures and Thoughts. Myths: PanGu created heaven and earth, NvWa made man, kingYu combating the flood, The Goddess Chang'E flew to the moon, the cowherd and the weaving maid.

Few historic stories: Taking Oath in the Peach Garden, Return the jade intact to the State of Zhao, Stand in the snow to wait upon Master Cheng respectfully, Every bush and tree looks like an enemy.

Prose poetry: *The book of songs, On the Goddess of Luo River, Orchid Pavilion, spring and Autumn, Peach Blossom Spring.*

Philosophy: *the book of changes, Analects of Confucius, Sutra, Moral classics*, Neo Confucianism.

Unique Artistic Expressions of Chinese Characteristics. Traditional art: painting, calligraphy, Chinese rubbing, fan carving.

Traditional music: musical instruments such as Guqin, guzheng and erhu, music *high mountain and flowing water, house of Flying Daggers, plum blossom, spring snow* and others.

Traditional opera dance: Beijing opera, Shaoxing opera, Henan opera, *Peach Blossom Fan, Mu Guiying, Snow* command.

Folk and folk paper-cut patterns: folk such as antithetical couplet, lanterns, patterns such as the knot, dragon beast, Chinese auspicious clouds, etc.

Religion, Medicine, Food, Agriculture, Traditional Festivals and Other Fields Closely Related to Our Lives. We do not realize that they nourish us and play essential roles in our lives.

4 Popular Mobile Marketing Methods in China - Mainland at the Present Stage

According to CNNIC 37th China Internet report, December 2015, the number of Chinese Internet users reached 688 million and the number of Chinese mobile phones users reached 620 million. The use of mobile Internet users among the population accounted for 90.1 % in 2015, up from 85.8 % in 2014. For desktop computers, laptops and tablet PCs the user rate declined, the phone constantly diverting other personal Internet uses.

During the marketing process, 35.5 % of the enterprises carry out marketing promotions through the mobile Internet. 21.9 % of the companies used to pay for promotions. Due to the user's behavioral move to mobile terminals, as such, mobile marketing will be taken by enterprises as an important channel for promotion. At the current time, China is generally using the following types of mobile marketing.

4.1 App Advertising

App advertising, also known as In-App advertising, refers to smart phones and tablet PCs or this type of mobile devices in the third party applications built-in advertising, belonging to the sub category of mobile advertising.

Thanks to the popularity of carrier Applications, the rising of App advertising and the widespread use of tablet computers and large screen touch mobile phones and other hardware, Wi-Fi, 3G, 4G that liberate the restrictions of cellular data flow, and Apple App Store ecosystem brought by the new interactive experience, prompted the significant increase of app audiences and app developers. For App developers, there is a need for the cellular data flow to be cashed. For the brand business, advertising needs to be changed in accordance with consumer attentions. As a result, App built-in advertising came into being. If we classify App advertising according to the advertising performances, APP advertising can be categorized into text ads, image ads, Animation advertising, advertising video, audio advertising; in column can be divided into banner ads, start screen advertising and plaque advertising, recommended wall, integral wall and video advertising.

4.2 H5 Advertising

H5 advertising is the use of HTML5 coding techniques to achieve digital advertising. It not only refers to the generation using HTML5 technology to produce Web advertising pages, but also covers for HTML5 and other related social media that utilizes the HTML5 technology of interactive advertising. Currently, mobile phones and tablet are the main routes of transmission. And in theory, computer or digital TV and all of the mobile platforms can be the entrances.

Compared with traditional advertising media, H5 advertising has the following advantages:

- Demonstrate quickly, can be infinitely modified
- Feedback in a timely manner, with accurate results
- Not limited by the time of delivery and the number of delivering times
- It has greater influence and greater potential of influence
- The rich dynamic effect can be interactive, and the mode of sound and picture transmission is more mature.

4.3   The Promotion of Wechat Public Accounts

The Wechat public account is applied and used by developers or merchants on the Wechat public platform. Through public accounts, businesses can communicate and interact with particular groups of individuals by text, images, audio, video in the micro channel, which are now mainstream online and offline micro interactive marketing methods.

According to Tencent official data, as of January 2015, the number of Wechat public accounts has reached 7,500,000 with growth of 15 thousand accounts per day.

4.4   Viral Video

Viral video can be regarded as the latest form of virus transmission, with the latest media channels, making video clips on the Internet to get a large area of communications. According to the style of production, viral video is usually very humorous and funny, some of which are natural and grassroots. Accidentally, viral video will obtain lots of attention and reproduce with the formation of the spread of the virus. There are some commercial short videos that resonate with audiences emotionally and achieve viral propagation by creating creative commercial packaging.

4.5   Digital Picture Marketing

In some of the private or public platforms, individuals or businesses strategically publish pictures and convey obscure or explicit and visual information to audiences in order to reap economic benefits.

4.6   Others

5   Concrete Case Analysis

5.1   Local Brand

Baidu. A large scale of high traffic pressure is happening in China every year before and after the lunar New Year. The Spring Festival transport time lasts from the last month of the lunar year to next January 25th.

The Spring Festival is in the middle of the period and lasts for around 40 days. Spring Festival transportation problem is always an important issue for the Chinese people; it has even been called the largest periodic migration in the history of mankind. In the last 30 years, the size of the population taking rate in this migration grow from 37 million to 100 million passengers in 2015. It is equal to the combined population of Africa, Europe, the Americas, and Oceania. Due to the reasons of a huge migrating population, relatively short migration time and the time of year, this transportation period often causes sea, land and air transportation peaks. Therefore, it becomes a common phenomenon that train ticket becomes "hard to get".

From queuing in the train station to buying tickets online nowadays, grabbing tickets has become a tricky tactic. There are many different online ticket purchasing systems. Mobile Baidu, an application launched by Baidu, is a convenience tool for mobile phone users to use Baidu search service at anytime, anywhere. Let's look at how mobile Baidu showcase their highlighted features:

Mobile Baidu combines the myth story which the Chinese people are familiar with the train tickets online purchasing systems to convey to audiences that the Mobile Baidu has functions to help them enhance the purchase success rate and to reserve tickets quickly.

The mobile communication project uses the plane of Chinese style picture (mythological figures, Xiangyun pattern, carving fonts, plain rice paper background color) as well as the patterns of the dynamic effects (immortals display their skills) in order to create a kind of antiquity and modern humorous coexisting situation. For example, Erlangshen is an immortal figure from the Taoist legend, *FengShenYanYi*. He is infinite and unpredictable and has seventy-two metamorphoses, a third eye on his forehead is said to be able to see what happened thousands of miles away, and can turn all illusions into truth. Here he can see many train tickets through the Internet which greatly enhances the success rate of the purchaser. His ears are able to catch sounds sent by winds. He is a God in ancient Chinese mythology, with a pair of long ears, and can hear sounds a hundred miles away. In the picture, he is seriously asking about the news of the train ticket. This tells the users that after they use the Mobile Baidu cloud to buy tickets they can immediately receive a message notification and pay for it as soon as possible to secure tickets. Another example is Guan Yu. He is a famous fellow in the Eastern Han dynasty. In the masterpiece *Romance of the Three Kingdoms,* Guan Yu is portrayed as a loyalty general figure. His legendary story has been eulogized widely for thousands of years. He was honored as Guan Gong in folk tales. In the picture, Guan Yu is riding his beloved red horse and highlights that Mobile Baidu has the advantage of securing tickets three days in advance. Nezha, Zhuge Liang, Avalokitesvara also show the fast and intelligent performance of products by their speed, wit and "Buddhism" respectively.

By using the myths characters who carry auspicious meaning to promote product features, it is easy for the customers to feel the "blessing" meaning of the products and realize that Mobile Baidu pays attention to people's livelihood and sincerely helps them solve the difficulties encountered in their daily life. The form is full of warmth, wisdom and without losing fun.

5.2   Localized Promotion of Overseas Brands for the Chinese Market

McDonald's. This year is the twenty-fifth year of McDonald's in China. Over these twenty-five years, western style fast food as represented by McDonald's is becoming more and more adaptable to Chinese tastes. This can be show by McDonald's new products in recent years.

Their series posters have a lot of Chinese daily supper symbols, like steamed bread and a steamer. These elements are very familiar to the Chinese people. And this picture combination shows that the products are combined with Chinese and Western characteristics. In another group of marketing pictures which are filled with Chinese folk characteristics, you can see McDonald's grasp of folk culture such as a Steamer, dustpan, tea tray, basket, small-sized artworks (it is also living articles) exudes a strong flavor of life. With exquisite bamboo, it can easily evoke memories for the native people. Looking at the green MACARON and attractive COFFE, audience appetites will be aroused quickly.

For traditional festivals and solar terms, lots of brands will launch the corresponding marketing behaviors during the ins and outs of the festival. The next example is McDonald's micro-blog photo released on the day of the *Chushu*: The pronunciation of the first word Chinese "potato chips" (Shu Tiao) and "Summer heat"(Shu Qi) is the same. In the day of *Chushu*, McDonald's using homophone to sell potato chips, and making the copy akin to a calendar appearance, it's very creative.

6   Marketing Effect

6.1   Brand Social Impact

Putting the elements of traditional Chinese culture into brand marketing activities, and mingling with enterprise images, enables the integration of business philosophy and corporate cultures so as to create a unique style of enterprise marketing. Behind this kind of marketing phenomenon, traditional culture is changed into a spirit and a blessing, because the Chinese people respect cultures and pursue the embodiment of beauty. It is also about overseas business contacts that understand and accept the Chinese culture in a good way. This is an important way for Chinese culture to spread outwardly.

To integrate the traditional elements into the brand's mobile marketing, various kind of media can be compared with this approach in diffusion, influence and penetration. It makes the brand fresh and more vital. People can feel the meaning and significance of the brand through the marketing activities. This self-sustaining native culture significantly helps to promote consumers from passive understanding of Chinese culture to taking the initiative of understanding it. It also enhances people's sense of national identity and makes the whole society advocate traditional Chinese good habits.

6.2   Public Perception of the Brand (Public Praise)

In the process of shaping the brand image, traditional culture plays a catalytic role. It makes the brand carry more classical charm, advocates a noble way of life and a life attitude and a consumption concept that are full of humanistic feelings. It also allows consumers to remember the brand in their minds. Compared to contemporary marketing that often directly copies western aesthetics, it makes the brand become more unique and improve the awareness, visibility, reputation and market share of the brand. Via the use of elements in traditional Chinese culture, it conveys to the audience that the brand is of good local cultural heritage, and bring people spiritual enjoyment and spiritual comfort. As such, the brand narrows the distance with the audience and create a good reputation among the consumers.

6.3 Promotion of Sales

The use of traditional Chinese elements to shape the brand with deep cultural atmosphere, is to convey an important message to the consumers: "I'm native, I have rich cultural connotations, you and I are the root homology. I am able to touch the Chinese feelings that are lying deep down inside you." Its audiences is very obvious, those who are curious about Chinese culture and have a strong interest in and strong recognitions of traditional Chinese culture.

The current local mobile marketing linked online and offline, across music, animation, video, interactive and other media. With the mixture of traditional Chinese elements, it burst into new diverse forms of creativity, attracted to the majority of young people in the local audience. Today's young people are addicted to smart devices and the Internet, they have their own social circles and love to share, and they have strong demands to the novelty of the games. In recent years, the spending of younger consumers is growing rapidly and the attention of young consumers will be able to maximize the realization of economic income has been noticed by the business sectors.

This way mobile marketing can spread through the complex information chain. No matter which modern city or remote country, and regardless of local or foreign, people can quickly get and spread those brand messages through a smart device. With the use of the existing convenient online payment systems and efficient logistics systems that can respond to consumer behavior, brand owners will be able to benefit from the effect of communication. Additionally, Data can be checked, which will result in greater economic benefits than traditional sales channels.

7   Conclusions

The combination of Chinese traditional elements and the social marketing of mobile terminals have enriched the consumer culture. In recent years, it has become even more competitive in the promotion of the brand. It is also a marketing method that has potential capacity. Brands and consumers generally recognize this form of marketing style, which is a product of the development of the rapid consumption era.

DUXU for Social Innovation
and Sustainability

A Review of Intervention Studies Aimed at Domestic Water Conservation

Nicholas Benzoni and Cassandra Telenko[✉]

Georgia Institute of Technology, Atlanta, USA
nbenzoni3@gatech.edu, cassandra.telenko@me.gatech.edu

Abstract. We must overhaul how we view and use water to ensure that there is enough potable water to meet the rising global demand. To achieve such changes, many researchers have developed intervention methods aimed at promoting water conservation in the home. Single or combined styles of intervention, applied from a range of a few days to eight months, achieve a wide range (2 % to 28 %) of water savings. However, what factors play the biggest roles in achieving such savings remain as of yet unclear. Two factors are highlighted in this review: an intervention's visibility and the climate context in which the intervention was conducted. This paper provides a comprehensive review of intervention methods; in doing so it summarizes findings of current research and provides recommendations for future work.

Keywords: Water · Conservation · Intervention · Feedback · Behavior

1 Introduction

Worldwide, 663 million people do not have access to clean water, and over 1.5 billion are affected by water-related disease each year [1]. To exacerbate the issue our demand for water has grown at double the rate of the global population. Further, our ability to supply clean water to the rapidly growing global population is quickly decreasing. Despite these figures, water is largely treated as an infinite resource by wealthy nations. Many first-world consumers do not understand the process water must go through before exiting the tap in one's home, the high associated environmental cost of these processes, nor the dwindling supply of per capita potable water.

This misunderstanding of water's value, coupled with the hidden water costs of many in-home processes, leads US consumers to demand far more water than is necessary for a comfortable life. The average American uses about 98 gallons per day *at home,* including irrigation [2]. In comparison, the average European consumes about 53 gallons per day municipally, and the average Sub-Saharan citizen consumes 3-5 gallons per day. Peter Gleick [3] concluded that the basic water needs for a human to reasonably, drink, bathe, prepare food, and maintain a clean environment is about 50 l a day, or 13.2 gallons. This figure does not account for the production of one's food, nor the maintenance of exotic landscapes.

How so much water is used is an important question, with a unique answer for each person and region. Mayer *et al.* [4] reported that indoor water usage in the US is generally

© Springer International Publishing Switzerland 2016
A. Marcus (Ed.): DUXU 2016, Part II, LNCS 9747, pp. 427–438, 2016.
DOI: 10.1007/978-3-319-40355-7_41

broken down as such; leaks 13.7 %, showers 16.8 %, clothes washer 22 %, toilets 26.7 % and faucets 15.7 %. Additionally, about 50-70 % of total domestic water is used outdoors for watering lawns and gardens [4].

Though at-home water use only accounts for about 11 % of the total US freshwater withdrawals [5], this type of usage is generally the most *intimate*, thus affecting the residential sector may result in significant savings in *other, larger,* sectors of use – more informed consumers may increase demand for water conservation by industry and government. However, even if far reaching effects are not accomplished, there are still massive savings to be had in the domestic sector alone. Amy Vickers estimates that a 30 % reduction in US household water usage would result in a savings of more than 5.4 billion gallons a day [5].

In recent years many new technologies for saving resources in-home have been developed and commercialized [6]. For water, these methods primarily take the form of water-efficient appliances and appliance "add-ons", such as faucet and shower aerators. Though ten states in the US now require new housing to be built with water-efficient appliances, there are still tens of millions of inefficient, old-fashioned appliances being used in the U.S. [7]. Thus it is important to motivate and enable homeowners to conserve water as effectively as possible. A system or device that "reaches out and affects" a user is termed an *intervention*.

Interventions in this review take two primary forms: before-use, termed antecedent, and after-use, termed consequential. Common antecedent interventions are educational, such as pamphlets containing water-saving tips, and consultation, such as goal-setting. Consequence interventions primarily take the form of usage tracking and comparison (feedback), and may sometimes take the form of reward/penalty systems. Feedback is a complicated mechanism and has many facets which may affect a consumer's response. How one displays data can have a large effect on the overall success [8]. Further, usage feedback is reliant on some system of monitoring a consumer's water usage. Monitoring poses a technological/infrastructural barrier to feedback systems, which may be overcome through the use of many types of systems, pre-existing and novel. Figure 1 illustrates, generally, how and when each method affects the subject.

This paper aims to create an accessible review of interventions for water consumption. Though many of the same strategies are used when dealing with water and electricity [6], the nature of the resources are rather different; one cannot see a kWh, but can generally envision or observe a gallon of water. The ways in which people interact with water and electricity differ greatly. These differences reasonably separate electricity and water, meaning that conclusions drawn about the conservation of one may not be true for the other. This review is distinguished from reviews of water conservation [9, 10], limited to smart metering systems as it focuses on all types of intervention systems and methods.

This review is intended to provide insight into what methods have been most effective, and what work is still to be done. Section 2 describes the method and criteria for including publications in this review. Sections 3 and 4 summarize and analyze antecedent and consequential intervention studies, respectively. Section 5 summarizes trends found in the previous sections and discusses the need for the consideration of mental

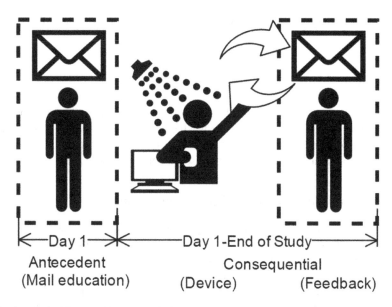

Fig. 1. Antecedent intervention occurs before the activity, consequential occurs during and after.

context and visibility in design. Lastly, Sect. 6 provides concrete recommendations on designing interventions, and on material which is useful to include in papers about such.

2   Method

The goal of this paper is to provide the reader with some idea as to why some water interventions succeeded while others did not. This paper also serves to provide a summary of a range of interventions. To find the papers reviewed here various databases were employed – Google scholar, Georgia Tech library system, Wiley Online – leading to many journal and conference papers associated with interventions for water conservation. The references of each paper were examined in order to find relevant publications, as was the list of "cited-by" papers. This is called the "snowball" method and has been shown to effectively reveal high quality papers [11].

In order to be included in this review a study had to either propose a product design with a functioning prototype, with results, and/or the study had to develop and test an intervention system aimed specifically at household water behaviors. The one exception to this criteria is a work which examines the great success of a governmental campaign [12]. Due to the consistency and quality of peer-reviewed academic studies, all reviewed studies are published academic papers.

To evaluate how effective an intervention was, studies generally measure the change in net water consumption versus a control, and/or rely on subject-reported changes in behavior or consumption. The inclusion of a behavior change survey provides insight into what the intervention succeeded or failed in affecting. These reported behavior changes imply some activities have a higher elasticity than others and provide insight into how a system may be optimized.

3   Antecedent Interventions

Antecedent interventions inform user behavior before the behavior is carried out. They work by supplying information in order to change the user's attitude towards water usage, teach how an individual's actions affect the big picture (i.e. one's locus of control) or provide action strategies that enable the user to conserve water [13].

3.1   Studies Providing Antecedent Tips and Information

Five studies were found that provided an experimental group with antecedent intervention [14–18]. In these studies, only water-saving tips and/or water related education were provided. The first four studies, summarized in this section, failed to achieve savings using only the antecedent education, but the fifth had measurable success.

The first study examined the difference in effectiveness of forms of education [17]. Researchers examined behavior of two education groups; one focused on water-use impacts on society, and the other oriented towards financial concerns. These groups were compared with two control groups, one of which was not informed when their usage information was being recorded. Although inconclusive, the results indicated that long-term consequence education was more motivating than economic education.

The second study, by Schultz et al. [15], examined the relative impacts of three information types. Only one of these was antecedent: tips for saving. The other two were consequential: social comparisons, and 'injunctive' comparisons (i.e. with an associated happy/sad face). Their ANOVA revealed no difference between the group given only information and tips compared with the control group. The feedback aspect of this study is discussed later in the consequence intervention section.

In the third study [14], 26,000 residents of Cobb County, GA were split into three groups and sent a single letter: (1) one with tips and information, and a message imploring conservation of water, (2) another given the same as (1) but with message stating that the participant was either higher or lower than average and (3) the final group was given both of the previous conditions along with a strong social comparison, detailing exactly how much more or less water a participant used compared with the average. In the first year the groups' savings were 0.5 %, 2.7 % and 4.8 % respectively, but the following year this diminished to 0 %, 0 %, and 1 %, respectively.

In the fourth study, 166 households were divided up into three groups, one was given attunement labels to place on water-intensive appliances, the second was given social-comparative feedback, the third was given only information pamphlets containing the same information as the labels from group one [18]. While the attunement labels group achieved 23 % total savings, the ANOVA tests revealed no significant reductions for the other two comparison groups. This indicates that information, if consumed out of the context of usage is much less effective than having that same information displayed at the point of use.

The fifth study, with a successful antecedent-only group, had results which starkly contrast with the previous results [16]. Studying behavior in a drought-stricken region of southeast Queensland, Australia, researchers divided 221 households into three groups: (1) an information only group, (2) a social norm (i.e. "X % of people conserve water") plus information group and (3) a group given tailored end-use feedback from smart meters with information. During the 3-month intervention period all groups achieved about 10 % total water usage reduction (11.3 l/person/day). After the intervention, all groups continued to reduce consumption, however group one, the information only group, achieved the highest peak savings of about 13.3 % (15 l/p/d) three months *after* the intervention. The groups eventually returned to pre-intervention usage levels, possibly due to flooding the area experienced after the study was completed. The discrepancy between the Queensland study's 13 % and the much lower savings of previous four studies' indicates that the *context* of intervention plays into its effectiveness, which is discussed further in Sect. 5. This fifth study [16] additionally stands out because it occurs after a campaign conducted by the Queensland Water Commission (QWC) from 2006 to 2009 [12].

The Target 140 Campaign (T140) was an eight month campaign to promote water conservation in response to "the worst drought in 100 years" [12]. The objective of the campaign was to reduce the per capita water usage of the Queensland area to 140 l per person per day. The T140 campaign eventually succeeded in reducing average consumption from about 165 L/p/d to of 129 L/p/d. Further, once the restrictions were lifted and the campaign over, residents continued to use less than 140 l/p/d, implying that there had been a durable shift in the values and attitudes of the people. In order to get residents to cooperate, the QWC ran commercials showing the dams at low capacity, ran billboard advertisements and targeted a single big behavior, 'the four minute shower'; by distributing over 1.1 M shower timers.

3.2 Cognitive Dissonance

Cognitive dissonance is the uncomfortable sensation of having inconsistent beliefs, attitudes, and/or actions, and may motivate an individual to change in order to make them consistent [19]. Two studies reviewed used cognitive dissonance to motivate water savings. Both of the studies used surveys to invoke cognitive dissonance in the participants. The first study [20] showed that people subjected to cognitive dissonance proceeded to take 26.9 % shorter showers than the control group while those who were only exposed to either a pledge, or a survey of usage habits were only 18 % shorter. Both groups showed significant shower habit changes compared to the control.

Aitken, McMahon *et al.* [21] hand-delivered surveys to 273 households containing tips on water saving. These surveys were either structured to invoke cognitive dissonance or they were paired with social comparative feedback. Both groups were shown artificial averages, 10 % lower than actual averages, to enlarge the gap attitude and performance. The participants' water usage was then recorded over a three-week period, and once again after this period. Directly after the intervention, the participants in the dissonance group who started at high usage levels lowered their water usage by 7.5 % while the participants with initially low usage levels achieved 2.8 % savings. In contrast, the comparative feedback groups achieved a 4 % reduction, and a 7 % *increase* respectively. After three weeks the high usage groups had reduced total usage by 6 % and 4 % for cognitive dissonance and comparative feedback respectively, while the low usage groups both returned to pre-intervention levels. These results imply that cognitive dissonance is more effective at motivating immediate behavior change than commitment or mindfulness of usage.

3.3   Antecedent Interventions: Conclusion

Information distribution is the most common form of antecedent intervention and has nominal effects. In contrast, information within a drought context was more effective at motivating change [15, 18]. In the drought context of the Queensland Target 140 campaign, residents had already reduced usage from an average of 300 to 165 l per person per day before the T140 campaign, and the changes were lasting. The studies indicate that when a population directly understands the need or benefit of water conservation, they are more willing to change their water behaviors [12, 18].

Thus people need to be both motivated *and* taught how to conserve water. Motivation may come in the form of education, climate necessity, social pressures, or by inciting a state of cognitive dissonance.

4   Consequence Interventions

Consequence interventions utilize "feedback" and come in two primary forms: negative/positive-reinforcement, and information. Informational feedback means that a user is simply given data about his or her usage. Attari *et al.* [22] and Beal [22, 23] have independently confirmed that people often have little idea of how much water they use, or what the most effective means of conservation are. Thus informational feedback may inform people of the consequences of their actions, enabling them to better their habits.

Erickson *et al.*'s [24] 2012 study used a website that allowed 303 households to monitor their water usage in near real time over a 15 week period. The website provided water saving tips, as well as social and historical comparisons of usage. Participants achieved an overall 6.6 % reduction in consumption compared with the experimental control data acquired during first 9 weeks of pilot study. However, only 35 % (106 of 303 households) of the participants reported logging into the portal website. Of these users, 61 % reported making a change to their household's water infrastructure.

Schultz *et al.*'s [15] 2014 study had 301 households; each household received either no feedback or one of two types of feedback by web or mail. One feedback group received personalized information about their water usage and a comparison of their usage to that of similar households. The other feedback group received identical information with an additional happy/sad face expressing social approval/disapproval. Each group only received a single packet of information. The first group achieved 26 % savings, while the group with the approval/disapproval face saved only 16 % over the following week compared with control.

Geller *et al.*'s 1983 study [25] provided daily and weekly written feedback to 129 households. This feedback contained the previous day's water usage compared to the median, the percentage change compared with the baseline data, and smiling/frowning faces. This feedback was given alone, or paired with water-savings devices, antecedent educational handbooks, or both devices and education, for 5 weeks. The feedback-only group increased water consumption by 1.36 %, while the no-intervention group managed to reduce consumption by 3.4 %. In this study the devices only group achieved the highest savings (9.5 %), followed by devices and feedback (7.7 %), and devices and education (6.9 %). Educational handbooks alone had almost no effect (0.7 % reduction).

4.1 Feedback Device Interventions

Device interventions allow users to monitor their water consumption during the time of use. These devices are either ambient, meaning the user gets an abstract idea of his/her usage, or indexical, meaning s/he receives an actual numerical value of his/her usage. Some of the devices below do not have experimental data justifying the design. All of the devices reviewed here are intended to reduce water consumption either in the shower or at the faucet, each of which accounts for about 20 % of the water used in home, and both are believed to be high elasticity activities [26].

Arroyo *et al.*'s Waterbot was a forerunner of device-oriented water intervention systems [27]. Waterbot attached to the spigot of a faucet, and included a two bar display (indicating current usage and average usage respectively), a speaker, and colored LED's that changed color according to the water temperature. Waterbot combines many strategies to affect the user's water usage: positive and negative reinforcements, 'just-in-time prompts' accomplished by audio feedback, and social/historical comparison via the bar graph (with other users of the same faucet). The pilot study of Waterbot took place over two months in a laboratory environment with 15 users, the change in water usage was not reported. Overall the users reported *not* becoming annoyed with Waterbot; 12 of 15 were still engaged after two months, and some wanted more sounds integrated into the system.

"Show-me" by Kappel *et al.* [28] is an attachment to showers which causes a tower of LEDs to illuminate proportionate to how much water has been used. This method of feedback is non-intrusive, non-judgmental, and allows users to set goals however they prefer, such as reducing a shower by 2 LEDs – corresponding to a 10 L savings. The pilot study of Show-me was conducted in 4 households, where it was installed for 3 weeks. The average shower was reduced about 20 % (10 L) and the device prompted discussion about usage among the participants.

Willis *et al.* conducted a similar experiment in Australia with 151 households over 2 years [29]. Forty-four of the households were equipped with the indexical display, showing exactly how much water was used in each shower, attached to their showerheads. Participants given the displays achieved an average of a 27 % reduction in shower volume, which equates to about 10 % of total water usage.

In their study "UpStream", Kuznetsov *et al.* [30] developed three unique displays for the shower; one ambient, one semi-ambient, and one indexical, as well as a bar graph indicator which attached to a faucet. They used microphones attached to microcontrollers to monitor flowrates at 0.2 gallon resolution with less than 10 % error. The pilot studies took place in a semi-public dorm setting and in four private single homes. In the semi-public setting, many users were attracted by the novelty of the devices, increasing faucet usage by 33–125 %. In the privatized setting the ambient shower display reduced shower volume by 17 %, while the numeric display achieved an 8 % reduction. Results for faucet usage were not reported in the private setting.

4.2 Conclusion: Consequence Intervention

For the three non-device feedback interventions, the biggest barrier to success seemed to be the medium of communication. Only 35 % and 18 % of the groups provided with web resources actually logged into them at least once [15, 24]. This low usage rate implies that the average water savings each study achieved may not have been 'maximized', and that there is potential for improvement. The results of Schultz *et al.*'s study [15], despite web usage rates, show that people are motivated to reduce their water usage when shown their own usage rates in the context of similar households (26 % reduction), though they are de-motivated by feedback with judgment embedded in it (16 % reduction). This same 'de-motivation' may also be responsible for the failure of Geller *et al.*'s feedback [25], which always included a smiling or sad face.

Device interventions have been shown to consistently have significant impact on the targeted behavior. This consistency may be due to the fact that a device reminds the user to care about water at the point of use, and often allows the user to track her conservation. The feedback given by the participants using the UpStream devices indicated that ambient displays are more pleasant to interact with regularly than are indexical. This result is corroborated by Ham *et al.*'s work on ambient displays' cognitive load [31].

5   Discussion

A few trends are evident when all the papers are analyzed together. Specifically, success may be attributed to visibility and context. Visibility refers to the timeliness and access to information, such as having information at the point of task. Context refers to situational awareness, such as a user who is aware of the consequences because of their experiences. For example, information and tips on how or why to conserve water provided as antecedent measures are generally ineffective for changing a user's behavior. However, when info/tips are administered in a drought context the participants achieved significant water savings.

Context of performance is also important; in Aitken *et al.*'s [21] work the participants who were shown that they used a lot of water were motivated to conserve, whereas the participants shown to use less water were not motivated, and in some cases used *more* water. These results may be due to the social pressure to conform, and/or due to a state of cognitive dissonance incited by one's realization that his/her usage is higher than average. Perception of peers' water usage has been shown to affect one's own usage habits. Verdugo *et al.* [32] showed that those who perceived their peers 'wasting water' tended to have worse conservation behaviors. Thus social feedback may only be useful to show a participant that her usage is above the norm.

The success of devices such as the "Show-me" may be attributed to the visibility of such a system; the user is automatically made aware of his or her usage, and the potential to conserve. An alternative explanation of the curtailments could be the Hawthorne effect; the participants were aware they were in a study and that their actions were being recorded so they acted in a way that would satisfy the researchers [33]. Though the Dubuque Portal achieved some degree of success, its information was not displayed easily (low visibility) and the participants in the study largely did not use it *at all* [24]. The use of attunement labels on appliances (high visibility) achieved high savings, whereas the same information in packet form achieved none [18].

Thus the two factors which seem most important for the success of an intervention are the context in which it is deployed, and its visibility. The context may be the user's predisposition to conservative behaviors, or foreknowledge of environmental consequences bestowed on her by living in a drought-stricken region, or by an educator. The visibility of an intervention is simply how easily and frequently a user is affected by an intervention (very high with labels, devices, or large campaigns, very low with a web-portal requiring a password). Lastly, these two factors do not constitute the intervention itself, but are attributes of any intervention.

6   Recommendations

In order to achieve maximum efficacy, intervention designers should consider mental context and visibility. With respect to mental context; He *et al.* [34] discuss how one may apply the trans-theoretical (stages of behavior change) model to persuasive technologies, specifically discussing electricity savings. Differing approaches to subjects at different points in their paths to behavior change may have the best results. They cite five specific phases; pre-contemplation, contemplation, preparation, action, and maintenance.

In the successful information-only studies the wide-spread drought seems to have primed the participants to begin conserving water. Similarly, the handful of studies whose information-only groups showed no change may have been unprepared to save water, thus providing details on how to do so was ineffectual at motivating behavior change. It may be more effective to first simply give participants information about the environment, and the current successes of conservation, perhaps a few times, before then giving them tips about how to conserve water. This phased approach may emulate the effect of living in a drought-stricken region by heightening one's awareness of the problems associated with water usage.

Providing objective information and allowing the subjects to draw their own conclusions before trying to change their behavior more accurately reflects *persuasion* defined by Brynjarsdottir *et al.* [35]. Coercion has been shown to actually attenuate results, shown by Schultz *et al.*'s where the experimental group whose feedback had an opinion expressed on it conserved significantly less than the group given an identical feedback *without* any opinion [15]. Thus any feedback should be given in a positive or neutral manner. As briefly stated in the discussion section, social feedback is effective though it should place the participants in a position where the pressure to conform acts in such a way that s/he uses less rather than more water.

Interventions should be very easily accessible, requiring little or no effort on the subject's part in order to communicate any information effectively. Both web-based feedback studies observed the intrinsic barrier to information posed by accessing a web medium. These extra steps may be ameliorated by integrating a passive widget, or plug-in to a sensor system. This barrier is not as strong in mail-based feedback, and is non-existent in devices. Mail has the obvious shortcomings of delay, bulk, and inconvenience of opening/reading the contents. Devices and attenuation labels are extremely visible; websites with user accounts and passwords are fairly invisible. People are generally unwilling or unable to regularly access internet portals, even when they *volunteer* to partake in a study known to be about conservation and the internet medium as in the Dubuque Portal.

Finally, when the study has been concluded, researchers should perform follow-up surveys to determine what factors the participants felt were most/least effective. They should also monitor participants' usage well after the intervention, to evaluate the durability of any changes made, as this is facet was surprisingly sparsely reported, though may be the most important effect of an intervention.

References

1. WHO/UNICEF: 2015 Update and MDG Assessment, p. 4 (2015)
2. United States: Environmental Protection Agency, Water on Tap - What You Need to Know, Water, p. 33 (2009)
3. Gleick, P.: Basic water requirements. Water Int. **21**(2), 83–92 (1996)
4. Mayer, P.W., Deoreo, W.B., Opitz, E.M., Kiefer, J.C., Davis, W.Y., Dziegielewski, B., Nelson, J.O.: Residential end uses of water. Awwarf, p. 310 (1999)
5. Vickers, A.: Handbook of Water Use and Conservation. WaterPlow Press, Amherst (2001)
6. Abrahamse, W., Steg, L., Vlek, C., Rothengatter, T.: A review of intervention studies aimed at household energy conservation. J. Environ. Psychol. **25**(3), 273–291 (2005)
7. Water-Efficient Plumbing Fixtures: http://www.ncsl.org/research/environment-and-natural-resources/water-efficient-plumbing-fixtures635433474.aspx. Accessed 08 Feb 2016
8. Froehlich, J., Findlater, L., Ostergren, M., Ramanathan, S., Peterson, J., Wragg, I., Larson, E., Fu, F., Bai, M., Patel, S., Landay, J.A.: The design and evaluation of prototype eco-feedback displays for fixture-level water usage data. In: Proceedings SIGCHI Conference Human Factors Computing System, pp. 2367–2376 (2012)
9. Inman, D., Jeffrey, P.: A review of residential water conservation tool performance and influences on implementation effectiveness. Urban Water J. **3**(3), 127–143 (2006)
10. Sønderlund, A.L., Smith, J.R., Hutton, C., Kapelan, Z.: Using smart meters for household water consumption feedback: knowns and unknowns. Procedia Eng. **89**, 990–997 (2014)
11. Greenhalgh, T.: Effectiveness and efficiency of search methods in systematic reviews of complex evidence: audit of primary sources. BMJ **331**(7524), 1064–1065 (2005)
12. Hume, M., Walton, A.: Creating positive habits in water conservation: the case of the queensland water commission and the target 140 campaign. Int. J. Nonprofit Volunt. Sect. Mark. **16**(3), 215–224 (2011)

13. Kollmuss, A., Agyeman, J.: Mind the gap: why do people act environmentally and what are the barriers to pro-environmental behavior? Environ. Educ. Res. **8**(3), 239–260 (2002)

14. Ferraro, P.J., Miranda, J.J., Price, M.K.: The persistence of treatment effects with norm-based policy instruments: evidence from a randomized environmental policy experiment. Am. Econ. Rev. Pap. Proc. **101**(3), 318–322 (2014)

15. Schultz, P.W., Messina, A., Tronu, G., Limas, E.F., Gupta, R., Estrada, M.: Personalized normative feedback and the moderating role of personal norms: a field experiment to reduce residential water consumption. Environ. Behav., pp. 1–25 (2014)

16. Fielding, K.S., Spinks, A., Russell, S., McCrea, R., Stewart, R., Gardner, J.: An experimental test of voluntary strategies to promote urban water demand management. J. Environ. Manage. **114**, 343–351 (2013)

17. Thompson, S.C., Stoutemyer, K.: Water use as a commons dilemma. Environ. Behav. **23**(3), 314–333 (1991)

18. Kurz, T., Donaghue, N., Walker, I.: Utilizing a social ecological framework to promote water and energy conservation: a field experiment. J. Appl. Soc. **35**(6), 1281–1300 (2005)

19. Aronson, E.: The theory of cognitive dissonance: a current perspective. Adv. Exp. Soc. Psychol. **4**(C), 1–34 (1969)

20. Dickerson, C.A., Thibodeau, R., Aronson, E., Miller, D.: Using cognitive dissonance to encourage water conservation. J. Appl. Soc. Psychol. **22**, 841–854 (1992)

21. Aitken, C.K., Mcmahon, T.A., Wearing, A.J., Finlayson, B.L.: Residential water use: predicting and reducing consumption. J. Appl. Soc. Psychol. **24**(2), 136–158 (1994)

22. Attari, S.Z.: Perceptions of water use. Proc. Natl. Acad. Sci. U.S.A. **111**(14), 5129–5134 (2014)

23. Beal, C.D., Stewart, R.A., Fielding, K.: A novel mixed method smart metering approach to reconciling differences between perceived and actual residential end use water consumption. J. Clean. Prod. **60**, 116–128 (2013)

24. Erickson, T., Podlaseck, M., Sahu, S., Dai, J.D., Chao, T., Naphade, M.: The Dubuque water portal: evaluation of the uptake, use and impact of residential water consumption feedback. In: Proceedings 2012 ACM Annual Conference on Human Factors Computing System (CHI 2012), pp. 675–684 (2012)

25. Geller, E.S., Erickson, J.B., Buttram, B.A.: Attempts to promote residential water conservation with educational, behavioral and engineering strategies. Popul. Environ. **6**(2), 96–112 (1983)

26. Kenny, J.F., Barber, N.L., Hutson, S.S., Linsey, K.S., Lovelace, J.K., Maupin, M.A.: Estimated use of water in the United States in 2005. Circular **1344**, 53 (2009). Circular 1268

27. Bonanni, L., Arroyo, E., Lee, C.-H., Selker, T.: Exploring feedback and persuasive techniques at the sink. Interactions **12**(4), 25 (2005)

28. Kappel, K., Grechenig, T.: "Show-Me": water consumption at a glance to promote water conservation in the shower. In: Persuas 2009, Proceedings of 4th International Conference on Persuasive Technology, pp. 1–6 (2009)

29. Willis, R.M., Stewarta, R.A., Panuwatwanich, K., Jones, S., Kyriakides, A.: Alarming visual display monitors affecting shower end use water and energy conservation in Australian residential households. Resour. Conserv. Recycl. **54**(12), 1117–1127 (2010)

30. Kuznetsov, S., Paulos, E.: UpStream. In: Proceedings of 28th International Conference on Human Factors Computing System, CHI 2010, vol. 3, p. 1851 (2010)

31. Ham, J., Midden, C.: Ambient persuasive technology needs little cognitive effort: the differential effects of cognitive load on lighting feedback versus factual feedback. In: Ploug, T., Hasle, P., Oinas-Kukkonen, H. (eds.) PERSUASIVE 2010. LNCS, vol. 6137, pp. 132–142. Springer, Heidelberg (2010)

32. Corral-Verdugo, V., Frias-Armenta, M., Perez-Urias, F., Orduna-Cabrera, V., Espinoza-Gallego, N.: Residential water consumption, motivation for conserving water and the continuing tragedy of the commons. Environ. Manage. **30**(4), 527–535 (2002)
33. Adair, J.G.: The Hawthorne effect: a reconsideration of the methodological artifact. J. Appl. Psychol. **69**(2), 334 (1984)
34. He, H.A., Greenberg, S., Huang, E.M.: One size does not fit all: applying the transtheoretical model to energy feedback technology design. In: Technology, pp. 1–11 (2009)
35. Brynjarsdottir, H., Håkansson, M., Pierce, J., Baumer, E., DiSalvo, C., Sengers, P.: Sustainably unpersuaded: how persuasion narrows our vision of sustainability. In: Proceedings of 2012 ACM Annual Conference on Human Factors Computing System, CHI 2012, p. 947 (2012)

Financial Literacy in China
as an Innovation Opportunity

Jan Brejcha[1]([✉]), Cong Wang[2], Xiaotong Wang[2], Ziwei Wang[2],
Li Wang[2], Qing Xu[2], Cheng Yang[2], Liangyu Chen[2], Yuxuan Luo[2],
Yijian Cheng[2], Shaopeng Zhang[2], Shuwen Liang[2], Xinru Liu[2],
Huitian Miao[2], Bingbing Wang[2], Nilin Chen[2], and Zhengjie Liu[2]

[1] Independent Researcher, Prague, Czech Republic
jan@brejcha.name
[2] Sino-European Usability Center (SEUC), Dalian Maritime University,
Dalian 116026, People's Republic of China
gutmannwc@live.com, {707706121,944084267,1271593115,
2318743061,861350580,850612479,1012644045,
1142765153}@qq.com, {chenliangyu,liuzhj}@dlmu.edu.cn,
{18765906978,15004112169,tianlidemiao}@163.com,
18840866738@139.com, cn10015@126.com

Abstract. The purpose of the study was to get insights of the financial knowledge, behavior, and attitudes of the young generation of Chinese (Millenials or Little Emperors, i.e. born between 1980–1995), in order to find and exploit design opportunities to improve the financial wellbeing of our target group. Our paper presents an introduction to the research area, the current technological trends, the results of our initial study, and further directions both for research and design of solutions targeted at our tentative users. Our results suggest that there is a strong growth in smartphone adoption and a growing availability of mobile applications targeted at managing finances, and conducting payments. However, the young Chinese have a middle-to-low level of financial literacy, and mimic the conservative behavior of their parents and family, who prefer to hold cash (or gold) in favor of investment instruments. There is a number of design opportunities to leverage our insights to improve the financial health and wellbeing of our target user group presented in our work.

Keywords: Cross-cultural research · Cultural markers · Design patterns · Design philosophy · Design thinking · DUXU in developing countries · Emotion · Financial competence · Financial inclusion · Financial literacy · Future trends in DUXU · HCI · Innovation · Methodology · Mobile products/services · Motivation · Persuasion design · Semiotics · Service design · Sustainability · User-interface

1 Introduction

The purpose of the study was to get insights of the **financial knowledge, behavior, and attitudes** of the young generation of Chinese (Millenials or Little Emperors, i.e. born between 1980–1995), in order to find and exploit design opportunities to improve their financial wellbeing.

© Springer International Publishing Switzerland 2016
A. Marcus (Ed.): DUXU 2016, Part II, LNCS 9747, pp. 439–450, 2016.
DOI: 10.1007/978-3-319-40355-7_42

Our results from the above three areas were then compared with data gathered in the Czech Republic [9] to provide some initial hints about the level of financial literacy in our target group across cultures. The Czech Republic was chosen as an example of a developed OECD-member country, and because of the availability of the latest survey data (courtesy of the Czech ministry of finance, and the University of Economics in Prague). China represents a contrasting example of a developing country.

We assume that by comparing the level of financial literacy in different cultures with the tools and products available in each culture we could provide a better guidance for the improvement of the financial wellbeing. This paper shows an initial progress in this direction.

Our paper presents an introduction to the research area, the current technological trends, the results of our initial study, and further directions both for research and design of solutions targeted at our defined user group.

1.1 Financial Literacy

Financial literacy is defined as follows: "A combination of awareness, knowledge, skill, attitude and behavior necessary to make sound financial decisions and ultimately achieve individual financial wellbeing" [1].

By improving financial literacy, we can improve the overall financial wellbeing of users. [22] There is also a positive effect of financial inclusion in general: "Financial inclusion has been broadly recognized as critical in reducing poverty and achieving inclusive economic growth. (…) Studies show that when people participate in the financial system, they are better able to start and expand businesses, invest in education, manage risk, and absorb financial shocks. Access to accounts and to savings and payment mechanisms increases savings, empowers women, and boosts productive investment and consumption. Access to credit also has positive effects on consumption—as well as on employment status and income and on some aspects of mental health and outlook" [5, page 2].

We start with the following research problem: "In developing economies [such as China] 110 million adults with an account—5 percent of account holders—are savers but save only semiformally, by using a savings club or a person outside the family. Designing appropriate savings products tailored to their needs could encourage these account holders to use their account for saving" [5, page 68].

We seek to address the problem by leveraging positive behavior modification techniques. Our rationale is based on previous research highlighting, that "a large proportion of individuals who could benefit from initiatives designed to change their behaviour. In almost every country surveyed, at least 3 in 10 respondents exhibited fewer that 6 of the 9 positive behaviours discussed" [1, page 12].

Positively modifying user's behavior is especially important, because people are exposed to the cognitive biases of instant gratification and loss aversion, which prevents them from saving, or saving enough for their needs. Also, millennials in particular face problems of low financial literacy, and of not having enough money to save.

The research also has cross-cultural potential, in that financial attitudes are cultural markers that can be studied in different cultural and linguistic environments (e.g., the factor of time and its representation in grammar). Thanks to global surveys on financial literacy (e.g. by the World Bank, OECD, various financial institutions) we can quickly compare the data across cultures.

Financial Capability. People are, in the words of influential behavioral economist Dan Ariely, predictably irrational. And because we can predict user's behavior, the design should take it into account.

Financial Capability: expressed through actions or behavior. If we plan to improve people's financial capability, we need to decide which aspects of their behavior we would like to see changed, as discussed by Spencer, Niboer, Elliott. [19] According to the authors, these consist of the following:

- **Maintaining a budget** can be thought of as 'making ends meet'. It means that people know how much they can spend and ensure they don't fall short on a regular basis.
- **To manage debt well** is to plan for 'inevitable' purchases on credit, such as buying a house or education. It involves securing good credit terms, making use of tax incentives and ensuring there is enough room within a budget for repayment.
- **Protecting dependents** means that partners, children and other dependents are protected in case anything happens to the main household income earner. Examples: critical illness insurance, life insurance and joint pensions.
- **Achieving financial resilience by protecting assets** means being financially prepared for unexpected events – e.g., medical emergencies, burglaries or car breakdowns. Examples: insurance, reduce key risks and have a 'rainy day fund'.
- **Saving regularly** means putting some money aside (beyond an emergency fund), such as setting up a savings fund for holidays and household appliances.
- **Saving for retirement** includes behaviors such as forecasting future outcomes, ensuring enough money is saved to guarantee the desired pension and selecting the right 'mix' of investments for retirement savings.

1.2 Technological Background

Technology is a vehicle of positive change in our domain, since there is a correlation between financial exclusion and the digital divide [7]. According to the latest report by the GSM Association [8], the mobile industry continues to scale rapidly, with a total of 3.6 billion unique mobile subscribers at the end of 2014. In the developed world there is already a very high penetration (at 79 % at the end of 2014), while the penetration rate in the developing world is below half the population (at 44.6 % at the end of 2014).

The GSMA report further suggests that mobile in the developing world is the predominant infrastructure compared to other services, such as electricity, sanitation and financial. "As a result, mobile is already helping to address a number of pressing social, economic and environmental challenges". From the financial services perspective, mobile money helps with the financial inclusion of a growing number of the previously unbanked and underbanked, and are now available in over 60 % of the world's developing markets, according to the report.

According to Shrader [18], there is a pronounced effect of social media on the use of money in China, where people use them to research and buy products and services.

1.3   Financial Inclusion Opportunities

There is a number of opportunities to leverage the mobile infrastructure, including mobile insurance, savings and credit. According to the GSMA, there are 32 mobile credit services available in 15 countries globally. Mobile insurance services have reached a total of 100 live services. Some operators are even paying interest on the money in mobile wallets, offering thus also saving facilities [8].

While many banked people already use mobile banking in China, there is untapped potential to draw on low-cost, accessible channels, such as mobile wallets, particularly for younger, technology-savvy populations, according to Shrader and Duflos [17].

"New models must be supported by meaningful products and viable business models to drive a new phase of technology-enabled rural growth and poverty alleviation" [17].

Importantly, the utility financial services through social media could be a driver to reach the unbanked (such as Alipay or Tencent), as discussed by Shrader [18].

According to the Economist Intelligence Unit, "[c]hallenges still remain in developing an inclusive financial environment in China, although a lot of progress has been made. Microfinance in China is mainly focused on micro-, small- and medium-sized-enterprise (MSME) lending, instead of providing services to the low-income population" [23, page 31].

2   Research Rationale

To address the above trends, to contribute to the current state of knowledge, and to build a basis for comparison with future surveys, namely the upcoming OECD INFE report due in March 2016 [15]. Currently there are no directly comparable results from other surveys, although a number of similar ones exists. Among these ranks the pilot OECD questionnaire [1], which has been carried out in the 14 participating countries around the world. Another survey of financial literacy, this time focused on students (15–16 years old), was run as a part of the PISA project [14] comparing the performance between the OECD countries and some emerging regions including the Shanghai area in mainland China. The S&P Global financial literacy survey provides comprehensive results on the basic financial concepts, such as numeracy (debt), risk diversification, inflation, and compound interest (saving) [12].

3   Research Methods

To pursue our goal, we identified the following research questions, and hypotheses:

Research Questions.

- What is the level of financial knowledge in our target group?

- What are the behavioral patterns related to managing finances?
- What are the attitudes towards money in general?
- What is the level of financial inclusion?
- What are the ways UX design can improve the above?
- What are the cross-cultural implications of designing financial applications?

Hypotheses.

- H1: Despite rapid economic growth, rising wealth and disposable income and higher consumption rates Gen Y [b. 1980–1995] consumers are still very much collectivists with a high need for security, conformity and benevolence, as is reflected in the Chinese cultural values [24].
- H2: Predominantly a fear of debt [in China] hinders excess spending and the use of credit cards. This is linked to a perceived guilt when spending 'future money' that has not yet been earned [24, page 6].
- H3: There is a very low participation rate of the formal financing sector, but very active informal finance.
- H4: People are risk averse – a large portion of their financial asset is riskless [6].
- H5: Languages with obligatory future-time reference lead their speakers to engage in less future-oriented behavior. On savings, the evidence is consistent on multiple levels: at an individual's propensity to save, to long-run effects on retirement wealth, and in national savings rates. [Mandarin is only a weakly future reference language, in contrast, e.g., to English or Czech]. [4] We expect therefore a high saving rate in China.
- H6: [US] millennials have financial goals. However, it appears many are not seeking guidance and advice from the appropriate sources. [11] We expect similar results in China.
- H7: Gen Y [in the USA] saves less than Gen X [b. 1965-1980]. The only savings vehicles young people today use more, than the previous generation did at the same age are transactional accounts. [25] We expect similar results in China.

Questionnaire Methodology. We constructed our questionnaire using varied guidelines, such as OECD [15] (areas include financial knowledge, behavior, attitudes), [20] (financial attitudes), [10] (UCD interview), as well others designed to better understand the user's needs. Therefore, we based our methodology on the suggestions by OECD [15], mainly:

- Follow the interviewer's instruction in different parts of the questionnaire
- The interviewers should ask the questions in the order that they are laid out in the questionnaire, without changing the wording and they should immediately record the responses. If necessary, they can go back to previous questions to make a correction or clarify a point (such as when asking about the product chosen most recently).
- Participants will not be expected to read any of the questions or write down their answers, and whilst it is important to reassure them that their responses are confidential and encourage them to participate, they must never be put under pressure to

answer anything that they don't want to answer – doing so is unethical and is also likely to significantly bias their responses.

Then we built a questionnaire for user interviews using an online reporting tool [21]. The study was conducted in November 2015, both on a qualitative and qualitative basis. 31 respondents were interviewed on ~ 50 questions (closed and open), and each session lasted 35 min. The respondents were recruited at the Dalian Maritime University (DMU) using a simple screener (they should be born in China between 1980–1995, be evenly split between males and females, be evenly split between lower, middle, and higher income). Local moderators conducted the study, because they shared the language and cultural background of the target group. After the interviews all the data was checked and translated, when appropriate.

4   Results

We organized our basic findings according to the main topics of our research as follows: Financial knowledge (Table 1), financial behavior (Table 2), and financial attitudes (Table 3). Each table contains a column presenting the topic, the question asked, and the result. The topics provide a structure for further comparison with other research.

To evaluate our dataset, we used a margin of error of 17.9 % (5 respondents) for the whole group of 31 respondents [16]. To limit the role of chance (50 %) we showed in percentage only the results higher than 67.9 % (50 % + 17.9 %). Results with a lower percentage were still taken into account, but confronted against qualitative responses to achieve maximum plausibility.

4.1   Triangulation of Results

In order to validate our data, we shall compare similar results from similar research in our target group. We expect to have the opportunity for a comprehensive comparison of our data with the upcoming results from the OECD INFE 2015 survey [15], both in our target cultures, and across cultures.

At present, we can triangulate the financial literacy data from different sources in the below table (Table 4) showing correct responses. The S&P results are based on a global survey from 2014 with more than 150000 respondents. The Czech data are based on data collected by the University of Economics and the Ministry of Finance in 2012 (212 university students of non-economic fields).

By triangulating the results, we can notice a pattern between the Czech and Chinese data. The data from student's research rank higher than the general population in each of the compared countries. Also, the data from the Czech students show a higher score compared to students in China, which is mirrored in the comparison between the general population. Our data has thus passed this plausibility check.

Table 1. Financial knowledge

Topic	Question	Results
Time-value of money	Five brothers are going to be given a gift of $1,000 in total to share between them. Now, imagine that they have to wait for one year to get their share of the $1,000 and inflation stays at X percent. In one year's time will they be able to buy: (a) More with their share of the money than they could today; (b) The same amount; (c) Or, less than they could buy today. (d) It depends on the types of things that they want to buy.	28/31(87 %) [response: C and D combined]
Interest paid on a loan	You lend $25 to a friend one evening and he gives you $25 back the next day. How much interest has he paid on this loan?	28/31 (87 %) [response: no interest paid]
Calculation of interest plus principle	Suppose you put $100 into a savings account with a guaranteed interest rate of 2 % per year. You don't make any further payments into this account and you don't withdraw any money. How much would be in the account at the end of the first year, once the interest payment was made?	27/31 (87 %) [response: 102 %]
	And how much would be in the account at the end of five years? Would it be: (a) More than $110; (b) Exactly $110; (c) Less than $110; (d) Or is it impossible to tell from the information given	24/31 (77 %) [response: A]
Risk and return	An investment with a high return is likely to be involving high risk	23/31 (74 %) [response: True]
Definition of inflation	High inflation means that the cost of living is increasing rapidly	25/31 (81 %) [response: True]
Diversification	It is usually possible to reduce the risk of investing in the stock market by buying a wide range of stocks and shares.	17/31 (−%) [response: True]

5   Discussion

Apart from the quantitative data we gathered useful qualitative data about the challenges in achieving financial wellbeing. We were able to confirm all our initial hypotheses, except H5 (the relation between language and savings rate).

We found out that although our respondents were used to make their day-to-day decisions about money usually themselves, even though most of them see their financial knowledge about or below average. The majority of our respondents would welcome obtaining advice from expert, or friends. This is especially true when pondering buying decisions of products or services. Respondents mostly understand, how interests and inflation works, but are prone to cognitive biases, such as loss aversion.

Table 2. Financial behavior

Topic	Question	Results
Timely bill payment	I pay my bills on time	26/31 (84 %) [response: Completely agree]
Keeping watch of financial affairs	I keep a close personal watch on my financial affairs	25/31 (81 %) [response: Completely agree and agree]
Long term financial goal setting	Some people set themselves financial goals, such as paying university fees, buying a car or becoming debt free. Do you (personally, or with your partner) have any financial goals?	19/31 (−%) [response: No]
	I set long term financial goals and strive to achieve them	13/31 (−%) [response: Completely agree and agree]
Responsible, has a household budget	Does your household have a budget? A budget is used to decide what share of your income will be used for spending, saving or paying bills	17/31 (−%) [response: Yes]
Active saving	In the past 12 months, have you been [personally] saving money in any of the following ways, whether or not you still have the money?	24/30 (80 %) [Most save in a bank account, or at home]
Choosing products	and which of the following statements best describes how you made your choice? (a) I considered several options from different companies before making my decision; (b) I considered the various options from one company; (c) I didn't consider any other options at all; (d) I looked around but there were no other options to consider	21/29 (72 %) [response: A]
Borrowing to make ends meet	If you, personally, faced a major expense today – equivalent to your own monthly income – would you be able to pay it without borrowing the money or asking family or friends to help?	21/31 (68 %) [response: Yes]
	What did you do to make ends meet the last time this happened? (a) Existing resources; (b) Creating resources; (c)Access credit by using existing contacts or resources; (d) Borrow from existing credit line; (e) Access additional credit; (f) Fall behind/go beyond arranged amount	16/27 (−%) [response: C]

(Continued)

Table 2. (*Continued*)

Topic	Question	Results
	Sometimes people find that their income does not quite cover their living costs. In the last 12 months, has this happened to you, personally?	19/31 (−%) [response: Yes]
Loss aversion	I am prepared to risk some of my own money when saving or making an investment	18/31 (−%) [response: Completely agree and agree]

Table 3. Financial attitudes

Question	Results
I find it more satisfying to spend money than to save it for the long term	14/31 (−%) [Disagree and completely disagree]
I tend to live for today and let tomorrow take care of itself	16/31 (−%) [Disagree and completely disagree]
Money is there to be spent	24/31 (77 %) [Completely agree and agree]

Table 4. Triangulation of financial literacy data, cross-cultural comparison between Czech (CZ) and Chinese (CN) respondents.

	CZ (OECD)	CZ (S&P)	CN (our)	CN (S&P)
Risk diversification	89 %	56 %	(−%)	37 %
Inflation	73 %	64 %	87 %	36 %
Numeracy (interest)	97 %	71 %	87 %	45 %
Compound interest	73 %	54 %	77 %	45 %

Perhaps given their lower financial literacy most of the students were tricked to provide financial information to scammers.

The preferred method of saving is in cash or in a bank/savings account, and the mostly known and used products are bank accounts, insurance, and mobile payments. Although the students are willing to take some risk with their money when saving or investing, they keep a close watch on their finances, pay bills on time, and avoid debt whenever possible.

Most students budget under 1875 RMB a month (about 290 USD), and spend usually half on food. The financial situation limits their ability to do things important to them, but most of them are rather satisfied with their situation. Less than half of the respondents have some financial goals, the most frequently cited goals were traveling, buying a house, or a car. Planning for retirement is obviously not a current issue, also because the students will rely· on their workplace pension plan together with the governmental one.

When it comes to keeping track of income and expenses, which would be helpful in attaining financial goals, only around half the students keep a budget. However, most of the respondents would be able to cover an unexpected expense. Sometimes however, the income does not quite cover the living costs, and when that happens, users tend to borrow from family or friends, rather than from institutions. Their income usually covers the expenses of 1–4 weeks.

Our findings show that there is a need among the young generation of Chinese students for solutions that would help them cope with their financial matters, and make the most of the money they have at disposal. Given the high proliferation of mobile technology in our user group, a mobile-based solution would have a potentially high impact. According to our competitive analysis of 21 mobile applications, the currently available apps in the financial domain in China do not quite address the pressing problems our users face. Those applications that address them are not designed to appeal to our users, nor to provide all of the tools that our users need.

To tackle these problems, we identified an opportunity for innovation in the following areas: Comparison/recommendation of financial products, budgeting, improving financial literacy and financial capability. We conducted a series of sessions using exploratory design methods to define the proposed solutions to help users change their behavior in a positive way. A similar work applying persuasion and gamification techniques in the financial domain was done by Aaron Marcus [13].

6 Future Work

Future work consists in analyzing the full results from the OECD INFE 2015 survey related to our target audience and cultures, adopting our cross-cultural semiotic framework [2, 3] to the financial cultural markers (e.g. price, value, mental models leading to specific financial behaviors and attitudes), and in proposing research-based tools and/or products (mobile application) to benefit our target audience. We plan to summarize our work based on the current paper in a future publication.

Acknowledgements. The authors wish to thank for the assistance of the Sino-European Usability Center (SEUC).

References

1. Atkinson, A., Messy, F.: Measuring Financial Literacy: Results of the OECD/International Network on Financial Education (INFE) Pilot Study. OECD Working Papers on Finance, Insurance and Private Pensions, No. 15, OECD Publishing (2012). http://dx.doi.org/10.1787/5k9csfs90fr4-en
2. Barber, W., Badre, A.: Culturability: the merging of culture and usability. In: Proceedings of the 4th Conference on Human Factors and the Web (1998)

3. Brejcha, J.: Cross-Cultural Human-Computer Interaction and User Experience Design. CRC Press, Boca Raton (2015). ISBN: 978-1-4987-0257-7
4. Chen, K.: The effect of language on economic behavior: evidence from savings rates, health behaviors, and retirement assets. Am. Econ. Rev. **103**(2), 690–731 (2013). http://dx.doi.org/10.1257/aer.103.2.690
5. Demirguc-Kunt, A., et al.: The Global Findex database 2014: measuring financial inclusion around the world. The World Bank (2015). https://openknowledge.worldbank.org/bitstream/handle/10986/21865/WPS7255.pdf
6. Gan, L.: Findings from China household finance survey. Southwestern University of finance and economics, January 2013. http://econweb.tamu.edu/gan/Report-English-Dec-2013.pdf
7. Geach, N.: The digital divide, financial exclusion and mobile phone technology: two problems, one solution. J. Int. Trade Law Policy **6**(1), 21–29 (2007). http://bileta.ac.uk/content/files/conference%20papers/2007/The%20Digital%20Divide,%20Financial%20Exclusion%20and%20Mobile%20Phone%20Technology%20-%20Two%20Problems,%20One%20Solution.pdf
8. GSMA: The Mobile Economy, Copyright © 2015 GSM Association (2015). http://www.gsmamobileeconomy.com
9. Hradil, D.: Empirické ověření gramotnosti studentů vysokých škol [Empirical Validation of Literacy in University Students]. Academic reseach project IGA 2012 (27/2012). University of Economics, Prague (2012)
10. IDEO.org: The Field Guide to Human-Centered Design, 1st edn. © 2015 (2015). http://www.designkit.org/resources/1, ISBN: 978-0-9914063-1-9
11. Iquantifi: Millennial Money Mindset Report (2015). http://iquantifi.com/2015-millennials-money-mindset-report/
12. Klapper, L., Lusardi, A., van Oudheusden, P.: Standard & Poor's Ratings Services Global Financial Literacy Survey (2015). http://www.FinLit.MHFI.com
13. Marcus, A.: The money machine: combining information design/visualization with persuasion design to change baby Boomers' wealth management behavior. In: Marcus, A. (ed.) Mobile Persuasion Design, pp. 79–161. Springer, London (2015)
14. OECD: PISA 2012 Results: Students and Money: Financial Literacy Skills for the 21st Century, vol. VI. OECD Publishing, Pisa (2014). http://dx.doi.org/10.1787/9789264208094-en, ISBN: 978-92-64-20809-4
15. OECD INFE: Measuring Financial Literacy: Core Questionnaire in Measuring Financial Literacy: Questionnaire and Guidance Notes for conducting an Internationally Comparable Survey of Financial literacy. OECD, Paris (2015). http://www.oecd.org/daf/fin/financial-education/2015_OECD_INFE_Toolkit_Measuring_Financial_Literacy.pdf
16. Sauro: Confidence Interval Calculator for a Completion Rate. Measuring Usability (2005). http://www.measuringusability.com/wald.htm. Accessed 19 Oct 2012
17. Shrader, L., Duflos, E.: China: A New Paradigm in Branchless Banking? CGAP (2014). https://www.cgap.org/sites/default/files/Working-Paper-China-A-New-Paradigm-in-Branchless-Banking-March-2014_0.pdf
18. Shrader, L.: Killer Apps in China: Social Networks and Financial Inclusion. CGAP, 19 May 2014. http://www.cgap.org/blog/killer-apps-china-social-networks-and-financial-inclusion
19. Spencer, N., Nieboer, J., Antony, E.: Wired for imprudence: behavioural hurdles to financial capability and challenges for financial education. RSA Action and Research Centre, 29 May 2015. https://www.thersa.org/discover/publications-and-articles/reports/wired-for-imprudence/Download
20. Statman, M., Weng, J.A.: Investments across cultures: financial attitudes of Chinese-Americans. J. Investment Consult. **11**(1), 37–44 (2010). http://papers.ssrn.com/sol3/Delivery.cfm/SSRN_ID1691236_code510892.pdf?abstractid=1691236&mirid=1

21. Survey Gizm: Widgix, LLC dba SurveyGizmo, ©2005–2016. http://www.surveygizmo.com
22. Taft, M.K., Hosein, Z.Z., Mehrizi, S.M.T.: The relation between financial literacy, financial wellbeing and financial concerns. Int. J. Bus. Manage. **8**(11), 63–75 (2013)
23. The Economist Intelligence Unit (EIU): Global Microscope 2015: The enabling environment for financial inclusion. Sponsored by MIF/IDB, CAF, Accion and the Metlife Foundation. EIU, New York, NY (2015). http://www.eiu.com/microscope2015
24. Thompson, F., Worthington, J.: 'Future money' and its impact on the attitudes of young Chinese towards saving. In: ANZMAC Annual Conference 2010 (Dave Fortin and Lucie K Ozanne 29 November 2010 to 1 December 2010), pp. 1–7. Department of Management University of Canterbury (2010)
25. Zumbrun, J.: Younger generation faces a savings deficit. Wall Street J., 09 November 2014. http://www.wsj.com/articles/savings-turn-negative-for-younger-generation-1415572405

Beyond Innovation Within the City Limits

Pavel Farkas[(✉)]

Faculty of Humanities, Charles University in Prague, Prague, Czech Republic
pf@pfarkas.com

Abstract. Although *vitalism*, denoting a dismissed concept in biology (life sciences), is a term rooted in the late 18th century, we still may abstractly think of vitalism even today — in a very different context. The use of this term has changed in the course of centuries, and has been used across different disciplines. Reflecting texts of modern philosophers as well as architects, urban planners and thinkers, this essay is setting the term of vitalism into urban environment and aims to examine the philosophical qualities of space, rationalization, function and beauty in the 21st century. Cities are viewed here as interfaces to interact with. At the same time, Interaction Design (IxD) has tools for making the world a better place from the viewpoint of users: User-Centered Design is widely established and used term. I propose that *urban vitalism* may stand on qualities valued in Human-Computer Interaction (HCI) and I am trying to open paths for new concepts in understanding urban life by actualizing the patterns of interaction with the technological layer in our environments.

Keywords: Cities · Design · Interaction · Philosophy · Semiotics · Usability · Vitalism · Wayfinding

1 Introduction

What would our life be like if we were to spend the rest of our lives on an isolated island in the middle of nowhere? In one of numerous versions on Robinson Crusoe, the French writer/philosopher Michel Tournier turns it into a novel where he also underlines the human need for organization and rationalization of space. He makes Robinson think of the island as "covered by the network of interpolations and extrapolations that differentiate the landscape and make it intelligible." His character found that the way to cope with "the disruptive effect" of absence of other people on the island was "to build, organize and make laws" [22]. Similarly as designers of interactions do.

2 Rationalization and Vitalism

This kind of rationalization is well apparent in modern cities of today, emphasizing the effectiveness of circulation, transportation and communication. We have seen modernist approaches as in Le Corbusier's work *Radiant City* [12] for three million inhabitants,

© Springer International Publishing Switzerland 2016
A. Marcus (Ed.): DUXU 2016, Part II, LNCS 9747, pp. 451–460, 2016.
DOI: 10.1007/978-3-319-40355-7_43

where the frequent term is the standardization[1]. We also can appreciate the civil and pragmatic approach, let's here say user-centered, as in Alexander's *Pattern Language* [1] applied to a human scale town. And by establishing those laws, he encouraged the physical environments to provide functions for its users resulting in, let's say *vital* lives (*lat.: vita*, life).

We need to remember, though, that progress in the right direction is not the only option. Saarinen [18] once wrote that: "Many achievements have been ignored because they took place in such slowly growing communities as were looked upon with disdain in a time when rapid growth was regarded by the prevailing attitude of materialism as the only acceptable sign of vitality. Let's not confuse vitality for speed and growth, or as transportation means for economic prosperity." Vitality may take forms of small improvements, as I suggest further in the text.

In another part of his grand work on the city, Saarinen remembers Haussmann's life project of rebuilding Paris: He sees as a positive fact that Haussmann was not a scholar of architectural orders, but a clearly thinking realist. Yet, at the same time, Saarinen does not forget to add that the exterior aspect of the city was of greater importance to Haussmann than were the vital needs of the population.

2.1 Users of Cities

Many aspects of city life are not at all spectacular and extraordinary; instead, they are ordinary, implicit and in fact hardly noticeable. And Michel de Certeau [6] sees central quality exactly in the everydayness of our being the inhabitants of cities. As I would like to stress, being the *users* of cities. Like De Certeau, I am interested in pragmatic side of everyday life of such users and am interested in finding out how to make their interaction with their city effective, possibly drafting paths to innovation of communication and interaction in urban environments.

When De Certeau talks of Concept-city functions, he mentions a place of *transformations* and *appropriations*. This way, a city is the object of various kinds of interference but also a subject that is constantly enriched by new attributes: it is simultaneously *the machinery and the hero of modernity*. And the driving force of this city life is—people. Their *intertwine paths* that give shape to spaces. In other words, it is how people use the city what defines it.

2.2 Users Versus Designers

Here comes the difference and at the same time the responsibility of designers, who are also users of cities. How does a user actually *appropriate* the interaction in a city?

---

[1] It needs to be said, though, that while the notion of standardization may have mechanist connotations, at the same time in his book, Le Corbusier does considers vital qualities as sound pollution, natural sunlight, population density, even human scale or harmony… and he adds: "What moves me in Paris is its vitality." [12, p. 99] In fact, there are many biological references in his book, including such as "urban biology" [12, p. 255].

If De Certeau compares pedestrian processes to linguistic formations and provokes with the idea that:

...the geometrical space of urbanists and architects seems to have the status of the "proper meaning" constructed by grammarians and linguists in order to have a normal and normative level to which they can compare the drifting of "figurative" language...," [6]

then interaction designers inevitably play a key role in creating such a "language of the city". They co-create what De Certeau calls the *urban fabric*. And at the same time, they are gaining certain amount of power over the processes in the city[2].

2.3   Does Perfect Design Make Perfect Cities?

Design of communication within our cities may easily imply the idea of actually designing of the society. Vacková [24] reminds us that the perfectly functioning society as the result of perfect design is in fact utopian. Yet, she claims, cities and utopia are firmly bound together: she defines cities as "the space from which grows the civilization and culture; space where the innovations take place, causing social and cultural changes and the richness of social world." But the question remains how the ideal city should actually look like. Can we view a city – and the design of information and interaction within – so that we discover the relationship intersecting these spaces? Like more or less visible "field lines"? How are they indexed? And can we then view the innovation as the enterprise in truly user-centered fashion?

The concept of *Space of Flows* elaborated by Castells [5] offers support for considering in urban relationships. Further, Castells urges to find new concepts of understanding the processes within them: "analysis of networked spatial mobility is another frontier for the new theory of urbanism. (...) How we relate to airports, train and bus stations, (...) are part of the new urban experience of hundreds of millions" [3].

2.4   Vitalism in Biology and Philosophy

To live in a *vital* city may sounds like a goal of every dweller and every local government. We could see above, that the term *vital* was casually used by respected architects. While vitalism is considered long abandoned idea in biology, we still can see it being mentioned to this day in historical studies in that field. "While the term of vitalism does not come into actual use until the late eighteenth century, many of the ideas and concepts embodied in the word are as old as medical and biological thought," summarize Normandin and Wolfe [16]. This allegedly outmoded and transcended philosophy of biology shows a remarkable endurance and vitality so much so that it has proven to be able to perform several resurgences, and to provoke attacks and refutations by mainstream reductionist

---

2   As Deleuze reminds us of Foucalt's approach to power, it is more of a strategy than an ownership. The effects of power cannot come out of appropriation but rather from "disponing of, maneuvering, tactics, techniques and functions...". Power is practiced rather than owned, it is not a privilege gained or protected by the governing class, but rather a general consequence of strategic positions of such a class [7].

science as late as the twentieth century [21]. Normandin and Wolfe [16] further note that vitalism again comes to the fore, as it does every time when the question of *boundaries* arises. But most notably, they also bring our attention to this straightforward dichotomy as pronounced by Ritchie in 1940:

"The mechanist is the kind of person who feels that everything important is known already, in principle at least, and that only minor details remain to be discovered. The vitalists feel that existing knowledge is only of minor details, and everything of importance is undiscovered" [17].

The concept of (neo)vitalism in philosophy took approach in several directions; and while Stollberg [20] reminds us that it is not a homogenous concept, number of modern philosophers are often viewed in context of the vitalist tradition: Driesch, Bergson, Deleuze, to name a few. But they may be known more for other provoking developments: Bergson for example, whose vitalism was not accepted by many scientists or philosophers [9], generalized vitalism into a comprehensive metaphysics applicable to all phenomena. [2] And as Marks points out, Deleuze evinces confidence and optimism with regard to the vitality of philosophy *itself*: Philosophy may have its rivals, in the form of advertising and information technology, but it retains a unique role in the world, "because philosophy is about *inventing concepts*," quotes Marks [15].

My interest in vitalism certainly does not lay in the extra-natural vital force in the organic world, but rather in the concepts demonstrating the life and humanity in the cities. Just as Marcelli [14] finally puts it, in the idea of vitalism attributed to the mobility and human circulation in modern cities. In his view, vitalism is not really aiming to explain life, but it is more of a reflection of processes taking places in modern cities: it demonstrates itself in doubts about enclosing the urban masses, populations and multiplicities into the framework of mechanist production of life.

2.5 Vital Layer of City Interaction

The basic presumption for my thinking exists that the need for effective function of city "organism", to prevent chaos in transportation, circulation and every day activities of its users, is desirable. Criticism may appear toward this presumption that the pursuit of effectivity and function might go to the extreme of futuristic novels[3], which would make people – the basic vital component – in fact disappear. Answering this kind of worries stretches, nevertheless, beyond the length of this essay.

In the second half of the 20th century, the number of inhabitants in large cities rose along with the need for controlling their flow in public spaces. For example, we saw first graphic manuals and wayfinding systems in transit networks[4], resulting in introducing

---

[3] As in The Brand New World by Aldous Huxley (first published in 1932), about developed but permanently limited society [11].

[4] To name a few examples, the origins of current information system in Chicago transit system are traceable to the late 1960's for the project of prolonging lines to Kennedy and Dan Ryan stations. The wayfinding system used there, designed by sub-consultants of original designers – Skidmore Owings & Merrill, was aesthetically and conceptually similar to other new systems in public transit, like New York (designed by Unimark) or Boston (designed by Cambridge Seven Associates) [8].

environmental graphic designs. This kind of interaction (or displaying information rather) is affordable, easy to maintain and quite effective. Some of the numerous purposes are designing the function of objects, providing wayfinding information, or control the traffic flow (see Fig. 1).

Fig. 1. Aside from aesthetic function, the mosaic decoration in New York subway stations provides information on different kinds of trains (express/local) serving the station.

With the rise of affordable electronic solutions by the end of the 20th century, another layer of city communication emerged. One that adds more or less interactive approach to the user. It aims to supplement the existing public communication, not to merely replace the older means. Keeping in mind the interaction design focus or my thought, I can state that these devices provide the kind of quality not otherwise achievable by static systems. Their signs are that they:

(A) Are implicitly present in the environment
(B) Use electric current
(C) Provide variable information
(D) Refresh automatically or semi-automatically
(E) Typically employ sensors
(F) Make it possible for user to interact
(G) May issue a restrictive instruction, but they are not invasive (over-ruling of their recommendation is possible by user)
(H) Are not computers per se

Semiotic analysis and design purpose of these devices are in the core of my thinking on this topic. Examples of systems for illustration are shown on Figs. 2, 3, and 4. The purpose of these systems is self-evident: to make the interaction with the environment more effective for the user of urban environments.

2.6   Smart Cities and Information Wayfinding

Interestingly, Harrison and Donnelly also reach to biology[5] when drafting what impact information technologies may have on norms of behavior, in their Theory of Smart Cities. But from the social point of view, they are stressing, that:

> *"An important question, especially for developers charged with creating a new city or a new district within a city, is how to make it attractive to the target tenants.*
> *Various tangible facilities, such as public wireless networks, electric vehicle charging stations, bicycle lanes, and so forth have been fashionable in such new developments based on the premise that other, attractive cities have these facilities..."* [10].

Fig. 2. Garages of the mall at Chodov subway station in Prague. Sensor above every carport reports the number of overall free position in the garage and its approximate position.

<hr/>

[5] They refer to findings of WEST, who "has spoken of the scaling of both biological and urban systems is being governed by the structures of connecting networks." In biological systems, these networks may be the nervous system or circulatory system and in urban systems, Harrison and Donnelly hypothesize, they may be the social and economic networks.

Fig. 3. Elevator at CDG airport in Paris. Elevator issues green LED light inside of the door while opening and red light while closing. Sensors are present so that passenger is not hurt if coincidentally present in the area of door closing.

Fig. 4. A crosswalk in San Diego, CA. Implicit information on the time remaining for crossing the street by pedestrian is issued and visible for both, the pedestrian and driver of a car. Audible information is employed and counting the time remaining, which is especially beneficial for blind citizens. Feedback after pressing the request button is provided by audibly and visually.

While the trend of self-promoting as *smart city* may be a way for communities to promote their uniqueness and compete for new inhabitants, we need to realize first of all, that we cannot simply leave our old city and build a brand new, start afresh next day, like Calvino [4] describes in his beautiful story of City of Eutropia, a city left by the whole citizenry for the next city,[6]

> "...which is there waiting for them, empty and good as new; there each will take up a new job, a different wife, will see another landscape on opening his window, and will spend his time with different pastimes, friends, gossip."

Most of us live in existing cities and we fit into the physical constrains. There, we can retrofit existing environments. Sensibly introducing a functional technological layer of information and interaction is what Smart Cities idea represents for me.

The complexity of the task makes it difficult, but existing trends in on-line and mobile communication design like *foreword affordances* or *spatial awareness* may be considered here and applied to cases in urban environments while keeping the logical structure of the whole system [23]. I also consider valid approaches, patterns and metaphors known from architecture and urbanism that may be applied to treat the added information in public environment, for example those defined by Lynch [13]. Yet, the way we search for and relate to information and interact in the built environment deserves an actualized approach. Following the ways that users of cities appropriate "their" space and finally drafting these actualized patterns of interaction remains in the very center of my interest.

2.7   Future and Trends in Cities

Significant area of interaction design research inevitable in the near future reflects the implementation of the trend of *Internet of things* (IoT). In a way, this is the new layer of vitality of post-modern and increasingly eclectic cities. Devices and sensors as extensions of city landscape being part of the sensing and reporting network in order to support the more effective functions of city departments: waste management, light management, traffic control, etc.

Le Corbusier was also speaking of the revolutionary fact back in 1930's, about the new arrangement of machine-age society: „In truth, the profound transformation of secular customs, the intervention of new customs and the probability of still more new ones." [12] Less than hundred years later, these expectations are reaching state which could be labeled either *Innovation* or *Surveillance*. "Big Data" is the new currency of commerce, as Sadowski and Pasquale [19] remind us; while the cities are becoming *cocoons of connectivity*. These authors are trying to raise awareness saying that this aim to evoke positive change and innovation via digital Information and Communication Technologies (ICT) is taking place for a wide range of different purposes[7]. "The seductive rhetoric of smart cities," they write, "have the potential to colonize the urban landscape and produce new forms of surveillance." [19] Notably, they also draw a conceptual

---

[6] In addition, not every user of the city has a smart phone at hand, or has the competences to use it (as debated in the sociological concept of *Digital Divide*).

[7] In their Social theory of the smart city [19], Sadowski and Pasquale further develop Deleuzian concept of the Spectrum of Control.

link between the ideology of smart cities and the ideology of the 20th century high-modernist architecture.

3 Concluding Thoughts

The central idea of this contribution is driven by thinking on how the types of interactions with urban environment change in the course of time. That is inevitably linking to more questions. Where lays the border of innovation in our cities? Where is the line between user-centered design, usability and the control of our lives? And most of all: How to make our cities *vital*? In life sciences, *vitalism is always on the borderland of thought* [16], and I wanted to point out that philosophy has been working with the idea of vitalism, on different levels, as well. Most interestingly, as Deleuze formulates it, *the vitality of philosophy is in inventing concepts* [15]. This short essay aimed to survey the conceptual bases for our thinking about cities in the digital age and to mention several approaches across the disciplines as a starting-point for further developments. I wanted to show that it is not unusual to cross boarders of one's discipline to grasp an unusual methodology; which our cities (equally built on the intersection of philosophy, sociology, and technology) may need at the end, to remain – or become – *vital*.

While the 21st century appears to be fast adopting terms as big data, connectivity, surveillance, social networks…, there is the physical aspect of the cities that won't change as fast as the increasingly dominating world on-line. We, nevertheless, can learn from the digital world and try to apply similar principles of interaction to enrich the physical environment. Still, I believe that cities must remain non-discriminatory environments for inhabitants/users of all ages, while maintaining the basic rights to privacy. Coming to understand the field lines of relations within vital urban environments shall be most interesting – and applying the knowledge in intuitive interaction design most gratifying.

References

1. Alexander, C., Ishikawa, S., Silverstein, M.: A Pattern Language: Towns, Buildings, Construction. Oxford University Press, New York (1977). xliv, 1171 p. ISBN: 0195019199
2. Beckner, M.O.: Vitalism. In: Borchert, D.M., ed. Encyclopedia of Philosophy. 2nd ed., vol. 9, pp. 694–698. Thomson/Gale, New York (2005). ISBN 0028660722
3. Braham, W.W., Hale, J.A., Sadar, J.S.: Rethinking Technology: A Reader in Architectural Theory. Routledge, Taylor & Francis Group, New York (2007). ISBN: 0203624335
4. Calvino, I.: Invisible Cities, 1st edn. Harcourt Brace Jovanovich, New York (1974). ISBN: 0151452903
5. Castells, M.: Networks of Outrage and Hope: Social Movements in the Internet Age, 2nd edn. Polity Press, Malden, MA (2015). ISBN: 9780745695761
6. de Certeau, M.: The Practice of Everyday Life. University of California Press, Berkeley (1984). xxiv, 229 s. ISBN: 978-0-520-27145-6
7. Deleuze, G., Hand, S.: Foucault. University of Minnesota Press, Minneapolis (1988). xlviii, 157 p. ISBN: 0816616752
8. Garfield, G.: Transit Chicago Contact Us – Visiting CTA Archive & Information Design Specialist (personal correspondence). Chicago, Illinois (2011)

9. Gunter, P.A.Y., Bergson, H.L. In: Audi, R. (ed.) The Cambridge Dictionary of Philosophy. 2nd edn. Cambridge University Press, Cambridge (2006). ISBN 9780511074172.
10. Harrison, C., Abbott Donnelly, I.: A Theory of Smart Cities. New York (2011). http://journals.isss.org/index.php/proceedings55th/article/view/1703. Accessed 20 Feb 2016
11. Huxley, A.: Brave new world, 1 Harper Perennial Modern Classics. Harper Perennial, New York (2006) ISBN: 9780060850524
12. Corbusier, L.E.: The Radiant City: Elements of a Doctrine of Urbanism to be Used as the Basis of Our Machine-Made Civilization. Faber, London (1967). ISBN: 0571080820
13. Lynch, K.: The Image of the City. The Technology Press & Harvard University Press, Cambridge (1960)
14. Marcelli, M.: Mesto vo filozofii (City in Philosophy), 1st edn. Kalligram, Bratislava (2011). 188 s. ISBN: 978-80-8101-400-0
15. Marks, J.: Gilles Deleuze: Vitalism and Multiplicity. Pluto Press, Sterling, VA (1998). ISBN: 0745308732
16. Normandin, S., Wolfe, C.T. (eds.): Vitalism and the Scientific Image in Post-Enlightenment Life Science, 1800-2010. Springer, New York (2013). ISBN: 978-940-0724-440
17. Ritchie, A.D.: Vitalism: its history and validity. Nature **145**, 6–7 (1940). Normandin, S., Wolfe, C.T. (eds.) p. 2 (2013)
18. Saarinen, E.: The City: Its Growth, Its Decay, Its Future, 1st edn. Kingsport Press, Kingsport, Tenn (1943)
19. Sadowski, J., Pasquale, F.: The spectrum of control: a social theory of the smart city. First Monday [S.l.], June 2015. ISSN: 13960466. doi:10.5210/fm.v20i7.5903. <http://journals.uic.edu/ojs/index.php/fm/article/view/5903/4660>. Accessed 09 Feb 2016
20. Stollberg, G.: Vitalism and Vital Force in Life Sciences: The Demise and Life of a Scientific Conception. Bielefeld. http://www.uni-bielefeld.de/soz/pdf/Vitalism.pdf. Accessed 20 Feb 2016
21. Szántó, V.: Vitalistic approaches to life in early modern England. Theory Sci. **37**(2), 209–230 (2015)
22. Tournier, M., Denny, N.: Johns Hopkins paperbacks (ed.) Friday, p. 235. Johns Hopkins University Press, Baltimore (1997) ISBN: 0801855924
23. Ussai, R.: The Principles of UX Choreography, Medium.com. A Medium Corporation, Chicago (2015). https://medium.com/@becca_u/the-principles-of-ux-choreography-69c91c2cbc2a#.wb2okialy. Accessed 09 Feb 2016
24. Vacková, B.: Prostor, moc a utopie: ideální město a jeho společnost (Space, Power and Utopia: Ideal City and its Society), 1st edn. Masarykova univerzita, Mezinárodní politologický ústav, Brno (2010)

Why Energy Consumption Feedback
Is not (Only) a Display Issue

Myriam Fréjus[1](✉) and Dominique Martini[2]

[1] EDF Research & Development, Paris-Saclay, France
myriam.frejus@edf.fr
[2] ITG, Paris, France
dmi@dmartini.fr

Abstract. This paper presents the results of a longitudinal study of the appropriation of a consumption display. Our results show that feedback on household energy consumption is contextually interpreted according to personal energy history, other available resources for managing energy issues, including resources for actions and human resources, and in relation with the occurring activity. We show that feedback use is an evolving process co-determined by the actors' preoccupations and their activity context. Consumption feedback should be considered as part of a system of assistance designed to enhance user engagement with energy control. To be appropriable, it must have at least three main characteristics: scalability, complementarity, and operationality.

Keywords: Sustainability · Energy consumption · Field study · Consumption feedback · User-centered design

1 Introduction

Sustainability has become an important issue in HCI research. Displaying consumption information is a way to make energy visible and engage people in self-reflective processes that prompt changes in domestic practices and thereby lower consumption. However, this "ideal path" to sustainability does not seem to correspond to observations in smart grid experiments and user research.

The earliest work in this field sought to modify behavior and convince consumers to change their habits. Yet the experiments designed to quantify the impact of displays on consumption often showed contradictory results [4]. The most frequent results were then retained in the literature to define an average range of lower consumption, thus obscuring the wide diversity in the results [3]. The focus on cost savings was linked, especially in the persuasive approach, to a view of the actor as a rational consumer, sensitive to influences and willing to change behaviors in order to control energy use [26].

The limitations of this approach were first noted by researchers in the human "behavior" sciences: social sciences [18, 23], psychology [21] and cognitive ergonomics [8].

© Springer International Publishing Switzerland 2016
A. Marcus (Ed.): DUXU 2016, Part II, LNCS 9747, pp. 461–471, 2016.
DOI: 10.1007/978-3-319-40355-7_44

The domination of the persuasive approach [17] has nevertheless resulted in many studies to evaluate consumption display types (functionalities, usages) [10], and the impact of functionalities on behaviors has guided the design of displays [1]. Yet both the designs and the evaluation methods remain questionable.

Feedback system design necessarily focuses on functionalities linked to energy use and cost, including consumption at various time scales, normal use compared with that of other households, desirable behaviors (eco-gestures), or the most likely energy bill [16]. Much of this information is too often disconnected from the contexts in which behaviors occur and energy is consumed [27]. Many of the questions about how to monitor and control energy depend on personal and familial contexts (domestic practices and activities, family organization), as well as technical (material, means of action, etc.) and social (skills, preoccupations, expectations, financial means, etc.) contexts. Moreover, the feedback display system is often considered apart from other solutions, like other information sources and ways of remoting appliances.

Another limitation of the experiments has been the focus on before-after behaviors. Perhaps because of experimental or methodological constraints (before/after questions) [25], the actual evolution in behavior has rarely been examined [15]. Yet an interpretation at the end of the experiment can be questioned if nothing is known about the course of the behavior over time and how it was affected by factors that obstructed or facilitated the appropriation of feedback. Increasingly, studies now describe the actual use (or nonuse) of feedback displays over time [2, 5, 17, 20]. These studies, which evaluate the long-term impact of energy monitoring, have shown results that differ from those of short-term studies. Notably, they indicate that user engagement with monitoring gradually lessens or disappears [13, 22, 24].

[13], for example, noted a drop in engagement over a 12-month study, despite an initial phase of interest. This drop was attributed to a lack of new information that might have held consumers' interest. Other authors have tested feedback displays with richer functionalities and observed no drop in engagement, but rather a shift from regular use to more occasional use [11, 17]. This has been interpreted as reflecting the shift from novelty to utility rather than a lack of interest, or from a discovery phase to a maintenance phase [14]. The growing competence of users who are quite aware of their energy use ("energy literacy" [17]) suggests that the information supply should be regularly enriched and renewed to respond to increasingly sophisticated user questions [9]. However, these user needs and their evolution have rarely been described in the literature, especially in relation to their socio-technical context, in addition to the feedback function. The impact of feedback displays is also a particularly complex issue because a better understanding of energy consumption does not necessarily result in energy-conserving actions [5] and may even limit action, with household members assuming that their energy use falls within the norms and should therefore merely be maintained [20].

Recent HCI findings have underlined the importance of enlarging the issue of energy savings to include consumer commitment [12], evolving competence [17], the development of reflective processes [7] and the contextual factors of domestic [8, 23] and familial [2, 19] activities. The above-cited studies confirm the need for in-depth analysis of the appropriation phase of feedback to determine how it can be made a part of daily preoccupations and domestic activities. This analysis can be accomplished by considering feedback use at the familial scale as an evolving process co-determined by the preoccupations of household members and their contexts of activity [9].

In this paper, we describe the first results from a study of the appropriation of an electrical energy consumption display that takes into account its context for use and questions anew its role in the evolution of household preoccupations and engagement with energy control.

2   The Study

We assumed that a longitudinal study would provide a better picture of consumer histories with feedback and energy control and help situate the use (or non-use) of feedback within its context of emergence. Individual users are studied in terms of their growing competence, understanding of energy issues, and changes in personal energy practices.

Description of the feedback. The study is being conducted in France, where a smart grid meter is currently being deployed. We are testing an application that can be downloaded onto iOS and Android smartphones or tablets (Fig. 1). The application receives energy-use data via Bluetooth 4 (low energy) from the smart meter, transmitted by a flash drive in the meter's USB slot. The application shows household customers the fluctuations in their energy use: current power usage and consumption in euros per month updated every 2 s; average, peak and purchased power; and standby consumption. They can see the peak and off-peak periods, with a summary table presenting their aggregate consumption over several time periods, as well as graphical presentations (in Wh or euros). They can measure consumption over a set period and even measure the consumption of certain appliances (estimating consumption per second, per hour or per euro).

Fig. 1. (from left to right) Start screen showing instantaneous power and consumption, graphical history (daily consumption), consumption information per appliance (measurement underway), consumption results per appliance.

The application was previously tested with users to verify and improve its usability.

Participants. The study has recruited individuals who are not currently participating in other smart grid studies by phone or in the energy supplier boutique. At the beginning of the study, the obstacles to technical eligibility were substantial (specific type of electricity meter, limited number of smartphone models) and these were the main filter for recruitment. We assumed that the willingness to participate in the experiment was the only complementary criterion, the idea being that we would complete the sample later with any missing profiles (type of lodging, family composition, etc.). Of the ten households, eight include children (two adolescents), one couple has no children, and one is a divorced man. All live in detached houses (six had them built) with electric heating (alone or with wood burning) and areas ranging from 80 to 200 m2. Nine are homeowners and one is renting. All have time-of-use pricing plans for peak/off-peak hours. The ten houses were equipped between the autumn 2013 and summer 2014. As of December 2015, all were still participating in the study. They have all been compensated on the basis of the length of their participation (70 euros for two visits and phone follow-up, 100 euros for three visits, etc.).

Method. On the first visit to the households, the system is installed, application use is explained, and an interview is conducted. An autobiographical interview provides a history of the participants in their homes as it relates to energy use. The longitudinal study alternates between home visits to gather in-depth information from the customers and document past usage, and remote follow-up to determine ongoing usage. The participants use the application for several months, as and when they choose. They are invited to inform us whenever they use the application (their choice of phone, email or text message). If they do not do so (most often), we send a reminder by phone or email, based on the remote tracking system. Display usage is reconstructed with the users to help us to understand the context that motivated the usage, and according to the sequencing of actions that they report. More home visits are planned for every three to six months. Whenever possible, in situ interviews are conducted with the couples.

Modeling. The interviews are fully transcribed, as are any filmed uses. The collected data are used to build the history of customers as they appropriate the system and to model the course of their reflections about energy use before, during and after we introduce the system.

Any person using the application is assumed to be an actor. As thus far this has often been only one person in the home, we initially analyzed data from his/her point of view, but we distinguished between energy questions or decisions that were personal and those shared with other family members. We intend to separate the evolution of each individual, but analysis will necessarily be partial because of differences in engagement level. This limitation will be addressed in future studies.

Data were formalized to produce a horizontal timeline showing the sequence of decisions, actions (or non-actions) and problems. Associated elements include material contexts (housing type, family composition, work routines, type of heating, insulation, electricity plans and options, electricity bills), resources used (electricity retailer, customer advisors, advertising campaigns, feedback and functionality used), and the underlying concerns expressed from the actor's point of view along with any actions taken or obstacles encountered. This formalization allows us to track questions and problems and their overlaps and interactions. Also, every problem related to consumption or housing (building a house, cost of electric heating, etc.) is addressed specifically to focus on how the actor dealt with it and to identify his/her needs.

3   Results

Our results show that consumption feedback is part of a global context linked to the life situation that produced the consumption, the family history about energy questions that are a source of particular preoccupations, and the role of other available resources that respond to energy concerns. We present our main results on the basis of our observations.

Energy consumption fits into a past or present "happening situation". The feedback gives rise to different usages according to the underlying questions and the stage of using the application, and these usages evolve with application use. For example, the participants sought to observe and understand their consumption. This is the first time that users actually see the installation in real time. Although first interested in the cost, they gradually focus on the relationship between the volume (in watts) and the cost, and progress toward increasing attention to volume, which has the advantage of fluctuating with the appliances being used and thus brings more information on the "life" of the household. By gradually integrating the notion of consumption in watts, users define a profile of their home and become able to estimate the cost of an appliance or identify a malfunction: avoiding peaks, not going beyond certain values, or looking for values that are too high or a peak at the start of the hot water system, for example. They then try to figure out what is causing the consumption pattern and think back to recent activities to find the source of the "over"-consumption. The history of consumption, especially the curves, also helps to retrospectively associate consumption with times of activity. The maximum power reached provides information on the adequacy of the power contracted for and the volume of consumption. Some participants have reported conducting tests on appliances by plugging them in or unplugging them to see their impact on consumption. These tests bolster them in their belief that the device in question uses either a lot of energy or very little. They give information on how appliances work (wash cycles, electric heaters, stoves, etc.). To find answers to their questions as they emerge, participants sometimes use different functionalities for similar objectives, seeking answers by employing various means.

The evolution of these uses and user concerns indicate the appropriation of the data and the application. This appropriation in itself results in a change in home behavior. Greater understanding about their consumption leads users to want to change, sometimes to "hunt down waste": systematically turning off the standby function of certain appliances (coffee machine, printer, etc.) after seeing the difference in the displayed values, identifying an appliance that has been left on (auxiliary heating) because of higher consumption than usual, and so on. For one couple, the possibility of measuring appliance use helped them to focus on only using the washing machine at off-peak hours, systematically turning off lights when leaving a room, and turning off standby functions, verifying with the application that all was off before leaving for work or going to bed.

But finding the cause of elevated use can be more complex when it is not the result of "forgetting" but rather of a malfunction. For example, after checking the display one morning out of curiosity, one participant observed higher consumption than "normal." Not finding the origin of this consumption, he then consulted the display several times throughout the day and in the following days, until he made the connection between this rise, taking his shower and his hot water heater. Contrary to what he thought, it was not an off-peak heater and used full energy as soon as it was turned on. He solved the problem by connecting the system to a timer, and took advantage to schedule limited-use periods in order to consume as little as possible.

However, this level of appropriation is not systematic and the evolution in behaviors is subject to conditions. Acquiring consumption data does not always mean understanding the data and the causes of fluctuations. Some questions remain unanswered. When they showed us their consumption summaries, some participants admitted that although they could see that they had used more or less energy in a given period, they could not always easily find the cause. These difficulties indicated functional limitations and the need for support to certain users or on the basis of certain data.

In addition, family contingencies (especially when there are children or adolescents) take precedence over energy conservation. This was the case, for example, of a family with teenagers that changed its control practices as the children got older. The adolescents were more demanding and their activities less easy to control, and the parents admitted to sometimes doing the ironing or washing during peak hours to meet a specific need or to triggering the water heater to work outside of off-peak hours to meet a need for more hot water. These were contextual uses that were incompatible with the predefined, anticipated and regular control actions.

Last, the most engaged households were those with financial worries (such as the divorced man living alone with diminished financial resources in an outmoded and poorly-insulated house, or families with young children who had just bought their home). The need to limit spending is a key variable in user engagement and contributes as much to the situation as the current activity.

Appropriation is thus encouraged or hindered by conditions not directly related to the "happening situation" of domestic activities, but instead influencing them. Thus, the happening situation is not sufficient to understand feedback use and user needs. It is important to take into account the context, as it is marked by a history of energy questions and problems that are more or less resolved.

Energy feedback is situated within a history of learning about energy issues.
Energy feedback is given in a preexisting situation that comprises the socio-technical environment and personal learning and experience. All households have energy concerns linked to past events. These concerns are more or less present (actualized) because of financial worries and/or the experience of discomfort (rarely for environmental reasons).

For example, all the homeowners who had had their homes built had chosen electric heaters of poor quality, uncomfortable and expensive to run. Some wanted to change the heating system but could not afford to. They had to handle the heating problem by seeking auxiliary solutions and by developing more competence to make decisions about a supplementary heating mode, changing radiators, or installing an energy manager. They sometimes consulted professionals who proved less than competent, which engendered distrust. One participant had to manage the repeated breakdown of an obsolete and costly fuel-based heating system and an antiquated electrical installation. The most expensive work was deferred (single-phase meter, insulation). Several households were aware that the insulation in their homes needed improvement. Not knowing what work was most relevant or unsure of the prospective costs, they dealt with high consumption for heating, discomfort (low temperature or limited to certain rooms) and high bills. These homes were also pioneers in the installation of smart electricity meters because of their geographical location. Unfortunately, malfunctions occurred: the new meters are more sensitive to power overloads and often caused the circuit breakers to shut off power in one of the homes. Two other households found that the new meters had been installed without notice or consideration. They remain wary and monitor their bills and outages.

These issues affect the users' engagement with energy control, their energy questions, and their personal repertories of feasible energy management actions. The commitment to dealing with energy issues provides the context for the appropriation of feedback. It encourages the use of feedback and affects the expectations for specific functionalities: knowing what costs can be reduced (standby, appliance use, off-peak hours, consumption while out of the home), alerts for "abnormal" consumption, responses to questions about heating systems by comparing the consumption of different types of systems. However, the application is insufficient for this type of testing. To avoid further unpleasant surprises on the bill, they monitor consumption over a billing period and expect that this consumption history will prepare them for the next bill. Last, they try to avoid tripping the circuit breaker by monitoring the maximum and average power used.

Conversely, if the proposed functionalities do not give users a better understanding of their actions or a new source for savings, use can become less frequent. Users on a tight budget who are already trying to reduce consumption (systematically turning off lights and standby systems, unplugging chargers) feel less room to maneuver with the feedback display. Moreover, when functionalities do not actually allow the expected calculations, users can draw erroneous conclusions. Thus, a household wanting to know the difference in cost of running a washing machine in peak and off-peak periods based their conclusion on a historical measure distorted by the use of other appliances running at the same time (hot water and heating). They concluded that off-peak was more expensive and did not see the interest of doing laundry at off-peak hours. Promoting the appropriation of feedback means providing enough functionalities to address concerns. It also implies articulating the feedback with other modes of assistance that help users throughout their learning and questioning.

Energy feedback is a part of a system of assistance. The design and evaluation of feedback systems are often considered apart from other devices that consumers can use. However, we note that feedback is part of a set of systems, as a complement, substitution or control.

All consumers obviously receive bills, which are often the first (or only) way to monitor consumption. Often, the billing frequency is not considered sufficient to anticipate mistakes or excesses in consumption. Thus, a couple with young children considered enrolling in a plan to follow consumption (with monthly paper reports) to have more detail on their energy use. But the offer was not free (2 euros per month) and they concluded that the solution was expensive for the expected gain. They thus remained without a solution until the application was proposed to them free of charge. Another household on a monthly plan (fixed payment every month based on an annual estimate, with an adjustment made in the last month based on actual consumption) used the application to anticipate the amount of the adjustment bill: they knew they had consume less than the estimate made by the energy company (by adding wood heating) and monitored their monthly consumption to estimate the annual amount and stay within budget. Several households also created their personal space on the site of their energy company. They can find their past bills and the main elements of their contracts (power, peak periods, etc.). In this case, there is additional information to that proposed by the smartphone display.

Digital systems are nevertheless not sufficient to respond to users' energy issues. User support should be thought of as a system of support for their engagement, with the offer of multiple resources, including human resources. In the histories of all our participants, we found that they have called on intermediaries for help in the past: friends, people knowledgeable about electricity, electricians and heating specialists. Yet they might have called their energy distributor or stopped by one of its boutiques. The man living alone in his energy-obsolete house was well supported by a customer advisor, first by telephone and then with a home visit, as he sought to understand the reasons for his high bills despite behavioral changes. The need for monitoring and personalized advice for deciding on concrete actions means that feedback displays should be seen as part of a much broader network of assistance, wherein other components may be deficient and thus compensated by the feedback display (in detecting that the water heater is not set for off-peak because the electrician forgot to set it, for example).

To bring about actions to control energy use, the display must be supplemented by other technologies. Although it detects problems, solving them often requires concrete actions such as equipment changes (heating manager, remote control outlets, power strips, controllers, etc.). However aware users become (publicity and information campaigns that help to improve competence and engagement), the willingness to act still requires the means for acting and technical assistance in adapting practices. Thus, our most active participants learned about, acquired and managed programmable outlets and standby power controllers.

Last, we have seen that financial constraints are an obstacle to action: consumers have to determine what they can do themselves, but they also should be able to obtain low-cost assistance or even financial aid.

Energy feedback is a resource among others for making decisions, learning and acting: human resources (family, personal relationships, customer advisers), information and advertising, financial resources and the concrete means for acting (control systems). The households request these resources according to their evolving preoccupations, competences and experience.

4   Conclusion

Our study shows that a focus on the appropriation of feedback provides insight into the determinants of the shift to active control of energy use.

This study has limitations, one of which we identified as the need to consider all household members in order to investigate collective appropriation. It will also be important to study the households that themselves opted for the feedback systems, in addition to those that were specifically recruited. We also plan to study a population that is energy-insecure. A new version of the application that includes missing functionalities and a complementary application for budget monitoring are also under development.

Analysis of the appropriation process shows that feedback use is determined by specific questions that vary over time and according to evolving user competence. This explains why the device was used differently over time. A consumption display cannot be the only way for consumers to engage with energy control because engagement depends on many factors that feedback alone cannot address. Changing behavior cannot be reduced to influence or persuasion; it must be seen as depending on a response to concerns through technical and cognitive resources, of which feedback is clearly one.

Consumption feedback is contextually interpreted and must be designed to fit into the user's context. The context must be defined from the user's point of view and considered as distributed over time: in connection with ongoing activities and questionings already experienced, resolved or persisting, all of which have needed diverse resources in the past. It therefore must take into account user development and the acquisition of new competences.

This means that consumption feedback must have at least three main characteristics to be appropriable: scalability, complementarity and operability. Thus, it must be functionally rich (to respond to evolving needs and capacities): the link to activity makes information essential – in real time, historically and per appliance. Effective feedback should contain multiple feedback options, not limited to a value unit (e.g., money), a timescale or a type of measure. The structure of feedback should allow for more in-depth uses as new questions and needs emerge. It must also be complementary with other forms of assistance: feedback cannot meet all consumer needs. It is important to differentiate the needs for assistance that can be met by a display from those needs best met by other resources, with the ultimate objective being the design of global support for user engagement. Last, it should allow for action: information alone is not sufficient. Feedback must allow the prediction of the impact of an action. Comparisons between situations and simulations of "what if" scenarios are needed. These should be extendable with the means for acting.

These contextual and operational constraints broaden the issue beyond the display. It will be important to design aids for a process in construction using diverse resources from the perspective of complementarity as users evolve and grow in commitment.

References

1. Abrahamse, W., Steg, L., Vlek, C., Rothengatter, T.: A review of intervention studies aimed at household energy conservation. J. Environ. Psychol. **25**, 273–291 (2005)

2. Barreto, M., Karapanos, E., Nunes, N.: Why don't families get along with eco-feedback technologies? a longitudinal inquiry. In: Proceedings of the Biannual Conference of the Italian Chapter of SIGCHI (CHItaly 2013). ACM, New York (2013)
3. Darby, S.: The Effectiveness of Feedback on Energy Consumption: A Review for Defra of the Literature on Metering Billing and Direct Displays. Environmental Change Institute, University of Oxford, Oxford (2006)
4. Electric Power Research Institute: Residential Electricity Use Feedback: A Research Synthesis and Economic Framework. Palo Alto, CA (2009)
5. Erickson, T., Li, M., Kim, Y., Deshpande, A., Sahu, S., Chao, T., Sukaviriya, P., Naphade, M.: The dubuque electricity portal: evaluation of a city-scale residential electricity consumption feedback system. In: Proceedings of the CHI 2013. ACM Press, Paris (2013)
6. Fischer, C.: Feedback on household electricity consumption: a tool for saving energy? Energy Effi. 1, 79–104 (2008)
7. Fréjus, M., Cahour, B.: Reflection processes in energy regulation situations assisted with reflective tools. In: MobileHCI 2015 Adjunct, August 25–28, Copenhagen, Denmark (2015)
8. Fréjus, M., Guibourdenche, J.: Analysing domestic activity to reduce household energy consumption. Work 41, 539–548 (2012)
9. Fréjus, M., Martini, D.: Taking into account user appropriation and development to design energy consumption feedback. In: CHI 2015 Extended Abstracts, April 18–23, Seoul (2015)
10. Froehlich, J., Findlater, L., Landay, J.: The design of eco-feedback technology. In: Proceedings of the SIGCHI Conference on Human Factors in Computing Systems (CHI 2010). ACM, New York (2010)
11. Grønhøj, A., Thøgersen, J.: Feedback on household electricity consumption: learning and social influence processes. Int. J. Consum. Stud. 35(2), 138–145 (2011)
12. Hargreaves, T., Nye, M., Burgess, J.: Making energy visible: a qualitative field study of how householders interact with feedback from smart energy monitors. Energy Policy 38, 6111–6119 (2010)
13. Hargreaves, T., Nye, M., Burgess, J.: Keeping energy visible: exploring how householders interact with feedback from smart energy monitors in the longer term. Energy Policy 52, 126–134 (2013)
14. Li, I., Dey, D.K., Forlizzi, J.: Understanding my data, myself: supporting self-reflection with ubicomp technologies. In: Proceedings UbiComp 2011, Beijing, China (2011)
15. Pierce, J., Fan, C., Lomas, D., Marcu, G., Paulos, E.: Some considerations on the (in)effectiveness of residential energy feedback systems. In: Proceedings DIS 2010 (2010)
16. Pierce, J., Odom, W., Blevis, E.: Energy aware dwelling: a critical survey of interaction design for eco-visualizations. In: Proceedings of OZCHI 2008 (2008)
17. Schwartz, T., Denef, S., Stevens, G., Ramirez, L., Wulf, V.: Cultivating energy literacy - results from a longitudinal living lab study of a home energy management system. In: Proceedings CHI 2013, Paris (2013)
18. Shove, E., Lutzenhiser, L., Guy, S., Hackett, B., Wilhite, H.: Energy and social systems. In: Rayner, S., Malone, E. (eds.) Human Choice and Climate Change. Battelle Press, Columbus, OH (1998)
19. Snow, S., Brereton, M.: When an eco-feedback system joins the family. Pers. Ubiquitous Comput. 19(5), 929–940 (2015)
20. Snow S., Buys L., Roe P., Brereton, M.: Curiosity to cupboard: self-reported disengagement with energy use feedback over time. In: Proceedings of the OzCHI 2013. ACM Press, pp. 245–254 (2013)
21. Stern, P.C.: What psychology knows about energy conservation. Am. Psychol. 47(10), 1224–1232 (1992)

22. Strengers, Y.: Beyond demand management: co-managing energy and water practices with australian households. Policy Stud. **32**(1), 35–58 (2011)
23. Strengers, Y.: Smart energy in everyday life: are you designing for resource man? Interactions **21**, 24–31 (2014)
24. Van Dam, S., Bakker, C.A., van Hal, J.D.M.: Home energy monitors: impact over the medium-term. Build. Res. Inf. **38**, 458–469 (2010)
25. Wallenborn, G., Orsini, M., Vanhaverbeke, J.: Household appropriation of electricity monitors. Int. J. Consum. Stud. **35**(2), 146–152 (2011)
26. Wilhite, H., Ling, R.: Measured energy savings from a more informative energy bill. Energy Buildings **22**, 145–155 (1995)
27. Wilhite, H., Shove, E.: Twenty years of energy demand management: we know more about individual behavior but how much do we really know about demand. In: Proceedings. ACEEE, pp. 435–453 (2000)

Chances for Urban Electromobility

Field Test of Intermodal Travel System and Effect on Usage Intention

Simon Himmel[1][(✉)], Barbara S. Zaunbrecher[1], Martina Ziefle[1], and Markus C. Beutel[2]

[1] HCIC, Communication Science, RWTH Aachen University, Aachen, Germany
{himmel,zaunbrecher,ziefle}@comm.rwth-aachen.de
[2] Information Systems, RWTH Aachen University, Aachen, Germany
beutel@dbis.rwth-aachen.de

Abstract. With growing cities, challenges of climate change, and ambitions for energy transition, innovations in urban mobility are inevitable. On the one hand, fossil-fueled vehicles are polluting the cities and could be substituted with electric cars. On the other hand, the sheer number of vehicles has to decrease and public transport needs to be enhanced. A possible solution addressing all challenges in one fully integrated concept is "Mobility Broker", which combines electric car and bike sharing with public transport in one intermodal traveling system. However, adoption and changes in mobility behavior are crucial for implementing new concepts. In this research, a prototype evaluation by 10 participants using the system for 2 months is presented. The usability of the system as well as the change in attitudes and usage intention before and after the hands-on experience is analyzed. The overall evaluation for intermodal traveling was positive but usability and a reliable infrastructure are crucial factors for usage adoption.

Keywords: Car-sharing · Bike sharing · Usability · Field test · Future mobility

1 Introduction

Most western societies face the challenges of urban mobility as cities everywhere are expanding tremendously [1]. Cities are confronted with environmental problems due to emissions as well as infrastructural problems caused by too many vehicles. With a change to electric car and bike sharing, both challenges could be met at once [2].

First of all, electromobility would mean decreased emissions in urban areas. Second, the implementation of electric car and bike sharing would make this technology available to a wide audience, as the transition from fossil-fueled to electric cars and e-bikes has, so far, only reached a very limited number of households. One reason for this are the higher acquisition costs of an electric car compared to a conventional one. Using electric cars as part of car sharing, however, is available at a much smaller cost [3].

To further reduce the actual number of cars in use, the next step would be the improvement of multimodal mobility options. To facilitate multi- and intermodal

© Springer International Publishing Switzerland 2016
A. Marcus (Ed.): DUXU 2016, Part II, LNCS 9747, pp. 472–484, 2016.
DOI: 10.1007/978-3-319-40355-7_45

mobility behavior, an encompassing information system was developed. This system integrates heterogeneous mobility services by independent providers on one platform that the user can access to book a journey, for example. To achieve a holistic integration, services needed at various stages of the travels, e.g., travel information via user interfaces, tariffs, and available infrastructure, were combined, thus eliminating the need to manually patch together an itinerary and pay each provider individually. This system, called "Mobility Broker," allows users to query, book, and utilize different modes of transportation within one trip, free from barriers like different platforms for booking and information, different tariffs, etc. (see Fig. 1). In this paper, we report initial observations of test persons interacting with the system in its first practical usage phase, including renting stations on site, the app, and tariffs.

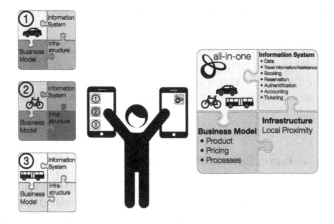

Fig. 1. Isolated mobility systems (left) vs. integrated "Mobility Broker" system (right)

1.1 The Intermodal Traveling System "Mobility Broker"

In past decades, the development of travel information systems moved from stand-alone solutions to integrated and complex information systems. Nowadays, advanced travel information systems (ATIS) use information and communication technology to provide travel information to a wide range of users who use various modes of transportation with a diversity of characteristics [4]. Beyond the provision of information, modern systems reduce the complexity of planning, booking, and utilization of intermodal travel chains [5].

As such, "Mobility Broker" manages heterogeneous modes of transportation offered by different mobility providers [6]. The respective system components, architecture, and information flows are described in [7]. Travelers interact with the system using a mobile application for android smartphones or a web portal which connects to the back-end using standardized APIs (see Fig. 2). A specific communication adapter is responsible for the communication with second party mobility providers. It exchanges travel information using a variety of open protocols, i.e., IXSI (Interface for X-Sharing Information).

Fig. 2. Intermodal planning, routing, and traveling within the "Mobility Broker" app

IXSI connects vehicle rental systems with travel information systems and allows an asynchronous exchange of vehicle sharing information, e.g., availability [8]. In its current state, the system provides travel information concerning public transportation modes and enables the utilization of two e-cars and up to five e-bikes connected to associated charging stations.

1.2   Usability of Travel Information Systems

Travel information systems are a prominent research field [9–11]. Projects and applications vary significantly in a multitude of aspects [12]. Some related research is aimed at the effects of integrated solutions on the mobility behavior: Huwer [13] investigated synergies of combining car sharing and public transportation services in the German regions of Aachen and Mannheim. Although the technical integration was not the main focus of these studies, beneficial synergies could be observed. Moreover, Hoffmann et al. [14] evaluated integrated mobility services from the user's perspective. They offer a smart card solution as integrated authorization method, combined with a mobile application to provide travel information. Although these studies examined integration on various layers, they did not have an application with advanced functionalities, e.g., integrated accounting and booking. In addition, car sharing and public transportation services were provided by the same mobility provider.

What we know so far is that the increase of technology acceptance depends on the perceived usefulness and ease of use of a technology (Technology Acceptance Model, TAM) [15]. But will the acceptance of the multimodal mobility system and its components actually influence travel behavior? Recent research has shown that for public transport systems adequate user interaction is crucial for acceptance and usability [16]. Similar results were drawn for car sharing in combination with intermodal traveling [14]. To assess the actual usage intention of new intermodal traveling systems, the UTAUT2 model [17] provides valid dimensions used in similar contexts [18] and was adopted for this research.

To investigate effects of travel information systems, we examined test-person's reactions, using different scientific instruments. In [6], we evaluated "Mobility Broker" via an online survey, primarily focused on integration factors of the system. Within this work, we investigate some aspects even further. In contrast to previous studies, we concentrate on subsequent changes in the test-persons' attitudes towards specific transportation services resulting from using the system. As central, distinctive feature of this work, we investigated a test-group intensively by data collection at the beginning and the end of a field test, as well as monitoring user interaction with the system.

The research focuses on three aspects: (1) the usability of the multimodal mobility system (infrastructure and ticketing), (2) the willingness to use such a system in the future, and (3) the influence of using such a system on the actual mobility behavior.

2   Method

First, in a **pre-questionnaire**, the participants had to provide general attitudes towards electromobility (e-bikes and e-cars), intermodal traveling, and their usage intentions towards those new technologies by evaluating given statements on a 4-point Likert scale (see Sect. 3.2). They were also asked to describe their average mobility behavior, stating types and frequency of used means of transportation.

Afterwards, they were introduced to the intermodal traveling system "Mobility Broker" and its rental and ticketing processes. The app was installed on their mobile phones and the card needed for the rental process handed out. Then they were familiarized with the infrastructure (see Fig. 3). Participants were instructed on how to book, rent, and return e-bikes and cars at the stations. Afterwards, they were asked to perform these actions on their own in groups of two. They were voice recorded during this process to capture questions and comments (see Sect. 3.1).

Fig. 3. Bike-sharing (left) and car-sharing (right) rental procedure with "Mobility Broker"

The participants used "Mobility Broker" in a **field test** for two months. They were instructed to use the system in their daily mobility routines as much or as little as they liked. To compare the usage frequency of means of transport with the system and use without the system, the participants documented their daily mobility behavior in a diary. They also wrote down any experience with the entire system. This onsite observation served as additional input for the usability analysis.

At the end of the field test, the participants filled in a **post-questionnaire**. In its *first part*, the users had to evaluate "Mobility Broker" by UTAUT2 [17] dimensions (see Sect. 3.2), with the exception of price values, as the field test app was a free trial. In the *second part*, the statements of the pre-questionnaire concerning electromobility, intermodal traveling, and usage intention were presented once more. The comparison of the pre- and post-items measured the attitude change influenced by actual hands-on experience of the system in everyday life (see Sect. 3.3).

Ten **participants** (9 male, 1 female) aged 21 to 30 took part in this study. The sample was quite homogenous: All participants were students of computer sciences and interested in technology. As the station for bike- and car-sharing was located near the department of informatics, close to lectures and their daily student life, all participants had the same initial conditions to use the system.

3   Results

The results are presented in three sections. First, usability of Mobility Broker is evaluated using the comments from the field test and the pre- and post-questionnaire (qualitative data). Second, UTAUT is evaluated for the system as well as changes in mobility behavior (quantitative data). First of all, the general mobility usage (means of transportation and usage frequency) did not change within the field test study. The hypothesis that the opportunity to use an intermodal mobility system with new means of transport such as e-bikes and e-cars leads to an increased usage of intermodal traveling has to be rejected for this field test. Why and if this might change will be analyzed in the qualitative and quantitative results.

3.1   Qualitative Results – General Comments and Usability Concerns

General Comments. Most users reported that using the electric vehicles was fun; some explicitly mentioned the "good conscience" because of the electric engine. Participants wished for more stations and vehicles in Aachen. Due to the test phase character of the study, only one station could be used at the time. However, there are plans to expand the network of stations.

The sample saw great potential, especially for an e-bike system, in Aachen where university buildings are spread all across the city and, therefore, considered students one of the major target groups. Although participants reported that general handling of the app was easy, its functionality was sometimes restricted due to software problems, for example, concerning reservations. Users demanded a back-up solution for returning the e-car should the system malfunction. They also suggested that "favorites" from the app should be saved to a user profile so that they do not need to be recreated manually should a re-installation be required. In addition, users demanded a specific contact person whom they could turn to if the system did not work as required. Because of the test status of the station, responsibilities for repairs were sometimes not clear.

Unfortunately, the system experienced some problems during the test phase, for example, a crashed app or problems at the charging station (e-car) and with the e-car itself. One participant reported that he had not been able to use e-cars during the entire test phase due to issues at the station or with the car.

Reservation. Participants asked for the possibility of reserving e-bikes several hours or days in advance but were told that this was only possible for e-cars. In this context, it was also of interest to them if costs were attached to the reservation itself or if they were only charged when actually driving the car. Furthermore, they wanted to know whether the app showed the charging status of e-bikes and cars in the reservation phase, as to plan their travels more reliably. This was named as essential prerequisite to be able to use the system as intended.

Handling at Station. *E-bike.* The handling of e-bikes was problematic for some, as the bikes were hard to detach/attach from and to the station and participants were afraid to damage the locking mechanism.

The significance of the number indicating the available e-bike in the app was not clear to the participants: while they thought it referred to the number of bikes available, it was actually its designation (e.g., 2 did not mean that two bikes were available, but bike no. 2 was available). Further confusion was caused by the incongruence of slot numbers and bike numbers (e.g., bike no 2 was in slot number 3, so it was mistaken for bike no. 3). Sometimes, it was displayed that no bike was available although there was one at the station. Participants expressed that, should this be the case, they would want more information on why the bike was not available to them, e.g., that it was already reserved, broken, etc. This was also mentioned with regard to the app, which sometimes displayed error messages without further details on the cause of the error.

E-car. Generally, handling of the e-car at the renting station proved to be much more complicated to the participants than the e-bike. This was mainly due to the many steps required for usage, including detaching the charging cable which was locked separately.

First, it was not clear to the participants that they had to take the charging cable with them once they had unlocked everything. It was also hard for them to know whether the locking mechanism was deactivated: they had to be instructed to listen to the cable unlocking. (Un-)Locking the car with the card instead of a conventional key also caused some confusion. First, because it was counterintuitive to the participants and, second, because they knew other car-sharing systems that use the key.

Participants also expected a visual or acoustic signal when the car had been (un-)locked with the card. They were unsure about the time necessary to hold the card near the sensor for it to work. The visual feedback for locking the charging pole was also not intuitively understood ("blue" for "ok"/"start" instead of, e.g., green). It was also not readily understandable to the participants why the charging cable had to be unlocked using the card. Participants wishes for a combined solution that allowed to unlock both car and charging station simultaneously.

Participants sometimes experienced hardware malfunctions, for example, it was not possible to re-connect the car to the charging station, the car could not be used despite reservation, gears did not work, etc. The reliability of the e-car system was thus criticized. Furthermore, questions were raised as to when the app had to be used: some functions were only available via the app, others only at the station itself. It was not clear that, once participants had reached the station, they did not need the app anymore.

Handling During Renting Period. Participants reported that, in general, they had no problems handling the e-cars and e-bikes.

E-Bike. For the bikes, participants complained that there was no lock available to secure the bikes when they were not attached to the station. This locking system should also allow to check whether it had been used correctly, so if the bike was stolen, the users would not be held accountable. Questions were also raised regarding the distribution of bikes across different stations and how it would be handled if the bikes were concentrated at one station and therefore not available at others.

E-car. It was asked whether it was allowed to cross borders with the car. (Aachen is close to both the Netherlands and Belgium.) During the instruction, the car did not start for one participant. He speculated that the key was in the wrong position, because there was no acoustic feedback that the engine was running. Another point of criticism was the short range provided by the battery's limited capacity.

3.2   Quantitative Usage Evaluation

After the trial period, participants were asked to evaluate "Mobility Broker" in general, using the UTAUT2 scale [17] (Fig. 4). Agreement to the statements was measured on a 4-point Likert scale from −1.5 (do not agree) to 1.5 (fully agree). As the sample size with n = 10 was too small, the effects of different evaluation dimensions on usage intention by UTAUT2 was not measured statistically.

The **Performance Expectancy** was not overly positive, although its value for the participants' lives was favorable. **Effort Expectancy** was valued best of all dimensions. The system itself was referred to as easy to learn, clear, and understandable. Except for ease-of-use, all participants valued Mobility Broker positively. The **Social Influence** was overall low. Concerning the **facilitating Conditions**, it can be said from the data that the system seems to be well-designed to meet users' level of expertise. This underlines the positive comments on the usability of the app. Concerning the **Hedonic Motivation**, it is noteworthy that participants did not overly enjoy using the system but were generally positive towards it. Regarding the **Habit** to use "Mobility Broker" in the future, the participants could imagine using an intermodal traveling system in their daily life. Only the imperative use of the system was rejected. In a second test, with a bigger sample size, this item should be modified or left out. Finally, the **Behavioral Intention** to use the system in the future was also not particularly high.

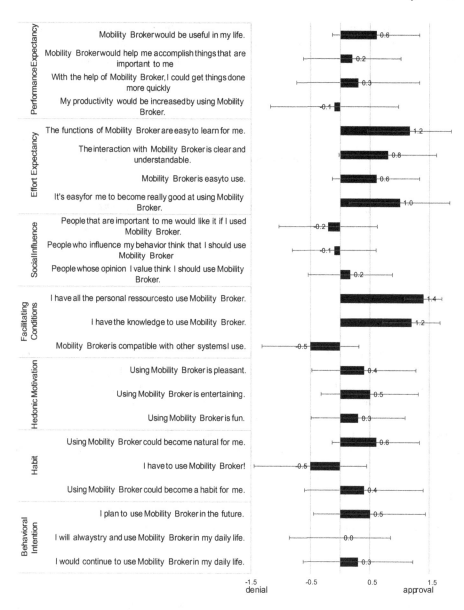

Fig. 4. Acceptance of "Mobility Broker" system, UTAUT dimensions (n = 10)

3.3 Attitudes Towards Electromobility and Intermodal Traveling – Before and After

The sample size was too small to report statistically significant findings. However, the results showed tendencies underlying the qualitative findings and are reported descriptively. The actual use of **electric car- and bike-sharing** (over a longer period) did influence the attitude towards these systems. Figure 5 shows mostly distinct differences between before and after the field test. Car- and bike-sharing were regarded positively for flexibility in mobility but while the test period improved the view of bike-sharing, the attitude towards car-sharing worsened, indicating the car-sharing process needs improvement.

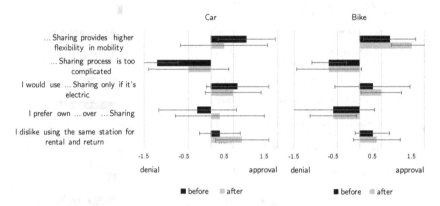

Fig. 5. Statements regarding car- and bike-sharing before and after test period (n = 10)

But although the participants determined several problems with the system, the overall sharing process for cars and bikes was appraised to be not too complicated. The amplification factor of the electric drive was negligible for the usage intention. While the test period had no effect regarding bike-sharing, the preference of an own car compared to car-sharing was strengthened. The concept of bringing the shared vehicle back to the same rental station was evaluated worse for the car, especially after the test period. Regarding the intermodal traveling process itself, the overall evaluation worsened a little after the hands-on experience. While the evaluation of an app did not change before and after the test period, again the infrastructure should be improved. More participants could imagine using multimodal traveling to transport heavy items after two months of testing. The perceived positive impact of multimodal traveling on traffic and the city climate remained unchanged after the field test (Fig. 6).

4   Discussion and Recommendations

The evaluation of the intermodal system "Mobility Broker" and its effect on usage behavior of new mobility concepts (electromobility and sharing services) shed light on users' perception of the system, usability issues and its potential to increase the use of sharing services.

With regard to the infrastructure, the communication of problems needs to be improved to prevent frustration of the users. Instead of stating that something was not available or wrong, knowing the reason would be greatly appreciated by the participants. In addition, notifying users when problems are detected and resolved would be beneficial. In general, system reliability needs to be ensured to make it attractive to use,

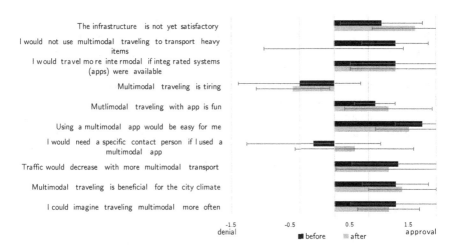

The infrastructure is not yet satisfactory

I would not use multimodal traveling to transport heavy items

I would travel more intermodal if integrated systems (apps) were available

Multimodal traveling is tiring

Mutlimodal traveling with app is fun

Using a multimodal app would be easy for me

I would need a specific contact person if I used a multimodal app

Traffic would decrease with more multimodal transport

Multimodal traveling is beneficial for the city climate

I could imagine traveling multimodal more often

-1.5 denial   -0.5   0.5   1.5 approval

■ before   ▨ after

Fig. 6. Evaluation of statements regarding intermodal traveling before and after test period

especially concerning e-cars. A step-by-step guide for the renting station would also be helpful to the participants and could avoid confusion related to the right order of the required actions. This could, for example, be realized by a display at the station showing instructions. Furthermore, visual and acoustic feedback should be improved for some of the actions required at the station, and color codes should be more intuitive. One solution could be a small screen visible from the outside of the car displaying "locked"/"car returned" after locking the car. Although the comment did not refer to "Mobility Broker" itself, the missing engine sound of the e-car confused one participant, as he had no feedback whether he had started the car correctly. This means that not only the novelty of the renting system but also of e-cars need to be considered, and that there may still be barriers to using e-cars.

Concerning the e-bikes, the interactive display at the station at the time of renting should indicate the bike number instead of slot number of the bike to be rented out to avoid confusion with the information given in the app at time of reservation. A smoother locking/unlocking mechanism for the bikes is also needed, especially when considering that future users can be considerably older than our test group and might not be strong enough to release the bike from the tight lock easily. It is of great importance for the future success of the bike-sharing system that a transportable lock is offered and insurance issues are resolved. This could be a major hindrance, as one participant remarked he did not dare to leave the bike anywhere in case it would be stolen. Insurance also needs to cover usage other countries, especially in cities close to borders.

Concerning the analysis of UTAUT applied to the system, the results need to interpreted against the background of the specific setting and some limitations. The low performance expectancy is most likely due to the unreliable performance of the system at times, as reported by the participants (see Sect. 3.1). The low social influence is probably a result of the fact that the system is not yet commercially used, so the social network of the participants did not know about it and thus could neither recommend nor criticize its use. A lack of fun was also observed, which could be attributed to problems with reliability and lack of communication and contact persons when problems occurred. Most interestingly for the future usage of the system was the behavioral intention, which was low for the sample under study. From the qualitative data, it became clear that participants liked the idea of "Mobility Broker" in principle but criticized that the system was still too faulty to be used on a regular basis. This is also due to the trial character of the study. Regarding the app itself, the system is already well constructed, and has a good usability and ease-of-use. But for an intermodal traveling system, the travel routine itself is much more important. Therefore, more focus should be on the hardware and infrastructure.

5   Conclusion

The aims of the study were twofold: First, the interaction of the users with the system should be investigated to detect possible usability problems. Second, it was assessed in how far the trial period of "Mobility Broker" increased participants' intention to use shared and electric modes of transport.

An obvious limitation to the study was the lack of more stations to rent and return e-bikes and e-cars. Regarding usability, the whole system was assessed. Although the app was evaluated quite positively compared to the reliability and the infrastructure of the whole system, another research approach could focus specifically on the app.

Finally, to gain general and statistically relevant results, the rather small sample size has to be enlarged. The very small and homogenous group of participants was a first step to evaluate an early prototype. The next step has to be the evaluation of a better functioning, improved intermodal traveling system with a broader sample to include effects of user diversity. These next research approaches could give deeper insights into the impact of actual hands-on experience with electric intermodal traveling systems on future mobility. Nevertheless, all participants enjoyed their experience with electric cars and bikes. Through this field test, they were made aware of the potential of electromobility as well as car- and bike-sharing. It is projects such as this, and having people interact directly with these systems, that can have a positive impact on urban mobility of the future.

Acknowledgements. Thanks for research support and help with data collection to Anaïs Haberman and thanks to Sean Lidynia for valuable remarks and support. This work was partially funded by German Federal Ministry of Economic Affairs Energy for the project Mobility Broker (01ME12136) as well as the Excellence Initiative of the German State and Federal Government (Project Urban Future Outline).

References

1. United Nations: World urbanization prospects: the 2011 revision. UN Proc. United Nations Department of Economic and Social Affairs/Population Division, New York (2012)
2. Lerner, W., Van Audenhove, F.-J.: The future of urban mobility: towards networked, multimodal cities in 2050. Public Transp. Int.-Engl. Ed. **61**, 14 (2012)
3. Benevolo, C., Dameri, R.P., D'Auria, B.: Smart mobility in smart city. In: Torre, T., Braccini, A.M., Spinelli, R. (eds.) Empowering Organizations, pp. 13–28. Springer, Cham (2016)
4. Chen, B., McQueen, R., Schuman, K.: Advanced Traveler Information Systems. Artech House Inc., Norwood (2002)
5. Beul-Leusmann, S., Jakobs, E.-M., Ziefle, M.: User-centered design of passenger information systems. In: Professional Communication Conference (IPCC), 2013 IEEE International, pp. 1–8. IEEE (2013)
6. Beutel, M.C., Zaunbrecher, B.S., Himmel, S., Krempels, K.-H., Ziefle, M.: Evaluating an integrated offering for intermodal traveling. In: Conference Proceedings of 5th International Conference on Smart Cities and Green ICT Systems, Rome, Italy (2016, in press)
7. Beutel, M.C., Gökay, S., Kluth, W., Krempels, K.-H., Samsel, C., Terwelp, C.: Heterogeneous travel information exchange. In: 2nd EAI International Conference on Mobility in IoT, Rome, Italy (2015)
8. Kluth, W., Beutel, M.C., Gökay, S., Krempels, K.-H., Samsel, C., Terwelp, C.: IXSI - interface for X-sharing information. In: 11th International Conference on Web Information Systems and Technologies (2015)
9. Beutel, M.C., Gokay, S., Kluth, W., Krempels, K.-H., Samsel, C., Terwelp, C.: Product oriented integration of heterogeneous mobility services. In: 2014 IEEE 17th International Conference on Intelligent Transportation Systems (ITSC), pp. 1529–1534. IEEE (2014)
10. Samsel, C., Beul-Leusmann, S., Wiederhold, M., Krempels, K.-H., Ziefle, M., Jakobs, E.-M.: Cascading information for public transport assistance. In: Proceedings of the 10th International Conference on Web Information Systems and Technologies (WEBIST 2014), pp. 411–422 (2014)
11. Wells, S., Forbes, P., Masthoff, J., Gabrielli, S., Jyllha, A.: SUPERHUB: integrating digital behaviour management into a novel sustainable urban mobility system. In: Proceedings of the 27th International BCS Human Computer Interaction Conference, p. 62. British Computer Society (2013)
12. Urban ITS Expert Group, European Commission: Best Practices in Urban ITS – Collection of Projects (2013). http://ec.europa.eu/transport/themes/its/road/action_plan/doc/2013-urban-its-expert_group-best-practice-collection.pdf
13. Huwer, U.: Public transport and car-sharing – benefits and effects of combined services. Transp. Policy **11**, 77–87 (2004)
14. Hoffmann, C., Graff, A., Kramer, S., Kuttler, T., Hendzlik, M., Scherf, C., Wolter, F.: Evaluation of integrated Mobility Services with electric vehicles from users' perspectives (orig. Bewertung integrierter Mobilitätsdienste mit Elektrofahrzeugen aus Nutzerperspektive). Ergeb. Begleit. Im Proj. BeMobility-Berl. ElektroMobil InnoZ-Baustein. 11 (2012)
15. Davis, F.D.: Perceived usefulness, perceived ease of use, and user acceptance of information technology. MIS Q. **13**, 319–337 (1989)
16. Mügge, H., Lüke, K.-H., Eisemann, M.: Potentials and requirements of mobile ubiquitous computing for public transport. GI Jahrestag **2**(110), 237–246 (2007)

17. Venkatesh, V., Thong, J.Y., Xu, X.: Consumer acceptance and use of information technology: extending the unified theory of acceptance and use of technology. MIS Q. **36**, 157–178 (2012)
18. Wolf, A., Seebauer, S.: Technology adoption of electric bicycles: a survey among early adopters. Transp. Res. Part Policy Pract. **69**, 196–211 (2014)

Disruptive UX for Sustainability

Radically Resolving User Needs Is Good for Business and Environment

Tao Huang[✉]

Southern Illinois University at Carbondale, Carbondale, USA
thuang@siu.edu

Abstract. The paper provides a brief discussion of the basic concepts of sustainability, disruptive innovation, systems thinking theory, and design for behavior change literature. It analyzes several business and design cases closely related to UX and HCI that demonstrated various degrees of success in changing user behaviors to improve the quality of our environment and strengthen communities in the following aspects: reducing pollution from fossil fuel based transportation; reducing waste; providing meaningful and gainful employment; and raising awareness, etc. The paper argues that UX/HCI, being the bridge between hardware and software, is fundamental in ensuring the success of any sustainability initiatives. The paper contemplates the cultural shift of material to immaterial by sharing economy in the internet age, which is one of the promising ways to help our society move towards sustainability. The paper also identifies certain challenges and room for improvement in user experience research and design for sustainability. In the end, this paper suggests four directions for radically rethinking user experience and human/computer interaction design for sustainability.

Keywords: User experience design · Systems thinking · Sustainability · Disruptive innovation · Sustainable design · Design for behavior change

1 Introduction

Technology has disrupted many sectors of the business world and in some cases, directly or indirectly made those new forms of businesses good for the environment. This paper presents the concept of "Disruptive UX for Sustainability", an approach in user experience research and design that radically rethinks the paradigms of business with the main focus of making people consume less and recycle more, business pollute less and profit more from new revenue. It goes beyond the usual function of user experience design and research: UX is not only necessary for adding value to any business, but it can also change the landscape by creating new business opportunities that can satisfy the triple bottom lines of sustainability: good for the economy, our society and the environment.

Though in the past two decades, the term "user experience design" (UXD or XD) has been more closely associated with the field of human-computer interaction design,

© Springer International Publishing Switzerland 2016
A. Marcus (Ed.): DUXU 2016, Part II, LNCS 9747, pp. 485–493, 2016.
DOI: 10.1007/978-3-319-40355-7_46

designers in all fields have been defining and resolving user experience issues for years. For instance, industrial designers must make three dimensional objects more usable for a better user experience. Thus, the study of human factors and ergonomics is a well-established field. As early as 1955, one of the founders of the Industrial Designers Society of America, Henry Dreyfuss, called for industrial designers' attention to anthropometric research and its important role in design [1]. Since then, design considerations of the physical measurements of human bodies have been expanded into cognitive ergonomics and organizational ergonomics [2].

As information technology permeates our daily lives, the research and advancement of UX has real world consequences beyond its usual two dimensional confinement. Generations of thinkers and designers have led the design community towards recognizing the environmental impacts of mass manufacturing. In the age of Industry 4.0, more and more products and services exist in both the physical and digital realms [3]. User experience design is inseparable from all the other design fields and it needs to be concerned of both the physical and cognitive limitations of humans.

In this paper, I propose to use systems thinking to examine how to design for behavior change to build a more sustainable future. There are four directions of rethinking: breaking the path dependency by disruptive innovation, automation to remove barrier, creating platforms to connect people and business, and visualizing information to change perceptions. I focus on business and design examples and possibilities in developed countries, as there is a more urgent need for these countries to adjust their life styles and consumer behavior to ensure a sustainable future for all mankind.

2   Sustainability by Design

The modern concept of sustainability emerged in the environmental movements in the 1960s and the term *sustainability* was adopted by The World Commission on Environment and Development in 1987. The Commission's report defines *sustainable development* as development that meets the needs of the current generation without compromising the ability of future generations to meet their needs [4].

One of the earliest advocates for sustainable design was Victor Papanek [5, 6]. In his ground-breaking books, he wrote that "there are few professions more harmful than industrial design...but only a very few of them... In this age of mass production when everything must be planned and designed, design has become the most powerful tool with which man shapes his tools and environments (and, by extension, society and himself). This demands high social and moral responsibility from the designer. It also demands greater understanding of the people by those who practice design and more insight into the design process by the public... Design must become an innovative, highly creative, cross-disciplinary tool responsive to the needs of [humankind]. It must be more research oriented, and we must stop defiling the earth itself with poorly designed objects and structures...."

Since Papanek, the design community by and large has gradually embraced the concept of sustainable design. There are many tools that can help designers conduct life cycle analysis such as the cloud-based software Sustainable Minds. CAD software giants such as Autodesk also invest heavily in sustainability solutions such as Auto-CASE (triple bottom line analysis) and Rapid Energy Modeling for buildings. Autodesk also launched a "design-led revolution" for sustainability [7] where they claim "This is the era of design, where human intention, empowered by technology, is reshaping everything."

In the field of HCI, Eli Blevis is another advocate for sustainable design. In one of his papers, Blevis coined the term Sustainable Interaction Design (SID) [8], stating that "sustainability can and should be a central focus of interaction design." This means that HCI should be more than helping to sustain the current "invent and disposal" model in technology. It needs to encourage more sustainable behavior ("renewal and reuse") [9, 10].

Therefore, the key question we should ask in the field of UXD or HCI, is not that what technology can achieve, but how to apply our arsenal of new tools to change human behavior. Rather than letting business or technology drive the direction of innovation, we must frame and define our problems based on human needs.

3   Disruptive Innovation

Politicians and advocates for sustainability such as Al Gore and David Blood [11] call for a more responsible form of capitalism for a sustainable future (sustainable capitalism), while some sees sustainable capitalism as an oxymoron [12]. While this paper does not intend to expand on that debate and discuss a structural change of the current economic system, it makes the assumption that user experience design must operate within the current economic system where sustainability initiatives are often resisted by the established market.

This led us to the concept of "disruptive innovation". Since Joseph Bower and Clayton Christensen coined the term "disruptive innovation" in 1995 [13], the term has become widely used in describing technological innovations that change the existing market and create new markets. Some disruptive innovations unexpectedly but eventually take over the existing market, such as in the case of Wikipedia (replacing traditional encyclopedia).

Many believe that disruptive innovation is the key to transform the current system and achieve the sustainability goal at a large scale [14]. Especially for the under-served population around the world, this bottom-up approach might create new markets and completely bypass the current unsustainable system. Mosaic, a company established in California in 2012, is a recent example for a startup business with sustainability in mind. As a crowdfunding platform, it connects investors with home owners who need funds to install solar plants. Residential solar installers can also access their finance products. Being such a young company, and with the recent plummeting global oil price having a detrimental effect on the development of clean energy industries, Mosaic's success remains yet to be seen. Nonetheless, Mosaic aims to disrupt the loan market controlled by banks for the sake of sustainability.

Despite the large amount of literature written about disruptive innovation over the years, there is no magical formula that can turn out disruptive ideas or make these ideas applicable to all businesses or markets. Some scholars also warned that disruptive inno-vation is "a double-edge sword" because replacing the old system might be expensive and might generate tremendous waste [15]. It might also cause social instability (as in the case of Uber's conflict with the traditional taxi industry).

4   Immateriality of User Experience Design

4.1   Material Reality of Technology

Compared to other forms of design such as industrial design and interior design, user experience design seems to generate fewer physical forms, but is nonetheless supported by a heavily material base [12]. It is important to remember that user experience design creates artifacts (interfaces) and they are sustained by hardware. While the experience might be immaterial or even invisible, it is not detached from the physical reality and has physical consequences. Therefore, there is a design opportunity to modify the user experience to impact the physical world beyond the hardware that hosts it.

4.2   Cultural Shift from Material to Immaterial

Fueled by technology, the recent emergence of sharing economy is one of the most discussed topics in human computer interaction community as well as the ecological economy field because sharing economy is not only framed as an example of disruptive innovation, but also viewed by many as a path that might help the capitalist society to reduce consumption [16, 17]. Sharing economy takes many forms and could be viewed as a part of the overall cultural shift from material to immaterial.

To understand the systematic impact of the sharing economy, this paper will discuss two examples of digital platforms that provide services for sharing items, Uber and Divvy. Unlike its car-sharing predecessors such as ZipCar and Car2Go, Uber, one of the most recognizable, highly valued, and controversial startups in the world, does not own any cars. It encourages the peer to peer sharing of transportation resources, therefore indirectly reduces the desires or needs to own cars individually. It also, arguably, provides gainful employment for the under-employed urban dwellers.

Similar to European companies such as Vélib' in France, Divvy is a business of rental bicycles in a large city (Chicago). It was launched in June 2013 by the Chicago Depart-ment of Transportation and operated by Motivate. On Divvy's website, the company shares with the public the data of its operation, including trip start day and time, trip end day and time, trip start station, trip end station, rider type (Member or 24-H Pass User) and members' gender, etc. Since the beginning of their data collection (June, 27, 2013), 759,788 trips were logged in 2013 [18], 2,454,634 trips were logged in 2014 [19, 20], and 2,621,494 trips in 2015 [21], which shows a growing acceptance to the bike sharing system. A larger study analyzing this data with other variables, such as gender, age and most heavily used stations, should yield further insightful results, which is beyond the scope of this paper. Rental bike business like this reduces urban pollution and traffic jams. It encourages exercises and thus helps improve public health.

Another recent noteworthy example for sharing economy is Generation Tux. George Zimmer, the founder of Men's Wearhouse, has launched this new venture at Dreamforce in September 2015. He also launched another business called zTailor, trying to bring the century old business into the startup scene.

These new startups are successful not because they have provided new solutions to common human needs, but because they provide a smooth, easy, and affordable experience to fulfill these needs by connecting people via technology.

Furthermore, sharing economy has social implications as Ezio Manzini has pointed out that designing for sharing could make connections more visible [22, 23]. This might help address the social aspect of sustainability beyond the environmental and economic impact.

5   Radically Redesign the System

5.1   Systematic Changes to Break Path Dependency

Causes and effects in any human society is so complex that to claim that anyone can replicate others' disruptive innovations is naïve. However, it is important that we have an understanding for the long term impacts of design on a system. General systems thinking is a holistic approach to the solution of complex problems such as sustainability [24].

The best example to illustrate a key characteristic of a system, path dependency [25, 26], is the design of computer keyboard. Based on the QWERTY layout of typewriters invented in the late 19th century, the technical issues resulted in this layout has no relevance to the modern design any more. Millions of people spent millions of hours learning to type on this layout. Inefficient? Probably. But because the layout has been a standard for typewriters for over a century, it is impossible to break this path dependency. Even the keyboards on our smart mobile devices follow the same design. The solution, is not to design a new layout of the computer keyboard, but to radically rethink the design of Input/Output device. Virtual reality devices such as Oculus Rift presents such opportunity.

Indeed, disruptive innovation should create new paths, instead of trying to break the old path dependency. Since the early dawn of graphic interface design, there has been the notion that the virtual appearance must match the physical reality so our users can navigate in the digital environment. Though Apple's iOS 7 (launched in 2013) and beyond practically announced "the death of skeuomorphism" in design, references to the physical world in the digital environment will and should never go away entirely. But the future of user experience design depends on the majority of technology users develop the cognitive understanding of a digital interface, supported by the touch screens or motion capture devices or whatever new technology. I have seen young children try to swipe the information boards erected in a Nashville zoo, pretending they were interacting with these static objects like they would with smart phones and tablets. These "digital natives" as Sir Ken Robinson called them [27], will increasingly blur the lines between digital and physical worlds. Their reality might always be "augmented reality".

5.2 Automate Behavior Changes

There is a common notion in UXD that good user experience should be intuitive and unobtrusive [28–31]. I propose that designing an optimal user experience for sustainability might mean designing away the interactions entirely. So the "disruptive innovation" does not disrupt the users.

Because wasteful behavior are most likely created by habits (under cultural influences), not by intention [32]. However, changing these behavior takes conscious efforts. Design can change these behavior by automation, making changes much easier to perform, instead of demanding for additional efforts that always makes changing our lifestyle for a more sustainable future feels like a lot of work. Whatever devices or software it may be, it should give the users the cue to call for changes, eliminate the obstacles to accomplish the changes, and provide satisfying feedback to encourage the users to stay on track [33]. Indeed, automatic energy and resource saving devices have been in use for decades, such as faucets and toilets equipped with infrared sensors or simple mechanical timers. Passive house movement also has been around since the late 1980s. The challenge for user experience designers is to identify the behavior that could be automated and fit that automation seamlessly into users' everyday routines.

It is also worth mentioning that this invisibility of technology might backfire in some user scenarios, therefore it is important to still offer the option for user controls [34]. In Kara Pernice's article about her experience with Nest [35], she states several of the energy-saving automatic device's flaws, including the difficulty to adjust the routine schedule. While the design of the device is praised by many, its experience leaves some users unsatisfied. In addition, privacy is also a major concern in the age of ubiquitous computing.

5.3 Platform Generation

Many examples of disruptive innovations are about creating platforms to connect people and business, such as the aforementioned Mosaic. What user experience design can achieve, is to ensure a platform created for sustainability is easily accessible and usable. The business and design opportunities often lie in the connections that are previously overlooked.

For example, one of the main problems faced by the electronic car producers, is trying to build a large public charging network to satisfy users' charging need. From the user experience point of view, electrical car owners have the most difficulty charging their cars on longer road trips, away from their home or office charging base. This routine often coincides with the need to find lodging. Therefore, it makes sense to involve hotels in the building of these charging station networks. Star Charge [36], a company based in Changzhou China, established a crowdsourcing platform to allow businesses (such as parking lots and hotels) to provide spaces to install charging stations as a form of partnership. As partners, these businesses share the profits of the charging service, while also earning the additional benefit to their main business. The company has the goal of establishing 10,000 charging stations for electric cars all over Mainland China in the first two quarters of 2016.

5.4   Make Decisions and Outcomes Visible

Nicholas Makelburge states that "the global economy has taken us far from the real impact and consequences of our decision [37]". It is easy to fall under the illusion of the immateriality of technology if what it takes to support such an infrastructure is hidden from users. People are more willing to make behavior changes when they clearly see the outcomes of their decisions [38]. In this age of big data, visualizing data might have surprisingly effective impact on sustainability.

One of the leaders in the Home Energy Management (HEM) [39] market segment is Opower [33], which helps utility company reach their customers with more understandable bills and encourage them to be more energy efficient by comparing their energy usage with neighbors and their previous year's usage. By visualizing the previously hidden information (comparison among users), Opower claims that they are able to achieve up to 3 % energy savings. The noteworthy part of Opower's success is that its design philosophy is based on user centered design principles, focusing on "the touch points that matters the most".

Following the same line of thoughts, banks or financial management websites such as mint.com can easily add functions to allow user to generate a reliable and accurate carbon footprint report for a household from utility bills and credit card bills, instead of relying solely on self-reporting. Such reports can also include comparison with other users and suggest improvements. While no physical intervention is delivered in this process, the change of user perception will clearly benefit the users as well as the environment.

6   Conclusion

Sustainability is not radical, it is a mandate for our survival. It is also not anti-business or anti-prosperity [12]. Radically redesigning user experience for sustainability is not only about redesigning websites or software so that they will be more efficient to use, or redesigning technology-driven hardware so that they are more energy efficient, but is about to create the behavior changes that is desperately needed to promote sustainability in human society.

References

1. Dreyfuss, H.: Designing for People, p. 240. Simon and Schuster, New York (1955)
2. Association, I.E.: What is Ergonomics? 2013. http://www.iea.cc/whats/index.html. Accessed 11 Feb 2016
3. Group, T.B.C.: Industry 4.0: The Future of Productivity and Growth in Manufacturing Industries (2015)
4. World Commission on Environment and Development: Our Common Future, Oxford University Press, New York (1987). xv, 383 p
5. Papanek, V.J.: Design for the Real World; Human Ecology and Social Change, 1st American edn., Pantheon Books, New York (1972). xxviii, 339 p

6. Papanek, V.J.: The Green Imperative: Natural Design for the Real World, p. 256. Thames and Hudson, New York (1995)
7. Autodesk: The Design-Led Revolution (2016). www.autodesk.com/sustainable-design/revolution. Acessed 27 Feb 2016
8. Blevis, E.: Sustainable interaction design: invention and disposal, renewal and reuse. In: Proceedings of the SIGCHI Conference on Human Factors in Computing Systems. ACM, San Jose (2007)
9. Bonanni, L., et al.: Visible - actionable - sustainable: sustainable interaction design in professional domains. In: CHI 2011 Extended Abstracts on Human Factors in Computing Systems. ACM, Vancouver (2011)
10. Odom, W., et al.: Understanding why we preserve some things and discard others in the context of interaction design. In: Proceedings of the SIGCHI Conference on Human Factors in Computing Systems. ACM, Boston (2009)
11. Gore, A., Blood, D.: A Manifesto for Sustainable Capitalism: How Businesses Can Embrace Environmental, Social and Governance Metrics, 15 February 2012
12. Porritt, J.: Capitalism as if the World Matters, Rev. pbk edn., Earthscan, London, Sterling (2007). xxiv, 360 p
13. Bower, J.L., Christensen, C.M.: Disruptive technology: catching the wave. Harvard Bus. Rev. **73**(1), 43–53 (1995)
14. Hart, S.L.: Innovation, creative destruction and sustainability. Res.-Technol. Manag. **48**(5), 21–27 (2005)
15. Hall, J., Vrendenburg, H.: The challenges for innovating for sustainable development. MIT Sloan Manag. Rev. **45**(1), 60–68 (2003)
16. Botsman, R., Rogers, R.: What's mine is yours: the rise of collaborative consumption, 1st edn, Harper Business, New York (2010). xxii, 279
17. Matin, C.: The sharing economy: a pathway to sustainability or a nightmarish form of neoliberal capitalism? Ecol. Econ. **121**, 149–159 (2016)
18. Divvy: Divvy_Trips_2013 (2014). https://www.divvybikes.com/data
19. Divvy: Divvy_Trips_2014-Q4 (2015). https://www.divvybikes.com/data
20. Divvy: Divvy_Trips_2014-Q3-0809, Divvy_Trips_2014-Q3-07, Divvy_Trips_2014_Q1Q2 (2014). https://www.divvybikes.com/data
21. Divvy: Divvy_Trips_2015-Q1, Divvy_Trips_2015-Q2, Divvy_Trips_2015-Q3Q4 (2015). https://www.divvybikes.com/data
22. Weaving designs in time and space to create a sustainable service society. Ezio Manzini. Future News (2004). www.changedesign.org/Students/Changes/Enabling/Enabling%20Docs/ffmanzini.pdf
23. Manzini, E., et al.: Product-service systems and sustainability: opportunities for sustainable solutions. UNEP, Paris, p. 31 (2003)
24. Huang, T.: Reforming Industrial Design Education in Mainland China: For Sustainability, p. 252. VDM Verlag, Saarbrücken (2009)
25. Sterman, J.: Business Dynamics: Systems Thinking and Modeling for a Complex World, Irwin/McGraw-Hill, Boston (2000). xxvi, 982 p
26. Meadows, D.H., Wright, D.: Thinking in Systems: A Primer, Chelsea Green Publishing, White River Junction (2008). xiii, 218 p
27. Robinson, K.: Do schools kill creativity? TED (2006)
28. Krug, S.: Don't Make Me Think, Revisited: A Common Sense Approach to Web Usability, Rev. edn., New Riders, Berkeley (2014). xi, 200
29. Krug, S.: Rocket surgery made easy the do-it-yourself guide to finding and fixing usability problems. In: Voices That Matter, p. 1. New Riders, Berkeley (2010). Online resource, v, 161 p

30. Anderson, S.P.: Seductive Interaction Design: Creating Playful, Fun, and Effective User Experiences. New Riders, Berkeley (2011). Pearson Education distributor, London
31. Bell, G., Dourish, P.: Yeseterday's tomorrow: notes on ubiquitous computing's dominant vision. Pers. Ubiquit. Comput. **11**(2), 133–143 (2007)
32. Duhigg, C.: The Power of Habit: Why We Do What We Do in Life and Business, 1st edn, Random House, New York (2012). xx, 371
33. Wendel, S.: Designing for Behavior Change: Applying Psychology and Behavioral Economics, 1st edn, O'Reilly, Sebastopol (2013). xxxvi, 355
34. Arnall, T.: Exploring 'immaterials': mediating design's invisible materials. Int. J. Des. **8**(2), 101–117 (2014)
35. Pernice, K.: Emotional Design Fail: I'm Divorcing My Nest Thermostat (2015). https://www.nngroup.com/articles/emotional-design-fail/. Accessed 28 Dec 2015
36. http://chuneng.bjx.com.cn/. Electrical Charging Stations in China in 2015 (2016). http://www.chinaev100.org/index.php?option=com_content&view=article&id=759:2016-1-6-1&catid=12&Itemid=126&lang=cn
37. Makelburge, N.: Computing against the grain. Des. Philos. Pap. **1**(4), 175–181 (2003)
38. Wakefield, M.A., Loken, B., Hornik, R.C.: Use of mass media campaigns to change health behaviour. The Lancet **376**, 1261–1271 (2010)
39. Leuschner, P., Strother, N., Callaway, L.: Navigant Research Leaderboard Report: Home Energy Management Assessment of Strategy and Execution for 16 HEM Vendors 2015. Navigant Consulting, Inc. Boulder, CO (2015)

Pitfalls and Potentials of Home Energy Monitoring Feedback: An Information Experience Critique

Marlen Promann[1,2], Zhenyu Cheryl Qian[1(✉)], and Yingjie Victor Chen[2]

[1] Interaction Design, Purdue University, West Lafayette, USA
{mpromann,qianz}@purdue.edu
[2] Computer Graphics Technology, Purdue University, West Lafayette, USA
victorchen@purdue.edu

Abstract. Our ageing energy grid, the fundamental resource for human activity, remains one of the great societal challenges. Governments and the energy industry are visioning a future of an engaged society that sustainably produces and consumes energy via a shared multi-directional Smart Grid. This vision; however, depends on our current efforts to increase public's awareness and comprehension of energy as a limited consumer product, involving personal choice. Energy monitoring and feedback, along with home automation, are fast emerging markets to support this vision. We reviewed 75 currently available home energy-monitoring systems (HEMS) and discussed their pitfalls and potentials. We hope to encourage discussions about the role user experience design could play in personal information visualization, and in addressing fundamental societal problems. We call for experience centric explorations into HEMS' design to address the energy feedback needs of the future.

Keywords: Home energy monitoring · Eco-feedback · Information displays · User interface · Information visualization · User experience

1 Introduction

The current usage of limited natural resources (e.g. coal, oil and natural gas), rising concern over global warming, steadily increasing energy demand, and ageing power grid hardware, all pose significant concerns on our ability to sustain our current ways of energy consumption [1]. In the United States, one of the largest energy producers and consumers energy demand is expected to grow 30 % by 2030, but our ageing grid structure, suffers increasingly from outages, costing $500 per person per year [3].

In an effort to avoid a sustained crisis in the long run, world governments have been seeking for feasible and effective ways to incentivize demand for renewables [3]. The lack of user awareness and comprehension of energy is the key roadblock in engaging people to care for the public good. Besides choosing a utility provider, people have had no avenues to get involved with the energy industry. Utilities have offered little feedback and so, little reason for users to be interested. This is persisting against the emerging findings, that people who live in eco-developments perceive their life quality and happiness higher than residents of traditional developments [4].

© Springer International Publishing Switzerland 2016
A. Marcus (Ed.): DUXU 2016, Part II, LNCS 9747, pp. 494–506, 2016.
DOI: 10.1007/978-3-319-40355-7_47

A new global market for home energy management systems (HEMS) has emerged with a 27 % growth rate [5]. The traditional heating, ventilating, and air conditioning (HVAC) or advanced central controllers, are complemented with smart thermostats, HEMS and automated monitors that form increasingly automated ecosystems that talk to each other over the Internet.

HEMS are important because their real-time feedback has the potential to increase awareness via self-reflection, and their two-way communication with utility providers can empower users to help manage the energy load in the Smart Grid. In-home displays used to function as the important feedback loops for HEMS; however, the physical displays are disappearing into clouds, accessible via third party smart devices [6]. New ways are needed in which to think about personal data visualization in users' casual home environments. We discuss the limitations of the current feedback solutions and call for new user experience centered information designs.

2   The Problem

Utilities and grid operators have argued for years that it is necessary to reduce peak consumer usage to ease the operation costs of the U.S. power grid [7]. Current energy demand response programs, that is, *"changing electric use by demand-side resources from their normal consumption patterns in response to changes in the price of electricity, or to incentive payments designed to induce lower electricity use at times of high whole-sale market prices or when system reliability is jeopardized* [8]", while limited, are the starting-point for this vision of real-time multi-directional energy platform. HEMS function as the gateway for this real time communication between the demand and the supply. With more than a half of the U.S. population (66 %) unaware of what the Smart Grid even is, the challenge of how to bridge the gap and engage users in this commu-nication, remains.

For decades, studies have reviewed behavior change literature and the adoption of feedback technologies to identify pro-environmental behaviors and to understand what incentivizes people [9–11]. The national energy labeling program 1992 in the U.S. proved influential on purchasing decisions, but only when consumers comprehended their meaning and impact on their life [12]. It worked, because it was added value at the point of purchase. The home energy consumption is not as susceptible, because it is not a conscious purchase decision.

Mechanisms that have repeatedly shown to deliver desirable results include: goal-setting, commitment, cognitive dissonance, and financial rewards, none of which grant perfectly positive results [10]. Discount price and savings-based incentives seem to be the most reliable ways to encourage behavior change [13], reported to save households between 5 and 15 %. The resulting argument that real-time energy consumption feedback will motivate users to change their behavior is certainly true in some, mostly experi-mental settings. The life context presents many more barriers, including users' state of mind, other cost variables, ease of use, and design [11, 12].

Despite the fast growth of the HEMS industry, the energy consumption feedback (i.e. feedback displays) has not become compelling enough to get past the tipping point in market adoption [14]. Given their mediating role between demand and supply of the energy grid, exploration into their limitations and potentials is required [15].

With the proliferation of HEMS in the market, a number of reviews have compared the product and technologies [11, 16], evaluated their functionalities [16, 17] and feedback capabilities [11, 15]. The needs for easy interface access, good aesthetic quality and enjoyability have been noted, yet no review has focused on the interface details. We set forth to study the data presentation features of HEMS' feedback and evaluate their limitations and potentials against the future energy vision.

3   Method

To understand the strengths and weaknesses of current HEMS' feedback displays, we reviewed the feedback interfaces of currently available HEMS products and software. We used Google's Chrome web browser to conduct two searches: "home energy monitoring" + "product" and "home energy monitoring" + "software" + "app". We used the general Google search, which revealed mostly businesses, and Google News, which led to several news sites' recommendation lists.

We sampled feedback displays that met the following criteria: (1) it was designed to or could be used to gain feedback on ones' home energy usage, (2) it had an interface (on a product or as software), and (3) it was designed for the residential consumer. The second criterion was important, as it excluded any home energy meters without its own data display (e.g. Aeon Labs Home Energy Meter) or other more basic products (e.g. Plug-In Power Meters or Amp Meter Analyzers) that are a part of the HEMS, but not the feedback solution.

Each product's website was visited, screen captures were collected, and data was manually coded in Excel. We took a grounded research perspective, evaluating the HEMS from three perspectives: (a) **what data** do they present; (b) **what visual** methods do they utilize; and (c) what **interaction** mechanics do they leverage. We established 83 variables (many beyond display descriptors) that were coded for each HEMS display. We grouped them into four categories:

1. *Corporate descriptors* (e.g., company, url, year, price, tagline, functions, etc.)
2. *Physical product* (item, shape, color, interface and its features, interactions, etc.)
3. *Software outside of the physical product* (e.g. platforms; interface; reporting, monitoring, and engagement features; status and history presentation, ratings, etc.)
4. *System features* (e.g. icons, metaphors, aesthetics, consistency, style, color, etc.)

Given the length-limitation of this paper, we shall limit our results and discussion sections to the most pertinent part of the HEMS feedback, namely what **data is presented** and **visualized** for feedback.

4   Results

We identified 75 currently on the market HEMS that have one or more feedback displays (N = 194) across multiple platforms. Most of the 62 products do not have a physical display, but are supported by feedback software on the web (N = 52) and/or mobile (60 iOS, 43 Android and 11 smart watch applications). Our sampled HEMS displays date from 2002 (Elgato's Eve) to 2016 (Sense), with 75 % (N = 55) launching in 2011 or later. Peak launch years were 2011 (N = 14) and 2014 (N = 16) (Fig. 1).

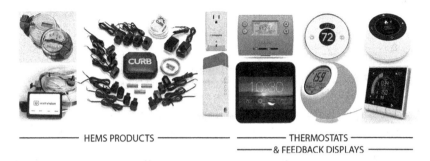

————————— HEMS PRODUCTS ————————— ————— THERMOSTATS —————
—————— & FEEDBACK DISPLAYS ——————

Fig. 1. Some sampled HEMS hardware (Blue Line Innovations, Wattvision, Curb, Smappee, Sense), thermostats (Energate, Lyric, Cosy) and feedback displays (Sentri, Energy Orb, Minim)

62 of the covered HEMS include **physical products**, costing between $25 and $300. Current homes require add-on products to smart meters (e.g. Blue Line Innovations) or fuse boxes (e.g. Neurio) to capture the energy consumption data. Some products include physical feedback displays (e.g. Sentri, Ambient Devices, Geo) and/or smart thermostats (e.g. Nest, Ecobee, Honeywell's Lyric), while others are a more technical set of gateways and Wi-Fi transmitters, with smart-plugs (e.g. WeMo, EnergyUFO, iDevices) or energy current sensors (e.g. Neurio, WattVision, Curb).

Data on in-home **feedback displays** is minimal and focused on the current consumption, occasionally production status. Contextualizing data in the different in-home feedback displays includes time, date, indoor and outdoor temperatures (F) and humidity levels (%), weather condition (icon), air quality (parts per million), current and next appliance status (e.g. on, off, idle, and schedule modes, such as auto, sleep, wake up, cozy or away), current hour's energy rate (kWh), if it is off- or on-peak, daily and monthly cumulative and estimated consumption volume (W, kWh) and costs ($), PV power generation (kWh, kW or W), if one is saving or not ($), and today's trend (in comparison to the day before, average, or other households). The physical become aesthetically pleasing, but still only a few have graphic interfaces.

Most **web** (N = 52) and **mobile** (N = 114) **applications** come free with HEMS products (e.g. Lyric, Sentri, SiteSage Energy Monitor), solar panels (e.g. SunEdison Echo, MySolarCity, OutBack Power's OpticsRe), or utility providers (e.g. Opower, Direct Energy, SimpleEnergy). Only a few function independently, compatible with the independent hardware (e.g. MiraWatt's T5K mobile app, Electricity Monitor by M. Tarmastin). The mobile applications function on iOS (N = 60) and Android (N = 43) platforms, with 11 smart watch apps (e.g. Honeywell's Ecobee, Nest and iDevices) (Fig. 2).

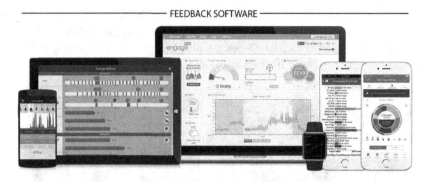

Fig. 2. Some sampled feedback software: Smappee (history), Nest (scheduling), Efargy Energy (dashboard), iDevices (pre-heating oven), Curb (live itemization), Direct Energy (monthly bill)

The **feedback software** builds on in-home displays in terms of information complexity, but each platform has its unique functions, varying their data accordingly. Data is most comprehensive on the web where current status, progress, history, estimation and other feedback information is presented for analysis and long-term decision-making. Mobile applications focus on the current status and afford users remote short-term controls beyond energy monitoring. Smart watches, available with some thermostats, connected devices and recently with energy monitors, relay only numeric statuses (e.g. levels, modes and active appliances) and alerts (e.g. fridge door open or kids arrived home), which are readily editable or actionable.

All feedback software are dashboards with small tiles or pages that communicate a specific data point. Common topics include current consumption summary (kWh, $, averages, comparisons, breakdown of biggest consumers), usage history over time (hourly, daily, weekly, monthly, and some even compare years), projections, bill estimation and whether the user is on target (with personal or social goals), real time energy demand that determines the hourly energy prices and affects items opted into demand response programs (approximate four price tiers are $0.04, $0.13, $0.25, and $0.47 for a kWh), appliance manager (i.e. scheduling and/or automating thermostats, lights, security cameras, washers, fridges, and other appliances), and personalized energy saving recommendations. Most data is presented numerically or in classic data charts. Varying visualizations are used for different data:

Representation of current status: Most display statuses are presented in raw units (e.g. KWh, $), though ambient use of colored light appears in about one third of the product displays. Feedback software focuses more on cost-savings, commonly presented as radial doughnut graphs around aggregated numeric values. Speedometer type gauge visualizations are also common for showing the Grid's status on the web. iDevices is the only watch app that uses a line graph to show a pre-heating oven.

Icons for good-bad status: Only a few displays use graphic icons to help relay the current status. Visual icons are commonly used for weather conditions, time, and good-bad status. A green leaf and tick mark are common signifiers of efficient hourly consumption rates. Red icons, strips or other alerting labels are used to warn users of pricey on-peak times (e.g. United Energy).

Color-coding information: Thermostats often use cool blues and warm oranges to signify cooling and heating process, respectively. Ambient lights from blue (off) and green (normal) to yellow (heads up) and red (warning) are used for current consumption levels, or to differentiate between the peak and off-peak rates. Same colors are also used on historical graphs to point out lowest and highest consumption points. Many solar apps prefer to use sun-related warm colors like orange and yellow.

Comparative status graphs: Only some displays have radial or gauge graphs to show the current consumption as a proportional value (e.g. Sentri, Geo's Soto III and Cisco's CGH-100 Tablet). Geo's Chorus II PV, the only in-home display for solar production, uses colored bars to compare users' production to their consumption, showing immediate money made or lost (solar sold or energy bought). A common benchmarking measure is the concept of '*always on*,' which refers to a house's baseline consumption. It is visualized as a dash on bar or radial consumption graphs.

Social status benchmarking: Users' cost-savings data is often mapped against their previously set goals, past consumption or other households. Comparisons against one's own budget or anonymous households tend to be visualized by a marker positioning the user in an ordinary stacked horizontal bar (e.g. efficient-inefficient scale).

Status itemization: Most current status itemizations are presented as active ranks of rooms, appliances or circuits (that mix rooms and appliances). Some visualize the lists with horizontal or vertical bars comparing their relative activity and/or costs. Rare solutions show circuits as actively moving meter reader dials on a circle or currently active appliances as an animated bubble chart, where bubble's sizes cue to their relative consumption volume.

Historical graphs: Consumption, production, temperature, humidity and other historic trend data are typically the largest graphs and presented as line, area, bar or histogram charts over some time unit (hours, days, weeks, and months). Thermostats often visualize energy data as bars, while temperature and air quality data as a line. Pixel visualizations over a calendar month have also been used. Sentri is the only physical feedback display large enough to show history data for temperature, air quality and humidity. It uses a filled area chart with simple time filters for different periods (day, week or a month). Nest's small thermostat does not display consumption, but weekly heating or cooling schedules as long hourly bars with bubble markers.

Historical comparisons: Newer apps integrate energy rates into usage graphs as stacked or differently colored bar charts. Others map past usage against user's average consumption, personally set goals, or past year. These lines are either emphasized in full accent color, or dashed and blending into the background. Solar compatible software visualizes consumption, production, energy sold back to the grid, and at times even '*always on*' data all in one stacked or clustered bar, line, area or bubble graphs. Predictions for the day, week or year continue as dashed line graphs or add-on filters that cluster or stack the bar charts for current-past comparison.

Monthly billing: Bills are monthly snapshot reports available via software. Monthly cost at the heart of a radial chart itemizing the bill is typical. Further details on each room, circuit or appliance can be accessed by filtering all else from view or deep diving into their 24 h usage clocks where each hour is colored with light to dark intensity, corresponding to little and much usage, respectively.

User controls: All mobile applications allow users some remote controls and scheduling options. Interfaces list currently active devices allowing users to control their lights (on-off, but also hues and density levels), door locks, sprinklers, security cameras, thermostats, to name a few, and even to pre-heat ovens (iDevices). Scheduling interfaces are either line or column based, and use the conventional blue-red or orange colors to color in active hours of the day. These come with unusual pattern alerts, safety warning and saving recommendations.

HEMS and control systems are separate services, but the emerging smart thermostats, –plugs and HMS are integrating into energy aware control of one's home.

5   Discussion

We used Nielsen's website heuristics [18] to help organize the strengths and limitations. We preferred Nielsen's heuristics over other information visualization specific heuristics, because the casual everyday user of HEMS is more familiar with websites than executing rational analytical tasks on interactive information visualizations. Due to space limitation, we shall focus on the *data* and *visualization methods*, while only briefly noting *interaction mechanics* as we discuss potential directions.

5.1   Strengths: Reporting Data

Reporting is the most basic function of feedback and knowledge management. In personal energy consumption context it refers to the verification of one's home consuming energy, the 'invisible' product. Monthly energy bills used to relay our house consumption data in a few numeric measures (kWh) that no one could relate to. Todays' HEMS capture an increasing volume of energy consumption data, decode and itemize it with little delay. As such, the primary benefit of current HEMS is their ability to deliver visibility and awareness to: (1) the continuous nature of energy consumption, (2) how it costs and (3) users' position against benchmarks. Main presentation strengths include (1) flexible to look back in time, (2) correlate data for quick insights, and (3) intuitive and consistent use of color codes.

Visibility of system usage: The currently dyadic product – software ecosystem divides the data reporting into current and historical descriptors, making it readily available. The continuous in-home reporting together with mobile alerts helps user's to experientially become aware of the continuous nature of energy consumption. As such, current

HEMS have addressed key issue with retrospective billing that has been observed to lead to cognitive disconnect between energy and its consumption [19].

Visibility of system cost: While the kWh unit remains cumbersome, the visually relative breakdown of bill items allows users to make sense what they are using, and what adds up to their cost.

Help users recognize errors: The numerous benchmark comparisons to ideal standards (e.g. budget), personal, or social variables (e.g. neighbors) afford an important personal value that supports the effectiveness of one's goal setting [10].

Help users diagnose errors: Different time frames into past data, complemented with visual comparisons to goals, average and the past, offer users insights into their progress and behavior. Itemizing past data into a list of appliances and visualizing their consumption, allows users to see what adds to the *'always on'* level.

Error prevention: Seeing how much energy is used when and by which rooms or appliances, combined with anomaly recognition, allows users to identify savings opportunities and understand how their house consumes energy. Correlating different data, such as energy usage and outdoor temperature (Bridgely), helps users visually capture their inter-relations. More literally, HEMS also alert users when consumption, budget or individual appliance values exceed pre-defined thresholds, helping them with budgeting, excessive usage, inefficient appliances and product failures.

Recognition rather than recall: Icons, like the popular green leaf are popular signals for when the user is doing. Animating the icons to cumulatively fill with or empty from color adds proportional information that is actionable (e.g. low prepay needs payment renewal). It is a common standard for thermostats to use cool blues and warm reds to intuitively help users grasp the cooling and heating modes, respectively. Similarly, green-yellow-red or light-dark saturation increments, is an easy to comprehend proxy for low-high energy consumption and costs.

In summary, current HEMS do well at increasing awareness and some basic comprehension of one's energy consumption and cost, but comprehension of the Smart Grid and energy as a public resource, remain unexplained.

5.2 Pitfalls: The Dull Monitoring

Monitoring refers to users' active engagement with real-time and/or historical data display and involves gaining insights. Given HEMS' intermediary role between utility providers and users, they hold the potential to engage users in energy Grid management. Problematically, current HEMS do not support information adoption beyond simple awareness. The dull data-centric presentations fail to entice users in active engagement [11]. Comprehension is hindered by: (1) lack of feedback at the point of consumption, (2) meaningless units (Watt, kWh and low energy prices), (3) inefficient data presentation, (4) dull visualization techniques, (5) inconsistent data presentation, and (6) lack of feedback customizability.

Visibility at point of consumption: Current HEMS feedback is readily available when users seek it, but most in-home displays are clunky tablets, stuck in one location, and affording little utility beyond current status. As a result, it is easy for users to ignore the devices [11]. In the emerging HMS context, more immediate feedback is needed to engage users with their homes' energy [10]. Energy Star's success relied on the point of consumption presentation [12].

Match between system and real world: Studies have confirmed users' struggles to comprehend kWh [20], yet few alternative units have been proposed (e.g. CO_2 contribution, gas/mileage, light bulb hours) that could help users translate and comprehend the energy unit. Feedback should be presented in a format relevant to user needs and in an easy to comprehend way [10].

Lack of visual efficiency: Many interfaces have flawed layouts and lack information presentations. Current dashboards make it hard to correlate meaningful insights in ones' head, resulting in too heavy cognitive load for the casual home environment. In addition, the limited use of visual metaphors for numeric values and long incomprehensible lists are hindering understanding and users' interest in the data.

Aesthetics and minimalist design: The feedback interfaces have become more minimal over time; however, the data presentation has not. An alternative to long lists is a screen full of icons that leverages our visual capacity. Yet, only a few outliers use icons in place of numeric values that are significantly less engaging and graspable. Currently, users have to take many steps to open, launch and engage with the feedback data. Utilizing visual metaphors that users are familiar with from their daily life (e.g. calendar), can help interpret multidimensional data.

Lack of consistency: Presenting rooms and appliances in one itemization graph, causes legibility, comprehension and possibly misinterpretation challenges due to high unit variances (e.g. a living room may consume $7.8 a month, while hallway lights only consume <$0.01). Inconsistent graph orientations and colors, furthermore, break users' ability to track variables throughout the software (e.g. yellow and blue for solar and utility), adding to the cognitive load problem in gaining insights.

Lack of visual user freedom: In-home product mobility and screen customizability are rare among current HEMS displays. Yet, it remains an important user engagement and personalization features. Geo's Cosy thermostat is unique in its mobility and variety of materials (e.g. plastic, wood). Honeywell's VoiceControl thermostat and Sentri home display are starting to think about the added value that allowing users to choose vibrant pink backgrounds or upload personal photos can bring.

Overall, current HEMS have two major pitfalls that need addressing: (1) *"energy information is boring,"* worsened by inconsistency [21] and (2) current data presentations that do not help users comprehend what energy is, where it comes from and why one should care about it beyond personal cost-efficiency [1, 12].

5.3   Potentials: Engaging Integrated Interactions

The rapid blending of home control, automation and HEMS is giving rise to comprehensive energy aware home management systems (HMS) that go well beyond energy monitoring. Herein, interactions refer to users' manual or automated responses to behavior data feedback. Current display-centric data-heavy feedback is insufficient for the emerging integrated HMS, where comfort and automation drive interactions.

A user centered design perspective that would treat feedback data visualization as a possible platform for experiential engagement, could lead to promising enhancements in how users increase their awareness and comprehension of energy. Some ways include: (1) situational awareness, (2) redefining energy via familiar metaphors, (3) physical interactions, (4) inclusion of consumer choice, (5) redefining the Grid as community (that one has impact on), (6) preventative feedback, and (7) artifact aesthetics of documentation.

Situational visibility at point of consumption: HEMS feedback should ask less of the users and contextually deliver the message at the exact time of use. To achieve this, future products should be subtle feedback platforms that make energy consumption visible during consumption and so aesthetically pleasing that people would want to display, rather than hide them. For example, STATIC's disappearing-pattern for the bathroom lose their patterns when you shower too long in hot water [22].

Match between the system and the future real world: Exploring ways how visually describe the kWh unit, the unique appliance consumption patterns or to totally redefine the energy unit, could help users achieve better comprehension of energy. Some artistic approaches to energy feedback have explored the metaphor of plants and their wellbeing. Serenity conceptualizes energy efficiency as a plant that dries in excess heat and rots in too humid air [23].

Interactive user control: Nest's physical interaction control of the device has seen much praise. Future product designs should seek to think more physically rather than digitally, about user interactions. Infotropism, is a physical manifestation of Serenity's digital plant metaphor, that uses a living but robotic plant as an interactive in-home feedback display [24].

User control and freedom: Future HEMS should become the primary mediators between the utilities and the users, empowering the users to not only pay bills via their systems, but also allow them to become aware and active consumers of different utility service options.

Grid as community: A shared sense of purpose, values and principles found in sustainable communities have been proven to increase the peoples perceived life quality [4]. Future HEMS should seek to help users see the social collectiveness in the Smart Grid that we all share.

Preventative freedom (towards home well-being): Future energy feedback should move beyond individual price-centric statuses and contextualize users in the broader Grid demand and its ideal status, that is, a flat stable energy consumption that has no morning and evening consumption spikes.

Aesthetics of documentation: Home energy monitoring is not an analytical work task. Future HEMS should explore spatial, physical and more experiential information visualization techniques for historical analysis and documentation. Instead of the classic line, bar and histogram charts on the web or mobile, the historical output could manifest as a personal information mural or data art. Artists seeking to raise questions rather than offer answers, leverage different engagement mechanism from the traditional efficiency driven technology usability in HCI [25]. Well-designed user experience design driven products can be informative and joyful at once.

Given the trends towards home automation and multidirectional Smart Grid, the HEMS in future HMS need to become more contextualized and experience driven. After all, many agree that *"the "killer app" of HEM has yet to surface"* [16].

6   Conclusions and Future Work

Move to more sustainable patterns of energy consumption remains one of the great societal challenges. To see an 'energy turnaround' we need to reduce personal energy consumption and shift to sustainable energy aware living [19]. Governments and the energy industry agree on the importance of engaging the demand side to drive behavioral change towards balancing the grid. Energy monitoring and feedback systems (HEMS) are seen centrifugal to this process of rising awareness and comprehension.

Our review of current HEMS on the market revealed the potential of the new market, but also concluded that the current HEMS do not support the future vision for a multidirectional Smart Grid where empowered users can act as products and consumers [3]. While much of the needed data is already available, HEMS feedback needs to move beyond basic screen based data visualizations, and towards information as a contextual experience. Despite wealthy literature on sustainable behavior, design suggestions for future feedback experiences are limited.

We conclude that there is a lack of engaging user-centered feedback interfaces, and call for user experience centric explorations into information as a potential platform for experience design. Our research hopes to raise questions, more than it seeks to answer questions as we point to our need to solve fundamental societal problems.

Acknowledgement. This paper was inspired by and reports on some of the findings of a home energy monitoring benchmarking research project sponsored by the Whirlpool Corporation.

References

1. Armaroli, N., Balzani, V.: The future of energy supply: challenges and opportunities. Angew. Chem. Int. Ed. **46**(1–2), 52–66 (2007)

2. U.S. Department of Energy: The Smart Grid: An Introduction, U.S. Department of Energy. Industry Report AC26-04NT41817, Subtask 560.01.04 (2008)
3. Bayulken, B., Huisingh, D.: Perceived 'Quality of Life' in eco-developments and in conventional residential settings: an explorative study. J. Cleaner Prod. **98**, 253–262 (2015)
4. Technavio market research: Global Home Energy Management Systems Market 2015–2019, Technavio Market Research Company, Toronto, ON. Industry Report IRTNTR6913, August 2015
5. ReportLinker: Advanced Metering Infrastructure Market by Devices, Solutions, Services, by Regions - Forecast 2020, ReportLinker, Lyon, France, December 2015
6. MIT Energy Initiative: The Future of the Electric Grid, Massachusetts Institute of Technology, Cambridge, Mass. December 2011. ISBN 978-0-9828008-6-7
7. Reports on Demand Response and Advanced Metering, Federal Energy Regulatory Commission (FERC), Washington D.C., Assessment 1–30, December 2015
8. MacDonald, E.F., She, J.: Seven cognitive concepts for successful eco-design. J. Cleaner Prod. **92**, 23–36 (2015)
9. van Houwelingen, J.H., van Raaij, W.F.: The effect of goal-setting and daily electronic feedback on in-home energy use. J. Consum. Res. **16**(1), 98–105 (1989)
10. Yang, R., Newman, M.W., Forlizzi, J.: Making sustainability sustainable: challenges in the design of eco-interaction technologies. In: Proceedings of the SIGCHI Conference on Human Factors in Computing Systems, New York, NY, USA, pp. 823–832 (2014)
11. Burgess, J., Nye, M.: Re-materialising energy use through transparent monitoring systems. Energy Policy **36**(12), 4454–4459 (2008)
12. Hargreaves, T., Nye, M., Burgess, J.: Making energy visible: a qualitative field study of how householders interact with feedback from smart energy monitors. Energy Policy **38**(10), 6111–6119 (2010)
13. LaMarche, J., Cheney, K., Akers, C., Roth, K., Sachs, O.: Home Energy Displays: Consumer Adoption and Response, U.S. Department of Energy, Building America Program, Cambridge, MA, DOE/GO-102012-3805, December 2012
14. Riche, Y., Dodge, J., Metoyer, R.A.: Studying always-on electricity feedback in the home. In: Proceedings of the SIGCHI Conference on Human Factors in Computing Systems, New York, NY, USA, pp. 1995–1998 (2010)
15. LaMarche, J., Cheney, K., Christian, S., Roth, K.: Home Energy Management Products and Trends, Fraunhofer Center for Sustainable Energy Systems, Cambridge, MA. Industry Report 55819 (2012)
16. Karlin, B., Ford, R., Squiers, C.: Energy feedback technology: a review and taxonomy of products and platforms. Energy Effi. **7**(3), 377–399 (2013)
17. Nielsen, J.: Enhancing the explanatory power of usability heuristics. In: Proceedings of the SIGCHI Conference on Human Factors in Computing Systems, New York, NY, USA, pp. 152–158 (1994)
18. Schwartz, T., Stevens, G., Jakobi, T., Denef, S., Ramirez, L., Wulf, V., Randall, D.: What people do with consumption feedback: a long-term living lab study of a home energy management system. Interact. Comput. (2014)
19. Kempton, W., Layne, L.L.: The consumer's energy analysis environment. Energy Policy **22**(10), 857–866 (1994)
20. Steven Castle: Beyond Energy Monitors, GreenTech Advocates, 14 July 2010. http://greentechadvocates.com/2010/07/14/beyond-energy-monitors/. Accessed 11 Feb 2016
21. Backlund, S., Gyllenswärd, M., Gustafsson, A., Ilstedt Hjelm, S., Mazé, R., Redström, J.: STATIC! the aesthetics of energy in everyday things. In: Proceedings of Design Research Society Wonderground International Conference 2006, Lisbon, Portugal (2007)

22. Artefact: Serenity: A Home OS with a Heart, Artefact Blog (2012)
23. Holstius, D., Kembel, J., Hurst, A., Wan, P.-H., Forlizzi, J.: Infotropism: living and robotic plants as interactive displays. In: Proceedings of the 5th Conference on Designing Interactive Systems: Processes, Practices, Methods, and Techniques, New York, NY, USA, pp. 215–221 (2004)
24. Holmes, T.G.: Eco-visualization: combining art and technology to reduce energy consumption. In: Proceedings of the 6th ACM SIGCHI Conference on Creativity and Cognition, New York, NY, USA, pp. 153–162 (2007)

User Experience Design for Green IT Products Through Wearable Computing and Quantified Self

Jingyan Qin[✉], Sha Cao, and Xiaohui Wang

School of Mechanical Engineering, University of Science and Technology Beijing,
Beijing, People's Republic of China
qinjingyan@gmail.com, ustbcs77@126.com, xiaohui0506@foxmail.com

Abstract. Green IT products collect personal small data by wearable computing and Quantified Self, Internet of Things (IoT) and Internet of Everything (IoE) link the small data with the big data, and transform the user experience from User-Centered Design (UCD) into User Participated (Involved or engagement) Design (UPD). To collect the seamless and sustainable UPD small data, we use the wearable computing sensors and applications for small data mining, filter, information visualization and interaction design. By information sorting the wearable computing into five types (in me, on me, with me, around me, beyond me), we intend to design the user experience in a sustainable way by Quantified Self. With the context awareness, conscious awareness and emotion awareness, we use LBS (location-based service) to construct context awareness, set up big five personalities and Enneagram to deal with the data of conscious awareness. For the Green IT Products, we set up the eco system information architecture and agile interaction model for the user experience design, we also use pre-conscious, subconscious and conscious awareness big data to analyze and predict the long-term impaction factors for the user experience and users' intuitive interaction. From the strategy level, structure level, framework level and visual level, we point out the Meaning-Centered Design methodology to dig out the user experience design for the Green IT Products, green and live information architecture for the life cycle evaluation for the Green IT products, figure out the stakeholder and interaction logic moving line by mapping the mental model for the diversified users' agile transformation needs, emotions and interaction feedback, provide the mass customization and crowds innovation contents to support the Green IT products and Product Service System (PSS), modify the quality of the real physical products and enrich the virtual reality digital information contents to prolong the life cycle of the Green IT Products. By decreasing the carbon footprint and increasing the three flows (information flow, logistics, financial flow) chain touchpoints, we find the painpoints and design the good user experience for the real people. We construct the user engagement innovation platform and transform the users' function with duality role player with user and designer. For the evaluation of the user experience, we change the scenario role player design into 'real design for real people', and with the agile interaction and intuitive interaction, we modify the user experience with the real time high-fidelity prototype and iterative usability testing. In the pilot study, we design the smart clothes and interactive stage, props to collect the dancer's small data about the heart-beat, EMG, EEG, motion, body gesture, emotion and the audience feedback such as the sound of clapping, the environment light change, the audience moving line and the air smog haze index.

© Springer International Publishing Switzerland 2016
A. Marcus (Ed.): DUXU 2016, Part II, LNCS 9747, pp. 507–515, 2016.
DOI: 10.1007/978-3-319-40355-7_48

We use the module and separate design for the clothes and sensors, memory metal, fiber-optical to balance the clothes light change, clothes form transformation and small data visualization. On the one hand, the clothes can collect the dancer's action data in an active way, at the same time, the clothes also interact with the dancer, the audience and the stage environment to support the digital contents of the dance. One clothes can express the five scenes of the dance in a sustainable way. And because of the separate design, the clothes and the sensors play the role in a parallel way to leave the dancer plenty of free uncertainty expression space. That win-win design support the real and virtual parts life cycle for the Green IT Products. We use the expert review, heuristic evaluation, big data visual analytics and usability testing for the user experience design evaluation and design the third version for the smart clothes and interactive stage.

Keywords: Smart clothing · Interaction design · Quantified self · Small data · Wearable computing · Participatory design

1 Introduction

Green IT (Green Computing, Green ICT or ICT sustainability), is the study and practice of environmentally sustainable computing or IT [1]. According to San Murugesan's notes, the goals of Green IT are "designing, manufacturing, using, and disposing of computers, servers, and associated subsystems—such as monitors, printers, storage devices, and networking and communications systems — efficiently and effectively with minimal or no impact on the environment" [2].

The research is the collaboration between the modern dancer and the interaction designer. We chose the smart clothing as the costume for the dancer as the container and medium of digital information, selected the pressure sensor, infrared sensor and other sensors to collect the dancer's behaviors pattern data, and transmission the data to the display OLED and Optical Fiber which are embedded in the dress, also the memory metal in the bamboo leaf hat to change the shape of the hat according to the data-driven sensor trigger. In order to reduce the use of hazardous materials (optical fiber, energy supply for the interactive smart clothing, memory metal transformation in the hat), maximize energy efficiency during the clothing's show time and wearing lifetime, and promote the recyclability or biodegradability of defunct products and waste, the user experience design has green computing initiatives to reduce the environmental impact of the smart clothing from the three aspects. One is the materials for the clothing and the whole stage, the second factor is the energy supply for the smart clothing and the dancer's small data collection. The third one is the data analysis center for the Quantified Self [3] of the dancer and the online and offline audience.

The project chose the smart clothing as the solo dancer's costume to map the metaphor of the modern dance *The Data Dance of Sunyata*. The dancer would experience the four stages which include *Data, Explore, Chaos, Out of Control/Lost* and *Free* as a Tree lives eternity. Throughout the five scenes, the dancer should wear the smart clothing and interact with the clothing to change the color and shapes of the clothing, to show the human (tree)'s growing up, constructing the human (tree)'s own eco system and branches, persistence and collision chaos with the environment, lost and out of control, finally in the peace of epiphany Freedom. In the process of Human-Clothing Data Inter-action, the smart clothing needs to collect the dancer's moving pattern data through the heart rate, blood pressure and skin conductivity. The change of the body's data leads to the transformation and color change of the clothing. In some scenarios, the data change also connects with the props and the scenario screen video changing.

The key findings in the consideration of Green Computing and user experience during the 90 min dance come from the smart clothing and props materials, the energy supply for the transformation and clothing light changing, and the dancer self-quantified data collection and audience interaction feedback which is the trigger of the clothing color shape changing.

1. The clothing material is woven by optical fiber. The clothing's lifecycle should last long to save the fiber, easy to clean and easy to be replaced by new cut or new shape, whereas the LED lights, the battery, the chips, the sensors and the wires should be easy to remove and recharge, easy to be replaced or maintenance by the new version. The clothing itself has different colors. When the LED lights glows, the optical fibers embedded in the clothing would glow with the LED lights, of which color is much stronger than the clothing color itself. To compare with the natural sunshine, the color of the clothing would not be obvious even in the strongest LED light.

2. The dance drama would take 90 min, in order to support the HCI interaction, the battery and energy supply would last over 120 min at least. And the battery should be taken away and change the new one easily. The rechargeable batteries should be minimize and provide no more than 10 mA electric current for the sake of the danc-er's safety.

3. The clothing shape and color change would be transformed by the sensor's data change. One part of the data comes from the dancer's behavior pattern and physio-logical data, another data resource comes from the environment change which include the air conditions, haze smog data, the audience's reaction such as claps, hurrah, hug with the dancer, etc. In order to interact with the complex stage micro environment, the algorithm about the data interaction and data visualization should be deep learning, prepared the default data and error tolerance design.

4. The clothing's color and shape change should be designed according to different drama, dance, music and shows. Diversified sensors should be tailored with the clothing in different scenarios. The context awareness challenges are what action and semi-improvisational performance should stimulate the sensor's data collection, and how data's change should stimulate the clothing and props color shape change.

Currently the development of smart hardware, wearable devices and ubiquitous computing makes a collection of personal small data possible, along with the analysis of Quantified Self [4]. Through context awareness and consciousness awareness [5], small data associated with big data, the products will have intelligent features. The requirement of lightweight, portable, mobility and self-collected data and real-time data collection appears increasingly important. People are gradually concerned about their personal data, including exercise, diet, sleep, mood and other individual data. Today, the data has penetrated into every aspect of our daily lives. The emergence of Quantified Self awaken individuals to take the initiative self-knowledge through data. Wearable devices achieve user's own data detection by using a variety of data indicators to analyze personal small data which include the pedometer, calories, heart rate, blood pressure, skin conductivity, etc. [6]. With the continuous development of smart mobile technology and micro-sensors, the features of wearable device increased and provide more convenience, efficiency and accuracy for personal data collection. Smart clothing followed the natural relationship between clothing and full-body contact, and become one of the most promising categories among the wearable devices. Through the user experience design and interaction design of smart clothing, people collect individual small data to achieve the vision of wearing small data and merging big data.

Through a variety of network, Internet of Things (IoT) [7], Internet of Everything (IoE), ubiquitous computing links personal small data with big data. In the era of data-driven Algorithm Economy, designers inform the personal small data artificial intelligence through interaction design, and use innovation thinking which include Big Data + Internet + Intelligent + Innovation to transform the non-intelligent entity into incorporeal ecological smart environment of the big data [8].

2 User Experience Design and Interaction Design of Smart Clothing

2.1 The Meaning of Smart Clothing

Smart clothing refers to the life simulation system which has perception and feedback of clothing. Smart clothing can sense changes in internal and external environmental conditions, as well as make real-time or near-time self-report feedback. The three elements of a smart clothing are perception, reaction and feedback [9]. The user experience design and interaction design of smart clothing relies on the multi-disciplines cooperation of computer science, electronic information technology, sensor technology, textile science, materials science and fashion design.

In 1990s, MIT's Media Lab developed wearable multimedia computer [10]. Wearable technology and smart clothing gradually become the research concern. As the improvement of the people's living standards, people are no longer confined to the requirements of comfort and fashion of the clothing, but to achieve the purposes of personal health management or entertainment through the clothing [11].

MIT Tangible Media Group developed a smart clothing which is embedded with the bacillus subtilis natto in the clothing fabric conducive to realize the fabric volume expansion or contraction transformation with the natto humidity change [12].

Intel and architectural sportswear designer Chromat [13] developed two responsive clothing: sports underwear and dresses. These two smart clothing which is embedded Intel Curie wearable device change the shape according to user temperature, adrenaline or pressure to produce level deformation. This clothing is embedded Intel Curie wearable device that can be used for health, fitness, social, etc.

Except for the smart clothing, NUI with wearable computing [14] is another key factors for the user experience in the dance. In February 15th, Lady Gaga collaborated with Intel at the 2016 Annual Grammy Awards for the performance which is supported by the Intel's wearable computing sensors [15].

In our project, the costume and props for the dancer should be made of the smart clothing materials, solar energy to support the rechargeable battery, data visualization and data analysis center to deal with the information contents and algorithm for the information visualization design, wearable computing sensors to support the data mining and collection. To support the live interaction between the dancer and the environment, the design team transform the user experience from User-Centered Design (UCD) into User Participated (Involved or engagement) Design (UPD) and Meaning-Centered Design (MCD) [8]. The designer analyzed the dance drama contents meaning with the dancer and choreographer, adjusted the dance scene sequence to match the interaction model and information flow and props logistics, information sorted the dancer's body languages into the information architect according to the dance contents meaning and metaphor functions, constructed the dancer's moving line, navigation on the stage and interaction feedback with the audience, did the layout of the props, video media contents, collected the dancer's personal small data such as the identity information, the action pattern and the meaning of the body gestures and languages. We used the LBS (location-based service) to track the dancer's locus to inspire the clothing's color and shape change. And we pre-designed the default color change in case of feedback failure and error tolerance performance according to recall randomly the dancer's action and stored the dancer's most types of dancing patterns before the show and used the algorithm according to context awareness, conscious awareness and emotion awareness computing which are judged by the dancer's Enneagram [5, 6] to predict the dancer's agile inter-action.

In the series of the dancing shows, we set up the eco system information architecture and agile interaction model for the user experience design from the perspective of Green IT Products design, we also use pre-conscious, sub-conscious and conscious awareness big data to analyze and predict the long-term impaction factors for the user experience and users' intuitive interaction. From the strategy level, structure level, framework level and visual level, we point out the Meaning-Centered Design methodology to dig out the user experience design for the Green IT Products, green and live information architecture for the life cycle evaluation for the Green IT products, figure out the stakeholder and interaction logic moving line by mapping the mental model for the diversified users' agile transformation needs, emotions and interaction feedback, provide the mass customization and crowds innovation contents to support the Green IT products and Product Service System (PSS) [16], modify the quality of the real physical products and enrich the virtual reality digital information contents to prolong the life cycle of the Green IT Products.

2.2 Interaction Design of Smart Clothing

Wearable device has a progressive approach to the relationship with the individual, worn on different parts of the body to collect different data of the body. Clothing as the most natural medium in contact with people has become one of the best choices for wearable devices.

This research will demonstrate the smart interactive clothing developed and designed by Dr. QIN Jingyan and her design team. Smart clothing is composed of black dress, red garment and white dress. We combined the LED lights with the optical fibers woven into the clothing. RGB values define the various types of lighting changes and feedback the collected data of dancer's body movements. This is a process of accumulating data, merging small data with big data and self-realization. Black clothing, named "Data", representing no light, is a process of data accumulation. The dancer dressed in the clothing perform zen dance. *The Data Dance of Sunyata*: When you get deep personal fulfillment, you are in the presence of your body dancing. Who want to complete self-realization, need through the body, heart, mind awakening and true to yourself, to your mind naturally expand. Red clothing, named "Explore", on behalf of the brave, is a process of exploring life. Three lights on the smart clothing means moral Sansei III - Cheng pulls, this life, the afterlife. This clothing equipped with bamboo hats. When bring bamboo hats, the dancer had the feeling like a explorer on the way. People do not have enough power in the world so they have courage to bare in the world. Bamboo hats' memory metal can pull red yarn which will automatically receive red yarn into bamboo hats. Then the dancer's face gradually unfolded. White clothing has three parts of "Chaos", "Out of Control/Lost" and "Free". White can absorb all colors, on behalf of the moment out of control and self-confession. By more and more rapid rotation of the dancer, the magnetic pieces of clothing reduced, thereby departing from the body.

Traditional clothing is mainly made from ordinary fiber and the main function is body cover protection, beautiful and stylish. But the smart clothing is mainly made from smart materials, such as sensors, intelligent information receptor, optical fiber and other bio molecular materials. Making smart clothing needs to consider the configuration of electronic components. It is necessary to ensure intelligent, as well as comfortable to wear. The user experience and interaction design for the smart clothing and props use the iterative dancer prototyping and usability testing. The design process include information sorting, interactive behavior pattern analysis, feedforward and feedback consideration, wayfinding design on the new media stage, navigation design on the smart information space, information design and visual design for the smart clothing and the whole dance environment. It consists of three types of information which lead to differences in behavior patterns of interaction. Feedforward (Hints) and feedback [17] guided the live sub-conscious intuitive interaction.

At the same time, we combined the smart clothing and modern scenery play with the interactive stage arena. We built a 4 m × 4 m × 4 m cube as the show stage and dance video display screen. Big stage represents the symbol of social relationships and the living environment. The dancer is as an individual and integrated into the stage. Her choreography and dance movements are recognized by the sensors which are embedded in the smart clothing and triggered the digital data contents shown on the big cube stages. The dancer's body movements interact with the virtual digital images on the stage screen. The dancer embraced a 50 cm × 50 cm × 50 cm cube as the interactive prop, which is a container and switch to open the cube on the track. It is a symbol of individual and metaphor of knowledge data accumulation as a subject to integrate into society.

3   Smart Clothing Quantified Self and Accumulate Data

"Wired" magazine editor Kevin Kelly and Gary Wolf [18–20] proposed the concept of Quantified Self in 2007. The meaning of Quantified Self is that through wearable sensors, mobile applications, software interface or online communities to track individual physiology, physical, behavioral or environmental information, then it can collect individual small data. Many different fields can be tracked and analyzed, such as weight, heat, mood, time, sleep quality, health, cognitive behavior, movement, and learning skills [21].

Mark Weiser at American Palo Alto Research Center (PARC) proposed that mankind will eventually enter the "ubiquitous computing" [22] stage that people can at any time and at any place, access and process information. A variety of wearable sensors [23] and mobile devices can collect, transport and calculate data and then form an information network. Data gradually infiltrated into our daily lives by detecting individual daily physical, physiological data and even environmental data around to help people better context awareness and conscious awareness [24] comprehension.

We designed the smart clothing to detect the body data and collect the individual's small data to monitor user's body. The lights of the smart clothing can produce corresponding changes through information visualization [25] with the NUI(natural user interface) [14] interactive action. By decreasing the carbon footprint and support the three flows (information flow, logistics, financial flow) chain touchpoints, we dig out the painpoints and design the good user experience for the real people. We construct the user engagement innovation and participatory design [26] platform and transform the users' function with duality role player with user and designer. For the evaluation of the user experience, we change the scenario role player design into 'real design for real people', and with the agile interaction and intuitive interaction, we modify the user experience with the real time high-fidelity prototype and iterative usability testing [27]. In the pilot study, we design the smart clothes and interactive stage, props to collect the dancer's small data about the heart-beat, EMG, EEG, motion, body gesture, emotion and the audience feedback such as the sound of clapping, the environment light change, the audience moving line and the air smog haze index. We use the module and separate design for the clothes and sensors, memory metal, fiber-optical to balance the clothes light change, clothes form transformation and small data visualization [25]. On the one hand, the clothes can collect the dancer's action data in an active way, at the same time, the clothes also interact with the dancer, the audience and the stage environment to support the digital contents of the dance. One clothes can express the five scenes of the dance in a sustainable way. And because of the separate design, the clothes and the sensors play the role in a parallel way to leave the dancer plenty of free uncertainty expression space. That win-win design support the real and virtual parts life cycle for the Green IT Products. We use the expert review, heuristic evaluation, big data visual analytics and usability testing for the user experience design evaluation and design the third version for the smart clothes and interactive stage.

4   Conclusion

The design team designed the costume through Modular Design and draping (Dimensionally cutting) to combine the digital parts (sensors, chips, memory metal, display system, energy supply, interactive installations, etc.) with the non-digital parts(clothing, props, stages) separately to deal with the different life cycle and design targets of digital parts and non-digital parts.

There are two energy supply designs to support live interactive show and static smart clothing exhibition. The user experience and interaction design try to find out the tripping point among the pain points, highlights and balance points opportunities. Next step for the research would rely on the power and energy supply ways.

The dancer's behavior patterns motivate the interactive patterns in the smart digital stages and wearable computing support HCI environments. And how to build the small data analysis center to design the show based on the dancer's body architecture and interaction pattern database? And how to map the show theme, the meaning of the behavior patterns, and contextual awareness with the metaphor and No-Metaphor design are the challenge for the future research.

Self-Quantified by ICT which is the record of life logging, personal genomics, location tracking, biometrics, and other personal small data needs the big data analytics and algorithm to support the long-term Green IT [2] research. The digital way to core is still a long way to go.

Wearable computing with Quantified Self is promising in Algorithm Economy. In the era of big data information, we wear the small data with the smart clothing and linked with the big data as a unity.

Acknowledgments. This work is funded by the National Natural Science Foundation of China (Grant No. 71173012) and the Fundamental Research Funds for the Central Universities (FRF-TP-14-004C1). The clothing was designed by Dr. QIN Jingyan, Sun Bohan and Zhou He. The project was technically supported by Xiao Wenpeng and Xian Feng's companies, and our design team provided the product service system (PSS) to the dancer Shi Jingxing. Over thirty master's candidates, Ph.D. candidates and post-doctoral researchers took part in the design project. We would like to express our gratitude to all those who helped us during the three years.

References

1. Murugesan, S.: Harnessing Green IT: Principles and Practices, IEEE IT Professional, pp. 24–33, January–February 2008
2. Kounatze, C.R.: OECD Conference on ICTs, the environment and climate change, Helsingør, Denmark, 27–28 May 2009. www.oecd.org/sti/ict/green-ict
3. Wolf, G.: The Data-Driven Life, The New York Times, 28 April 2010
4. CES 2013: The Year of The Quantified Self? Forbes. CES 2013: The Year of the Quantified Self? Accessed 15 Sept 2013
5. Card, S.K., Moran, T.P., Newell, A.: The Psychology of Human-Computer Interaction. Taylor & Francis, Moran (1983)
6. Ellis, A., Abrams, M., Lidia, D.A.: Personality Theories: Critical Perspectives. SAGE, Thousand Oaks (2008)

7. Swan, M.: Sensor mania! the internet of things, wearable computing, objective metrics, and the quantified self 2.0. J. Sens. Actuator Netw. **1**, 217–253 (2012)
8. Jing-yan, Q.I.N.: Grand Interaction Design in Big Data Information Era. Packag. Eng. **36**(8), 1–5 (2015)
9. Kiekens, P., Langenhove, L.V., Hertleer, C.: Smart clothing: a new life. Int. J. Clothing Sci. Technol. **16**(1/2), 63–72 (2004)
10. Mann, S.: Smart clothing: wearable multimedia computing and personal imaging to restore the technological balance between people and their environments. In: Aigrain, P. (ed.) The Fourth ACM International Conference on Multimedia, pp. 163–174. ACM, Boston (1997)
11. Tian, M., Li, J.: Design mode and development tendency of smart clothing. J. Text. Res. **35**(2), 109–114 (2014)
12. Yao, L., Ou, J., Cheng, C.-Y., Steiner, H., Wang, W., Wang, G., Ishii, H.: bioLogic: natto cells as nanoactuators for shape changing interfaces. In: CHI 2015, pp. 1–10 (2015)
13. Ildeniz, A.: Intel and Chromat Reveal Technology's Possibilities for Fashion on the Runway. [EB/OL]. (11 September 2011) [05 March 2016]. http://tech.huanqiu.com/news/2015-09/7486255.html
14. Wigdor, D., Wixon, D.: Brave NUI World, Designing Natural User Interfaces for Touch and Gesture. Morgan Kaufmann, Burlington (2011)
15. The Lady Gaga + Intel Collaboration Experience, 15 February 2016. http://www.cbs.com/shows/grammys/
16. Van Halen, C., Vezzoli, C., Wimmer, R.: Methodology for Product Service System Innovation, p. 21. Uitgeverij Van Gorcum, Assen (2005)
17. Cooper, R.: About Face 2.0: The Essentials of Interaction Design. Wiley, New York (2003)
18. Singer, E.: The Measured Life. MIT. Accessed 05 July 2011
19. Wolf, G.: Quantified Self. Archived from the original on 26 March 2012. Accessed 26 March 2012
20. Quantified Self Blog, oldest entries. Archived from the original on 26–03–2012. Accessed 26–Mar–2012
21. Augemberg, K.: Building that Perfect Quantified Self APP: Notes to Developers, Part 1 (2012). www.measuredme.com/2012/10/building-that-perfect-quantified-self-ap. Accessed 20 Mar 2013
22. Weiser, M.: The computer for the 21st century. Sci. Am. **265**(3), 94–104 (1991)
23. Dourish, P.: Where the Action Is: The Foundations of Embodied Interaction. The MIT Press, Cambridge (2001)
24. Shettleworth, S.J.: Cognition, Evolution, and Behavior. Oxford, New York (2010)
25. Card, S.K., Mackinlay, J., Shneiderman, B.: Readings in Information Visualization: Using Vision to Think (Interactive Technologies), 1st edn. Morgan Kaufmann, Burlington (1999)
26. Levy, J.: UX Strategy: How to Devise Innovative Digital Products that People Want, 1st edn. O'Reilly Media, Sebastopol (2015)
27. Nielson, J.: Usability Engineering, 1st edn. Morgan Kaufmann, Burlington (1993)

Proposal on Service Design for Social Innovation: Self-expression of Adolescent to Parents

Jae Sun Yi[✉]

Department of Contents Convergence Design,
Handong Global University, Pohang, South Korea
creative1@handong.edu

Abstract. As a proposal to contributing to lessening of teenage suicide rate in South Korea, this study aimed to find a solution for conflict between teenage children and parents, the essential factor for juvenile delinquency, via an improved communication method between the two groups. Juvenile delinquency, still increasing despite new programs and systems conducted by governments and organizations, was approached in the perspective of family. Through surveys, it was shown parents' poor attitudes towards their children, such as demand for coercive submission, constant nagging and interrupting by directly cutting children off to speak over, were main obstacles to better communication. Thus this study proposes a communication service, preventing one-sided communication of parents' and providing space for adolescents to express their personal issues and problems, in which in response parents could only give positive feedback.

Keywords: Service design · Social innovation · Self-expression of adolescent to parents · Mobile application · Human-computer interaction

1 Introduction

Despite living in a world more affluent than ever, diverse social problems are caused by rapid social changes and changes in values. Hearing media reports on addictions, suicides, sexual trafficking and youth crimes, people are only getting more anxious about such issues as they are emerging as serious matter. Among them, juvenile delinquency is growing constantly, with more than 10,000 teenagers leaving home annually in South Korea [1], suffering on their own, leading to extreme measures such as suicide.

According to OECD Health Data 2014, South Korea was ranked the highest on the list of suicide rate with considerable rate of teenage suicide contributing to the statistic [2]. One in five adolescents in South Korea have felt suicide urge, and it was reported conflict with parents to be the main reason for the urge and drop in school grades as the second reason, which is another factor for parent-children conflict (see Figs. 1 and 2). According to a social service conducted by Statistics Korea done in 2014 [3], teenagers struggled the most with studying (52.6 %). In fact, it is the biggest reason for the

© Springer International Publishing Switzerland 2016
A. Marcus (Ed.): DUXU 2016, Part II, LNCS 9747, pp. 516–526, 2016.
DOI: 10.1007/978-3-319-40355-7_49

conflict between the parents and children. On the same note, Professor Jingon Jeong of the Department of Education, Hanyang Univeristy quoted; "Korean parents are only interested in their children's academic performances, not in children's wants" [4].

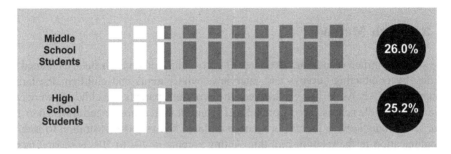

Fig. 1. Middle school and high school students' suicide urge rate

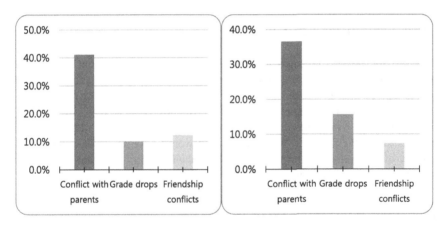

Fig. 2. Reasons for suicide urge

A major conflict factor lies on the difference between the way for communicating; parents, used to obedient relationship, demanding coercive submission from adolescents, whom self-expression is important. This caused absence of communication at home, leading many shapes of juvenile delinquency. Moreover, even though the rapid industrialization and urbanization in South Korea played firm scaffolds for stable education system and economic growth, interestingly with craze for education and the government's policy of education, the parent's pressure for better academic performance and success in life on teenagers made them unhappiest children in the world and worsened parent-children relationship [5]. The governments, only into numbers happening, funded programs and counselling that prevent adolescents from committing suicides, not being able to identify underlying cause for the happening. As a matter of fact, 7 out of 10 teenagers that committed suicide in Gyeonggi-do Province, had taken 'wee class', a counselling program, prior to the act [6]. Fragmentarily this shows how the government's confrontational policy does not help. Thus, with hypothesis that solution to the problem of juvenile delinquency is improving parent-child relationship, the smallest relationship unit in society, this study proposes a communication service design that able teenage children to express themselves to parents without any conflict.

2   Research Method

This study identified communication state of parent-children through stats, examined its validity by conducting surveys and interviews with parents and children; the target groups for service. As the age gap between the two users, parents and children, were big, children in middle school, aged from 13 to 15, and in high school, aged from 16 to 18, were set as main service users. For teenage children shows most frustration to lack of communication in the relationship, thus setting parents in 40s to 50s as second target group. Through data analysis, an optimum service platform was selected, followed by contents structure and flow.

3   Research on Present-Condition

Survey on Adolescent Condition in 2014 (Table 1) shows the amount of time spent between parents and teenage children in communication weekly. As shown, spending less than half an hour per week for communication is most popular, with less than an hour per week being the average. Table 2 also shows how often teenage children talk to parents about their issues and concerns. In statistics below, 34.6 % children never talk to parents about their concerns and 32.7 % answered once to thrice a month. The frequency of children speaking to parents about their concerns are 'almost none'. As years go by fewer children are talking to their parents.

Table 1. Time spent on parent-children conversation per week

Time spent	Father	Mother
Never	0.0 %	2.0 %
Less than 30 min	48.1 %	22.4 %
Btw 30 min – 1 h	21.7 %	20.0 %
Btw 1 – 2 h	11.0 %	10.2 %
More than 2 h	12.0 %	23.0 %
None above	0.5 %	0.1 %

Table 2. Frequency of children sharing their concerns to parents

Frequency on conversation	2011	2014
Never	34.1 %	34.6 %
1 ~ 3 a month	35.8 %	32.7 %
1 ~ 3 a week	18.6 %	18.9 %
4 ~ 6 a week	4.1 %	5.0 %
Everyday	6.4 %	8.5 %
None above	1.0 %	0.3 %

Table 3 shows 89.6 % of the parents show satisfaction in their relationship with children. Not only that, 80.6 % of them think they are having 'enough conversation with children' and 71.0 % that they 'respect children's opinions'. Despite the short

Table 3. Parents' satisfaction on relationship to teenage children

Questionnaire/answer	Not at all	Not so much	To some degrees	Always
Have enough conversation with children	1.1 %	19.3 %	59.3 %	20.3 %
Usually respect teenage children's opinion	0.7 %	7.0 %	70.2 %	22.1 %
Satisfy with relationship with children	0.9 %	8.6 %	59.6 %	30.9 %

amount of time spent and decreasing frequency of conversation sessions between parents and teenage children, parents' satisfaction on parent-children relationship is high.

The professional counselors indicate that students, who are going through puberty, regard parents, who are able to listen to them until they finish, as the most favorable ones. On the other hand, parents in South Korea believe that providing their children to make sure children do not fall behind when compared to other peers is the role they are assigned to do [7]. As such, not only do they have generation difference, but also they lack in understanding of each other. Table 4 below shows differences in list of concerns between parents and teenage children. As shown in the career category, both parents and children show concerns for finding out career, however shows the difference, in which children have vague anxiety over their future, while parents have concerns over children's lack of preparation for their future. In addition to that, in the academic category, both parents and children feel burden on steady performance management and fear grade drops. Not only that, but they also show worries and big burdens on competition between friends in academic performances. Moreover, children feel pressure to get prepared for University enrollment, while parents think that the children have issues on not being able to do what they want to do due to studying. Children, in friendship category, show difficulty in adapting to communal living, concern over getting bullied and other similar notes. Meanwhile, parents show most concern over external issues, such as amount of time their children spend with the peers and the kids' difference in physical development with other peers. Finally, in family category, teenage children show dissatisfaction over their siblings' and parents' attention on them and over parents' constant emphasis on academic performances, while parents have conflicts regarding their children within themselves on top of conflicts with children. Like wise, parents and children show different range of conflict factors and concerns; what parents thought their children were going through were not always in accord with what the children actually going through.

From above research few insights were learned. (1) The amount of time spent on parent-children communication and the frequency of it are low and teenage children experience difficulty in expressing their concerns to their parents. (2) On the contrary, parents think they are having enough amount of conversations with children and think they show respect to their children, and are satisfied with the overall relationship with children. (3) Both children and parents have different concerns and factors that they regard as conflict starters.

Table 4. Categories of adolescence concerns recognized by teenage children and parents

Category	Sub-category	Teenage children	Parents
Career	Experiencing difficulty in figuring out future career path	V	V
	Having vague anxiety about future career	V	
	Lacking preparation for decided career		V
	Struggling with role of parents and expenses in career exploration		V
Academic	Not studying (lack of academic interest)		V
	Feeling burden on steady performance management	V	V
	Having fear of low grades	V	V
	Discontent at not having free time		V
	Feeling burden on competition and comparison with peers	V	V
	Feeling pressure to get prepared for university enrollment	V	V
Friendship	Spending unnecessary amount of time with peers		V
	Experiencing difficulty in friendship		V
	Anxiety about different physical development than other peers		V
	Lacking friendship skills	V	
	Experiencing hardship on friendship due to grades	V	
	Feeling alienation from the crowd	V	
	Having heterosexual relationship issues	V	
Family	Having marital disputes, due to their children		V
	Relationship with parents		V
	Parent-children relationship growing apart	V	
	Feeling discontent with parents attitude on children	V	
	Lacking attention from parents	V	
	Dissatisfaction with emphasis academic performance	V	

4 Surveys and Results

A survey was conducted to teenagers aged from 13 to 18, from 10th to 17th April in 2015. Online survey and printed survey were distributed to each school and handed in accordingly. In total 219 persons were involved in this survey, and 217 valid answers were selected and then carefully analyzed. Among the respondents, 114 were middle school students, making 52.1 % of the whole, and 103 were high school students, making 47.1 % of the whole. 80 male students, taking up 38.2 %, and 137 female students, taking up 62.8 %, were involved in this survey. The first survey investigated on the intimacy teenagers felt they had with their parents, whether there are conflicts with parents, and on factors that hindered further conversation with parents. The second survey investigated to search for an effective method of communication between the parents and children.

From the first set of survey, about parent-children communication in the last one-year period, 70.7 % reported 'I can talk about my thoughts and beliefs without hesitation to my parents', 77.9 % 'My parents are good listeners', 70.6 % 'We spend good amount of time for communication', 72.5 % 'Parents are ones I can depend on the most', and 63.7 % reporting 'I believe my parents are well aware of how I live'. On the scale from 1 to 10, 1 being 'very intimate' with parents and 10 being 'very far' from parents, 172 answered between 'very intimate' to 'close', taking up 78.5 % of the whole. (see Fig. 3) Teenagers, in overall, showed positive feedback concerning their relationship with parents and conversation satisfaction.

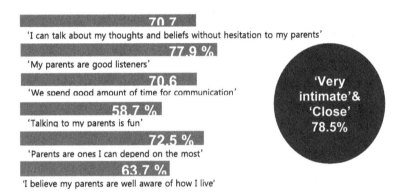

Fig. 3. Subjects conversed in last one year period and intimacy with parents and respondent

Regarding the frequency of parent-children communication, it is shown that children on average have 8.267 conversation sessions a week talking to their fathers, with an average of 22.9 min for each conversation, while children have 13.096 conversations a week with mothers, with each lasting 33.43 min on average. The figures are low considering that children spend, excluding hours of sleep, 3.75 h a day on average with their parents at home (see Table 5).

Table 5. Frequency of parent-children conversation sessions and minutes spent in average

	Time spent (per day)	Frequency (per week)	Duration (per session)
Father	3.75 h	8.26 session	22.9 min.
Mother	3.75 h	13.09 session	33.43 min

Figure 4 shows conflict ration of parent and teenage children. 80.3 % answered that they are 'experiencing conflict' with parents, and when asked for methods of expressing feelings and thoughts while in conflict with parents, 71 % answered they 'Talk directly in person', 44 % expressing through 'Use letters, texts and Kakao Talk (a messenger application)', while 5 % 'Talk on the phone', yet 65 % of them still 'experience frustration for not being able to express as wanted to parents'. When asked why they could not express as wanted, they said 'scared' 'fear of not being understood' 'one sided demand from parents' 'knowing that they would not be heard anyway' 'fear of getting scolded at more' 'fear of disagreement' 'their thoughts being ignored' 'being cut while talking' and 'parents not opening to new opinions'(see Fig. 4).

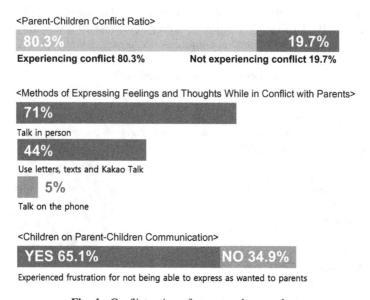

Fig. 4. Conflict ration of parent and respondent

In the second set of survey, 66.1 % answered that they had expressed their thoughts and feelings via Social Networks System(SNS), and 56.9 % answered that they had used other measures to do so, including conversation, writing poems, diaries, secret notes, letters, composing songs and etc. Moreover, 61.9 % is not 'friends with parents' on SNS, due to parents not using SNS, taking 43.6 %, but more than half wished not to share SNS with their parents (see Fig. 5).

5 Surveys Analysis

Even though the data analysis shows that the actual amount of time spent for communication is rather short, and the attitudes of parents, of pushing their thought to children and not being good at listening, while having conversations were not welcoming enough for children to fully speak of their issues to their parents, the teenage children think that they are having well-rounded communication with their parents. The rooting problem of it all is; children not expressing themselves to parents to avoid conflicts and yet defining the relationship as 'intimate'. In addition, large percentage of parents think that they respect children's opinion and are very satisfied with their

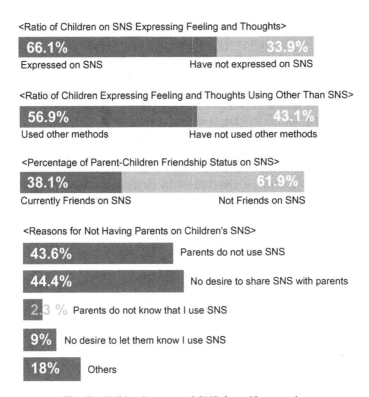

<Ratio of Children on SNS Expressing Feeling and Thoughts>

66.1%   33.9%
Expressed on SNS   Have not expressed on SNS

<Ratio of Children Expressing Feeling and Thoughts Using Other Than SNS>

56.9%   43.1%
Used other methods   Have not used other methods

<Percentage of Parent-Children Friendship Status on SNS>

38.1%   61.9%
Currently Friends on SNS   Not Friends on SNS

<Reasons for Not Having Parents on Children's SNS>

43.6%   Parents do not use SNS

44.4%   No desire to share SNS with parents

2.3 % Parents do not know that I use SNS

9% No desire to let them know I use SNS

18%   Others

Fig. 5. Children's usage of SNS for self-expression

relationship to teenage children. Therefore, there is need for an effective measure for communication, in which children would not be hindered by the parents' attitude or negative real-time responses, that allows children to fully deliver what is on their mind and clearly sees where the relationship to their parents is.

Analyzed, the second survey showed that many adolescents use Social Network Service(SNS) to express their feelings and thoughts, while also using other measures such as conversation, writing diaries, secret notes, letters, poems, and composing songs outside of SNS, which translates that children use writing as most preferred way of expressing their thoughts and feelings. Furthermore, many teenage children showed negativity on being 'friends with parents' and sharing their lives on SNS for they did not wish to expose their privacy to their parents. These adds to a conclusion; the need for a third space where children can freely communicate via SNS, yet not having to worry about their privacy being exposed to parents.

6 Proposal

Except direct conversation, writing is one of the main communication method that is frequently used between teenage children when delivering their thoughts and emotions. This study chose social media, particularly, mobile application as a communication platform taking into account the preference and acquaintance of social media to the teenage children. The study proposes a closed-type of social media of novel design to prevent privacy issues of the teenage children as previous social media may contain private details the children may not wish to disclose to their parents. Taken into account of parents who are reluctant to using complicated mobile application, the proposed application contains simple contents with user interface and graphic user interface designed specifically for the sub target users, parents.

Along with shared album and small-group chatting services, there are three main features to this application. First, instead of bilateral communication, the study proposes unilateral communication, enabling single-sided delivery system from children to parents to prevent miscommunication caused by negative reactions from parents. The social media suggested by the study enables the children to become an active subject, whereas the parents are limited to only present passive reactions. In other words, the

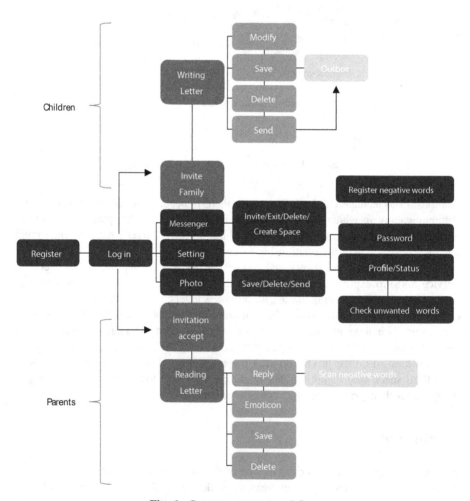

Fig. 6. Contents structure and flow

teenage children may send long writings or letters, but the parents are only allowed to write up to one sentence and are offered only with positive emoticons to send.

Second, this platform contains a feature to block words, registered in advance, that teenage children do not wish to hear from their parents. This feature automatically filters negative words and recommends positive expressions with similar context upon responding to their children.

Lastly, in the surveys, despite the short communication time and conflicts between parents and teenage children, both target users showed satisfaction in the relationship. For this reason, the third main feature is added; visual data showing interaction; counts of text messages, total length of calls and more, between the parents and teenage children in a set period of time, to help understand visually how close or distant they are(see Fig. 6).

7 Conclusion and Limitation

This study proposed a closed-type of one-way SNS mobile application, where teenage children can freely communicate to the parents by setting children as main users, allowing them to lead conversation. Furthermore, parents were set as second users, however giving them only limited options for response to ensure that children would not be discouraged to communicate, making parents to truly listen. It is worth anticipating, with the study results and content outputs and future yet-to-be-made mobile application, improvements in family communication leading to alleviation of youth crimes in future.

There are limitations to this platform. First, if there is no active attitude and involvement from the main user, communication problems cannot be alleviated. Second, surveys and interview of parents were referenced only during the process, but were not used to fulfill the needs of parents as users in the actual service. Finally, the survey and research were conducted on population of a specific region, thus certain customs may reflect on results.

Acknowledgments. This research was supported by No. 20150124 of Handong Global University Research Grants. I would like to thank team MEME for all the data collected by observations, interviews and surveys.

References

1. National Youth Policy Institute: Youth Research Brief, vol. 25 (2015)
2. OECD Health Data: Health at a Glance 2011. 1.6.1 Suicide mortality rates (2009)
3. Statistics Korea: Social Service Survey. #27 Reasons for the conflict (2014)
4. Jeong, J.G., Ill-bo, J.: http://newshyu.com/news/articleView.html?idxno=16934. 19 March 2015
5. OECD: PISA database, Table III.2.3a (2012)
6. Kukje News: http://www.gukjenews.com/news/articleView.html?idxno=165634. 24 November 2014

7. Narangaerell: Counsel on Conflict between Parents and Teenage Children (2015)
8. Studies on Korean Youth, vol. 16, no. 1, pp. 5–34 (2015)
9. Kim, H.J.A.: Study on the Operation and Improvement of Adolescents' Shelters in Korea (2006)
10. Lee, E.K.A.: Study on the Effect of Parents-Children Dysfunctional Communication and Social Anxiety Perceived by Teenagers on School Adjustment (2012)

The Third-Type Settlement: Research of Unified Urban and Rural Living Organisms and Its Interaction Design

Wei Yu[1] and Xinyu Jiang[1,2(✉)]

[1] East China University of Science and Technology, Shanghai, China
[2] DongHua University, Shanghai, China
jiangxinyu@dhu.edu.cn

Abstract. Throughout human inhabit history and future development there exists many practical problems in urban and rural construction and human settlement, especially under the complicated situation that China is experiencing rapid industrialization and urbanization but with huge urban-rural binary opposites and lack of organic interaction. It is urgent for us to explore new human settlement patterns and the implementation way for their interaction design.

This paper argues that it will be the inevitable development mode for future human settlement to change from the first kind of race-gathering mode in the agrarian age, to the second kind of profit-gathering mode in the ministry era, and then head for the third kind of kindness-gathering pattern that heaven and people integrate. Man and man, man and society, man and nature will interact with each other in a friendly way. This third mode will have a positive role to play in natural harmony and human sustainable development, especially for the research and practical application of green, organic, living and cultural theory. As an organic system, interaction design of unified urban and rural areas here especially refer to mutual interaction design between population and natural environment, social relations, public products and so on, with the aim of planning and describing the system of interaction between people and people, people and things, people and the environment as well as people and system, and then lay outing and conveying these organic system interaction in a reasonable and art way.

As the third class inhabit, unified urban and rural living organism becomes the best settlement mode for being green ecological, organic harmonious, life-healthy and cultural prosperity. Taking heaven-and-human harmonious interaction ecological nature as maternal background, living healthy state as interactive operation mechanism, the growth of the continuous development of science as the fundamental purpose, the truth of technology, the goodness of human and the beauty of the art as the design pointer, this model follows the nature of justice but higher, imitates the wisdom of the ancients but sublime it to fit today, studies the laws of science but makes best use of the advantages and bypass the disadvantages, and truly achieve the vision of "Better life for all living beings".

Keywords: Three kinds of settlement patterns · Unified urban and rural living organisms · System interaction design

© Springer International Publishing Switzerland 2016
A. Marcus (Ed.): DUXU 2016, Part II, LNCS 9747, pp. 527–536, 2016.
DOI: 10.1007/978-3-319-40355-7_50

1 Introduction

For China and even global city, the rapid development always brings out the result that advantages and disadvantages coexist. At the same time of enjoying the city modernization, people also have to face many complex settlement problems resulting from the widening gap between the urban and rural areas and the process of urbanization. While the existing architecture and urban planning study lacks of practical and effective solution for many real problems. China is in rapid industrialization and urbanization, while is in the complicated situation that there are huge urban-rural binary opposites, and lacks organic interaction. We urgently need to explore new human settlement patterns and the implementation way of system interaction design for many practical problems in urban and rural construction and human settlement.

2 Three Types of Human Society Settlement Pattern Division

Human populations, first of all follow the universal law of gravity in the physics sense. Gravity is a motive force of the human settlement or birth, which is called the first motive force in this article. It is determined by the force that human settlement must be an integral part of nature, not exclusive in nature. Anthropology gravity or veins close force like human blood, clan and nation in the sense psychological is the drive for the steady development of human settlement, which is called the second force in this article. The power is based on human groups' dear cardiac power, making condensation of human populations continue. The third power source of human inhabit is the political, economic, social and other social field effect in the sense of culture gravity (here the culture is the human culture, including politics, economy, literature and art, science and technology, etc.), which is objective outside drives that keep the mode of human groups in changing and is called the third force in this article. The third force keeps human settlement mode in continues changing for imbalance of the development in time and space, which can be either negative or positive. Human settlement is the result of the interaction and balance of these three forces.

Through the ages, the human settlement history is watershed with the industrial revolution under the action of the three forces from tree-dwelling, cave, villages, cities, villages and towns, castles to metropolitan circle, etc. It basically can be summed up as the first settlement and the second settlement shape or pattern. The long time from human birth to the industrial revolution may be called the era of the first kind of settlement patterns, which was mainly settlement of primitive hunting and farming methods. The settlement pattern in this long stage plays a leading role in the first and second force. Time from industrial revolution to now could be called the second pattern in the history of human settlement era, mainly characterized by the modern industry and post-industrialization. During this time, the third force mentioned above is the main force while because of the unbalanced development of human culture and immature at this stage, the force is in increasingly negative effect.

In 1687, Newton wrote in his book the Mathematics Principle of Natural Philosophy that "any two objects in the universe are attracted to each other ... all celestial bodies must follow the law of universal gravitation". Gravitation constitutes the basic logical order of the universe celestial bodies and the universe universal, which also directly or indirectly provides relatively stable polymerization existence and inhabitation surviving relationship for everything inside or among each other.

Microscopic particles in universe makes up atoms molecules, molecular component objects (the body), celestial body, which then compose celestial universe galaxies, and finally form a total system in the universe. Universe has the feature of similarity, circles-like and settlements. They are closely related with each other and abide by the same evolution rules, and similar morphological change development rules. Although occasionally there exist randomness and disorder but in general the existence and evolution of the universe adhere to the unified principle. In the infinite loop movement pattern it observe its evolution rules, procedures, rules, and form a group existing system with settlement pattern characteristics. Take the inorganic polymerization existing mode as an example, that rotary motion around the core of the macro cosmic objects such as stars, thus forming a group existing system of settlement characteristics. The natural rules will be reminiscent of a similar social law. Confucius said in The Analects of Confucius Political Discourse that to run a country with morality wins a ruler the respect that the Pole Star gets, circled by numerous other stars. According to records, the ancients had seen the north celestial pole star surrounded by two "Francisco" wall composed of numerous stars, known as "purple msi walls". "Purple msi walls" is above the north heaven, where emperor of heaven live and the corresponding positions of the earth is the center of the country- purple palace, from which the Forbidden City takes its name. In the 60–70 s of the 20th century, American engineers Hugh Harleston, Jr. conducted field exploration for the ancient city of Chios Huakan aid based on mathematical principles. It was reported by him that, obviously there are certain mathematical relationship among the main building listed on both sides of the Ghost Road. The size of each part and the solar system has certain accurate proportion relationship.

Rotary motion around the core of microscopic particles such as molecular electronic structure forms a group exist system of settlement characteristics. Also, as for survival mode of plants and animals inhabit, whatever cell, microscopic flora, trees, forest or grassland vegetation, and so on, all groups existing system with the characteristics of polymerization or cluster. And like animals inhabit survival mode, ant societies, the bee nest, birds, fish, primate family, their survival mode is complete survival system of settlement characteristics.

As mentioned above, whether the human settled as city or country, they all follow the first force on macro, namely gravity. On microscopic family blood relationship, the aggregation of the clan, raising the folk custom, etc., stems from the blood affinity; throughout the change of settlement modes, such as the change from religious to military city, political, economic and cultural city, etc., it is all because of the power of culture. These three forces promote human populations and their evolution. Because of the strength of the positive or negative power, the human settlements are presented in three kinds of modes: the first kind is eco-friendly and health settlement patterns in original and natural farming stage. The second category of settlement is the heaven-against-people alienated settlement model after the industrial revolution that become prosperous float world even an ailing state.

This paper argues that in the future, human will play up strengths and avoid weaknesses in the former mode and head for the third type of settlement that featured by modern ecology, healthy life, continual growth, which is drove by these three forces, especially the third force to play a positive role. It is the unified urban and rural living organism that will make life better in the third class inhabit mode.

3   The Third-Type Settlement—Unified Urban and Rural Areas in the Future

As the main form of human settlement, city and country are different parts of the macro social, economic and cultural structure; the two is of homologous symbiotic relationship, undivided from each other. Although the first kind of settlement pattern is good, but it is the beauty of the original primary stage after all, not suitable for the current era of human society and the future development needs. Featured by modern industrial city, heaven are against with people in the second type of settlement pattern, which is of high entropy high carbon, and ailing. The pure interest orientation of market economy, the indifference and lack of cultural values and the alienation of human spirit and aesthetic is the cause.

Based on the analysis above, this article put forward the third settlement pattern, namely the unified urban and rural living organism that inherit ancient harmony, overcome the ills of modern urban and rural settlement and satisfy the future social development of the third kind of pattern from the perspective of organization ecology, life science, system science, city culture and design art by following the principle of green organic life inhabit, focusing on ecology, life and growth, and taking the best mankind inhabit mode as an organic unity on the basis of ecosystem healthy growth of unified life system.

Unified urban and rural living organism is of the organic characteristics, the type of life can be summarized as three categories of life type from background system to its own native and to future derivation subsystem, which form a complete structure functionalism theory in the sense of complete giant life system. Background system categories: the subject itself of unified organism is an organic system in ecology sense, rather than a simple machine product system, let alone the rigid material of architectural space composition. Native categories: in biological sense, all human and related plants and animals, including the object form of a living system, they friendly live together to form an organic biosphere system, instead of splitting between each other like fire and water. Future derived classes: they are intelligent life based on the information of the intelligent building, on the artificial intelligence system such as cloud computing and Internet of things; they are huge human inhabit intelligent robot system. In time, unified urban and rural areas follow the law of life that develops from birth to recession throughout. In space, it corresponds with the physical systems, tissues, organs and cells. Inner signs system of life structure, external guarantee system, and urban and rural areas, as well as the formation mechanism of unified urban and rural living organism are included, which achieve its function and role through the imitation (bionic) design, system design and interaction design methods. Its basic connotation should include composition of organic ecological system (natural environment, unified organism, people, and systems), the dialectical unity between urban and rural areas (urban and rural areas discard the disadvantages to blend organically), and the concrete embodiment of vital signs (brain, central nervous, life signs and mechanism). The basic mechanism is as follows:

3.1   Inner Signs System of Unified Urban and Rural Living Organism's Life Structure

"Life" is organic composition created by the accident of natural. All "life" refers to individual life that of stable substance and energy metabolism. And the most complex life form is "people" itself. People is not only with a visible nature, but also has the intangible vital signs "thought", and at the same time it is influenced by the social, cultural, ideology, values and other aspects, which is a magic and energetic individuals. Urban and rural can also be seen as living organisms with stable physical form and energy metabolism. Similar to the human body, it is also made up of different cell body, and different cells form tissues and organs, which is with signs of life and vitality.

As is known to all, the human body inner signs are made up of four large organizations and eight systems. The author believes that the inner structure of unified urban and rural areas is also made up of different organization and system, corresponding with the human body inner signs system.

3.2   External Support System of Unified Urban and Rural Living Organisms

Unified Urban and rural areas running needs external support system to support. The author will analyze external support system of unified urban and rural from three aspects, micro, meso and macro.

- External micro support system

"people" is the main body in unified urban and rural living organisms, which can also be seen as micro core part of unified urban and rural areas. Because people themselves have subjective initiation so they play a main role in understanding and transforming the objective world. One reason for the increasingly problems in the unified urban and rural dual structure is the failure in coordinating the contradiction between people and heaven. The essence of many economic problems and social problems is for neglecting the guarantee of the survival and development and the support of natural rights. So the construction of unified urban and rural life system should pay attention to the microcosmic support system construction and planning. External micro support system can be briefly summarized by eating, wearing, living, transporting, learning, working, leisure, queuing and recycling.

- External medium support system

External micro support system takes the guarantee for the survival and development of people as the fundamental starting point, while for the medium support system takes support and guarantees the unified urban and rural life in industrial layout, system arrangement and so on economic construction as the core. From the static perspective, the industry layout refers to the elements of different industries and departments in space distribution and combination; from the dynamic perspective, the industry layout is flow and restructuring of all sorts of industry resources in space. Industrial layout is one of the important factors that affect the industry and the regional competitiveness, which decides the development structure and of industry.

- External macro support system learns from theory of structural functionalism.

From the perspective of system theory, populated area, residents of passengers in the unified urban and rural areas can be seen as different subsystem in the macroscopic system environment that supported by the nature, society, economy and culture, and carry out philosophical structure adjustment. Oriental philosophy thought promote the harmony concept, thinking geographical and human conditions are the foundation of all things. It is thought by author that, from the macroscopic level, external support system of unified urban and rural areas can be divided into the integration of three parts, time-liness, favorable geographical position, and popular support.

3.3   Mechanism Analysis of Unified Urban and Rural Areas Living Organism

Organizational structure system of unified urban and rural living mechanism:
  Space hardware structure collection organization (objects)

- The structure of the space facilities (static) organizations collection: hardware 1 - class material hardware system of public facilities.
- Motor products (dynamic) run linkage groups: hardware 2 - traffic moving material hardware system.

Organic life system running: Wetware (human life) – interact, link, network, and organization among populated and management server.
  Spiritual culture system design organization. Software

- Urban cultural style and brand image (such as Beijing Shanghai style culture, etc.). Software
- Virtual digital information, the wisdom of city science and technology and the "wisdom" of culture. Software
- Non-material cultural inheritance, colony gene mapping, memory, nostalgia rings birthmark, etc. Software
- Social memory time keeping system: settlement context inheriting the emotional design mechanism and the legal safeguard system.

Mechanism analysis of unified urban and rural living organisms:
  Living organisms: the life of urban and rural areas drove on the basis of natural ecological life and prime life force combination drive.
  Science and technology leading mechanism: intelligent and information of urban and rural areas, the driving and traction force of productivity of modern science and technology civilization.
  Cultural governance auxiliary mechanism: aesthetics of urban and rural culture:

Production relations of force and the traction on the basis of humanity: culture function and function of art that the government, society and the individual work in autonomy, which has a similar effect with firewall buffer isolation belt and massage chair, and purifier.

In short, people is the advanced form of life, is the experience and the embodiment part of the macroscopic forms of life, is the true main body of organic constitution of the depth of life system 4D, 3D plus time dimension, and zero distance immersive interactive. The urban and rural characteristics combine with their respective advantages and learn from each other, organic life system that $1 + 1$ is greater than 2 has the characteristics of the activity of life. Therefore, unified urban and rural design is a dynamic process of history, is the longest time dimension in the design of all design. It almost keeps company with the whole of the human life in unified settlement system between urban and rural areas. And at the same time, it is a green organic life constitution system; the unified life system constitutes the following four hierarchies:

- Layer of urban and rural ecological environment (mainly outer ring, primary, background, and first natural ecological features).
- Layer of architectural landscape space (mainly include 2 laps, level 2, skeleton, the second natural design in fixed form).
- Layer of public life product (mainly 3 laps, level 3, media, mobile media and tool system, including the real and virtual ones).
- Layer of human life movement (core, level 4, the main body, life, ecological features mainly).

Unified urban and rural living organisms are a composite system, which has organic link between each other. Therefore, it requires a systemic interaction design to achieve.

4 Interaction Design of Unified Urban and Rural Living Organisms

As an organic system, interaction design of united urban and rural life referred to especially is the interaction between population and the natural environment, social relations and systems such as public goods, with the aim of planning and describing interaction way between people and people, people and things, people and the environment, and then layout and convey these interactions in a reasonable and art way. Specific is as follows.

4.1 Interaction Design of the Objective Nature and Tool System

People here refer to the ones from different scale and the level from individuals to segmentation and public. First is the interaction between human and nature. Nature is the foundation of human survival while barbarous development and unlimited use of ecological environment and nature resources since the industrial civilization has finally been revenged by nature, leading to the global ecological crisis. How to overcome the ecological crisis and realize the harmonious coexistence of man and nature is the urgent questions need to explored and solved. Tool is an extension of the human body, human actively invent and escalate tool system evolution, making person increasingly close with tools that tool system has become the second floor, the third layer of body and skin. Interaction design of people and tools are mainly the UI and UE design and experience design between individual people and fixed tools and mobile digital products. To sum up, it includes multiple levels of interaction design at least from macroscopic to micro-cosmic: first of all, it is interaction design between people and the dynamics of unified urban and rural life in macro level, natural ecology and static real estate) inhabit and the architectural design. The second is the interaction between people and medium measure dynamic tools such as all kinds of traffic tools, or other public interaction between household furniture. The third is interaction between portable mobile terminal infor-mation tools or network equipment in micro level. It is also the interaction of bioengin-eering implantable or immersive interaction tools, represented by biological chips or superfine sensor in the human body. It fuses people and tools organically together.

4.2   Interaction Design Among People

From micro level of individual human interaction level, it should emphasize on face-to-face interactive communication mode, such as in the tenement yard and courtyard, interaction is smooth and people integrated well emotionally in the past. Also great importance should be paid interaction platform of interaction patterns like WeChat, as well as virtual and real interaction design. As the most advanced intelligent life with strongest social relations and social feature, individual person's survival and develop-ment must be established on the basis of good interaction with society. Wisdom city has the characteristics of life, interaction design methods such as Internet, Internet of things, melting networking related to today's wisdom city construction must be applied to unified urban and rural areas settlement design. From group of interaction design that across trade or industry in the macro level, attention must be paid to the coordinated development of productivity and production relations to promote the overall progress of human civilization and health fast development. So the coordination and innovation, fusion between related industries is definitely the organic composition of the human interaction design that for adjusting and perfecting production relations.

4.3   Interaction Design of City and Countryside

Construction of unified urban and rural areas is not a simple assembling of city and country combination, but healthy living system of organic interaction and fusion, which as fully explained by this article in chapter 6 that has the characteristics of healthy mechanism of living systems. In the organic integration of interactive process of city and countryside, the design service concept and the user experience ideas are reflected. Let the user experience pleasure, satisfaction and happiness through the unified urban and rural service life design. Users here is the diverse organisms in broad, make all things grow, vitality and prosperity through interaction design. Make the service system of unified living areas more humane, more secured and meticulously through interaction design. The specific design should include at least two aspects in the form and content:

The first is the interaction design of form and ecology. Interact towns and villages with beautiful shape and high-quality ecology, such as settlement building integrated into the landscape green net, which is inhabit environment with garden and orchard. This is the embodiment of city and countryside's external beauty and truth. The second is the interaction design of humanism and human. It need to break the traditional rigid system between urban and rural areas at the first to make urban and rural gentry literati organic exchange cost reduced, new interactive mechanisms sound. Such as under interactive, open and shared adjacent architectural form, people come to and fro, culture exchanges, ideas are touched. Material heritage and intangible cultural heritage and the heritage of people here will be the bridge and medium, which is the deep inner spiritual interaction between city and countryside based on the purpose of good and beauty. It is also rendering and expression of service design and interaction. Organic fusion and interactive design of green ecological, organic life of unified urban and rural living will be a fundamental improvement in the collapse disorder of the city and hollowing of country.

As the explanation of Lai Zhide, the Zhouyi scholars in Ming dynasty, for the sentence that "If heaven and earth communicates, then everything circles; if emperor and his subjects communicates, then the up and down thought is consistent" from the Zhouyi-Tai-Tuan Analects, Heaven and earth communicates by gas, gas exchange and things pass, heaven and earth is also peaceful. Up and down communicates by heart and have the same goals, it's good for both of the high and low levels. This is the highest goal and level of unified urban and rural life interaction design in the future.

5   Conclusion

Although the third-type settlement: unified urban and rural living system and interaction design research are proposed for the first time both at home and abroad, it will inevitably be the future human settlement development mode by looking to the human settlement history and future development to change from the first kind of race-gathering mode in the agrarian age, to the second kind of profit-gathering mode in the ministry era, and then head for the third kind of kindness-gathering pattern that heaven and people integrate. It will definitely play a positive role in natural harmony existence and Human sustainable development, especially in human green, organic, life and culture of theoretical research and practical application.

As the third class inhabit, unified urban and rural living organism becomes the best settlement mode for being green ecological, organic harmonious, life-healthy and cultural prosperity. Taking heaven-and-human harmonious interaction ecological nature as maternal background, living healthy state as interactive operation mechanism, the growth of the continuous development of science as the fundamental purpose, the truth of technology, the goodness of human and the beauty of the art as the design pointer, this model follows the nature of justice but higher, imitates the wisdom of the ancients but sublime it to fit today, studies the laws of science but makes best use of the advantages and bypass the disadvantages, and truly achieve the vision of "better life for all living beings".

References

1. Ignatieva, M., Stewart, G.H., Meurk, C.: Planning and design of ecological networks in urban areas. Landscape Ecol. Eng. **7**(1), 17–25 (2011)
2. Carmona, M.: Public Places, Urban Spaces: The Dimensions of Urban Design. Routledge, London (2010)
3. Aspray, T.J., Mugusi, F., Rashid, S., et al.: Rural and urban differences in diabetes prevalence in Tanzania: the role of obesity, physical inactivity and urban living. Trans. R. Soc. Trop. Med. Hyg. **94**(6), 637–644 (2000)
4. Tacoli, C.: Rural-urban interactions; a guide to the literature. Environ. Urbanization **10**, 147–166 (1998)
5. Zhang, J., Inbakaran, R.J., Jackson, M.S.: Understanding community attitudes towards tourism and host—guest interaction in the urban—rural border region. Tourism Geographies **8**(2), 182–204 (2006)
6. Pickett, S.T.A., Cadenasso, M.L., Grove, J.M., et al.: Urban ecological systems: linking terrestrial ecological, physical, and socioeconomic components of metropolitan areas. In: Marzluff, J.M. (ed.) Urban Ecology, pp. 99–122. Springer, New York (2008)
7. Rapoport, A.: Human Aspects of Urban Form: Towards a Man—Environment Approach to Urban Form and Design. Elsevier, Burlington (2013)
8. Aspray, T.J., Mugusi, F., Rashid, S., et al.: Rural and urban differences in diabetes prevalence in Tanzania: the role of obesity, physical inactivity and urban living. Trans. R. Soc. Trop. Med. Hyg. **94**(6), 637–644 (2000)

Usability and User
Experience Studies

Analysis of Product Use by Means of Eye Tracking and EEG: A Study of Neuroergonomics

Rafaela Q. Barros[1(✉)], Ademário S. Tavares[1], Wilson Albuquerque[1],
Jaciara Clarissa da Silva[3], Isaltino Abel de Lemos[4],
Raísa Lorena Siqueira de Albuquerque Cardoso[5],
Marcelo Márcio Soares[1], and Marcelo R. Cairrao[2]

[1] Post-Graduate Program in Design, Federal University of Pernambuco, Recife, Brazil
queirozdebarros@hotmail.com
[2] Post-Graduate Program in Physiology and Pharmacology,
Federal University of Pernambuco, Recife, Brazil
[3] Unifavip DeVry, Caruaru, Brazil
[4] Undergraduate Program in Interior Design, Unifavip DeVry, Caruaru, Brazil
[5] Post-Graduate Program in Public Health, Unifavip DeVry, Caruaru, Brazil

Abstract. Studies related to measuring user satisfaction with soft drinks PET packaging are still scarce, especially when related to users' actual performance in the act of opening screw caps. Although there are usability techniques that evaluate a user's experience by using the process for conceptualizing and evaluating consumer products, the researcher does not always have factual knowledge about whether or not the experience reported by the user at the time of the research fully matches what the user actually experienced. This study conducted a usability evaluation of how a sample of users manually handled PET bottles for soft drinks by making a comparison between the experience as reported by the user and the real experience that the user underwent by using three techniques to measure them, namely usability analysis, eye tracking and electroencephalography (EEG).

Keywords: Ergonomics · Usability · Neuroergonomics · EEG · Eye tracking

1 Introduction

Packaging materials are consumer products which have interfaces with everyday life that are frequently used. However, many such materials do not satisfy aspects related to usability and safety. For this reason the design of packaging must provide the user with safety, comfort, efficiency and aesthetic satisfaction. In addition, the user's capabilities should be taken into consideration especially in relation to usability and accessibility when opening the product. This question, when it involves seniors and children, should be a priority for the designer.

In this case, the interface problems harm users when accidents occur, which, among other causes, can be due to improper sizing of the strength needed while handling product packaging [1, 2]. Thus, individuals considered strong as well as those considered weak

© Springer International Publishing Switzerland 2016
A. Marcus (Ed.): DUXU 2016, Part II, LNCS 9747, pp. 539–548, 2016.
DOI: 10.1007/978-3-319-40355-7_51

may suffer adverse effects in the motor performance of this task. Furthermore, the difficulty of opening a PET bottle may lead to waste and even the ruin of the product.

Thus, studies related to measuring user satisfaction with PET bottles for soft drinks are still scarce, especially when related to the user´s actual performance at the moment when he/she opens screw caps.

Bevan [3] explains that even though usability is a tool used to improve the development of products and interfaces, this is still not enough for optimizing the human-product interface. Tullis and Albert [4] explain that usability uses metrics to measure a user's experience and that this takes place during the design and evaluation process which helps to identify possible usability problems. Moreover, some measures are taken to facilitate the analysis and the conduct of usability tests, such as by applying usability models.

However, the researcher does not always have factual knowledge about whether or not the experience reported by the user at the time of the experiment is fully consistent with the actual experience that the user feels. The difference between what is reported and, in fact, felt becomes an unknown to the researcher.

In this perspective, ergonomics studies associated with neuroscience have given rise to Neuroergonomics which studies the brain and its behavior in various work activities [5, 6]. This area enables cognition and human behavior in various activity sites to be analyzed. This research set out to conduct a usability evaluation of a sample of users when they were manually handling soft drink PET bottles by comparing the experience the user reported and the real experience felt by measuring them using the techniques of eye tracking and electroencephalography (EEG).

2   Methodology

The methodology of this study was of a quantitative character, consisting of a field study, comprising 12 participants for the usability study who are from different age groups and are higher education students. As for the Electroencephalogram (EEG) study, initially seven volunteers were recruited.

To select the sample for the usability study, the inclusion criteria were: individuals about whom no pathological condition of the upper limbs had been reported in the previous year and the exclusion criteria were patients who had a reported pathological condition of the upper limbs in the previous year. This exclusion criterion was justified since, for this study, those having limitations in their upper limbs cannot manipulate the PET bottles.

For the neuroergonomics study, the inclusion criteria were: no fluid intake, the intention being to cause the volunteers to feel thirsty when they first saw the soft drinks packaging. In addition, the volunteers were asked not to use alcohol or illicit drugs, caffeine, colas for 24 h before the experiment.

As to the exclusion criteria, these were: not to present any kind of neurological lesion or dysfunction, such as traumatic brain injury, epilepsy, stroke or psychiatric symptom, such as bipolar disorder, schizophrenia and cyclothymia. Also excluded were those who had artifacts or unusual changes in their pattern of electrical activity, as well as participants who did not match up to the inclusion criteria.

The results of the steps of the experiment were analyzed using software corresponding to each technique and compared with each other by conducting usability analysis to investigate whether the opinion reported by means of the questionnaire that evaluated usability was similar to the experience felt and measured on using eye-tracking techniques and EEG.

3   Field Study on Usability

For the first step of the experiment, PET bottles packaging were selected in accordance with the study by Silva [7]. In this study, the author assessed the level of difficulty of opening five types of soft drinks PET bottle. For this, the Likert scale was used to assess the level of user satisfaction. According to the results of this research, PET bottle 1 (Fig. 1a) and PT bottle 2 (Fig. 1b) were selected because these were considered easy and difficult to open, respectively.

1a   1b

Fig. 1. PET bottles considered easy (a) and hard (b) to open.(Source: Authors)

Thus, 12 users were asked to open the top of the two PET bottle models for soft drinks (Fig. 2). Then, a usability evaluation was conducted to analyze the user's satisfaction level as to the level of difficulty of opening them based on the Likert scale by Tullis and Albert [4].

The choice of this scale enables an analysis of the user's satisfaction regarding the opening of the two models of PET bottle to be made. This scale has extremes corresponding to the degree of positive or negative affirmation to which respondents assess their level of agreement or disagreement with what was requested. Five options were presented: very satisfied, satisfied, moderately satisfied, dissatisfied and very dissatisfied.

Thus, this scale let the participants express their satisfaction in degrees of agreement with a positive affirmation or in disagreement with a negative affirmation, thereby

Fig. 2. Participants in the act of opening the soft drinks PET bottles.(Source: Authors)

enabling them to compare and define which of the PET bottles was the most or least difficult to use.

Analysis and Results of the Experiment. The responses to the usability evaluation were organized according to the participants' level of satisfaction and presented the following results: as to PET bottle 1, seven respondents reported being very satisfied and satisfied four. As for PET bottle 2, one respondent reported being very satisfied, three were satisfied, five stated that they were indifferent (moderately satisfied), two were dissatisfied and one was very dissatisfied.

Thus, it can be seen that as to PET bottle 1, the responses were clustered at two levels of positive satisfaction, thus indicating that it was less difficult to open, while as for PET bottle 2, the responses were more spread out among the alternatives presented. Thus, we can conclude that in this study, most respondents preferred PT bottle 1 as this was easier to open.

4   Eye-Tracking Field Study

We used the Tobii Pro TX 300 equipment was used to record the position and the fixations of the patients' eyes in accordance with what PE bottle the user chose as having "liked" and "disliked", at a sampling rate of 300 Hz.

The experiment used two sets of stimuli for cognitive activity. The first set consisted of an image with both PET bottles against a white background (Fig. 3) and the second set was represented by the same content of image and background. The images had a resolution of 648 × 1080 and were established with average luminance and equal sizes.

In the second phase, the volunteers were asked verbally by the moderator to initially close their eyes for one minute. Soon after, the record of cognitive activity was started when they opened their eyes and this was followed by a fixed gaze activity, for five seconds, at the PET bottle that "you did not like" the photo with the PET bottles 2 and 1.

The presentation of this image was interspersed with neutral 20 images for 20 s, followed by displaying the photo with PET bottles 1 and 2 and asking the participant to

Fig. 3. Image of the PET bottles displayed in Tobii.(Source: Authors)

gaze fixedly at the PET bottle that "you liked" for five seconds. Finally, 20 neutral images were shown again for 20 s. The total time of this experiment was 50 s.

Five seconds was considered as the time needed to make a decision and so was chosen as the time needed to analyze the PET bottles the user "liked" and "did not like". This would define the user's preference for PET bottle 1 or 2.

Analysis and Results of the Experiment. By using Tobii® Studio 3.2.1 software, the exact moment that the user made a decision was identified as being the moment at which the fixed gaze was longest on the PET bottle that he/she "liked" and "did not like", namely, long periods of fixed gazing at PET bottles 1 or 2 shown in red.

Identifying the length of time (start and end) of fixed gaze and glances in the area that represents the PET bottle image that the user "did not like" and "liked" is the means by which the user´s preference between these two options is determined.

With respect to PET bottle 1, 11 participants were identified as casting long fixed stares at it. As to PET bottle 2, only one volunteer had the longest fixed stare at it. Therefore, in accordance with the highest total number of fixed stares, it was PET bottle 1 which individuals "least liked" and PET bottle 2 that they most "liked".

5   EEG Field Study

In the second stage of the experiment, the recording of electrical brain activity with EEG (Fig. 4) was carried out at the same time as capturing the Eye Tracking with 12 participants.

The EEG analysis aimed to record the electrical oscillations of the brain while the PET bottles were being displayed when this was associated with the command to fix a stare at the bottle that the volunteer did not like, and then following the same pattern analysis, the stare at the bottle liked.

The electrical signals of the brain were obtained by placing a cap with 64 gold chloride channels. The size of the cap was based on the measurement of the circumference of the brain. Placing the electrodes followed the 10-10 international system and

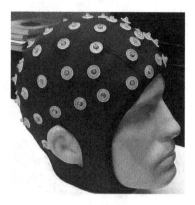

Fig. 4. Image of EEG cap produced by NeuroUp Company.(Source: www.neuroup.com.br)

the reference electrodes are sited in the linked-mastoids of the temporal bones, and earthed in the AFz position. A conductive gel was applied to each of the 64 electrodes.

For analysis of the EEG offline data, first of all, a visual inspection was made to identify the artifacts, and then the automatic removal using Neuroup/Matlab software aided by Independent Component Analysis - ICA and the Multiple Artifact Rejection Algorithm - MARA.

After removing the artifacts, the record of the following regions was selected and sent in ASCII format to sLORETA software in order to analyze the current density in the time domain of the cognitive tasks: FC6, FC4, F8, F4, F6, AF8, O2, P8, PO 4, PO8, FT8, C6, T8, CP4, CP6, TP8, P4, P6, Oz, C4, FC2, FCz, FC1, F2, Fz, F1, AF4, Fp2, Fpz, Fp1, Iz, C1, C2, CP1, CPZ, CP2, P1, Pz, P2, AF3, Cz, C3, C5, T7, FC3, FC5, FT7, F3, F7, AF7, PO3, TP7, CP3, P7, P5, P3, PO7, POZ, O1, F5, CP5.

The EEG recording began with the volunteer resting for one minute with his/her eyes closed and then open for one minute to capture the basal electrical activity. Immediately thereafter the activity of choosing the bottle they "did not like" and "liked" was recorded in accordance with what was obtained from applying the eye tracker.

Results of the Experiment. Using sLORETA software, 61 electrodes were selected, with 250 times, a 512 Hz sampling rate. The 10-10 system was used as coordinates to create the transformed matrix. Thus, in accordance with the intensity of the current, only values greater than 2.5 (MaxLor) were selected.

In accordance with the software, the records of the individuals corresponding to the two classes of those who "liked" and "disliked" what PET bottles were analyzed. Thus, in Class 3, the Brodmann areas (BA) that were activated were 18, this being located in the occipital lobe and median occiptal gyrus and AB 7 which is located in the parietal lobe and median occipital gyrus. Class 4 activity activated Brodmann areas 5 (parietal lobe and post-central gyrus), 6 (frontal lobe and medial frontal gyrus), 7 (parietal lobe and post-central gyrus), 11 (frontal lobe and median frontal gyrus) and 47 (frontal lobe and lower front gyrus).

In addition an analysis was performed on the record of a volunteer per individual in order to investigate more specific results on the satisfaction of the activity of choosing the PET bottle in the two classes of "liked" and "disliked" (Fig. 5a and b). As to Class 3, the areas of the brain activated were 1 (post-central gyrus) and 7 (precuneus and superior parietal lobes) both in the parietal lobe. Class 4 activated Brodmann areas 5 and 07 both located in the parietal lobe and post-central gyrus (Fig. 6).

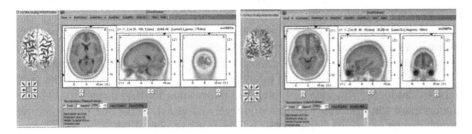

Fig. 5. Images from sLORETA with the 3D representation of classes 3(a) and 4(b) and the respective transversal sections of the brain.

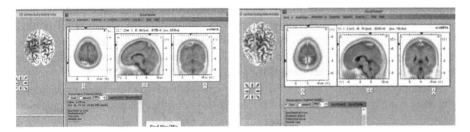

Fig. 6. sLORETA image of individual 01 of the class that did not like (a) (AB 7) and the class that liked (b) (AB 1) schematized in the 3D map, and in the displays of anatomical sections of the brain.

Results of the Experiment. We believe that the EEG records of Classes 3 and 4 do not show significant results in the brain areas activated by choosing the sections of the times that had been analyzed after the process for selecting the PET bottles (decision making) had taken place which is when we synchronized the EEG with the activity of the eye tracker.

Therefore, according to [8], we can say that the area of the precuneus and the parietal lobe that were activated in both classes are related to the voluntary control of staring, the task of spatial visual attention and saccadic movements when tracking the accompanying oculomotor movements. However, the objective of this study was not to check staring in itself or to see if the individual managed to plan and perform the activity requested.

To do so, an additional analysis was conducted to understand the process by which users select PET bottles. During this further analysis, it was observed that individual 01 of the (disliked) class had activated the primary somatosensory cortex, which is formed by the post-central gyrus in the parietal lobe and its operation of Brodmann area 1. This system is involved in the central processing of tactile stimuli and of noxious (aversive or aggressive) stimuli [9].

Thus, we can suggest that the somatosensory cortex, especially in Brodmann area 1 was activated at the time when an individual is likely to have associated the activity of opening the bottle with an aggressive stimulus, as mentioned by [9]. In this reasoning, the nociceptive stimuli found may be related to the difficulty of opening PET bottle 1, this being perhaps what causes less satisfaction in using it. This suggests that the user preferred PET bottle 2.

As to individual 01, in class 4, what was activated was his tertiary somatosensory cortex that consists of the superior parietal lobe and relates to the posterior parietal association area which corresponded to the workings of Brodmann Areas 5 and 7.

Area 5 is related to the tactile information from mechanoreceptors of the skin, muscles and joints. This area also integrates information for both hands [10, 11]. The authors cited add that area 7 is related to receiving visual, tactile and proprioceptive stimuli that let visual and stereognostic information to be identified.

According to neurologists, the property known as stereognosis has the capacity to perceive/recognize or identify shapes and objects with one´s hands and is also responsible for processing cognitive information in the brain [10].

Therefore, we can suggest that as a result of activating Brodmann area 5, the individual obtained tactile information while performing the activity with the PET bottles. As to activating area 7, what was received was visual and tactile stimuli for the process of identifying and probably selecting the PET bottles. In this case, no activities in the brain related to this user's preference for PET bottle were observed.

Attention should be drawn to the need to carry out new randomized experiments with displaying images with the PET bottles so as to clarify or confirm these results.

6   Conclusions

The findings were obtained arising from the two hypotheses that underpinned this research study. The first put forward the possibility that "The experience *reported* by the users of the soft drink PET bottles can be analyzed by means of the score for satisfaction obtained from the Likert scale (usability assessment) and compared with the experiences *felt* by the users (eye tracking and EEG)."

Given this hypothesis, the field study of usability evaluation succeeded in proving that it is possible to analyze the experience *reported* by users. Likewise, it was also possible to analyze the experience *felt* by the user on using ET and EEG techniques which were compared with the usability evaluation. Thus, this hypothesis was confirmed.

The second hypothesis stated that "The results obtained by the eye-tracking techniques and EEG are effective for measuring the satisfaction (felt experience) of the users of the soft drinks PET bottles."

In eye-tracking we obtained a response that was in line with our objective. The volunteers, by fixing their gaze, selected the bottle that they preferred. The objective of this technique, which captures the participant's attention, is to filter the individual's oculomotor behavior while performing a given cognitive activity (selecting a PET bottle that he or she liked or did not like).

When choosing which bottle he/she liked, the volunteer had fixed his/her gaze on this one and developed a cognitive activity. This procedure reinforces our hypothesis that this technique reveals the experience felt by the volunteer.

It was also possible to identify the experience *felt* while the PET bottles were being opened by using Electroencephalography (EEG) techniques. In this case, the user's mental performance was captured by the EEG during his/her cognitive and physical work. In the eye tracking activity, the EEG recording was associated with the volunteer choosing the PET bottle that he/she liked. This choice, at the mental (cognitive) level, with subsequent selection at the visual (physical) level characterizes an activity related to the experience that the user *felt*felt by the user, confirming the hypothesis presented.

Thus, the tools used confirmed the hypotheses that (1) the *reported* experience can be compared to the experience that the user *felt* and (2) that the tools used are appropriate to measure the experience *felt* and consequent satisfaction of the user.

Attention should be drawn to the fact that the Usability Field Study presented a result that is contrary to other studies. In this field study, volunteers said they liked PET bottle 1 best, while in other field studies, PET bottle 2 was chosen.

These results may suggest that the opinion reported by the user at the time of a usability evaluation by using a questionnaire, can be totally different from his/her thoughts/feelings or impressions regarding the use of a product.

Therefore, what our brain perceives and remembers may be different from the things that we say we understand and record when we are asked about this [12]. Thus, it is extremely important to use techniques that can compare the experience felt and the experience reported by the user. Another point of interest is that users can carry out correlations with their own unconscious processes with the meaning of their answers, the reasons for their preferences, their beliefs, and the analysis of their experiences [13].

References

1. Razza, B.M., Paschoarelli, L.C.: Avaliação de forças de preensão digital: parâmetros para o design ergonômico de produtos, vol. 4, p. 77 (2009)
2. Paschoarelli, L.C., Menezes, M.S.: Design e ergonomia: aspectos metodológicos, 1st edn., vol. 1, p. 279. Cultura Academica, São Paulo (2009)
3. Bevan, N.: Measuring usability as quality of use. J. Softw. Qual. **4**, 115–140 (1995)
4. Tullis, T., Albert, B.: Measuring the User Experience: Collecting, Analyzing and Presenting Usability Metrics. Elsevier Inc., Waltham (2008)
5. Parasuraman, R.: Neuroergonomics: research and practice. Theor. Issues Ergon. Sci. **4**(1–2), 5–20 (2003)
6. Parasuraman, R., Rizzo, M.: Neuroergonomics: The Brain at Work. Oxford University Press, Oxford (2007)
7. Silva, D.C.: A influência do design na aplicação de forças manuais para abertura de embalagens plásticas de refrigerantes. Dissertação (Mestrado em Desenho Industrial) - Universidade Estadual Paulista Júlio de Mesquita Filho, Fundação de Amparo à Pesquisa do Estado de São Paulo (2012)
8. Berman, R.A., Colby, C.L., Genovese, C.R., Voyvodic, J.T., Luna, B., Thulborn, K.R., Sweeney, J.A.: Cortical networks subserving pursuit and saccadic eye movements in humans: an FMRI study. Hum. Brain Mapp. **8**, 209–225 (1999)

9. Gallace, A., Spence, C.: Touch and the body: the role of the somatosensory cortex in tactile awareness. Psyche **16**(1), 30–67 (2012)
10. Purves, D., Augustine, G.J., Fitzpatrick, D., Hall, W.C., Lamantia, A., White, L.E.: Neuroscience, 5th edn. Sinauer Associates, Sunderland (2011)
11. Mcglone, F., Reilly, D.: The cutaneous sensory system. Neurosci. Behav. Rev. **34**, 148–159 (2010). Elsevier
12. Pradeep, A.K.: Can neuromarketing research increase sales? (2010)
13. Berry, L.L., et al.: Managing the total customer experience. Sloan Manag. Rev. **43**(3), 85–90 (2002)

A Survey for Monitoring the Users' Profile and Information Technology Needs in Biodiversity Information Systems

Thiago Adriano Coleti[(⊠)], Marcelo Morandini,
and Pedro Luiz Pizzigatti Correa

University of Sao Paulo, São Paulo, Brazil
{thiagocoleti,m.morandini,pedro.correa}@usp.br

Abstract. The biodiversity monitoring activities are considered as meaningful to ensure a great worldwide environment. In Brazil, a biodiversity monitoring program is being performed and due to this reason Information Systems are needed to support the collect, storage, management and delivery of data. The Information System's users are usually environmental analysts that perform several administrative and technical tasks. Thus, to know this user is essential to develop a appropriate software interaction that allow them to fully perform their task with satisfaction. This paper presents a survey performed in Conservation Units in order to collect data from users that present their tasks and so produce a user's profile to be used as parameters in the interaction development process. This survey was performed after in loco visits in some units and the final data were used to support the development of the first release of the proposed software interface.

1 Introduction

The biodiversity is one of the main Brazilian concerns and means the variety of all kind of alive organisms such as animals, microorganisms and plants in the terrestrial, marine and aquatic ecosystems. The biodiversity has a really meaningful task in order to provide food, medicines and feedstock beside to serve environmental services such as pollination, carbon storage and others task some time not visible for human begins [7].

Performing biodiversity monitoring activities can be considered as a meaningful activity to ensure a great worldwide environment and an appropriate balance among economy tasks, industries and the preservation of biodiversity patrimony. The knowledge and information management about the use, preservation and state of nature is other government needs that encourage a group of systematic activities in order to monitoring the biodiversity [7].

Brazil has one of the most important biodiversity areas considering the scale and the amount of species that live in the several Brazilian forests. Brazilian government partnership with international entities, universities and other organizations provide a group of activities that aim to monitor the biodiversity in preserved areas as known as Conservation Units.

A Biodiversity Monitoring Program proposed by Brazilian Ministry of Environment aims to use computational resources such as Information System to collect,

A. Marcus (Ed.): DUXU 2016, Part II, LNCS 9747, pp. 549–559, 2016.
DOI: 10.1007/978-3-319-40355-7_52

process, store, maintain and publish meaningful information about biodiversity. The project main resource is composed by a group of software that is proposed to work as the basis of this process, i.e., in the Conservation Unit supporting the data gathering, visualization, standardization, updating and recuperating data about the monitoring process. A second software tool aims to support management and executive decisions providing information based on a monitoring data mining. Also, a popular tool to be used by every people whose want to know about biodiversity was proposed.

Before starting this system development, the developers and stakeholders identified some issues that should be solved. One of the concerns related to this project was about users and software interaction features in the Conservation Units since they should perform an important task to support all the biodiversity monitoring process and provide data for analysis about Brazilian Biodiversity conservation. Besides the interaction features, we also concerned about external items that could interfere the data gathering process such as: (1) Internet Service: Some Conservation Units are located far from cities and may not provide internet service and this can affect the data gathering process; (2) External Activities features: it is necessary to understand how the data gathering should work in order to provide interface and interaction resources to ensure an appropriate computational process; and (3) Extra users tools: understand whether other activities (related or not to the monitoring program) could interfere in the use of the system and so, adapt the interface to solve or support it.

Based on these requirements doubts and aiming to provide the best interface and interaction environment to support the data gathering process, we proposed three research questions:

- Who are the users that work in the Conservation Units and what are their features?
- How should be the interface and the interaction process in the Conservation Unit software to support the data input?
- How is the hardware infrastructure?

This research was performed in two stages: (1) composed by three *in loco* visits to know and understand the Conservation Unit working process; (2) a survey that was answered by several Conservation Units.

The survey results were used to guide the Biodiversity Information System Human Computer Interaction (HCI) development, mainly, the collect data software. Also, the data were used to improve the Conservation Unit's information management.

The next section presents the bibliographic review used in this work.

2 Bibliographic Review

This section presents the bibliographic review about subjects that are meaningful for this research.

2.1 User Profile

Users are the most important concern of the Human Computer Interaction (HCI) development team. The variety of needs, preferences, knowledge, physical and mental features from one person to another can interfere in software HCI capacity, making a tool easy, difficult or impossible to be used. For example, features as vision, hearing, touch and other can define a pleasurable interaction to one user and a not so good for another user [1].

The environment, tasks, relationship and age are features that must be observed by the designer before creating a software HCI. For example, if a user will use software for many hours per day, the system must have a interface with light colors [1, 5, 6].

Thus, by understanding the user's features, their environment, limits and knowledge, the design is more likely to achieve a correct interaction strategy that may allow the users to perform their task with effectiveness, efficiency and satisfaction, i.e., the software will present a great level of usability [6].

2.2 Interviews and Surveys

There are several techniques to support the identification of users' profiles and tasks [1, 6]. Two widely used techniques are: Interviews and Surveys.

The interviews are dialogs established between user and interviewer (can be the designer) and the interviewer uses questions created previously in order to obtain information about a subject. Two interviews approaches can be used: Structured or semi-structured [1].

The structured interview is composed by questions created previously and the interviewer must only use these questions and follow a specific guide to ask and manage the answers. The interviewer cannot change the interview guide and all the answers are limited to specific options proposed [1, 6].

The semi-structured interview is similar to the structured interview, but the interviewer can use no previously prepared questions or can guide the interview to a not planned strategy. Whether the user answers a question and this answer provides some relevant data, the interviewer can use this data to create new questions or to establish a more complex dialog and so, collected more data about the user [1].

No structured interviews can also be used when it is necessary to minimize the design pre concepts or when the designer do not have any information about the users, context or environment that the software will be used.

The interviews are techniques that the interviewer is close to the user, usually, face to face. However, not always this situation is allowed due to the reason that sometime it is necessary to interview a great number of people that are not accessible or the users are far from the interviewer. When this situation happens, it is necessary to use the survey technique.

The surveys are an optimized way to collect data from a great amount of users/participants or from participants that are not geographically close to each other [1]. Preparing a survey is not a trivial and/or easy task because it is necessary to analyze, design and test the survey. A survey validation, with other professionals such as administrators, can improve the quality of the survey [1]. An appropriate survey takes time to be created and should be:

- Comprehensive;
- Unequivocal;

- Collect relevant data to the evaluation context;
- Easy to analyze.

The terms to be used should be carefully chosen in order to allow the participant to understand the questions and provide relevant answers. Closed and Open questions can be used [1, 5, 6]. Closed questions contain specific answers where the user should choose one or more answers. Open questions allow the user to write any text about the answer.

The data analysis is a complex task that requires availability and attention from the analysts. Open questions require more effort to be analyzed since there is no default in the answers guide in order to identify standards or relevant data. Considering Closed questions, the analysis can be easier due to the reason that each answer has a scare or scale indicating the confidence level of answers. However, process all the possible answers combination to create relevant information is also a complex and extensive task.

The next section presents the activities performed during the visits (mainly interviews with the users) and the survey application.

3   Data Collect Process

This section presents the data collect process that is composed by the following stages:

- Visiting the Conservation Units and Interviews;
- Survey preparation; and
- Survey Application.

3.1   Visit to Conservation Units and Interviews

The survey preparation was preceded by three in loco visits performed in three different Conservation Units. The visits were performed to support the requirements and users profile gathering in real conditions of work. Also, data about hardware and software infrastructure, business process and boundaries were also registered.

These three Conservation Units, controlled by Brazilian Environment Ministry, were chosen: (1) Rio de Janeiro State; (2) Mato Grosso do Sul State; (3) Amazonas State.

The Conservation Units chosen are located far from each other and it were selected based on their particular aspects such as: ease of access, number of staff, technology services available, distance from the forest where the monitoring happens, biome. Figure 1 presents the Brazilian Map with the visited Conservation Unit locations. The Conservation Unit 01 was considered the best unit since its infrastructure was really good, Unit 02 presented middle level because it did not have the same infrastructure but was acceptable and was the common scenario presented in most Conservation Units in Brazil. Unit 03 was considered as a critical scenario due to the distance from cities and the difficult with services such as Internet, hardware equipments, transport and staff.

For each visit we used the following techniques to achieve specific goals: The Ethnography technique [1] was used to understand the administrative and operational process, to learn about daily activities and their impacts on the monitoring program and

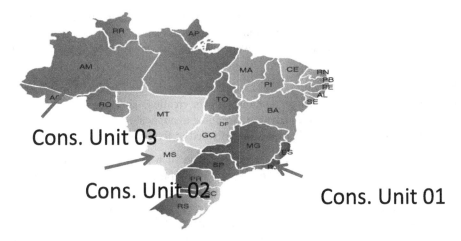

Fig. 1. Brazilian Map and Conservation Units location

consequently on the software. Besides ethnography, a semi structured interview [1] was used to understand details about the biodiversity monitoring process in each unit. The interviews also supported the gathering of data about technology resources and the knowledge, expectation and interest of the staff about the biodiversity monitoring.

During the visits, the researchers also verified and tested previous releases of the survey in order to support the deployment of the final version that should be applied to the selected units. Three versions (one per unit visited) were analyzed to improve the next survey releases. So, the improvements were applied considering the questions and suggestions proposed by previous answers during the discussions of the issues that were identified by the researchers and considered meaningful to the software/HCI development process.

After the visits and the three previous survey releases, we established the final release that was send to the units and a process to select a group of participants was also started by stakeholders.

In the next section we present the survey preparation and deployment.

3.2   Survey Deployment

This section presents the participant selection process, the survey deployment process and the survey final release structure.

Selection of Survey Participants. The process to select the participants was performed by the project sponsors due to the reason that they knew all the users that could really contribute to the project. Seventeen Conservation Units were chosen to answer the survey and, for each unit, two or three future software users participated. The users presented different qualifications and performed different tasks leading to a condition to provide more consistent data based on several views. The unit's employees were advised about the research and oriented to answer the survey correctly.

All the selected units were located in different areas such as South, North and Coast of Brazil assuring that cultural differences and qualifications were assured in the development of the HCIs. The surveys were answered by environmental analysts and units managers.

Survey Deployment. The survey was created using a tool named Lime Survey[1]. The Lime Survey is an open source tool that allows creating, applying and managing surveys. Also, this tool provides advanced resource to application and to data analysis. The survey final release had fifty questions divided in five groups:

Personal Profile: Questions related to personal data such as age, education and previous knowledge about basic skills of using the computer. This group of questions aimed to identify personal issues about the future users that could interfere in the software and also to provide data to the development team identify the features of future users and try to adequate the software and its HCIs to specific characteristics. Questions such as: "Does the software need to have resources to conduct lay people or we can provide the basic computing resources considering that all the users had basic computing knowledge?" is an example.

Technical Profile: Questions related to the use, preferences, needs and restrictions considering the daily use of the software. This group was created aimed to identify the user interfaces requirements. All the questions guided to issues that must be a concern to the HCI development team. To support the questions and improve the results, we required the participants to indicate examples of software and web sites that they know and consider the interaction as good or bad.

The technical profile survey also provided questions about new technologies that the development team intended to use. The questions were about: mobile technologies; touch technologies; use of mobile in the external areas; and new interfaces approaches. The participants answered with really nice suggestions about HCI requirements and provide a great discussion about the use of mobile technology that was an approach desired by the stakeholders. Unfortunately the participants/users did not presented good perspectives about the use of this resource.

Monitoring Profile: Questions related to the knowledge about biodiversity monitoring protocol and how the software could support the monitoring process. This was the smaller group of questions because there were provided questions that just aimed to know about the participants monitoring knowledge. Thus, questions such as: "what is the monitoring protocol?"; "how is performed the monitoring protocol?" were applied.

Information Management: Questions related to the information management of the unit and about the tools that supported this management. One of the main stockholders' concern was related to the management of biodiversity data and correct support to the decisions that should be taken. Thus, questions about which the users considered important to support the biodiversity information management and how biodiversity information could be applied in daily work were presented. The questions had content

---

[1] https://www.limesurvey.org/pt/.

such as: suggestions to data visualization; opinions about system that were used daily; data/information considered relevant; forms of data use and delivery.

Infrastructure: One of the main concerns of the development team was the information technology infrastructure due to the reason that some stakeholders notified the team that some units had precarious computers and Internet Service and this limitations could lead to software failure. Considering this, the questions proposed about the computer configuration, Internet power, computers amount, quality of hardware and hard disk capacity. In the survey there was a question that asked to the participant to input data about support service (some units pay for external hardware support).

These five groups composed the survey and each group was presented in a different webpage previously announced by a "welcome page".

Survey Apply. The survey was applied using the Lime Survey tool. A web link was sent to the participants by the stakeholders and the deadline for the participants to answer the survey was 15 days.

After the surveys were responded, the data were stored in the administration system in the Lime Survey. Some participants reported problems to answer, but they were just related to Internet service.

4   Results

The visits, interviews and surveys were proposed in order to provide data to support functional and non-functions biodiversity information system requirements quality and identify users' profile. In this paper, we are just considering the data analysis to support the HCI development and the data provided by final survey release.

The data analysis was performed based on two approaches: Specific Groups Analysis; and General Analysis. The results are presented both in qualitative and quantitative approach due to the reason that some the questions were not created qualitative or quantitative oriented.

4.1   Individually Groups Analysis

For each group of questions we performed an individual data analysis. This section presents the analysis performed by group individually.

Personal Profile Analysis. The personal profile analysis presented that the participants are typically computer users and they would have no difficulty to use software. The answers presented that all the users has, at least, the undergraduate education and most of them are master degree and/or PHD.

The use of software is common for business and personal tasks for 100 % of the participants. Also, the users were familiar to mobile devices and 40 % answer that learned informatics using and learning alone, and 60 % learned in courses or other people teaching.

These questions presented that there is no restrictions in the development of a new tool to be used by the participants considering that the lack of knowledge of basic computing would not interfere in the activities and, also, do not require special training or preparation.

Another important issue analyzed was the period of daily use of computers by the users. All the participants answered that they use the computer at least 8 h by day. This information leads to a HCI requirement focused on an easy and clear interface and interaction that should not affected or tire the users. Also, considering that all the participants work with computer several hours per day, it means that they could had several tasks to be performed and so, new activities should not create stress or delays for monitoring or existing activities.

Thus, as a final personal profile created based on presented information, we established that users may:

- Have basic computing Knowledge;
- Have good and easy learning ability;
- Have knowledge about new technologies; and
- Work many hours by day with computer for business activities.

Technical Profile Analysis. The technical survey was analyzed in order to identify the HCI features desired by users. We aimed to identify whether the user preferred typical interface, more interactive interface or new HCI approaches (few used until now). This survey stage was considered the most important for HCI requirements since it should provide data to support the HCI software development.

For this research we assumed typical interfaces with a default layout usually applied to Microsoft Windows or Linux, Desktop or Web approaches. A more interactive interface refers to a software interaction with more interactive components, bigger buttons and labels, movements on the components, highlights and other issue that provide a more dynamic interaction. As new HCI approach we assumed new concepts such as Natural User Interface [8] or Internet of Things [9].

The first profile group was composed by three groups of questions: (1) Type of interface; (2) Knowledge about interaction components; (3) Users' behavior in the use of HCI systems.

The type of interface questions were composed by three questions such as: preferences about colors and contrast; Size and shape of objects on the screen; and a open question that required to be filled about the user opinion about a perfect interface. This question also accepted suggestions about software to be used as prototype or to exemplify user answer.

The results presented that 90 % of the participants clearly preferred the traditional interface layout with simple text labels and formats; also they prefer the interface with a background light color and dark labels and fonts. The use of highlights components or nonstandard objects was not accepted for 88 % of the participants due to the reason that different components could make them do not interact properly with the systems. The open question presented a common list of users' suggestion that contained:

- Easy to use;
- Intuitive;
- Support use activities with auto complete, suggestions and errors handling; and
- The software should just contain the enough items to accomplish the tasks.

The last suggestion was justified with the fact that actual software presents many components, resources and interfaces that are not used, but interfere in the daily tasks.

The second profile group was composed by five questions related to user experience and aimed to collect data about: Interaction devices preferences, information distributions on the screen; and interaction facilities preferences.

The questions related to devices preferences presented that the users did not desired new components such as touch screen or voice recognition. 90 % presented that they never used these devices and 10 % presented that use rarely but did not agree with the use in the new software. The use of traditional keyboard and mouse was the answer of 100 % of the participants. The questions related to the information distribution presented the result of 100 % of participants that preferred an interface with the components and interaction distributed/grouped by context. This feature ensured that the users found and used the software components easily.

A security group with two questions was applied and these questions asked about the users readability, i.e., "do the users read the messages presented by the software". This question was applied because the developers should know the level of security and error prevention that should be necessary. The results presented that the developers are concerned about security issues on the interface due to the reason that 70 % of the participants answered that they do not read messages provided by computer and 20 % read the messages quickly and do not pay attention to the message content. Just 10 % answered that they read carefully the messages. Thus, we assumed that a complex security interaction approach should be deployed in order to avoid that the users perform incorrect activities or take decisions based on a advertisement that were not read by the user. Confirmation messages and text confirmations were used to support these activities. Figure 2 present an advertise interface example. The text is in Brazilian Portuguese.

Fig. 2. Advertise interface example

All the questions should present the focus on a non-destructive activity to avoid the wrong call of a function, i.e., case the user desired to execute an activity, he/she must move the mouse or input some text by the keyboard to select the action. We proposed this approach because we considered that making a complex action using mouse or keyboard, they could read the message and take the decision about the tasks before perform any action.

Lastly, we present a question about the user of Wizard Standard to support the interaction. Wizard Standard is an interaction feature usually known as "Next, Next, Previous", i.e., all the process is based on a sequence of interface where the user go a specific next screen or return to a specific previous. There is no way to go to another screen since it does not be the sequence of the process. All the participants answered that known this standard and agree with the applying in the projects.

Thus, considering the results presented by the technical survey, the development team could analyze technical interface issues in order to provide a HCI final product that really meets the user's needs and allows them to perform the biodiversity monitoring task appropriated and safe.

The next section presents the Monitoring Protocol data analysis.

Information Management Data Analysis. As meaningful data for HCI development we considered some answers related to the use of Microsoft Office and Microsoft Excel to accomplish most tasks and due to this reason, the users are really familiar with these tools.

Thus, we identified a users' desired that future software should present a resource to import/transform Excel data in software data besides create interfaces similar to Excel could improve and facilitate user experience.

Infrastructure Information Data. The infrastructure survey aimed to gathered data about hardware and network capacity. For HCI development this group of questions provided data in order to support the development of HCI to work with traditional computers because the Conservation Units did not have supercomputers or computer with high performance, so any resource that required computers with more power could not work correctly.

4.2 General Analysis

Considering the results of the surveys presents in the previous section and considering a project to support the biodiversity monitoring we proposed the HCI requirements present at Table 1. The requirements are classified as:

In the next section we present the conclusions.

Table 1. HCI requirements proposed

Type	Description
User profile	Basic computing Knowledge
	Good and easy learning ability
	Knowledge about new technologies
	Participants work many hours by day with computer for business activities
	Prefer traditional HCI components and resources
	Prefer a kind of organization in information and components presented by interface
HCI requirements	Interfaces with information organization by context
	Security resources: software should handle erros
	Basic interfaces without any different or exotic component
	Interface with positive contrast (light background)
	Easy to use, learn and memorize
	Supporting use activities with auto complete suggestions and other resources that can reduce user effort
	Software containing just the enough items to accomplish the tasks

5   Conclusions

This paper presented a survey performed in Conservation Units in Brazil in order to collect data to support the development of a software to support the biodiversity monitoring system. This paper focused on the collect and analysis of data related to users' profile and HCI requirements.

The results were used in the development and supported the HCI project. These results were used to support the design decisions aiming to present an interface that can be used by the users in the best strategy to achieve theirs goals with efficacy and efficiency. Also, some decisions about the software were taken based on the needs the users presented such as a better visualization of the system information and the needs for the biodiversity monitoring activities.

References

1. Benyon, David: Interação Humano Computador, 2nd edn. Pearson Prentice Hall, São Paulo (2011)
2. Pressman, R.S.: Engenharia de Software: uma abordagem profissional, 7th edn. AMGH, Porto Alegre (2011)
3. Engholm Jr., H.: Engenharia de Software na Prática. Editora Novatec, São Paulo (2010)
4. Engholm Jr., H.: Análise e Design orientados a objeto. Editora Novatec, São Paulo (2013)
5. Preece, J., Rogers, Y., Sharp, H.: Design de Interação. Além da interação homem-computador, 5th edn. Bookman, Porto Alegre (2005)
6. Cybis, W., et al.: Ergonomia e Usabilidade. Editora Novatec, São Paulo (2010)
7. Pereira, R.C., Roque, F.O., Constantino, P.A.L., Sabino, J., Uehara-Prado, M.: Monitoramento in situ da Biodiversidade. Proposta para um Sistema Brasileiro de Monitoramento da Biodiversidade, Brasilia, DF, Brazil (2013)
8. Peterson, N, Stricker, D.; Continuos natural user interface: reducing the gap between real and digital word. In: Proceedings of the IEEE International Symposium on Mixed and Augmented Reality – Science and Technology Proceedings, Orlando, USA, pp. 17–22 (2009)
9. Zara, A., Zamora-Izizuierdo, M.A., Sharmeta, A.F.: Interconnection framework for mHealth and remote monitoring based on the internet of things. IEEE J. Sel. Areas Commun. 31(Suppl. 9), 49–65 (2013)

Learnability Testing of a Complex
Software Application

Cheryl L. Coyle[1(✉)] and Mary Peterson[2]

[1] SAS, Cary, NC, USA
cheryl.coyle@sas.com
[2] University of Massachusetts Lowell, Lowell, MA, USA
mary.e.peterson@gmail.com

Abstract. As part of a small team of user experience designers at an enterprise software company, we created designs for a full-featured business application, and included usability testing in our design cycle. As we delved into the creation of tasks, we realized that we needed to assess the learnability of our design concepts, in addition to their usability, to best direct our design efforts in the immediate future.

We conducted an extensive assessment of the learnability of the application. Our testing included unstructured time for exploration of the software, participant-led training with a moderator who was knowledgeable about the software, repeated sets of virtually identical tasks, multiple breaks, and a lengthy distraction task. This testing method provided us with necessary information about which parts of the user interface needed iteration and which parts were learnable.

Keywords: Learnability · User testing · User experience design · Usability of complex applications · Designing for enterprise software · Testing methods

1 Introduction

Many articles on user experience design and usability are focused on websites, e-commerce, consumer applications, and even gaming [1–4]. The design for a retail site must be simple and straightforward, or sales may be lost. The design for a service-provider site must capture the user's attention immediately, or a short-attention-span user will go elsewhere. Mobile applications, games, and social media sites have the potential for exceedingly large revenue when designed to engage users in a way that keeps them coming back again and again.

Enterprise software, however, is different than consumer software. Users of enterprise software rarely, if ever, get to choose which applications they will use at their workplace. Business users' tasks, experiences, and duration of use are different than private users' motivations, needs, and goals. The design of the user experience of complex enterprise software should be approached differently than the design of other applications.

As effective designers realize, the design of any product should focus on its users, their tasks, and usage scenarios [5–7]. Accordingly, usability evaluations should focus on users, tasks, and scenarios, and should be conducted in contexts as similar as

© Springer International Publishing Switzerland 2016
A. Marcus (Ed.): DUXU 2016, Part II, LNCS 9747, pp. 560–568, 2016.
DOI: 10.1007/978-3-319-40355-7_53

possible to real-world situations. Walk-up-and-use testing methodology is frequently used for consumer applications and websites; however, enterprise applications are more robust and intricate. These designs require a different kind of usability testing. Enterprise software that is used daily by skilled technicians needs to be both usable and efficient. Evaluating its usability via walk-up-and-use methods is ill-advised.

During the design phase of a multifaceted business application, we started to organize usability testing of the user interface. As we began drafting tasks for the usability test, it quickly became obvious that the tasks our end users would do with our software could not be easily evaluated with walk-up-and-use testing methodology. In order for us to properly assess the efficiency and intuitiveness of our user interface, we needed to measure both the learnability and the usability of our design concepts.

2 Related Work

One documented process for how to create usable enterprise software [8] includes creation of user interface guidelines, standards, and style guides, along with prototyping and conducting user studies. Think-aloud protocol, field observation, and user interviews are encouraged as methods that developers can employ to improve the usability of their products [9], and strategies can be found for assessing the usability of business intelligence applications [10], focusing primarily on heuristic evaluation and user surveys.

A literature review [11] of learnability factors in software applications provides insights on various techniques to improve learnability, and proposes providing help systems to aid users, but it does not explicitly describe methods for assessing the learnability of a software application and implications for design. A model for understanding the factors that contribute to learnability [12] was defined and tested with a future goal of specifying requirements that would improve the learnability of software; however, the focus is on the attributes of learnable software rather than the process for testing learnability in software. Although learnable software is desired, and is recognized as a critical component of usability [13], it is challenging to find a generally accepted methodology for assessing the learnability of an enterprise software application. One survey of research on learnability [14] details the various ways learnability has been defined and assessed, including 25 learnability metrics that have been used in usability evaluations. In addition, a method of "coaching" was used in a study and compared to think-aloud protocol [14]. None of the learnability testing in this body of related work compared task completion times of users over time. We sought to do just that.

3 Procedure

We recruited six user-surrogates, whose job experience and skill sets matched our target users. Each participant was tested individually. Sessions lasted three-and-a-half to four-hours each. Each session was recorded, including all participants' comments and all screen interactions.

Sessions began with formal instructions that were read aloud by the moderator. The instructions consisted of a high-level overview of the application, a description of the testing scenario, and details about two distinct and separate concepts that are introduced in the application. Included in the explanation of the two new concepts was a comparison between them. The goal of the instructions was to give participants as much information as possible about the user interface before they began to interact with the application. Participants were given the opportunity to ask questions.

After the instructions were read, and any questions answered, users were given approximately 15 min of unstructured time to interact with the application. Participants were told to browse through the application on their own, with no specific tasks to attempt. The moderator was not present during this time. The intention of the unstructured time was to simulate what many business users do with new software: explore it before attempting to use it. Participants were allowed to click and explore the set-up of the software as they wished, while alone in the testing room. This allowed the user to become familiar with the interaction patterns and explore parts of the software that appealed to them. After the unstructured time, participants were given tasks to complete.

Tasks were conducted in three rounds. Each round consisted of 6 primary tasks. Round 1 was positioned as a participant-led training exercise. The moderator acted as a trainer, answered questions, explained how the product worked, and assisted with problems. Participants were required to read each task aloud, and attempt to complete it. If participants experienced difficulties completing a task, asked for help, or simply did not know what to do next, the moderator assisted. The moderator answered all questions, directed the users, explained the interaction paradigm, and helped users move on to their next step. This part of our procedure contrasts sharply with usability testing in which users are given no assistance while attempting to complete a task. Participants were informed that the moderator would assist with tasks only during Round 1. The moderator acted as a trainer or colleague who was knowledgeable about the application. Participants were encouraged to ask as many questions as possible during Round 1 because the moderator would not answer questions or help with the tasks during Rounds 2 or 3.

Following Round 1, participants were offered snacks and beverages, and given a 15 min break. They were escorted outside the testing room and encouraged to talk about other subjects. Our objective was to disrupt participants' focus on the software and distract them from what they had been doing.

Round 2 consisted of the same 6 tasks as in the training round, but performed on different objects. Our intention was to emulate what a real workday could look like for those who use our product. The primary difference between Rounds 1 and 2 was that the moderator did not assist participants in Round 2. As with the training round, participants were required to read each task aloud, and attempt to complete it. However, if a participant struggled with a task, the moderator, though present in the room, did not provide help. Participants were encouraged to try to figure out, or remember, how to complete the tasks on their own. If a user could not successfully complete a task after a lengthy attempt, the moderator redirected the user to the part of the application where he/she needed to be, but did not provide any instruction or explanation. After Round 2, participants were given another 15 min break outside of the testing room.

After their second break, and prior to Round 3, participants were given a 45 min elaborate distraction task followed by their third, and final, break. The intention of the distraction task was to introduce interference, preventing users from rehearsing the previous tasks. The objective of the distraction task was similar to that of the breaks. We wanted our participants to stop thinking about the part of the software we were testing. The distraction task used a part of the application that had no crossover to the main test series.

Round 3 included the same tasks as Rounds 1 and 2, but again with different objects. The moderator was present but, again, did not support participants. With each round of tasks, the moderator played less of a role. In the first round the moderator served as a trainer, and in the subsequent rounds only provided guidance or support when the user could not otherwise complete the task.

Table 1 presents an overview of the entire testing session. The user activities are listed in order, along with their duration.

Table 1. Session Overview

Activity	Description	Duration
Introduction	Welcome and formal instructions	5 min
Exploration time	Unmoderated time to explore the application	15 min
Round 1	Participants completed 6 tasks, each with sub tasks	17–34 min
	Moderator answered all questions and assisted in task completion	
Break	Location change and refreshments	15 min
Round 2	Participants completed 6 tasks, each with sub tasks	10–22 min
	Moderator did not assist; redirected only when necessary	
Confidence Scale	Participants rated how confident they were that they had successfully completed the tasks	5 min
Break	Location change and refreshments	15 min
Distraction task	Participants were given a new set of tasks for a different part of the UI, supervised by a different moderator	30–50 min
Break	Location change and refreshments	15 min
Round 3	Participants completed 6 tasks, each with sub tasks	7–18 min
	Moderator did not assist; redirected only when necessary.	
Confidence Scale	Participants rated how confident they were that they had successfully completed the tasks	5 min
Open-ended questions	Participants answered 2 open-ended questions about their experience with the application	5 min
System Usability Scale	Participants rated their agreement with 10 statements.	5 min

4   Metrics

4.1   Task Completion Times

Two observers timed participants while they were attempting to complete the tasks. Observers started timing as the participant began to read the task, and paused timing for any application errors. After all sessions were completed, one observer watched the 24 h of video recordings multiple times to accurately collect the time on task.

4.2   Moderator Redirects

The two observers made note of all redirection provided by the moderator in Rounds 2 and 3. These data were verified again with the video recordings.

4.3   Confidence Ratings

At the conclusion of Rounds 2 and 3, participants were asked to rate each task on how confident they were that they had completed it correctly. The 7-point Likert scale went from 1 (not at all confident) to 7 (extremely confident).

4.4   Open-Ended Questions

After Round 3, participants were asked to provide written responses to two open-ended questions. The goal of these questions was to solicit qualitative feedback about the experience of using the software and to capture ideas for improvement. The questions were, "Considering your entire experience today: (1) List a few things you liked about this application; and (2) List a few things about this application that could be improved."

4.5   The SUS

The System Usability Scale (SUS) is an easy-to-apply tool that provides a usability score for a software application [15]. It has been in use for more than two decades and has been found to be both reliable and valid [16]. After participants completed all three rounds of testing, rated their confidence of success, and answered the two open-ended questions, we asked them to complete the SUS as our final measure of usability.

5   Results

5.1   Task Completion Times

All participants demonstrated learning from the beginning of the test session to the end of the session, as evidenced by faster task completion times. As shown in Fig. 1, all 6 participants completed their tasks faster in Round 3 compared to Round 1. Five of the six participants completed the Round 2 tasks more quickly than the Round 1 tasks. The lone participant who had a slower time in Round 2 than in Round 1 spent a lot of time talking about the application while completing tasks during Round 2.

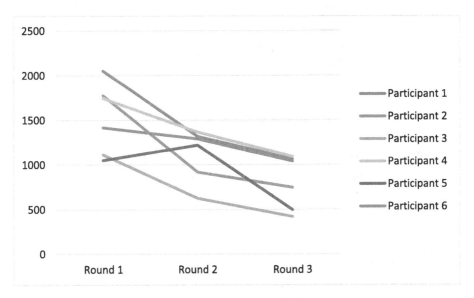

Fig. 1. Time (in seconds) to complete all tasks per round, per participant (Color figure online)

All 6 participants completed the tasks more quickly in Round 3 compared to Round 2. The improvement in task completion times is evidence that the overall design paradigm of our enterprise application is learnable.

To identify the features which were not easily learned, and therefore may warrant redesign efforts, we calculated average percent improvement for each task across participants. Since participants all work at their own pace, looking at raw overall times provided very little context to determine if improvement was consistently happening across the board. Instead we looked at the percent improvement so we could compare the times across participants. We calculated the percent improvement in completion time, for each task, per participant, across rounds. We then determined the average percent improvement across all participants to uncover any differences in learnability of tasks.

Participants improved their task completion times for all tasks except one. For that particular task, comprehension of two new concepts was needed. As shown in Fig. 2, completion time for Task 6 did not improve between rounds. In fact, participants were slower with this task during the last round of testing than they were during the training round.

The average percent improvement data illustrate an underlying problem with two new concepts we were trying to introduce into the application. Task 6 required participants to understand our conceptual model and interact with new structures.

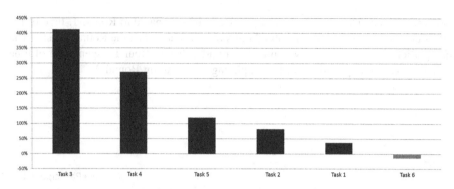

Fig. 2. Average percent improvement in task completion time from Round 1 to Round 3

5.2 Moderator Redirects

The total number of moderator redirects was 16 for Round 2, and 7 for Round 3. Of the 16 redirects in Round 2, 11 involved the two new concepts, as did 4 of the 7 redirects in Round 3.

5.3 Confidence Ratings

The Confidence Scale ratings indicate that participants were mostly confident they had completed tasks successfully: 89 % of the tasks were rated a 5, 6 or 7, with 7 = extremely confident that they completed the task successfully. The task for which participants rated their lowest confidence of success was that which involved the two new concepts, with most participants rating it a 4 or 5.

5.4 Open-Ended Questions

Among the six participants, there were a total of nine items listed in answer to the question: List a few things about this application that could be improved. Five of the nine items mentioned the design of our two new concepts.

5.5 The SUS

According to generally accepted standards [17], products with a SUS score above 68 is considered usable. The SUS score for our software was 67.86. This score was higher than what we expected, since the version we tested did not have complete functionality. However, a SUS score of 68 is not high enough for software that will be delivered to our end users. The good news was that, because of our other metrics, we knew where the problems were in our application.

6 Discussion

Based on task times across rounds of testing, confidence ratings, and SUS scores, our product is a usable and learnable enterprise software application, with some room for improvement.

Several subtasks proved challenging to participants in Round 1. For example, participants struggled adding text to a page. The moderator had to point out an icon which needed to be selected before participants could complete the task. In a typical usability session, this observation may have led to a redesign of the text feature, or a repositioning of the icon. However, adding text was quickly performed by all participants in Rounds 2 and 3, indicating that it did not need to be redesigned. If we had conducted only one round of testing, we would not have been able to distinguish between the parts of the design which were confusing versus those which were unfamiliar but quickly learned.

Participants were able to learn the navigation, menus, and object model of our application. However, they were unable to grasp the two new concepts we had hoped to introduce in our software. In addition to a lack of improvement in task completion time for these concepts, participants expressed frustration when interacting with them. They did not understand where they were in the application, where they were putting objects, or how to move objects between different sections of the user interface.

Participants were given explicit instructions about the concepts at the beginning of the session. They were taken through a series of tasks, given feedback and guidance. Despite multiple attempts to communicate and educate, participants could not understand the distinction between these two concepts. This critical finding guided our subsequent design efforts. Instead of merely debating whether or not our end users would grasp the general ideas of these two new concepts, we had evidence that these concepts were vague and overlapping, and the design for them needed to be revisited and revised. Our testing methodology provided a clear direction for the user experience design team. This finding would not have been clear with only one round of testing, particularly if we had followed a walk-up-and-use method. If participants of a single test session struggled with our new concepts, one could contend that the concepts would be learned quickly enough, even if not immediately intuitive. Our testing procedure demonstrated that other aspects of the design were indeed learnable, but these concepts were not.

Enterprise applications are often used daily by some business users. Learning will take place as business users interact with the application to perform tasks. Identifying the design concepts which can be quickly learned versus those which cannot may have a substantial effect on the overall ease of use of the product. For complex software, conducting an evaluation of the learnability of the design - in addition to its initial usability - can help uncover deeper usability issues.

References

1. NN/g Nielsen Norman Group. http://www.nngroup.com/articles/
2. Smashing Magazine. http://www.smashingmagazine.com

3. UX Matters. http://www.uxmatters.com
4. UX Magazine. https://uxmag.com/
5. Nielsen, J.: Usability Engineering. Morgan Kaufmann, San Francisco (1993)
6. Schneiderman, B.: Designing the User Interface: Strategies for Effective Human-Computer Interaction. Pearson, New York (2009)
7. Sherman, P.: An introduction to usability and user-centred design. In: Sherman, P. (ed.) Usability Success Stories: How Organizations Improve by Making Easier-To-Use Software and Web Sites. Gower House, Hampshire (2006)
8. Moallem, A.: Enterprise applications can be both feature rich and easy to use. Ergon. Des. Q. Hum. Fact. Appl. **19**(2), 6–13 (2011)
9. Holzinger, A.: Usability engineering methods for software developers. Commun. ACM **48** (1), 71–74 (2005). ACM Press
10. Jooste, C., VanBiljon, J., Mentz, J.: Usability evaluation guideline for business intelligence applications. In: SAICSIT 2013, pp. 331–340. ACM Press (2013)
11. Shamsuddin, N.A., Syed-Mohamad, S.M., Sulaiman, S.: Learnability and understandability factors in software applications: a systematic literature review. Int. J. Softw. Eng. Technol. **1** (1), 25–31 (2014)
12. Rafique, I., Jingnong, W., Abbasi, M.Q., Lew, P., Wang, X.: Evaluating software learnability: a learnability attributes model. In: IEEE International Conference on Systems and Informatics, pp. 2443–2447. IEEE Press, New York (2012)
13. Dix, A., Finlay, J.E., Abowd, G.D., Beale, R.: Human Computer Interaction. Prentice Hall, Englewood Cliffs (2003)
14. Grossman, T., Fitzmaurice, G., Attar, R.: A survey of software learnability: metrics, methodologies and guidelines. In: Computer Human Interaction, pp. 649–658. ACM Press (2009)
15. Brooke, J.: SUS: A "Quick and Dirty" usability scale. In: Jordan, P.W., Thomas, B., Weerdmeester, B.A., McClelland, I.L. (eds.) Usability Evaluation in Industry, pp. 189–194. Taylor and Francis, London (1996)
16. Brooke, J.: SUS: a retrospective. J. Usability Stud. **8**(2), 29–40 (2013)
17. Measuring Usability with the System Usability Scale (SUS). http://www.measuringu.com/sus.php

Usability Testing Results for a Mobile Medical Transition Application

Jeremy Dixon[1(✉)], Josh Dehlinger[1], Shannan DeLany Dixon[2],
and Joyram Chakraborty[1]

[1] Department of Computer and Information Sciences,
Towson University, Towson, MD, USA
jdixon6@students.towson.edu,
{jdehlinger,jchakraborty}@towson.edu
[2] Department of Pediatrics,
University of Maryland - School of Medicine, Baltimore, MD, USA
smdixon@som.umaryland.edu

Abstract. The use of mobile applications to assist with healthcare management is becoming increasingly present today. Healthcare consumers are demanding technologies that promote self-directed healthcare management; additionally, healthcare practitioners are utilizing these technologies to share ownership of healthcare responsibility. One aspect of healthcare that is common is the process of medical transition. Medical transition is when an individual shifts from a pediatric to adult healthcare team. As an individual's medical history becomes more complex, often due to a chronic medical condition, the medical transition process is often complicated. To address this, a mobile application was designed and developed to assist patients undergoing medical transition. This paper extends previous work by presenting the results of the first round of usability testing on the mobile application.

Keywords: Mobile applications · Differently-abled technologies · Human-computer interaction · Accessibility

1 Introduction

The process of medical transition from pediatric-based care to adult-based care has been studied, developed and implemented in the medical community for a number of years [1]. Although caregivers emphasize the process of transition, it is not universal in practice [2]. Those individuals who are best prepared for medical transition, and ultimately succeed with the process, are those who receive care and direction from a team that helps to anticipate transition issues [3, 4]. Orchestrating the transition from a pediatric team to an adult team requires a significant amount of planning and execution. Many of the guides provided to assist with transition process are paper based, and there is significant variation from practice to practice, and on a wider scale - state to state.

The goal of the larger project is to investigate how technology can assist with the traditional paper-based pediatric-to-adult medical transition process. Specifically, this work extends [8, 11] and seeks to:

© Springer International Publishing Switzerland 2016
A. Marcus (Ed.): DUXU 2016, Part II, LNCS 9747, pp. 569–577, 2016.
DOI: 10.1007/978-3-319-40355-7_54

- Investigate the state-of-practice related to how the pediatric-to-adult transition process is currently managed
- Design and develop a mobile application that aids with the transition from pediatric-to-adult healthcare
- Evaluate the mobile application to determine the level of comprehensiveness as compared to the traditional paper-based resources
- Improve the application throughout a series of iterative usability studies to help prepare the application for additional testing or release

Since inception, the medical transition process has been inconsistently managed and has been supported by tools such as paper-based checklists, forms and questionnaires, such as those created by the North Carolina Health and Transition Organization, the GotTransition – Center for Health Care Transition Improvement and the Children's Hospital Boston Transition Toolkit [5–7]. As these tools are paper based, they are not readily accessible at all times. Additionally, as most of the individuals who undergo transition are digital natives, the use of paper tools may be considered antiquated or cumbersome.

One of the ways that healthcare services are being more successfully managed is by the use of mobile applications to help inform, instruct, record, display, guide, remind and communicate with patients [3]. The mobile medical transition application was designed to help an individual track important information related to their personal information, medical condition(s), insurance information, and special considerations to aid with the transition process [8, 11]; however, it is not designed to act as a replacement for their medical record (either paper or electronic) [4]. By encouraging the patient to track information that is important to their own healthcare and personal status in the application, they will learn about their own medical history, the responsibilities related to their medical situation and how to best advocate for their own medical needs. This is important as the individual works through the transition process.

The mobile application was designed, to track a comparable amount of data that the traditional paper-based checklists contained. In many instances, the mobile application was able to store additional information in a more organized fashion than traditional checklists.

After the application requirements were identified and analyzed, a fully-functional prototype mobile application was developed. The mobile application was designed to replace and improve upon, existing paper-based medical transition processes. A list of skills that patients should be able to demonstrate at the time of transition, as well as a task list was created based on a review of the literature and existing tools. The tools and skills were organized into themes based on evaluation of paper-based transition tools. Finally, semi-structured interviews were conducted with three medical geneticists to review completeness and importance [4].

The final phase of this research, which this paper focuses, is the first phase of iterative usability testing. This usability testing will evaluate the application and provide the feedback to improve future iterations of the application. The details of the usability testing including the results are included in Sect. 3.

2 Mobile Transition Navigator Application

The mobile application, the Mobile Transition Navigator Application (MTNA), was built using Sencha Touch 2 which is a model-view-controller (MVC) framework that uses JavaScript to build cross-platform mobile applications thereby allowing it to be compiled and used on a variety of mobile device platforms (i.e., Android and iOS-based platforms). Additional critical considerations include: limitations of the differently-abled, native accessibility features of the operating system and data security [9, 10]. Although this development framework allows for cross-platform implementation, the first round of usability testing only used Android-based tablet computers.

Table 1 shows the tab organization of the MTNA as defined by the design analysis done in early phases. As the table indicates, the MTNA includes all major features as listed in each of the paper-based transition checklists and each of the three geneticists interviewed.

3 Usability Testing

The complete usability study will consist of three rounds of iterative usability testing. Following each round of testing improvements will be incorporated in the application in order to improve the user experience. For round 1, candidates were determined to meet eligibility criteria based on the following:

Table 1. Tab organization of MTNA [4]

	Aplastic Anemia and MDS	Got Transition?	Children's Hospital Boston	Seattle Children's	Missouri Resouce Center	New York Health Transitions	North Carolina Health and Transition	Rhode Island Transition Checklist	Geneticist 1 Opinion	Geneticist 2 Opinion	Geneticist 3 Opinion	MTNA Tab
Personal Information	No	Yes	Yes	Yes	Yes	Yes	Yes	No	Yes	Yes	Yes	Patient Data
Health Care Team	No	Yes	Yes	Yes	Yes	Yes	Yes	No	Yes	Yes	Yes	Health Care Team
Insurance Information	No	Yes	Yes	Yes	Yes	Yes	Yes	No	Yes	Yes	Yes	Insurance
Support Circle	No	No	No	Yes	Yes	Yes	No	No	Yes	Yes	Yes	Network of Support
Emergency Contact Information	No	Yes	Yes	Yes	Yes	Yes	Yes	No	Yes	Yes	Yes	Network of Support
Medical Conditions	No	Yes	Yes	Yes	Yes	Yes	Yes	No	Yes	Yes	Yes	Conditions
Past Medical History	No	Yes	No	Yes	Yes	Yes	No	No	Yes	Yes	Yes	Conditions
Family Health History	No	No	No	No	Yes	No	No	No	Yes	Yes	Yes	Care Management
Medications	No	Yes	Yes	Yes	Yes	Yes	Yes	No	Yes	Yes	Yes	Medical Products
Allergies	No	Yes	Yes	Yes	Yes	Yes	Yes	No	Yes	Yes	Yes	Patient Data
Immunizations	No	No	Yes	Yes	Yes	Yes	Yes	No	Yes	Yes	Yes	Patient Data
Pharmacy Information	No	No	Yes	Yes	Yes	Yes	Yes	No	Yes	Yes	Yes	Health Care Team
Special Considerations*	No	Yes	No	Yes	Yes	No	No	No	Yes	Yes	Yes	Care Management
Transition Checklists	Yes	Yes	Yes	Yes	Yes	Yes	Yes	Yes	Yes	Yes	Yes	Transition Checklist

*Includes School/Work Information, Care Schedule, Advanced Directives etc.

1. Participants must be between the ages of 18–30
2. Participants must have a strong working knowledge of medical transition and the process that individuals undertake medical transition
3. Participants must be enrolled in an academic institution with a minimum of a Bachelor's degree

Inclusion criteria was selected so that the study participants were able to understand the questions and content being asked with regards to transition tasks, thereby minimizing researcher input in explanations of why the skill was being assessed. To obtain a baseline understanding of the overall functionality and usability of the application and

Table 2. Round 1 task list

Task No.	Task	Level	Priority	Question	Topic
1	Login to the tablet computer (username: test and password: password) and start the MTNA application	*Application Level*	High	From 1 to 5 (1 worst and 5 best), how satisfied were you with the login and startup process?	Login and App Start
2	The little tabs at the bottom of the application are used to navigate around the application. Take a few minutes and explore the application.	*Application Level*	High	From 1 to 5 (1 worst and 5 best), how easy is it to navigate through the application?	Navigation
3	As you explore the application, take notice of the icons, the fonts, and the colors. Take a couple of minutes to examine the details of the application.	*Application Level*	High	From 1 to 5 (1 worst and 5 best), do you think that the icons are appropriate? What about the fonts? What about the colors?	Aesthetics
4	This application has two primary functions - first - to help store personal information and second - to help educate an individual about their medical condition(s). Find the personal data tab and enter your personal information.	*Scenario Level*	High	From 1 to 5 (1 worst and 5 best), what did you rate the data entry experience?	Data Entry
5	Based on your previous data entry, change your name to something else (John or Jane Doe).	*Scenario Level*	Medium	From 1 to 5 (1 worst and 5 best), how would you rate the data editing process?	Data Editing
6	In the Evalute Transition Checklist, there is a task called, "I know my full-name, birth date, home address, and telephone number" under the Self-Awareness tasklist. Find it and change your result to "True".	*Scenario Level*	Medium	From 1 to 5 (1 worst and 5 best), how easy was it to complete that checklist item?	Checklist
7	Now that you have populated the application with some data, close the application. Open the application again. Navigate to the personal data.	*Scenario Level*	High	Was all of your previously entered data still there? Is it correctly stored?	Data Persistence

the tasks being demonstrated, participants were required to have a working knowledge of medication transition as well as report having completed transition.

The usability testing for round 1 included three main parts: 1. Demographic Survey; 2. Task Completion; and, 3. Exit Interview. The demographic portion ensured that the participants met the round requirements both based on age and experience. For the task completion, participants were asked to conduct a series of seven standardized tasks, detailed in Table 2, on an Android-based tablet. The exit interview provided the users the opportunity to provide open ended answers to questions. Often, these open-ended questions yielded important feedback regarding observed application characteristics.

As this was the first time that this application was tested, some basic functionality testing was conducted including the login and app start testing and the data persistence testing. Since these tasks test fundamental data (data persistence) storage and operating system (login and application starting), they were only scheduled to be tested during round one.

4   Results

The first round of usability testing was completed in March 2015 at Towson University using six individuals. The demographic details are summarized as part of Table 3. The quantitative task results from round 1 were collected and presented as part of Table 4. The exit interview results were collected and presented as part of Table 5.

In this particular case, the demographic results provided little additional information beyond ensuring that the individuals met the minimum testing candidate requirements although in future rounds of testing it would be ideal to have a more

Table 3. Demographic survey results

	Demographics	A1	A2	A3	B1	B2	B3
		3/25/2015	3/25/2015	3/25/2015	3/27/2015	3/27/2015	3/27/2015
1	Gender	Female	Female	Female	Female	Female	Female
2	Age	27	26	24	26	23	29
3	Highest Degree	Bachelor's Degree	Bachelor's Degree	Bachelor's Degree	Bachelor's Degree	Bachelor's Degree	Master's Degree
4a	Desktop	18	15	14	18	17	20
4b	Laptop	14	10	6	9	13	11
4c	Smartphones	6	5	3	3	8	4
4d	Tablets	2	5	3	2	5	2
5	Industry	Healthcare	Healthcare	Healthcare	Healthcare	Healthcare	Healthcare
6	Current Position	Student	Student	Student	Student	Student	Student
7	Physical Impairments	No	No	No	No	No	No
8	Visual Impairments	No	No	No	No	No	No
9	Additional Limiters	No	No	No	No	No	No
10	Medical Transition?	Yes	Yes	Yes	Yes	Yes	Yes
11	Personal Transition?	No	No	No	Yes	Yes	Yes
12	Touch-Based Keyboard?	Yes	Yes	Yes	Yes	Yes	Yes
12b	TBK Frequency	Daily	Hourly	Hourly	Hourly	Hourly	Daily

Table 4. Summary of task results

Task Number	Task	Expected Outcome	Average Score	Range	Success
1	Login to the tablet computer (username: test and password: password) and start the MTNA application	100% of users will be able to use the touch-based keyboard to log into the device	5	5	Yes
2	The little tabs at the bottom of the application are used to navigate around the application. Take a few minutes and explore the application.	80% of users will rate the navigation a 4 or above on a rating scale.	4.66	4-5	Yes
3	As you explore the application, take notice of the icons, the fonts, and the colors. Take a couple of minutes to examine the details of the application.	80% of users will rate the navigation a 4 or above on a rating scale.	Icons: 4.667 Fonts: 5 Colors:5	Icons: 3-5 Fonts: 5 Colors: 5	Yes
4	This application has two primary functions - first - to help store personal information and second - to help educate an individual about their medical condition(s). Find the personal data tab and enter your personal information.	80% of users will rate the navigation a 4 or above on a rating scale.	4.667	4-5	Yes
5	Based on your previous data entry, change your name to something else (John or Jane Doe).	80% of users will rate the navigation a 4 or above on a rating scale.	4.833	4-5	Yes
6	In the Evaluate Transition Checklist, there is a task called, "I know my full-name, birth date, home address, and telephone number" under the Self-Awareness tasklist. Find it and change your result to "True".	80% of users will rate the navigation a 4 or above on a rating scale.	4.667	4-5	Yes
7	Now that you have populated the application with some data, close the application. Open the application again. Navigate to the personal data.	100% of the users will have the data successfully stored.	Yes	All	Yes

gender varied testing pool. The quantitative results of the testing indicated that there was a problem with the icons. Several people commented that the icons for the application were to small and difficult to read. In general, the exit interview results continued the overall positive comments made during the task completion.

Table 5. Summary of exit interview questions

	A1	A2	A3	B1	B2	B3
	3/25/2015	3/25/2015	3/25/2015	3/27/2015	3/27/2015	3/27/2015
What were you overall impressions of the application?	Useful and it would be food for communicating with doctors. Easy to navigate	Easy to use Clean interface Houses important data	Useful and potentially easy "no problem" to track data. Good store of data.	Pretty easy to use. Tabs were clear (although small)	Great. Easy to use. Asked if doctor would have access to this - Good for anyone going through transition.	Good for storing information. Easy to navigate (pretty obvious).
Can you please rate the application from 1 to 5? (1 = least usable and 5 = most usable)	5	5	5	4	5	5
What aspects of the app did you find frustrating or confusing?	Checking for the initiate checklist. Good to have check validation.	Nothing just getting used to it.	Edit button was small but not actually frustrating.	Nothing confusing although when entering data the screen not being visible was annoying.	None	Not sure with the checklist (and checkmarks)
What would you change to improve the navigation in the application?	Icons and text larger	Perhaps use a homepage with all icons (large icons on the main page for navigation)	Nothing	Larger icons	Making sure they can see it. Bottom icons.	Nothing but size of icons and fonts.
If you could change anything about the application what would it be?	Icons and text larger Edit/save buttons larger	Navigation with large icons	No.	Nothing.	Size of bottom icons.	Help icons and edit buttons larger. Update instructions, edit/new, and sentences
Is there anything else you would like to say about this experience?	No problems and it was easy to use	Important niche not being filled "Great job!"	I think it is very useful and we can encourage teenages to take control of their transition.	Pretty easy to use. A lot of access to useful information.	Nope.	Nothing.

5 Discussion

Following round one of usability testing and participant interviews, several themes were apparent. Based on feedback, users suggested that modifications to text and screen formatting, including increased icon size, larger fonts, and improved contrast for other graphics would further enhance the application. Specifically, five of the six users indicated that the icons were too small. Users also suggested that understanding of the completion of tasks was not intuitive. In order to indicate that a checklist item was complete, the users had to touch on a checkbox. After they had completed the task it was difficult to see that task had been completed. The testing indicated that the checkboxes should be changed to red upon completion. Users shared that while minor, these modifications would add to the ease of use of the application.

6 Conclusion

Based on the results of the first round of testing, there were a number of trends that were identified and analyzed for possible application improvements. The participants of the first round of testing were familiar with medical transition and were able to provide important feedback on the effectiveness and efficiency of the application. The quantitative results of the testing also provided some clues as to how easy to learn the application is. Based on the results of round 1, there were 16 changes were identified made to the application, prior to the recruitment and completion of round 2 testing.

Overall, the results of the usability testing suggested that the overall design was good for the MTNA. The changes that were incorporated included some very minor such as making the check items in the checklist turn red when checked to some more significant such as adding a check to save when changing tabs. The hope is that after the complete usability testing, the application will be ready for a longitudinal study to see how effective the application is though the transition process.

As the first round of testing was only done on Android tablet computers by six individuals, it is our hope that the second round (when the n increases to 30) will yield some additional constructive criticism.

References

1. American Academic of Pediatrics: Supporting the transition from adolescence to adulthood in the medical home. Pediatrics **128**, 182–200 (2011)
2. Lotstein, D., McPherson, M., Strickland, B., Newacheck, P.: Transition planning for youth with special health care needs: results from the National Survey of Children with special health care needs. Pediatrics **115**(6), 1562–1568 (2005)
3. Strickland, B., et al.: Access to the medical home: results of the National Survey of Children with special healthcare needs. Pediatrics **113**(5), 1485–1492 (2004)
4. Scal, P., Ireland, M.: Addressing transition to adult health care for adolescents with special health care needs. Pediatrics **115**(6), 1607–1612 (2005)

5. North Carolina Division of Public Health: Carolina Health and Transition Program, 10 November 2014. http://mahec.net/?/innovation-and-research/special-initiatives/chat-project
6. American Academy of Pediatrics: Got Transition, 31 March 2014. http://www.gottransition.org/
7. Children's Hospital Boston: Children's Hospital Boston Transition Toolkit (2010). http://newenglandconsortium.org/brochures/Transition-Toolkit-Complete.pdf
8. Dixon, J., Dixon, S., Dehlinger, J.: Medical transition checklists for mobile applications. Presented at the 65th Annual Meeting of the American Society of Human Genetics, Baltimore, MD (2015)
9. Dehlinger, J., Dixon, J.: Mobile application software engineering: challenges and research directions. In: MobiCase 2011 - Mobile Software Engineering Workshop, Santa Monica, CA (2011)
10. Sencha Inc.: Sencha Touch Build Mobile Web Apps with HTML5, 10 January 2016. https://www.sencha.com/products/touch/#overview
11. Dixon, J., Dehlinger, J., Dixon, S.D.: Designing, implementing and testing a mobile application to assist with pediatric-to-adult health care transition. In: Kurosu, M. (ed.) HCII/HCI 2013, Part II. LNCS, vol. 8005, pp. 66–75. Springer, Heidelberg (2013)

How Serif and Sans Serif Typefaces Influence Reading on Screen: An Eye Tracking Study

Berrin Dogusoy[1(✉)], Filiz Cicek[2], and Kursat Cagiltay[2]

[1] Department of Computer Education and Instructional Technology,
Mersin University, Mersin, Turkey
berrindogusoy@gmail.com
[2] Department of Computer Education and Instructional Technology,
Middle East Technical University, Ankara, Turkey
{fcicek,kursat}@metu.edu.tr

Abstract. This study aims to investigate how serif and sans serif typefaces influence reading from screen. 10 graduate students voluntarily participated in the study. The data were collected in a laboratory setting. Participants were asked to find the misspelled words in two different texts written in serif and sans serif typeface. The participants tried to find the misspelled words in the texts, during the data collection there was no time limitation. Participants' eye movements were recorded by Tobii 1750 eye tracker device. The data were analyzed according to the accuracy and eye behavior metrics. The findings showed that participants read from sans serif typeface faster and more accurate than serif typeface. The findings suggest that participants fixated on the misspelled words more on serif typeface than sans serif typeface, in terms of the total visit duration participants spent more time on serif typeface than sans serif typeface.

Keywords: Reading behavior · Reading from screen · Eye movement · Serif · Sans serif · User interface

1 Introduction

In recent years, there is a transformation in reading habits from print to screen arising from the advent in digital reading devices (Banerjee et al. 2011; Mangen et al. 2013). The change in individuals' reading behavior in digital platforms and why people have difficulties during reading from screen took attention of the researchers (Dyson and Haselgrove 2000; Dyson 2004; Rose 2011; Jeong 2012). As Liu (2005) explained, reading from screen is not a single process, even people starts reading from screen the process usually includes spending time on activities like browsing, scanning and spotting (Liu 2005). Horton et al. (1996) also pointed out that skimming is more frequent while reading from screen than in-depth reading.

In the literature, many studies have been conducted to understand on why people read slower from screen than from a paper (Jorna and Snyder 1991; Gould et al. 1987). The reasons found for reading faster on paper were; poor image quality displayed on the screen (Gould et al. 1987; Dillon et al. 1988), font type as serif and sans serif

© Springer International Publishing Switzerland 2016
A. Marcus (Ed.): DUXU 2016, Part II, LNCS 9747, pp. 578–586, 2016.
DOI: 10.1007/978-3-319-40355-7_55

(Beymer et al. 2008; Bernard et al. 2001; Mackeben 1999; Tullis et al. 1995), and size which have an influence on readability and legibility of the text (Franken et al. 2015). (Gould et al. 1987) found that with the improvements of the screen resolution, proofreading performance are not differed on paper and screen when the same font used. Although proofreading and reading processes are differed from each other, proofreading studies contribute the reading studies as well (Schotter et al. 2012). Schotter et al. (2012) expressed that proofreading may differ from reading process in terms of the similarity of the nature of the visual search tasks. The proofreading process also differed from reading that during proofreading tasks people tend to skim instead of trying to understand the text. Exploring the reading and other information processing tests by using eye behavior are well researched issues among researchers (Clifton et al. 2007; Rayner 1998; Rayner and Morris 1992; Just and Carpenter 1980). In order to understand reading process and legibility of a block of text, researchers focus on eye movements (Franken et al. 2015; Rello and Marcos 2012; Beymer et al. 2008; Rayner and Pollatsek 1989). Moreover, eye tracker-based method might provide more reliable results for a very precise measurement of reading speed (Franken et al. 2015).

Even the developments in screen resolutions and various research on how reading process occurred, investigating readability of texts and reading process still taking attention of the researchers. Font size and type are the other mostly focused variable for investigating readability in reading process, different findings were found for the preferred font size and type. Bernard et al. (2002a) found that in terms of reading efficiency there was no significant difference between font typeface in different size but in terms of the relation between font type and size there was a difference when considered the font legibility. They explained that people read faster in 12 point size than 10 point size fonts during online reading (Bernard et al. 2002b). According to Banerjee et al. (2011) legibility of the serif fonts (Times New Roman, Georgia and Courier New) is better compared to the sans serif fonts (Arial, Verdana and Tahoma). Moret-Tatay and Perea (2011) mentioned the advantage of texts in sans serif fonts compared to serif fonts during reading. They also mentioned about choosing sans serif typeface while preparing texts in computers screen. On the other hand, Tullis et al. (1995) found no difference between the serif and sans serif fonts considering reading speed in a proofreading task. Interestingly, in the study, the participants preferred sans serif fonts over serif fonts. Similarly, Boyarski et al. (1998) reported that reading speed of sans serif (Verdana) and serif (Georgia and Time New Romans) fonts did not differ for comprehension. Moreover, Bernard and Mills (2000) couldn't find any difference between sans serif (Arial) and serif (Times new roman) fonts regarding reading speed and detection of word errors. In general, serif fonts performed better than sans serif fonts (Banerjee et al. 2011; Beymer et al. 2008; Bernard et al., 2001), not statistically significant however. Most people seem to prefer the sans serif fonts of Arial and Verdana rather than serif fonts (Banerjee et al. 2011; Beymer et al. 2008; Bernard et al. 2002b). However, these preferences as different font size and types may subject to the different age groups and needs (Darroch et al. 2005; Bernard et al. 2002b; Kawasaki et al. 2008; Tullis et al. 1995).

Despite the developments in the screen resolution and attempts on making the screens more readable, making the screens more preferable than printed versions is yet not a solved issue for researchers and designers. Since, nonetheless, there was not a definite assent regarding using serif or sans serif in electronic environments, improving the reading performance still is a concern for designers. In this regard, the purpose of this study is to investigate speed and accuracy of participants while proofreading texts written in serif and sans serif with misspelled words on computer screen. Participants' eye behavior patterns during reading the misspelled text were compared in serif and sans serif typefaces during the proofreading process and task completion period and accuracy of the participants were compared. The research questions of the study as follows:

- Do participants' eye movement behavior changes in the serif and sans serif font styles while detecting the misspelled words?
- Is there any difference in the accuracy of finding the misspelled words with serif and sans serif typeface?
- Is there any difference in task completion time of the participants of finding the misspelled words with serif and sans serif font styles?

2   Method

A case study design was used to explore how participants' eye behavior differed according to the serif and sans serif typeface during proofreading task. 10 graduate students (4 female and 6 male) from Computer Education and Instructional Technology department participated to the experiment voluntarily. The participants' age was ranging from 21 to 43 (M = 27.5). Each participant proofread two six-page articles written in Serif and Sans Serif typeface for finding the misspelled words from screen. Researchers informed the participants about the ethical issues by a consent form including information regarding the process. In addition, all participants were informed about they are free to end the session whenever they feel uncomfortable or disrupted. Before starting the data collection, pilot study which consists of two pages text with misspelled words was conducted before the experiment to enable participants familiar with the apparatus and the experiment.

2.1   Apparatus and Procedure

During the experiment, each participant proofread two six-page articles taken from a novel for finding the misspelled words while reading from an LCD screen. The articles selected from the novel include 1548 to 1694 words. While determining the articles, it was our concern to find articles including no digital number or symbols. Each participant proofread one article in Serif typeface (Times New Roman) and one article in Sans Serif (Arial) typeface. Each article has about 24 lines for both font styles, 12-point version, and double space line spacing option was used. The proofreading sessions were recorded and each session took approximately 15 min. The main task in this study was to proofread the pre-determined misspelled words in the text to compare the speed and accuracy of the participants. Participants were informed that there were one to ten misspelled words in the texts and they would be evaluated by their accuracy and speed during the proofreading. In the experiment, four types of misspellings were used in each article; letter omissions, letter substitutions, letter transpositions and letter additions. Eye movements were measured by using Tobii 1750 eye tracker device in a laboratory setting, which has voice and video recording equipment. The data analyzed by Tobii Studio 3.2.1 software. The reading distance was set to 60 cm by the researchers for providing the best eye movement catching ability to the eye tracker device. Participants were informed about keeping the distance from screen as much as possible to prevent the eye behavior lost. Before the experiments each participant's eye movements were calibrated. For each experiment instead of scrolling, participants were asked to press any button for continuing the next page to keep the similarity as much as possible. During the experiment, the participants were asked to tell the misspelled word aloud to the researcher. There was no time limitation in the experiment and were tracked by using a stopwatch and recorded by the cameras settled in the laboratory setting (Fig. 1).

Böyle dersen pek bir keyiflenir, çiçeklenirler." Asya başka soru sormadan boyamasına geri

döndü. Palyaçosunun elbisesini turuncuya, dişlerini yeşile boyadı. Tam ayakkabılarını kan

kırmızıya boyayacakken aniden durup, şımarık bir edayla anneannesini taklit etmeye başladı.

"Canım canım! Aman da aman! Toprak annen, su baban. "Gülsüm Nine'nin kaşları çatıldıysa

da bir müddet durumu fark etmemit gibi davrandı. Bu kayıtsızlıktan cesaret bulan Asya

taklitçiliğinin dozunu arttırdı.

Süpermarketler asabı bozuk ve kafası karışık kadınlar için tuzaklarla dolu tehlikeli

yerlerdir. En azndan Rose gibi kadınlar için. Ne zaman süpermarkete girse ihtiyacı

olmayan bir sürü ıvır zıvır sepetine dolduruyor Rose. Ama bu sefer aynı hatayı

tekrarlamamaya kararlı. Bu kez hakikaten ihtiyacı olan şeylerden başkasını

almayacak. Söz verdi kendine. Bu kararlılıkla bebek bezlerinin bulunduğu koridora

yollandı. Hem oyalanmanın zamanı değildi.

Fig. 1. Screenshot from the texts written in serif and sans serif typefaces

3 Findings

Before the experiment, demographic information regarding the computer, internet usage experience and reading preferences were gathered. The results showed that all participants have at least 5 years of experience on computer usage (M = 12.8, SD = 3.45) and using the internet at least 4 h in a day (M = 8.5, SD = 3.26). Most of the participants (N = 8) did not take a training for speed reading. Participants were also asked about their preferences in which environment they were feeling more focused during reading. Most of the participants (N = 7) expressed that they were focusing better on paper than screen. They were also asked to compare the screen and paper medium in terms of non-stop reading activity, most of the participants (N = 6) preferred paper than screen (N = 1). Some participants (N = 3) explained that both medium are the same for them during non-stop reading activity (See Table 1). Participants' reading experiences and their mostly preferred media (screen and paper) for reading (newspaper, article, and books) were explored. Most of the participants (N = 7) preferred to read books from paper instead of screen. On the other hand, they preferred to read articles (N = 6) and newspaper (N = 8) from screen than paper (Fig. 2).

Table 1. Demographics of the participants

		N
Internet usage (day/hour)	3–5 h	1
	5–7 h	3
	More than 7 h	6
Training for speed reading	Yes	2
	No	8
Focusing better during reading	Screen	3
	Paper	7
Non-stop reading time comparison	Screen	1
	Paper	6
	Same	3

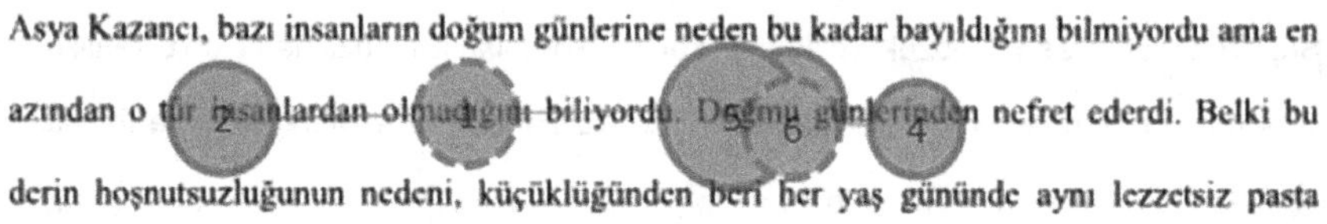

Asya Kazancı, bazı insanların doğum günlerine neden bu kadar bayıldığını bilmiyordu ama en azından o tür insanlardan olmadığını biliyordu. Doğum günlerinden nefret ederdi. Belki bu derin hoşnutsuzluğunun nedeni, küçüklüğünden beri her yaş gününde aynı lezzetsiz pasta

Fig. 2. A gaze plot from the misspelled word search process

In terms of the accuracy between these two typefaces during proofreading, participants found more misspelled words in total in sans serif (M = 16,4) than the serif typeface (M = 14,7). Moreover, they had completed the tasks in sans serif in a shorter period of time (M = 9,10) than the serif typeface (M = 9,96) (See Table 2).

The eye behavior analysis showed that participants fixated more on serif typeface texts (M = 264, 55, SD = 58) than sans serif typeface text (M = 241, 66, SD = 43). In that vein, participants spent more time on serif typeface text (M = 91, 97, SD = 23, 33) while proofreading the document than sans serif typeface text (M = 85,23, SD = 18,2) (See Table 3).

Participants' accuracy in finding different types of misspelled words was also explored. In serif typeface participants found the "letter transposition" (70 %) and letter addition (67 %) types of misspelling more than the other types. In sans serif typeface,

Table 2. Mean proofreading rate (words/min) and accuracy (% hits) in serif and sans serif typeface.

	Serif (TNR)		Sans serif (Arial)	
	M	SD	M	SD
Accuracy	14,7 (61 %)	3.5	16,4 (68 %)	3,71
Task completion time	9,96*	3,73	9,10*	4,96

Table 3. Eye movement parameters comparison for Serif and sans serif typefaces

		Fixation count		Total visit duration		Fixation duration	
		M	SD	M	SD	M	SD
Serif	Misspelled AOI (all)	264,55	58	91,97*	23,33	0,25	0,02
Sans serif	Misspelled AOI (all)	241,66	43	85,23*	18,2	0,25	0,03

*sec

letter addition and letter substitution types were mostly recognized misspelled words in the text than the other misspelled words. The eye behavior metrics showed that in specific types of misspelled words fixation count numbers were differed in serif and sans serif typeface (See Table 4).

Table 4. Accuracy (% hits) and fixation counts on the misspelled words AOI for serif and sans serif typeface.

	Serif (TNR)			Sans serif (Arial)		
	(% hits)	Fixation count		(% hits)	Fixation count	
	N	M	SD	N	M	SD
Letter substitution	26 (43 %)	60	26	45 (75 %)	70,8	13
Letter addition	40 (67 %)	81	26	45 (75 %)	61,5	24
Letter omission	37 (61 %)	56,5	14	34 (57 %)	56,5	21
Letter transposition	42 (70 %)	67	28	39 (65 %)	52,8	19

4   Discussion and Conclusion

In this study, reading electronic text in serif and sans serif typefaces were compared In general it was found that participants read from sans serif typeface faster and more accurate than serif typeface. According to findings, there was no difference in participants' fixation duration in serif and sans serif typeface while proofreading task. This might be a result of the limited number of participants, which could not provide a significance among these two typefaces. Even though the total fixation durations on the whole texts were not differed, the fixation duration values for misspelled words and fixation counts on misspelled word AOI and in the whole document differed. The longer fixation durations might be related with having trouble or difficulty in eliciting information (Just and Carpenter 1980). Accordingly, the difference in total fixation duration also might be an indicator for revealing the cognitive process (Salvucci 2001). On the other hand, the total visit durations and fixation count numbers of the participants differed in serif and sans serif typefaces. The increase in fixation count number is considered as an interest to a specific area or cognitive processing (Holmqvist et al. 2011; Doherty et al. 2009). Accordingly, the total visit duration during the proofreading was higher in serif typeface than sans serif typeface. This might be a result of the struggle in the serif typeface while recognizing the misspelled words. Of course this single study cannot prove that one typeface is definitely better than other. However, the findings show some similarities with the previous recent studies (Tullis et al. 1995; Boyarski et al. 1998). So, practitioners may use those user performance scores to make decisions on their typeface selections for electronic text. The major limitation in eye-tracking research is the limited number of participants and lack of demographic diversity. This study may be replicated with a larger number of participants from various demographic diversity and reading experiences to compare the reading patterns through electronic environments. Additionally, different parameters like reading from different media can be another future study to explore how people read from environments like mobile phone and tablets.

References

Banerjee, J., Majumdar, D., Pal, M.S.: Readability, subjective preference and mental workload studies on young Indian adults for selection of optimum font type and size during onscreen reading. Al Ameen J. Med. Sci. **4**, 131–143 (2011)

Bernard, M., Mills, M.: So, what size and type of font should I use on my website? Usability News 2.2 (2000). http://usabilitynews.org/so-what-size-and-type-of-font-should-i-use-on-my-website/

Bernard, M.L., Lida, B., Riley, S., Hackler, T., Janzen, K.: A comparison of popular online fonts: which size and type is best? Usability News 4.4 (2002a). http://usabilitynews.org/a-comparison-of-two-computer-fonts-serif-versus-ornate-sans-serif/

Bernard, M.L., Chaparro, B.S., Mills, M.M., Halcomb, C.G.: Examining children's reading performance and preference for different computer-displayed text. Behav. Inf. Technol. **21**(2), 87–96 (2002b)

Bernard, M.L., Mills, M.M., Peterson, M., Storrer, K.: A comparison of popular online fonts: which is best and when? Usability News 3.2 (2001). http://usabilitynews.org/a-comparison-of-popular-online-fonts-which-is-best-and-when/

Beymer, D., Russell, D., Orton, P.: An eye tracking study of how font size and type influence online reading. In: People and Computers xxii: Culture, Creativity, Interaction: Proceedings of HCI 2008, the 22nd British HCI Group Annual Conference, vol. 2. Presented at the 22nd British HCI Group Annual Conference, Liverpool John Moores University, UK: British Computer Society (2008). http://www.bcs.org/upload/pdf/ewic_hc08_v2_paper4.pdf

Boyarski, D., Neuwirth, C., Forlizzi, J., Regli, S.H.: A study of fonts designed for screen display. In: Proceedings of CHI 1998, pp. 87–94. ACM, New York, NY (1998)

Clifton Jr., C., Staub, A., Rayner, K.: Eye movements in reading words and sentences. In: Van Gompel, R., Fisher, M., Murray, W., Hill, R.L. (eds.) Eye Movement Research: A Window on Mind and Brain, pp. 341–372. Elsevier Ltd., Oxford (2007). Invited chapter

Darroch, I., Goodman, J., Brewster, S., Gray, P.: The effect of age and font size on reading text on handheld computers. In: Costabile, M.F., Paternó, F. (eds.) INTERACT 2005. LNCS, vol. 3585, pp. 253–266. Springer, Heidelberg (2005)

Dillon, A., McKnight, C., Richardson, J.: Reading from paper versus reading from screens. Comput. J. **31**(5), 457–464 (1988)

Doherty, S., O'Brien, S., Carl, M.: Eye tracking as an MT evaluation technique. Mach. Translat. **24**(1), 1–13 (2009). Springer

Dyson, M.C.: How physical text layout affects reading from screen. Behav. Inf. Technol. **23**(6), 377–393 (2004)

Dyson, M.C., Haselgrove, M.: The effects of reading speed and reading patterns on the understanding of text read from screen. J. Res. Read. **23**(2), 210–223 (2000)

Franken, G., Podlesek, A., Možina, K.: Eye-tracking study of reading speed from LCD displays: influence of type style and type size. J. Eye Mov. Res. **8**(1), 1–8 (2015)

Gould, J.L., Alfaro, L., Finn, R., Haupt, B., Minuto, A.: Why reading was slower from CRT displays than from paper. ACM SIGCHI Bull. **17**, 7–11 (1987)

Holmqvist, K., Nyström, M., Andersson, R., Dewhurst, R., Jarodzka, H., Van De Weijer, J.: Eye Tracking a Comprehensive Guide to Methods and Measures. Oxford University Press, New York (2011)

Horton, W., Taylor, L., Ignacio, A., Hoft, N.L.: The Web Page Design Cookbook. Wiley, New York (1996)

Jeong, H.: A comparison of the influence of electronic books and paper books on reading comprehension, eye fatigue, and perception. Electron. Libr. **30**(3), 390–408 (2012)

Jorna, G.C., Snyder, H.L.: Image quality determines differences in reading performance and perceived image quality with CRT and hard-copy displays. Hum. Factors **33**(4), 459–469 (1991)

Just, M.A., Carpenter, P.A.: A theory of reading: from eye fixations to comprehension. Psychol. Rev. **87**, 329–354 (1980)

Kawasaki, Y., Sasaki, H., Yamaguchi, H., Yamaguchi, Y.: Cognitive conditions in text reading on a visual display terminal by different age groups. In: 10th WSEAS International Conference on Mathematical Methods and Computational Techniques in Electrical Engineering, Sofia, Bulgaria (2008)

Liu, Z.: Reading behavior in the digital environment: changes in reading behavior over the past ten years. J. Documentation **61**(6), 700–712 (2005)

Mackeben, M.: Typefaces influence peripheral letter recognition and can be optimized for reading with eccentric viewing. In: Paper Presented at the Vision 1999, New York (1999)

Mangen, A., Walgermo, B.R., Bronnick, K.: Reading linear texts on paper versus computer screen: effects on reading comprehension. Int. J. Educ. Res. **58**, 61–68 (2013)

Moret-Tatay, C., Perea, M.: Do serifs provide an advantage in the recognition of written words? J. Cogn. Psychol. **23**(5), 619–624 (2011)

Rayner, K.: Eye movements in reading and information processing: 20 years of research. Psychol. Bull. **124**, 372–422 (1998)

Rayner, K., Pollatsek, A.: The Psychology of Reading. Lawrence Erlbaum Associates, Hillsdale (1989)

Rayner, K., Morris, R.K.: Eye movement control in reading: evidence against semantic preprocessing. J. Exp. Psychol. Hum. Percept. Perform. **5**, 522–526 (1992)

Rello, L., Marcos, M.-C.: An eye tracking study on text customization for user performance and preference. In: The 8th Edition of the Latin American Web Congress, Cartagena, Colombia (2012). http://www.taln.upf.edu/system/files/biblio_files/laweb2012.pdf

Rose, E.: The phenomenology of on-screen reading: university students' lived experience of digitized text. Br. J. Educ. Technol. **42**(3), 515–526 (2011)

Salvucci, D.D.: An integrated model of eye movements and visual encoding. J. Cogn. Syst. Res. 1, 201–220 (2001)

Schotter, E.R., Bicknell, K., Howard, I., Levy, R., Rayner, K.: Task effects reveal cognitive flexibility responding to frequency and predictability: evidence from eye movements in reading and proofreading. Cognition 131, 1–27 (2012)

Tullis, T.S., Boynton, J.L., Hersch, H.: Readability of fonts in the windows environment. In: Proceedings of CHI 1995, pp. 127–128. ACM Press, Denver, CO (1995)

Usability Evaluation of a Gestural Interface Application for Children

Valéria Farinazzo Martins[1(✉)], Paulo N.M. Sampaio[2],
Andrea Niedermeyer[3], and Marcelo de Paiva Guimarães[3]

[1] Computing and Informatics Program, Mackenzie Presbyterian University, Sao Paulo, SP, Brazil
valeria.farinazzo@mackenzie.br
[2] Computing and Systems Graduate Program, Salvador University (UNIFACS),
Salvador, BA, Brazil
Pnms.funchal@gmail.com
[3] Master Program of Faculty, Brazilian Open University - Federal University of São Paulo,
Campo Limpo Paulista, SP, Brazil
andreaniedermeyer@yahoo.com.br, marcelodepaiva@gmail.com

Abstract. One of the main difficulties of this literacy process is the question of the spelling of the Portuguese language, which has no regularity in relation to issue of letter-sound conversion. The advancement of technology in the educational environment has become the most dynamic and engaging lessons for students and teachers. The use of natural interfaces makes it the simplest and easiest applications to interact. This paper presents the development of an educational game covering the issue of misspellings of children in the literacy process and the use of the interface by gestures, such as motivation and attraction to the educational environment. The application developed was tested with children of the second year of elementary education at a private school in São Paulo, Brazil, and usability rating is described in this paper. The main contribution of this work to the educational environment is the experience of children with new ways to interact with the computer and the motivation for using the application in everyday school life.

Keywords: Literacy process · Natural interface · Game · Gesture

1 Introduction

During literacy process children face several difficulties, as long as they consolidate this process and become able to read, write and understand what they read and write. Within literacy studies, make children to understand the relation between letters and sound is a challenge [1]. This is due each letter would represent a sound and each sound a letter in a written alphabetical system. However, this correspondence is not straightforward. Within Portuguese language, as with another languages, these relations between the spoken sound with the written letters is quite complex, since there are some cases where two or more letters represent the same sound. This scenario ends up by having the students to make several orthographical mistakes during the literacy process.

© Springer International Publishing Switzerland 2016
A. Marcus (Ed.): DUXU 2016, Part II, LNCS 9747, pp. 587–596, 2016.
DOI: 10.1007/978-3-319-40355-7_56

Therefore, in order to deal with these orthographic drawbacks, teachers search for mechanisms and activities that would be helpful for children to make them understand the language's orthographical subtleties and overcome these literacy challenges.

In this context, the goal of this work is to present an application (educational game) to assist the learning processes of words likely to cause orthographical difficulties. For this purpose, a natural interface (using Kinect [2]) is applied in order to motivate and attract children to use the application. In order to validate the proposed work, some usability tests were carried out with elementary school students under literacy process.

The current work is organized in the following sections: Sect. 2 presents the main concepts related to the developed work; Sect. 3 discusses some related work regarding the use of Kinect within educational applications; Sect. 4 introduces the development model applied for the proposed application; Sect. 5 discusses some tests evaluation results; and, finally, Sect. 6 presents some general conclusions and future perspectives.

2   The Human Language and Its Relation with the Written Word

We define the human language as a code inside which a set of linguistic forms is related to a given meaning, used to express a particular language task (or skill): speech, auditory comprehension, reading and writing [3].

The spoken language is acquired spontaneously as children grow up, interact and communicate with other people; as children expose themselves to the speech, they improve their acquisition process and their communication skills. In opposite, the acquisition of the written word requires an explicit instruction process, a systematic learning effort [4].

Alphabetic systems are applied to represent the abstract structures of the spoken language, such as the phonemes (smallest linguistic unit of a language's phonology). The conversion between graphemes (smallest unit in a writing system) and a phoneme is quite variable from alphabet to another alphabet, since some sounds (phonemes) can be represented by several letters, or the opposite, a letter being represented by different sounds, depending on the context of the whole word [3].

The Portuguese language alphabetic orthographic system is classified as irregular, its means that the graphemes do not possess a direct relation with the phonemes. These irregularities within the alphabetic system reflect directly on the learning drawbacks, leading to longer and larger rates of orthography misspelling [3, 5].

Cristofolini [6] claims that there is a close relation between speech and literacy, since that the literacy process relies on carrying out a mapping between a sequence of sounds and a written code. This mapping affects directly the orthography domain, since repro-ducing Portuguese phonetic sequences in written expression requires the utilization of graphical signals representing these sounds, or the so-called graphemes or letters. When someone speaks, this person produces phonemes and, when he/she writes, these sounds should be described as graphemes. Therefore, since there is no one-to-one correspond-ence between Portuguese's graphemes and phonemes, orthography misspelling reflects this lack of correspondence between these two systems.

According to Zorzi [5], orthography has been one of the issues constantly discussed during literacy process, since learn how to write implies in understanding the relations between sounds and letters, in other words, one has to master the conventional words writing. Thus, the orthographic mistake has been a major issue, which has not been given the proper attention and understanding during writing acquisition. The author suggests a classification regarding the types of mistakes commonly made by children at elementary school:

- Modifications or mistakes due the possibility of multiple representations: The alphabetic writing systems present as essential feature correspondence between sounds and letters. Regarding the Portuguese language, it is possible to find several types of correspondences: A stable relation, within which just one letter is always applied to write a given sound (as in the case of letter f which always describes the sound of / f/); A non-stable relation, within which the same letter can represent several sounds (the letter c, for instance can represent the sounds /k/ and /s/) and, at last, another non-stable correspondence, which is characterized by the fact that the same sound can be characterized by several letters (for instance, the sound /s/ can be represented by s, ss, c, ç, x, z, sc, sç, and xc). Therefore, it possible to make an assumption of the amount of mistakes generated by this non-stable correspondence between letters and sounds, as it is illustrated by the written form of the word "*cabeça*" with letter "*s*" or "*ss*", resulting in "*cabesa*", "*cabeça*" or "*cabessa*".
- Replacements related to the spelling of the unvoiced and voiced phonemes: some pairs of phonemes can be differentiated by their sound trace; it means that some of them are unvoiced, others are voiced. The phonemes /p/, /t/, /k/, /f/ and /s/ are considered unvoiced since they do not present vibration of the vocal cords when they are reproduced in Portuguese. In turn, the phonemes /b/, /d/, /v/ and /z/ are produced in Portuguese with the vibration of the vocal cords, being considered, therefore as voiced phonemes. The sound traces is related to an important distinction between pairs of phonemes, such as /p/x /b/; /t/x /d/; /f/x /v/; /s/x /z/. The orthographic modifications considered as "unvoiced/voiced switches" regard the words presenting replacements between the letters that describe the following phonemes *p/b*; *t/d*; *q-c/ g*; *f/v*; *ch-x /j-g* and the set of letters that represent the phoneme /s/ when replaced by those related to the sound /z/. For instance, this type of replacement can be found in the following words: "*tijolo*" – "*ticholo*"; "*filme*" – "*vilme*" and "*gato*" –"*cato*".

Similar letters: some letters or even a set of letters that compose words can be considered similar if we consider their graphical shape. In other words, the similar drawing of these letters can take to misspelling, for instance, as in "*maçã*" being written as "*naçã*".

3   Related Works

Several contributions have presented the development of applications for the educational environment focusing on learning drawbacks [7]. Guerra [8] developed an application for teaching color blending using Kinect as interaction resource. The developed application proposed colorful circles where children are encouraged to select colors using natural gestures and blend them in order to observe the resulting colors.

Alves et al. [9] developed an application that uses Kinects to assist in the literacy process. The application provides a user interface that presents to the user a letter, a word and an image; each one with a particular geometric shape. The user should move these objects around screen in order to position them correctly (association).

Kawamoto and Martins [10] developed a game, also using Kinect, to automatize the Corsi test [11]. This test verifies the short-term memory. In this game, a sequence of squares is presented to the user who should select them in a given order. The sequence presented to the user is constantly modified and improved, in order to verify the user's level of short-term memory. The tests with this application were carried out with an elderly target public.

Homer et al. [12] conducted an experiment comparing language and reading outcomes for children who had a story read to them by an adult, to those who had the same story read to them by a character in a prototype of a Kinect game, either with or without the addition of in-game activities. Their findings encourages the next generation of digital literacy games.

4 Development of the Application

The game developed provides interaction through Kinect [2], or mouse. The main concept is related to the presentation of an image and the pronunciation of the respective word represented by the image. The child should choose, with the hand if he/she is using a Kinect otherwise with a mouse, the initial letter of the word he/she has just heard. The option of the initial letters is related to the level of orthographic difficulty within Portuguese language, detailed in Sect. 2. When the child selects the incorrect option, a sound alert is triggered informing the user has made a mistake, and he/she will have another opportunity to select the correct option. Consequently, the child will learn how to write the first letter of the word.

During the development, an interactive approach was adopted, where several versions were generated. Improvements and corrections were implemented using pilot versions. The final version was tested with children under literacy process. The functional and non-functional requirements are discussed in the following sections.

4.1 Functional Requirements

For the definition of functional and non-functional requirements, there were several meetings with pedagogy and psychology professionals with large experience with learning drawbacks in childhood. The following requirements were identified:

- The game should allow, in case the children do not listen or have doubt about the pronunciation of a word, to repeat the reproduction of the sound or the word.
- If the children select an incorrect answer, the application should notify them with a pleasant sentence: "Try again, you are almost there" or "Keep trying".

- Every time the game is executed, it should generate a report with the following information: image visualized by the child; the correct initial letter; the time the child selected the correct letter; how many times the child listened to the pronunciation of the word, and; how many mistakes the child made before selecting the correct letter.
- In order to select the options of the game, the child will use his/her hands and to select (click) he/she has to push his hand forward.
- The application should allow the children before starting the game, to train how to interact using hands gestures.
- The words should be presented randomly during the execution.
- When all the words are made available and the user concludes the word successfully, a textual and audio message should be presented saying: "Congratulations, you completed all the stages of the game".

4.2 Non-functional Requirements

The non-functional requirements identified during the requirements phase were:

- The time to complete each task of the game, that is, to select the initial letter of the presented word, cannot be too long or demanding. It should be easy and intuitive for the children.
- Only one click should be enough to select an answer. More than one click should be difficult for the children to interact.
- The distance between the objects on the screen should not be large, so that user can move the mouse and click easily over the object.
- The game should not last too long, since this can be too demanding and exhaustive for the children.

4.3 Design and Implementation

The game was implemented using the programming language C# in order to apply the platform .NET Framework [2]. Also the development kit Kinect SDK 1.7 [2] was applied, besides the Kinect device.

In this game the hands gesture recognition was implemented in order to simulate a "click" (selection). Figure 1 illustrates one of the screens of the developed application. In this picture, the user's hand is already depicted; however the interaction was not yet available.

4.4 Assessment Methodology with Final Users

Initially, a private school in the city of São Paulo (Brazil) was contacted, and the developed project was presented in order to have their permission to run an application usability evaluation with their elementary school students (k2), which are already literate (can read and write), but still can make some misspelling. After this request approved by the school board, the consent letter was sent to the parents clarifying the content of

Fig. 1. A screenshot of the application

the evaluation to be carried out, and requesting their approval so that their kids would participate in the evaluation.

Out of 35 children invited to participate in the evaluation, only 16 kids were authorized. The experiment was carried out at the school's multimedia room, which was equipped with a projector and an appropriate sound system (Fig. 2).

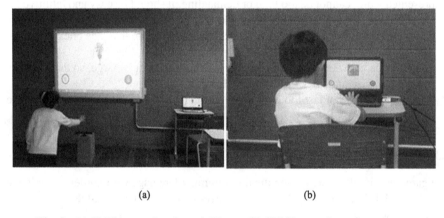

(a)   (b)

Fig. 2. (a) Child interacting through Kinect. (b) Child interacting using a mouse

Before starting the tests, a short interview was carried out with the users in order to characterize their profile, where some questions were made such as sex, age, previous experience with computers and if they were already familiar with the Kinect motion sensor.

Children were invited to interact with the application using Kinect (Fig. 2a) and also interact using the computer's mouse (Fig. 2b). The tests were executed randomly, using Kinect or mouse, so that kids were not suggested to think that one or another interaction solution was better than the other.

After the interactions, children were invited to answer a quiz in order to provide further information related to usability and to their acceptance regarding the proposed application. In the quiz the Likert scale of 3 points [13] was applied with some images support to facilitate children's understanding. The quiz proposed after the interaction using a mouse and Kinect was composed of the following questions: (a) Do you think the size of the image was good?; (b) Do you think it was easy to click on the image?; (c) Did you think the images were beautiful?; (d) Do you think the size of the letters was good?; (e) Did you like the sound?; (f) oud you play this game again using mouse/Kinect?

Running a pilot test, it was possible to verify that it would be necessary, in average, 1 min for explanations and profile interview, 3 min for executing the application using mouse interaction, 2 min for the quiz after test with mouse, 5 min for the execution of the application with Kinect, 2 min for the quiz after test with Kinect and 2 min of the interview after test.

5 Results

The usability evaluation was carried out with fourteen children from the school, eight girls and six boys, all of them with six years old. The result of the profile quiz indicated that all the participants had previous contact with computers, from which eight informed that are used to use the computer up to twice a week; four informed that they use the computer up to four times a week and two children everyday.

As for the utilization of the computer for entertainment purposes (games), thirteen children informed that they play with the computer, from which nine answered that they play with the computer up to twice a week; two informed that they play up to four times a week and two play everyday with the computer. Regarding Kinect, the profile quiz indicates that only six children had already previous experience with this type of interaction, mainly with Xbox Kinect console [14].

5.1 Results of the Usability Tests Using Mouse for the Interaction

Based on the answers provided by the children on the quizzes, it was possible to verify the usability of the application interacting with the interface with the mouse. The quiz revealed that only one child agreed partially about the size of the images in the application, and the remaining agreed that the size of it was good. Two children thought it was difficult to click on the image using the mouse, while the remaining considered this action straightforward. Also, it was possible to verify that twelve children thought the images beautiful and two partially agreed.

As for the size of the letter, thirteen kids informed that the size was good; one child answered that it was not good. Regarding the sound of the application, eleven children answered that it was good; one informed it was partially good, and two thought the sound was bad.

When they were questioned if they were likely to play again using mouse, just one kid informed negatively, the remaining answered yes.

As for the interaction with the mouse, we could conclude that the application met children's expectations. As for the kid that informed that probably would not play again, it was not possible to observe the reason that caused this reaction since he/she did not inform the reason for his/her answer.

5.2   Results of the Usability Tests Using Kinect for the Interaction

After interacting with the application using Kinect, children answered usability assessment quiz, where it was possible to verify that thirteen kids agreed that the size of the image was good, and just one thought it was partially good.

As for clicking, nine children thought it was easy, two partially easy and three considered it difficult. We could observe that the children that did not considered it easy, or partially easy, had never interacted before with Kinect. Nevertheless, these kids claimed that they enjoyed using this kind of interaction.

Regarding the images, thirteen kids considered the images beautiful and only one answered that he/she though the image partially beautiful. All the kids answered that the size of the letter on the answers alternatives was good. Thirteen kids considered the sounds of the application good and only one informed that the audio quality was reasonably good.

In the question related to the application approval, twelve children liked to apply Kinect to play; one child liked partially and one didn't like it. As for the question if they would ever play again the game using Kinect, twelve children answered affirmatively; one was undecided and one answered that would not play again using Kinect.

During the tests with Kinect, all the kids demonstrated interest and joy to be executing this activity. No child required assistance to use the application with Kinect. After explanations and the initial training, all the children concluded the activity successfully.

In addition, it was not possible to observe if any child felt irritated or tired with the game, however, we verified the successful conclusion of the activity by all the children.

During the tests, we could observe that six children selected any answer by mistake, that is, they selected a letter with a non-intentional push movement.

5.3   Comparative Between the Obtained Results

By the utilization of Kinect, children needed in average six minutes, and with the mouse, just three minutes. Since it was for the kids, in general, their first experience with a gesture-based interface, a longer duration to conclude the activity could be justified. Children that already had previous experience with a mouse required less time to conclude the activity.

After having used the game with two different forms of interaction - conventional with a mouse and gesture-based with Kinect, children answered an interview in order to verify which form was more attractive for them. Seven children preferred Kinect; five enjoyed both forms and they could not define which one pleased more and two children enjoyed most using the mouse to interact with the application.

When questioned what they liked most about the application, children replied that Kinect as the interaction solution since they were using their own hands to play with the computer. Just two children claimed that they got tired with the motion required by their arms and hands in order to interact and play.

6 Conclusions

The application developed in this work applied words which children under literacy process most likely have misspelling difficulties with. These words are in general related to unvoiced-voiced switches and multiple representations. Besides this, the developed game provided students with focus when studying, the first experience with natural interface for the interaction with the computer.

Through the usability tests carried out with K2 children in a private school of the city of São Paulo (Brazil), we were able to verify that children indeed make misspelling in this stage (in average, 19 % of mistakes). Therefore, we were able to conclude that the proposed application can be very useful during literacy process since help children in the written acquisition process.

As for the gesture-based interface with the utilization of Kinect, it was possible to verify children's acceptance, demonstrating that it is not only viable but also useful to apply this kind of technology within classroom, helping teachers to make their classes more attractive, interactive and motivational within learning process.

Nevertheless, a minor issue was raised regarding Kinect which had difficulties to recognize children's small hands. Therefore, kids needed to have their hands wide opened, with fingers away one from the other, so that Kinect could recognize the open hand gesture for the selection of objects on the screen. With adults this drawback could not be verified.

As for future works, it is interesting to add in the application other common misspelling mistakes that children usually make during literacy process, such as accentuation mistakes and spelling verification of the whole word, not only the first letter. It is also interesting if the application recognizes other motions and gestures, once that through the usability tests we could verify how motivated children were to interact with the computer though natural gestures. Another possibility would be to adapt the application to work with other idioms.

References

1. DePriest, D., Barilovits, K.: LIVE: xbox Kinect©s virtual realities to learning games. In: 16th Annual TCC Worldwide Online Conference, Hawaii, pp. 48–52 (2011)
2. Microsoft: Kinect para Windows. http://www.microsoft.com/en-us/kinectforwindows/develop/. Accessed 10 Sept 2015
3. Barton, D.: Literacy: An Introduction to the Ecology of Written Language, 2nd edn. Wiley, New York (2007)
4. Scribner, S., Cole, M., Cole, M.: The Psychology of Literacy, vol. 198, issue 1. Harvard University Press, Cambridge, MA (1981)
5. Zorzi, J.L.: Aprender a escrever: a apropriação do sistema ortográfico. Artes Médicas, Porto Alegre (1998)
6. Cristofolini, C.: Trocas ortográficas: uma interpretação a partir de análises acústicas. Doctoral dissertation. Universidade Federal de Santa Catarina, Centro de Comunicação e Expressão. Programa de Pós-graduação em Linguística (2008)

7. Boutsika, E.: Kinect in education: a proposal for children with autism. In: 5th International Conference on Software Development and Technologies for Enhancing Accessibility and Fighting Info-Exclusion, pp. 123–129 (2014)
8. Guerra, L.L.I.R.: Interação gestual em jogos educativos utilizando o sensor de movimentos Kinect. Monografia de graduação em Ciência da Computação. Instituto de Informática. Universidade Federal do Rio Grande do Sul, Porto Alegre, Brasil (2013). http://www.lume.ufrgs.br/handle/10183/77274. Accessed 1 May 2014
9. de Alves, R.S., de Araujo, J.O.A., Madeiro, F.: AlfabetoKinect: Um aplicativo para auxiliar na alfabetização de crianças com o uso do Kinect. In: Anais do Simpósio Brasileiro de Informática na Educação, vol. 23, issue 1 (2012)
10. Kawamoto, A.L.S., Martins, V.F.: Application designed for the elderly using gestural interface. Revista Brasileira de Computação Aplicada 2, 96–109 (2013). Edition 5
11. Corsi, P.M.: Human memory and the medial temporal region of the brain. McGill University (1972)
12. Homer, B.D., Kinzer, C.K., Plass, J.L., Letourneau, S.M., Hoffman, D., Bromley, M., Hayward, E.O., Turkay, S., Kornak, Y.: Moved to learn: the effects of interactivity in a Kinect-based literacy game for beginning readers. J. Comput. Educ. 74, 37–49 (2014)
13. Likert, R.: A technique for the measurement of attitudes. Arch. Psycho. (1932)
14. Xbox. http://www.xbox.com/pt-BR/HomeLATAM. Accessed 10 Sept 2015

Improvement Design of the Clinical Upper Extremity Rehabilitation Product for Stroke Patients

Lan-Ling Huang[1], Hsi-Hsun Yang[2], Chang-Franw Lee[3], and Mei-Hsiang Chen[4(✉)]

[1] School of Design, Fujian University of Technology, No. 3 Xueyuan Road, University Town, Minhou, Fuzhou City, Fujian Province, China
Lanlingh@gmail.com
[2] Department of Digital Media Design,
National Yunlin University of Science and Technology, 123 University Road, Section 3, Douliou 64002, Yunlin, Taiwan, ROC
jimmy@yuntech.edu.tw
[3] Department of Industrial Design,
National Yunlin University of Science and Technology, 123 University Road, Section 3, Douliou 64002, Yunlin, Taiwan, ROC
leecf@yuntech.edu.tw
[4] Department of Occupational Therapy,
Chung Shan Medical University/Chung Shan Medical University Hospital,
No. 110, Section 1, Jianguo N. Road, Taichung City 40201, Taiwan
cmh@csmu.edu.tw

Abstract. The purpose of this study was to survey the usage problems and needs of the traditional UERE and commercial digital videogames applied in rehabilitation, and summarize a guideline for improvement design of the digital UERP. According to the guideline, this study was to design a Hand-rehab product design with treatment needs, and evaluate its acceptability with a questionnaire. The hardware design features includes: (1) the shapes and sizes of the operation objects can be chosen by the users to fit their own hand dimensions, (2) weight of the object can also be adjusted accordingly. The software design features are: (3) it displays visual and verbal cues, game scores, and operation times to the patients in each stage, notifying whether or not their action succeeded, (4) it allows adjustments of the reaction time to movements and the scope of sensing area of the objects. (5) The scope size of sensing area of the object can be adjusted. A total of 52 post-stroke patients were invited to assess the acceptability of Hand-rehab product. For the acceptability, most patients, after a trial with this product, reported had a positive and high satisfaction (mean 6.7, SD 0.6) with Hand-rehab product for rehabilitation.

Keywords: Physical disabilities occupational therapy · Upper extremity equipment · Rehabilitation product design

© Springer International Publishing Switzerland 2016
A. Marcus (Ed.): DUXU 2016, Part II, LNCS 9747, pp. 597–605, 2016.
DOI: 10.1007/978-3-319-40355-7_57

1 Introduction

Upper limb motor deficit is one of the main symptoms of stroke patients. Between 55 % and 75 % of survivors continue to experience motor deficits associated with diminished quality of life (Saposnik et al. 2010). Many daily living tasks are performed with the upper limbs; therefore, rehabilitation treatment of the upper limbs is very important for stroke patients. Upper extremity rehabilitation equipment (UERE) are essential tools in the occupational therapy (OT) practice and are frequently used in most of Taiwan's OT clinics. Their individual strengths and weaknesses may affect treatment effectiveness and safety for the patient (Huang et al. 2013). Therefore, UERE must be designed with users in mind.

The most fundamental principle in motor learning is that the degree of performance improvement is dependent on the amount of practice (Krakauer 2006). Practice at its simplest, which is just performing the same movement repeatedly (Krakauer 2006; Sabari 1991), may be the most effective way to improve performance during the training session itself (Krakauer 2006). Patients at each session of therapy take about 15–20 min in repeated use of the equipment, which are common in Taiwan because a therapist usually has to take care of two to three patients at a session. A therapist has to try to motivate patients, for example, by embedding meaningful occupations with the UERE. The outcomes of OT would be best when the tasks employed for patients are meaningful to patients. Many UERE are employed for the purpose of preparing the body for future integrated work. For example, many clinicians begin OT for patients with stroke with a UERE and range of motion therapy prior to engaging the patient and move on to functional reaching tasks. These prior or preparatory activities are part of the treatment process. However, a skilled therapist knows that these tasks are not the end goal of therapy. These tasks are required components and are often only the short-term goals. These short-term goals contribute to longer-term goals like being able to independently do upper-body dressing. Therefore, the functions of the traditional UERE are needed to remain and redesign for user needs (Huang et al. 2013).

A key challenge for a clinician is to motivate a patient through/during the more routine preparatory activities in anticipation of future meaningful occupations. The meaning component in OT is how a therapist utilizes an individual success with the UERE and clearly ties these successes to future purposeful activities. Most existing clinical UERP provides no feedback to the patients. Patients may find that repeating the same activity can be boring and monotonous and thus develop a negative attitude toward the therapy process (Chen et al. 2015). In order to increase the mental satisfaction and physical vitality of rehabilitation therapy, some therapists have using off-the-shelf video game systems in rehabilitation. A better designed piece of equipment with variable options to choose and fun to use may also be helpful for therapists to plan the therapy activities with interaction and feedback. These therapy activities may raise clients' motivation to participate in the activities. With the increase of clients' motivation, both patients' levels of participation in therapy activities and the therapeutic effectiveness might also increase as a result.

Our study was to survey the usage problems and needs of the traditional UERE and commercial digital videogames applied in rehabilitation, then summarize a guideline for improvement design of the digital UERP. According to the guideline, this study was to design a digital UERP with treatment needs, and evaluate its acceptability with a questionnaire. In this study, we choice one pieces of equipment commonly used for OT in Taiwan hospitals - Stacking cones (Table 1-A) as improvement design case.

2   Methods

The study includes three parts: (1) a questionnaire was developed to survey the usage problems and improvement needs of the existing UERE and commercial digital videogames used in Taiwan hospitals. (2) According to the results of the usage problems and improvement needs, summarize a guideline for improvement design of the UERP. (3) Redesigning the Stacking cones. (4) Evaluating the acceptability of the Stacking cones.

2.1   The Usage Problems and Improvement Needs of the Existing UERE

Subjects. The target sample of this study was therapists working in OT departments of hospitals at the time of survey. One hundred and thirteen hospitals having OT units with three or more full-time therapists were selected and surveyed.

Procedures. The researchers mailed the questionnaires to one therapist at each selected hospital with an OT department, and then he or she gave the questionnaires to other occupational therapists to fill in. The questionnaire description included the purpose of the study, the definition of the surveyed items, a description of the fill-in questionnaire and the deadline for returning the questionnaire to the researchers. The therapists were asked to check the appropriate items according to their personal experiences and opinions. The questionnaire was written in Chinese. It consisted mainly of four parts: therapist personal profile, questions about usage problems, improvement needs of the eight different types of UERE and suggestions for new designs for UERE.

Each therapist was asked two kinds of questions about the equipment: (1) usage problems and (2) improvement needs. The usage problems and adding new design for UERE items were listed on a 5-point Likert-type scale with 1 signifying "strongly disagree" and 5 being "strongly agree". A multiple-choice checklist concerning features needed for improvement in the new design was also provided. Furthermore, the therapists were also asked to provide additional information not mentioned in the questionnaire.

Results. For the Stacking cones, a total of 184 valid questionnaires were received. The usage problems of Stacking cones were easily damaged (mean 3.6, SD 1.1), Uninteresting (mean 3.0, SD 0.9), Base unstable (mean 3.1, SD 1.1) and Height not adjustable (mean 2.2, SD 0.8). For the improvement needs, a higher value signifies a more urgent need for improvement. The Stacking cones, the top two features with the

Table 1. Design features of the Hand-rehab product

A. The Stacking cones commonly used for OT in Taiwan hospitals.

B. The touch screen is used to display the tasks of Hand-rehab product.

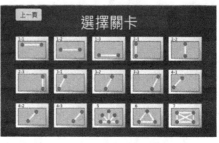

C. The shapes and sizes of the operation objects.

D. The menu of the tasks in Hand-rehab product.

E. Weight of the object can also be adjusted.

F. It displays visual and verbal cues, game scores, and operation times to the patients.

(*Continued*)

G. It allows adjustments of the reaction time to movements and the scope of sensing area of the objects.

H. The scope of sensing area of the object is about 60 mm in diameter.

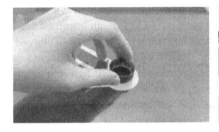

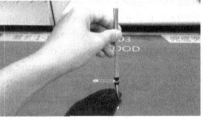

I. The scope of sensing area of the object is about 36 mm in diameter.

J. The scope of sensing area of the object is about 2 mm in diameter.

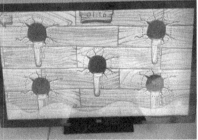

K. The menu of the tasks with scenario in Hand-rehab product.

L. A new series of the tasks - Block holes.

highest percentages were the following: (1) interchangeable components (57 %) and (2) durable material (51 %).

2.2 The Usage Problems and Improvement Needs of the Commercial Digital Videogames

Subjects. Stroke patients were recruited from an outpatient occupational therapy department of Chung Shan Medical University Hospital in Taiwan. Inclusion criteria were as follows: (a) hemiparesis with upper extremity dysfunction following a single unilateral stroke; (b) a history of first-time stroke (3–24 months post-stroke); (c) a need for upper extremity rehabilitation to convalescent levels of Brunnstrom stages III to V; (d) ability to communicate, and to understand and follow instructions; and (e) ability to maintain sitting and standing balance unsupported for two minutes under supervision (score ≥ 3 on the Berg Balance Scale). Exclusion criteria were as follows: (a) engagement in any other rehabilitation studies during the study; and (b) serious aphasia or cognitive impairment. Each patient gave informed consent. This study was approved by the Human Research Ethics Board of a local hospital.

Procedures. This part was a single-blind clinical trial. First, clinical therapists reviewed their patients with the inclusion criteria and asked about their willingness to participate in this trial. Subjects who accepted were asked to sign an informed consent form. All subjects were sequentially allocated into three groups (the XaviX®Port group, the Nintendo Wii group, or conventional group) by the researcher according to the order of recruitment (i.e. patient one goes into group A, patient two into group B, patient three into group C, patient four into group A, and so on). The functional ability of each subject's affected upper extremity was assessed by one of the assessors in two stages: (1) prior to the interventions, and (2) immediately after completing all the training sessions. All subjects were asked to complete a total of 20 training sessions over eight weeks, scheduled at three 30-minute sessions per week (excluding set-up time). In addition to the training sessions in this study, all subjects also received at least one hour of occupational therapy and physical therapy, respectively. After the post-training assessment, each patient also completed the improvement needs, motivation and enjoyment questionnaire.

Results. A total of 24 consecutively screened stroke patients completed all the training sessions. Each group had 8 patients. For the improvement needs of the Nintendo Wii and XaviX®Port games were: (a) To increase the response time of the games. (b) To increase difficulty levels of the games in order to better suit the various patients with different abilities of upper extremity functions. (c) To expand the sensor's sensing scope. (d) To be able to record movement data, such as: reaction time, operating time. (e) To improve the ways to fix the controller on the user's hand. (f) To fit the controllers size for different hand dimensions of the patients. (g) To provide better correspondence between the game and real-life movements. (h) To provide controllers for body control training, such as chest strap and belt. (i) To simplify the controller's operation. Regarding motivation and enjoyment, patients in the Nintendo Wii and

XaviX®Port groups reported that using video games in treatment increased their treatment motivation. Enjoyment was significantly greater in the Nintendo Wii and XaviX®Port groups than in the conventional group (F2, 21 = 18.55, p < 0.001).

2.3   A Guideline for Improvement Design of the Stacking Cones

In terms of the improvement needs of existing UERE and the commercial digital videogames, we can synthesize a design guideline for Stacking cones as follows: (a) To provide interchangeable components. (b) To use durable material. (c) To increase the response time of the games. (d) To increase difficulty levels of the games in order to better suit the various patients with different abilities of upper extremity functions. (e) To provide better correspondence between the game and real-life movements. (f) To be able to record movement data, such as: reaction time, operating time.

2.4   Evaluating the Acceptability of the Stacking Cones

The acceptability of using the digital UERP in rehabilitation was assessed with a questionnaire by stroke patients after a trial with this product. Inclusion criteria were the following: (a) Hemiparetic with upper extremity dysfunction following a single unilateral stroke, (b) the required upper extremity rehabilitation convalescent levels were Brunnstrom stage III to IV, i.e., having basic upper extremity synergies to perform joint movement voluntarily, (c) ability to communicate and follow instructions. Each patient was asked to use the product 15 min, then to fill in a questionnaire. The items of the questionnaire were drafted according to the Technology Acceptance Model (TAM). The items were scored on a 7-point Likert-type scale, with 1 signifying "strongly disagree" and 7 being "strongly agree".

3   Results

The Stacking Cones Redesign. Based on these preliminary results, a design proposal for a digital UERP with treatment needs in mind was proposed, named as Hand-rehab product. The Hand-rehab product has a touch screen to display the game contents and it incorporates objects from daily live in its operation.

The hardware design features includes (Table 1): (1) the shapes and sizes of the operation objects can be chosen by the users to fit their own hand dimensions (Table 1-C), (2) weight of the object can also be adjusted accordingly (Table 1-E). The software design features are: (3) it displays visual and verbal cues, game scores, and operation times to the patients in each stage, notifying whether or not their action succeeded (Table 1-F), (4) it allows adjustments of the reaction time to movements and the scope of sensing area of the objects (Table 1-G). (5) The scope size of sensing area of the object can be adjusted (Table 1-H-J).

The Acceptability of Hand-Rehab Product. A total of 52 post-stroke patients (34 males and 18 females) were admitted from the occupational therapy department of Chung Shan Medical University Hospital. The mean age of the patients was 54.1 years (SD 14.4). 28 (54 %) patients ever used computer, and 24 patients (46 %) never used computer. 17 patients (33 %) ever used touchscreen, and 35 patients never used. 9 patients ever used digital games for rehabilitation, but 43 patients never used.

For the acceptability, most patients, after a trial with this product, reported had a positive and high satisfaction (mean 6.7, SD 0.6) with hand-rehab product for rehabilitation (Table 2).

Table 2. Stroke patients used the Hand-rehab product

4 Conclusion

This study proposed the initial design of the Hand-rehab product. It is still debatable whether treatment with video gaming systems can effectively facilitate upper extremity functions, and this area still needs more research.

Two suggestions are proposed for future studies: (1) it will be better if the views of those therapists who use Hand-rehab product were also further surveyed. (2) In order to make this product more suitable to use in rehabilitation, it would be necessary to survey the therapeutic effectiveness of the Hand-rehab product.

Acknowledgment. This study is supported by the Ministry of Science and Technology with grant No.: MOST 104-2221-E-040-008.

References

Chen, M.H., Huang, L.L., Lee, C.F., Hsieh, C.L., Lin, Y.C., Liu, H., Chen, M.I., Lu, W.S.: A controlled pilot trial of two commercial video games for rehabilitation of arm function after stroke. Clin. Rehabil. **29**(7), 674–682 (2015)

Huang, L.L., Lee, C.F., Hsieh, C.L., Chen, M.H.: Upper extremity rehabilitation equipment for stroke patients in Taiwan: usage problems and improvement needs. Occup. Ther. Int. **20**, 205–214 (2013)

Krakauer, J.: Motor learning: its relevance to stroke recovery and neurorehabilitation. Curr. Opin. Neurol. **19**, 84–90 (2006)

Sabari, J.: Motor learning concepts applied to activity based intervention with adults with hemiplegia. Am. J. Occup. Ther. **45**, 523–530 (1991)

Saposnik, G., Teasell, R., Mamdani, M., Hall, J., McIlroy, W., Cheung, D., Thorpe, K.E., Cohen, L.G., Bayley, M.: Effectiveness of virtual reality using Wii gaming technology in stroke rehabilitation: a pilot randomized clinical trial and proof of principle. Stroke **41**(7), 1477–1484 (2010). The Stroke Outcome Research Canada Working Group

Assessing the Cooperation Portal's Usability Based on the Proposition of Users' Needs

Clarissa Lins[✉], André Pinho, and José Guilherme Santa Rosa

Department of Arts, Professional Design Master's Program UFRN, Natal, Brazil
clarissalorena@gmail.com, alsdepinho@gmail.com,
jguilhermesantarosa@gmail.com

Abstract. This research is about identifying the Cooperation Portal users' needs for information. The Cooperation Portal was created and implemented by the Superintendence of Informatics of the Federal University of Rio Grande do Norte (UFRN) aiming to propose a collaborative environment that would facilitate the process of transferring UFRN's Integrated Management Systems (SIG-UFRN), which is done through cooperation agreements that are signed by federal educational institutions (IFES network) and the direct administration (CYCLE network). It is a qualitative and quantitative case study performed using log analysis and application of a questionnaire to members of the IFES and CYCLE networks. As a result, it was identified that although the interfaces are simple and well structured, with menus, self-explanatory images and search systems that help find information, the users' real needs are not met, causing dissatisfaction when using the tool.

Keywords: Design · Ergonomics · Interaction

1 Introduction

The Superintendence of Informatics (SINFO), an executive body held by a superintendent appointed by the university's president, was established in 1999 and is responsible for: (i) planning, coordinating, organizing, executing and evaluating activities related to informatics, based on the Institutional Development Plan [1] and the Management Plan [2]; (ii) managing UFRN's infrastructure network; and (iii) managing and developing UFRN's information and management systems.

In 2008, the Federal Rural University of The Semiarid (UFERSA) showed interest in UFRN's Integrated Management Systems (SIG-UFRN), meaning to implement them in their organization. Therefore, in the second semester of 2008, the first cooperation agreement was signed aiming to broaden UFERSA's administrative and academic processes' computerization as well as its data management through systems developed by UFRN and adapted and maintained by UFERSA with the aid and the assistance provided by UFRN, which establishes a technology transfer process.

In the following years, there was an expansion of this business and technical transfer process to the institutions in the CYCLE and IFES networks (Fig. 1).

Each year, these networks come together in an event called Workshop, conducted by SINFO with the goal of exchanging experiences between partner institutions, as

A. Marcus (Ed.): DUXU 2016, Part II, LNCS 9747, pp. 606–617, 2016.
DOI: 10.1007/978-3-319-40355-7_58

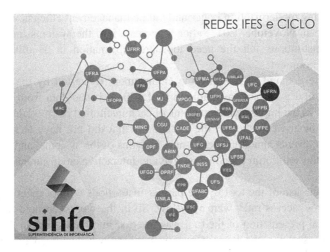

Fig. 1. Partner institutions in CYCLE and IFES networks

Fig. 2. Cooperation **Portal**

well as discussing modernization issues and public management efficiency. In the event that took place in November 2013, after four years into the systems implementation process, the institutions felt the need to share information in a collaborative and interactive environment.

To meet the demand of building the environment requested by the partners, the Cooperation Portal was made available in 02.12.2014. It had data from partner institutions, as well as the implementation status of each institution per module; information on companies licensed to support the institutions that did not have technical staff; a space for news; events announcements; new versions of the systems; and a forum tool that served as the solution for a collaborative and interactive environment, as shown in Fig. 2.

However, the use of the tool by the partner institutions did not meet expectations, since the forums' access rates were very low. So in the workshop held in November 2014, an official presentation of the tool was inserted into the lineup. In the following months, when assessing the Portal's access numbers, we continued to notice a low demand, which led, in April 2015, to the insertion of a Google Analytics visitation statistic tool to help understand the users' access behavior in the Cooperation Portal.

In this sense, the present work aims to identify and prioritize the need for information according to the Cooperation Portal's users, and then set the page scope, proposing a new way to organize the information, a wireframe definition and a new choice of colors and typography.

2 Usability Evaluation

Usability is the extent to which a product can be used by specific users to achieve specific goals with effectiveness, efficiency and satisfaction in a specific use context [3]. Depending on the rule, the usability can be measured according to how easy it is to learn, memorization and users' low error rate when handling the system.

According to Nielsen and Loranger [4], usability is a quality attribute related to the easiness of using something. More specifically, it refers to the speed at which users can learn how to use something, their efficiency when using it, how they remember it, their level of tendency to errors and how much they enjoy using it. The authors complement by saying that if people cannot or do not use a resource, it may as well not exist.

The software acceptance is directly related to the user's satisfaction when using it. Ergonomically user-centered interfaces tend to increase the positive assessment of the system's use. Researches in Human-Computer Interaction (HCI) seek to evaluate the quality of an interface project even after it is ready. According to Nielsen [5], this quality is related to attributes of learning easiness, efficiency, easiness to remember how to perform a task after a period of time, how fast a task can be done, low error rates and subjective user satisfaction.

For Rogers et al. [6], the usability ensures that interactive products are easy to learn how to use and are effective and pleasant in the user's perspective. For these authors, this involves optimizing the interactions established by the people with the products.

3 Methodology

A qualitative and quantitative case study considers log analysis from April/2014 to December/2015 and an online questionnaire sent on September 04th, 2015 with a seven day term to answer questions about the need for information and the easiness to use the "Cooperation Portal" tool. Triangulation of the information collected in this exploratory study proves to be adequate to enrich the data and propose improvements in the access to information.

The target population is made up of 30 active partners in the IFES and CYCLE networks. 11 (36.67 %) partners who did not respond were excluded.

In order to analyze the research responses, an Affinity Diagram was created with the Portal users' insights on the need for information in order to well perform the implementation of the SIG-UFRN systems.

4 Results

Users' Profile. In order to outline the investigated partners' profiles, the partnership period, the period of access to the Cooperation Portal, the partner's institution of origin and the partner's position in the institution were determined.

Of the 30 active institutions, being 22 from the IFES network and 8 from the CYCLE network, 19 answered, from which 6 were from the direct administration (CYCLE network) and 12 from the IFES network.

Institutions with 1 to 7 years of partnership answered the questionnaire. Of all of the institutions, 14 began to use the tool in 2014, when it was launched; 6 institutions began to use the Cooperation Portal in 2015; and two of them still did not have access to it.

Regarding the participants' position in the institution, it was found that all of the respondents are in Information Technology (IT), being directors, coordinators, technicians, leaders and analysts.

Cooperation Portal's Usability Log Analysis. The system usage satisfaction can be evaluated indirectly through log analysis, in which the user's interactions are analyzed through log files generated while using the system [7]. Log analysis can help understand the user's behavior with the systems' interfaces, allowing to identify how people arrive at the website, the bounce rates and how the system is being used in mobile applications in order to improve the interfaces' quality.

By using Google Analytics' analysis from April/2014 to December/2015, a reject rate of around 57 % in the use of the tool was found, as shown in Fig. 3:

By looking at Fig. 4, it is clear that a percentage of 70 % of the users use Android to access the Cooperation Portal and 22.67 % use iOS, which demonstrates considerable use via mobile application.

Cooperation Portal Use. It was noticed that 74 % of the users rarely or never use the system created as a collaborative environment for experience exchange between the

Fig. 3. Google **Analytics Graph** (Color figure online)

Sistema operacional	Sessões	Porcentagem do Sessões
1. Android	105	70,00%
2. iOS	34	22,67%
3. Windows Phone	8	5,33%
4. (not set)	3	2,00%

Fig. 4. Google **Analytics Graph**

partner institutions. Those who use it on a weekly and monthly basis accounted for 37 %, as shown in Graph 1:

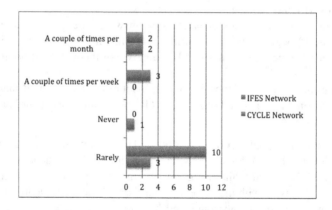

Graph 1. Use frequency (Color figure online)

As for the purpose of the use of the Cooperation Portal, the "See the institutions' implementation status per module" option reached a higher percentage - 68 % - when compared to the other options presented, demonstrating that there is an interest in knowing what other institutions are implementing in order to share experiences.

Following the option that reached 68 %, the options with the highest percentages presented were "See news about available versions, new features/modules, institutions' visits to UFRN and/or events that took place in UFRN" and "Access to the systems' forum" with 58 % and 53 %, respectively.

The "See what institutions are UFRN's partners and see their contact information" and "See licensed companies and their contracts" options obtained a percentage of 26 % each.

Only 5 % of the tool's users indicated other purposes for use, as follows: "Exchange of information, Solving common problems, Establishment of joint demands from all of the cooperative institutions" (Graph 2).

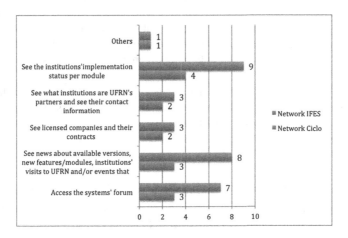

Graph 2. Cooperation portal's purpose of use (Color figure online)

Regarding interaction with the Cooperation Portal, 89 % of IFES and CYCLE networks institutions responded positively to issues related to the accessibility of navigation features. As for performing the required tasks, there was a divergence between the opinions of representatives of both networks. While the IFES network showed a positive percentage of 92 %, the CYCLE network showed a higher negative percentage of 83 %, as shown in Graph 3.

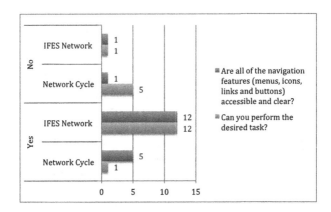

Graph 3. Accessibility of resources available in the portal (Color figure online)

Users' Opinions in the Questionnaire. The questionnaire's open questions sought to understand the need for information and the users' level of satisfaction when using the Cooperation Portal. The following table and figures represent the Affinity Diagram with users' opinions on the Cooperation Portal and their need for information.

According to Santa Rosa and Moraes [8] regarding usability and the definition of the project's requirements, the "Affinity Diagram" method can be used after focus group sessions, interviews, questionnaires, brainstorms and usability tests - providing discussion, categorization and ranking of large amounts of qualitative data. According to the authors mentioned above, the method is characterized by a bottom-up approach in which specification, elements classification and use of many levels of categories help to emphasize data interposition and data grouping that are often not apparent or noticed during raw data analysis.

When analyzing the responses related to the attractiveness to search for the wanted information, most users found that the idea was appropriate. The suggestion to use the forum was considered interesting, but the tool was seen in a negative way because the news were outdated since there was insufficient contribution in the forum, mainly because the Skype tool is predominantly used for one-off and one-way communications

Table 1. Is the Cooperation Portal attractive to search for the wanted information?

It is a very good idea. I do not use it often enough because many of the questions that I have are answered via Skype and the many demands of the institution end up making me forget the importance of using this tool, which allows greater interaction between the partner institutions. It is unattractive because it does not contain relevant content related to the systems (UNILAB)
Yes (IFPR, PRF, INSS, UFRA, UFPE, UFG, UNIFEI)
First, the Portal should be made public in other SIG's communication tools. There is only one link in the top menu of the sinfo.ufrn.br website, but there are no banners or links in the Wiki systems. As for being attractive, I believe that **news released at least on a weekly basis motivate frequent visits to the Portal** (CGU)
It could be better used by the users. It is **important to identify the usage rates and find out why we find only a little amount of data being fed to the forum** (CADE)
Yes, the forum model is interesting, however many users do not have the habit of using this type of tool (UFS)
No. Sometimes it's difficult to find the information we are looking for (UFSB)
Honestly, **it's not attractive**. The forum has only a few contributions and very outdated news (IFSC)
Yes, when it is updated (IFC)
I believe that it is **simple and serves well the purpose for which it was created** (UFRR)
We have not been using UFRN's Cooperation Portal (ABIN)
In this first moment, what we want most is information on how the systems works, **which we usually seek in Wiki. Maybe it would be interesting to centralize the information in the Portal**. Insert a link to Wiki and everything that is related to the systems (UFGD)
Apparently, the model is unresponsive. Perhaps using a format similar to the social media's model would tend to give the Portal more "life" (UFAL)
Yes, the idea is very interesting, but it needs to be used by the teams in the partner institutions, who will feed the forum with information (MJ)

between partners and UFRN - harming the use of the collaborative environment (forum). This indicates that there is a need for more participation and interaction among institutions, as shown in Table 1.

When asked about the available information they would like to have and their order of priority, users answered: (1) technical information from patterns, workflows performed by UFRN to bug corrections and code merge tips; (2) uptodate documentation of new technologies, tutorials, link to wiki, list of difficulty in the implementation process in the institutions; (3) collaborative environment for exchange of experience, new features, FAQs, success cases and improvement in the forum's use permission. In Fig. 5 we observe the affinity diagram of priorities.

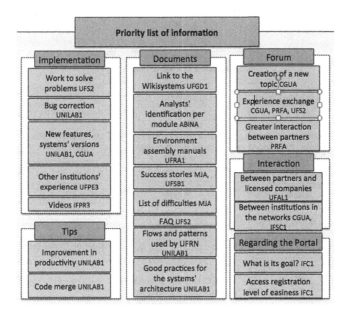

Fig. 5. Cooperation Portal's priority list

Regarding the important information found in the Portal, most respondents mentioned the forum, systems' versions and implementation by module, as shown in Fig. 6.

Regarding the need for unavailable information, the institutions need more technical information such as experienced errors and their solutions, FAQs, tutorials, videos and manuals, as shown in Fig. 7:

As for the location of the information in the Cooperation Portal, 53 % of the partners in the IFES and CYCLE networks said they did not find it difficult to locate the information, which indicates good organization in the distribution of information. However, comments were made regarding the large amount of static information and the little amount of data updates, as well as the difficulty in interacting with partners and in accessing the Portal, since institutions must ask SINFO to register them instead of being able to do it directly in the system or to use the same access information used

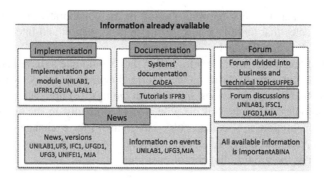

Fig. 6. Important information already available in the Cooperation Portal

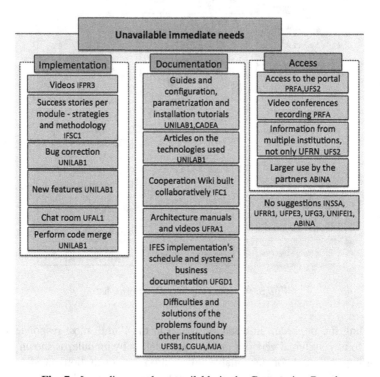

Fig. 7. Immediate needs unavailable in the Cooperation Portal

in the corporate project management tool called iProject. The institutions indicated the menu, self-explanatory images, simple and well structured layout, keywords, ongoing implementations and information on licensed companies as aspects that facilitate the location of information in the Cooperation Portal. Moreover, they reported the need for: greater usability; making information available online; having news on the home page; a search and classification system; and an environment to centralize the information in only one address. As a solution to remove unclear resources, an institution in the IFES network suggested to use a single link to access the forum and from which the user could access other information, as shown in Fig. 8.

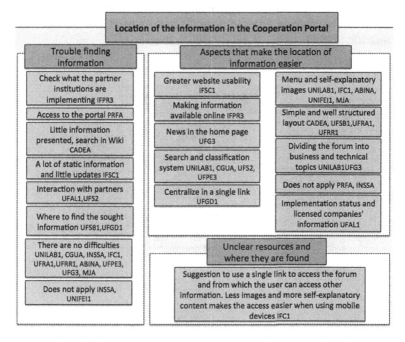

Fig. 8. Location of the information in the Cooperation Portal

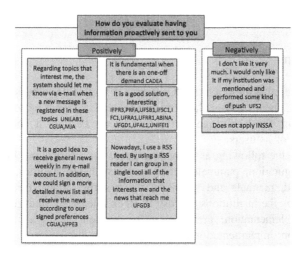

Fig. 9. Sending information proactively

When analyzing the answers on information proactivity, most of the partners evaluated it positively. Although they mentioned e-mail as a source of information feed, since it was found in the log analysis a noticeable percentage of use, and since they also mentioned the information they are interested in receiving proactively, an investment could be made in order to optimize the use of the tool, as seen below in Figs. 9 and 10:

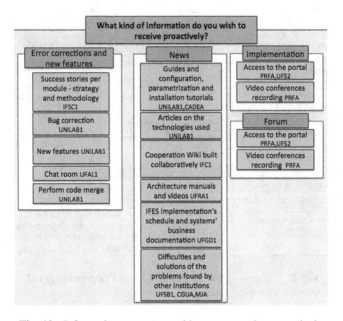

Fig. 10. Information partners would want to receive proactively

5   Conclusions

The research found that although the "Cooperation Portal" presents a simple and well structured layout, menu, self-explanatory images and a search system that helps to locate information, the low usage of the tool occurs because it does not meet the immediate needs of its users.

Results show the following as immediate needs for information: bug fixes; documentation (configuration, parameterization and installation tutorials, articles on the technologies used, manuals and videos of the systems' architecture, solutions and problems found by the institutions that use UFRN's Integrated Management Systems - SIG-UFRN); implementation; greater user involvement; news about the versions; events information; implementation per module; forum discussions; and improvement in access to the Portal. Moreover, the percentage of users accessing the tool through mobile apps draws attention to the development of a Cooperation Portal to serve this audience, mainly because they find it relevant to proactively receive information.

Finally, by knowing that much of the information wanted by partner users are also needed by other users such as licensed companies, university community and SINFO employees, we intend to reformulate the Cooperation Portal, incorporating this information to SINFO's webpage in an organized way in a wireframe, taking into account not only information priority, but also typography and colors so that the webpage can be more accessed and used.

References

1. PDI: Plano de Desenvolvimento Institucional (2010–2019). http://www.sistemas.ufrn.br/portal/PT/pdi/#.VeIOjXu7yf4
2. Plano de Gestão (2011–2015). http://www.sistemas.ufrn.br/portal/PT/plano_gestao/#.VeIPA3u7yf4
3. ISO 9241-11: Ergonomic requirements for office work with visual display terminals (VDTs), Part 11 — Guidelines for specifying and measuring usability. International Standards Organisation, Gènève (1997)
4. Nielsen, J., Loranger, H.: Usabilidade na web. Tradução Edson Furmankiewicz & Carlos Schafranski, Docware Traduções técnicas. Elsevier, Rio de Janeiro (2007)
5. Nielsen, J.: Usability Engineering. Academic Press, Boston (1993)
6. Rogers, Y., Sharp, H., Preece, J.: Design de interação [recurso eletrônico]: além da interação humano-computador. Tradução: Gasparini, Isabela; revisão técnica: Pimenta, Marcelo Soares. – 3. Ed. Dados eletrônicos. Bookman, Porto Alegre (2013)
7. Winckler, M., Pimenta, M.: A avaliação da Usabilidade de Sites Web. Escola de Informática da SBC SUL (ERI 2002) ed. Porto Alegre: Sociedade Brasileira de Computação (2002). http://www.irit.fr/~Marco.Winckler/2002-winckler-pimenta-ERI-2002-cap3.pdf
8. Santa Rosa, J.G., Moraes, A.: Design Participativo - técnicas para inclusão de usuários no processo de ergodesign de interfaces. Rio Book's, Rio de Janeiro (2012)

What Do Users Prefer: Concrete or Abstract User Interface?

Abbas Moallem[✉]

UX Experts LLC, Cupertino, CA, USA
Abbas@uxexperts.com

Abstract. In a previous study we reported that 71 % of the participants who created a UI for light control used a nonfigurative image of the object expressing an abstract meaning while 29 % used a concrete vision of a lighting fixture to illustrate the on and off functions. For the temperature control group, the breakdown was 52 % abstract and 48 % concrete.

In this follow-up study we first replicated an enhanced version of the previous study with 33 graduate students. Then we expanded the survey to the general population asking them to choose between the two options: Concrete and Abstract. The survey was administrated online and on paper to a population in Silicon Valley, California. The results show a 44 % preference for concrete designs versus 56 % for abstract designs. Thus, overall the abstract design preference was still higher. However, a slight difference was observed among older participants.

Keywords: UI design · Paradigms · UI designer · Mental image

1 Introduction

User interaction with computers is now a constant in our lives, an active part of our daily routines. We not only use computers to perform tasks but also use them to manipulate remote Internet access and control devices such as home security devices, camera surveillance, and temperature or light controls. All users, from young to old, count on user interface to work in their favor, helping them successfully complete their essential tasks. One issue that has been observed concerns the way in which interface design reflects how users want to view the devices they are remotely managing. In other words, what kind of mental image should the design trigger when a user views the user interface? The knowledge as to how this mental image matches the real concept of user interface is the key to creating a capable design.

A variety of researchers have investigated the mental image, imagery, perception, and effects on how we interact with our world [1]. To just mention a few sources for example, Norman suggests that people form internal representations or mental models of themselves and the objects with which they interact to create predictive and explanatory powers for understanding the interaction [2]. Gentner and Stevens support the concept that mental models are based on the way people understand a specific knowledge domain [3]. Johnson-Laird believes that mental models play a central and

© Springer International Publishing Switzerland 2016
A. Marcus (Ed.): DUXU 2016, Part II, LNCS 9747, pp. 618–624, 2016.
DOI: 10.1007/978-3-319-40355-7_59

unifying role in representing objects, states of affairs, sequences of events, the way the world is, and the social and psychological actions of daily life (397) [4].

Much research is focused on how the mental image differs among the designers and users. Overall, two mental models have been distinguished: a user's mental model, referring to what an end user believes about a system [5], and a designer's mental model, which refers to the conceptualization invented by a design [6]. Nielson believes that "what users believe they know about a UI strongly impacts how they use it. Mismatched mental models are common, especially with designs that try something new". Several studies tend to investigate, understand, and use mental representations to analyze design interfaces that are based on users' mental and propose frameworks [7].

Athavankar's study illustrates that designer create virtual models in their "mind's eye," then manipulate and alter them, and make them behave according to their wishes during the development of their ideas [8]. Waren reports that users develop a mental model of the new system that is analogous to the old one [9].

In a previous study [10] we tried to understand what user interface would be easier for users to manipulate or control through UI, whether an abstract or concrete representation would be better received. For example, to turn a light on and off, would it be easier to click on a representation of a lighting fixture, such as a light bulb, or simply check a box? Another example is temperature regulation. Would it be better to manipulate a virtual representation of thermometer or enter a set temperature? We have shown that 71 % of the participants who created a UI for light control had a more abstract approach, using a nonfigurative image of the object, 4 % had a semi-concrete approach (somehow visualizing the light), and only 25 % had a very concrete view of a lighting fixture to illustrate the on and off functions. For the temperature control group, the breakdown was 52 % abstract, 32 % semi-concrete and 16 % concrete.

In this follow-up study, two user studies were conducted. In the first, the previous study was replicated with 33 graduate students. In the second study, we expanded the survey to the general population asking them to choose between the two options: Concrete and Abstract.

2 Method

Two user studies were conducted. In the first study, the previous study was replicated with 33 graduate students. The participants were a mixture of human factors and software engineering students (13 males and 20 female). The students were mid-way through the course and already had acquired fundamental knowledge of HCI and user interface design. The exercise is given during the class time where 10 min were given to provide a 1-page paper prototype (low fidelity) of the design case. No other instruction beside what was written on the exercise description was given (Table 1). Upon collection of the prototypes they were classified into following categories: Virtual (Concrete), and Abstract (See Figs. 1 and 2). After conducting this experiment we then gave the same group two design options: Abstract and Concrete (Figs. 3 and 4) asking them to select the one they prefer. We wanted to see whether participants were consistent in preferring their own design type when offered the alternate option.

Table 1. Design exercise description

Design Exercise: A new service application offers people an online account where they are able to login and use a browser to view and remotely control one's home lighting and temperature. 6 Wi-Fi sensors are already installed on five lighting controls and one has been placed on the home temperature control device.

The requirements are:

• After logging in to the account through a browser (not needed for this exercise) the user should be able to see.

• Date and time

• 5 light switches and their status (i.e. on or off at the present time) with the ability to changed their statuses

• Home temperature at the present time with the ability to change the temperature

• Users: All home owners have different levels of computer knowledge

• Expectations: An extremely easy to use and robust system

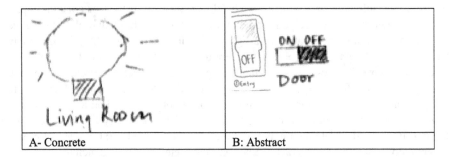

| A- Concrete | B: Abstract |

Fig. 1. Classification of the design categories for light control

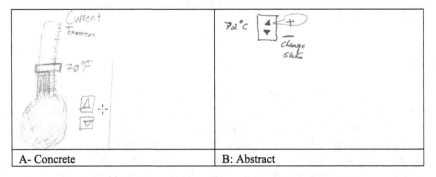

| A- Concrete | B: Abstract |

Fig. 2. Classification of the design categories for temperature control

For the second study we designed a survey that was administrated online and on paper to a population in Silicon Valley, California. The participants were asked to select their preference between two design options: Abstract and Concrete (Figs. 3 and 4). 130 people took this survey. The demographics were 48 % (58) female and 52 %

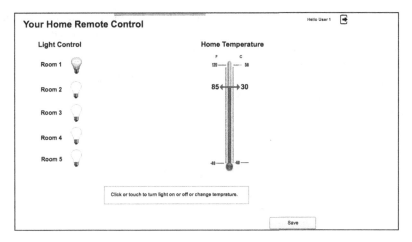

Fig. 3. Concrete design option

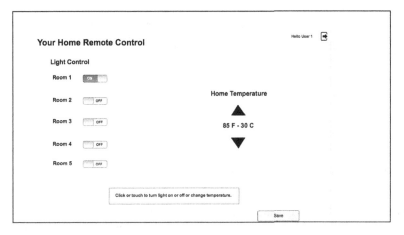

Fig. 4. Abstract design option

(63) male. The age range of the participants was as follows: 44 % 18 to 25 years old, 22 % 25 to 35 years old, 7 % 36 to 45 years old, 11 % 46 to 55 years old, 14 % 56 to 65 years old, and 2 % over 65 years old. The level of education was 6 % high school, 63 % college, and 31 % graduate school.

3 Results

The results on the replication of the first experiment were consistent with the previous study [10]. 73 % of the participants' designs were classified as abstract (compared to 71 % in the previous study) and 27 % concrete (29 % in the previous study). When the participants were asked to choose between abstract and concrete designs, 42 %

preferred concrete designs versus the 58 % who chose abstract design. This illustrates that some participants preferred the concrete option when offered the two design options, despite the fact that their own design was considered to be abstract.

The results of the second survey asking general population preference between the two design options (Figs. 3 and 4) are shown in Charts 1, 2 and 3. The results show that 56 % of participants preferred an abstract design while 44 % preferred a concrete design (Chart 1).

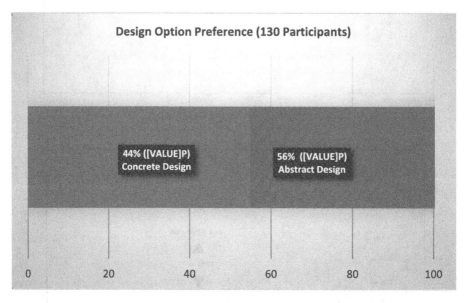

Chart 1. Preference of the general population between abstract and concrete design options

We also tried to understand if the preference might change across gender and age groups. Chart 2 shows the design preference based on gender. 53 % of female participants prefer the abstract design compared to 59 % of the male participants (Chart 2).

47 % of female participants and 41 % of male participants prefer the concrete design (Chart 2). This illustrates that overall, female participants are more likely than men to prefer concrete designs.

The design preferences differ when we analyze the data based on age groups. Interestingly, the design preference for concrete design rises in correlation with participant age. The preference for concrete design among the 18–25 year age group is 38 %, while it is 29 % for ages 25 to 36, and 60 % for those over 36 years (Chart 3).

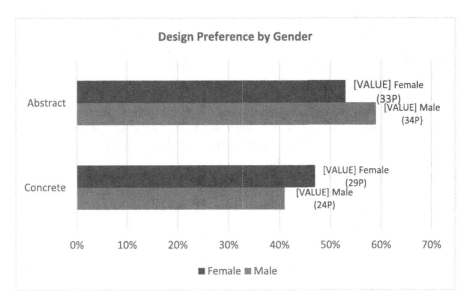

Chart 2. Design preference by gender (Color figure online)

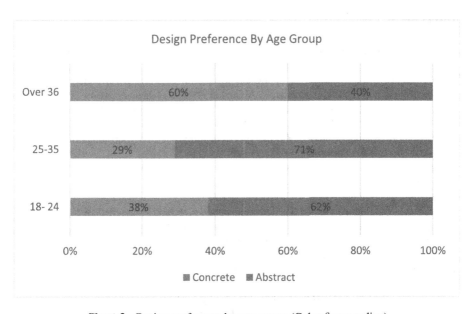

Chart 3. Design preference by age group (Color figure online)

4 Discussion

The results of this study suggest the preference among the general population (male and female participants of all age groups) is for abstract UI design (59 % versus 47 %). However, female participants tend to prefer concrete design more than male participants (47 % female versus 41 % of the male participants).

The preference for concrete designs seems to rise with age, as older adult prefer the concrete design.

It is hard to draw more general conclusions due to the limited sample size, the fact that the participants were choosing the design on static page (screens shots) and a real application web application. Having said this, the study does seem to show a trend. For example, should one extrapolate Piaget's theory of stages of intelligence: sensorimotor, preoperational, concrete operational and formal operational to this finding one might think that the accessibility of the concrete object might be more attainable to older adults who are utilizing more concrete thinking [11]. Again, the data set is too limited to expand in that direction.

Further studies should investigate children of younger ages and older adults to see if the results would support the results of this study.

This result would be applicable when designing user interfaces for and applications that target older adults.

Acknowledgements. Thank you to all of my students who took part in this exercise.

References

1. Gerrit, C., et al.: Mental model. In: Jacko, J., Sears, A. (eds.) The Human Computer Interaction Handbook, pp. 52–80. Lawrence Erlbaum Associate Publisher, Mahwah (2003)
2. Norman, D.: Some observation on mental model. In: Gentner, D., Stevens, A.L. (eds.) Psychology, p. 352. Taylor & Francis, Abingdon (1983). 14 January 2014
3. Johnson-Laird, P.N.: Mental models. Harvard University, Cambridge (1983)
4. Gentner, D., Stevens, A.L.: Psychology Press, p. 352 (1983). 14 January 2014
5. Nielson, J.: Mental Models, 18 October 2010. http://www.nngroup.com/articles/mental-models. Accessed 2 Feb 2015
6. Staggers, A., Norcio, A.F.: Mental models: concepts for human-computer interaction research. Int. J. Man Mach. Stud. **38**(4), 587–605 (1993)
7. http://userpages.umbc.edu/∼norcio/papers/1993/Staggers-MM-IJMMS.pdf
8. Qian, X., Yang, Y., Gong, Y.: The art of metaphor: a method for interface design based on mental models. In: VRCAI 2011: Proceedings of the 10th International Conference on Virtual Reality Continuum and Its Applications in Industry (2011)
9. Athavankar, U.A.: Mental imagery as design tool. Int. J. Cybern. Syst. **28**(1), 25–42 (1997)
10. Waren, Y.: Cognitive Aspect of Computer Supported Tasks. Wiley, New York (1989)
11. Moallem, A.: Concrete or abstract user interface? In: Kurosu, M. (ed.) Human-Computer Interaction. LNCS, vol. 9169, pp. 390–395. Springer, Heidelberg (2015)
12. Piaget, J.: Origins of Intelligence in the Child. Routledge & Kegan Paul, London (1936)

Printed Matter as an Interactive System

Marco Neves[1,2(✉)]

[1] CIAUD – Research Center for Architecture, Urban Planning and Design,
Faculty of Architecture, University of Lisbon, Rua Sá Nogueira,
Pólo Universitário, Alto da Ajuda, 1349-055 Lisbon, Portugal
mneves@fa.ulisboa.pt
[2] CITAD – Research Center in Territory, Architecture and Design,
Lusiada University, R. da Junqueira 188-198, 1349-001 Lisbon, Portugal

Abstract. An interactive system is usually considered to be a computer process based on a group of possible interactions between computer and humans. Whenever interaction is discussed, only digital artifacts are mentioned. This is largely due to the fact that they are inherently interactive.

Unlike their digital counterpart, most print material is not considered interactive, but something static and two-dimensional. There has been no research about a relation between the conception of printed materials for various purposes with the feature of interaction.

Through a case study method in digital artifacts, we reach a list of interaction categories to compare with print production, crossing ways in which we may examine the creation of interaction.

As a consequence of this connection, we must be able to define the means by which we can understand, or try to produce interaction in printed matter.

Keywords: Interaction · Printed matter · Digital · Graphic design

1 Introduction

Interaction is not exclusive of digital systems, if we regard studying it as a concept. Digital artifacts are built in a way where both software and hardware are prepared from the start to allow action-reaction. But the majority of them are actually based on a physical use that precedes the digital universe. What we use today within any digital electronic device is mostly a replication of our material, concrete tasks into a virtual setting. However, it is undisputed that the environment produced by digital artifacts became a very specific experience, yielding phenomena which otherwise would not be possible.

Nevertheless, this capacity has not been adequately explored in the opposite direction. By having served as the basis for the digital development, printed matter has been influenced only sparingly by the involvement with the binary system. The study of interaction in printed matter can bring a purpose not yet obtained, which is the understanding of behavior within this technology and related areas, namely graphic design.

© Springer International Publishing Switzerland 2016
A. Marcus (Ed.): DUXU 2016, Part II, LNCS 9747, pp. 625–637, 2016.
DOI: 10.1007/978-3-319-40355-7_60

In this sense, we may retrieve information from digital artifacts and their interactive possibilities to compare with printed matter, in order to understand how can print be considered an interactive system and in which way can it be conceived in accordance.

We follow a qualitative methodology for exploration and description, comprising a case study method based on a review of the main literature and on participant observation. This allowed us to perform a multiple cases group for digital artifacts. The observation of elements and actions that shape interaction in graphic systems arising from digital artifacts, allows us to generate a framework of results. Some of these artifacts are the GUI (Graphical User Interface) for operating systems in personal computers, the influence of hypertext on the Web or the development of online applications. All of them allow various interactive options and also user participation. They can be compared to objects, whose production technology is print and that carry with them a strong visual tradition used in graphic design.

Printed matter already has a strong visual organization and hierarchy. What is missing in a lot of production is the ability to reach their users in an interactive way, and to enable a set of solutions that make printed matter innovative. Thus, the existing graphic organization and materialization can be considered the working basis, where we may conceive an interactive system.

2 Static and Dynamic Systems

Objects that undergo a printing process are often referred to as just 'prints'. They are mostly the work result that graphic designers carry out and are based on a large tradition of graphic arts and printing techniques. They are nonetheless, objects in their own right that we can use through their material presence. Still, they have not been conceived in a way to include an interactive concern and the straightforward understanding of these objects leaves to visual creation the responsibility to distinguish them [1–3], focusing on visual elements, mainly pictures, typography, shapes and colors [4–7]. This, somehow narrow perspective, inhibits an analysis of the material relationship printed matter has with any user. Graphic designers, who develop most of printed materials, do not usually consider any disruption in most outcomes [8]. But there are still space and time factors not well thought-out and consequently, no way to improve them. This seems a neglected aspect, since printed matter is tactile and requires a certain amount of time to be useful.

To discuss whether or not printed matter can be an interactive system, we should first understand the concept of interaction and what sort of interactive characteristics would be considered.

Bonsiepe [9] argues that interaction is something present in every design activity, in order to connect the user and an artefact, thus forming the context for user participation [10, 11]. But Heeter [12] does not consider the newspaper, for instance, as interactive, since its audience is passive. Both Davis [13] and Buchanan [14] envision an understanding of interaction in many design projects and Tapia [15] even relates some printed materials with hypertext organization, but there is no study or sufficient information about the notion of interaction when considering print. Dubberly et al. [16]

take it even further, claiming a difference must be made between interaction and reaction, placing an opposition between static and dynamic systems.

If printed matter is static and non-interactive, is there ways to create, interfere or modify it, in order to pursue an interactive existence? We can seek to explore a relation between printed matter and the establishment of an interactive capacity. However, this relation implies a different approach to printed matter. No longer based on the exclusive graphic assessment of the object in hand, since design will no longer be about creating the object, but rather conceiving an encounter [17]. The attention should be transferred from the relationship between graphic elements to the relationship that the design may have with people who use those objects [18], or a shift may occur, from designing artifacts to experiences [19].

Digital media provide a rich source for the observation of these features, [20–22], since interaction is immediately implied in them [10, 22]. Also Stolterman [23] suggests improving research in HCI in order to contribute to design related areas. The user is understood as a central point in planning actions and functions and his presence in front of graphic interfaces dictates the real meaning of a digital artifact.

This paper discusses the ways in which we can envision an interactive approach for objects that use print technologies for their production. This interpretation is enabled by two specific and complementary situations. First we draw an understanding of interaction as a context, rather than an end by itself, linked with the need for user participation. Second, we studied some of the ways in which digital technologies have been producing interaction, in order to know their suitability for printed matter.

3 Interaction and User Participation

Different perspectives on interaction exist, depending on the field of study. Designers tend to consider interaction as a part of the relation artifacts establish with people; while in human-computer interaction is regarded as a feedback based process.

Interaction design brought something not considered by other design practices, the focuses on behavior [19]. This area can be explained as a process of giving the user control over the machine [20]. Although being mainly dedicated to computer systems, interaction design became aware of how to interpret its users [24].

When using an object or a system, we fulfill a number of steps that determine a certain experience. We make objects function through several requests and they serve us through their form, material and behavior. We interact with them and we do so through a continuing exchange of messages or actions. It is something that happens in time and is not related to visual composition [25]. We may consider interaction, not as exclusive or prevalent in a specific area of expertise, but rather as a context that can be enabled in several situations [26, 27].

The purpose of interaction however, is for the user to become somehow content generator [11]. This allows for the inclusion of the user in the final stages of object development. But it can also refer, in same cases, to a participation of the user in modifying or handling the object. An experience supposes a participation of someone in a certain time and space [10]. Being that interaction is positioned in time and in the ability to make a narrative construction in the relation our body has with the surrounding environment, then it is interaction that allows in fact such participation.

Technologies, in their own way, allow a mediated interaction, which can be understood as a designed experience [24], where a person is participant through the affordances present in a system. Some technologies, as digital ones make full advantage of the possibilities of interaction and consequently make us aware of the experiences they provide. Others, like printing technologies, originate from a time where interaction was not an issue and perhaps not considered.

4 Print as Devoid of Interaction

The invention of the printing press with movable types defined printed matter ever since. The printing press, which marked an important technology transition, dictated a status of reproduced product. From this point, printed material would be repeatable and equal in every copy [28].

It also influenced a shift from the use of multiple senses to a preponderance of vision. This predominance is reflected nowadays in the importance that graphic designers establish in developing their projects and consequently, in assuming what makes their business relevant. It is essentially a creation for the eye. As a result, there is little study of a three dimensional, time-driven set of actions to engage a user in what we can call, an experience.

Objects such as books, magazines, newspapers, letterheads, posters, signage, are a traditional printed accomplishment, conceived with procedures that are based on a long track record of examples and that take for granted a certain production and distribution to people. They fulfill several functions individually and yet have so much in common. They all have a potential to enhance the level of interaction, so any user can be a physical part of discovering information and increasing the emotional attachment to the object in hand. Of course print technology must rely on graphic elements to convey messages and to make them distinct. But their qualities and effects do not end here.

If printed matter that arises from the practice of graphic design has a concern for formal organization [2, 3] but disregards interaction; digital artifacts are becoming increasingly personal and well prepared not just to be viewed or received.

5 Digital Interaction

What can best define a digital artifact is to be available to the demands of users, to execute a request and send the response to that request. The electronic encoding for all information allows that all graphic elements in a system can be connected [14]. This experience is improved almost from the start by offering user choices instead of an imposed order.

We can observe this in personal computers operating systems. They have a rich set of interactive features, added along their history with a strong visual composition, that allow the use of the personal computer through the desktop, by means of manipulation of graphics. They do however present an imposed limitation, which are the computer resources where it works.

In a different way, the Web enables movement. Browsing implies going from screen to screen, with connections between them. This happens with Web 2.0 and its expansion of interactive possibilities, as well as user participation in Internet. Digital cases such as blogs and social networks change the perception and the need for interaction. From a common thing they become a requirement. This ability that users now have to save, create and spread information, translates a strong presence of interaction, made possible by a broad set of characteristics, such as search within digital artifacts; to create and update content in different formats; or to categorize information [29].

As printed matter and consequently graphic design can become more interactive, we are able to use these digital media cases to know how can we include interaction in print media and in what way.

6 Case Study

In order to reach a relevant knowledge of interaction features, a case study method was developed to analyze three digital artifacts. These cases provide a group of common categories of interaction. These categories may be the simplest and basic when considering their presence in digital media, but may be of relevance in the use of printed matter in a near future. The choice of cases was done to be representative of important ways to produce interaction and to indicate a transverse characterization of it [20, 29, 30]. So by comparing different cases we can summarize close ideas employed in a significant number of digital artifacts.

The main reason of using the case study method is to realize how digital artifacts are made available to users, allowing alternating messages, constant action and reaction and how they permit the generation of content by any user. This method aims to understand and interpret and it is based on the collection and comparing of relevant information, especially the one retrieved from observation as user.

The method was structured from Yin [31], supported by Tellis [32] and Baxter and Jack [33] and adapted to the specific needs of this study. As a principle of quality, each individual case is presented by a description and an explanation, synthesized from an examination on a diverse set of sources.

The information processing of each case and its transposition for a comparative conclusion of all the cases is based on the notions of grounded theory as described by Strauss and Corbin [34] and explained by Gibbs [35]. Thus, codes are given to groups of information collected in each case, which aggregate in common concepts and produce categories. The encoding process relies on identifying collected excerpts, accompanied by their designations and descriptions. Then, relationships are formed between the various codes, looking for similarities that help to explain certain experience. Finally, we try to explain what develops around these created categories.

6.1   Case 1 – Operating System

For the first case we regard Mac OS X, an operating system of Apple®. As an operating system it is based, like others, in the desktop metaphor, presenting the elements that suit this notion.

The first action in which it was possible to verify interaction is a routine in several computer media and executable via a pointing device, commonly the mouse. The operation we call 'point and click' allows tasks with a click, double click, select and drag or drop movements. It became trivial, but it is profoundly effective. Such as 'drag and drop', that allows any element, once selected, to be placed in a different location.

The system includes different types of menus that provide access to information. They display lists of items that the user can select without having to memorize the information contained therein. One of the most important is a set of pull down menus on top of the screen in the system's desktop. By pressing them we are offered commands and tasks options. After pointing and selecting an item it becomes highlighted and an action will occur after pressing the mouse.

A different menu, called Dock, is located at the bottom or at the side of the screen and consists of icons that act as shortcuts to open files, folders or applications. Each user can compose the Dock with the icons he wants. The row of icons will be adjustable to the amount of elements in it, to stay within the limits of the screen. By going through this menu with the cursor, each icon is enlarged.

Some of the most used elements are windows, as a resource for the presentation and organization of documents, applications and panels. There are several types of windows, which are distinguished by appearance and behavior. Windows have a title bar, important to move the window and a button to close it. They may also have buttons to minimize and expand, a scrollbar and a control to resize it. Main windows in Mac OS X are usually accompanied by source lists or sidebars, which are lateral and separate areas that indicate and enable browsing. The selection of an element in on of these sidebars, displays the information contained in it, in the larger area of the window.

The idea of revealing what is contained in a given element was expanded to the concept of 'quick look'. In the desktop the user can select a file and press the spacebar on the keyboard and see the contents of that file. This is possible without having to open any application to do so.

The ease in controlling the work and tasks is also allowed by the use of the keyboard, in which almost all keys have assigned roles. In terms of interaction, this feature is not significant, with the exceptions of F9, F10 and F11 function keys, which the company refers to as Exposé. When you press each key, the screen rearranges to show all windows in use on the computer, all windows within an application, or to hide all windows in the sides of the screen, respectively.

From the gathered information, it is possible to identify and bring together a group of actions and elements that introduce interaction. Table 1 presents each by its name, with a description of the provided interaction and user participation.

Table 1. Actions and elements of interaction in Mac OS X

ID	Designation	Description	
		Interaction	User participation
Ma01	Point and click	Using a pointing device to select, open and work with the content	Defining the following arrangement of elements
Ma02	Drag and drop	Moving elements in the workspace	Defining the following arrangement of elements
Ma03	Visualization (Quick Look)	Select file, press the spacebar on the keyboard and a translucent window opens	Decision on how to access the files, even ones with multiple pages. Use of mouse and keyboard The window can be resized
Ma04	Visualization (Exposé)	Using the F9, F10 and F11 keys gives it a new arrangement of the workspace	Decision on how to access content. Use of mouse or keyboard
Me01	Horizontal menu	Browsing (search, presentation and selection of information)	Horizontal search movement
Me02	Pull down menu	Pressing the horizontal bar at the top of the screen, a list of commands and tasks is presented	The user sees and points without having to memorize the information contained therein
Me03	Dock	Magnifies icons by sliding the cursor	Horizontal or vertical movement between the icons
Me04	Windows	Unfolding of the content. When you open a folder, you have access to the information inside	Control of the size and location with the mouse
Me05	Source Lists and Sidebars	Separate areas in the windows that allow browsing	Selection of information accompanied by a scrollbar

6.2   Case 2 – Website

The chosen case to present a website example was the BBC's® homepage, available between 2008 and 2010. It was first launched as a beta version in 2007 and later replaced by a new one in 2011. The interesting aspect of this homepage was to be based on a module system, similar to widgets that allowed a high level of customization. Each module contained information about certain subject areas and each user could choose and compose the group that would form the homepage. The analysis was done only on this homepage and on the various elements that improve interaction.

The layout of the homepage demonstrated a dominance of horizontal browsing for the key information, compiled into a horizontal menu. A smaller, secondary menu named 'More' was placed to the right of the screen, completing the information not present in the main menu.

The most important visual element was the group of modules, which could be changed to different arrangements. Each user could change, through drag and drop, the position of a given module. The similarity with typical elements of an operating system and non-standard in the Web continued with attributes, such as a cross to close the module on the right side and an arrow to minimize it on the left. In each of these modules, information was customizable by choosing the 'Edit' option that allowed adding or removing information topics.

Customization was enlarged by the presence of a panel through which the user could modify the information modules, in number and order. The user could also pick the color for the homepage. After performing these individual choices, changes should be saved and then the 'reset homepage' option should be pressed. Table 2 presents the main actions and elements present in this homepage.

Table 2. Actions and elements of interaction in BBC's homepage

ID	Designation	Description	
		Interaction	User participation
Ba01	Point and click	Using a pointing device to access content	Defining the next screen display
Ba02	Drag and drop (Module)	To move modules to another location on the homepage	Movement with the pointing device
Be01	Hyperlink	Possibility communicated through rollover and change in the cursor shape	The choice of certain titles and photographs establishes an access to new information
Be02	Horizontal menu	Browsing (search, presentation and selection of information)	Allows access to several websites
Be03	"More" menu	By pressing the horizontal bar at the top of the screen, a larger list of access options is presented	The user sees and points without having to memorize the information contained therein
Be04	Edit (module)	Selecting different content, they become visible in the respective modules	Selection through checkbox. Selected options need to be saved in order to be seen
Be05	Customization panel	Selection of various options, content and formatting style, that become visible	Checkbox selection of each module that will form the homepage. The same action for color choice

6.3   Case 3 – Social Network

The chosen case was Twitter's® profile page. This case was chosen because it is an example of Web 2.0. The analysis was developed on what came to be called 'New Twitter', available online through a website, between 2010 and 2011.

The interface had a structure defined by three areas: a horizontal menu at the top; below this, the screen was divided by a vertical timeline and an area for various information such as the list of users that follow us, users that we follow, most discussed topics and more links related to the service.

Both the horizontal menu and the timeline were permanent, while the area on the right could be filled with other information, such as for visualizing a selected message. Each message (tweet) was possible to be pressed and if so, on the right side, it would appear with additional aggregate information, such as the profile data of the author or recent tweets.

All users could customize some visual elements that would make up their interface and communicate to others their profile. The color code, as well as the background could be controlled and depending on these options, profiles would be presented in very different ways.

Despite the limited number of available characters, terms were created to fit some needs. For instance, placing '@username' in a tweet, automatically generates a hyperlink to another user profile. Another example is the hashtag, words preceded by the symbol '#' that have become markers of concepts. The hashtag phenomenon represents a strong way for users to participate. They have identified a need, came up with a solution and the company incorporated it.

Table 3 lists and summarizes the main actions and elements that enhance inter-action in this case.

Table 3. Actions and elements of interaction in Twitter's profile page

ID	Designation	Description	
		Interaction	User participation
Ta01	Text insertion (tweet)	Writing a message in the field below the question "What's happening?"	Production of content through individual writing
Ta02	@username	Automatically converted into a link to the user's profile	The user must type the name directly in the tweet
Ta03	Hashtag	Creates searchable categories	Placing the "#" sign before an expression
Te01	Hyperlink	Possibility communicated through rollover and colour change	The choice of certain headings and photographs establishes an access to new information
Te02	Horizontal menu	Browsing (search, presentation and selection of information)	Allows access to various contents of our account and is always present
Te03	Follow	Enables us to receive messages from a chosen origin in a timeline	Selection of other users
Te04	Profile	Through selection, various options of content and formatting style become visible	Possible customization of colours and images

6.4   Case Study Results

One of the difficulties involved in comparing the various cases was to group the interaction factors around its characteristics, since these, although sometimes similar, are present with different names in each case.

The three tables of codes and descriptions were then reviewed. Similar descriptions in different cases were matched and their ID codes put together to form a single category. This has resulted in Table 4 of interactive categories. Each one of these comprises the descriptions that came from different actions and elements of the studied cases and are now defined by a set of properties.

Table 4. Interactive categories from the case study

Categories	ID's	Properties
Point and click	Ma01 Ba0 Te03	- Use of a pointing device - Organization of the following information - Access to information desired by the user, through its request
Drag and drop	Ma02 Ba02	- Moving and reorganizing elements
Visualization	Ma03, 04	- Modify the way of observing an element or information - Details on the elements
Browsing	Me01, 03, 05 Be02 Te02	- Horizontal disposition of accesses - Presentation and selection of information
Pull down menu	Me02, 04 Be03	- Unfolding options: the user runs through information without having to memorize it - The desired item, differs visually from the other - Manage the amount of information
Hyperlink	Be01 Ta02, 03 Te01	- Access to different information - The concept of hypertext, although expanded to other elements - Differentiation of the visual element that will allow access
Customization	Be04, 05 Te04	- Availability of a set of options for content and/or visual formatting - Modification of the visual aspect by the user

This table confirms the existence of common characteristics among the various cases. Some notions of interaction seem to be common in all, although different actions unfold. But it is always a user decision, to reorganize information and advance to fulfill a certain task.

The horizontal browsing menu seems to be the preferred solution to make available a set of several accesses to extend the experience, promoting a space saver.

Elements arranged in the GUI have both spatial and time concerns. Several areas of the screen appear and disappear, depending on the needs to increase information view and consequently, more browsing possibilities. But they also show an anticipation of desirable functions to perform, giving all the options and sometimes, transforming elements in order to execute actions.

Also helpful is the amount of entries related to the unfolding of options when hidden at first. The pull down menu is perhaps the most notable one. By accessing a visual element, it extends to various directions, showing several options to accomplish tasks or to access new information.

Most situations show the course of a task from an initial request. This demonstrates the preparation of the artifact to execute. But we can also note that interaction is not only due to existing elements in the system or interface, but also and especially due to activities, which require user participation.

7   Conclusion

Considering printed matter as an interactive system may benefit print technology and graphic design. While product and interaction design are almost combined from the very beginning, the large production of printed matter has been keen on deploying such an interactive approach. Their nature and technologies have origins in many past habits that do not seem to encompass concerns we have in present days. And yet, the everyday purpose of most printed matter is still to reach its users.

Digital artifacts deviate from a purely visual concern, unlike printed matter. Never denying the importance of visual elements, digital artifacts are more concerned with time of action and behavior. We can observe it in the studied cases and in the list of interactive categories hat we present, which function as principles for inclusion in graphic design.

The main condition of interaction seems to be the availability for use and therefore, interaction requires the proximity of a person. Printed matter should become a material result able to respond, to transform the information contained in it and its configuration in order to reach and relate to people.

To carry out this transformation, printed matter may adopt the mentioned categories. Not in the sense of a graphic transposition, but a behavioral one. Printed matter can then be an interactive system if it allows users to reorganize information and move elements of the layout; if it takes advantages of folding and unfolding schemes to communicate and most of all, if it conceives time and space for user to became a participant in completing the experience.

These interactive categories are instrumental in pursuing the research intention, but they are however still basic. The results derive from a set of cases that are representative, but the digital realm is increasing everyday. We can expect to further develop the study in other digital media, especially in mobile devices and probably obtain more specific results. They also need to be tested in a print media model, with its own properties.

We have generated an initial source for the development of print interactive-based solutions by studying digital media in some detail. From this point it seems possible to develop print media, in different dimensions, formats or materials and to improve its material connection to its users.

Acknowledgements. The author would like to thank the funding support by the Foundation for Science and Technology of the Ministry of Science, Technology and Higher Education of Portugal under the projects UID/EAT/04008/2013 (CIAUD) and UID/AUR/04026/2013 (CITAD).

References

1. Meggs, P.: A History of Graphic Design. Wiley, New York (1998)
2. Hollis, R.: Graphic Design: A Concise History. Thames and Hudson, London (1997)
3. Heller, S.: Design Literacy: Understanding Graphic Design. Allworth Press, New York (2004)
4. Müller-Brockmann, J.: Grid Systems in Graphic Design. Niggli Verlag, Switzerland (2012)
5. Haslam, A.: Book Design. Laurence King Publishing, London (2006)
6. Tschichold, J.: The New Typography. University of California Press, Berkeley (1998)
7. Spiekermann, E., Ginger, E.M.: Stop Stealing Sheep and Find Out How Type Works. Adobe Press, Berkley (2003)
8. Ambrose, G., Harris, P.: The Fundamentals of Graphic Design. AVA Publishing, Lausanne (2009)
9. Bonsiepe, G.: Interface: An Approach to Design. Jan van Eyck Akademie, Maastricht (1999)
10. Heeter, C.: Interactivity in the context of designed experiences. J. Interact. Advertising **1**(1) (2000). http://jiad.org/article2. Accessed 5 May 2010
11. Richards, R.: Users, interactivity and generation. New Media Soc. **8**(4), 531–550 (2005)
12. Davis, M.: Toto, I've got a feeling we're not in Kansas anymore.... Interactions **XV**(5), 28–34 (2008)
13. Buchanan, R.: Design research and the new learning. Des. Issues **17**(4), 3–23 (2001)
14. Tapia, A.: Graphic design in the digital era: the rhetoric of hypertext. Des. Issues **19**(1), 5–24 (2003)
15. Dubberly, H., Haque, U., Pangaro, P.: What is interaction? Are there different types? (2009). http://www.dubberly.com/articles/what-is-interaction.html Accessed 18 July 2012
16. Julier, G.: From visual culture to design culture. Des. Issues **22**(1), 64–76 (2006)
17. Frascara, J.: Graphic design: fine art or social science? In: Margolin, V., Buchanan, R. (eds.) The Idea of Design, A Design Issues Reader, pp. 44–55. MIT Press, Cambridge (1995)
18. Davis, M.: Why do we need doctoral study in design? Int. J. Des. **2**(3), 71–79 (2008)
19. Cooper, A., Reimann, R., Cronin, D.: About face 3: The Essentials of Interaction Design. Wiley Publishing, Indianapolis (2007)
20. Moggridge, B.: Designing Interactions. The MIT Press, Cambridge (2007)
21. Saffer, D.: Designing for Interaction: Creating Smart Applications and Clever Devices. New Riders, Berkeley (2007)
22. Manovich, L.: The Language of New Media. MIT Press, Cambridge (2001)
23. Stolterman, E.: The nature of design practice and implications for interaction design research. Int. J. Des. **2**(1), 55–65 (2008)
24. Bolter, J., Gromala, D.: Text rain: the digital experience. In: Windows and Mirrors: Interaction Design, Digital Art, and the Myth of Transparency, pp. 8–28. MIT Press, Cambridge (2008)
25. Neves, M.: Printed interactivity: towards a new understanding of graphic design. Iridescent: Icograda. J. Des. Res. **2**(2), 22–37 (2013)
26. Rafaeli, S.: Interactivity: from new media to communication. In: Advancing Communication Science: Merging Mass and Interpersonal Processes, pp. 110–134. Sage, London (1988)

27. Hallnäs, L.: On the foundations of interaction design aesthetics: revisiting the notions of form and expression. Int. J. Des. **5**(1), 73–84 (2011)
28. McLuhan, M.: The Gutenberg Galaxy: The Making of Typographic Man. University of Toronto Press, Canada (1962)
29. O'Reilly, T.: What is web 2.0: design patterns and business models for the next generation of software. http://oreilly.com/web2/archive/what-is-web-20.html. Accessed 21 Oct 2010
30. Mugge, R., Schifferstein, H., Schoormans, J.: Personalizing product appearance: the effect on product attachment. In: Kurtgözü, A. (ed.) Proceedings of the Fourth International Conference on Design and Emotion. Ankara (2004)
31. Yin, R.: Case Study Research: Design and Methods. Sage Publications, Thousand Oaks (1994)
32. Tellis, W.: Introduction to case study. The qualitative report 3(2) (1997). http://www.nova.edu/ssss/QR/QR3-2/tellis1.html. Accessed 9 July 2010
33. Baxter, P., Jack, S.: Qualitative case study methodology: study design and implementation for novice researchers. The qualitative report, vol. 13, no. 4, pp. 544–559 (2008). http://www.nova.edu/ssss/QR/QR13-4/baxter.pdf. Accessed 22 Mar 2010
34. Strauss, A., Corbin, J.: Basics of Qualitative Research: Techniques and Procedures For Developing Grounded Theory. Sage Publications, Thousand Oaks (1998)
35. Gibbs, G.: Grounded theory. University of Huddersfield. http://www.youtube.com/watch?v=Dfd_U-24egg&feature=related. Accessed 6 Aug 2011

How Do the User Experiences of Everyday Content Differ from Those of Academic Content?

Emine Sendurur[✉]

Department of Computer Education and Instructional Technologies,
Ondokuz Mayıs University, Samsun, Turkey
eminesendurur@gmail.com

Abstract. This study aims to compare the user experiences in a web search context. Within the scope of the study, 15 voluntary students participated in the sessions in a fully equipped human-computer interaction laboratory. Two different tasks were assigned, which varied in the context: everyday vs. academic. There was no time limitation to complete the tasks. All sessions were recorded by Tobii software, which allowed recording eye movements. Collected data were analyzed both quantitatively and qualitatively. Findings suggest that searching for everyday content can be less complicated than that for academic content. Participants shared some common beliefs for the everyday content. They trusted a website including real travelers' reviews, and do not need to visit any other website, but for academic task, they first judged the seriousness of the website. They did not prefer to visit blogs, wikis, or news web sites while they were looking for academic information.

Keywords: Web search · Search engines · Academic search · Travel search

1 Introduction

The World Wide Web provides people with various sources of information, but one might get lost easily within enormous resources. It is not always easy to find the exact information at once, in a short duration, with one keyword, or by typing an exact URL. Web search engines are the tools helping us to eliminate the unrelated information within the vast majority of candidate resources. That is why; people utilize them as the primary search strategy (Hsieh-Yee 1998). The earliest search engine named Archie was very limited with regards to the resources it offered (Koster 1994). From Archie to Google, many features have changed. The former were listing the resources in an index-like fashion, but the contemporary search engines have much more space to access and list the detailed information of the found resources. Compared to the earlier examples, today, the users have much more freedom to customize the queries, including image search. Nonetheless, general-purpose search engines may not be useful all the time for all types of users. As a result of certain safety concerns, the safer search engines emerged for kids in time. Yahooligans, KidRex, Gogoligans, etc. are some examples to this kind. In addition, such search engines as scholar.google are also

© Springer International Publishing Switzerland 2016
A. Marcus (Ed.): DUXU 2016, Part II, LNCS 9747, pp. 638–646, 2016.
DOI: 10.1007/978-3-319-40355-7_61

available for more specific audiences. Those efforts can be considered as important initiatives to manage the related resources more easily.

Although the range of Internet users is very expansive, the university students constitute the major part of the search engine users since they use those for their projects, especially at the beginning of the process (Biddix et al. 2011; Colon-Aguirre and Fleming-May 2012; Hsieh-Yee 1998). This may be due to the fact that accessing electronic resources is more convenient than accessing printed ones. Utilizing a search engine can bring about timesaving with less effort. The user may hope to find the exact information within one click after typing the keyword, but this is not generally the case. Depending on the searched information, the clicks can be more than one, whereas, some information can be found on search engine results page (SERP) without any clicks, i.e. just scanning or reading the title or explanation listed on SERP. Today, one more challenge has been added to web search process, which is the fact that the browsers allowing working with multi-tabs can make the process more sophisticated. The user needs to manage both SERP and the content opened in different tabs.

The type of a search task can shape the search patterns of users. While a close-ended (or ready-to use) task is considered as easy to search, an open-ended task is the exact opposite (Sendurur and Yildirim 2015; White and Iivonen 2002). According to Hogan et al. (2011), Google as a search engine is not appropriate for complex tasks because these tasks require collection of various resources with heterogeneous interfaces. A close-ended task can be readily found with simple queries, however, open-ended tasks demand customized search, more than one query sessions, or the comprehension of visited sites' contents, which may in turn result in the keyword changes. Although general-purpose search engines provide advance search features, users generally do not prefer to use them (Moukdad and Large 2001). In addition, including customization within the web search process does not always guarantee reaching at the target content. In short, the user experience with search engines have multiple facets including pre-search decisions, interaction with the interface, examination of SERP, locating the related pages or information, and so on.

Initial interfaces of search engines seem very simple. For example, Google's search engine has a quite simple design, which is exemplary in terms of white space usage. The user only needs to type a keyword, but the complexity of the search process begins before deciding on the appropriate keywords, therefore, the user experience during a web search can be somewhat sophisticated. For some users, SERP can turn into a maze. In terms of cognition, searching the web is much more beyond just typing a keyword. According to Wu et al. (2008), a search process includes certain cognitive stages: "recalling and inputting a query, navigating the query results, understanding the query results, judging the relevance of the results, learning the new information contained in the results, and refining the query if necessary" (p. 1831). If the task is complicated, then these stages can become harder to accomplish in a smooth fashion.

People use search engines to explore many things. As well as academic purposes, people also frequently use them for everyday issues, such as health problems, news, addresses, etc. One of the significant examples for daily use may be the case of travellers, who generally search the web for various purposes such as planning where to stay (Xiang and Gretzel 2010). There are many popular web sites containing real travelers' comments, pictures, ratings, and so on. When one includes such keywords as

"X city hotels" or "X city attractions", the top ten on the SERP list will probably include such web sites. For a traveler, planning stage is considerably complex if she/he has never previously been to the city/country. A user might not want to feel over-whelmed while experiencing the web search, content of which is already challenging, so she/he might expect the interface and the overall context to let the search flow. On the other hand, while searching for an academic content, the cognitive load might be higher, but the expectations from the web search can be similar to everyday content search.

Although the process, interaction, expectations, decisions, keywords, scanning, filtering, reading, and selecting actions seem to be similar for both types of web searches (everyday vs. academic), there might be differences in terms of user experi-ence. In this study, the search patterns were compared by using two different contents, therefore, the main research question of this study is:

"How do academic search patterns differ from everyday content search patterns?"

2 Method

The research design is a single-case study (Yin 2009), in which graduate students are the units of analysis. 15 undergraduate and graduate students from various departments voluntarily participated in the study. The researcher contacted participants online, and then scheduled the sessions, each of which took approximately 25 min. Before starting the data collection, each participant was informed about rights and ethical issues. They were allowed to leave whenever they want without any excuse. When they agreed on the both screen and voice recordings, the sessions started. 8 female (2 graduate; 6 undergraduate) and 7 male (2 graduate; 5 undergraduate) students were assigned to two web search tasks within two scenarios:

Scenario 1: The University is funding a 3-day trip to London for high-honor students and you are one of them. All expenses are going to be funded by the uni-versity, but you need to decide where to stay with a maximum budget of 500 Sterlin *(Note that 500 Sterlin should be all spent for accommodation!)*.

Task 1: With the assigned budget (500 Sterlin), find three best accommodation options to stay between the given dates (1–4 Feb. 2016).

Scenario 2: For one of the courses you attend, the instructor assigned you to prepare a presentation about "Scientific Ethics and Plagiarism". You can search the web and use maximum 3 web resources.

Task 2: In order to prepare your class presentation, find three best resources about "Scientific Ethics and Plagiarism" topic.

Participants were encouraged to search the web as they do in daily life. The starting point for both tasks were Google search engine. The order of the tasks was the same for all participants. There were no time restrictions for the tasks. During the whole ses-sions, all participants were encouraged to think aloud about the search process. Their eye-movements, speeches, gestures, and mimics were all recorded in the Human-Computer Interaction Laboratory. Eye tracking data can provide rich, realistic, and real time data (Webb and Renshaw 2008), for that reason, the main data collection and analysis techniques in this study were all based on the collected eye tracking data. Tobii 1750 Eye Tracker with 50 Hz sampling rate was utilized for data collection. Tobii Studio 3.4.0 software was used to analyze the recorded data. Participants' think aloud data were analyzed qualitatively in order to shed light on their criteria or any action on the web search experiences.

3   Findings

3.1   Task 1

The first task was a regular task that anyone can perform while planning a trip, thus it is considered as an everyday web search task. For this task, the majority of the participants completed the session with keyword entry at once and there were certain popular keywords. Two common phrases were: '*hotels in London*'; and '*accommodation London*'. Only two female participants tried more than one keyword entries. These included '*booking.com*', '*cheap stay London*', '*London hostels*' etc. They explained that the reason why they used these phrases was so that they would find either the cheapest or the highly rated hotels or hostels.

Except for five participants, the majority opened more than one tab on the browser ($N = 10$). The maximum number of tabs was 8. The number of visited sites also differed among participants. Nine participants performed only one web site visit and this was 'booking.com', however, all of the participants visited this web site as well ($N = 15$). The maximum number of visited sites was 5 ($N = 2$). The participants who worked with multiple tabs explored the hotels by opening them on another tab. Before making their final decision, they all navigated across tabs, and compared the ratings, images, prices, and other features and comments. Those who worked within one tab first explored the hotel, then immediately decided to choose or not to choose the hotel as an option.

While experiencing the web sites, the participants searched the best places to stay. Their selection criteria were similar, yet differed in terms of priority. From the think aloud data and eye tracker screen recordings, the overall criteria for this task can be listed as follows: photos ($N = 14$); budget ($N = 13$); ratings ($N = 10$); name ($N = 5$); and special offers ($N = 2$). When eye-tracking data were investigated qualitatively together with the think aloud data, the first or most preferred criterion of their hotel selection was found: budget ($N = 6$); photos ($N = 3$); travelers' reviews ($N = 2$); ratings ($N = 2$); location ($N = 1$); and free Wi-Fi ($N = 1$).

Related to the listed criteria, some areas in booking.com website were pointed as Areas of Interest (AOI), because this site was visited by all participants. Price, photo, hotel name, rating, and stars were the main AOIs (Fig. 1). Time to first fixation, fixation count, visit duration, and percentage-fixated metrics were calculated with the help of Tobii software. The summary of the metrics is displayed in Table 1. As soon as the web site opened, it took shorter for price and rating AOIs to be fixated ($M = 1.41$ s for both), whereas it was longer for photo ($M = 8.79$ s) and hotel name ($M = 13.61$ s) AOIs. The highest fixation count belonged to price AOI ($M = 8$) with the longest visit duration ($M = .75$ s). In addition, the highest percentage fixated also belonged to

respectively; price AOI ($M = 57$ %), photo ($M = 50$ %), and hotel name ($M = 36$ %) and rating ($M = 36$ %) AOIs came.

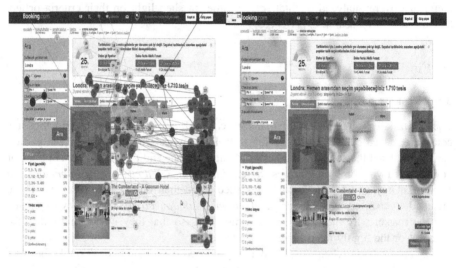

Fig. 1. Gaze plot and heatmap of main AOIs of booking.com: price, photo, hotel name, rating, and stars.

Table 1. Metrics summary for task 1

Metric	Price	Rating	Photo	Hotel name
Time to first fixation (sec)	1.41	1.41	8.79	13.61
Fixation count	8.00	3.00	3.43	3.40
Visit duration (sec)	.75	.44	.27	.32
Percentage fixated (%)	57	36	50	36

3.2   Task 2

The second task was very similar to regular academic tasks, since university students generally start their projects with the exploration of the web with the utilization of search engines (Biddix et al. 2011). For this task, most of the participants entered more than one keyword ($N = 10$). Only five participants entered keywords once, but the rest of the participants' entries had a range between 2–8 times. Interestingly, 'scientific ethics and plagiarism' was the first keyword phrase of all participants.

Most of the participants preferred to work with multiple tabs on the browser ($N = 10$), but some of them explored the pages within one tab ($N = 5$). The maximum number of tabs was 7. The students working with multiple tabs visited more pages, and focused less on the main parts of the documents. On the other hand, those working within one tab visited less web site, but were more tended to read the main body of the pages.

For this task, minimum number of web site visits was 4 and the maximum number was 10. Although the number of visits varied among participants, there were some common web sites visited: '*yok.gov.tr*', '*researchgate.net*', '*uvt.ulakbim.gov.tr*', '*biotek.ankara.edu.tr*'. Moreover, most of the participants reached the same document from different web sites. For example, a scientific article was available on both biotek.ankara.edu.tr and researchgate.net. This situation enabled the examination of the same documents in terms of eye movements' comparison of different users.

During the examination of the electronic resources, the participants tried to eliminate the unrelated content, thus they set certain criteria to select the best ones. Their selection criteria were similar, however, differed in terms of priority. The overall criteria for the selections can be listed as follows: published article ($N = 11$); title of the author ($N = 7$); gov and edu extensions ($N = 7$); well-organized ($N = 4$); and the number of citations ($N = 2$). From either think aloud data or eye-tracking data, it could be inferred that among the listed criteria, the primary concern or criterion of participants can be summarized respectively: title of the author ($N = 4$); rich content ($N = 4$); being a published source ($N = 4$); simple and organized content ($N = 2$); and edu and gov extensions ($N = 1$). One of the common websites visited for this task was biotek.ankara.edu.tr. Considering the popular criteria, the AOIs for this web site were title, author, abstract, keywords, and name of the journal (publisher) (Fig. 2). It took shortest to the first fixation of *title* ($M = 1.43$ s) AOI and longest to the first fixation of *keywords* ($M = 8.33$ s) AOI. The highest fixation count was within *abstract* AOI ($M = 12$) with the longest visit *duration* ($M = 1.05$ s). In terms of percentage fixated metric, the abstract AOI had the highest *percentage* ($M = 43$ %), then *title* ($M = 36$ %), *author* ($M = 21$ %), *keywords* ($M = 21$ %), and *journal* ($M = 14$ %) AOIs came respectively (Table 2).

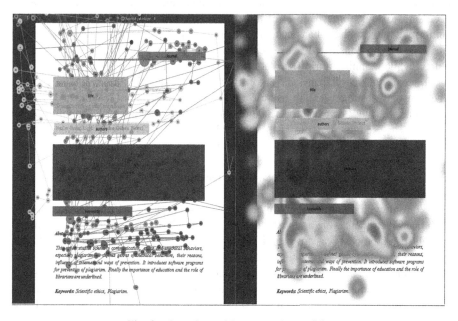

Fig. 2. Gazeplot and heatmap of an article

Table 2. Metrics summary for task 2

Metric	Title	Name of journal	Abstract	Author	Keywords
Time to first fixation (sec)	1.43	4.62	7.12	7.12	8.33
Fixation count	7.00	3.00	12.00	2.00	5.00
Visit duration (sec)	.33	.25	1.05	.37	.49
Percentage fixated (%)	36	14	43	21	21

4 Discussion and Conclusion

The findings point that web search for everyday content can be less complicated than that for academic content. Keyword entries and visited websites differed in number for academic search. Although common keywords were observed for either task, participants used more keywords for the academic task. Moreover, the number of web site visits was also higher for the academic task. On the other hand, participants visited generally booking.com website in order to decide on the best three hotels, and they did not feel the necessity to check the hotel (with regards to pricing, photos, features, etc.) somewhere else. This was not the case for academic search, because they find it necessary to check whether the information they obtain is reliable.

While participants trust the reviewers on a web site for travellers, they are more apprehensive to trust any academic content, i.e. they consider who the author is. Reviewers have either nicknames or real names with profiles showing the number of reviews. Their reviews are listed on a well-known web site, which may be the reason why participants rely on the reviews on the site; another reason may be because booking.com is located generally at the top of the SERP. The rank of a page can be sign of how prestigious the site is (Witten 2008), therefore, they might not consider it necessary to look somewhere else. In other words, this site can be perceived as an authority like the author of an academic paper or the publisher of an article. Such a web site can also be considered as a social networking site, so the power of reviews is crucial while planning a trip (Kim et al. 2014; Xiang and Gretzel 2010).

It seems that participants have some common beliefs for the everyday content. They trust a website presenting real travelers' reviews, and do not feel the need to visit any other website; however, for academic task, they first judged the formality of the website. They did not prefer to visit blogs, wikis, or news web sites. Such small pieces of information as budget (or price) were the main concern or primary selection criteria for the everyday task; whereas it was the origin of the sources for academic task. The users all valued where it was published, who the authors were, and the extension of the web site providing access.

Working with multiple tasks can be a sign of multitasking, which was observed for both tasks, yet, there were a few students searching within one tab. The one-tab users' overall search process was not very detailed for everyday task, whereas, they read main body of the documents more than others. Comparing this situation for either tasks may demonstrate that academic search may demand more comprehension; because in everyday task, small pieces of information may be enough to evaluate whether it is a good option or not. Since the web search is a way to distinguish what we do not know within a vast majority of information (Witten 2008), not only multitasking but also single tasking can be overwhelming during any search process.

For the everyday task, participants' most priorities criterion was budget (or price); which did photographs of the hotel, and travelers' reviews follow respectively. The eye tracking data asserted that it took less time to the first fixation to the price AOI, then rating (or review) AOI. Price AOI had also the highest fixation count and percentage fixated was higher. In short, all data about criteria for the everyday task were consistent. Although the photos of hotels seemed important at first sight, which was inferred from participants' responses, that AOI did not strike too much attention. It came after price or ratings, which might mean that when the search task has limits, the visual attention can be shaped along with that.

For academic task, participants' primary criterion was the title of the authors; which was respectively followed by content and its publishing status. However, the eye tracking data did not support it; since the title of the article was the AOI stroke attention first. On the other hand, the abstract AOI had the most frequently fixated location, which may mean that participants wanted to understand the content in a deeper way. The overall meaning should be extracted from the whole text, and it is possible through reading the text.

The findings of the study are limited to 15 participants. Although the direct observation and eye tracking data, which is objective in nature, gave insights of web searchers, more detailed analyses with more participants are required. A true experimental design can be appropriate in order to compare the tasks or to see how different level searchers conduct the web search.

Acknowledgement. I would like to acknowledge the support of everyone at METU Human-Computer-Interaction Lab. The technical supports of Nihan Ocak and Elif Cakir Turgut were of vital importance for me. Her efforts were critical during data collection period.

References

Biddix, J.P., Chung, C.J., Park, H.W.: Convenience or credibility? A study of college student online research behaviors. Internet High. Educ. **14**, 175–182 (2011)

Colon-Aguirre, M., Fleming-May, R.A.: "You just type in what you are looking for": undergraduates' use of library resources vs Wikipedia. J. Acad. Librarianship **38**(6), 391–399 (2012)

Hogan, A., Harth, A., Umbrich, J., Kinsella, S., Polleres, A., Decker, S.: Searching and browsing linked data with SWSE: the semantic web search engine. Web Seman.: Sci. Serv. Agent World Wide Web **9**(4), 365–401 (2011)

Hsieh-Yee, I.: Search tactics of web users in searching for texts, graphics, known items and subjects: a search simulation study. Ref. Librarian **60**, 61–85 (1998)

Kim, K.-S., Sin, S.-C.J., Tsai, T.-I.: Individual differences in social media use for information seeking. J. Acad. Librarianship **40**, 171–178 (2014)

Koster, M.: ALIWEB - Archie-like indexing in the WEB. Comput. Netw. ISDN Syst. **27**(2), 175–182 (1994)

Moukdad, H., Large, A.: Users' perceptions of the web as revealed by transaction log analysis. Online Inf. Rev. **25**(6), 349–359 (2001)

Sendurur, E., Yildirim, Z.: Students' web search strategies with different task types: an eye-tracking study. Int. J. Hum.-Comput. Interact. **31**(2), 101–111 (2015)

Webb, N., Renshaw, T.: Eyetracking in HCI. In: Cairns, P., Cox, A.L. (eds.) Research Methods for Human-Computer Interaction, pp. 35–69. Cambridge University Press, Cambridge (2008)

White, M.D., Iivonen, M.: Assessing level of difficulty in web search questions. Library Q. **72**(2), 205–233 (2002)

Witten, I.H.: Searching … in a Web. J. Univ. Comput. Sci. **14**(10), 1739–1762 (2008)

Wu, L.-L., Chuang, Y.-L., Chen, P.-Y.: Motivation for using search engines: a two-factor model. J. Am. Soc. Inf. Technol. **59**(1), 1829–1840 (2008)

Xiang, Z., Gretzel, U.: Role of social media in online travel information search. Tourism Manag. **31**, 179–188 (2010)

Yin, R.K.: Case Study Research: Design and Methods, 4th edn. Sage, Thousand Oaks (2009)

Animation on How to Take Medicines: A Study of Electronic Patient Leaflets in Brazil

Carla Galvão Spinillo[✉]

Department of Design, Federal University of Parana, Curitiba, Brazil
cgspin@gmail.com

Abstract. Animation has been proved to facilitate content learning. However, in Brazil the electronic Patient Information Leaflets (e-PILs) do not employ animation, but static images, to show medicine usage to patients. By considering animation a beneficial communication resource to PILs, a study was conducted with 80 participants on comprehension and simulated tasks of using the medicines: vaginal cream, insulin syringe, inhaler and nasal spray. The results ratified the assumption, however, suggest that (a) participants' perception of their understanding and task performance are related to their satisfaction with the animation, and (b) there is a gap between users' understanding of medicine animation and their task performance when using a medicine. Recommendations are proposed based upon the literature and the outcomes of the study.

Keywords: Animation · Medicine usage · Comprehension · Task performance

1 Introduction

In Brazil, patients may access information about medicines in printed leaflets or in electronic ones. The latter is referred to as e-PIL (electronic Patient Information Leaflet) and is made available by the Ministry of Health in the governmental medicine database *Bulário Eletrônico* (www4.anvisa.gov.br/BularioEletronico/). However, information on medicine usage in the Brazilian e-PILs is shown through static images in the same way as printed PILs. Thus, technological resources of digital media, such as animation, are not employed to represent medicine usage in e-PILs, despite their contributions to content learning [1–3]. Figure 1 shows a detail of an e-PIL presenting a static pictorial sequence on using a medicine, which is the same used in printed version.

The graphic representation of animated instructions may vary in pictorial style (e.g., design in 2D, 3D), represented participants (e.g., agent, object), camera position (e.g., zoom, close shot); and text position (e.g., caption, labels for parts of the image) [4]. Regarding animation on medicine usage, emphasis on graphical representation of the steps should also be considered for satisfactory content learning. This is particularly relevant to the manipulation of objects, such as syringes and dosing devices which require special attention from patients so as to prevent misuse or dosage error.

For the information content, it can be procedural (steps) and non-procedural, such as warnings and introductory information [4]. Among the non-procedural content, inventory information is of relevance, as it is the necessary material or components to undertake a task [5], as for example an insulin bottle, syringe, and alcohol for hygiene,

© Springer International Publishing Switzerland 2016
A. Marcus (Ed.): DUXU 2016, Part II, LNCS 9747, pp. 647–654, 2016.
DOI: 10.1007/978-3-319-40355-7_62

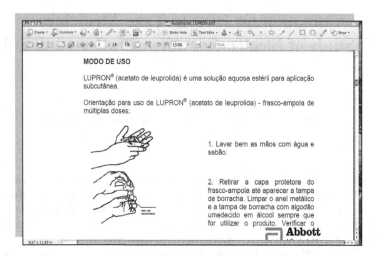

Fig. 1. Detail of an e-PIL presenting the same images as for the print format

which are necessary to take an insulin injection. The inventory information, together with the depiction of the steps to be carried out, may also aid to build a mental representation of the task. This regards the action plan one develops to perform a task [6]. Thus, lack of accuracy and/or of completeness in the representation of procedural and non-procedural contents may jeopardize their comprehension and/or the task performance.

As for learning contents, studies show that animation facilitates cognitive processes and motivates learners [7], as well as promoting visualization of processes and procedures [8]. Accordingly, it can be said that the animation is appropriate to convey a sequence of steps to be performed, as it is the case in medicine usage. Mayer and Moreno [1] proposed principles to design animation as an instructional tool based upon the Cognitive Theory of Multimedia Learning [9]. This theory considers that the human cognitive system has two subsystems acting in an integrated manner to enhance information processes: the verbal (processes auditory stimuli) and non-verbal (processes visual stimuli). Hence, Mayer and Moreno's [9] animation principles mainly advocates that audio/narration and animation (moving images) should be employed simultaneously, and convey the same messages in a coherent manner to promote learning.

Thus, medicine usage represented through animation (image and audio) may ease comprehension and therefore may support task performance, contributing to the medical treatment of patients. Having this as a premise, a study was conducted in Brazil to verify the effectiveness of animation on comprehension and on task performance of using medicines, which are available in the *Bulário Eletrônico*. This study intended to meet the demand for information design research on animation conveying instructional messages in health care, particularly on medicine usage in e-PILs in Brazil.

2 The Research Design of the Study on Animation of Medicine Usage

Four e-PILS of medicines varying in their way of use (i.e., pharmaceutical presentation) were selected for the study: (a) insulin syringe, (b) vaginal cream, (c) nasal spray and (d) inhaler. An animation was produced to for each medicine, based on the literature recommendations. The animated images were in drawing style, employed arrows to stress the actions, and color to emphasize particular parts of the images. The images next are screenshots of the animations vaginal cream and inhaler (Fig. 2).

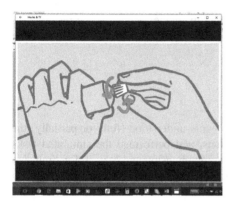 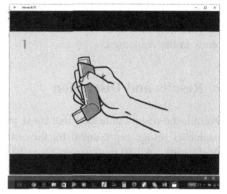

Fig. 2. Screenshots of the animations tested (vaginal cream and inhaler). Source: The author's archives.

The animations were tested with a total of 80 adult participants varying in gender and age, being 20 participants per medicine animation. The animation of the vaginal cream medicine was tested with women only, due to the nature of the task. The dependent variables (X) were comprehension of the animations and participants' task performance. The independent variable (Y) was the animations of the medicines' usage. Participants were equally divided into two groups: (a) Comprehension (40 = 10 participants per medicine animation) and (b) Simulated medicine usage (40 = 10 participants per medicine animation) as shown in Table 1.

Table 1. Participants' distribution across groups and medicine animations tested

Medicine animation	Group (a) comprehension	Group (b) simulated medicine usage	Total
Vaginal cream	10	10	20
Insulin syringe	10	10	20
Nasal spray	10	10	20
Inhaler	10	10	20
Total	40	40	80

The animated procedural pictorial sequence of each medicine was presented to the participants, individually and in isolation. For the comprehension test, participants were asked to watch the animation, and then, to answer questions related to the steps represented and to their level of satisfaction with the animation they watched. For the task performance test, participants were asked to watch the animation, and then, to use the medicine in a simulated manner. They were informed that they could watch the animation as many times as they considered necessary, and were encouraged to verbalize their actions during task performance. Afterwards, they were asked to answer questions related to their performance and to their level of satisfaction with the animation. The data was collected through observation and recorded in written protocols by the researchers.

Due to the limited number of participants per medicine animation, the results were analyzed qualitatively only. However, figures are considered herein to indicate possible trends in the responses.

3   Results and Discussion

Overall, the results indicated that most participants understood (fully or partially) the medicines' usage represented by the animations, and performed the simulated tasks satisfactorily. All 80 participants (N = 40 for comprehension and N = 40 for simulated tasks) agreed that audio and animation together helped them to understand and to perform the tasks on the medicines usage. This is in line with the Cognitive Theory for Multimedia Learning [9]. When asked what could be improved in the animations, participants' main suggestion was to enhance clarity of the audio, followed by the animation's presentation speed (e.g., faster for the insulin injection and slower for the inhaler). The results on each medicine animation per group are summarized next.

Comprehension. The results showed that all participants (N = 40) believed they had a high degree of comprehension of the tasks, and were satisfied with the animations. The majority of the participants (N = 9 out of 10) answered the questions on how to use an insulin syringe properly. However, when asked to explain the task, few participants mentioned how to pinch the skin (N = 3 out of 10) and to angle the needle to inject insulin (N = 2 out of 10). Similarly, the animation on how to use a vaginal cream was fully understood by more than half of the woman participants (N = 6 out of 10). It is worth mentioning that all of the participants (N = 10) answered the questions on how to attach the applicator to the cream tube in a satisfactory manner.

Differently, the results of the animation on how to use nasal spray show that 9 out of 10 participants did not fully understand the represented task. When asked to describe the task, most participants did not mention the steps shaking the nasal spray bottle and positioning the head down when spraying the medicine. However, participants satisfactorily understood how to angle the nasal spray bottle to avoid touching the nose bone (N = 5 out of 10), and to breath via the mouth after spraying (N = 8 out of 10). Figure 3 shows a screenshot of the step of the nasal spray animation. The animation on how to use an inhaler produced similar results. It was partially understood by all 10

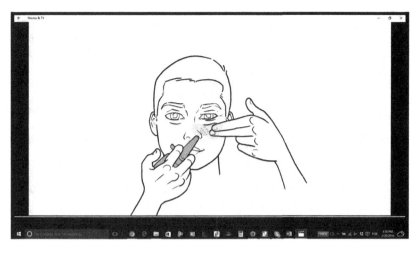

Fig. 3. Screenshot of the step showing how to angle the nasal spray bottle. Source: The author's archives.

participants. Their main difficulty regarded the animated step of positioning the inhaler bottle in between the lips. On the other hand, 8 out of 10 participants fully understood the steps of exhaling air from the lungs before inhaling, and holding the breath for 10 s when inhaling.

Task performance. All 40 participants completed (fully or partially) the tasks of using the medicines in a simulated manner and most of them responded positively when asked if they had succeed in performing the steps represented in the animations. Nevertheless, the majority of participants have not mentioned the hygiene procedures and the inventorial content when explaining the procedures after they had performed the tasks. Also, errors occurred when participants undertook each one of the tasks of the medicines' usage.

Participants (N = 10) made errors in simulating the use of the insulin syringe, mainly regarding measuring the glucose level (N = 7). Rubbing the insulin bottle against the hands and positioning the bottle correctly to withdraw the insulin with the syringe were also not properly done by the participants when carrying on the task. Similarly, the results on how to use vaginal cream show that 8 out of 10 woman participants made errors, which were mostly related to hygiene procedures (e.g., wash the hands before the task).

As for the task of using a nasal spray, 9 out of 10 participants made errors. The most frequent errors were to shake the nasal spray bottle before using the medicine, to properly angle the bottle so as not to touch the nose bone, and to put the head down to spray the medicine. Participants also suggested to improve the illustrations of the animation and to reduce the number of represented steps as they found there were too many steps, making it difficult to remember them all. Likewise, errors occurred when participants (N = 7) conducted the task of using an inhaler. These errors were related to

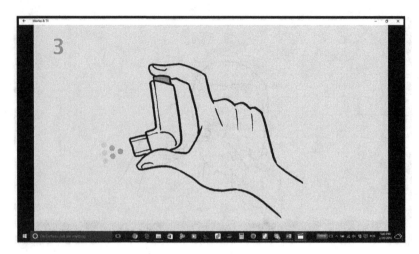

Fig. 4. Screenshot of the step showing how to press the inhaler to release the medicine. Source: The author's archives.

shaking the inhaler before using it, pressing the inhaler bottle to release the medicine (Fig. 4), exhaling air from the lungs before inhaling, and holding the breath for 10 s when inhaling.

By comparing the results of comprehension to those of simulated tasks, discrepancies were found. Participants performed better in the comprehension test. This suggests that understanding a procedural animation of medicine usage may not lead to success in task performance. Thus, there may be a gap between understanding and performance in medicine usage.

Despite the drawbacks in the comprehension of the animations tested and in task performances, all 80 participants considered that they had understood and successfully performed the tasks. They also found the animations satisfactory. These results indicate participants' misperception of their understanding and task performance, as they seem not to realize the occurrence of errors.

Moreover, the inventorial content was not mentioned by several participants when asked to describe the procedures in all animations tested. This is perhaps, because (a) the inventorial content is not a step (procedural content) and/or (b) it is displayed at the very beginning of the animations, which may make recalling inventorial content difficult. This indicates that participants' perception and recall of different kinds of contents in procedural animation may play a role on task comprehension and description. However, these issues are beyond the scope of this study, demanding further investigation.

Despite the above-mentioned concerns, the results on comprehension and satisfaction are aligned to the literature on the beneficial effects of animation in motivation and learning [1, 2, 7], and in the visualization of processes and procedures [3, 8].

Furthermore, the outcomes of this study suggest that some aspects are not fully accounted for in research on procedural animation: the time presentation speed; the presentation of inventorial content; and the relation between task performance and comprehension. Thus, it is pertinent to consider not only what but also how to represent medicine usage through animation to reach effectiveness in communicating procedures.

4   Conclusions and Some Recommendations

Although the qualitative approach of the study does not allow generalizations, the results make it possible to conclude that animation facilitates the understanding and the use of medicines. In addition, the study's outcomes suggest that (a) participants' perception of their understanding and task performance are related to their satisfaction with the animation, and (b) there is a gap between users' understanding of medicine animation and their task performance when using a medicine. These findings call for future studies.

Taking into account the findings presented herein together with the literature, the following recommendations are proposed with view to improve the design of animation of medicine usage for e-PILs in Brazil:

1. Present both procedural and non-procedural contents in medicine animation, as this may facilitate users' information processing and their action plan to carry out the tasks
2. Consider users' satisfaction with an animation and their understanding together with their task performance, to decide on how to represent medicine usage
3. Consider users' information needs regarding the presentation speed and the use of emphatic devices in the animation
4. Present information through audio text and animated images in an integrated manner, as this promotes comprehension
5. If inventorial content is represented in medicine animation, make sure that users' understand it and recall its communicational role (e.g., comprehension test)

Needless to say that the above-mentioned recommendations are not meant to supplant the verification of the success of the animation in communicating medicine usage and supporting task performance. Thus, the recommendations for medicine animation are intended to aid the designers' decisions, and should be tested with users to guarantee their effectiveness.

Acknowledgement. The author would like to thank The National Council for Research and Development of Brazil (CNPq) for supporting this research, and the participants who volunteered to this study. Special thanks are due to the research assistants: Amanda Gomes, Elissandra Pereira, Larissa Asami and Tathianne Ferreira; and to Leandro Alburquerque for producing the illustrations.

References

1. Mayer, R.E., Moreno, R.: Animation as an aid to multimedia learning. Educ. Psychol. Rev. **14**, 87–99 (2002)
2. Tversky, B., Morrison, J.B.: Animation: can it facilitate? Int. J. Hum.-Comput. Stud. **57**(4), 247–262 (2002)

3. Ainsworth, S.: How do animations influence learning? In: Robinson, D., Schraw, G. (eds.) Current Perspectives on Cognition, Learning, and Instruction: Recent Innovations in Educational Technology that Facilitate Student Learning, pp. 37–67. Information Age Publishing, Charlotte (2008)

4. Buba, D., Spinillo, C.G.: How animated visual instructions can be analyzed? A study of the graphic representation of procedures through animation. In: Coelho, L.A.L., Farias, P.L., Spinillo, C.G., Tori, R. (eds.) Selected Readings of the 4th Information Design. Theories, Methods and Applications, vol. 1, 1st edn, pp. 33–46. Novas Ideias, Teresópolis (2011)

5. Bieger, G.R., Glock, M.D.: Comprehending spatial and contextual information in picture text instructions. J. Exp. Educ. **54**, 181–188 (1986). 1985/1986

6. Ganier, F.: Les apports de la psychologie cognitive a la conception d'instructions procedurals. InfoDesign- Braz. J. Inf. Des. **1**(1), 17–28 (2004). http://infodesign.org.br

7. Schnotz, W., Lowe, R.K.: A unified view of learning from animated and static graphics. In: Lowe, R.K., Schnotz, W. (eds.) Learning with Animation. Research Implications for Design, pp. 304–356. Cambridge University Press, New York (2008)

8. Hoffler, T.N., Leutner, D.: Instructional animation versus static pictures: a meta-analysis. Learn. Instr. **17**, 722–738 (2007)

9. Mayer, R.E.: Multimedia Learning. Cambridge University Press, Cambridge (2001). Age Publishing (2008)

Usability Evaluation of the Cockpit Display System

Hong-jun Xue[✉], Xiu-bo Yu, and Xiao-yan Zhang

School of Aeronautics, Northwestern Polytechnical University,
Xi'an 710072, China
xuehj@nwpu.edu.cn, 603649479@qq.com

Abstract. The cockpit display system is the most important source for the pilot to obtain information, so its usability has a great significance. However, the relevant research is very rare and inappropriate for the moment. Therefore, in order to improve the cockpit display system, this paper proposes five evaluation factors and a series of evaluation indicators, and build a set of evaluation method. Firstly, this paper adopt Analytic Hierarchy Process to confirm the weight of each factor and its indicators. Secondly, this paper adopt expert scoring method to obtain all indicators' usability score. Finally, this paper integrates the usability score and corresponding weight of every indicator to give a overall usability score of the cockpit display system. Besides, using the above method, we invite five graduate students to make a cockpit simulator display system's usability evaluation, the evaluation result is between good and very good, demonstrating that the method of this paper indeed can make a quantitative evaluation for the usability of cockpit display system. Fortunately, this will be the first time in the history of the whole cockpit display system's usability evaluation, undoubtedly, it will also accelerate the development of the whole cockpit display system's usability rapidly. Similarly, we can also generalize this method to the whole cockpit or even the whole aircraft's usability evaluation.

Keywords: Cockpit display system · Usability evaluation · Analytic hierarchy process · Expert scoring method

1   Introduction

The concept of usability arises from the internet industry in North America and some developed countries in Europe at the end of 1980s, now it has become one of the important research contents in the field of man-machine interaction by now. The international standards ISO9241 defines the usability as Extent to which a product can be used by specified users to achieve specified goals with effectiveness, efficiency and satisfaction in a specified context of use.

The cockpit is the terminal for pilot and aircraft interaction directly. Just like other interactive devices, the cockpit's usability is directly related to the flight safety. 80 % of the information in flight is provided by the display system, and the information on the display system is numerous and complicated, especially in emergency, various visual

© Springer International Publishing Switzerland 2016
A. Marcus (Ed.): DUXU 2016, Part II, LNCS 9747, pp. 655–662, 2016.
DOI: 10.1007/978-3-319-40355-7_63

or auditory alarm signals appear at the same time. There is no doubt that the pilot will bear great psychological pressure, not only may slow down the effective operation, may also make errors in busy. So the usability design of cockpit display system should be effectiveness, efficiency and satisfaction.

Wang Haibo from Southeast University (Nanjing, P.R. China) made an eye movement experiment to evaluate the usability of the fighter cockpit digital interface. By analysing four kinds of quantitative data of the eye movement which include the pilot's gaze point coordinate, the gaze point number, the pupil frequency and the event time of each layout, they confirmed the optimal layout since all the eye movement's date of this one is better than all others.

Besides, Wang Haibo made another experiment to compare the digital interface's usability of F18 and a new 4th-generation fighter. They offered the cockpit digital interface prototypes by computer simulating, and then noted down the task complete ratio, errors, task time and assists in the same task. As a result, all the four data of the new fourth-generation fighter were better than the F18's. So they drawed a conclusion that the new fourth-generation fighter digital interface's usability was higher.

There are at least two methods to layout the information on the display. One is Multi Criteria Decision Making (MCDM) that is employed as a quantitative tool. Firstly, experts give a importance's sequence of all information, then according to the importance's sequence of all positions on display, put each information onto the corresponding position. Another is Card Sorting that is used as a qualitative tool for the same problem. Firstly, each information is written on one of the cards, then users put all cards with information onto the positions of the display, explaining every choice's reason, finally, confirm the information's layout on the display on the basis of these reasons recorded. We can evaluate a certain layout's usability of the information on the display according to the above methods' result.

Wei Hengyang from Beihang University think the situation awareness (SA) is a very important factor for the aircraft cockpit display interface (CDA)'s design. Based on the simulation environment, they carry out a human-in-the-loop experiment to measure the SA by the situation awareness global assessment technique (SAGAT) and find the SA can serve as an objective way to evaluate the design of CDI. That is to say, the SA will affect the CDA's usability.

Williams and Ball from Office of Aerospace Medicine conducted a study to assess the impact of advanced navigation displays on instrument flight procedures for general aviation, single pilot operations and found the advanced display in flight performance was advantaged under high-workload conditions. So the advanced display has a better usability under high-workload conditions.

The above researches just focus on someone aspect's usability of the display system, such as the information layout, instead of the whole display system, in addition, the above evaluation methods have a same latent shortcoming: It can't confirm which one is the best when there is no one group whose all date are better than others. So this paper is devoted to solve these problems, we focus on the usability evaluation of the whole cockpit display system, including information representation, information layout and information updating and so on. Differently in the method, this paper adopt Analytic Hierarchy

Process to confirm the weight of each factor and its indicators, and then integrates the usability score and corresponding weight of every indicator to give a overall usability score of the cockpit display system, thus avoiding the above shortcoming.

2 Methodology

A. Evaluation factor and its indicators

Factor1: The layout rationality of the whole display system
Its indicators: installation angle, importance principle, common use principle, function principle, sequential use principle
Factor2: The layout rationality of the information on display
Its indicators: importance principle, accordant motion principle, adjoin inter-related information principle
Factor3: Comprehensibility
Its indicators: icon simplicity, icon figurativeness, icon distinction
Factor4: Visibility
Its indicators: resolution, brightness, icon size, color settings, signal reaction time, visual angle
Factor5: Information updating rate
Its indicators: PFD, ND, ECAM/EICAS

Some annotations are as follows:

Importance principle: put the most important display in the most convenient location for the pilot.

Common use principle: put the display of highest use frequency in the most convenient location for the pilot.

Function principle: put displays which have relevant function together.

Sequential use principle: the layout of displays should be coincident with their usual use sequence in the task execution.

Accordant motion principle: when the pilot manipulates the aircraft during the flight, all the pilot, the aircraft and the aircraft's icon on the display should be accordant in the direction of motion.

Adjoin interrelated information principle: the principle of proximity to the specific processing of the structure of the display problem. Generally should be related to the information displayed in space close to. Relevance or similarity of the display depends on the correlation of the task and the system. Therefore, the related display components should be placed together with the integration of the system.

Signal reaction time: it reflects pixel points' response speed to input signals of the liquid crystal display, the smaller the signal reaction time is, the better the picture's changing-over effect will be.

Visual angle: the maximum angle that one can clearly see all the contents of the screen from different directions.

B. Evaluation procedures

   (1). Adopt Analytic Hierarchy Process to confirm the weight of each factor and its indicators. That is to say, every user fills in a judgment matrix of factors, and then we take the mean as a final factors' weigh. In the same way, we obtain each factor's indicators' weighs.

   (2). Establish a set of numerical indicator evaluating system whose score is from 1 to 9 that corresponds to extremely bad, very bad, bad, slightly bad, neutral, slightly good, good, very good, extremely good respectively. And then users score the indicators according to their performance in use. This paper take the mean score as a final evaluation result.

   (3). Integrate some factor's all indicators' usability scores and corresponding weights to give a usability score of the factor. As such, we can obtain other factors' usability scores. And then integrate all factors' usability scores and corresponding weights to give a overall usability score of the cockpit display system.

3   The Usability Evaluation Experiment of a Cockpit Simulator's Display System

A. Participants

There are 5 participants including both undergraduate and graduate students from Northwestern Polytechnical University in this test. Among which there are one woman and four men students. They are 23.2 years old in average, ranging from 22 to 25. All the participants have plentiful experience of using computer, but didn't familiar with the cockpit display system, so they can evaluate its usability by their experiences without mindset. That is to say, they are appropriate participants.

In this experiment, we only employ 5 users, because the key point of this article is to provide a method, of course, the more the user's number is, the better.

B. Apparatus

The test is provided with a cockpit simulator, which is a simplified version, but the basic functions on the display are complete (Fig. 1).

C. Tasks

In order to exhibit the display system's performance in work, we will manipulate the plane in the simulator take off, cruise and land. Experimenters look at the display carefully, fill the judgment matrix of factors and the ones of each factor's indicators, and give their usability scores to all the indicators.

D. Results

The experimenters are marked (A), (B), (C), (D), (E) respectively. Due to the experimental data is massive, we only list some of the data as follows (Table 1):

We can work out A's factors' weights by using MATLAB after putting the above judgment matrix into computer, the result is as follows (Table 2):

Fig. 1. The cockpit simulator

Table 1. A's judgment matrix of factors

	F actor1	Factor2	Factor3	Factor4	Factor5
Factor1	1	5	7	7	9
Factor2	1/5	1	5	5	3
Factor3	1/7	1/5	1	1	2
Factor4	1/7	1/5	1	1	2
Factor5	1/9	1/3	1/2	1/2	1

CR = 0.0623 < 0.1

Table 2. A's factors' weights

Factor1	Factor2	Factor3	Factor4	Factor5
0.59	0.22	0.07	0.07	0.05

Table 3. The average of factors' weights

Factor1	Factor2	Factor3	Factor4	Factor5
0.39	0.12	0.22	0.18	0.09

We can obtain B, C, D and E's factors' weights in the same way, the results are not listed. The following is the average of all the participants' factors' weights (Table 3).

Similarly, we can obtain each factor's average weights of corresponding indicators as follows (Tables 4, 5, 6, 7 and 8):

We can acquire each factor's indicators' scores with the same processing procedure, and this paper just take the factor(1) for a example (Table 9).

We can figure out the factor(1)'s usability score since its each indicator's weight and each indicator's score is known (Table 10).

Table 4. Factor(1)'s average weights of indicators

Installation angle	Importance principle	Common use principle	Function principle	Sequential use principle
0.08	0.36	0.26	0.18	0.12

Table 5. Factor(2)'s average weights of indicators

Importance principle	Accordant motion principle	Adjoin interrelated information principle
0.32	0.43	0.25

Table 6. Factor(3)'s average weights of indicators

Icon simplicity	Icon figurativeness	Icon distinction
0.24	0.41	0.35

Table 7. Factor(4)'s average weights of indicators

Resolution	Brightness	Icon size	Color setting	Signal reaction time	Visual angle
0.2	0.18	0.12	0.18	0.16	0.16

Table 8. Factor(5)'s average weights of indicators

PFD	ND	ECAM/EICAS
0.63	0.24	0.13

Table 9. Factor(1)'s indicators' scores

	Installation angle	Importance principle	Common use principle	Function principle	Sequential use principle
A	8	7	8	7	5
B	8	8	7	9	7
C	8	8	7	7	6
D	9	7	8	7	6
E	8	8	8	7	8
Average	8.2	7.6	7.6	7.4	6.4

Table 10. Factor(1)'s usability score

Indicator	Installation angle	Importance principle	Common use principle	Function principle	Sequential use principle
Indicator weight	0.08	0.36	0.26	0.18	0.12
Indicator score	8.2	7.6	7.6	7.4	6.4
Factor score	7.47				

Table 11. Cockpit simulator display system's usability score

Factor	Factor1	Factor2	Factor3	Factor4	Factor5
Factor weight	0.39	0.12	0.22	0.18	0.09
Factor score	7.47	7.59	7.5	7.11	7.79
Cockpit simulator display system's usability score	7.46				

Similarly, we can obtain all the factors' usability scores. Finally we'll work out the cockpit simulator display system's usability score (Table 11).

Thus it can be seen the cockpit simulator display system's usability score is 7.46 (the full mark is 9), which is between good and very good.

4 Conclusion

This paper proposes five evaluation factors and a series of evaluation indicators, and build a set of cockpit display system's usability evaluation method. Moreover, we verify this method is feasible by a experiment. And our work will be the first time in the history of the whole cockpit display system's usability evaluation, undoubtedly, it will also accelerate the development of the whole cockpit display system's usability rapidly. Similarly, we can also generalize this method to the whole cockpit or even the whole aircraft's usability evaluation.

We will continue to optimize this method by regulating the evaluation factors and indicators with the development of the cockpit display system's technology.

References

McCall, J.A., Richards, P.K., Walters, G.F.: Factors in Software Quality: Concepts and Definitions of Software Quality, vol. 1. Information Service, Springfield, VA (1977)

Mo, C., Chengqi, X., Haiyan, W., Jing, L., Jiang, S.: The analysis of virtual product based on the usability. Ind. Eng. Manag. **03**, 135–140 (2014)

Saffeh, A., Kececi, N., Donyaee, M.: QUIM: a framework for quantifying usability metrics in software quality models. In: Second Asia - Pacific Conference on Quality Software, APAQS 2001, Hong-Kong, pp. 311–318 (2001)

Van Welie, M., Van Der Veer, G.C., Elins, A.: Breaking down usability. In: Proceedings of INTERACT, Amsterdam, The Netherlands, pp. 613–620 (1999)

Tang, L., Yang, M., (Wuhan University of Technology Wuhan, 430070): Research of usability engineering based on the design process of product. The industrial design institution of Chinese Mechanical Engineering Society. In: Proceedings of the 2007 International Conference on Industrial Design, vol. 2/2. The Industrial Design Institution of Chinese Mechanical Engineering Society, May 2007

Wang, H., Xue, C., Liu, Q.: The eye movement experiment and the usability evaluation of the fighter cockpit digital interface. In: 2010 2nd International Conference on Information Engineering and Computer Science (ICIECS), pp. 1–4. IEEE (2010)

Wang, H., Xue, C., Wang, Z.: The quantitative usability evaluation of fighter cockpit digital interface. In: 2010 IEEE 11th International Conference on Computer-Aided Industrial Design and Conceptual Design (CAIDCD), pp. 384–387. IEEE (2010)

Senol, M.B., Dagdeviren, M., Kurt, M., et al.: Evaluation of cockpit design by using quantitative and qualitative tools. In: IEEE International Conference on Industrial Engineering and Engineering Management, IEEM 2009, pp. 847–851. IEEE (2009)

Wei, H., Zhuang, D., Wanyan, X., et al.: An experimental analysis of situation awareness for cockpit display interface evaluation based on flight simulation. Chin. J. Aeronaut. **26**(4), 884–889 (2013)

Williams, K.W., Ball, J.D.: Usability and effectiveness of advanced general aviation cockpit displays for instrument flight procedures. Usability and Effectiveness of Advanced General Aviation Cockpit Displays for Instrument Flight Procedures (2003)

Based on High Order Aberration Analysis of Influence Index of Vision Fatigue by Watching 3D TV

Fan Yang[1(✉)], Jianqi Cai[2(✉)], Ya Guo[2], Qianxiang Zhou[1], and Zhongqi Liu[1]

[1] School of Biological Science and Medical Engineering, Beihang University,
Beijing 100029, China
{BY1210115,zqxg,liuzhongqi}@buaa.edu.cn
[2] Visual Health and Safety Institute, China National Institute of Standardization,
Beijing 100088, China
{Caijq,Guoya}@cnis.gov.cn

Abstract. The purpose of this study was to assess the visual fatigue after watching 3D TV in wave-front aberration (WFA) test methods. The evaluation method is different from the previous visual fatigue test method (such as accommodation response, subjective assessment and electroencephalography). The self-developed wave-front aberrometer used to collect the data. 60 participants were recruited, who watched 3D TV by wearing two glasses respectively. SPSS18.0 was used for analysis and significance is defined as $p < 0.05$. The results show that MTF (Modulation Transfer Function) and means of WFA (3rd to 5th) of before and after watching 3D TV had significant differences ($p < 0.05$) and consistent trends. The RMS (root mean square) of WFA had no significance. Meanwhile, we found that the result of MTF of wearing different glasses had significant differences ($p < 0.01$). In conclusion, MTF and mean of WFA (3rd to 5th) can be used as the evaluation index of visual fatigue. In follow-up studies, more relationship between changes of higher-order aberrations (6th–35th order) and visual fatigue will be studied.

Keywords: High order aberration · Visual fatigue · 3D

1 Introduction

With the development of 3D picture production technology, a large number of excellent films such as Avatar and Titanic have showed successively, which leads to the rapid increase in the number of audience. And 3D display technology (3D film, 3D TV, etc.) has been the main trend of Screen Display Technology. At the same time, the long-time watching 3D films will lead to the problem of visual quality descending, which has been paid more and more attention by people. So developing a set of reliable and accurate index to evaluate visual fatigue has a very important and urgent effect on people optical health.

In recent years, a lot of scholars have made pre-explorations in this respect. Yano et al. explored the comfort of watching 3D HDTV/HDTV picture by testing the accommodation response of eyes [1]. Kuze et al. evaluated visual fatigue led by watching

© Springer International Publishing Switzerland 2016
A. Marcus (Ed.): DUXU 2016, Part II, LNCS 9747, pp. 663–669, 2016.
DOI: 10.1007/978-3-319-40355-7_64

3D video in five aspects (visual fatigue, general discomfort, nausea, difficulty of focusing, headache) by means of subjective evaluation [2]. Ntuen et al. discovered that the growth rate of visual fatigue led by watching 3D video is higher than 2D by expression of human vision [3]. Mun et al. carried out the research of electroencephalography (EEG), and discovered that steady-state visually evoked potential (EEVEP) and event-related potential (ERP) were related to the cognitive fatigue after watching 3D video [4]. Previous research indicated that long-time watching 3D TV will lead people to visual fatigue, headache, nausea and other fatigue symptoms [5–7]. However, these evaluation methods don't consider of the physiological essence of eyes. Furthermore, methods such as subjective evaluation and EEG, are unable to quantize assessment index effectively.

Measuring wave-front aberration is to analyse the visual quality of human eyes. It mainly uses Zernike polynomial, which is an orthonormalized function, to describe the optical aberration of pupillary zone in ocular [8, 9]. With the development of exploration to optical aberration of Ocular, people pay more and more attention to high order aberration, and the change of high order aberration is very important to the improvement of the quality of visual in ocular. And the modulation transfer function (MTF) decided by wave-front aberration is the total response of eyes to spatial video. Research of Yang showed that there was hope to realize evaluating the visual quality of corneal refractive surgery by the MTF of wave-front aberration [10]. From the physiological optics characteristics of human eyes, this study summarizes and evaluates the effect of watching 3D TV to visual health, by means of testing the wave-front aberration of participants while they were in the course of watching 3D TV.

2   Methods

2.1   Participants

Total 60 subjects (age: 31.4 ± 7.1; sexuality ratio: 1/1) were recruited, who were told about the detailed experimental process before the test and signed a volunteer agreement. Avoiding the disturbing of fatigue, all the subjects had enough sleep and were arranged half an hour's rest with eyes closed before the test, ensuring all the subjects had a good mental and physiological state during the test.

2.2   Methods

2.2.1   Human Eyes Screening
Before the test, subjects were tested by optometer (NIDEK AR-310), dominant eye and wavefront aberration analyzer, in order to eliminate the high degree of myopia, big visual acuity difference between left and right eye and poor stereopsis feeling.

2.2.2   Testing Process
TV type in this study was 42 in. polarizing LED-3D (LG 42LW5500CA). Screen resolution is 1080 p. There were two types of 3D glasses (The degree of polarization of type A is 98.8 %, attaching angle is 125°–127°; The degree of polarization of type B is 99 %,

attaching angle is 109°–112°, optical index of type A is better than type B's), their photos are shown in Fig. 1. Schematic testing diagram is shown in Fig. 2: the entire test is in the darkroom environment, distance between subjects and TV is 3500 mm, video is the 3D standard sample.

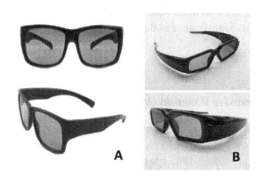

Fig. 1. Glasses style (A and B)

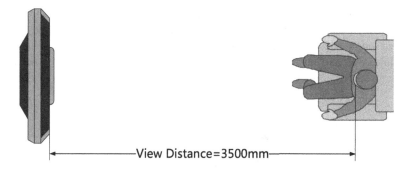

Fig. 2. Test site arrangement diagram

At first, after having a rest of half an hour with eyes closed in a darkroom, subjects were tested by wavefront analyzer, and the value of wave-front aberrations of subjects are collected. Then they began on the 3D standard samples' watching. The whole watching time was 90 min, and there was an aberration test every 45 min. In two days subjects had done the all test, and assured that everyone has worn the two kinds of glasses, A and B.

2.2.3 Test Equipments

Using the self-developed wave-front aberrometer (calibrated by The measurement test research institute of Beijing, Calibration certificate No.: H413Z-G0125) to test, and parameters are include overall wave-front aberrations and the 7th order and 35th term value of aberration calculated by Zernike function.

2.3 Statistical Methods

Statistics were performed using SPSS (Version 18.0 for Windows). Means and standard deviations were calculated for the total 60 subjects for wave-front aberrations. Paired t-test was used to describe the differences of the data before watching, 45 min after watching and 90 min after watching. And the two kinds of 3D glasses are also conducted by paired sample t test. Significance is defined as $p < 0.05$.

3 Results

3.1 Modulation Transfer Function (MTF)

MTF is one of the most important and visual evaluation index of video quality in applied optics. In this study, we synthesize 35 terms aberration indices, and calculate the MTF value of human eyes at various time spans. Results of the three MTF tests can be seen in Fig. 3, among them, "before watching" is the test result after subjects having a rest with the eyes closed on test site for 30 min, "45 min after watching" is the test result of the subjects who had viewed 3D film for 45 min, and "90 min after watching" is the test result after watching 3D film for 90 min. As Fig. 3 shows, "before watching" and "45 min after watching", "before watching" and "90 min after watching", are conducted by using the paired sample t test respectively, $p < 0.05$, and the difference in statistics is obvious. Meanwhile, we can find that the MTF value is gradually lowered (as the red arrow shows).

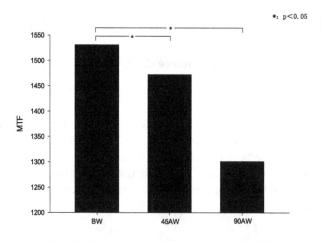

Fig. 3. The paired sample t-test results of MTF

3.2 The Root Mean Square (RMS) of Higher-Order Aberration

The RMS value of higher-order aberration is always used to evaluate the visual quality [11]. This study is analysing the variation trend of the 3rd, 4th and 5th order aberrations. All samples from 3rd–5th orders aberrations of 'before watching', '45 min after 'watching', and 'before watching' and '90 min after watching', are conducted by using the paired sample t-test. No obvious difference in statistics exists ($p > 0.05$). And variations of each order aberration are not consistent (As shown in Fig. 4).

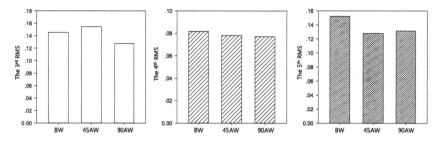

Fig. 4. The paired sample t-test results of RMS for the 'before watching (A)', '45 min after watching (B)' and '90 min after watching (C)'

3.3 The Mean of Higher-Order Aberration

This study begins statistical analysis from the variation trend of 3rd, 4th and 5th order aberration mean (as show in Fig. 5). The 3rd–5th orders aberration means of 'before watching', '45 min after watching', and 'before watching', '90 min after watching', are conducted by using the paired sample t test. Among them, 'before watching' and '45 min after watching in 3rd order ($p < 0.01$) and 5th order ($p < 0.05$) show 'Before watching' and '45 min after watching' in 3rd, 4th order ($p < 0.05$) and 5th order ($p < 0.01$) also have statistically significant. With the increase of watching time, we can find that 4th and 5th order aberration means are in the upward trend, as the red arrow shows in Fig. 5.

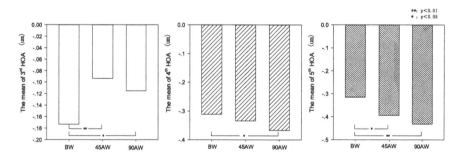

Fig. 5. The paired sample t-test results of means for the 'before watching (A)', '45 min after watching (B)' and '90 min after watching (C)'

3.4 Comparing of A and B 3D Glasses

The range of MTF changes of the two types glasses was compared by the analysis of the difference of MTF value between the time of 45 and 90 min after watching and the time before watching. The two changes were conducted by using Paired Sample T test.

The results are shown in Fig. 6. The parameters of the glasses A is superior to B in this study, and test results show that the MTF decline of wearing B glasses is significantly (p < 0.01) greater than A. The longer it was worn, the shaper it changed.

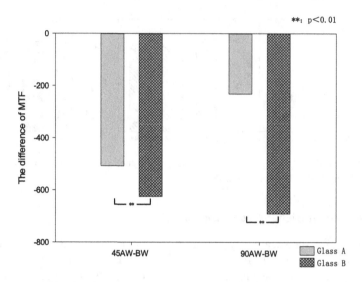

Fig. 6. The comparing result of MTF of A and B glasses

4   Discussion and Conclusion

4.1. In this study, MTF (Modulation Transfer Function) can be used as an analysis index for evaluation of visual comfort after watching 3D TV. With the increase of viewing time, MTF is gradually increasing.

4.2. From the result of study, we can conclude that RMS of higher order aberration has no significant difference before and after watching, and the change trend has no consistency. The index cannot be used to assess the visual health quality.

4.3. In this study, the changing trend of average value of 4th and 5th order aberration gradually grows with the increase of viewing time, and there is a significant difference between times before and after watching. So the parameter can be used to evaluate the visual health quality after watching the 3D TV.

4.4. Wearing different types of 3D glasses for watching 3D TV, the quality of glasses greatly affected the viewing quality of eye imaging after the view. Glasses with poor parameters caused higher eye fatigue level than glasses with better parameters.

4.5. This research just analyzed and compared aberrations of 3rd to 5th order, In follow-up studies, more relationship between index changes of higher-order aberrations (6th–35th order) and visual health will be studied. We will supply data and technical support for the formulation of visual health evaluation standards in the future.

Acknowledgments. This work is supported by the National Major Scientific Instrument Development Special Project of Ministry of Science and Technology of the People's Republic of China (2012YQ12008001).

References

1. Yano, S., Ide, S., Mitsuhashi, T., Thwaites, H.: A study of visual fatigue and visual comfort for 3D HDTV/HDTV images. Displays **23**, 191–201 (2002)
2. Kuze, J., Ukai, K.: Subjective evaluation of visual fatigue caused by motion images. Displays **29**, 159–166 (2008)
3. Ntuen, C.A., Goings, M., Reddin, M., Holmes, K.: Comparison between 2-D & 3-D using an autostereoscopic display: the effects of viewing field and illumination on performance and visual fatigue. Int. J. Ind. Ergon. **39**, 388–395 (2009)
4. Muna, S., Park, M.-C., Park, S., Whang, M.: SSVEP and ERP measurement of cognitive fatigue caused by stereoscopic 3D. Neurosci. Lett. **525**, 89–94 (2012)
5. Ukai, K., Howarth, P.A.: Visual fatigue caused by viewing stereoscopic motion images: background, theories, and observations. Displays **19**(2), 106–116 (2008)
6. Lambooij, M., Fortuin, M.F., IJsselsteijn, W.A., Heynderickx, I.: Visual discomfort associated with 3D displays. In: Fifth International Workshop on Video Processing and Quality Metrics (VPQM) (2010)
7. Lambooij, M., IJsselsteijn, W.A., Heynderickx, I.: Visual discomfort of 3DTV: assessment methods and modeling. Displays **32**(4), 209–218 (2011)
8. Maeda, N.: Wavefront technology in ophthalmology. Cur. Opin. Ophthalmol. **12**, 294–299 (2001)
9. Thibos, L.N., Applegate, R.A., Schwiegerling, J.T., et al.: Standards for reporting the optical aberrations of eyes. J. Refract. Surg. **18**, S652–S660 (2002)
10. Yan, W.: Research on visual and optical quality evaluation based on wavefront aberration and Modulation Transfer Function (MTF) before and after corneal refractive surgery. Doctor thesis, Tianjin Medical University, Tianjin, China (2006). (in Chinese)
11. Liu, F., Yong, J.H., Xu, M., Xu, H.W., Wei, F., Jing, C.L.: High-order aberration and visual quality. Int. J. Ophthalmol. **7**(4), 1113–1115 (2007)

User Experience Studies Based on Expectation Dis-confirmation Theory

Zhigang Zhang, Wangshu Cheng, and Zhenyu Gu[✉]

Interaction Design Lab, Shanghai Jiao Tong University, Shanghai, China
zygu@sjtu.edu.cn

Abstract. In order to measure and predict user experience (UX) more accurately, researchers have proposed a variety of models to integrate various factors affecting user experience. However, the complexity of user experience research is due to the dynamically changing factors of user and environment. The user expectation is not only affected by social communication and media, but also formed by his\her previous experience of similar products. To study user experience in the temporal dimension, we must consider the dynamic nature of user expectation and take the interaction between user expectation and user experience into account.

In this study, we first discuss the definition of user expectation, and then explore how the previous user experiences to existing products influence the present user expectation, and thereby affect the successive user experience on a new design.

Keywords: User experience · User expectation

1 Introduction

User experience (UX) refers to a person's emotions and attitudes about using a particular product, system or service (Wikipedia). User experience includes the practical, experiential, affective, meaningful and valuable aspects of human–computer interaction and product ownership. Additionally, it includes a person's perceptions of system aspects such as utility, ease of use and efficiency. User experience may be considered subjective in nature to the degree that it is about individual perception and thought with respect to the system. User experience is dynamic as it is constantly modified over time due to changing usage circumstances and changes to individual systems as well as the wider usage context in which they can be found. International Standard Organization (2008) defined the user experience as "a person's perceptions and responses that result from the use or anticipated use of a product, system or service". According to the ISO definition, user experience includes all the users' emotions, beliefs, preferences, perceptions, physical and psychological responses, behaviors and accomplishments that occur before, during and after use.

In the light of the definition, we consider user experience a multi-aspect feeling which based on the interaction between the user and the product (Roto 2006b), including the perception of product attributes (such as full-featured, innovative design, etc.), emotional change (such as satisfaction, pleasure, etc.), formation evaluation (such as

© Springer International Publishing Switzerland 2016
A. Marcus (Ed.): DUXU 2016, Part II, LNCS 9747, pp. 670–677, 2016.
DOI: 10.1007/978-3-319-40355-7_65

easy to use, value for money, etc.), behavioral changes (such as avoidance, re-purchase, etc.) and other aspects (Hassenzahl 2004).

So what factors determines or influences our overall experience in using a product or system? Many researchers studied from the one or several perspectives in the user experience, trying to find the determinants of the user experience; other researchers are trying to establish structure theory and process models from the theoretical level. Norman (2004) divided the product experience into three levels, named as visceral level, behavioral level and reflective level. Hassenzahl and Tractinsky (2006) proposed a user experience model which analyzed three main factors of user experience: the present state of the user, the properties of the system and the context of use (Fig. 1).

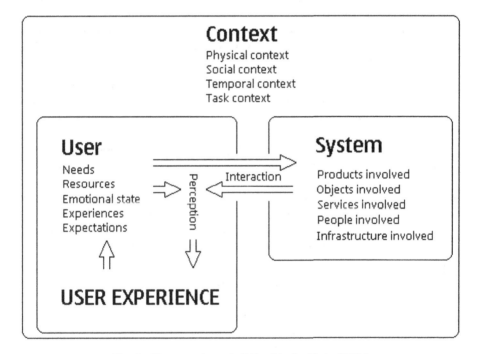

Fig. 1. User experience building blocks (Roto 2006a)

As we can see, these factors truly play a significant role in user experience. Additionally, time also influences the user experience. Single experiences influence the overall user experience. For example, the experience of a key click affects the experience of typing a text message, the experience of typing a message affects the experience of text messaging, and the experience of text messaging affects the overall user experience with the phone. The overall user experience is not simply a sum of smaller interaction experiences, because some experiences are more salient than others. This paper gives a report of how the previous user experience to a similar product affects the existing user experience with the expectation dis-confirmation theory.

2 Related Works

One of the difficulties of user experience researches is that the user inner state and the environment are changing over time. More and more researchers study user experience in longitudinal perspectives. Karapanos et al. (2009) used the DRM (Day Reconstruction Method, namely the users record usability problems and feelings by diary documentaries) to record and qualitatively analyze six mobile phone users within 8 weeks. The regression analysis of different stages of the user experience has revealed that factors playing the major roles in different stages of the user experience are different: early stage of the user experience is mainly affected by the impact of the hedonic properties of products, while the later stages of the user experience depend on the pragmatic values of products.

Karapanos et al. (2009) divided the product (or service) life cycle into three periods, namely orientation, incorporation, and identification. In each period, there is a key factor that decided the merits of the user experience.

(1) In the orientation period, when user gets more familiar with the product, the feeling of freshness gradually declines, and problems come out. Key factors affecting the user experience are the attraction of the product and user's learning cost.

(2) In the incorporation period, dependence helps the product integrate into people's daily life scenes gradually. During this period, availability and effectiveness are more important for the formation of the user experience.

(3) In identification period, people's mental recognition of the product gradually increases. It requires products to meet users' social and emotional needs, individuality, self-highlighting, and community sense. Thus, the degree of products' social and personalization mainly affects user experience (Fig. 2).

Hassenzahl (2004) also pointed out that some aspects of user experience are based on the intuitive feelings, such as satisfaction after using.

Other researchers studied the user's perception from the perspective of the individual attributes of user experience. Mendoza and Novick (2005) made a longitudinal study of software usability with school employee during eight weeks. They analyzed the crux of the availability and the change of user confusion degree. While the time of using the product increases, that the degree of user confusion declines and the proficiency is on the rise. They believed that the current research on usability paid too much attention to problems encountered by novice users while ignoring many important issues emerging in late period. The researchers should thoroughly analyze problems encountered by users of all time.

The formation of user experience is mainly the accumulation of past events (i.e., experience) and the outlook of unhappened events. Happened and unhappened events superimposed on the happening events on temporal dimension, and users' behavior to achieve goals will guide and restrict the formation of experience. These interrelated events form a specific experience. In time series, the formation of an experience, whether conscious or unconscious, is an important node in the event. Events are the pauses of experience. It can be described as a specific interaction process for a

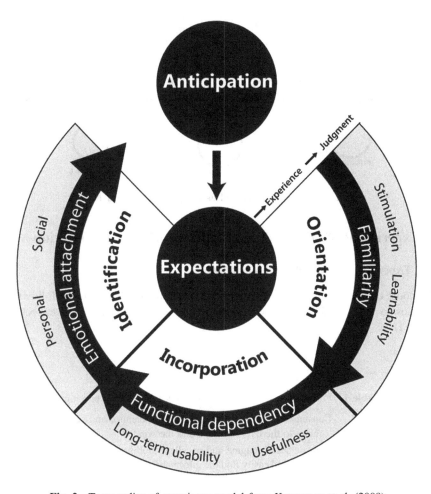

Fig. 2. Temporality of experience model from Karapanos et al. (2009)

particular task. The end of each event will be accompanied by a real-time experience. Homogeneous parts of those events are retained from similar experiences and eventually form an overall experience (Sun and Wu 2014) (Fig. 3).

In business, customer satisfaction plays an important role in service evaluation. Researchers believe that there are a number of factors that affect customer satisfaction: customer expectations, customer perception of quality, price, customer perceived value, etc.

Oliver is the first scholar who takes the expectation into the research of the customer satisfaction analysis. He takes the expectation of service quality as the base point of evaluation after purchase, and puts forward that customer satisfaction is the function of customer expectations and "expectation dis-confirmation". Oliver's "expectation dis-confirmation" is the difference between perceived quality and expected quality. When customers perceive the qualities less than their expectations, they tend to feel disappointed, and otherwise they feel rejoicing (Zhigang et al. 2011).

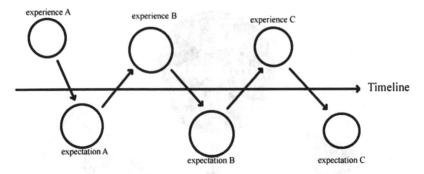

Fig. 3. User experience and user expectations interaction

3   Experiment of Dis-confirmation Effect of User Expectation

3.1   Experiment Materials and Variables

We choose online shopping apps as experiment material. We also select the following 8 variables to analysis the interaction between user experience and user expectation (Table 1):

Table 1. Variables to evaluate user experience and user expectation

Design feature of the app	Consumers perceived shopping app appearance and aesthetic feeling, refers to the overall image and the wind
Usability of operation	Website search engine and excellent mobility can help consumers simply and easily find the information or product they want when self operation
Product quality assurance	The degree of consistency with the online store selling products operators promise
Network security	Consumers in the shopping site in financial payment and the privacy of personal information on the safety degree of feeling
price advantage	Online store to save a lot of costs, customer expects to buy cheaper products through the online store
Convenience	Internet to break the boundaries of space and time, consumers can buy things online fast
Network interaction	Online stores and consumers continue to dialogue, mutual communication, and through the continuous feedback and correction get to know each other and improve the efficiency of the service, turn to a timely response to customers
Personalize	Online store provide personalized service for every customer, according to customer preferences, history, and identification

3.2   Tests and Data Collection

Step 1: To compare with previous findings, this paper takes the existing methods of questionnaire.

Step 2: Before the formal experiment and questionnaire, we post the questionnaire to 15 students, in order to test the variables. There is 37 questions in the original questionnaire. Four failed questions are removed.

Step 3: There are two android apps (app A and app B). Before the formal experiment, we conduct a pre-test in order to compare the user experiences of the two apps. Then 60 young students who have never used these two apps before participates in the formal experiment. They are divided into two groups. The first group uses the apps in the order from app A to B. The second group tests in the reverse order as a control group. Before using the apps, the two groups are asked to fill in the questionnaires to give the current expectations. Then after using the first app, the two groups fill in the questionnaires once again and participated in the interviews to report their experiences of the apps and the updated expectations for the next app. After using the next app, the user experiences of the last one are measured. The data of two groups have been compared to find the changes of user experience and user expectations.

Data Collection. We selected 105 university students in Shanghai. A total of 105 questionnaires were distributed, among them 96 were fully completed, and 60 were valid questionnaires. After analyzing the data collected, we visualize the results in Figs. 4, 5, 6 and 7.

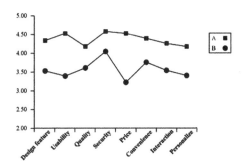

Fig. 4. User experience comparison of A and B

As shown in Fig. 4, the user experiences of app A and app B are compared on eight dimensions. It is indicated that the user experience of app A is better than the app B. Figure 5 shows that after using app A or app B, user expectations are changed. It is indicated that app A improves the user expectation to the next app, while app B reduces the user expectation to the next app. Figure 6 shows the experience of using app B after using app A and the experience of using the app B without using app A before. It is apparently that the user experience of app B after using app A is worse than the

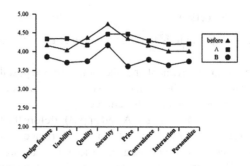

Fig. 5. User expectation comparison of A and B

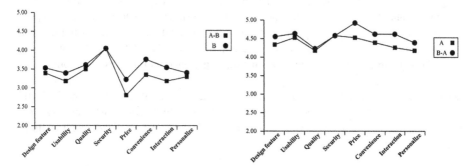

Fig. 6. User experience comparison for B

Fig. 7. User experience comparison for A

experience of using app B directly. Figure 7 shows the user experience of using app A after using app B and the experience of using app A without using app B in advance. It is indicated that after using app B, the user experience of app A is better than the experience of using app A directly.

4   Results and Conclusions

The experiment shows that the existing user experience will affect the subsequent user experience by changing the user expectations in between. Good user experiences will raise user expectations for the future uses of products, and poor user experiences will reduce user expectations to future uses of product.

User experience is now the core competitiveness of services and products. User experience determines the entire satisfaction of products.

Evaluation of user experience is not only judged by the perceived value, but the diffidence between perceived value and user expectation. That is what the study of user expectations contributes to user experience research. When the perceived value is larger than user expectation, user experience is positive and the product is satisfactory.

When perceived value is less than user expectation, user experience is negative and the product might fail on the market.

Former similar products will directly affect user expectations to new products. Therefore, to do a good experience design, designers must investigate what similar products the targeted users have already used and make sure that the new product goes beyond the users' expectations.

References

Hassenzahl, M.: The interplay of beauty, goodness, and usability in interactive products. Hum.-Comput. Interact. **19**, 319–349 (2004)

Hassenzahl, M., Tractinsky, N.: User experience – a research agenda. Behav. Inf. Technol. **25**(2), 91–99 (2006)

ISO (International Standards Organization): ISO 9241-210. Ergonomics of human system interaction. In: Part 210: Human-Centred Design for Interactive Systems. ISO, Geneva, Switzerland (2008)

Karapanos, E., Zimmerman, J., Forlizzi, J., Martens, J.-B.: User experience over time: an initial framework. In: Greenberg, S., Hudson, S.E. (eds.) Proceedings of 27th Annual SIGCHI Conference on Human Factors in Computing Systems - CHI 2009, pp. 729–738. ACM, New York, USA (2009)

Mendoza, V., Novick, D.: Usability over time. In: Proceedings of 23rd Conference on Computer Documentation, pp. 151–158. ACM, Coventry, UK (2005)

Norman, D.A.: Emotional Design, Why We Love (or Hate) Everyday Things. Basic Books, New York (2004)

Roto, V.: User experience building blocks. In: Conjunction with Nordi CHI 2006 Conference (2006a). http://research.nokia.com/files/UX-BuildingBlocks.pdf. Accessed 4 July 2010

Roto, V.: Web browsing on mobile phones -characteristics of user experience. Ph.D. dissertation, Helsinki University of Technology, Espoo, Finland (2006b)

Sun, L., Wu, J.: Total user experience design based on time dimension. Packag. Eng. **2**, 009 (2014)

User Experience (Wikipedia). https://en.wikipedia.org/wiki/User_experience

Zhigang, S., Feng, W., Jianmin, W.: The measurement of cumulative satisfaction: an analytical model based on dynamic customer expectation. Nankai Bus. Rev. **3**, 142–150 (2011)

Accessibility and Usability of Websites Intended for People with Disabilities: A Preliminary Study

Emilene Zitkus[(✉)], Aline C. Brigatto, Ana Lya M. Ferrari, Gabriel H.C. Bonfim,
Idinei F.P. Carvalho Filho, Thaís D. Reis, Fausto O. Medola, and Luis C. Paschoarelli

Department of Design, Universidade Estadual Paulista, Bauru, Brazil
emilenezitkus@gmail.com,
{fausto.medola,paschoarelli}@faac.unesp.br

Abstract. This paper reports a preliminary study evaluating accessibility and usability of a Brazilian government website - the national digital catalogue of assistive technology (CNPTA). Although since 2004 e-government information should be broadly accessible, several studies indicate that web accessibility has not been accomplished in many government websites. This study is part of a research project that analyses whether this negative outcome replicates on government websites intended for people with disabilities. The website was assessed by automated testing and the results were compared to the outcomes from user testing. The paper discusses the findings compared with past studies and not only proposes specific aspects to enhance the website, but also it outlines several points to be considered in the next steps of the research project, as well as in other research that considers web accessibility and usability for blind people.

Keywords: Blind user · Brazilian government website · Visual impairment · Web development · Accessibility guidelines · Universal design · Inclusive design

1 Introduction

According to the last Brazilian census 23.9 % of the population have at least one type of physical or sensorial disability [1], with 18.6 % of the population being visually impaired. Although, the visual disability is the most predominant disability among the population, there is a number of barriers and challenges that these individuals have to face in their everyday life. Access to information is one of them; mainly for those with severe disability or blind people.

Globally speaking, societies have become dependent of the information and the communication provided by digital technologies. For the people with disabilities, the internet represents an opportunity to access information that would be unavailable otherwise. However, websites that are difficult to access and use are countless, excluding most of the visually impaired people [2–4].

Similarly, in Brazil, the internet is an acknowledged source of general information and service, including those provided by the government. Since 2004 it is compulsory for any Brazilian government websites to comply with accessibility guidelines established in the e-MAG - Brazilian web accessibility standard for e-government [5, 6].

© Springer International Publishing Switzerland 2016
A. Marcus (Ed.): DUXU 2016, Part II, LNCS 9747, pp. 678–688, 2016.
DOI: 10.1007/978-3-319-40355-7_66

The intention of such resolution is to enable people with disabilities, including blind individuals, to access any government information. However, some studies indicate that these websites have not accomplished this standard [7–10]. More recently the government has used the web to inform people with disabilities regarding their rights and to assist them in the purchase of assistive technology. In this case, specifically, it is essential to ensure that a diverse range of people is able to access the information available in such websites. Thus, this study evaluates the accessibility and usability of a government website developed to inform disabled people about assistive technologies available on market. It is called the national digital catalogue of assistive technology (CNPTA) – http://www.assistiva.mct.gov.br.

Nevertheless, the relationship between web accessibility and web usability is often understood in two distinguished ways. The former as the problems encountered by users with disabilities which prevent them from using the website; and, the latter as the issues found by non-disabled people [14]. Following this concept in 1994 the World Wide Web Consortium started to develop web accessibility guidelines which became a global reference of guidelines, the WCAG - Web Content Accessibility Guidelines [15].

Since it was first created the WCAG has progressed towards promoting universal access. The guidelines have improved the way to evaluate accessibility by adopting different methods, including usability methods, like user testing [12]. This improvement may be a response to past studies that indicated the need to connect website usability with disabled people [14, 16–19]. As highlighted by Theofanos and Redish (2003),

> *"observing, listening to, and talking with representatives of the target audience in this case, users of screen readers are critical. To truly meet the needs of all users, it is not enough to have guidelines that are based on technology. It is also necessary to understand the users and how they work with their tools."*

In the case of blind users, web accessibility is dependent of screen readers. This type of assistive technology translates the information provided in the website in audio outputs. Most of them use standardised protocols to identify icons, texts, hyperlinks, menus, and other graphic interfaces [15]. Hence, the efficiency of such assistive technologies combined with the design of the website are fundamental to allow the use of the website by blind people.

The present study analysed whether the catalogue complies with the WCAG 2.0 through automated and user testing. Although the legislation indicates the Brazilian guidelines e-MAG, we understood that the e-MAG cover the same criteria established in the WCAG 2.0, but the e-MAG are in Portuguese what makes the guidelines more accessible for web-developers in Brazil [6, 11]. However, the WCAG 2.0 are more detailed and up-to-date guidelines, which is important for the purpose of the research project that this study is one part. Moreover, the WCAG 2.0 guidelines cover different types of web-accessibility evaluation, such as inspection methods, automated testing, screening techniques, subjective assessments and user testing [12, 13].

Considering the WCAG 2.0 conformance requirements [20] the study presented here explores the usability test and the automated accessibility test in order to answer the following question: In the website under investigation, is there any relationship between the score in the automated testing and the results of the user testing with blind users?

2   Methods

New studies on digital interface design consider accessibility in use, taking into account evaluation tools such as those used for usability [13, 14]. In this preliminary study we evaluated the national digital catalogue of assistive technology (CNPTA), which is shown in Fig. 1.

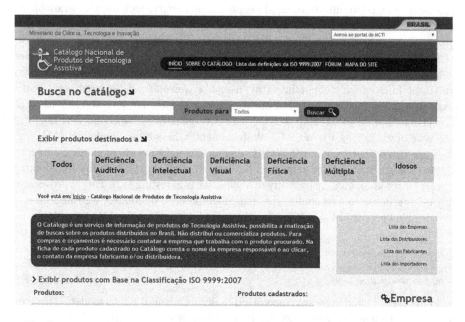

Fig. 1.   National digital catalogue of assistive technology http://www.assistiva.mct.gov.br

2.1   The Website

The research group belongs to the Ergonomics and Interface Laboratory (UNESP-Bauru, Brazil) in which several research projects are related to assistive technology. The researchers are familiar with the website chosen. In fact, this was the reason for choosing the website. The research group found many usability problems every time they accessed the CNPTA searching for some assistive technologies. Five of the issues are the following:

1. lack of information regarding the assistive technologies available in the catalogue;
2. products without any image, or images are in very low resolution;
3. the information supplied do not follow the same structure. Some products are described in details, others are briefly described and others do not have a description. In other cases, some products require a login to access the information;
4. some of the products in the CNPTA are out-of-date, in some cases they are out of the market;

5. a faulty searching system:
   - users cannot filter the options by the type of products they are searching for;
   - the suppliers' links offered in the website are not links to connect to the products they found in the catalogue, it links to the home page of the supplier, which means that users have to do all the search again in the website of the supplier. In some cases, the product is no longer available. As a result, the user is only linked to another catalogue;

Many of the problems encountered by the research group were visually identified and thus, a question was raised to understand whether the website would be accessible for the intended users - people with disabilities.

2.2 User Testing

Blind people are the users who encounter the most difficulties in using the web [14]. Thus, they can potentially highlight accessibility and usability problems whenever a website is developed [17]. In the present study, the participants were volunteers who receive professional training in an institute for blind people - Lar Escola Santa Luzia para Cegos - based in the city of Bauru (SP-Brazil). Two blind individuals who are familiarised with online resources and frequent users of the internet participated in the study.

Procedure. Before we run the test a consent form was read to each participant, complying with the ERG BR 1002 - ergonomist code of practice [21]. The form assured the following aspects of the study:

1. the evaluation was to test the website, not their skills to use the internet;
2. the data collected would be coded to protect their anonymity;
3. their right of leaving the study anytime without the need to explain the reason for doing so.

We asked their permission to record all evaluation sessions by using a digital camera for later viewing and analysis. Both participants gave permission to record and signed the consent form.

The tests were conducted in the institute where the participants use the computers, which means that they were familiarised with the equipment, including the keyboard and the screen-reader (NVDA screen reader).

Two types of questionnaires were applied: one at the beginning and another at the end of each task. The former was applied just before we run the test, in which the participants shared personal data, like age, computer experience, including familiarity with the internet (years of use), their expertise, the frequency of use, etc.; whilst the latter was applied after each task, in which we enquired about their opinion regarding the accessibility and usability of the website.

We divided the usability tests into four distinguished activities to be performed by the participants. All activities were designed to be brief and to ensure that it would not cause any embarrassment to them.

The Tasks. We gave the four tasks one at a time:

1. the first activity involved to find the website of the national digital catalogue of assistive technology – http://www.assistiva.mct.gov.br.
2. the second activity was to seek for supporting products of communication and information on the initial page of the website. Among the products encountered, the participant should find products for reading and among them, the one of interest.
3. the third activity was to seek for packs (game cards) or Braille printers on the website and then, based on the information available to choose one of interest.
4. the fourth activity involved searching among the products related to visual impairment on the page four of the catalogue, the product most interesting to them.

The ISO 9241 principles were used to evaluate effectiveness, efficiency and satisfaction, which were measured by the following criteria:

- effectiveness: the objectives successfully achieved;
- efficiency: the tasks completed correctly within the variables of time and degree of difficulty - measured by the number of errors made, and;
- satisfaction: the answers given in a questionnaire.

2.3 Automated Testing

We chose the WAVE accessibility checker to run the automated testing. Initially, the accessibility checker was chosen based on the resources available online and the easy-of-use [22]. It also counted in the selection, the type of outcomes provided by the checker, whether oriented to issues encountered by blind people - like the sequence browsed by screen readers [23]. We ran the test on all the WebPages accessed in the user testing.

3   Results

The results of the automated testing were compared with the results of the user testing ran with two blind people.

3.1 User Testing

Both participants are expert users, who works with computer. They teach blind or people with severe visual impairments to use the computer and the internet. Their experience in using the internet is over 10 years, which includes using it to socialise, to search, for shopping, to work, etc. Although they heard about the CNPTA website, they were not familiar with the website, neither had ever accessed it.

The first participant (P1) used the web browser Mozilla Firefox, while the second (P2) used the Internet Explorer. Both used an open source screen readers named NonVisual Desktop Access - NVDA. Although, they navigated in the website through different keyboard commands, the outcomes of the user testing were very similar. For example, P1 used a searching tool provided by the screen reader that helped him to search for the products, listing them by their initials; whereas P2 navigated the website following the sequence established for the screen reader in the page.

According to the participants, they performed the tasks without much effort. The amount of time spent by them in each task is shown in Fig. 2. In the third task, when the first participant sought "packs in Braille" he could not find the packs available in the website. The time spent performing this task is shown in Fig. 2, which represents his difficulty to find the product. Although he was not able to finish the task he was still satisfied with the majority of the features of the website, apart from the searching system.

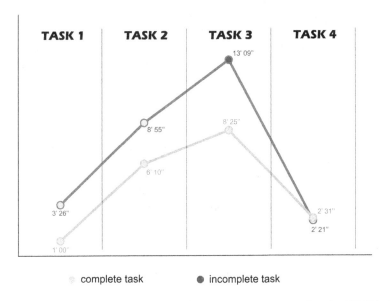

Fig. 2. Participants (P1 - dark line; P2 - light line) performance accessing the CNPTA. (Color figure online)

Similarly, although the second participant for few times found himself navigating in another website, due to unexpected links in the heading of the website, he was satisfied with all the features of the website (structure, navigability, searching system and information).

For many times, during the second and third tasks, both participants tried the searching form and did not succeed. They typed the word correctly but, due to an error that occurs in the searching system, the results were unrelated, incomplete or incorrect. However, both mentioned that the amount of time spent is the usual time when navigating and exploring new websites. Moreover, both explained that although the website presents some issues, they were satisfied with it. The reason gave, in their words, is:

> "*among the websites available, it* [the type of problems in the CNPTA] *is just normal. We could say* [that this is a problem], *but it is present in all websites, for example, every time we come back to the page it* [the NVDA] *reads all the headings text by text. This is something that cannot change, it would break the website structure, it cannot change. So, it* [CNPTA] *is just an average website*". P1 - 00:22:50.

"[generally we have problems if] *the structure or links are not specified, or a function or infor-*
mation is in Flash, or other issues [i.e. as mentioned later, security codes do not have audio]
that cause problems during the navigation. These type of problems I haven't found in this website
[CNPTA]*"*. P2 - 00:42:01.

Additionally, in the third task, the second participant chose a product of interest, but the
product could not be accessed, due to another error that occurs in the website. Some
products do not have any information, any description and any link to suppliers; they
are listed there only or; in some cases, they are in the CNPTA, but not in the market
anymore. However, when asked, the participant described himself as satisfied with the
information provided.

For P2 the most important and positive aspect of the website is that he was able to
use it without asking any help. Moreover, for him it was important that all products listed
in the website are ISO certified, which is a guarantee of their quality. However, he
pointed out some issues in the website based on his experience in teaching people with
visual impairment: the website do not offer accessibility features, such as the ones to
increase the size of the text or to increase the contrast level between text and background.
He also mentioned that he benefits from keyboard shortcuts, that are available in some
websites, which allow the user to skip to the content; to go to the searching form; to go
to the initial page; to skip headings. He mentioned some websites that makes good use
of such resources (i.e. http://www.fundacaodorina.org.br).

At the end of all tasks P1 mentioned that the products' descriptions could be better
if they provide more details about the products, suppliers and price.

3.2   Automated Testing

The WAVE accessibility checker were used in every page the participants accessed to
understand the relationship between the issues indicated in the automated testing and
the ones found in the user testing. Figure 3 shows an example of the pages assessed.

Among all the pages the WAVE evaluated the majority of the results are alerts instead
of errors. The errors are divided into two types: one error is a missing form label in the
main search bar, and; twelve errors are empty links throughout the initial and secondary
pages. The latter issues are not directly related to the problems encountered in the user
testing. The former, however, can be one of the reasons for the difficulties found by the
participants whenever they used the search bar, added to the fault in the searching system
itself.

The automated accessibility checker highlighted the issues encountered in the
website. It does not offer a checklist for web developers to check if some essential
features to improve accessibility and usability are available. This may explain the low
rate of errors encountered.

4   Discussion

This study confirmed the need to establish usability tests with disabled people to enhance
website accessibility, as suggested in past studies and proposed by WCAG 2.0 [14, 16–19].

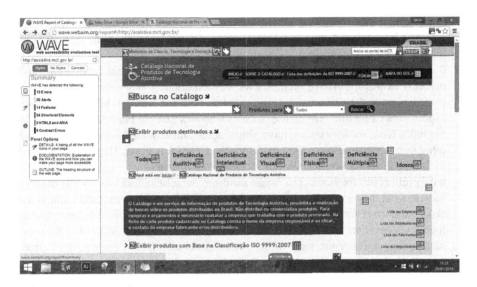

Fig. 3. Results of WAVE test in the initial page of the CNPTA

User testing not only evaluates what is in the website, but also elucidates the user needs based on problems encountered. Based on this preliminary study, we can underline that only the use of automated testing would not highlight accessibility features that are missing in the website. For example, the possibility of changing text size or contrast level is missing in the CNPTA, but the WAVE evaluates the website content, not what is omitted. In reality, in this study, the user testing indicated more needs and features to improve than the errors highlighted in the automated checker.

Based on the preliminary findings, we cannot affirm whether there is a relationship between the score in the automated testing and the results of the user testing with blind users. If on the one hand, the twelve 'empty link errors' indicated in the automated checker did not seem to us that directly affected the use of the website, on the other hand, the single 'missing form label error' in the main search bar affected both participants. In fact, this error related to the search bar was the only error highlighted in both tests - automated and user. The participants had difficulties whenever they tried to search in the website. In the case of the first participant the problem unable him to finish the task. The second participant were challenged by the feature also, though he tended to alleviate its performance by saying that the time spent is normal.

In reality, in both user testing the responses gave by the participants were highly positive (they were very satisfied with the website in most aspects); whereas the performance observed were rather more difficult (with low efficiency in most of the tasks and in one case ineffective). There may be many reasons for the disparity between the difficulties found by the users (recorded in the observation), and the positive responses (gave in the questionnaire); here we discuss three of them:

1. it possibly highlights the inadequate use of ranking questions at this stage. We understood that the use of ranking questions in the questionnaires used after tasks did not add much, comparing to the comments that the participants made at the end

of the study. The comments elucidated their needs and problems when accessing websites in general. A more qualitative approach will be taken in the next steps of the research.

2. it indicates that the participants have low expectation regarding the accessibility and usability of websites based on their everyday experience. When the second participant explained the reasons for being satisfied with the website, he outlined many aspects that cause difficulty to use, such as websites that use Flash®; do not specify the links; have security codes; have plugs incompatible with the screen reader; and other issues. Comparing to these websites the CNPTA is good. They are habituated to finding usability problems when accessing the internet.

3. it may reflect that they expect to "make mistakes" which can take time to find the way back to what they are seeking. Both participants highlighted that the time spent in the tasks are normal for first access. Comparing to the usability issues we (researchers) found whenever we had accessed the CNPTA, we can say that, differently from the participants, we attribute most of our unsuccessful attempts to the website's errors (messages that we see when accessing) and lack of information in it.

In summary, although we cannot state that there is a direct relationship between the automated testing and the user testing, we can affirm that the user testing with the two blind people brought to light several aspects for improvements that would not be recognised or even indicated through automated testing. The next section describes some of them.

5   Recommendations

In this section we outline some recommendations to improve the accessibility and usability of the CNPTA website:

- an efficient searching system, with a label identifying the main search bar - currently it does not work if the type of disability is not identified, and; it is too difficult to search for a category of products;
- features that allow adjustments on text size and contrast level;
- features that allow shortcuts through keyboard keys - in the case of government websites intended for people with disabilities, the shortcuts could be the same, avoiding variations that could affect the usability of these websites;
- the use of high resolution images;
- the use of standardised information to be provided by the suppliers;
- features that allow automate update of the catalogue if products have changed by suppliers or are unavailable in the market;
- adjustment of the links of the products in the catalogue, connecting to the same products on the suppliers' websites;
- change the sequence of the main menu, with the visual disability being the first option.

6 Conclusions

A careful search for methods to assess the accessibility and usability of websites has to be considered when preparing a study or developing a website. Mainly, in cases of websites intended for people with disabilities. Based in this preliminary study, we can underline that only the use of automated testing would not highlight accessibility features that are missing in the website. In this case, user testing is fundamental to understand usability problems that drives to inaccessible information, or in other words to accessibility problems. Thus, it is difficult to distinguish where accessibility ends and usability starts when discussing website accessibility for disabled people. User observations and open questions that encourage the user to speak their needs are resources that highlight the real problems and help web developers to translate accessibility guidelines to needs and practical solutions. Consequently, such methods are complementary and should be broadly used in accessibility test.

Acknowledgments. The authors would like to thank the institute for blind people - Lar Escola Santa Luzia para Cegos and the participants for their time and highly appreciated comments. Also, we gratefully acknowledge CNPq (National Council for Scientific and Technological Development - Brazil, Process N. 458740/2013-6), CAPES (Coordination for the Improvement of Higher Level Personnel – Brazil - PGPTA 59/2014 - Project 10) for the financial support.

References

1. IBGE - Instituto Brasileiro de Geografia e Estatística. Censo Demográfico 2010 - Características Gerais da População, Religião e Pessoas com Deficiência. Rio de Janeiro: Ministério do Planejamento, Orçamento e Gestão (2010). (Translation from Portuguese: Brazilian Census)
2. Raufi, B., Feratia, M., Zenunia, X., Ajdaria, J., Ismailia, F.: Methods and techniques of adaptive web accessibility for the blind and visually impaired. Proc.- Soc. Behav. Sci. **195**, 1999–2007 (2015)
3. Guimarães, I.J.B., Sousa, M.R.F.: Acessibilidade em websites de comércio eletrônico: avaliação através da interação com usuários cegos na Paraíba. Pesq. Bras. em Ci. da Inf. e Bib., João Pessoa **10**(1), 185–197 (2015). (Translation from Portuguese: Accessibility of e-comerce websites: interactive evaluation with blind users.)
4. Scatolim, R.L.: A importância da acessibilidade como mediadora da informação na internet para os deficientes visuais. In: XXXII Congresso Brasileiro de Ciências da Comunicação (2009). (Translation from Portuguese: Accessibility of internet content to visual impaired people)
5. Decreto nº 5.296 de 2 de Dezembro 2004 (2004)
6. e-MAG: Modelo de Acessibilidade em Governo Eletrônico (2014). http://emag.governoeletronico.gov.br/#s3. Accessed 23 Dec 2015
7. Pereira, A.S., Machado, A.M., Carneiro, T.C.J.: Web accessibility evaluation on Brazilian institutions in higher education. Inform. Soc. **23**(3), 123–142 (2013)

8. Silveira, D.S., Silveira, M.A.A., Andrade, S.R.P., Cunha, G.R., Ferreira, A.F.: Acessibilidade de Informações em Portais Governamentais para Deficientes Visuais: O Caso da Receita Federal do Brasil. In: XI Encontro Nacional de Pesquisa em Ciência da Informação Inovação e inclusão social: questões contemporâneas da informação (2010). (Translation from Portuguese: Accessibility of e-gov information: the case of Brazilian Revenue website)

9. Freire, A.P., de Castro, M., Fortes, R.P.M.: Accessibility of Brazilian state government websites: a quantitative analysis between 1996 and 2007. Revista de Administracao Publica 43(2), 395–414 (2009)

10. Tangarife, T., Mont'Alvao, C.: Estudo Comparativo Utilizando uma Ferramenta de Avaliacao de Acessibilidade para Web. In: CLIHC 2005, pp. 313–318. ACM, Cuernavaca, Mexico (2005). (Translation from Portuguese: Comparative study of websites with the use of an accessibility evaluation tool)

11. Rocha, J.A.P., Duarte, A.B.S.: Diretrizes de acessibilidade web: um estudo comparativo entre as WCAG 2.0 e o e-MAG 3.0. Inc. Soc. 5(2), 73–86 (2012)

12. W3C/WCAG2.0: General Techniques for WCAG 2.0 (2014). https://www.w3.org/TR/WCAG20-TECHS/general.html Accessed 23 Dec 2015

13. Brajnik, G., Yesilada, Y., Harper, S.: Is accessibility conformance an elusive property? A study of validity and reliability of WCAG 2.0. ACM Trans. Access. Comput. 4(2), 8 (2012)

14. Petrie, H., Kheir, O.: Relationship between accessibility and usability of web sites. In: SIGCHI Conference on Human Factors in Computing Systems, pp. 397–406. ACM Press, New York (2007)

15. Chiang, M.F., Cole, R.G., Gupta, S., Kaiser, G.E., Starren, J.B.: Computer and world wide web accessibility by visually disabled patients: problems and solutions. Surv. Ophthalmol. 50, 394–405 (2005)

16. Petrie, H., Fraser, H., Neil, K.: Tension, what tension? Website accessibility and visual design. In: International World Wide Web Conference, pp. 13–18. ACM, New York (2004)

17. Theofanos, M., Redish, J.: Guidelines for accessible and usable web sites: observing users who work with screen readers. Interactions 10, 36–51 (2003)

18. Shneiderman, B.: Promoting universal usability with multi-layer interface design. In: Proceedings of the 2003 Conference on Universal Usability. ACM Press, New York (2003)

19. Shneiderman, B.: Universal usability: pushing human-computer interaction research to empower every citizen. Commun. ACM 43, 84–91 (2000)

20. W3C: Understanding Conformance (2015). https://www.w3.org/TR/UNDERSTANDING-WCAG20/conformance.html. Accessed 05 Jan 2016)

21. ABERGO: Norma ERG BR 1002 - Código de Deontologia do Ergonomista Certificado. Associação Brasileira de Ergonomia (2003)

22. W3C/WAI: Web Accessibility Evaluation Tools List (2014). https://www.w3.org/WAI/ER/tools/index.html. Accessed 21 Dec 2015

23. Youngblood, N.E., MacKiewicz, J.: A usability analysis of municipal government website home pages in Alabama. Govern. Inf. Q. 29(4), 582–588 (2012)

Passenger Friendly Bus Stop Signs Design by Integrating Kano's Model into Riding Needs Analysis

Chuan-yu Zou[1(✉)], Guangxin Wang[2], Yijun Chen[3], and Yongquan Chen[1]

[1] Research Group of Way Guidance,
China National Institute of Standardization, Beijing 100191, China
zouchy@cnis.gov.cn
[2] Psychology Department, Beijing Forestry University, Beijing 100083, China
[3] School of Design, Central Academy of Fine Arts, Beijing 100102, China

Abstract. **Objective:** Based on the result of passenger satisfaction survey of the bus transportation signs, three signs that scored highly unsatisfied were picked out. The 13 riding information carried by those three signs and in urgent need were extracted. And then Kano questionnaire were made to analysis the attribute of 13 riding information. **Methods:** 558 volunteers participated in the passenger satisfaction survey. 400 volunteers participated in the Kano questionnaire survey. **Results:** There are six must-be information, one one-dimensional information, three attractive information and three indifferent information. **Conclusion:** An optimized plan and the corresponding suggestions were put forward to improve the design and setting of bus stop's signs.

Keywords: Bus stop · Sign · Public transportation sign · Kano model

1 Introduction

As one of the most important key nodes in public transit network, bus stop is the basic infrastructure that helps passenger riding along bus routes [1, 2], and also bears the responsibility of transferring with pedestrians (including bike riders) and other transportations. In addition, the bus transportation has more choices in setting bus stops and lines. The density of bus transportation network is much higher than the density of urban rail transit network (see Table 1). As a result, the riding information that different kinds of signs (for example, bus stop board, neighborhood map and bus operating diagram, etc.) set at bus stops covers a much wider effective radiation range and influences more people. The information service level of bus stops has direct influence on passenger satisfaction both for bus services, and for the entirety city transportation.

The bus travelling information often conveys to passengers and pedestrians by various public transportation signs, e.g. bus stop board, neighborhood map and bus operating diagram, which combined by graphical symbols, text, numeral and color. Public transportation signs are the essential public information communication system that guides passengers travelling safe, well ordered [3].

© Springer International Publishing Switzerland 2016
A. Marcus (Ed.): DUXU 2016, Part II, LNCS 9747, pp. 689–698, 2016.
DOI: 10.1007/978-3-319-40355-7_67

Table 1. Station numbers of bus and urban transit of major cities in China*

	Beijing	Tianjin	Shanghai	Guangzhou	Nanjing	Wuhan	Shenzhen	Xi'an	Hongkong	Taipei
Ratio of bus stations and subway stations (times)	17	15	24	50	14	23	26	24	65	28

*Note: Data is collected from online map.

1.1   Public Transportation Signs

The construction of bus stops in China, take Beijing as an example, the public transportation signs used at bus stops are two kinds: bus stop board and city map (see Fig. 1), they are often centralized set, that is, the majority travelling information in passengers' needs are provided by bus stop boards. The advantages of centralized setting are easy to read without searching. But the disadvantages are also obvious. First, it does not fit well with the changed bus lines and bus services. In 2014, the reform of bus fare and subway fare were launched in Beijing, 40234 bus stop boards needed to be changed [4], a lot of manpower and material resources were cost as only one piece of price information should be changed. Second, the bus boards' setting positions are easy to become the localized congestion points and impede passengers boarding or alighting.

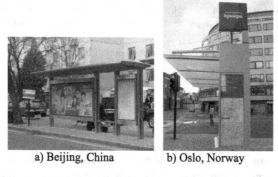

a) Beijing, China   b) Oslo, Norway

Fig. 1. Photos of bus stops

The public transportation signs used at abroad bus stops are various: circuit board, current station sign, bus stop board, neighborhood map, bus operating diagram and bus operating time table (see Fig. 1). Those signs are modularized designed and set, that is, according to the needs of observing in far or close distance, they are set at different positions. As the bus stops are divided into multiple information release spaces, the advantages of modularized design are easy to change information carried, easy to be read. But the disadvantage is that passengers need to find information that set at different position. They can't obtain information at one point.

The current Chinese national standard [5] only specifies one kind of bus transportation signs — bus stop board, while does not mention others. Moreover, the design patterns specified haven't widely used in various regions. As results, the bus transportation signs used are various; information carried can't meet passengers' needs, the design patterns are inconsistent. Extracting the information of bus stops carried, classifying the information in terms of passengers' needs, we can arrange the information appropriately according to the degree of association and passengers' interests when making the plan of bus stops. It can facilitate passengers' travelling, also ease the bus stop congestion, and improve the service level of bus transportation.

The current studies on bus transportation signs often focus on the existing problems of the bus stop boards' design and improvement. In Chen [6] opinion, there are four main problems in the design of bus stop boards, e.g. unable to identify one-way or two-way lines, unable to find the bus stop position on the opposite side of the street, lack the transfer information, and lack the direction of the bus routing in the city. He also comes up with suggestions on design principles and methods. Wang [7] analyses the common visual elements used in bus transportation signs design, e.g. graphical symbol, diagram, text and color. He proposes the specifications in design the visual interface of bus transportation signs.

1.2   Kano Model

Sun [8] investigated the bus stop boards at Haidian District in Beijing using small sample size and found passengers unsatisfied with Beijing bus transportation signs. He summarizes existing five main problems. Ding et al. [9] conducted a survey on bus stop boards in Shanghai. The survey includes 12 aspects related with design and reading effect, e.g. color scheme, legibility, font size and Information comprehensive. They propose improvement of bus stop boards design based on survey results. But current studies do not analysis the attributes of bus riding information.

In his model, Kano et al. [10] distinguish five types of product or service quality attributes according to their objective performance and the feeling of users. The five quality attributes are must-be, one-dimensional, attractive, indifferent and reverse attributes.

Since 1984, Kano model is widely used in the management of various fields, e.g. hotel business (Chang and Chen [11]), commercial bank (Chen and Kuo [12]), stationery industry (Chen et al. [13]), the Internet Protocol Television industry (Jan et al. [14]), people management (Martensen and Gronholdt [15]), product development (Matzler and Hinterhuber [16]), and international airlines (Shahin and Zairi [17]). But, seldom studies use Kano model in the design of public transportation signage system.

In order to provide qualitative and quantitative suggestions for design and setting bus transportation signs, this paper analyses the common bus riding information at bus stops using Kano model, categories them into different information attributes, and then comes up with improvement technical suggestions. It would help to improve the information communication effect of bus stops, raise the efficiency of passengers boarding or alighting, and create a convenient and safe riding environment by using standardized designed and set bus transportation signs.

2 Methods

This paper aimed to improve the design of bus stops' signs in Beijing. Firstly, The passenger satisfaction for common signs at bus facilities was surveyed and analyzed by using questionnaires. Secondly, those signs that scored highly unsatisfied were picked out. The riding information carried by those signs and in urgent need were analyzed and categorized by using Kano's model. Finally, based on the possible improve aspects analyzed and good practices around the world, a new design of Beijing bus stop was provided.

2.1 Passenger Satisfaction Survey

Based on the field investigation of Beijing bus transportation signs, this paper conducts passenger satisfaction survey on bus transportation signs. The primary objective of the survey was to provide BMCT (Beijing Municipal Commission of Transport) with a means to identify passengers' concerns on bus signs. Seven kinds of signs which commonly used at bus facilities were surveyed, for example bus stop board, bus operating diagram, neighborhood map, vehicle sign, safety sign, price sign and accessible sign etc.

Respondents. This survey conducted from May to August 2014. A total of 558 questionnaires are collected, among which there are 549 valid questionnaires. The ratio of men to women was 56.5:43.5. Regarding the age distribution of the participants, those under the age of 25 was 25.5 %, those between 26 and 45 accounted for 50.8 %, those between 46 and 65 accounted for 20.9 %, while those over the age of 65 accounted for 2.7 %. Regarding the education level distribution, those under the education level of senior high school or technical secondary school was 9.1 %, those with undergraduate education level was 59.75 %, while those over the education level of Master degree was 9.65 %.

Questionnaire Preparation and Analysis. The questionnaire included two parts, respondent self-report part, and test part. In the respondent's self-report part, the following personal data was collected: age, sex, education level and riding frequency. There were 7 multiple-choice questions and 1 open question in the test part. The multiple-choice questions investigated passenger satisfaction on bus transportation signs that set at transport facilities (e.g. origin-terminal station, bus stop, bus vehicle). The open question collected respondents' ideas about existing problems and improvement suggestions.

From the result of the survey, three kinds of signs were scored highly unsatisfied. They were: bus operating diagram 58.11 %, bus stop board 44.99 %, neighborhood map 36.98 %. Passengers' urgent needs were: time of next bus, transfer with other transportations.

2.2   Kano Questionnaire Survey

Based on the result of passenger satisfaction survey, this paper chose the normal setting place of the three highly unsatisfied signs, made extended analysis on the riding information of the place, and then using Kano model to classify the information attributes. As the three highly unsatisfied signs are normally set at bus stops, we use Kano model to analysis the bus stop's riding information and the information attributes.

Respondents. The Kano questionnaire survey conducted from March to May 2015. 400 volunteers participated in the survey, 353 valid questionnaires were collected. The invalid questionnaires were those incomplete, or the number of R/Q category answers over 2. The total valid percent was 88.25 %. The ratio of men to women was 61.5:38.5. Regarding the age distribution of the respondents, those under the age of 18 were 5, those between 19 and 44 were 241, and those between 45 and 59 were 79, while those over 60 were 28. Regarding the education level distribution, those under the education level of middle school was 2.5 %, those with senior high school or technical secondary school was 9.3 %, those with junior college was 22.1 %, those with undergraduate education level was 51.1 %, while those over the education level of Master degree was 15 %.

Questionnaire Preparation and Analysis Method. According to Kano model, 13 riding information were included in the questionnaire, those information were mainly selected from three unsatisfied signs (bus operating diagram, bus stop board, neighborhood map), other common used signs and passengers' urgent needs. The questionnaire was formulated by questions in pair to which volunteers can answer in one of five different ways. By combining the two answers in the Kano evaluation table, the riding information can be classified. The functional form of the question was to collect volunteers' attitude when one specific information was provide at bus stop; while the dysfunctional form of the question was to collect volunteers' attitude when one specific information was not provide at bus stop. A sample-paired question for "Number of bus route" was given in Table 2. For the functional form and dysfunctional form of each information, there were 5×5 possible answers. And the combination of the questions in the evaluation table produces six different category A, O, M, I, R, Q (see Table 3) (Matzler and Hinterhuber [16]).

3   Result Analysis

The questionnaire is evaluated using the Kano evaluation table in Table 3. Combine two paired answers to the functional and dysfunctional questions in the Table 3. And the attributes of 13 riding information can be gained according to the frequency of answers (see Table 4). In Table 4, there were six must-be information, one one-dimensional information, three attractive information and three indifferent information. Furthermore, SI/DSI were calculated using the formula of Matzler and Hinterhuber [16]. A SI/DSI sensitivity matrix was drawn (see Fig. 2). The three riding information, i.e. Time of next bus, Neighborhood map, and Bus operating diagram, marked as attractive category, were in full accord with the passenger satisfaction survey.

Table 2. Functional and dysfunctional questions for "Number of bus route"

If you can find the number of bus route at the bus stop, how do you feel?	☐I like it that way ☐It must be that way ☐I am neutral ☐I can live with it that way ☐I dislike it that way
If you can **not** find the number of bus route at the bus stop, how do you feel?	☐I like it that way ☐It must be that way ☐I am neutral ☐I can live with it that way ☐I dislike it that way

Table 3. Kano evaluation table

Riding information		Dysfunctional form of the question				
		1. I like it that way	2. It must be that way	3. I am neutral	4. I can live with it that way	5. I dislike it that way
Functional form of the question	1. I like it that way	Q	A	A	A	O
	2. It must be that way	R	I	I	I	M
	3. I am neutral	R	I	I	I	M
	4. I can live with it that way	R	I	I	I	M
	5. I dislike it that way	R	R	R	R	Q

4 Discussion

4.1 Riding Information Attributes and the Design of Signs

Limited by road environment, the spaces of bus facilities are narrow. Based on the result of Kano questionnaire, when designing the bus transportation signs, we should arrange riding information rationally, i.e., the important information should be arranged at outstanding positions in the sign board, to ease passengers' difficulties in reading and comprehension.

Attractive information, one-dimensional information, and must-be information can improve passenger satisfaction highly. Those three attributes should be presented at

Table 4. Kano result table

Riding information (frequency)	A	O	M	I	R	Q	Category	SI	DSI
Number of bus route	7.9	31.2	**49.9**	9.6	0.6	0.8	M	0.40	−0.82
Name of origin and terminal stop	6.2	30.9	**50.4**	10.2	0.6	1.7	M	0.38	−0.83
Time of first and last bus	4.0	35.7	**44.8**	11.3	1.4	2.8	M	0.41	−0.84
All stops' name	7.1	34.8	**47.9**	7.1	0.6	2.5	M	0.43	−0.85
Price	6.8	25.2	**39.7**	26.9	0.8	0.6	M	0.32	−0.66
Direction of bus route	4.8	37.7	9.1	**47.3**	0.8	0.3	I	0.43	−0.47
Current stop's name	4.8	37.4	**46.2**	10.5	0.8	0.3	M	0.43	−0.85
Mileage	17.0	18.4	17.0	45.9	1.1	0.6	I	0.36	−0.36
Transfer	22.7	**35.7**	17.6	23.2	0.6	0.3	O	0.59	−0.54
Time of next bus	**32.3**	28.0	11.9	26.3	0.8	0.6	A	0.61	−0.41
Chinese pinyin of stop's name	12.5	8.8	10.2	**64.6**	3.4	0.6	I	0.22	−0.20
Neighborhood map	**35.4**	23.5	9.6	29.2	0.8	1.4	A	0.60	−0.34
Bus operating diagram	**30.3**	25.2	15.6	27.8	0.8	0.3	A	0.56	−0.41

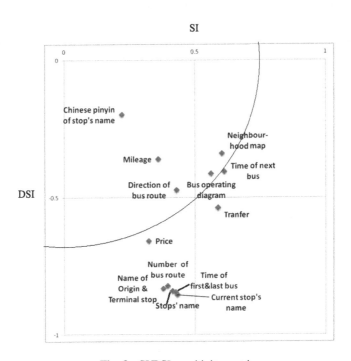

Fig. 2. SI/DSI sensitivity matrix

positions with visual dominance by using bigger font size, significant contrast color. Indifferent information doesn't much concern passengers at all, but it needs to be informed in bus operation. This attribute should be presented at unimportant positions with smaller font size.

4.2   Riding Information Attribute and the Setting of Signs

When setting the bus transportation signs, factors like information attribute, available positions, and observation distance should be taken into consideration. A vertical, stratified arranged bus transportation signage system could be constructed by presenting information at suitable positions and appropriate heights.

Attractive riding information can improve passenger satisfaction significantly, such information should be set at outstanding positions of bus stops, e.g. at the top of bus shelter, or at the back plate of bus shelter, as individual sign as possible.

One-dimensional information is linearly correlated to passenger satisfaction; such information should be integrated with other information as key information.

Must-be information is to meet the basic need when passenger travelling. If this attribute is overlooked, passengers will feel quite dissatisfied. It is essential to extract and integrate the "common factor" information, like price, which content is the same in different bus stops, and then present this kind of information at one position to save bus stop space and reduce maintenance cost.

Indifferent information is not the main passenger need; such information should be integrated with other information as auxiliary information.

Based on the above discussion, a new design and setting plan (see Fig. 3) for Beijing bus transportation signage system has been proposed and included in the Beijing local standard DB11/T 657.3 "Public transportation signs for passengers — Part3: trolley and bus".

Fig. 3. Modularized bus stop design

5 Conclusion

If one has investigated and studied comprehensively into the need of bus service and the characteristics of bus operation, the Kano model can give an accurate judgment on bus stop riding information service improvement: guarantee providing all Must-be information (e.g. Number of bus route, Name of Origin and Terminal stop, Time of first and last bus), improve actively the one-dimension information (Transfer), outstand those attractive information and SI > 0.5 information, that is, set those information at the top of bus shelter, or, set in large format.

Acknowledgement. This research was supported by China National Institute of Standardization through the "special funds for the basic R&D undertakings by welfare research institutions" (522014Y-3344) and the National Key Technology R&D Program (2012BAK28B03, 2014BAK01B01).

References

1. Zhang, X.D., Jing, X.: A study on reasonable size of urban bus stops, 城市公交中途站合理规模研究. J. Urban Transp. Chin. **7**(5), 68–71 (2009)
2. Shi, H.W., Luo, L.X., Bao, T.Z.: Research on the way to determine type and scale of bus stops, 公交中间站类型与规模的确定方法研究. J. Transp. Syst. Eng. Inf. Technol. **7**(2), 83–87 (2007)
3. Sun, M.: Study on public information guidance system of underground station of urban rail transit, 城市轨道交通地下车站标识导向系统研究. J. Railw. Stand. Des. **04**, 118–121 (2008)
4. The Beijing News. http://www.bjnews.com.cn
5. GB/T 5845.3—2008, Urban public transport sign - Part 3: stop board and line number plate of bus and trolley bus, 城市公共交通标志 第3部分:公共汽电车站牌和路牌. S. Standardization Administration of the People's Republic of China (SAC). 03.220.20 (2008)
6. Chen, Z.Z.: Improved design for indicating information on bus-stop boards, 公交站牌指示信息的改进设计. Sci. Technol. Inf. **03**, 190–207 (2014)
7. Wang, L.: Research on visual interface design with the sign of static public transport stop boards, 静态公交站点导向标识视觉界面设计研究. J. Packag. Eng. **04**, 23–27 (2012)
8. Sun, Q.: System research and the improvement measures of the bus stop in Haidian district Beijing city, 北京市海淀区公交站牌系统调研及改进措施. J. Art Des. **11**, 48–50 (2014)
9. Ding, H.Y., Zhu, W.Q., Guo, J.L.: Investigation and analysis of bus stop sign in Shanghai, 上海市公交站牌的调查与分析. Urban Public Transp. **12**, 37–39 (2009)
10. Kano, N., Seraku, N., Takahashi, F.: Attractive quality and must be quality. J. Jpn. Soc. Qual. Control **14**(2), 39–48 (1984)
11. Chang, K., Chen, M.: Applying the Kano model and QFD to explore customers' brand contacts in the hotel business: a study of a hot spring hotel. Total Qual. Manag. Bus. Excell. **22**(1), 1–27 (2011)
12. Chen, L., Kuo, Y.: Understanding e-learning service quality of a commercial bank by using Kano's model. Total Qual. Manag. Bus. Excell. **22**(1), 99–116 (2011)

13. Chen, S., Chang, L., Huang, T.: Applying Six-Sigma methodology in the Kano quality model: an example of the stationery industry. Total Qual. Manag. Bus. Excell. **20**(2), 153–170 (2009)
14. Jan, P., Lu, H., Chou, T.: Measuring the perception discrepancy of the service quality between provider and customers in the Internet Protocol Television industry. Total Qual. Manag. Bus. Excell. **23**(8), 981–995 (2012)
15. Martensen, A., Gronholdt, L.: Using employee satisfaction measurement to improve people management: an adaptation of Kano's quality types. Total Qual. Manag. **12**(7–8), 949–957 (2001)
16. Matzler, K., Hinterhuber, H.: How to make product development projects more successful by integrating Kano's model of customer satisfaction into quality function deployment. Technovation **18**(1), 25–38 (1998)
17. Shahin, A., Zairi, M.: Kano model: a dynamic approach for classifying and prioritising requirements of airline travellers with three case studies on international airlines. Total Qual. Manag. Bus. Excell. **20**(9), 1003–1028 (2009)

Author Index

Printed in the United States
By Bookmasters